Economics for Business

Palgrave Foundations

A series of introductory texts across a wide range of subject areas to meet the needs of today's lecturers and students

Foundations texts provide complete yet concise coverage of core topics and skills based on detailed research of course requirements suitable for both independent study and class use – *the firm foundations for future study.*

Published

A History of English Literature
Biology
Chemistry
Contemporary Europe
Economics
Economics for Business
Modern British History
Nineteenth-Century Britain
Physics
Politics

Forthcoming

British Politics
Maths for Science and Engineering
Modern European History
Sociology

Economics for Business

CHRIS MULHEARN, HOWARD R. VANE and JAMES EDEN

palgrave

First published 2001 by
PALGRAVE
Houndmills, Basingstoke, Hampshire R G 2 1 6 X S and
175 Fifth Avenue, New York, N. Y. 10010
Companies and representatives throughout the world

PALGRAVE is the new global academic imprint of St. Martin's Press LLC Scholarly and Reference Division and Palgrave Publishers Ltd (formerly Macmillan Press Ltd).

ISBN 0–333–91476–7

This book is printed on paper suitable for recycling and made from fully managed and sustained forest sources.

A catalogue record for this book is available from the British Library.

10   9   8   7   6   5   4   3
10   09   08   07   06   05   04   03

Typeset by Footnote Graphics, Warminster, Wilts
Printed and bound in Great Britain by J. W. Arrowsmith Ltd., Bristol

Contents

Preface

TODAY foundation courses in economics for business are taught on a range of undergraduate degree programmes, most notably business studies and management studies. While students on such degree programmes can turn to a number of well-established and respected introductory textbooks covering the core material, they are often intimidated by the sheer length of these texts.

The main aim of the present book is to meet the needs of business studies and management students taking an introductory course in economics by providing a rigorous yet *concise* coverage of the core material in a *user-friendly* and *accessible* fashion. The book will also prove useful to students on HND and MBA programmes.

The book is organized as follows. At the start of each chapter a set of questions indicates the main issues to be addressed. As they are introduced, key terms and concepts are highlighted in the text and defined in the margin. Examples of actual economic problems and phenomena are presented in boxes so that the reader can verify the immediate relevance of the analysis under consideration and confirm his or her understanding of it. Frequent cross-references are also made to material covered in other chapters so that the reader can see important links between the different aspects of economics. Each chapter ends with a summary of the main issues discussed; a list of key terms; a set of self-test questions (where appropriate); questions for discussion; and again, where appropriate, suggestions for further reading and links to the Internet. Answers to the self-test questions, a glossary and a brief bibliography can be found at the end of the book.

The book is conventionally divided between the two interrelated areas of microeconomics and macroeconomics. In its treatment of microeconomic material, in Chapters 1–8, attention is focused on the activities of business firms, operating in different market structures, in satisfying consumer wants and providing employment. This part of the book also explicitly looks at the relationship between business and the government. In the second half of the book, macroeconomic issues are interpreted as a series of problems that require elaboration as to their nature, their (competing) underlying explanations, and the range of policy options available for their resolution. Given the importance of the macroeconomic environment to business, it is crucial that students understand what causes change in the macroeconomy and what influence government policy has on the macroeconomic environment. The microeconomic and macroeconomic material is explicitly linked by the recurrent theme of the importance of government policy as a factor that influences business performance. In taking this approach we hope to demystify economics for business studies and management students, aid their understanding of how economic analysis can be applied to 'real world' issues, and demonstrate the relevance of economics for business and business activity in the economy.

In writing this book we have worked closely together, and benefited from a number of helpful and incisive comments made by a mutual friend and colleague, Steve Smith, to whom we should like to express our thanks. We are grateful to a colleague James Eden for writing the chapters on 'Firms' Costs and Revenues' (Chapter 4), and 'Investment Policy and Appraisal' (Chapter 6), in addition to a number of sections in the first half of the book, namely sections 3.6, 5.2–5.3, 5.8–5.10 and 8.6. We should also like to express our gratitude to the anonymous reviewers used by Palgrave for their helpful comments. However, above all, our thanks go to our families, who have been a constant source of support to us and to whom this book is dedicated.

CHRIS MULHEARN AND HOWARD R. VANE

Acknowledgements

The author and publishers wish to thank the following for permission to use copyright material:

The Boston Consulting Group for Box 8.2 (page 190); The Controller of Her Majesty's Stationery Office for Box 8.1 (page 189); *Financial Times* for Box 1.3 (page 16), Box 2.2 (page 30), Box 2.3 (page 32), Box 2.4 (page 34), Box 5.1 (page 112), Box 7.1 (page 151), Box 7.3 (page 153), Box 7.8 (page 165), Box 10.1 (page 242), Box 10.4 (page 254), Box 13.1 (page 318), Box 13.3 (page 323); *The Guardian* for Box 1.1 (page 7), Box 2.5 (page 44), Box 7.4 (page 155), Box 7.5 (page 156), Box 8.3 (page 192), Box 13.2 (page 319), Figure 14.6 (page 364), Box 15.3 (page 389), Box 16.2 (page 397); *The Independent* for Box 2.1 (page 29), Box 7.2 (page 152); OECD for Table 2.4 (page 46), Figure 8.4 (page 182), Table 9.2 (page 210), Table 9.3 (page 213), Table 14.5 (page 340), Table 14.6 (page 341), Table 15.2 (page 374), Table 15.4 (page 377); Office for National Statistics (ONS) for Table 3.1 (page 61), Table 8.1 (page 181), Table 8.2 (page 187), Figure 8.9 (page 186), Table 14.3 (page 336); Oxford University Press for Box 16.1 (page 395); Routledge for Table 7.1 (page 160); United Nations Conference on Trade and Development (UNCTAD) for Figure 15.1 (page 373), Table 15.3 (page 375), Box 15.1 (page 378), Table 15.5 (page 380), Table 15.6 (page 381), Table 15.7 (page 382), Table 15.8 (page 388).

Illustrations

Channel Tunnel Publications (page 140); Clive Farndon Photography (page 4); IKEA (page 305); The Littlewoods Organisation plc (page 64); Mercedes (page 72); *Private Eye* (for cartoons on pages 73, 107, 123, 242, 363, 394); Siemens (page 370); Unilever (page 112); Virgin (page 56).

Every effort has been made to contact all the copyright holders but if any have been inadvertently overlooked the publishers will be pleased to make the necessary arrangements at the first opportunity.

CHAPTER 1

Economics and Business

Key issues

▶ What are the basic questions that every economy must face?

▶ Why must business concern itself with economics?

▶ What does economics have to say about the respective roles of firms, consumers and government in the allocation of resources?

▶ What is resource scarcity, and what are its implications?

▶ What are microeconomics and macroeconomics, and why are they important for business?

Contents

1.1 Introduction: what is economics?

Most people can probably say what economics is about. It deals with issues such as inflation, unemployment, the profitability of firms, privatization, exchange rates, international trade and so on. But lists of this kind do not really tell us what the essence of the subject is. Economics is concerned with how societies organize the production and consumption of **goods** (physical commodities such as cars, books, food, and housing) and **services** (such as those provided by banks, barbers, teachers, or railway companies). More precisely, it tries to explain and understand:

- *what* goods and services societies produce
- *how* they produce them, and
- *for whom* they are produced.

Consider the society or economy in which *you* live. What are its production and consumption priorities? Table 1.1 lists a range of familiar goods and services. Are they all *produced* in your economy? If so, *how* are they produced – in a business setting by firms, or does the government assist or even take primary responsibility for the production of some of them? All of these goods and services are clearly available in the advanced 'Western' economies, but *to whom* are they available – everyone, or just those who are able to pay for them?

Goods: Tangible products.
Services: Intangible products.

Table 1.1 Produced in the society in which you live?

Produced in some industrial countries	Produced in most industrial countries but in uneven quantities	Produced in industrial countries in declining quantities	Produced in all industrial countries in large quantities
Cars	Tourist services	Clothing	Education services
Professional football	Books, magazines	Sports goods	Health care
Wine	Contemporary music	Toys	Housing
CDs	Food		Fast food
	Beer		
	Feature films		

Concept

Resource allocation

Resource allocation is the commitment of a society's productive endowments, such as labour and machinery, to particular uses or patterns of use. Thus, for a society to produce a particular good or service, it must allocate resources to the appropriate industry.

Table 1.1 categorizes our selected goods and services in terms of whether and in what relative quantities **resources** in the major economies[1] are **allocated** to their production. The following '*what*, *how* and *for whom*' patterns can be discerned.

What is produced?

- Some goods and services are produced only in certain of the advanced countries: the car, for example. Cars are manufactured in countries such as the United States, Japan, Germany and the UK but not in (say) Ireland or Iceland. Similarly, in France and Italy there is heavy investment in professional football but none in Canada or Australia.

- For a second category of goods and services, the production question is a matter of degree. Over the last 20 or 30 years, as international travel has become easier, many industrial countries have become tourist destinations and now produce the kinds of services that foreign tourists want. However, for some countries, the commitment to tourism is particularly marked: France and Spain are obvious examples. Similarly, although many major film productions are American in origin, other countries have their own but mostly more modest film industries.

- Clothing and footwear provide an instance of *reduced* production by most if not all the advanced countries. If you check your wardrobe, you will find that the labels on your clothes and shoes mostly indicate origins in the Far East and eastern Europe. Thirty or forty years ago Western economies produced much more of their own clothing and footwear.

- Finally, there is a fourth category of good or service that virtually all industrialized countries continue to produce in very large quantities: education and health services, for example.

We shall have more to say in this and other chapters (see Chapter 13, especially) about *why* patterns of country specialization in production arise, but for the moment let us proceed to the noted questions of *how* and *for whom* production takes place.

[1] We define classes of economy more carefully in later chapters. For the purposes of this introductory example, the 'major' economies are taken to be the long-established industrial economies such as those in western Europe and North America.

How is production organized?

The form taken by production – the *how* question – can actually be discussed at two levels:

- First, we might be interested in the particular *technicalities* of production in different economies: does the organization of (say) food production vary greatly between countries? For example, in some parts of the world agriculture is heavily mechanized; elsewhere it continues to use relatively large volumes of human labour instead of machinery.

- Second, as noted, we might ask to what extent *governments* involve themselves in production decisions. Since the early 1980s, in countries such as the UK and New Zealand, concerted attempts have been made to *reduce* the influence of government over economic activity, through the privatization of state-owned firms, for example. Elsewhere, experience has been divided: in the United States, to take the most obvious case, the economic impact of government has always been comparatively limited, and there is consequently a greater role for the private sector in the allocation of resources. By contrast, in the Scandinavian countries the role of the state in the economy is traditionally more pervasive. As we shall see, the balance between what the business sector does in an economy and what the state does is one of the key issues in economics.

For whom is production organized?

The *for whom* question is often closely linked to the latter form of the *how* question. Where governments involve themselves in production decisions, they may, among other things, choose to provide quantities of goods and services to citizens that otherwise might not have been available – and, moreover, provide them without charge or at a subsidized rate. For example, in the Netherlands, the government sponsors a major 'social housing' programme. This means that a large proportion of the housing stock in the Netherlands is publicly owned; houses are built by the government according to perceived general need, and rents are relatively cheap. As a result, few Dutch citizens are unable to find somewhere to live or find rents unaffordable. Here then, *for whom* means for most people, if not everyone. In the UK, to take a contrasting case, although there is investment in public housing, much more of the housing stock tends to be privately produced. Firms build houses in the expectation that they will be able to sell them at a profit. This means that the ability of an individual to become a consumer – the *for whom* question – turns not on need but on the ability to pay.

Positive and normative economics

To complete our introduction we need to mention one final issue. Economics seeks to be a **positive** discipline: that is, one concerned with matters of *fact* not opinion. That Britain's retail opening hours have become much more liberal over the last 20 years is a positive observation. Some shops now trade 24 hours a day, every day. Twenty years ago, very few shops opened on Sundays. Whether or not more liberal retail opening is a good thing is a **normative** question. The Archbishop of Canterbury probably has a view, one that is possibly at variance with the opinions held by the shareholders of Sainsbury's. Economists though do not claim to be able to answer such normative questions. What they *can* say is something about the impacts of this

Positive issues: Those that are factually based.

Normative issues: Those that are a matter of opinion.

change: on retail employment for example, on the profitability of retail businesses, on the changing form of retailing – the development of e-commerce – and so on. These are all positive issues.

1.2 Understanding the roles of firms, consumers and government in markets: why economics matters for business

In section 1.1 we learned that economics is concerned with understanding how a society allocates resources: what it chooses to produce, how it produces and for whom it produces. But how are these determinations made? Which individuals or agencies, exactly, decide *what*, *how* and *for whom*? We can identify three influences on resource allocation in most economies:

- firms
- consumers
- government.

A notable part of the market for live music: the Glastonbury Festival.
© Clive Farndon

Firms, consumers and government interact through **markets**. A market is simply a nexus, a means of connection for these different groups. It can of course, in the familiar sense, be a localized physical entity where buyers and sellers literally meet together – Billingsgate fish market in London, for example. More usually when economists speak about markets they are referring to the *process* of interaction between producers, consumers and, as we shall see, government – as in the European car market, the UK insurance market, and so on. Let us consider the role of each of the three key agents in the market, beginning with firms.

Market: A framework that brings buyers and sellers together.

The role of firms in markets

We examine the role of firms in markets and the wider modern economy in much more detail in Chapter 3; here, a brief introduction will suffice. Firms may have a number of objectives but their central purpose is generally recognized as the organization of production for profit. In a sense, with profit as its goal, the firm must ask *itself* the three basic economic questions: what should it produce, how should production be organized, and at which customers should the goods and services it produces be aimed?

As an example, consider the declared business strategy of *Tesco*, Britain's largest supermarket group. Tesco is a food retailer that has traditionally concentrated on the domestic market. Its answers to the *what*, *how* and *for whom* questions were simple: it sold food, in large stores, to British consumers. Now Tesco has announced rather more ambitious plans. Its intention is to become a global retailer, and not just of food. It wants to sell more non-grocery goods such as clothing, computers, electrical goods and even scooters. Tesco also plans to become much more internationally oriented: it expects to have 200 stores overseas by 2004; in 1997 it had two. The company will also move further into the rapidly expanding market for on-line shopping for groceries, household goods and books. Tesco's answers to the basic economic questions are thus beginning to look radically different: it will sell food and a growing range of non-food items, in large stores in Britain, overseas and over the Internet, to an increasingly global customer base (*Source*: *Guardian* 22 September 1999).

Why is Tesco adopting this new strategy? Firms cannot afford to be complacent: Tesco did not get to be Britain's premier food retailer by resting on its laurels; it is simply responding to changes in the marketplace. Food retailing in Britain was transformed over the last two decades of the twentieth century, becoming dominated by the large often 'out-of-town' stores of a small number of companies such as Tesco, Sainsbury's and Asda. As these firms opened more and more stores, the level of competition between them became increasingly intense and, importantly, the possibility of further expansion was limited, ultimately by the size of the British market. For Tesco (and the rest) then, two problems were apparent: rival firms threatening to 'steal' its customers, and a ceiling on the overall retail food customer base. Tesco's new strategy will, it hopes, allow it to make progress on both these fronts: it becomes a more attractive retailer than its competitors, selling a wider range of goods in new ways, *and* it simultaneously gains access to a much larger 'global' market with immense growth potential. This example demonstrates the importance of economics in a business context in two ways. First, it allows us, from the outside as it were, to make sense of the business strategy that Tesco has implemented: economics is useful in that it helps us to understand business decisions. Second, economic principles clearly inform Tesco's own strategy: they are, in other words, an *integral part of* business decision-making.

The Tesco case also shows that, in the pursuit of the objective of production for profit, firms are subject to two initial market-based constraints: competition from rival firms, and the potentially elusive demands of consumers. We shall consider what economists have to say about the role of consumers in a moment, but let us first briefly reflect on the importance of competition between firms.

For each firm, rivals are always significant because they represent a immediate threat to *its* continued presence in the market. A rival may improve a good or service, lower its price, practice more effective marketing, or even introduce an entirely new product that makes established ones obsolete. The point about all these eventualities is that they are best understood in the context of *resource allocation in a competitive market environment*. Every firm must ask itself what it should produce, how, and for whom – in the knowledge that other firms are out there asking themselves exactly the same questions. Again, this makes economics central to an understanding of the unfolding competitive process between firms.

The role of consumers in markets

Consumers too are certainly a major constraint on firms. In fact, it is ultimately consumers who effectively determine the way in which markets behave – whether they grow or decline and how fast they change. Consumers will even condition how quickly products are developed and improved in markets. How do they do this? Later today if you buy a CD you are entering a market as a consumer but you would hardly perceive yourself as a major player in the music business. And this is true: on its own, your interest in John Lennon or Boyzone doesn't count for much. However, expressed *collectively*, purchasing power is the most powerful force at work in any market. If people decide that John Lennon's songs have begun to sound a little twee and Boyzone are a bit old, then the firms that produce and sell their CDs will focus their efforts upon other more popular or potentially more popular artists.

Economists have a name for this notion of consumer power: **consumer sovereignty**. Consumer sovereignty suggests that individual consumers have ultimate control over what markets produce. As each individual chooses to buy a good or service, he or she is affirming the existence and provision of that good or service. On the other hand, if consumers generally choose not to buy something that was formerly in demand then producers will begin to withdraw it from the market. There is no point in trying to sell goods or services that people no longer want. Box 1.1 illustrates a case in point: the threat posed by changes in fashion to Levi jeans, until recently an apparently rock-solid brand with a 120-year history. All that past popularity now counts for little: consumer preferences have changed, the market has evolved, and Levi Strauss finds it uneconomic to produce jeans in accustomed quantities. The same principle applies if consumers become avid purchasers of a good or service: producers then have a reason to increase the amount they produce. The simple presence of consumers or potential consumers also gives firms an incentive to continually refine and improve the quality of their products. A firm that innovates – produces something better or cheaper – will be rewarded with more custom and thus with more profit. It *pays* firms to do as much as they can to please those who might buy their goods and services. Thus economics also matters in a business context because it is able to identify and understand the nature of the consumer-led *governance of markets*.

Concept

Consumer sovereignty

Consumer sovereignty implies that the consumption choices of individuals in competitive markets condition production patterns. Producers *must* follow the lead given by the purchasing decisions of consumers. If they produce goods and services that consumers do not want they will bankrupt themselves. Hence consumers exercise sovereignty over producers. The production of 'environmentally friendly' goods and services is an example of this kind of consumer power. The tuna fish producer who admitted to canning the odd dolphin would not remain in business very long.

Box 1.1

Jeans blues blamed for 700 job losses

By Terry Mcalister

Jeans manufacturer Levi Strauss's plans to cut nearly 700 jobs yesterday sent shockwaves through Scotland's industrial heartland. The company also admitted that other positions could be vulnerable.

The job losses [were] blamed on falling sales due to changes in fashion trends.

A recent survey found that UK sales of budget jeans, priced at £19.99 or less, had slumped by a quarter since 1995. Top brands such as Levi have also been hit hard as buyers have turned to brands such as Diesel and Dead or Red.

Popular with wearers from James Dean to Cindy Crawford, the Levi 501 has been an indispensable fashion item for 120 years. But of late it has become associated with less 'hip' public figures, such as Des O'Connor and Tony Blair.

Frank Ross, a Levi director, insisted the decision had been forced on Levi because of a fall in jeans buying by a shrinking population of young Europeans and a shift away from denim as a fashion fabric.

'Discretionary spending on electronics, computer games and accessories, leisure activities and travel has affected all jeans manufacturers, along with increased competition from 'sports brands' and own label brands,' he explained.

Source: *Guardian* 22 September 1999

The role of government in markets

One way in which economists characterize markets is according to the degree of influence that government has over them. A **free market** is one in which government has little or no influence. In a free market the key economic questions of what to produce, how and for whom will be decided mainly by interaction between individual consumers and private producers – usually business firms. Firms will respond to the demands or anticipated demands of consumers. However, where markets are not free, resource allocation usually becomes subject to some combination of influence by firms, consumers *and* government. State intervention in markets can take two broad forms:

Concept

Free market

A free market is one in which there is no government interference or intervention.

- The state may elect to produce directly some goods and services itself in tandem with or instead of production by private firms. Our earlier case of social housing provision in the Netherlands would be one example of mixed public and private provision: the Dutch government *and* private firms build houses in the Netherlands. An instance of wholly public provision arose in Britain after the Second World War, when coal and steel production were taken from the private sector and run exclusively for many years by state-owned firms.

- The state may choose not to produce goods and services directly in markets but to *regulate* markets in some way. There can be a wide variety of practice here. In the European Union agricultural production is heavily conditioned by financial subsidies paid by European governments to farmers. In fact, governments can and do choose to subsidize production by private producers in many markets. Conversely, instead of encouraging more production, governments may either try to limit what it considers to be harmful or undesirable forms of output, or it may seek to influence the quality of what is produced. For example, many of the world's governments have begun to show concern about environmental pollution, and have tried to regulate industry so that it pollutes less. There are more mundane illustrations of the same kind of activity: for instance the empowerment by

Concept

Mixed economy

A mixed economy is one in which there is some role for government in resource allocation.

Concept

Centrally planned economy

A centrally planned economy is one in which resource allocation is almost wholly determined by government.

Concept

Economy in transition

An economy in transition is one in which resource allocation by the state is being eroded in favour of allocation determined by private firms and consumers.

government of health inspectors as a means to ensure that restaurants meet certain hygiene and food preparation standards.

Fig. 1.1 broadly summarizes these categories of free markets and markets subject to forms of state intervention. In Fig. 1.1(a) the market is composed only of business firms and private consumers – it is a free market. In Fig. 1.1(b), the *production* side of the market is composed of both firms and government. Here then the state has involved itself in the production of goods and services either alongside or, in some instances, perhaps instead of private firms. In Fig. 1.1(c) there is a layer of state regulation of the market as a whole.

Using the illustrative categories in Fig. 1.1, can we say what a 'real' economy looks like – what is its typical form? In fact, **mixed economies** will be typified by the presence of markets represented by all three of the panels (a)–(c) in Fig. 1.1. Mixed economies are defined by the existence in them of some combination of public and private resource allocation: both private firms and government are involved in determining what society produces, how and for whom. Now, in the new millennium, most of the world's economies are like this but, prior to the late 1980s, economies in eastern Europe and some in Africa and the Far East were **centrally planned** rather than mixed. This meant that there was relatively little room for private firms, and resource allocation was primarily determined by the state. Bureaucrats rather than businesspeople decided what kinds of goods and services should be produced. They also decided how production would be organized, and controlled the way in which goods and services were distributed. Most of the old centrally planned economies are currently engaged in a process of **transition** to mixed status. This means that the influence of the state over resource allocation is being eroded in these economies and there are increasing opportunities for private firms to actively participate in economic decision-making.

So, the mixed economy is an arena in which key economic decisions are taken by business firms, consumers and government. It is also important to note that these decisions are seldom taken in isolation. Under the general imperatives of consumer sovereignty, firms, consumers and government continually *interact* with one another

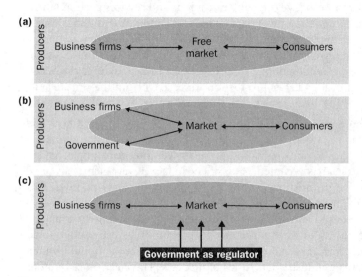

Fig. 1.1 The free market and state intervention in markets.

across most markets in the mixed economy. In terms of Fig. 1.1, this means that (b) and (c) are most prevalent, with (a) – the free market – in reality quite rare.

Consider, as examples, the UK markets for clothing, cars and top football matches. These might be thought to approximate reasonably 'free' markets in the sense that there appears to be relatively little government interference or intervention in them. The government does not, for example, try to provide clothing to its citizens in the same way that it provides, say, health care services. Nor does it pay 'clothing inspectors' to do an equivalent job to that of health inspectors. Thus, to understand the clothing business, we might suppose that most attention would have to be paid to clothing firms and their customers. Similarly, for clothing firms themselves, we might expect that *their* sole concern would be the demands of their customers and the business strategies of their rivals. In fact, the clothing market is more complicated than this, as are the markets for cars and football matches. We shall examine each in turn.

Clothing

The UK clothing market is not a free market, it is *protected*. We explain the economics of protectionism in more detail in Chapter 13, section 13.5. For present purposes a simple overview will do. Since the early 1960s, the advanced nations have arranged limits on the exports of textiles and clothing from the less developed parts of the world to their own economies. The purpose of these limits is simple: to protect domestic textile and clothing producers from foreign competition. By taking such action, governments in the advanced economies hope to safeguard 'their own' clothing firms and the jobs of those who work in them. In terms of Fig. 1.1, the UK clothing market would thus approximate (c) – the market is state regulated. Note that while protection may appear to help textile and clothing firms and their employees, it does so at the expense of UK consumers, who have their access to goods from abroad restricted.

Cars

Although the UK government does not itself produce cars, in the past it has done so through its ownership of Rover. However, the UK car market remains one that is conditioned by state intervention. This arises in two broad ways. First, like textiles and clothing, the UK car market has been periodically protected, in this case against car exports from Japan (protection is, however, administered at the level of the European Union). Second, the UK government has consistently elected to subsidize investments by big car manufacturers. Millions of pounds raised in taxes have been paid to the likes of Ford, Nissan and Honda as a means to obtain or retain their production interests in Britain. Again, the government's chief concern here is the creation and retention of jobs. Thus the car market, too, is state regulated. Historically, it has moved from an approximation of Fig. 1.1(b) (where government itself produces) to Fig. 1.1(c) (with an emphasis on government regulation).

Football

The Premier League might at first seem far removed from state concerns, but there have been notable instances of intervention here too, which have had important impacts on the market. As a result of the Hillsborough disaster in 1989, in which a large number of Liverpool supporters lost their lives, the Government decreed that all Premier League grounds should provide only seated accommodation. This safety measure has had the effect of reducing the capacity of many grounds, and prompted the building of a number of new stadia. The European Union has also imposed a significant change in the labour market for professional footballers. The so-called Bosman Ruling prevents football clubs in the EU from 'selling' footballers once their contracts have expired. This has vastly increased the negotiating and earning power of the best players at the expense of clubs. Taken together, there is little doubt that these two instances of state intervention in the football market have had a notable impact upon it. In terms of Fig. 1.1, (c) would be representative of this market.

These examples suggest that state intervention in markets in the mixed economy is more prevalent that it might at first appear. However, it is possible to go even further. The preceding discussion considered *discrete* forms of intervention in particular markets. Most governments in the advanced economies maintain, in addition, a regulatory brief in respect of markets *generally*. There are several reasons for this; here it will suffice to highlight one. For reasons that we elaborate fully in Chapter 5, it is a commonplace amongst economists that monopoly – defined for now as the presence of one firm in an industry or market – is undesirable, not least because it restricts consumer choice and impedes consumer sovereignty. Accordingly, to a greater or lesser degree, governments are concerned to prevent the achievement of monopoly status by any firm in most (not all, as we shall see) industries or markets. In a sense, then, the state regulation of markets can be said almost always to have particular and general forms: particular in terms of, say, discrete intervention to subsidize carmakers; and general as (and, to reiterate, this is but one example) in the watching brief to prevent the formation of monopolies.

On the basis of the discussion so far, we would argue that business operates in consumer-led market environments that are pervasively and sometimes subtly conditioned by government. Again then, economics counts for business because it understands this operating context. If you wish to understand business, or you are actually in business, you need at least some awareness of economics.

1.3 Scarcity, choice and opportunity cost

We have learned that economics concerns itself with the production choices that a society has to make: *what goods and services . . . produced how . . . for whom*? But we also need to know why these choices are so pressing. It is painfully obvious that many societies continue to struggle with the large-scale human tragedies of poverty, disease and malnutrition. The starkness of choice here needs little emphasis: people have basic needs for food, warmth and shelter, and will allocate what resources they have into producing these things first. But in affluent parts of the world the general levels of production and consumption are higher now than they have ever been. Food, warmth and shelter are largely taken for granted, as indeed is the availability of an at times seemingly boundless array of other goods and services. Is there really a problem here for economics to engage with? We might of course point out that poverty and want are still present in many sections of the advanced societies, but even if they weren't economics would still be given purpose by the notion of **resource scarcity**.

In everyday usage, scarcity is interpreted simply as a lack of ready availability: diamonds might be considered scarce and therefore highly prized but beer, for example, is not: you can get it relatively cheaply in quantities that you might the next

> **Concept**
>
> **Resource scarcity**
>
> Resource scarcity implies that *all* a society's resources are scarce in relation to the limitless wants present in every society.

morning live to regret. For economists, however, scarcity has a different emphasis: it is always placed in the context of the potentially *infinite* demands upon a society's scarce resources. It is true that the advanced societies currently enjoy previously unparalleled standards of living, but that does not mean that there are no unmet needs or wants in these societies. In a country as rich as the United States some people still lack comprehensive medical care, not everyone who wants one has a car, and many people would like to live in houses better than those they currently occupy. These are more than glib points: they suggest that a society's wants are in fact *limitless*. All resources must be considered scarce because of the vast range of competing uses to which they could be put.

Because, in an economic sense, resources are scarce every society is faced with a potentially huge spectrum of choice. Committing resources to one set of production and consumption patterns necessarily means that others must be forgone. In economics the essence of resource choice is captured in the notion of **opportunity cost**. The opportunity cost of a particular resource commitment is the value of the best alternative use that must consequently be given up. But opportunity cost is more than a fancy way of saying societies can't do everything; it allows us to understand why particular production choices are made.

Consider, for example, the issue of environmental pollution. In the advanced industrial countries of western Europe there is a relatively high standard of environmental protection, which is administered both by individual nation states and by the European Union. In contrast, protection standards in parts of Africa and South America are undoubtedly lower. Why? Is it simply a question of varying degrees of interest in and commitment to the environment, or are there other forces at work here? An economic analysis would suggest the latter. A society's view of the balance between the imperative of industrial production and what is tolerable in terms of consequent environmental despoliation must be tempered by the level of economic development of the society in question. In, say, the relatively affluent German economy it might be possible to raise industrial output by relaxing the controls over the ways in which firms dispose of liquid waste. Instead of investing in expensive plant that treated such material, it could be pumped straight into rivers such as the Rhine and the Danube. Here the balance between what would be gained and lost by such action becomes critical. How highly are clean rivers valued as against a *bit* more output in an already rich society? The likely answer is that the opportunity cost of the increase in output is too great: clean rivers are more highly valued, therefore there is an economic rationale for pollution control and a particular production choice can be understood. Now, in much poorer countries, the value attached to extra industrial output will undoubtedly be higher, and therefore the cost of some forms of environmental protection may be considered prohibitive in terms of the value of the output that much be sacrificed. If the extra output pays for necessary food or shelter, the priority it will be accorded is apparent. Here then the opportunity cost of environmental protection may be prohibitive, and the decision to pollute becomes an economically defensible one.

Although this example contrasts rich and poor countries in the new millennium, exactly the same analysis could be used to compare the production priorities set by contemporary rich countries and those same countries in the nineteenth century. *Then*, industrial interests triumphed over the environment in the West too. This was because, then, the opportunity cost of lost output was higher than the value that society put on the environment. Note also that, in those modern economies where

Opportunity cost: The cost of an action measured in terms of the best forgone alternative action.

the opportunity cost of pollution is deemed to be too high, it is the state that inter-venes in markets – usually by imposing fines on polluting firms – to ensure more satisfactory outcomes.

The concept of opportunity cost also allows us to understand why countries specialize in the production of particular goods and services. Switzerland, for ex-ample, has a reputation for high quality clock and watch-making. Why? There are no climatic or natural resource attributes that make Switzerland an obvious place in which to manufacture clocks and watches. However, having – over time – developed skills in the production of these items, it is evidently an efficient use of resources to exploit such skills fully. This is because, in economic terms, the opportunity cost associated with reallocating some resources away from the production of watches and clocks into, say, the manufacture of cars – where the Swiss have no particular pedigree – would be too great. Certainly, the Swiss could make cars, but they would have to switch a disproportionate volume of resources away from something they are much better at in order to do so – thus sacrificing the output of many (too many: this is the critically high opportunity cost) watches and clocks. The case is made all the more compelling by the possibility of international trade. The Swiss can special-ize in the production of watches and clocks and sell these on international markets in order to obtain the foreign currencies needed to buy cars and other goods and services produced more efficiently by other nations. The application of the concept of opportunity cost to international trade is discussed more fully in Chapter 13.

So economics is about understanding production choices in the context of resource scarcity and with an awareness of opportunity cost. Societies have limitless wants: which are to be satisfied and which neglected? Economics offers a range of arguments about these possible choices, which reflect the implications of doing this or that, in this or that way. Now, if we return to our earlier examples of the markets for clothing, cars and Premiership football – and, indeed, some of the others we used – it is apparent that one issue comes consistently to the fore: *the extent to which the state should be involved in resolving the key economic questions a society faces – what, how, for whom?* Indeed, it might be argued that this is *the* issue for economics. All societies aspire to be good producers: to have modern industries, comprehensive health care programmes, flourishing systems of education, good housing, efficient means of communication and transport and so on. It then becomes a question of the *balance* between state and private-market actors (firms and consumers) in organiz-ing the provision of these things.

Putting this another way, we can refer to the *freedoms* that the state allows private-market actors in resource allocation. In some markets in the UK, such as clothing, the state normally allows much more private decision-making by firms and con-sumers than it does, for example, in the provision of health care. In the market for health care, the state, in conjunction with the medical profession, has a major say in the kind of health services that are produced, how they are produced, and for whom they are produced. The National Health Service is largely funded using money from taxation. The government chooses how many health professionals to train and employ, how many hospitals to build, how long waiting lists for treatment can toler-ably be, and so on. It also provides health care to patients or consumers on the basis of clinical need. People do not pay directly for the treatment they receive. At the same time, the government does not prohibit private health care: in the UK there is genuinely dual provision by the public and private sectors. This means that the private sector is free to take up any opportunities it sees in the market for health care services. If private agents can identify any unmet health care needs on the part of private consumers they have an incentive – in the form of profit – to try to meet those needs.

From a business perspective, this example suggests that an understanding of the role of the state in markets and the freedoms and opportunities it allows private actors is crucially important. The modern mixed economy is a dynamic entity. The forms of control exercised by the state over markets will evolve and change over time, not least because the control of the state itself is subject to democratic check and political influence. For business firms, then, the freedom to act in markets will be subject to review and periodic modification; this means that new business opportunities will continue to present themselves. But market dynamism has another important source that we have already identified: consumers. Consumer demands are also subject to change, sometimes decisively so. Our Levi jeans case provides an instance of a firm taking dramatic action to cope with abrupt movements in what had been a long-established market. Thus, although business opportunities might be tempered by the interventionist and regulatory inclinations of the state, they are simultaneously conditioned by the imperatives derived from the sovereignty of consumers. Finally, of course, the shifting actions – real or anticipated – of rival firms are an additional consideration in business decision-making.

1.4 Microeconomics, macroeconomics and business

As we explain in more detail in Box 1.2, modern economics is conventionally divided into two complementary parts: **microeconomics** and **macroeconomics** (or micro and macro for short):

- Microeconomics deals with issues at the level of the *individual*: the individual consumer, producer, market or industry, worker and so on.
- Macroeconomics, on the other hand, considers the workings of the economy *as a*

Macroeconomics: The study of the behaviour of individual households and firms, and the determination of the relative prices of particular goods and services.

Microeconomics: The study of the economy as a whole.

Box 1.2

Microeconomics and macroeconomics

Microeconomics focuses upon *disaggregate* and *individualistic* economic issues. Macroeconomics, by contrast, looks at the behaviour of *the economy as a whole*.

The concerns of microeconomics include individual consumer and producer behaviour. It looks, for example, at factors that influence people's purchasing and firms' production decisions. Microeconomics also considers the behaviour of economic agents in particular markets, such as the labour market. Wage determination is therefore an example of a micro issue. Which factors influence the level of a worker's wage? Why do wages between different occupations vary? Would a government-set minimum wage affect the numbers of people employed in particular industries? These are all questions that micro analyses are able to address.

Macroeconomics studies the behaviour and performance of the economy as a whole. It is chiefly concerned with the four major aggregates of economic growth, unemployment, inflation, and the balance of payments. Macroeconomics seeks both to understand the factors that determine these aggregates and to inform the government policies that are used to try to influence them.

whole: inflation, the overall levels of employment and unemployment, the rate at which the economy grows, and how it fits into the international economic environment are all macro concerns.

In terms of our discussion so far an emphasis on *micro* issues has been evident. We have considered the interaction of firms, consumers and government in *markets*. Markets are arenas where particular resource allocation decisions are determined. For example, the present popularity of scooters among consumers in Britain is a boon for firms making or selling scooters, and may also be of interest to government for environmental reasons (scooters pollute less than cars, and don't contribute as much as cars do to traffic congestion). However, because what happens in the scooter market is not an issue for the economy as a whole or business in general this, along with developments in most other such markets, remains a focus of micro-economics.

From Chapter 9 onwards we shall turn our attention to macroeconomics. Our interest will still be in the three sets of actors we have identified – firms, consumers and government – but it will be situated at the more general level of the whole economy instead of in this or that particular market. Although it would be premature to enter into too detailed a discussion of the significance of macroeconomics at this stage, for illustrative purposes it is worth reflecting briefly on two macro concerns that impact heavily on business – *interest rates* and *exchange rates*.

Interest rates

Generalizing for the moment, we can say that interest rates are set by governments or their agents for some specific macroeconomic purpose. If, for example, a government wished to bring down the rate of inflation, or prevent it from rising, it might raise interest rates. This would make borrowing for firms and consumers in the economy more expensive, and encourage them to consume less. As we shall see in Chapter 10, section 10.4, moderating the demand for goods and services in the economy as a whole may cause a reduction in inflationary pressure. Interest rates are therefore a key tool of macroeconomic policy. Clearly, however, they cannot be used costlessly. Because higher interest rates increase the cost of borrowing they are burdensome to businesses that require finance for investment or other purposes. If interest rate increases also depress spending by consumers on the goods and services that firms produce they become a double bind on business.

However, despite these problems, the business community is usually one of the most supportive of government attempts to control inflation. Again, we explain fully why this is the case in later chapters (see, in particular, Chapter 9, section 9.4) but we can give a hint here. As we shall discuss in Chapter 2, markets are coordinated by *price signals*. Prices inform firms and consumers about conditions in markets. When prices are rising in a particular market this may signal to firms that demand in that market is buoyant and encourage them to produce more goods to sell in it. However, when significant inflationary pressures are also present in the economy as a whole, the price signals from all markets become less reliable as guides to conditions in those markets. Do rising prices in markets represent strong demand for particular goods, or are they just part of the general increase in prices across the economy as a whole? The problem for firms is that they cannot easily tell. In these circumstances it becomes easy for firms to make mistakes that may turn out to be costly: they might produce too much and be left with unsold stocks, or they might produce too little and miss an opportunity to make profits. One problem associated with inflation is therefore the degree of *uncertainty* that it introduces into economic decision-making. Firms prefer a low and stable rate of inflation because it minimizes such uncertainty.

So, despite the discomfort of higher interest rates for the business community, there is a recognition that this may have to be tolerated in order to control inflationary pressures. But this is not the end of the matter. Interest rates also have an important bearing on the exchange rate, and this too is important from a business perspective.

Exchange rates

We deal extensively with exchange rate issues in Chapter 14, sections 14.3–14.7. For present purposes we shall only highlight the significance of the exchange rate for firms selling goods or services in foreign markets. If the value of the pound sterling increases it becomes more difficult for British firms to sell abroad. Why? Simply, foreign residents have to spend more of their own currencies to obtain a given amount of sterling as the sterling exchange rate rises. For example, if the pound and the US dollar exchanged at parity (i.e. £1:$1), a British computer costing £1000 would retail in the USA for $1000. However, if the pound strengthens against the dollar to the point where £1 is worth $2 (£1:$2), it should be clear that the same computer will now retail at $2000 in the USA. In other words, increases in the exchange rate of a currency drive up the (foreign currency) prices of the issuing country's exports. One implication for business is immediately apparent: a strong currency makes exporting more difficult.

Now the unfortunate connection between interest rates – which, remember, business does not wish to see increase but has to put up with to keep inflation in check – and the exchange rate is that they tend to move together. In other words, an increase in interest rates may promote a strengthening of the exchange rate.[2] This is because higher interest rates encourage international investors to buy more British financial instruments as they now carry a higher yield in comparison with those in countries with unchanged interest rates. As investment of this sort in Britain increases, so too does the demand for sterling, thus driving up its value or rate of exchange.

In summary, then, an economy that has a perceived need to maintain interest rates at a robust level in order to keep inflation under control may experience some simultaneous strengthening of its currency. Both eventualities may be unwelcome from a business perspective. It so happens that the British economy has experienced this unhappy combination in recent times. Box 1.3 offers some details.

The box refers first to Eddie George's concern about the strength of sterling as expressed to another worried group, businesspeople at the British Chambers of Commerce Conference. Eddie George is the Governor of the Bank of England. He chairs the Monetary Policy Committee (MPC) of the Bank, which has responsibility for setting UK interest rates. The MPC's job is to set interest rates so as to meet inflation targets established by politicians in the government. Reading the box you will see that the MPC had at the previous day's meeting (it meets once every month) decided to leave interest rates unchanged, despite evidence that a rate rise might have been advisable in order to put a check on certain signs of inflationary pressure

---

[2]At least in the short term – we discuss exchange rate determination fully in Chapter 14, section 14.4.

Box 1.3

George does what he can to ease the plight of industry: but for the strength of the pound, there is no question that interest rates would have been raised yesterday

writes Ed Crooks

When Eddie George told businesspeople at the British Chambers of Commerce conference on Tuesday he was every bit as concerned about the strength of the pound as they were, few doubted his sincerity.

There was just one problem. 'What the hell can we do about it?' he asked.

Yesterday the governor of the Bank of England did what he could, by leading the Monetary Policy Committee to leave interest rates unchanged. It was a demonstration that their regular expressions of sympathy for the plight of manufacturers are not just empty words.

But for the strength of the pound, there can be no question that interest rates would have risen yesterday.

Even though the confusion caused by the turn of the millennium makes recent economic statistics difficult to interpret, domestic demand still seems to be growing strongly, as are wages and house prices. At some point that growth will have to slow if inflation is to be kept on target.

But the problems of Rover and other carmakers are only the most visible signs of the havoc caused by the strength of the pound.

'What we have been waiting for is the pound to have a real effect on the economy, and I think now that is starting to happen,' says Martin Weale of the National Institute of Economic and Social Research.

Exports of goods fell by more than £1.1bn in the fourth quarter of last year, and in the three months to February the output of manufacturing industry fell by 0.5 per cent.

Exporters and manufacturers have had a rough time since 1997, but the difference up until last year was that world markets were very shaky. To be struggling still now the world economy is roaring back to life is deeply disturbing.

The result has been a barrage of lobbying from businesses and unions, which would have meant that a rate rise, apart from its economic impact would have been politically disastrous.

'If the MPC had put up rates, they would have been lynched,' says Geoffrey Dicks of Greenwich NatWest. The Committee's members may not have to worry about winning votes, but they do need to think about their legitimacy in the eyes of the public.

None of this means the upward trend in rates is over. The Bank is about to go into the round of analysis and forecasting that will go into next month's Inflation Report, when it will, among other things, take its first really considered view of the Budget. Another 0.25 per cent rate rise next month is widely expected in the City.

Source: Financial Times 7 April 2000

in labour and housing markets. The central reason for this decision was the risk that higher interest rates would drive an already strong pound still higher, creating even more 'havoc' among beleaguered British exporters. The box cites the case of Rover as the ultimate example of the implications of the strength of sterling for British industry. After a particularly lean period Rover has been jettisoned by its former owner BMW, and is currently struggling to survive on its own.

For business, then, interest and exchange rates are clearly crucial issues. Our discussion in this section suggests that business needs to retain a focus on both microeconomic and macroeconomic issues. At the micro level, the short- and long-term conditions of the market in which the firm operates are its immediate concern, but no less significant will be factors operating at the macro level such as interest and exchange rates. To refine an earlier conclusion: if you are studying business or in business, you need to know about micro *and* macroeconomics.

■ Summary

◆ Economics is concerned with three basic questions: what goods and services a society produces, how these are produced, and for whom they are produced.

◆ Economics matters in a business context because it understands the respective market roles of firms, consumers and government.

◆ All resources are scarce in the context of the infinite demands that can be placed upon them. Society is therefore faced with a myriad of choices concerning how the resources it has should be used. The concept of opportunity cost allows us to begin to understand the choices that particular societies make at given times.

◆ Microeconomics deals with the economics of the individual; macroeconomics deals with the economy as a whole. Both are important from a business perspective.

■ Key terms

◆ Market
◆ Resource allocation
◆ Positive issues
◆ Normative issues
◆ Free market
◆ Mixed economy
◆ Scarcity and choice
◆ Opportunity cost
◆ Microeconomics
◆ Macroeconomics

■ Self-test questions

True (t) or false (f)

1. Economics tries to understand how a society uses its resources, all of which are considered scarce.

2. Because it is so plentiful, water is not a scarce resource.

3. Firms control markets.

4. Governments have some influence over most markets.

5. The UK clothing market is a free market.

6. Opportunity costs are borne only by firms.

7. The following is a normative statement: 'Because it is so important, health care should always be provided for everyone by the state.'

8. The following is a positive statement: 'Because they are inimical to consumers' interests, monopolies are usually regulated in some way by government.'

9. The rate of inflation is a microeconomic issue.

10. Macroeconomics deals with issues arising at the level of the economy as a whole.

Questions for discussion

◆ What is economics?

◆ Microeconomics suggests that successful businesses need to be dynamic. Can you explain the need for such dynamism?

◆ Explain how consumer sovereignty places consumers at the heart of economic decision-making in capitalist economies.

◆ How can the notion of opportunity cost help us to understand the production choices that a society makes?

◆ Why is some knowledge of macroeconomics important for business?

Reflective questions on 'boxed' material

◆ Box 1.1 describes market difficulties experienced by jeans manufacturer Levi Strauss. Levi Strauss may be depicted as a 'victim' of consumer sovereignty. Explain how. Using references in the box suggest what general business strategy Levi Strauss might adopt to try to improve its market position.

◆ Box 1.3 refers to business worries about high interest rates and a strong pound. Why can't the Bank of England simply cut interest rates, making British exports more competitive in foreign markets and reducing the cost of borrowing for British firms? To answer this question you may need to re-read the text around the box as well as the box itself.

Further reading

Jowsey, E. *100 Essay Plans for Economics* (Oxford: Oxford University Press, 1998). Offers a comprehensive summary of micro and macro issues, and is also a very useful revision guide.

Artis, M.J. (ed.) *The UK Economy* (14th ed.) (Oxford: Oxford University Press, 1996). Provides a thorough overview of UK economic performance and policy.

Ormerod, P. *Butterfly Economics* (London: Faber and Faber, 1998). Provides an interesting and critical perspective on modern economics, which has explicit implications for business.

For those with interests in *other* economies, a good starting point is the *OECD Economic Surveys* series. This offers regularly published updates on economic policy and performance in a large number of countries, including less developed economies and those in transition from central planning.

Using the Internet to study economics for business

The Internet, or more specifically the World Wide Web, provides a wealth of sources for anyone studying economics for business. At the end of each chapter, where appropriate, we suggest links to Internet sites that will help you to follow up on what you have learned. However, because in our experience a lot of time can be spent searching through the contents of sites (and as site addresses are prone to change) we do not think it worthwhile providing lengthy lists for you to work through. Instead, we highlight selected Internet sites that we think students new to economics will find especially useful. We provide a brief description of the contents of each recommended site, together with the relevant address. In any particular instance, should you find that the address we have given fails to provide a link, you should be able to locate the relevant site using a search engine. Better still, see the dedicated website that supports this book at: **http://www.palgrave.com/foundations/mulhearn**

■ Internet links

To complement the introductory chapter you have just read you might try the following:

The Economist offers a free digest of articles on contemporary economic issues, written in an accessible style for a wide audience. *The Economist* can be found at: **http://www.economist.com/**
The *OECD* also offers issue-based articles free of charge, together with useful data covering many economic issues and countries. The OECD is at: **http://www.oecd. org/**

CHAPTER **2**

The Market

Contents

Goods markets: Markets in which goods and services are bought and sold.

Quantity demanded: The amount of a good or service that consumers wish to purchase at a particular price, *ceteris paribus*.

Key issues

▶ Which factors determine the demand for a good or service?

▶ Which factors determine the supply of a good or service?

▶ How do demand and supply interact?

▶ How can market theory be applied to the real world?

▶ Which factors determine how consumers and business firms respond to price changes?

2.1 Introduction

In Chapter 1 we saw that an economy's scarce resources are allocated by the inter-action – in markets – of firms, consumers and government. In this chapter we offer a more detailed analysis of how the market is supposed to work in theory – and we see how real markets actually work in practice. We concentrate here on markets for goods and services: so-called **goods markets**. These are composed of two sets of economic agents: consumers who demand goods and services; and producers or firms who supply them. In order to understand how goods markets work, we need to begin by thinking about the respective aspirations and motivations of firms and consumers in the market process.

2.2 Consumers and demand

For a particular good or service, which factors influence the precise **quantity demanded** by consumers over a given time period? The obvious factor is *price*. If we assume that all other influences upon demand remain unchanged (the so-called *ceteris paribus* assumption), then higher prices will usually be associated with a lower quantity demanded. Similarly, lower prices will usually be associated with a greater quantity demanded. We can illustrate the *inverse* nature of the relationship between price and quantity demanded graphically.

In Fig. 2.1, the price of a good is depicted on the vertical axis, while the quantity demanded is depicted on the horizontal axis. At price P_1, the amount Q_1 is demanded. However, if the price increases to P_2, then the quantity demanded falls, or contracts, to Q_2. Conversely, if there is a reduction in price from P_1 to P_3, then the quantity demanded rises, or extends, to Q_3. If several such links between price and quantity demanded are established, it becomes possible to discern a *demand curve* (D_1), which shows *ceteris paribus* the *entire* relationship between price and quantity demanded for the particular good in question. It should be clear that the relationship is indeed an inverse one. In other words, higher prices are associated with **contractions** in the quantity demanded and lower prices prompt **extensions** in the quantity demanded. The convention in economics is to refer to **movements** along a single demand curve as either contractions (where the quantity demanded is falling) or extensions (where it is rising).

So the particular price of a good determines, over a given time period, the precise quantity demanded: 50 aircraft, 2 million cars, 50 million newspapers and so on. But, beyond price, there are other factors that have some bearing upon the **demand** for a good, again over a given time period. Here, demand refers not to a particular quantity and a particular price but to *all* possible prices and quantities demanded. Consider, for example, the influence of a change in the *incomes of consumers* on demand. If incomes rise, then *ceteris paribus* we would anticipate that the demand for a **normal good** would increase whatever its particular price. Conversely, a fall in consumer incomes would prompt a decrease in the demand for a normal good.

It is possible to illustrate the effects of a change in income on demand graphically. In Fig. 2.2, the demand curve D_1 represents the range of possible relationships between the price of a normal good and the quantity demanded at an initial level of consumers' income. For example, at price P_1 the quantity demanded is Q_1. Now, what happens if the incomes of consumers rise? The higher levels of income prompt consumers to increase their demand for the good. Note that this is the case *regardless of the level of the assumed price*: if it was higher or lower than our arbitrary selection,

Ceteris paribus: A commonly used assumption in economics. It means 'other things remaining the same'. Its purpose is to allow us to examine the influence of one factor at a time on something – in this case, price on quantity demanded – we are trying to explain or understand.

Contractions, extensions: Movements along a demand curve that result from a change in the price of the good are referred to as contractions or extensions in the quantity demanded.

Demand: The quantity of a good or service that consumers wish to purchase at each conceivable price (*ceteris paribus*).

Normal good: One for which demand increases when income increases.

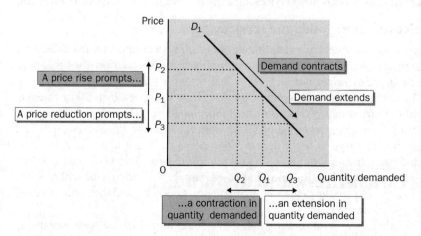

Fig. 2.1 The effect of a change in price on the quantity demanded of a particular good or service.

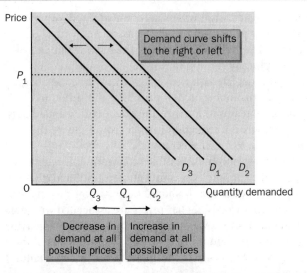

Fig. 2.2 The effect of a change in income on the demand for a normal good or service.

P_1, the outcome would be the same. The increase in *demand* that results from the higher level of consumer income is captured graphically by a *rightward shift* of the demand curve from D_1 to D_2. At each and every possible price, demand will increase. For example, at a price of P_1, quantity demanded increases to Q_2. Conversely, because it prompts a decrease in demand, a fall in consumers' income is associated with a leftward shift of the demand curve. In the diagram this is captured in the shift of the curve from D_1 to D_3. At price P_1 the quantity demanded is Q_3. To distinguish them from the extensions and contractions in the quantity demanded caused by a change in the price of a particular good, changes in demand that are associated with **shifts** in the demand curve are conventionally referred to as **increases** or **decreases** in demand.

In addition to changes in consumers' incomes, there are a range of other factors that also prompt shifts in the demand curve for a particular good or service and consequent increases or decreases in demand. Amongst the most important of these are the prices of other goods and services, and the preferences or tastes of consumers.

The prices of other goods and services

Some goods and services have **substitutes**: for example, viewing a rented video film at home might be thought of as substitute for a visit to the cinema to see the same film. Rented videos might not be *perfect* substitutes for the cinema – many people prefer the cinema 'experience', and new releases are shown exclusively in cinemas first – but they are certainly *close* substitutes. So, considering the demand for cinema seats, what would we expect to happen if the rental charges for videos increased? The answer is that, *ceteris paribus*, the demand for cinema seats should increase. In other words, following the logic of Fig. 2.2, the demand curve for cinema seats would shift to the right as demand by consumers increased. Similarly, if video rental charges fell, we would expect to see the demand for cinema seats decrease and the demand curve for them shift to the left.

On the other hand, some other goods and services are said to be **complementary**, in the sense that they are consumed jointly. For example, CDs are not much use on

Increases or decreases in demand: Refer to shifts of the demand curve.

Substitute: A good that can be substituted in place of another good.

Complement: A good that is used with another good.

their own; you need to have a CD player too. So, considering the demand for CDs, what would be the outcome of a fall in the price of CD players? The expectation is that, *ceteris paribus*, the demand for CDs would increase as more people demanded CD players and CDs too. In terms of Fig. 2.2, this would be reflected in a rightward shift of the demand curve (for CDs). Alternatively, a rise in the price of CD players would, *ceteris paribus*, lead to a fall in the demand for them and an associated decrease in the demand for CDs. In Fig. 2.2 this would be depicted by a leftward shift in the demand curve.

The preferences or tastes of consumers

At different times, consumers take different views as to the attractiveness of particular goods and services. In virtually every city in Europe over the last 20 years there has been an explosion in 'fast food': a relatively narrow product line of burgers, shakes, coffee and doughnuts, mostly served through the same restaurant chains. People clearly like fast food, so more and more of it is produced. There may, of course, come a time when it wanes in popularity. If and when this happens, the resources given over to its production will be reallocated to different uses. This is one example of the possible effects on demand (and resource allocation) of changes in consumer preferences, but other interesting cases are not hard to find. For instance, in recent years consumers have become much more aware of the environmental implications of some of their consumption decisions. This has prompted increases in the demand for goods and services that are, or are perceived to be, 'environmentally friendly' (demand curve shifts to the right). Political issues can also influence demand. During the years of apartheid in South Africa an effective consumer boycott of South African goods was enacted in other countries by people concerned to register their opposition to an odious regime (demand curve shifts to the left). Finally, in the UK in the 1990s, beef producers experienced a decrease in the demand for their output because of the BSE-related health worries of domestic consumers (demand curve shifts left).

A summary of the main factors influencing demand is given in Table 2.1.

2.3 Firms and supply

The second economic actor or agent in the market is the producer or firm. The role of the firm is to supply goods and services to the marketplace. So what influences firms' decisions in respect of the **quantity supplied** of a particular good or service?

Quantity supplied: The amount that firms wish to sell at a particular price, *ceteris paribus*.

Table 2.1 Factors that influence the demand for a particular good: a summary

Factor	Effect
• Price	Price changes cause movements along a demand curve. Price decreases are associated with extensions in the particular *quantity demanded*. Price increases are associated with contractions in the particular *quantity demanded*.
• Income • Tastes and preferences • Prices of other goods	A change in any one of these factors will cause a shift in the demand curve itself, with increases or decreases in demand at *every possible price*.

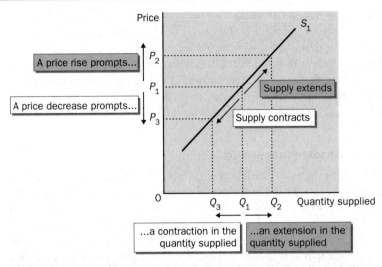

Fig. 2.3 The effect of a change in price on the quantity supplied of a particular good or service.

The question of price is again relevant here. The proposition is that the higher the price of a particular good, the greater the incentive for firms to supply it. What is the reasoning behind this statement? We know from Chapter 1 that the motive force of capitalism is self-interest. For firms this translates as profit. We shall see in later discussion that the standard assumption made is that firms seek to maximize the profits they earn, and they do this by producing as many profitable commodities as they can. The profit on an individual good is simply the price it fetches less the cost of its production. Now, it follows that if the price of a good increases then, *ceteris paribus*, more of it will become profitable to produce. Thus a higher price for a particular good will prompt firms to raise the quantity supplied.

The relationship between the price of a good in a market and the quantity supplied over a given time period can be illustrated graphically. In Fig. 2.3, as for our discussion of demand, price is depicted on the vertical axis. The horizontal axis depicts the quantity supplied. At price P_1, firms are motivated to supply Q_1 of the good or service in question. If price increases to P_2, then the quantity supplied extends to Q_2. Conversely, if price falls from P_1 to P_3, then the quantity supplied contracts from Q_1 to Q_3. If we examine a range of such links between price and quantity supplied, it becomes possible to distinguish a *supply curve* (S_1), which shows the *entire* relationship between price and the quantity supplied. It can be seen that the relationship is *positive* in nature: that is, price and quantity supplied move in the same direction. Increases in price prompt **extensions** in the quantity supplied; decreases in price prompt **contractions** in the quantity supplied (as for demand, the convention is that **movements** along a given supply curve are referred to as extensions or contractions).

So the particular price of a good determines, over a given time period, the precise quantity supplied: 5 ships, 2 million burgers, 5 million canned drinks and so on. But, as for demand, there are other factors beyond price that have some bearing upon the **supply** of a good, again over a given time period. Here, supply refers not to a particular quantity and a particular price but to *all* possible prices and quantities supplied. We have already noted that firms are interested in the profit yielded by their output, and that this is a function of both price and the cost of production. It follows that lower production costs will occasion increases in supply. If, for example, firms pro-

Contractions, extensions: Movements along a supply curve that result from a change in the price of a good are referred to as contractions or extensions in the quantity supplied.

Supply: The quantity of a good or service that producers wish to sell at each conceivable price, *ceteris paribus*.

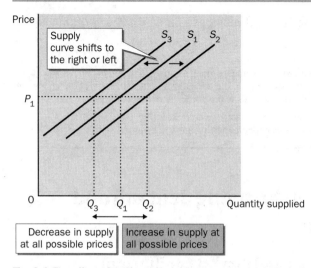

Fig. 2.4 The effect of a change in production costs on the supply of a particular good or service.

ducing baked beans find that the costs of **factor inputs** such as tin, beans, sugar or tomatoes fall, then, *ceteris paribus,* they will be motivated to supply more tins of baked beans at each and every possible price. This is because the higher ranges of output that were formerly unprofitable are less costly and now yield a profit.

The nature of the link between the cost of production and supply can be illustrated graphically. In Fig. 2.4 the supply curve S_1 represents a set of possible relationships between price and quantity supplied with a given set of production costs. Operating with this supply curve, it can be seen that at, say, price P_1, firms are motivated to supply Q_1. The effect of a fall in production costs is to shift the supply curve to the right from S_1 to S_2. Operating with the new supply curve, S_2, and the given price P_1, it can be seen that firms would wish to supply an increased output Q_2 to the market. Note that this would be the case regardless of the (given) price of the good. In other words, at each and every possible price, supply would increase. Conversely, an increase in production costs would reduce the number of profitable tins of beans that could be produced at any given price: so, if costs rise, firms will be motivated to decrease supply. In Fig. 2.4, higher production costs have the effect of shifting the supply curve to the left (from S_1 to S_3). With S_3 operating, at a price P_1 firms are motivated to supply Q_3 to the market. Note that the terms **increase** and **decrease** in supply refer to changes arising from **shifts** of supply curves, as opposed to extensions and contractions in the quantity supplied, which arise, as noted, from price related movements along given supply curves.

Changes in production costs that shift the supply curve for a good or service can also result from a change in technology. In terms of Fig. 2.4, an improvement in technology that reduces production costs will shift the supply curve to the right. This is because, at each possible price, more units of output become profitable, thus prompting increases in supply. For example, car production was revolutionized by Henry Ford's introduction of the mechanized assembly line in the early years of the twentieth century. Ford didn't invent the car, but his new method of production vastly reduced the cost of producing cars, first in America and subsequently worldwide, leading to a vast increase in supply (the supply curve shifted to the right). A summary of the main factors influencing supply is given in Table 2.2.

Factor inputs: Any goods and services used in the process of production.

Increases or decreases in supply: Refer to shifts of the supply curve.

Table 2.2 Factors that influence the supply of a particular good: a summary

Factor	Effect
• Price	Price changes cause movements along a supply curve. Higher prices are associated with extensions in the particular *quantity supplied*. Lower prices are associated with contractions in the particular *quantity supplied*.
• Input costs • Technology	A change in either of these factors will cause a shift in the supply curve itself, with increases or decreases in supply at *every possible price*.

2.4 The market: bringing demand and supply together

The equilibrium price and market equilibrium

Having reviewed the two sides of the market in isolation, we are now in a position to see how they interact: it is this *interplay* between consumers and firms – or demand and supply – that produces market conditions satisfactory to both. The necessary analysis is easiest to conduct graphically. Fig. 2.5 represents the market for a particular good or service. Price is again depicted on the vertical axis, while the quantities demanded and supplied are depicted on the horizontal axis. At price P_1 notice that the quantity demanded (Q_1), as given by the demand curve D_1, *exactly matches* the quantity supplied (also Q_1), as given by the supply curve S_1. Thus at price P_1 the market is said to **clear** in the sense that, in any given time period, all goods supplied are actually sold. This situation appears to have some intrinsic merit as there are no gluts or shortages in the market: no consumers are left with demand unsatisfied, and no firms are left with stocks they cannot sell.

Clear: A market is said to clear when all goods or services supplied in it are sold.

Equilibrium price: The price at which the quantity demanded equals the quantity supplied.

The price P_1 can also be shown to be an **equilibrium price**. In economics the term 'equilibrium' is used to describe a state of balance from which there is *no tendency to change*. How then does P_1 prompt an equilibrium? Consider the prices P_2 and P_3, also shown in Fig. 2.5. At P_2, the quantity supplied (Q_2) exceeds the quantity

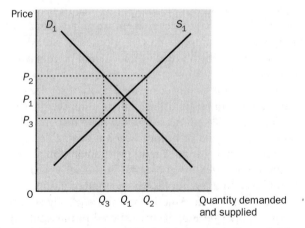

Fig. 2.5 The interaction of demand and supply in the market for a particular good.

demanded (Q_3), and there is said to be **excess supply** in the market. Now, because they are saddled with unsold stocks, this situation leaves some firms dissatisfied (those consumers in the market at price P_2 are able to buy all they desire, so we judge them content). In order to change things, the most obvious option open to firms is to reduce the price they charge. As this happens and price starts to fall below P_2, the quantity demanded begins to extend and the quantity supplied contracts. Eventually, as price falls to P_1, quantity demanded will have extended and quantity supplied contracted sufficiently to eliminate excess supply entirely, leaving demand and supply perfectly matched. We can draw an important general implication from this analysis:

Any price above P_1 will be a disequilibrium price so that there is a tendency for change to occur. Excess supply will encourage firms to initiate price reductions until demand and supply are harmonized.

When this happens, the market itself is said to be in equilibrium.

So much for prices above P_1, but what of those below it? Consider a price below P_1: P_3, for example. At price P_3 there is **excess demand** over the supply that firms choose to make available. Now, while firms are content with this situation (as they sell all they wish to offer to the market), the same cannot be said of consumers. At P_3, consumers wish to buy Q_2 of the good or service in question but only Q_3 is available: the demand of some consumers is left unsatisfied. Now, as their output is rapidly and avidly swallowed up by consumers, firms will be aware that there is excess demand in the market. This results in the price being 'bid up'. Notice that, as price rises above P_3, the quantity demanded begins to contract and the quantity supplied extends. However, it is only when price reaches P_1 that the excess demand in the market is entirely eliminated. Again, we can draw an important general implication from this analysis:

Any price below P_1 will be a disequilibrium price. Excess demand will encourage firms to initiate price increases until demand and supply are harmonized.

Moreover, it is now evident that P_1 is in fact a unique equilibrium price in the market depicted in Fig. 2.5. All other possible prices are associated with either excess supply or excess demand conditions, which prompt spontaneous movements back towards *the* equilibrium price.

Excess supply: Occurs when the quantity supplied exceeds the quantity demanded at some given price.

Excess demand: Occurs when the quantity demanded exceeds the quantity supplied at some given price.

Changes in the equilibrium price and market equilibrium

Let us now think about how the plans of consumers and firms are harmonized following changes in market circumstances. We shall do this using examples of the interaction of demand and supply in three 'real world' markets: those for *canned tuna fish*, for *coffee*, and for the metal *palladium*. Although the outcomes in each case are different, these examples demonstrate that markets do have the ability to respond to changed circumstances, and can readily produce new equilibrium positions.

The UK market for canned tuna fish grew from 1.3 million cases annually in the early 1980s to 9 million cases by the mid 1990s (a case contains 48 of the familiar 200 g cans). The market continues to increase by about 10 per cent per year (*Source*: *The Grocer* 12 April 1997). There is little doubt that this expansion is demand led. Research by the industry shows that consumers see tuna as a low-cost, high-protein food and an attractive alternative to meat. Diagrammatically, the increase in demand

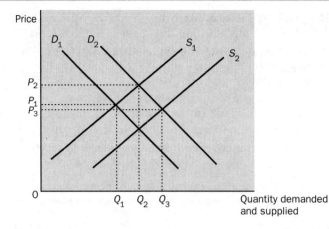

Fig. 2.6 A stylized representation of recent developments in the UK market for canned tuna fish.

can be represented by a rightward shift of the demand curve in Fig. 2.6, from D_1 to D_2. The outcome, *ceteris paribus*, would be an increase in the equilibrium price from P_1 to P_2 and a new equilibrium quantity Q_2 bought and sold. However, demand changes are not the end of the matter. Over recent years most major tuna producers have invested heavily in new modernized plant and equipment. Recall that technological improvements in a market have the effect of shifting the supply curve to the right (from S_1 to S_2). When we incorporate this feature into Fig. 2.6, the end result is given by the intersection of D_2 and S_2: an equilibrium price of P_3 and an equilibrium quantity of Q_3. This is broadly consistent with what has happened in the tuna market: a marked increase in the equilibrium quantity demanded and supplied with relatively little movement in price.

Recent developments in the world coffee market appear rather less benign. These are described in Box 2.1. In reading the box you should be able to discern *five* factors that have served to disrupt the market. Four of these are on the supply side, and all serve to *reduce* supply. They are:

- bad weather in Central and South America
- strikes by coffee bean farmers in Columbia (the world's second largest coffee exporter)
- higher input costs for Colombian coffee farmers as the cocaine trade competes for labour
- insect problems.

On the demand side, speculation in coffee (buying it in the anticipation that prices will rise) is also blamed for unwelcome price movements. The effects of these developments are summarized in Fig. 2.7. The supply influences produce a leftward shift of the supply curve (from S_1 to S_2), while rising speculative demand shifts the demand curve to the right (from D_1 to D_2). The end result is the 'surge' in the price of coffee anticipated in Box 2.1 (from P_1 to P_2). Incidentally, note that although our summary of influences on supply (see Table 2.2) mentions only technology and input costs, these can also be taken as proxies for some of the 'coffee specific' supply factors mentioned here. Thus the effects of bad weather and the broca pest are the equivalent of temporary *adverse* movements in technology: in their presence, a given

Box 2.1

There's not a lot of coffee in Brazil this year: prices will rise as farmers are ground down

By Phil Davison

Brace yourself for a surge in the price of coffee. And you can blame it on Colombian cocaine producers, a plague of insects, Brazilian showers or financial speculators.

Experts predict your coffee break is about to cost you considerably more within the next few days as supermarkets stick higher price tags on coffee beans, both ground and instant. They are distinctly less clear about the reason.

What we do know is that the price that the big roasting corporations pay to producers has rocketed 40 per cent since December and is about to be reflected on your supermarket shelves ...

Why? Take your pick. One factor is certainly bad weather during the recent harvesting season in Central and South America – particularly the world's top two producers, Brazil and Colombia. It is likely to cut their exports and further reduce dwindling stocks in the consumer nations.

Then there are reports of a pending strike by Colombia's coffee farmers. They are angered by the fact that the world price rise has not been passed on to them by their National Coffee Federation ...

On his farm ... Colombian coffee grower Fabio Zuluaga notes another problem. 'An experienced coffee bean picker earns around twice the minimum wage during the November–December picking season,' he said. 'But the traditional pickers can now earn five times that much by picking cocoa leaves for the narco-traffickers.'

Like other Colombian growers, Mr Zuluaga has also been battling a plague of insects known as broca, barely visible to the human eye but deadly to the coffee bean ...

But the International Coffee Organization's Director, Celsius Lodder, admitted that there was some confusion. 'The fundamentals are not explaining price variations 100 per cent,' he said ... He appeared to be referring to the speculation in the coffee futures market.

Source: The Independent 5 February 1997

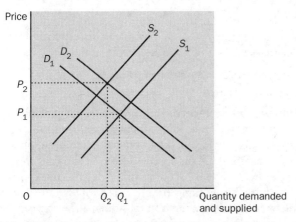

Fig. 2.7 An approximation of changes in demand and supply conditions in the world coffee market in 1997.

assemblage of coffee-growing equipment and infrastructure yields a lower output than would otherwise be the case.

Finally, we come to the market in palladium. As Box 2.2 explains, palladium is used to make components for portable electronic goods such as mobile phones. The demand for these goods and therefore for palladium itself continues to grow strongly. Unfortunately, however, supply has been constrained by the unreliability of the

Electronics industry warns of palladium shortage

Warning was given yesterday of a severe shortage of palladium, a metal essential for some components of portable electronic equipment such as mobile telephones and laptop computers, as well as for catalytic converters that remove pollutants from car exhausts.

'Palladium use continues to grow very strongly but production lags well behind. Soon after 2000 we could be in a very difficult situation unless industrial users take heed now,' said Mike Steel, research director at Johnson Matthey, the world's biggest platinum and palladium marketing group.

He said consumers had been relying on

Russia's palladium stocks to fill a substantial gap between demand and supply. JM believes these stocks will run out soon after the end of the century.

Mr Steel said there had been a preview of potential trouble earlier this year when Russia, which exports 70 per cent of the world's palladium, stopped exporting the metal for six months. This helped to drive the price to its highest level for eighteen years ... Although it has fallen back since Russian exports restarted, the price remains roughly double its level at this time last year.

Source: *Financial Times* 19 November 1997

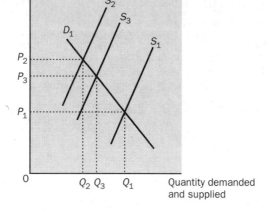

Fig. 2.8 The stylized effects of short-term changes in the supply of palladium.

world's major palladium producer, Russia. Indeed, Russian exports of palladium have actually been wholly suspended for a time. Such supply difficulties have seen palladium prices driven to record highs. In Fig. 2.8, the severe reduction in supply is represented by the decisive leftward shift of the supply curve from S_1 to S_2, prompting an increase in price from P_1 to P_2. As Box 2.2 reports, although Russian exports have since resumed, prices remain relatively high. In effect, the supply curve has begun to shift to the right again but only slowly (say to S_3, with price P_3).

2.5 Applying market analysis 1: the example of economic integration in the European Union

If markets can work as our theoretical arguments have so far suggested – prompting equilibria in the face of various forms of change and disruption – we might expect to see them promoted and supported in many 'real world' situations. Using policies adopted by the European Union (EU) towards the organization of markets as an example, let us now see if this is the case. In fact our findings will demonstrate that the EU appears to be somewhat *ambiguous* in its attitudes towards the free market. On the one hand, it has introduced the so-called **single market programme**, which seeks to use the market mechanism in a positive way, harnessing it to coordinate the production and consumption of many goods and services across Europe. On the other hand, however, in the market for agricultural goods in particular, the EU prefers intervention to *laissez-faire* or free enterprise. In what follows, we use the principles of demand and supply to explain such ambiguity.

The EU is currently composed of 15 member states. These are:

- Austria
- Belgium
- Denmark
- Finland
- France
- Germany
- Greece
- Ireland
- Italy
- Luxembourg
- Netherlands
- Portugal
- Spain
- Sweden
- UK.

> **Concept**
>
> ### The single market programme
>
> The single market programme is an attempt to create, across the EU, a unified market in goods, services, capital and labour. In an economic sense, national boundaries inside the EU were abolished at the end of 1992.

A central aim of the EU is to enhance the economic prospects of its members. This is to be achieved by binding their separate national territories together to form a *single market* in Europe. The result will be the creation of a unified economic space that, it is anticipated, will enjoy the kind of cohesiveness currently evident inside the separate national economies. Consumption and production decisions, decisions about where to live and work, decisions about where to invest – *all* will begin to be taken more and more at the European level. Technically, the single market has been in existence since the end of 1992. However, it is one thing to create the framework for a market; whether the single market actually flourishes will depend on the actions of European firms, consumers and state agencies.

The single market was born out of a concern that, over the 1970s and early 1980s, the existing form of the so-called European 'common market' was unable sufficiently to help its members to match the economic performances and potential of other advanced nations: the United States and Japan in particular. The source of the problem was thought to be the increasingly *fragmented* nature of the European economy. The European 'common market' was an economic space that provided for the free movement of goods and services between member nations. Since its creation in 1957 as part of the *Treaty of Rome*, citizens in member states all over Europe could buy and sell freely to one another, without the hindrance of any barriers to trade such as tariffs.[1] Commercial freedom of this form should in theory have brought substantial benefits. German citizens would not have to buy goods and services from mostly German firms, they could buy *just as easily* from French firms if these offered better or cheaper products. Similarly, (say) Italian and Dutch firms would be able to sell wherever in Europe their products merited a demand. In this way, a more open *European* market would allow European consumers to buy from European firms that offered them the best value. Moreover, because the best firms would tend to be rewarded with more custom, they would thrive at the expense of their inferior rivals. The long-term effect of the 'common market' would therefore be the encouragement and promotion of the best producers: Europe would become a more productive and competitive place.

Laissez-faire: Describes a situation in which there is little or no state interference in the market economy. Here all decisions are taken by individual firms and consumers.

[1] A tariff is a tax on internationally traded goods – see Chapter 13, section 13.5.

How then did the concern over the fragmentation of the European economy arise? The problem was that, in some important respects, Europe appeared by the late 1970s and early 1980s to be *retreating back* into its national economic components. For example, it was felt that the free movement of goods and services was increasingly hampered by various kinds of what we might term 'administrative' trade barrier, such as those concerned with national standards for certain classes of good. For example, both the Danish and German governments have, at times in the past, sought to prevent their citizens from importing foreign beers that did not match established domestic production standards. In addition, it was evident that despite their apparent commitment to European integration, national governments themselves tended to purchase along very nationalistic lines. Thus the British government usually bought from British firms, the French government from French firms, and so on. In this context the single market, introduced in 1992, is an attempt to *refresh the integration project*. Its intention is to sweep away all forms of trade barrier in the markets for goods and services and, in addition, to allow the free movement of labour and capital in Europe too. By opening up economic opportunity in this way, it is hoped that the single market will re-establish the EU's competitive edge *vis-à-vis* the United States and Japan.

Box 2.3

Brussels aims to speed pace of harmonization

Deborah Hargreaves reports

The European Commission is preparing an ambitious push to speed up efforts to harmonize European legislation on financial services, in a bid to meet the 2005 deadline for the creation of a single market in the sector.

There is clearly ground to make up. The fastest piece of legislation approved so far in the sector took 25 months. Even the directive that passed most quickly was too late. It was a three-page piece of legislation on how banks create market risks, aimed at enabling European banks to improve their competitiveness. The US agreed the same measure at the same time, passing it onto its statute books in just six months.

By the time the EU countries had reached agreement, all the relevant business had passed to the US. 'Our banks were very upset about it and were screaming at us, but now they've lost business and there's no way to get it back,' one Commission official said.

Banks and investors are urging the Commission to get a framework in place for a single market in financial services as they want to take advantage of the euro and sell across borders. 'We want this to move forward and we're very disappointed if we see delays at a major policy level and in the detail,' said Jaap Kamp, EU liaison officer at ABN Amro.

The chief executives of six leading EU banks wrote to EU economic and finance ministers in June urging them to agree a joint approach to online banking and how this can be integrated into the EU's overall strategy on electronic commerce. The European Commission will bring out an advisory paper in November to outline its views . . .

Over the next few months, the Commission will put together a detailed analysis of the benefits of an integrated EU capital market to try to inject more political momentum into agreement on legislation. The Commission wants to present governments with figures that show how much the EU is losing out by having a fragmented market for financial services. At another level, it is also compiling figures on the cost of mortgages, for example, in different member countries as well as wholesale financial products such as syndicated loans, to try and put pressure on governments to move towards a single market.

Frits Blokstein, single market commissioner, said recently countries were losing out by not having a single, integrated market for financial services: 'now is the time to accelerate efforts and create momentum'.

Source: *Financial Times* 5 July 2000

Box 2.3 offers a brief discussion of one particular European market where the benefits of the single market programme are apparent in theory but where progress needs to be speeded up. This is the market in financial services, such as banking and insurance. When national barriers in financial service provision disappear, consumers will certainly gain: a greater choice of services will become available at lower prices. The most efficient producers offering the best services will also gain: they will be rewarded with more custom. The only losers are likely to be weaker firms who are currently able to stay in business only because their customers find it difficult to access markets in other parts of the EU.

As Box 2.3 indicates, EU banks are concerned that the 2005 deadline for the creation of a single market in financial services may not be met. Continued fragmentation in this sector would permit the accentuation of two sets of difficulties. First, EU residents will still be denied the benefits of integration: for example, the box mentions intra-EU differences in the cost of mortgages. Second, the EU financial sector as a whole will continue to struggle against large, fully integrated rival providers: the box reports that the USA has recently secured business that EU banks might otherwise have had some claim on.

We can express the anticipated gains from a European financial services market using our knowledge of demand and supply. In diagrammatic terms, the movement towards a single market in financial services in Europe would resemble the case depicted in Fig. 2.9. Here, because the market becomes composed only of more efficient firms (the weaker ones having lost custom and left the market), the supply curve shifts to the right from S_1 to S_2. *Ceteris paribus*, this is associated with an increase in the quantity of financial services demanded and supplied (from Q_1 to Q_2) and a fall in price (from P_1 to P_2). Note that the origin of the movement in the supply curve is consistent with our earlier analysis. The fact that the market is served by only the most efficient firms means that the cost base of firms on average has fallen. This is the equivalent of a reduction in input costs – which, as we know from our theoretical discussion, shifts the supply curve to the right. In essence, the single market programme is about promoting changes such as this in as many markets in Europe as possible. However, as our next case illustrates, in some markets there is relatively little room for manoeuvre.

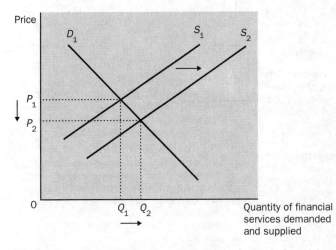

Fig. 2.9 The effect of the creation of a European market in financial services.

The European car industry provides a somewhat contrasting example of the potential of the single market to effect major changes in the organization of production and consumption in the EU. As Box 2.4 makes clear, the central problem currently facing Europe's car makers is essentially that of excess supply. In section 2.4 and Fig. 2.5 we argued that the usual reaction to excess supply in a market is for producers to lower prices until a market-clearing equilibrium is attained. There is some evidence (from the box) that this is happening in the European car market. However, there appear to be limits to the extent to which car makers are prepared to lower prices because of the tightness of profit margins. A second possibility is for car makers to decrease supply. Box 2.4 suggests that this too is something that they have been trying: for example, by introducing short-term working and partial factory shut-downs.

Box 2.4

Engine of demand splutters: mergers and joint ventures should top European carmakers' agendas as they face overcapacity and declining profits

It has been an inauspicious start to the year for Europe's carmakers . . . Excess production capacity and the poor outlook for car sales has reinforced the belief that Europe's car industry requires *structural changes to balance supply and demand*. Manufacturers have already taken limited steps to reduce costs by collaborating with each other. But the improbability of a long-term upturn in the market means that much more drastic steps – including big mergers – are again on the agenda.

'The essential problem is that long-run demand is not matched to long-run supply and Europe's carmakers have been too sluggish to react to the new realities in the market,' says Professor Garel Rhys, a specialist in motor industry economics at Cardiff Business School.

In spite of Western Europe's economic recovery after the recession, demand for new cars has been stalled . . . Lower demand and the need, in many cases, for expensive special offers to sell cars have been reflected in poor profitability. 'Europe's car market has become saturated. Demand is now on a replacement-only basis, and even that is fragile,' says Mr Graham Morris, of Volkswagen's Audi subsidiary.

Excess capacity is the main problem. Europe's carmakers have been loath to rationalize for fear of labour unrest, and governments have exerted pressure to minimize politically sensitive redundancies.

Many European carmakers have opted for short-term working and partial shutdowns to counter excess supply. But their efforts have been undermined by new capacity at other car companies. Toyota, Honda and Nissan, the three Japanese car companies which have set up in the UK, want to expand capacity to 650 000 vehicles a year by 1999 from 500 000 today.

The obvious answer to overcapacity, slack demand and tougher competition is rationalization and mergers. But Europe's carmakers have moved mountains to keep their independence . . . The industry's economic importance – it can contribute almost a sixth of a country's gross domestic product – means any merger is bound to have a big macro-economic impact. So not only private shareholders, but also trade unions and governments, are reluctant to make concessions when jobs and earnings are at stake.

In the absence of mergers, manufacturers have focused on reducing their production costs to compete with lower-priced rivals. 'Lean production' techniques, involving a plethora of measures to streamline organization on the shopfloor, have become ubiquitous.

Other tactics to achieve savings have included simplifying model ranges around a simple number of basic 'platforms' for vehicles and wresting price cuts from suppliers.

While such attempts to lower manufacturers' costs are understandable, motor industry analysts doubt [these] will be enough to overcome the long-term problems of excess capacity and insufficient demand.

Source: *Financial Times* 15 February 1996 (emphases added)

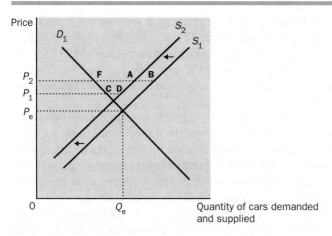

Fig. 2.10 Dealing with the problem of excess supply in the European car market.

Fig. 2.10 provides a demand and supply illustration of both options. Let us suppose that the market would be in equilibrium at price P_e and quantity Q_e, with demand curve D_1 and supply curve S_1. At price P_2, however, there is excess supply equal to FB. This is the disequilibrium position, which has been the focus for change. Short-term working and partial factory shut-downs, decreasing supply from S_1 to S_2, have reduced excess demand from FB to FA. As, in addition, prices have been bid down – in this illustration from P_2 to P_1 – excess supply has been squeezed still further: from FA to CD. The difficulty, however, is that – to date – these measures have been insufficient to deal *fully* with the problem of excess supply in the market. The longer-term solution suggested in the box is for the weaker firms to leave the industry or be taken over by the stronger ones, thus effecting a more sizeable reduction in supply in the long term (shifting S_2 further to the left and squeezing the remaining excess supply CD out completely) and leaving the European car market very much closer to, or even at, equilibrium. The main reason why this is not happening, or is happening only slowly, is that – as the box indicates – Europe's car makers, backed by national governments and powerful trade unions, are reluctant to concede their independence. In the European car industry, then, the single market appears less likely to have the sort of impact anticipated in financial services.

While car making and financial service provision offer examples of industries where, in its single market programme, the EU seeks to reap the benefits of *laissez-faire*, in other areas *intervention* in markets is the preferred option. As noted, heavily state-managed agricultural production in Europe is the most obvious and – with associated claims of 'butter mountains' and 'wine lakes' – notorious case. We can again use supply and demand here to follow what is going on.

Agriculture in the EU is regulated by the Common Agricultural Policy (CAP). The CAP is actually a determined attempt to *prevent* the operation of market forces in European agriculture. This, of course, must mean that a free market in agriculture would produce outcomes that the EU does not want. In effect, the CAP works to preserve the kind of localized production that, for the most part, the EU would like to sweep away in its single market programme. If the CAP were abolished, a free market in European agriculture would tend to drive less efficient farmers out of business and, in the search for **economies of scale**, encourage the creation of much

Concept

Economies of scale

Economies of scale arise when a larger output is produced without a proportionately equal increase in the costs of production. In agriculture this might involve, for example, the more intensive use of existing machinery as a farm extends its cultivated acreage. More output results but no new machines are required to help produce it, so unit costs fall.

larger farms. These would be necessary to compete with low-cost food producers outside Europe, who – given free market conditions – would be able to export greater volumes of output to meet European demand. So why does the EU wish to preserve relatively small-scale, fragmented and less efficient localized production? The simple answer is that it wants to protect the jobs and incomes of its farmers.[2] Let us see how this is achieved.

Fig. 2.11 depicts the EU market for a particular agricultural commodity, say cereals. The supply and demand curves therefore represent the dispositions of EU producers and consumers respectively. Assuming there is no possibility of trade between the EU and the rest of the world, the equilibrium in this market is given by price P_e and quantity Q_e. Now, let us also assume that cereals can be produced more cheaply in the rest of the world (which, as it happens, *is* actually the case) This means, of course, that the prevailing world price for cereals is lower than P_e. Thus, if free trade between the EU and the rest of the world were possible, European consumers could buy their cereals at the lower world price. In this case, the quantity demanded would be Q_4, but European producers would offer only Q_1. At the world price, therefore, cereal imports into the EU would amount to $Q_4 - Q_1$. In a completely free market for cereals, then, the relatively low world price would appear to benefit European consumers, who would pay less and, collectively, consume more. However, the EU's cereal output would fall and so, presumably, would the number of EU farmers in the now 'world articulated' cereals market.

This means that, for the CAP to fulfil its noted objective – the retention of the jobs and incomes of EU farmers – it must insulate or protect EU agricultural markets from those of the rest of the world. This done by setting a *target price* for each agricultural commodity to be protected (not all are). Target prices are decided on the basis of farm production costs in the EU, with a 'mark-up' to allow for profit. Clearly, in Fig. 2.11, there is a big difference between the world price for cereals and the EU's target price, which means that EU consumers must be prevented from obtaining cereals at the lower world price (because they would not then buy EU cereals). This is done by the imposition of a tariff on cereal imports into the EU. A tariff is a tax on traded

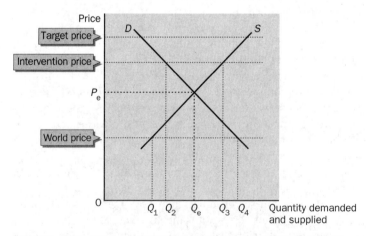

Fig. 2.11 Market intervention: the case of the Common Agricultural Policy.

---

[2] The origins of the CAP are to be found in the agricultural policies of the major European nations before and after the Second World War. These laid stress on self-sufficiency in food production.

goods, and in this case it has the effect of raising the price of the EU's cereal imports close to the level of the target price (if importers have to pay a tax on cereals they ship to the EU, the assumption is that they will pass the costs of the tax on to EU consumers in the form of higher prices).

In addition to the target price, the EU also sets an intervention price for the agricultural commodities it wishes to protect. This is a minimum price that the EU guarantees its farmers for the output they produce. In Fig. 2.11, note that at both the intervention price and the higher target price there is excess supply in the EU cereal market. As we have seen, disequilibrium prices of this sort are unstable. The accumulating unsold stocks they are left with should prompt farmers to sell at lower prices until the equilibrium price P_e is attained. To prevent this happening – and to prevent EU farmers from leaving the market – *the EU itself purchases whatever excess supply arises at the intervention price*. In Fig. 2.11 this amounts to $Q_3 - Q_2$. Purchases of this kind are the source of the infamous food 'mountains', for which the EU is often criticized. Because there is no demand for these agricultural surpluses, they are simply stored indefinitely at the EU's expense.

In summary, the effect of the CAP is to raise the prices of agricultural commodities in the EU. This encourages more farmers to remain in business than would be the case in a free market, fully integrated with the rest of the world. The positive outcome of the policy is therefore a higher number of farmers supported by subsidized incomes. The less attractive implications of the policy include the higher prices that EU consumers have to pay for agricultural produce, the sheer cost of the policy (alone it consumes over half of the EU's total budget), and its distortion of world trade (as, for example, the rest of the world has its capacity to export to the EU restricted).

On the basis of the examples reviewed in this section, the EU appears to have a rather inconsistent view as to the usefulness of the market mechanism. For industry in general, it anticipates that the articulation of market processes at the widest level will serve to enhance Europe's competitiveness in the world economy. However, for agriculture, the same market processes are judged to be harmful. Why the difference? The answer lies in the conditions of industry and agriculture in the EU *relative* to their conditions in the rest of the world. European industry *already* enjoys a level of overall competitiveness that is equivalent or very close to the world's best, and it is *currently* integrated into international markets in the same general way that, for example, American and Japanese industries are. Further progress for European industry might well be predicated on the market-based improvement of an existing highly creditable performance.

However, when compared with the rest of the world, the relative performance of the agricultural sector in the EU is generally inferior. The integration of European agriculture into the world market is therefore difficult for the EU to accept because it would expose the uncompetitiveness of European farmers, and many of them would be driven out of business. The reason why this has not been allowed to happen has much to do with the political and lobbying strength of agricultural interests in the EU: witness, for example, the familiar spectacle of European capital cities clogged by the tractors or sheep of demonstrating farmers. The agricultural community is an able defender of the CAP, while those who have most to gain from its removal – EU consumers who would benefit from lower food prices – are largely without a collective voice.

Price elasticity of demand: The proportionate (or percentage) change in the quantity demanded of a good divided by the proportionate (or percentage) change in its price that brought it about.

2.6 Elasticity in the market

The concept of elasticity is the final element to be introduced to our analysis of the operation of markets. What is elasticity? In sections 2.2 and 2.3 we reviewed the respective sets of factors that determine the demand for and supply of a particular good or service. For example, following the usual *ceteris paribus* assumption, higher prices reduce the quantity demanded, and lower prices push it up (the analytical terms we used were contractions and extensions of the quantity demanded), but what about the *strength of response*? When, for example, the price of a good increases by say 5 per cent, by *how much* does the quantity demanded contract – about the same, more, much more, or less? This is clearly a significant question, both for economists who want to understand how markets work, and particularly for firms who are active participants in them. If a firm is considering a price change for a product it makes, it will want to know the likely effect of the change. Will a price reduction allow it to sell a lot more units of output or only a few more, and what will be the effect upon the overall level of revenue? The concept of elasticity provides answers to such questions.

We conceptualize the response of supply and demand to other economic changes as the *elasticity* of supply or demand. When the quantity supplied or demanded is relatively unresponsive to a particular stimulus – such as a price change – they are said to be *inelastic*. Conversely, when they are more responsive and change substantially they are said to be *elastic*. We define and extend these categories more carefully below.

2.7 Price elasticity of demand

The most commonly used form of elasticity is **price elasticity of demand**. This measures the responsiveness of the quantity demanded of a particular good or service to changes in its price. More formally, the price elasticity of demand of a good or service (P_{ed}) is measured by the proportionate change in its quantity demanded divided by the proportionate change in price that brings this about:

$$P_{ed} = \frac{\text{Proportionate change in quantity demanded}}{\text{Proportionate change in price}} \tag{2.1}$$

Price elasticity of demand can be illustrated diagrammatically. In Fig. 2.12 we show a hypothetical market for new cars. Two among many possible prices are considered, together with the respective quantities demanded at each price. Now, we wish to use the concept of elasticity in this market, which means – following the equation above – that we have to find proportionate changes in quantity demanded and price. But there is a snag here. The proportionate change in price will depend upon whether we are considering a price *increase* (from £12 000 to £15 000 per car) or a *decrease* (from £15 000 to £12 000). When price increases, the proportionate change is one quarter, or 25 per cent (an increase of £3000 over the original price of £12 000). But if price falls from £15 000 to £12 000, then the proportionate change is one fifth, or 20 per cent (a decrease of £3000 on the original price of £15 000). In order to overcome this problem and arrive at the same number for a proportionate price change in either direction, we express the change in price as a proportion or percentage of the *average* price over the range in which we are interested. In this case, the average price is

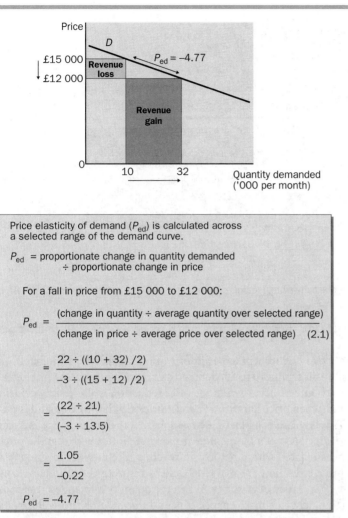

Price elasticity of demand (P_{ed}) is calculated across a selected range of the demand curve.

P_{ed} = proportionate change in quantity demanded ÷ proportionate change in price

For a fall in price from £15 000 to £12 000:

$$P_{ed} = \frac{\text{(change in quantity} \div \text{average quantity over selected range)}}{\text{(change in price} \div \text{average price over selected range)}} \quad (2.1)$$

$$= \frac{22 \div ((10 + 32)/2)}{-3 \div ((15 + 12)/2)}$$

$$= \frac{(22 \div 21)}{(-3 \div 13.5)}$$

$$= \frac{1.05}{-0.22}$$

$$P_{ed} = -4.77$$

Fig. 2.12 Price elasticity of demand in the market for new cars. (Note that, although our calculation is for a decrease in price, the same figure of 4.77 would result for a price increase. This is because we have expressed the change in price and quantity as a proportion of their average values over the selected range.)

£13 500 ((£12 000 + £15 000)/2). We follow the same procedure when calculating proportionate changes in quantity demanded.

We now have a slightly more sophisticated means of calculating price elasticity of demand. In Fig. 2.12, following equation (2.1), we arrive at a value for price elasticity of demand in our example of −4.77 (correct to two decimal places). But what does this number tell us? In fact, it indicates that, for the range in question, demand is **price elastic**: in other words, the price change (in either direction) will produce a *more than proportionate response* in the quantity demanded. Notice also that, as price is cut, there is an increase in the net revenue earned on the sale of cars. This increase is derived from the combination of the area of revenue loss (£3000 × 10 000 cars = £30 million per month) and the area of revenue gain (£12 000 × 22 000 cars = £264 million per month), and amounts to £234 million per month. For a price increase

Price elastic: Describes a situation in which the proportionate change in quantity demanded is greater than the proportionate change in price; elasticity is greater than 1.

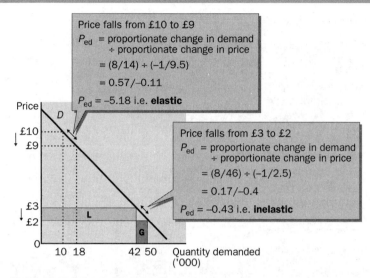

Price falls from £10 to £9

P_{ed} = proportionate change in demand
          ÷ proportionate change in price

= (8/14) ÷ (−1/9.5)

= 0.57/−0.11

P_{ed} = −5.18 i.e. **elastic**

Price falls from £3 to £2

P_{ed} = proportionate change in demand
          ÷ proportionate change in price

= (8/46) ÷ (−1/2.5)

= 0.17/−0.4

P_{ed} = −0.43 i.e. **inelastic**

Fig. 2.13 Variation in elasticity along a demand curve.

Price inelastic: Describes a situation in which the proportionate change in quantity demanded is less than the proportionate change in price; elasticity is less than 1.

Unit elasticity: Describes a situation where the proportionate change in quantity demanded is equal to the proportionate change in price; elasticity is 1.

Perfect inelasticity: Arises where the quantity demanded does *not* respond to a change in price; elasticity is 0.

Perfect elasticity: Describes a situation where the response of quantity demanded to a price change is infinitely large; elasticity is ∞.

from £12 000 to £15 000, there would be a net revenue loss of £234 million per month.

Fig. 2.13 presents two further worked examples of price elasticity of demand. In the first case, as price falls from £10 to £9, demand can again be seen to be price elastic. The gain in net revenue associated with the price reduction is also clearly evident in this case. However, when price falls from £3 to £2 price elasticity of demand is calculated at −0.43. This is a case of **inelastic demand**, in that the price change induces a *less than proportionate response in the quantity demanded*. Notice here that the price reduction is clearly associated with a net loss in revenue (the areas of revenue loss and gain for this price reduction are marked L and G respectively). We have now uncovered the two *main* classes of elasticity. When the quantity demanded responds more than proportionately to a price change it is said to be *elastic* and will carry a value *greater than 1*. On the other hand, when the quantity demanded responds less than proportionately to a price change it is said to be *inelastic* and will carry a value *less than 1*. Although, given the inverse relationship between price and quantity demanded, the values of price elasticity of demand are negative, the convention is to omit the minus sign to avoid any possible confusion. We shall follow this custom from now on.

Beyond the two main cases of price elastic and inelastic demand, the prescient reader may have anticipated other possibilities. The quantity demanded may respond *proportionately* to a change in price. Here $P_{ed} = 1$. This is known as **unit elasticity**. An example of unit elasticity is presented in Fig. 2.14(a). Notice, incidentally, that here the loss and gain in revenue resulting from changes in the price and quantity demanded are identical. Of course, it may be that quantity demanded is completely *unresponsive* to changes in price. In such cases demand is said to be **perfectly inelastic**. Or there may be a *perfect response*, inasmuch as the quantity demanded is infinitely large at one unique price and zero at all other possible prices. Here demand is said to be **perfectly elastic**. Fig. 2.14(b) and (c) also depicts examples of these two cases. Notice that, for the vertical perfectly inelastic demand curve, regardless of whatever price is set over the range of the curve, the quantity demanded remains static at Q_1.

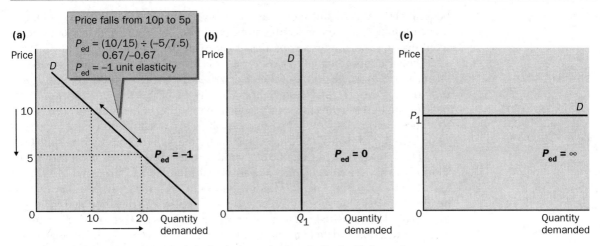

Fig. 2.14 (a) Unit elasticity, (b) perfectly inelastic demand, (c) perfectly elastic demand.

Here P_{ed} = zero, consistent with the complete unresponsiveness of quantity de-manded to a change in price. In the case of the perfectly elastic curve, at price P_1 there is an infinitely elastic demand for the good or service, but at all other prices quantity demanded evaporates completely. Here $P_{ed} = \infty$ (infinity), consistent with an infinitely large response of quantity demanded to the change in price.

In summary, then, price elasticity of demand can range in value from zero (per-fectly unresponsive) to infinity (perfectly responsive) as follows:

- *Perfectly inelastic demand*: Quantity demanded fails to respond to price changes ($P_{ed} = 0$).
- *Inelastic demand*: The response of quantity demanded is proportionately smaller than the price change ($P_{ed} < 1$).
- *Unit elastic demand*: The response of quantity demanded is proportionately equal to the price change ($P_{ed} = 1$).
- *Elastic demand*: The response of quantity demanded is proportionately greater than the price change ($P_{ed} > 1$).
- *Perfectly elastic demand*: The response of quantity demanded to the price change is infinitely large ($P_{ed} = \infty$).

Less than: The sign $<$ indicates less than.

Greater than: The sign $>$ indicates greater than.

2.8 Determinants of price elasticity of demand

The most important determinants of price elasticity of demand are:

- the availability of substitutes
- the proportion of income spent on a good or service
- time.

The availability of substitutes

Goods and services that have *close substitutes* tend to have relatively price *elastic* de-mand structures; those with only distant substitutes tend to be more price inelastic. There are, for example, many brands of chocolate bar sold in Europe, and most tend to be similarly priced. Manufacturers are generally unwilling to raise their prices for fear that custom will leak to their competitors' products. This is an implicit acknowledgement that the demand for any particular chocolate bar is price elastic and is so precisely because consumers enjoy a wide range of choice. Incidentally, where a market is characterized by a high degree of choice-driven price elasticity, producers have a great incentive to develop *brand loyalties*. Brand loyalty establishes the superiority of a particular good or service over its rival products in the mind of the consumer, and serves to reduce its price elasticity: people may be willing to pay a little more for it because of its perceived qualities. In the chocolate industry the *Mars bar* has such a reputation.

Oil is an often quoted example of a good with *few close substitutes* (at least in the short run) and, as a consequence, a relatively *inelastic* demand structure. In 1973–74 and 1979 a group of the world's leading oil producers – the OPEC nations, in what became known as 'oil shocks' – effectively quadrupled and then doubled the world price of oil. The industrialized non-oil-producing nations had little immediate choice except to meet the inflated oil prices, as their economies were highly oil-dependent. This, of course, led to significantly increased flows of revenue from oil-importing countries to the oil producers. We shall have more to say about the market for oil in section 2.10 below.

The price inelastic demand qualities of tobacco and alcohol are equally well known, not least by those governments that choose to tax these commodities in order to raise revenue. Such taxes are passed on by producers to their customers in the form of higher prices. The working assumption here, of course, is that the higher prices, because they brush up against inelastic demand, do not significantly reduce consumption. Again, inelastic demand arises in these cases because, for smokers and drinkers, there are few, if any, close substitutes for tobacco and alcohol. Governments could not tax, say, crisps or peanuts with the same degree of impunity: people would snack instead on the dozens of alternative savouries and confectioneries available over any sweetcounter.

The proportion of income spent on a good or service

When only a small portion of income is spent on a good, purchasers are thought to be relatively indifferent to price changes in terms of their demand for it: demand in such case will be more inelastic. Consider, for example, the little packets of sauce sold in fish and chip shops. These cost only a few pence. Will the quantity demanded be significantly reduced if say their price jumps from say 4p to 5p: a 22 per cent increase (on the average price principle introduced earlier)? The suggestion is that it will not – when the pubs shut and people are buying their chips or whatever, a penny extra won't lever many of them away from their usual order. Demand here then is *price inelastic*. However, what might be the demand reaction to an equivalent proportionate rise in the price of, say, a washing machine? Washing machines cost several hundred pounds, which is a much more significant slice of the average person's income. The same order of price increase here might involve the outlay of an extra £100 or so. This, it is suggested, would be more likely to significantly affect the quantity demanded: the response in other words would be more *elastic* in nature because the good in question takes up a greater proportion of the consumer's income.

Time

Demand patterns often do not respond instantaneously to price changes. Take, for example, the demand for national newspapers. Newspapers have substitutes readily available in the form of rival titles and rival news media. This suggests that the demand for particular newspaper titles should be price elastic, and this indeed is the case. However, demand is not *instantaneously* elastic. If the price of one title rises, those who customarily buy it may not notice at first because they have the paper delivered and pay for it weekly, or because they're not particularly alert in the shop first thing in the morning. They continue to buy it for these reasons and also perhaps because it reflects their views, they like a particular commentator whose byline it carries, and so on. However, some readers will notice the price rise – certainly after a day or two, or when they next pay their paper bill – and they may then begin to sample rival titles. This *gradual* change means that price elasticity of demand is likely to be more inelastic immediately after a price rise than later on. Once consumers have had time to register the price change in their minds they *then* begin to seek out close substitutes for the good or service in question.

2.9 Why firms need to know about price elasticity of demand

An awareness of price elasticity of demand is clearly essential for firms if they are to understand consumer responses to the pricing structures they set in particular markets. We are already aware that firms cannot afford to misread market conditions. If, for example, price is set above its equilibrium level, the market will fail to clear: there will be excess supply and firms will be stuck with unsold stocks. However, the extent of excess supply will increase as price elasticity of demand increases. This means that if firms fail to appreciate the nature of elasticity in the market they can make poor commercial decisions even in apparently very favourable general market conditions.

As an illustration of this possibility, Box 2.5 reviews the rather unimaginative pricing structures set by the English Football Association for the FA Cup semi-finals in 1996. These are compared with the much more nuanced pricing arrangements of the Royal Opera House. What the material in the box demonstrates is that the FA *assumed* that the price elasticity of demand for semi-final tickets was much more *inelastic* than was actually the case. For both games some of the tickets for the most highly priced seats were unsold, and at the ground with more seats in this category the attendance was only 80 per cent of capacity. Demand, in other words, was too elastic to permit the market to clear in the face of high ticket prices (and, most significantly, prices much higher than fans were accustomed to paying for the season's league games). So, what caused the FA to misread the elasticity conditions? In each football season there are only two FA Cup semi-finals. This might suggest that the availability of close substitutes is minimal. However, as Box 2.5 indicates, both games were screened live on television, which is certainly one form of substitute. In addition, other rarely available high-quality (and highly priced) football matches were to follow close on the semi-finals: most obviously the final itself but also the 31 international matches of the *Euro 96* championship, which were to be played in England. Taking these factors into account, the pricing structure for the semi-finals almost certainly needed to be closer to that set for normal league games. This would have ensured the traditional capacity attendances for FA Cup semi-finals. In the case of the Royal Opera House, the *much greater* variability of the pricing structure is intended to reflect the uneven level of demand anticipated for different kinds of performance. This is an explicit recognition that elasticity conditions must be

Box 2.5

The Football Association and Opera House share a worthy goal

Recent events . . . in football showed a total failure to appreciate basic supply and demand principles . . .

The Football Association came under fire for somehow failing to sell out one of the highlights of the soccer calendar, the semi-final between two of Britain's most passionately followed and on-form clubs. The game between Liverpool and Aston Villa should have been played in front of a capacity crowd. It was held at Old Trafford, the home ground of Manchester United and a modern, high-class stadium. It was within easy travelling distance of both visiting teams' fans.

Granted, it was on Sky television, but any good football supporter will tell you that watching the match on TV is not as good as being there. So why was the ground only 80 per cent full? Liverpool returned 6000 of their 23 500 tickets unsold and Aston Villa returned 4400 of their 23 004. The FA imposed a pricing structure at Old Trafford which took the average weighted price to £31.68. Almost all of the Old Trafford returns were tickets priced at the top level of £38.

But at Villa Park, the venue of the other semi-final played on the same day and televised live by the BBC, Chelsea sold all of their 18 500 allocation while Manchester United sold all but 700 of their 19 000. The 700 outstanding were all priced at £38.

The key difference seemed to be that the smarter Old Trafford ground had 86 per cent of its seats priced at £38 or £30, while Villa Park mustered 67 per cent of the better appointed [seats]. The market almost cleared at Villa Park but by the accident of its seating status rather than by the design of the FA.

The FA got it wrong in both cases. It assumed that demand was less [price] elastic than it proved to be and so the market did not clear.

Perhaps the FA could have learned a lesson from the Royal Opera House, an organization which has become used to the allegation of unjustifiable prices. On closer inspection the allegations seem a little harsh. The Opera House has a pricing system with 131 levels. The range depends on the performance. Thus, for Wagner's The Ring, which corporate affairs director Keith Cooper compared with an FA Cup semi-final as opposed to a Domingo concert which would be the final itself, the average price was £76 with the range starting at under £50 (800 of the 2000 tickets) and rising to £140 (for 124 of the total). Result: full house. But for a recent performance of three modern ballets, the average ticket price was £17.80 with a range of £2 to £34, and 800 of the seats available priced at £13.50 or less. Result: also full house. The comparison, like most, is flawed because the Royal Opera House's supply curve goes vertical at 2000 tickets whereas Old Trafford's has to reach almost 25 times that before no more seats are available. There are other factors to consider, such as popular appeal and income. Is opera's popularity as widespread as football's, and do most football fans enjoy the same earnings as opera devotees?

The logical step, economically speaking, would be for football and opera organisers to test the elasticity of demand until they discovered the price equilibrium.

Source: Guardian 8 April 1996

respected if markets are to clear. Assuming that capacity attendances are desired at semi-finals, the FA would do well to take heed.

2.10 Applying market analysis 2: OPEC and the market for oil

In section 2.8 we mentioned that, because it has few close substitutes, oil may be classed as a good with low price elasticity of demand. In the 1970s it became a commonplace that the possession of substantial oil reserves was a very welcome economic advantage for a country. As noted, in 1973–4 and 1979 OPEC, the group of major oil-exporting nations, imposed dramatic increases in the price of oil. These

Table 2.3 Sources of energy in the world economy:[a] 1973 and 1986

	1973		1986	
	MTOE[b]	**% of total**	**MTOE**[b]	**% of total**
Total energy use of which:	4045	100	4172	100
Imports of OPEC oil	1480	36.5	674	16.2
Other energy imports[c]	100	2.5	207	5.0
Indigeneous production of which:				
Oil	760	18.8	1191	28.5
Natural gas	765	18.9	741	17.8
Coal	805	19.9	1076	25.8
Other	135	3.3	283	6.8

[a] Excluding OPEC and the planned economies.
[b] MTOE = million tons oil equivalent.
[c] Oil, natural gas and coal imported from the centrally planned economies.

Source: Odell, P.R. 'The world petroleum market: the current situation and prospects' in K.I.F. Kahn (ed.) *Petroleum Resources and Development* (London and New York: Belhaven Press, 1987)

price increases greatly enriched OPEC members and caused major problems for economies that were highly dependent on imported oil. At first at least, oil importers simply had to pay more for this important commodity. But this is not the end of the story. Subsequent developments in the market for oil provide a good illustration of how market processes come to constrain even the most powerful producers. The possession of something as vital as oil to modern industrial economies is certainly desirable, but it does not allow producers to evade the ultimate sanction of the laws of supply and demand.

Table 2.3 captures the essence of this problem for the OPEC nations. The table describes energy consumption by the non-OPEC countries (excluding the then centrally planned or communist states) in 1973 and 1986. The selection of these particular years is intended to depict the state of the international energy and oil markets at the time of the first oil price shock and then again after the combined effects of this and the second shock in 1979 became clear. Consider the data for 1973. At this time OPEC oil accounted for 36.5 per cent of all energy used by the non-OPEC countries and about two-thirds of their oil consumption (they consumed 1480 + 760 = 2240 MTOE of oil; 1480 is approximately two thirds of 2240). By 1986 some significant shifts had occurred. Although total energy use increased only modestly, OPEC's oil now accounted for only 16.2 per cent of this total. Moreover, in 1986 the non-OPEC countries were able to produce about two thirds of their own oil requirements, as opposed to one third in 1973 (they consumed 674 + 1191 = 1865 MTOE of oil; 1191 is approximately two thirds of 1865). Notice too that these countries increased the contributions to energy use of coal and other non-oil fuels.

Table 2.4 tracks the influence of these shifts in forms of energy consumption for oil prices in the world's major oil-importing area – the Organization for Economic Cooperation and Development (OECD).[3] The table also reveals the extent of the initial

[3] The Organization for Economic Cooperation and Development (OECD), formed in 1961, is a body representing a number of rich industrial countries. Its primary purpose is to promote policy coordination amongst members.

Table 2.4 Oil market statistics: OECD area

	Import price of crude (c.i.f. $ per barrel)	Real oil price[a]
1970	1.7	14
1971	2.2	17
1972	2.5	17
1973	3.5	20
1974	11.6	56
1975	11.4	48
1976	12.9	53
1977	13.9	52
1978	14.0	46
1979	19.3	56
1980	32.9	89
1981	36.3	104
1982	34.2	100
1983	30.3	91
1984	29.2	91
1985	27.4	86
1986	18.5	52

[a] OECD import price of crude deflated by OECD export unit values, manufactured goods, 1982 = 100.

Source: OECD *Economic Outlook* 39, May 1986. Reproduced by permission of the OECD.

OPEC-inspired surge in oil prices. The effects of the 1973–74 and 1979 oil shocks are apparent in both the dollar price per barrel of crude oil (oil is priced in US dollars on the world market) and the real oil price, which is shown as an index number. The price per barrel and the real oil price in the OECD area reached a peak in 1981, but thereafter a sharp fall in oil prices occurred such that, by 1986 for example, the real oil price was approximately half its 1981 level.

Putting information from Tables 2.3 and 2.4 together, we can begin to summarize developments in the oil market over the 1970s and the first half of the 1980s. The two oil shocks were indeed a major problem for the non-OPEC nations. The price of an imported commodity, central to their established patterns of energy use, increased sharply. Because this commodity has relatively few substitutes, and therefore possesses a relatively low price elasticity of demand, the price increases simply had to be absorbed, at least in the *short term*. However, the rising price of oil itself stimulated changes in the international energy market. Oil-importing nations had a growing incentive to economize on the use of oil; to exploit their own and other non-OPEC oil deposits more intensively (in many instances, the previously low OPEC price had meant this was not worthwhile); and to develop further alternative energy sources, such as coal. Over time, then, the relatively price inelastic demand structure of OPEC's oil began to melt away as demand (for OPEC's oil) slackened and new non-OPEC oil and non-oil energy supplies became more economic and available. In effect OPEC, in 1973–74 and 1979, had attempted to impose its will on the long-run development of the market. It wanted permanently higher prices for its oil. This was, in other words, an attempt to 'buck the market'. Unfortunately for OPEC, markets are not amenable to this kind of manipulation much beyond the short term. All OPEC succeeded in doing was to encourage the development of new oil and energy supplies outside its jurisdiction. The laws of supply and demand in time simply reasserted themselves.

Before we leave this example, it is worth saying a few words about the *current* state of the oil market. From a low of $10 in 1999, the price of a barrel of crude oil had reached $30 by July 2000. Oil experts generally agree that a price of $25 is sufficient to encourage non-OPEC producers to invest in new oil exploration. With a high and rising oil price, OPEC may once again enjoy a short-term boom but only at the real risk of a re-run of the kind of collapse in oil prices witnessed in the mid-1980s. Indeed, there have been recent signs that some OPEC members are aware of this danger. At the time of writing, Saudi Arabia – the world's biggest oil producer – has just announced an increase in production, with the expressed intention of bringing the oil price down from its current level. It is probably not unreasonable to interpret this move as representative of an acceptance on the part of oil producers that they are subservient to market pressures in the long term.

2.11 Other forms of elasticity

Income elasticity of demand

In section 2.2 we considered a range of factors other than price that influenced the demand for a good or service. These factors too can be placed in an elasticity framework. We suggested, for example, that demand can vary positively with consumers' income: higher incomes, *ceteris paribus*, prompted the demand curve for a normal good to shift to the right, while lower incomes caused it to shift to the left (see Fig. 2.2). The question now arises: how *responsive* is the quantity demanded of a good to a change in income? We can resolve this issue using the concept of **income elasticity of demand**.

Income elasticity of demand (Y_{ed}) measures the responsiveness of the quantity of a good demanded to changes in income. It is calculated using an approach similar to that which allowed us to calculate price elasticity of demand. The equation for income elasticity of demand is

$$Y_{ed} = \frac{\text{Proportionate change in quantity demanded}}{\text{Proportionate change in income}} \tag{2.2}$$

Generally, we would expect Y_{ed} to be *positive*. In other words, higher incomes would be associated with an increase in demand (and vice versa). However, this is not always the case: in some circumstances, higher incomes can prompt a decrease in the demand for particular goods and services. In such cases Y_{ed} will be *negative*. For example, rising incomes in Britain over the last 30 years have substantially altered the way people spend their holiday time. As many more people can afford to travel abroad for longer periods, the demand for holidays in traditional seaside towns has declined. Where Y_{ed} is negative, the relevant goods and services are said to be **inferior**. In contrast, as noted in section 2.2, *normal* goods are those for which demand increases as income increases.

Income elasticity of demand: The proportionate change in the quantity of a good demanded divided by the proportionate change in consumers' incomes.

Inferior good: One for which demand decreases when income increases.

We can identify two sets of normal good:

- First, that for which Y_{ed} is *inelastic* (<1). An obvious example here is the demand for basic foods. In Europe, where incomes are already relatively high, the demand for basic foods is unlikely to increase much even when incomes rise still further. Consumers are more likely to spend their extra incomes on 'luxury' goods such as cars and foreign holidays. Of course, there may be changes in the *way* people consume food as incomes rise – they will be more likely to eat out, for example – but the actual level of basic food consumption will increase relatively slowly.

- The second kind of normal good possesses an *elastic* Y_{ed} (>1). Here, when incomes rise, there is a proportionately greater increase in demand. Examples of income elastic goods would typically include the kinds of luxury items mentioned above. In the richer societies, most basic needs – such as those for food and housing – are already amply met, and so further increases in income tend to be directed towards cars, foreign holidays and so on.

Applying income elasticity of demand

The concept of income elasticity of demand can usefully contribute to, amongst other things, an understanding of the patterns of specialization and development that have emerged in the international economy since the 1960s. Before this period there was a clear and long-established **international division of labour** within which, broadly speaking, the industrial countries produced manufactured goods while most other developing countries specialized in the production of agricultural output and raw materials. However, during the 1960s and 1970s a number of developing countries successfully reallocated productive resources away from old dependences on agriculture and raw materials and switched them instead into manufacturing. Foremost amongst these so-called *newly industrializing countries* (NICs) are South Korea, Hong Kong, Singapore and Taiwan. Now, the point here is that the economic success of the NICs is underpinned by their awareness of the pattern of *world* income elasticity of demand. Despite regrettably wide differences in economic growth between its different regions, the world itself is, as a whole, a richer place than it has ever been hitherto. This implies that, especially in its most advanced European, North American and Far Eastern economies, most basic needs are met. Any growth in incomes in these places is then inevitably translated into higher demand for *income elastic luxuries*, many of which are manufactured: cars, TVs, video players, cameras, hi-fi equipment, fridge-freezers, sports equipment, clothes, children's toys and so on. This of course means that the decision to switch resources into the production of this class of goods was extremely wise: the demand for them will continue to increase at a faster rate than the growth in world income. Meanwhile, the many countries that continue to rely on exports of agricultural goods and raw materials find the more sedate (*income inelastic*) demand for them constrains wider national prospects for faster economic growth and development.

Price elasticity of supply

Price elasticity of supply: The proportionate change in quantity supplied of a good divided by the proportionate change in price that brought it about.

As the reader will expect from our discussion in this section so far, **price elasticity of supply** (P_{es}) measures the responsiveness of quantity supplied to changes in price. It is given by the following equation:

$$P_{es} = \frac{\text{Proportionate change in quantity supplied}}{\text{Proportionate change in price}} \qquad (2.3)$$

Fig. 2.15 provides two worked examples of price elasticity of supply. These follow precisely the same general principles as those introduced in Fig. 2.12 for the calculation of price elasticity of demand. It can be seen from Fig. 2.15 that price elasticity of supply can vary along a single supply curve. In this case, we observe both an instance of price inelastic supply, where the proportionate response of quantity supplied is less than the proportionate change in price which brings it about; and an elastic response, where the proportionate change in quantity supplied is greater than the proportionate change in price. Instances of unit elastic, perfectly inelastic and perfectly elastic supply are also possible. These are depicted in Fig. 2.16. Notice that, as in Fig. 2.16(a), any supply curve that passes through the origin will have unit elastic supply characteristics. In Fig. 2.16(b) a situation of perfectly inelastic supply indicates that the quantity supplied will not respond, regardless of the scale or direction of any price change. Finally, in Fig. 2.16(c), where supply is perfectly elastic, all prices other than P_1 induce an infinitely large fall in the quantity supplied.

Determinants of price elasticity of supply

There are two principal determinants of elasticity of supply: time, and the elasticity of supply of factor inputs.

Time

We noted earlier that the demand for many goods and services does not respond instantaneously to changes in price; a similar constraint operates on supply. In some markets, such as that for newspapers, output may be increased (or decreased) relatively quickly in response to a new market price. It is simply a matter of extending the print run; all the requisite machinery and raw materials will already be in place. In other markets, however, the task is more difficult. A given season's total supply of seats at football matches is highly inelastic. The only way to increase the quantity of

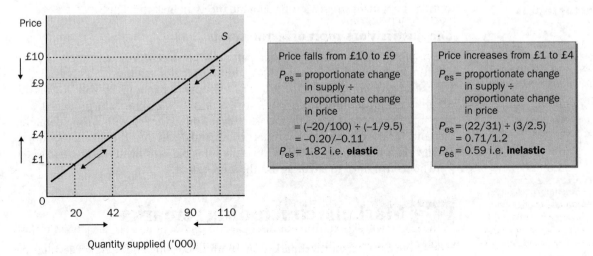

Price falls from £10 to £9

P_{es} = proportionate change in supply ÷ proportionate change in price

= (−20/100) ÷ (−1/9.5)
= −0.20/−0.11
P_{es} = 1.82 i.e. **elastic**

Price increases from £1 to £4

P_{es} = proportionate change in supply ÷ proportionate change in price

P_{es} = (22/31) ÷ (3/2.5)
= 0.71/1.2
P_{es} = 0.59 i.e. **inelastic**

Fig. 2.15 Price elasticity of supply.

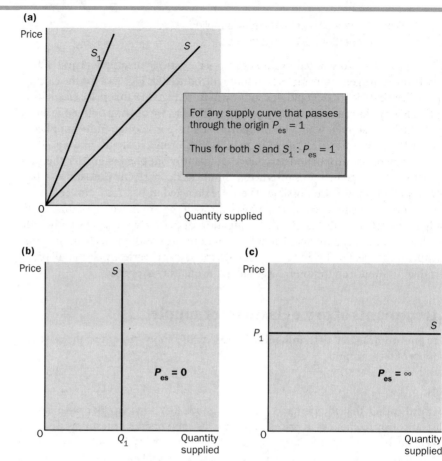

(a)

Price

S_1

S

For any supply curve that passes through the origin $P_{es} = 1$

Thus for both S and S_1 : $P_{es} = 1$

0   Quantity supplied

(b)

Price

S

$P_{es} = 0$

0   Q_1 Quantity supplied

(c)

Price

P_1

S

$P_{es} = \infty$

0   Quantity supplied

Fig. 2.16 (a) Unit elasticity, (b) perfectly inelastic supply, (c) perfectly elastic supply.

◆ **Concept**

Factor inputs

Economists generally recognize four factor inputs – or factors of production – some or all of which are required in order to supply a good or service. These are: land, labour, capital and entrepreneurial – or business – skill.

seats supplied is to extend football grounds or build new ones – a process that can take several years. Incidentally, this makes apparent the economic basis of ticket touting at popular games: a strong demand meets an inelastic supply.

The elasticity of supply of factor inputs

The responsiveness of the supply of a particular good or service to changes in price will also depend on the degree to which additional **factor inputs** are readily available. To take an extreme example, the prime factor input to paintings by Van Gogh is the labour of the artist himself. No more work by Van Gogh will ever be produced, and therefore its supply is perfectly inelastic (again this, coupled with strong demand, accounts for the high prices that his art commands). On the other hand, the supply of lolly ices is much more elastic because the principal ingredients – sugar and water – are not constrained to anything like the same extent.

2.12 Markets: concluding remarks

From a business perspective markets are both interesting and useful. They are the vital frameworks through which firms can reach their customers, but they are also the means by which consumers assert their authority over firms. It is impossible for any one firm, or indeed firms in general, to evade the basic operational laws of supply and demand in markets. Where this has been tried, as in the case of oil, the sovereignty of consumers reasserts itself in the end. The basic lesson for business seems to be that prosperity may follow where market priorities are respected; where they are not, there is missed opportunity.

We shall see later that there are some economic questions to which markets cannot provide answers. In such instances it is often the case that the state intervenes to restrict the commercial freedoms of firms or to otherwise moderate their behaviour, even to the extent that the state may act as a producer itself. However, before we move on to explore these possibilities we must first begin to examine the firm itself in much more detail.

Summary

◆ A market is a framework that allows firms and consumers to interact to their mutual satisfaction.

◆ For any given set of supply and demand schedules or curves, there is *one* equilibrium position where price, the quantity demanded and the quantity supplied are in balance. All other prices indicate positions of disequilibrium in the market, where firms and consumers are motivated to change their behaviour.

◆ The articulation of markets at wider levels raises the possibility of greater choice in production and consumption decisions.

◆ The EU's single market programme is an example of the wide-ranging application of market analysis to the real economic problem of slower growth in Europe over the 1970s and early 1980s.

◆ Nonetheless, where it feels it is justified and in response to strong producer lobbies, the EU continues to intervene heavily in certain agricultural markets.

◆ The concept of price elasticity of demand allows us to analyse the strength of the relationship between changes in price and corresponding changes in the quantity demanded. Similarly, price elasticity of supply allows us to analyse the strength of the relationship between price and quantity supplied.

◆ Income elasticity of demand measures the responsiveness of quantity demanded to changes in incomes. It may be used to understand the basis of contemporary shifts in the international division of labour.

Key terms

◆ Demand
◆ Supply
◆ Equilibrium
◆ Excess supply
◆ Excess demand
◆ Disequilibrium

◆ The single market programme
◆ Common Agricultural Policy
◆ Market intervention
◆ Price elasticity of demand
◆ Income elasticity of demand
◆ Price elasticity of supply

■ Self-test questions

True (t) or false (f)

1. A change in the price of a good causes extensions or contractions in the quantity demanded.

2. Demand and supply in a market are always equal.

3. A change in the price of a good causes a shift in its demand curve.

4. Excess demand and excess supply can coexist in a market.

5. Changes in consumer incomes influence supply.

6. If the price of sugar falls, *ceteris paribus*, more sweets will be produced.

7. There is a positive relationship between the price of a good and its supply.

8. Excess supply will usually prompt increases in price.

9. 'Butter mountains' in Europe are a product of the market mechanism.

10. The Common Agricultural Policy raises the prices of many agricultural products in Europe.

11. Price elasticity of demand measures the responsiveness of price to changes in demand.

12. When price elasticity of demand is less than 1, price reductions are associated with net losses in revenue for producers.

13. When demand is perfectly price inelastic the quantity demanded does not change, regardless of what happens to price.

14. Demand becomes more price elastic over time.

15. Supply becomes more price inelastic over time.

16. The supply of rare fossils is perfectly inelastic.

Complete the following sentences by inserting the missing word(s)

1. The amount of a good or service that consumers wish to purchase at a particular price is called ____.

2. A movement along a demand or supply curve is referred to as an ____ or ____.

3. A good used in conjunction with another good is called a ____.

4. When there is no tendency to change in a market, the market is said to be in ____.

5. When all goods are sold the market is said to ____.

6. The Common Agricultural Policy is an example of ____ in a market.

7. Butter and margarine are ____ for one another.

8. A price that fails to equate the quantities demanded and supplied in a market is said to be a ____ price.

9. Price elasticity of demand measures the ____ of the quantity demanded to a change in ____.

10. When price elasticity of demand is 1, it is said to be ____.

11. Goods with few ____ are more likely to be price inelastic in character.

12. Cars are likely to be in price inelastic demand because they absorb a greater proportion of consumers' ____.

13. If the income elasticity of demand for a good is negative then the good is said to be ____.

14. For any supply curve that passes through the origin, price elasticity of supply equals ____.

■ Questions for discussion

◆ What are the principal determinants of the demand for a particular commodity?

◆ What are the principal determinants of the supply of a particular commodity?

◆ Explain the process by which disequilibrium prices in a market give way to one unique equilibrium price.

◆ For a particular good, what will happen to the equilibrium price and quantity bought and sold following:

  an improvement in technology;

  a change in tastes away from the good;

  an increase in the cost of producing it;

  an increase in consumers' incomes?

◆ Using an analysis of markets, explain the basis of the single market programme in Europe.

◆ How can governments offset movements towards equilibrium in markets?

◆ Use the concept of price elasticity of demand to explain why governments are able to continually raise the tax they levy on tobacco.

◆ Why is a tax not levied on boxes of matches?

◆ Why can't firms 'buck the market'?

■ Further reading

If you have access to CD-ROM newspaper search facilities, you will be able to research conditions in many markets yourself. Try entering the keywords 'demand' and 'supply' together with the particular good you have in mind: 'apples', 'tea', 'wheat' or whatever. This is usually sufficient to locate material on recent developments in the markets for such goods. You will then be in a position to try to sketch out your own 'real world' market diagrams, much as we did in section 2.4.

Curran, J. *Taking the Fear Out of Economics* (London: Business Press, 1999). A step-by-step guide to micro, with plenty of examples.

Levacic, R. 'Markets as coordinating devices' in R. Maidment and G. Thompson (eds) *Managing the United Kingdom* (London: Sage Publications, 1993). Offers a brief overview of the basis of the operation of markets.

McDonald, F. and S. Dearden (eds) *European Economic Integration* (3rd ed.) (London: Longman, 1999). Provides a good summary of the economics of the European single market.

■ Internet links

More information about the European single market and other EU initiatives is available from the *European Union* website at **http://www.europa.eu.int/index-en.htm**

The Firm

CHAPTER 3

Key issues

▶ What is the role of the firm in the modern economy?

▶ Why do *firms* necessarily have to fulfil this role?

▶ What different kinds of firm exist in the modern economy?

▶ What is entrepreneurship and what is its significance?

▶ What difficulties are there for the firm in managing its affairs?

Contents

3.1 Introduction

The first two chapters of this book have been primarily concerned with the operation of markets. Markets allow producers to pursue their own economic ends by serving the consumption needs of others. Up to this point, however, we have neither considered in any *detail* how market processes actually influence producers nor, indeed, reflected upon the institution of the *firm*, the most common organizational form that capitalist production assumes. In the present chapter and Chapters 4 and 5 we fill in these gaps. Here we provide an overview of the contribution that firms make to answering the basic economic questions of what to produce, how and for whom. In Chapter 4 we introduce the parameters that economists use to interpret and measure the performance of firms: cost, revenue and profit. Chapter 5 offers a common framework for analysing the different kinds of **market structure** in which firms are located. It also considers the extent to which firms actually match up to the ideals that conventional economics supposes that they follow. There are, for example, serious doubts about whether consumer sovereignty can prevail in the presence of firms with **monopoly power**. Monopoly power, the argument runs, permits the firm – rather than consumers – to direct the general course of production. It is in Chapter 5, then, that we begin to encounter some of the *shortcomings* of the market system.

Market structure: Characterizes a market according to the degree of competition in it. Monopoly is an example of a market structure where there is an absence of competition.

Monopoly power: Exists where a firm has the ability to exclude competing firms from the market. Competition is the process that empowers consumers: each firm in a competitive market seeks to offer a better deal to consumers than its rivals. Monopoly power removes this incentive and may leave the firm less responsive to consumer interests.

3.2 What do firms do?

Firms are organizations that buy or hire *factors of production* in order to produce goods or services that can be sold for profit. As noted in Chapter 2, economic theory recognizes four factors of production. These are:

- land
- labour
- capital
- entrepreneurship.

We assume that a firm will require some combination of all four factors in order to produce goods or services. Let us reflect briefly on the nature of each factor.

- *Land* embodies all natural resources. Thus it includes not only the physical space in which production occurs but also all the unprocessed materials present in the environment. For economists, houses and factories are built on land; animals, minerals and vegetables can be reared, extracted and grown on it; even fish swim in it.

- *Labour* is the time and effort of people hired by firms to perform specialist production tasks and to increase the scale of production of the individual firm.

- *Capital* consists of all those production goods that are used to produce other goods and services. Thus machines, tools and factories are all forms of capital: their value lies not in immediate consumption but in what can be made with them.

- Finally, *entrepreneurship* – the ability to read the market, anticipate the demands of consumers and manage land, labour and capital to meet these demands – is *the* pivotal factor of capitalist production. If a firm is lacking in entrepreneurship, it risks destruction simply because it will fail to judge the market correctly. Most obviously, it may produce goods and services for which there proves to be little or no demand. By contrast, the entrepreneurial firm must, by definition, be profitable and therefore successful: it is effectively producing things that consumers want. Entrepreneurial skill enables firms, in their thousands, to dovetail production to incredibly complex patterns of demand; it also encourages them to continually refine what they produce and how they produce it so that they can better meet demand in the future. Because of its centrality to the market process, we elaborate upon the role of the entrepreneur within the firm in a later section.

Richard Branson.
Entrepreneurship: from music to airlines.
© Virgin

The particular *factor mix* – how much land, labour and capital – used by a firm will, of course, reflect the nature of the production process that the firm is engaged in. Economists recognize that certain forms of production favour particular **factor intensities**. For example, the manufacture of chemicals is a *capital-intensive* process in that the typical firm employs relatively more capital than labour or land. On the other hand, the manufacture of footwear and clothing is a *labour-intensive* activity, and most forms of agriculture are *land intensive*.

Finally in this section we should note the payments that firms make for the factors of production they employ. The returns paid to each factor are as follows:

- Land earns *rent*.
- Labour is paid a *wage*.

Factor intensity: Refers to the emphasis in production towards the use of one particular factor of production above others.

- Capital earns *interest*.

- Entrepreneurship is rewarded with *profit*.

We elaborate upon the earnings of land, labour and capital in Chapter 8; for the moment we concentrate upon profit. As noted, a firm's entrepreneurial ability is rewarded in the form of profit. If, by organizing land, labour and capital, the firm produces goods that consumers are willing and able to buy at a price that exceeds the cost of production, then the difference between price and cost is retained by the firm as profit. The conventional assumption is that firms attempt to *maximize profits*. Now, this might appear to place the firm and the consumer slightly at odds, given that higher profits could simply result from firms increasing the prices they charge. However, such a view neglects the significance of the *competitive environment* in which firms, in theory at least, operate. Because firms must compete with one another for customers, no single firm can risk speculative price increases for fear that its rivals will not follow suit and will maroon it in an uncompetitive position. At the same time, the competitive environment places a *cost control* imperative on firms. No firm can absolve itself of the need to produce as efficiently as possible for fear of the competitive disadvantage it would incur in the presence of more cost-conscious rivals. The competitive environment thus makes profit maximization advantageous both for the firm *and* the consumer. Recall also our discussion of the constraining influence of markets upon producers. Using the example of oil, we saw (in Chapter 2, section 2.10) that even a body as powerful as OPEC was unable in the long run to defy the laws of supply and demand.

3.3 Why are firms necessary?

We begin here with an obvious question: *what is the purpose of firms?* Why do markets not simply consist of large collections of individual (sole) producers and consumers? By way of an answer, consider the following example. If a person wishes to obtain a new house, one option open to him or her is to organize the details of its construction single-handedly. Land would need to be purchased and an architect commissioned to design the house. The requisite materials and tools would also have to be obtained, and a bricklayer, joiner, plumber, roofer and so on hired. Overall, the project might take, say, six months to complete, and it would probably require a good deal of management attention from our potential house owner; conceivably, he or she might have to work full-time in a managerial capacity. This kind of approach involves building the house through the *use of the market*: the consumer hires the skills and experience of individual producers and puts them to work on designated tasks. Now, in the UK, some houses might be built in this way but most are not. This is because most buyers of new houses find it more convenient and cheaper to rely on specialist building *firms* instead. In our example, the individual must devote six months of his or her time to construction management. The opportunity cost of this work would include the loss of income from employment that must be given up while building is going on. Moreover, the individual would have to have confidence in his or her ability to manage and coordinate the project effectively. Because few people find it possible to easily open up a six-month window in their working lives, and because few are likely to have the requisite building management skills, the favoured option for many is to turn to an established building firm.

But opportunity cost and the questionable managerial abilities of consumers are not the only factors that militate against market-coordinated production and therefore give rise to the existence of firms. Firms also offer a range of additional advantages as organizers of production that consumers would not otherwise benefit from. The most important of these are:

- savings on transaction costs
- the capacity of firms to extend the division of labour
- the potential of firms to innovate.

Savings on transaction costs

A building firm that constructs several thousand houses a year will contract for consistently large volumes of building materials; it will not order individual loads of sand, cement, bricks and timber for each house. To repeatedly order small loads in this way would clearly be less efficient: it would cost more in time and in paperwork. Similarly, the workers whom the firm employs will not be issued new contracts as they move from house to house, and the tools and equipment they use will not be re-hired each time a house is finished: *one* set of contracts or transactions would cover a year's work or more for the firm. Now, if the houses were built by their eventual owners through the market, as described above, the number of transactions taking place could be multiplied several thousand-fold. Therefore, in terms of transaction costs, firms appear to offer a much more efficient means of organizing production than a market without firms.

The capacity of firms to extend the division of labour

If production was predominantly organized by individuals through the market process then some or all of the signal leaps in productivity that have occurred over the last 250 years might never have been realized. Perhaps the most famous of these was the utilization, by Henry Ford in the early 1900s, of 'flow-line' car assembly. This process involved the fragmentation of car making into very simple tasks that could be repeated easily and quickly. The flow-line enabled the cars themselves to move at a given pace while the stationary workers repeated their allotted tasks on each unit. Ford demonstrated that cars could be made in their millions in this way at a *much lower cost per car than had ever been achieved before*. Subsequently, this method of production – sometimes known, after its originator, as *Fordism* – spread beyond car making to many other branches of industry, and provided the basis for a general and marked improvement in productivity in the advanced economies. The point here is of course that the flow-line principle, resting on an extended division of labour, could not have been put into practice outside the firm. To produce efficiently, Ford's output needed to be at least in *the hundreds of thousands* per annum. Car production (and, by implication, most forms of industrial production) on any meaningful scale is clearly most efficiently done by firms.

The motor industry also provides an example of the way in which firms can extend the *external* as well as their own internal division of labour. Although most of the world's cars are now produced by a fairly limited number of large **multinationals**, these firms usually rely on supplies of auto parts from other specialist producers. Car radios, tyres, windscreen wipers, upholstery and electrical components as well as other items are 'bought in' by carmakers. This arrangement allows the car firms to concentrate on the central tasks of design and body, engine and transmission pro-

Multinational: A firm that owns and controls assets (usually production facilities) in more than one country.

duction, as well as final assembly, while the specialist suppliers refine their own particular product contributions. Again, such a complex and highly integrated production system would be unlikely to emerge in the absence of the institution of the firm.

The potential of firms to innovate

Where do new products come from? How can we account for the vast array of goods and services that modern societies make available? The answer in each case is *innovation*. Innovation can, of course, be driven by solitary genius. For example, the vulcanizing process that makes rubber malleable and therefore usable in so many ways in heat or cold was discovered after a long and lonely struggle by one individual: Charles Goodyear. Innovation may also result from military imperatives. It is well known that the design and manufacture of aircraft was revolutionized as a result of pressures that emerged during the First and Second World Wars. Of course, research and development into new products and processes is also sponsored by firms: the manuscript of this book was prepared using the remarkable word processing software produced by the American Microsoft Corporation.

Innovation then has a variety of sources. Most importantly, however, in capitalist economies, it is usually firms that *apply* advances in technology to the marketplace, regardless of how these arise in the first place. Indeed, for many branches of production, it is difficult now to imagine how it could be otherwise. While an individual consumer might be capable of hiring the factors of production that he or she needs to build a house or repair a car, following the same process to obtain computer software or a television set would be immensely difficult. Indeed, it would be virtually impossible for a complex society to organize production as a whole in this way. Of course, though our reference here is to *private sector* firms, there are areas in capitalist economies where *public sector institutions* such as nationalized industries, hospitals and universities bear some burden of both production and innovation. However, it still appears reasonable to conclude that the firm is the uniquely important source of *marketable* innovation – the introduction of new goods and services to markets where individuals pay directly for what they consume. Note also that this still leaves the firm subservient to the market, and therefore preserves the central principle of consumer sovereignty. An innovation that fails to bring forth sufficient demand is itself destined for oblivion, regardless of any other considerations.

3.4 Different kinds of firm

In this section we describe the main kinds of firm that exist in the modern economy. Although the examples and data we use are primarily UK specific, the general patterns they reveal are applicable to other advanced capitalist economies, such as those in North America and other parts of western Europe.

Firms are legally distinguished by their forms of *ownership*. There are three main categories of ownership:

- sole proprietorship
- partnership
- companies.

Sole proprietorship

A firm owned by one individual is a sole proprietorship. The firm's owner receives all the profits it makes, but these are taxed as income, in the same way as wages and salaries. The owner is also responsible for any debts or losses that the firm may incur: in fact, he or she has **unlimited liability** for such losses. This means that the entire personal wealth – savings, a house, a car or any other asset – of the owner is at risk if losses are sufficiently large. Sole proprietorships are typically small, and are most common in the *service sector*, in areas of work such as retailing, property and business services (especially plumbing, electrical work and so on).

Partnership

A partnership *divides* ownership of the firm between two or more individuals. This is clearly a more complicated arrangement than that which obtains for the sole proprietorship, as the management of the firm and the disbursement of its profits must be the subject of agreement between the partners. However, partnerships also allow more individuals to participate in the firm, perhaps bringing in more money and a wider range of business expertise. As for the sole proprietorship, the profits of a partnership are taxed as the income of its owners. Partners are also subject to *joint* unlimited liability. This means that the personal wealth of all partners is at risk if the firm runs into financial difficulty. In the UK, partnerships predominate in retailing, agriculture and property and business services (typically in firms of accountants and solicitors).

Companies

Companies are owned by their *shareholders*. The more shares that are held, the greater the proportion of ownership that the holder enjoys. Shares in *private limited companies* can be bought and sold only when there is mutual agreement to do so amongst existing shareholders. By contrast, shares in *publicly quoted limited companies* may be bought and sold openly by anyone on the *stock exchange*. Shareholders also enjoy the important advantage of **limited liability**. This means that, unlike sole proprietors and partners, their financial exposure is limited to the value of the company itself. In the event of poor trading and a decision to wind up the company, any debts that cannot be covered by selling stocks of goods, plant and machinery etc. will remain unmet. Creditors of the company are not entitled to any claim on the personal wealth of shareholders. In the UK, the government levies *corporation tax* (currently at 33 per cent) on the profits earned by companies. After the payment of corporation tax, profits are disbursed amongst shareholders as *dividends* on each share held. For shareholders these dividends are then subject to a second *income* tax. One evident disadvantage of shareholding therefore is that profits may be subject to *two* taxes, compared with the single tax on income from profits that sole proprietors and partners pay.

Table 3.1 summarizes the distribution of the three main types of firm according to their respective annual turnovers for 1999. From the table it can be seen that sole proprietorship is the second most numerous in the UK, with almost 600 000 firms. Most sole proprietorships are relatively small: 66 per cent have a turnover of less than £100 000 per annum. Partnerships are the least numerous type of firm but have a greater proportion of larger firms compared with sole proprietorships. Finally, it is

Table 3.1 UK private sector firms by type and turnover, 1999

Turnover in £'000	Sole proprietorships		Partnerships		Companies and public corporations	
	Number	%	Number	%	Number	%
1–49	199 935	34	66 455	18	93 570	15
50–99	188 575	32	90 335	24	129 330	21
100–249	136 735	23	120 865	32	120 770	20
250–499	39 000	7	54 440	15	80 875	13
500–999	14 000	2	25 095	7	68 395	11
1000+	6 175	1	14 825	4	–	–
1000–1999	–	–	–	–	48 000	8
2000–4999	–	–	–	–	36 405	6
5000–9999	–	–	–	–	14 865	2
10 000–49 999					13 855	2
50 000+	–	–	–	–	4 245	1
Totals	584 420	100	372 020	100	610 310	100

Source: *Business Monitor* PA1003, National Statistics, © Crown Copyright 2000

amongst the slightly more than 600 000 companies and public corporations that the largest firms are to be found: 19 per cent (117 370 firms) in this category have turnovers in excess of £1 million as compared with only 2 per cent (21 000 firms out of almost 1 million firms) in the other two categories taken together.

The relative advantages and disadvantages of different forms of ownership

In sifting through the three main forms that a firm might assume, the decisive factors of choice are:

- the taxation of the firm's profits
- the extent of liability of the firm's owners for any losses that might arise
- how easily capital can be raised
- the way the firm is to be managed.

Let us consider each of these factors in turn.

The taxation of the firm's profits

As noted, the profits of sole proprietorships and partnerships are taxed – *once only* – as the personal income of the firm's owners. Company profits, by contrast, are subject to tax twice: corporation tax is levied initially and, subsequently, any dividends paid to shareholders are liable to income tax. Moreover, in the UK, as income tax commences at a lower rate than corporation tax, sole proprietorships and partnerships that make only modest profits will pay proportionately less in tax than companies.

Liability

Though tax arrangements might appear to favour sole proprietorships and partnerships over companies, the issue of liability works in the opposite direction. While shareholders risk nothing more than the stake that they own in a company, sole proprietors and partners lay open their entire personal wealth should their firms collapse. While this might appear to be a major burden under which to conduct business, it must also be remembered that most sole proprietorships and partnerships are relatively small, and their financial exposure is therefore limited (see Table 3.1). Moreover, as these firms are usually under the immediate supervision and control of their owners, any risk-taking will presumably not be done in a cavalier or reckless manner.

Raising capital

New and existing businesses need money for investment to help them grow. For sole proprietorships and partnerships, additional capital may come from the owners themselves, their families and friends or the bank. Generally, however, *large* injections of capital will not be available from these sources. This helps to explain why sole proprietorships and partnerships tend to be small. Companies, by contrast, find it easier to secure substantial amounts of new money. One way in which they can do this is by selling shares. These are attractive to individuals and investment institutions because, if the company performs well, the shares will yield a stream of dividends, and because the value of the shares may rise as demand for them increases. Note that limited liability underpins the attractiveness of shareholding as the purchaser shoulders a risk only equivalent to his or her investment. Indeed, this explains the origin of the principle of limited liability: it was devised as a means to help firms secure larger amounts of capital at minimal risk to investors.

The management of the firm

For sole proprietorships and partnerships, management and ownership of the firm are usually fused into one. In tandem with the generally smaller scale of operations, this makes for relatively simple management and decision-making. However, in the case of companies, both the typically larger scale of the firm and its diversified form of ownership may make for more complex and unwieldy management structures. Some economists, notably J.K. Galbraith, claim that this is a major source of weakness in advanced capitalism. We begin to introduce his views on this subject in section 3.5.

As Table 3.1 makes clear, in the UK, all three types of firm are well represented. *This suggests that no one type has an overwhelming advantage over the others.* We conclude this section with a brief review of the legal status of several well-known firms:

- the John Lewis Partnership
- Littlewoods
- Sunderland Football Club.

Our intention here is to reflect upon the reasons behind particular choices of status and to understand pressures that might favour a change in a firm's status. We begin with the John Lewis Partnership.

The John Lewis Partnership

The John Lewis Partnership is a department store group owned by its 39 000 staff. In the summer of 1999 it was in the news because of rumours that the firm might be floated on the stock exchange. A stock market flotation could bring windfalls to John Lewis staff of up to £100 000 each. Not surprisingly, many staff appeared to favour a sell-off. This example makes clear one of the possible advantages of a public listing: it realizes capital that the owners of a business have tied up in it. However, the sell-off has been resisted by John Lewis management. In its view it may be counter-productive in a business sense to sell the company. Management also point out that the partnership arose in the first place because of an act of generosity by the previous owner, Spedan Lewis. It would be legally difficult and morally questionable to break up the partnership he founded.

The business argument is easy to understand. The John Lewis shops have strong traditions and are patronized by many customers because of a jealously guarded reputation for quality and value. A change of ownership might well undermine all this. There is also the issue of what the John Lewis partners risk *losing* in a change of ownership. Shop staff enjoy a range of benefits unusual in retailing. After 5 years' service they are guaranteed a job for life; after 25 years there is six months' paid leave. All staff receive an annual bonus based on profits. In 1998 this was set at 22 per cent. John Lewis shops naturally open on Saturday, so all staff get Monday off instead. There is more, but the reader will get the general idea. It might be expected that new owners might quickly push working practices and staff benefits towards (i.e. *down* to) the more familiar level for retail employees. So, while flotation might bring its obvious immediate cash rewards for the John Lewis partners, it might also put at risk at least some of their jobs and possibly the whole basis of the business itself. The question of which legal status to adopt is clearly a more difficult one than it might at first appear.

Littlewoods

This sentiment can be echoed in the case of Littlewoods, Britain's largest *private* company. Littlewoods, the retailing and football pools group, is owned by 32 members of the Moores family. The company was founded in the 1930s by the late Sir John Moores. In common with other large retailing groups, the decade or so up to the millennium was not an easy period for Littlewoods. The growth of out-of-town shopping made city centre retailing a challenging business. On top of this, Littlewoods Pools faced intense competition with the launch of the National Lottery.[1] In 1995 Littlewoods was subject to two takeover bids. These were of particular interest because of the long-standing family-owned status of the business. Reports in the press suggested that some of the younger elements of the Moores family favoured selling, while others wished to retain ownership. In the end the business was not sold, and more recently there have been clear statements that a straight flotation is not on the family's agenda. Had the Moores family given up control of Littlewoods, ownership by others or a possible flotation would have provided a large amount of money for new investment in the firm's various divisions as well as substantial additional personal wealth for the family itself. In the case of Littlewoods, then, continued private ownership means that the Moores family have chosen not to realize the wealth tied up in the business, and indicated that they prefer to meet the challenges

[1] The pools business was subsequently sold to another firm.

Littlewoods: staying a private company.

of an increasingly competitive environment without recourse to the cash infusion that might come from a change in ownership.

Sunderland Football Club

For Sunderland Football Club, competitive pressures have brought a different answer to the question of whether or not to change the basis of ownership of a business. Sunderland was floated on the stock market at the end of 1996. This move was intended to help the club compete in the Premier League business alongside the traditionally bigger clubs, some of which had already opted for public company status. The capital raised by the sale was intended to help Sunderland strengthen its team *and* underpin investment in the wider business. The two go hand in hand. If Sunderland perform well in footballing terms then match attendances – at a completely new stadium – will increase, they will be on satellite television more (earning substantial fees), and they will sell more replica kits and other merchandise. In this case, then, the existing owners of a business are happy to sell some of their shareholdings in order to generate new monies for investment.

Note that, in each of our examples, there is no right or wrong solution. Decisions concerning the legal status of a firm will be taken by the owners of the firm in their perceptions of their own and the firm's best interests.

Finally, emerging evidence suggests that *combining* forms of ownership can make commercial sense. For example, consider the growth in *franchising* in Western economies in recent years. Franchising involves a firm's selling or leasing the right to produce and/or sell its brand of goods to a third party. In the UK, it has been estimated that 10 per cent of retailing is franchise based. Perhaps the world's most famous franchising operation is *McDonald's*: 85 per cent of McDonald's restaurants are actually run by franchisees. The attraction of franchising is that it can combine the resources, experience and expertise of a large company with the commitment of the franchisee. The franchisee can take the same kind of risks as (say) a sole proprietor but does so in the knowledge that he or she is treading on proven ground. At the same time, the franchiser is assured that each individual franchisee has a direct personal stake in the development of the business and is therefore highly committed to it.

3.5 Objectives of firms, and the principal–agent problem

Objectives of firms

As noted, the conventional assumption underlying orthodox microeconomic theory of the firm is that firms seek to maximize the profit that they earn. Firms compete with one another for the patronage of the consumer, profit being the indicator of success: those firms that neglect the profit motive risk bankruptcy at the hands of rivals who do not. The greater the degree of competition, the higher the likelihood that non-profit-maximizing firms will fail to survive. Pursuing the objective of profit maximization is seen as the best guarantee that the firm will continue in business and succeed. Profit is determined by the difference between the total revenue and total costs of the firm over a given period of time. In Chapter 4 we examine firms' costs and revenues, and specifically in section 4.6 discuss the level of output at which profit maximization is achieved. Before discussing the profit-maximization objective, which underlies traditional theory, it is worth briefly considering a number of *alternative views* on the objectives of firms that have appeared in the literature. We begin our discussion with an overview of the behavioural approach, in which firms do not aim to 'maximize' a 'single' goal (namely profits), but instead seek to achieve 'satisfactory' performance over a range of 'multiple' objectives.

According to R.M. Cyert and J.G. March, who developed their behavioural theory of the firm in the early 1960s, firms normally try to achieve five main goals involving targets for output, sales, inventory control, market share and profit. In this approach the firm is viewed as a *coalition* of various groups, which include managers, workers, shareholders, creditors and customers. These groups make competing demands on the firm. For example, workers may want high wages, whereas shareholders may want high dividends. Goals are set, and are modified over time, through a complex process of bargaining as managers try to contain and resolve the conflicting demands of different groups in the firm. In contrast to the conventional theory of the firm, firms are seen as *satisficers* with multiple goals, rather than 'maximizers' pursuing a single goal of profits.

We now turn to managerial theories that retain 'maximization' in objectives, but highlight objectives being maximized that are different from that of the conventional profit-maximization objective. In what follows we outline three such theories associated with the work of W.J. Baumol, O.E. Williamson and R. Marris. These theories are based on the separation of ownership (by shareholders) from control (by managers) of the firm and an understanding that the objective that is maximized depends on the motives of the top managers. The factors commonly highlighted that motivate managers are the desire for status, power, income and security.

In the early 1960s W.J. Baumol developed a theory of the firm in which some managers seek to *maximize sales revenue*, subject to a minimum level of profit being earned. Baumol based his theory on his experiences as a consultant for a number of large firms, in which he observed that some managers were more interested in expanding turnover than profits. The reason identified for this is that the status, power and income of top managers are often more closely related to sales revenue than they are to profit. It is, however, important to note that the objective of sales revenue maximization is subject to a minimum profit constraint that allows shareholders to be paid dividends that are high enough to keep them content and deter them from getting together to threaten the security of the management team.

Another theory developed in the early 1960s is that advanced by O.E. Williamson, involving 'managerial discretion', in which managers aim to *maximize* their own *satisfaction* or utility, subject to a minimum level of profit being earned that will keep shareholders content. Williamson argued that managers derive satisfaction, or utility, from certain kinds of expenditure, namely spending on emoluments, discretionary investment and staff. Managerial emoluments (for example, on such 'perks' as generous expense accounts and luxurious company cars) and discretionary investment (such as expenditure on new and expensive personal computers) are more likely to enhance image, rather than be justified on the grounds of profit maximization. Finally, increased expenditure on staff may also be undertaken to enhance the status, influence and standing of managers. Such expenditure is commonly referred to as 'empire building'. To summarize, in this approach managers will spend any profit that exceeds the minimum profit constraint on emoluments, discretionary investment and staff so as to maximize their own satisfaction or utility.

The final managerial theory we shall briefly outline is that put forward by R. Marris in the mid 1960s. According to this theory managers seek to *maximize* the *growth rate* of the firms they manage in order to increase their own status, power and income. As managers also desire job security they have an interest in minimizing the risk of mergers and takeovers which threaten their security. The danger of a firm being taken over will increase the lower is the market value of the shares of the firm compared with the capital or book value of the assets of the firm (such as buildings, capital equipment and land).Given that the risk that the firm will be taken over is greater the lower the **valuation ratio**, managers will need to pay shareholders adequate dividends to maintain the present market value of the firm's shares at a relatively high level.

Central to the three managerial theories we have outlined is the divergence in interest between managers and shareholders. As such these theories can be seen as an example of the so-called principal–agent problem.

The principal–agent problem

The basic premise of the principal–agent problem is that firms may not always behave in the profit-maximizing way anticipated by economic theory. This is because firms are often not simple organizations: their structures are riven by relationships between diverse economic groups that can effectively pull the individual firm in different directions. We have noted, for example, the possible tensions between a firm's managers and its shareholder owners, but probably the most quoted instance of the principal–agent problem concerns the relationship between the managers of a firm and its workers. Here, the managers assume the guise of principals and are responsible for setting the 'agenda' for the firm while the workers as their agents

Valuation ratio: The market valuation of a firm, expressed by the price of its shares divided by the book value of its assets.

essentially carry out major parts of that agenda. If the objective of the firm is indeed profit maximization, what happens when the worker-agents choose not to perform their allotted tasks as well as they might? Workers may not be as zealous about production or quality targets because it is managers who are directly responsible for these, not the workers themselves. Here again the firm's effectiveness and therefore its profits will be compromised by the establishment of two disparate agendas: the managers' (principals') and the workers' (agents').

The solution to the principal–agent problem in this case involves binding the objectives of the agents to those of the principals. This can be done in a variety of ways. For example, the distribution of shares to workers – giving them a direct stake in the firm – may serve to focus their attention on the performance of the firm. This means that the objectives of workers and managers run in parallel, and a degree of unanimity about the need for profit maximization in the firm can be achieved.

In recent years, a more common strategy to overcome the principal–agent problem in respect of workers as agents has involved the reorganization of work itself. In manufacturing industry especially, the introduction of computerized technology has allowed managers to define more autonomous and challenging roles for production workers. The objective here is to push more responsibility for the organization of work and for the quality and quantity of what is produced onto the worker-agents: in other words, to make them behave more like (self) managers or principals. Once again, the solution to the principal–agent problem is an attempt to fuse the agent to the principal.

A good early example of this kind of development is provided by the car industry and, in particular, innovative working practices amongst Japanese car manufacturers such as Nissan. Nissan opened its first car plant in Britain in 1986. The plant was located in Washington in the North-East of England – a place with no history of car making. This was no accident. Nissan wanted to make cars in ways not previously seen in Britain. It supposed that this would be best done in a place where traditional methods of manufacturing would not have to be challenged or 'unlearned'. The Nissan television advertisement in Box 3.1 gives a flavour of the working environment the firm had in mind for its new plant. Nissan wanted management and workers to meet daily to discuss possible improvements in car production. It saw work as achieving something, fostering a pride in the product. The firm had still further ambitions. It saw its employees – management and workers alike – as part of the same team. All employees at Nissan would wear the same uniform and eat in the same canteen. There would be no clocking on. Finally, Nissan recognized a single union at its plant. In exchange for recognition, the union agreed a set of protocols that made

---

Box 3.1

Nissan television advertisement

'Imagine a car factory where no one goes on strike, and where no one is made redundant either. Imagine if the managing director dressed just the same as the men on the line. Imagine if the management and workers got together every day to see how they could make things better. Imagine if work wasn't just about getting a better pay packet, but about working together to make something you could be proud of. Maybe then it would be possible to make a car so good, they'd have a 100 000 mile or three-year warranty. Or is this just a daydream?'

Source: Bassett, P. *Strike Free: New Industrial Relations in Britain* (London: Macmillan, 1986)

industrial action – strikes – the last option in a long process of negotiation and arbitration.

All this was a long way from traditional working arrangements and industrial relations in British car plants. In the 1960s and 1970s car manufacturing had represented an archetype of the principal–agent problem as far as car firms were concerned. Large numbers of workers were engaged in boring, arduous and repetitive tasks on an assembly line under the direct supervision and control of chargehands, foremen and managers. It was the job of these authority figures – principals – to *extract* work from those on the line. The result was a continuing antagonism between management and labour that translated into poor industrial relations and problems for car firms in their attempts to organize profitable production. Now, whether or not the attempts by Nissan and – following its lead – most other car producers *fundamentally* changed the organization of work is an open question, and not one we have the opportunity to explore further in a book of this kind. However, what we *can* say is that the Nissan case provides a useful illustration of how firms may confront the principal–agent problem in the context of workers as agents.

3.6 Takeovers and mergers: the market for corporate control

A merger occurs when two firms agree to join together. Sometimes one firm actually 'takes over' the other by buying a controlling interest in that firm. Not surprisingly this is known as a 'takeover' or an 'acquisition'. In practice there is little distinction between the two. Most of the larger firms that exist today will have achieved their present size via a merger or a takeover. Mergers often dominate the financial press, and there have been a number of large-scale mergers in recent years in many different industries. Examples include the merger of the Alliance Building Society and the Leicester Building Society, British Airways and British Caledonian in the air traffic industry, Price Waterhouse and Coopers and Lybrand in chartered accountancy, and the TSB and Lloyds in the banking industry.

In broad terms there are three types of merger. The first arises where two firms are in the same industry and at the same stage of production: for example the merging of Glaxo-Wellcome with SmithKline and Beecham in the pharmaceuticals industry. This is known as a **horizontal merger**. The second arises where two firms are in the same industry but at different stages of production: for example, a supplier such as a brewery takes over a retailer such as a pub. This is an instance of a **vertical merger**. Finally, **conglomerate mergers** arise where the relevant firms are in completely different industries: for example the merger of Cadburys and Schweppes.

Motives for merger

Why might two firms decide to merge? In the case of *horizontal mergers*, the main motivation is to lower overall costs. If two firms merge then, for example, only one marketing department is required. This means that overall expenditure on marketing can be reduced. Of course, reduced costs often come via redundancies. At the time of writing, National Westminster Bank is the target of a takeover bid by the Royal Bank of Scotland, and a large number of staff redundancies seem likely.

Horizontal merger: Arises when two firms in the same industry and stage in the production process merge together.

Vertical merger: Occurs when two firms in the same industry, but at different stages in the production process, merge.

Conglomerate merger: Occurs when two firms from different industries merge.

The merger of Commercial Union and General Accident in the insurance industry is another example of a horizontal merger. Horizontal mergers may also be the result of a desire on the part of both firms to reduce overall competition and to increase overall market share and market power. Market power is explored in more detail in Chapter 5.

The motivation for a *vertical merger* tends to be somewhat different. A supplier or manufacturer often merges with a retailer to ensure an outlet for its product. Furthermore, in doing so it reduces the number of outlets available to rival suppliers or manufacturers. A vertical merger can also work in the opposite direction when a firm merges with its supplier. This enables it to guarantee a supply of raw materials or components, and also allows it to control the quality of supply more easily. Such a merger would also tend to reduce the cost of inputs, as the supplier's profit margin would almost certainly be removed. An excellent example of a vertical merger in recent years is the Halifax bank's decision to purchase a large chain of estate agents.

The prime motivation for a *conglomerate merger* is diversification: when a firm chooses to develop a market in a completely different industrial sector. This may be because the market for its own product has become 'saturated'. It also gives a firm a form of insurance in that it can still prosper if the demand for its own product starts to decline.

There are, of course, a number of other motives for merger that we have not yet considered. One such motive is the desire to combine complementary resources, in such areas as design, marketing or production. Recently, Deutsche Bank acquired the investment bank Morgan Grenfell. This may well reflect a desire on the part of Deutsche Bank to gain a share of the large American investment market. Taxation considerations may also provide motivation for mergers. Firms that make a trading loss in one year can 'carry forward' these losses to offset against future profits. This will reduce that firm's tax liability. This is perfectly legal under US tax legislation, so that there is an incentive to acquire firms with large accumulated trading losses. The legislation in the UK, however, is far more strict. Losses incurred by the acquired firm *before* the merger takes place cannot be used to offset future trading profits of the newly merged firm.

A merger may also result from inefficient management. If the management of Firm A is more efficient that the management of Firm B then the merger will be beneficial if the management of Firm A is in control of the firm after the merger. This benefit will not be restricted simply to the new firm. The public at large may also benefit if the quality of the product is improved, or if it becomes available at a reduced price.

One firm may also seek to acquire another firm if it has a surplus of unused cash available. A firm will allocate resources to investment projects and to the payment of dividends to shareholders. It may be argued that any surplus cash should then be distributed to shareholders. However, management may be reluctant to do this, preferring instead to purchase another firm. It is worth pointing out that the threat of a takeover can act as a control on managerial behaviour. It may be that the management of a firm is pursuing its own interests and not acting in the interests of the firm's shareholders. In such cases the mere threat of a takeover may help to encourage managers to act in the interests of the shareholders. One final motive for merger, which should not be overlooked, is the managerial motive. Management will tend to benefit from a merger. They will be responsible for the running of a much larger enterprise and, in turn, will receive higher salaries and greater perks commensurate

Box 3.2

Merger in the British banking industry

At the beginning of October 1999 the Bank of Scotland launched a £21 billion bid to take over National Westminster Bank (NatWest). The Bank of Scotland announced that the merging of the two banks would result in cost savings of over £1 billion. These reduced costs would involve the closing down of NatWest's head office, rationalization of the treasury and computing departments, and almost certainly branch closures. In addition, the Bank of Scotland plans to close many of the older, larger premises and move to much smaller branches. These reductions in cost, associated with the increase in size, are known as *economies of scale* (see Chapter 4, section 4.4). If the bid is successful, the Bank of Scotland will have expanded its branch network and widened its customer base while simultaneously reducing costs. It will also increase its market power by reducing potential competition. An increase in profitability seems likely.

Merger in the European steel industry

In June 1999 British Steel announced plans to merge with the Dutch company Hoogovens. If the merger goes ahead it will form the third largest steel firm in the world. This is the latest in a series of mergers in the European steel industry. The motivation for such merger activity may be a response to falling steel prices following low market demand in recent years. It may also be a response to the availability of cheaper imported steel from Asia and Eastern Europe. Many European steel firms have reported large reductions in profits. As a result many are seeking partners in order to protect market share, become more efficient by reducing costs, and thereby safeguard future profits.

However, the case of British Steel and Hoogovens is slightly different. Both are in good financial health, and neither has experienced falling profits. The proposed merger is almost certainly designed to reduce costs through increased size of operations – that is, economies of scale. Furthermore, both firms, aware of the threat of competition from abroad, clearly feel that the increase in market power that comes from increased size will help them to compete in the world steel industry.

with an increase in their status. Box 3.2 looks at recent merger activity in two very different industries and considers some of the reasons behind it.

Patterns of merger activity

Fig. 3.1 illustrates merger activity in the United Kingdom between 1970 and 1998. The graph shows the total value of companies acquired in that time. Note that merger activity is not constant, but tends to come in 'waves'. Often mergers tend to increase when the economy is doing well. Firms will tend to have larger profits in such times and can more easily afford to purchase another firm. There is an obvious peak in merger activity in the late 1980s. During this period, the economy was expanding rapidly (the period is often known as the 'Lawson boom' after the Chancellor at the time); taxation and interest rates were low, and the value of property was soaring. Firms were able to obtain cheap finance with which to acquire other firms.

The main impact of merger activity is usually the creation of large firms with increased market share and power. This raises the issue of whether such growth in the size of firms is desirable. Market power and some of its implications are discussed in Chapter 5. Naturally, the government is keen to ensure that mergers do not act against the public interest, and therefore any proposed merger may be considered by the Competition Commission (previously known as the Monopolies and Mergers

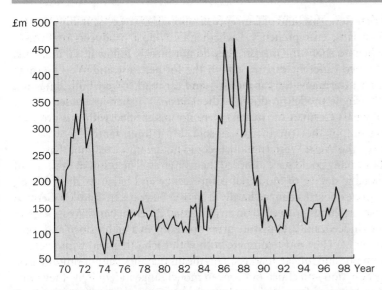

Fig. 3.1 UK industrial and commercial companies acquired – actual value.
Source: Datastream.

Commission). The Commission can advise as to whether or not any merger can proceed. We examine the regulation of competition more fully in Chapter 7, section 7.8.

3.7 Firms and entrepreneurship: an Austrian view

Earlier in this chapter we defined entrepreneurship as the capacity to organize the remaining factors of production: land, labour and capital. We also argued that it is the pivotal factor in capitalist production insomuch as it is uniquely able to discern the demands of consumers. This latter claim is derived from the *Austrian School* of economic thought, and merits further elaboration here. Austrian economics emerged in Vienna in the 1870s in the works of Carl Menger (1840–1921), Ludwig von Mises (1881–1973) and Friedrich Hayek (1899–1992). As a result of Nazism, the school's leading proponents moved abroad, especially to the United States. The major contemporary figure in Austrian economics is Israel Kirzner (b. 1930), who has written extensively on entrepreneurship.

For pre-Austrian economists, including Adam Smith, the *organizational role* of the entrepreneur was of primary interest: he or she assembled the necessary factors of production in the appropriate form and received the appropriate reward – profit – for so doing. With its emphasis on the attainment of market equilibrium (as detailed in Chapters 1 and 2), mainstream economic thought has tended to reinforce this view that the entrepreneurial task is not possessed of any particular dynamism. The market process balances supply and demand; all entrepreneurs have to do is produce the appropriate quantities of goods and services at the appropriate price while controlling their costs. Rather like an engine that has been set running, each firm can simply 'tick over', with the entrepreneur supplying the fuel and the occasional tune-up as required.

In the Austrian view, this kind of conceptualization of entrepreneurship is *far too passive*. For Austrians, entrepreneurs – whether individual producers or firms – anticipate and help to shape the market, they do not meekly follow it. To illustrate, think about the two different car markets in the former East and West German economies. In East Germany, the car industry and car market were both state-run. Demand for the single model produced – the *Trabant* – generally tended to run ahead of supply. East German car makers were not dissatisfied with this arrangement; whatever output they produced was sold. Most importantly there was no competition from the West; Western models could not be imported, not that many people in East Germany could have afforded them anyway. The result of this state of affairs was a notable degree of industrial complacency and lethargy: the Trabant, made partly from cardboard, changed hardly at all over 30 years. In the West German car market, however, things proceeded on an altogether different basis. West German car makers were (indeed, still are) private firms operating in a highly open and competitive environment. They must compete both with each other and with overseas firms for the domestic and foreign markets. This means that they cannot simply parcel up factors of production and churn out a given model range indefinitely: they must continually strive to outperform their rivals, both on price and in terms of the quality of product. In a word these firms must be *entrepreneurial*. The outcome is that names such as *Mercedes* and *BMW* have become bywords for quality and excellence, while Trabants, shorn of state protection following German reunification, are no longer made.

While this example gives us a flavour of what Austrians mean by entrepreneurship, it doesn't quite capture their interpretation completely. Entrepreneurial firms must certainly observe the imperatives of consumer sovereignty and follow the patterns of demand that consumers lay down. But, crucially from the Austrian perspective, they also help to *anticipate* demand. The key here is the ability of the entrepreneurial firm to *innovate*. For example, the impressive range of new computerized electronic goods that have emerged over the last two decades – personal computers, video, CD and DVD equipment, advanced communications technologies and so on – are all available because of the entrepreneurial skill of firms. Note again that this does not mean that all or even many firms have to *invent* new goods; their contribution is to *find market applications* for technologies as they emerge. Indeed, innovation does not necessarily have to embody sophisticated new technologies at

Mercedes: cars of quality from a highly entrepreneurial firm.

Unlikely entrepreneurs?

"Son, your Mother and I have decided to start an advertising agency."

all. For example, in the UK at present there is a phenomenal interest in cooking. All the major TV channels show cooking programmes, and there are numerous promotional spin-offs in 'book of the series' publications, specialized kitchen equipment, and even cooking holidays. The entrepreneurial skill here was to *anticipate* the level of popular demand for this kind of activity and to *persuade and even educate* people that cooking is something most of us can enjoy doing. Of course, however strong the persuasion, the consumer remains the final arbiter. If demand is not forthcoming, the product or products will inevitably fail.

Now, the Austrian version of entrepreneurship has some interesting implications for the notion of *market equilibrium*. Recall the definition of equilibrium we offered in Chapter 2: a position from which there is no tendency to change. At an equilibrium price, the quantities of a good demanded and supplied are perfectly matched. Accordingly, because both consumers and producers are satisfied with existing conditions, there is no pressure from either group that might result in changes in the quantities demanded or supplied. Yet entrepreneurs, in the Austrian view, are clearly *never* satisfied with the existing state of affairs in a given market. Prompted by the pressure of a competitive environment and the prospect of profit, they are *continually* seeking to engineer changes in the market, to introduce modified or wholly new goods and services to make consumers aware of wants and needs they did not know they had. In this sense, equilibrium is always just out of reach, and inevitably so. A market in equilibrium would be one in which entrepreneurship was dead: an impossibility under capitalism but a state of affairs that Austrians would recognize in (say) the former East German car industry. In the Austrian view then, markets are dynamic and uncertain arenas in which entrepreneurs innovate and compete under the ultimate sanction of the consumer; entrepreneurship is in effect the *motive force* of capitalism.

Summary

◆ Firms are a key institution in capitalism. They use factors of production to produce goods and services that can be sold for profit. Economic theory assumes that firms attempt to maximize profits.

◆ Profit maximization, while self-evidently beneficial for the firm, is also held to serve the interests of consumers. Firms operate in a competitive environment, and must produce goods and services that consumers demand at an appropriate price. Thus the most successful and most profitable firms are those best able to satisfy the consumer.

◆ Firms exist because they offer a number of advantages as organizers of production that individuals operating through the market cannot attain. Thus firms provide savings on transaction costs; they facilitate the extension of the division of labour; and they are accomplished innovators.

◆ There are three main categories of firm, as defined by ownership: sole proprietorships, partnerships, and limited companies. Sole proprietorships and partnerships are generally smaller, simpler to manage and taxed less than limited companies, but they find it harder to raise capital and their owners have unlimited liability for losses. Companies tend to be larger, more difficult to manage, and are subject to heavier taxes. However, they can raise capital more easily, as their shareholders' risk is limited to the size of their immediate investment. All three categories are well represented in most advanced capitalist economies, suggesting a fairly even balance of advantage and disadvantage between them.

◆ A number of alternative views on the objectives of firms have appeared in the literature. Aside from profit maximization these include: achieving satisfactory performance over a range of multiple objectives; maximizing sales revenue; maximizing managerial satisfaction; and maximizing the growth rate of firms.

◆ The principal–agent problem is an acknowledgement that, in the real world, firms may not always approximate the seamless profit-maximizing entities of economic theory.

◆ In the view of Austrian economists, the central attribute of the firm is its entrepreneurial skill. Motivated by profit, entrepreneurial firms operating in a competitive environment are at the dynamic and innovative heart of capitalism. This conceptualization of the firm leaves the consumer as the ultimate arbiter of the course of capitalist production, but it sits rather uneasily with the notion of equilibrium as defined by mainstream economic theory. For Austrians, equilibrium is always just out of reach as entrepreneurs consistently reshape what they produce and how they produce it in the search for more profit.

Key terms

◆ Firms
◆ Entrepreneurship
◆ Factors of production
◆ Profit maximization
◆ Limited and unlimited liability
◆ Objectives of firms
◆ Principal–agent problem
◆ Austrian approach to entrepreneurship

◼ Questions for discussion

◆ What is the prime function of the firm, and how is it motivated?

◆ What advantages do firms, as opposed to individuals, offer as organizers of production?

◆ What are the relative merits of the three main types of firm?

◆ What is the principal–agent problem, and what implications does it have for the firm?

◆ What perspective do Austrian economists have on entrepreneurship?

◼ Further reading

Putterman, L. and R.S. Kroszner, *The Economic Nature of the Firm* (London: Cambridge University Press, 1996). Offers a combination of classic papers and modern interpretations on the nature of the firm.

Kirzner, I. *The Meaning of Market Process* (London: Routledge, 1992). Collection of writings on Austrian economics by one of its leading exponents.

◼ Internet links

The *Financial Times'* website, which we further endorse in later chapters, is an excellent source of free company news: **http://www.ft.com/**

Firms' Costs and Revenues

Key issues

▶ How does the principle of diminishing marginal returns determine firms' short-run costs?

▶ What are the implications for costs of a change in the scale of production?

▶ How are firms' revenues affected by a change in quantity produced?

▶ How do firms determine the profit-maximizing level of output?

4.1 Introduction

In the previous chapter we discussed the role of the firm in the capitalist production process, and considered some specific advantages offered by firms as organizers of production. In the present chapter we examine how firms convert factors of production, such as land, labour and capital, into goods and services. In doing so we look closely at the different costs that arise in production, and analyse why costs are so important in the identification of the profit-maximizing quantity of production. As we shall see, firms seeking to maximize profits try to maximize the difference between costs and revenues. Therefore we also need to examine firms' revenues, and the way in which revenues are related to price and quantity.

At the outset we need to make a distinction between the short run and the long run.

- The **short run** is that period of time for which at least one of the factors of production, usually land or capital, is fixed. In this chapter, for simplification, we refer to land and capital collectively as capital. Our assumption means that, in the short run, if a firm wishes to produce more of a good it will only be able to do so by hiring more labour. It is difficult to define the short run as a precise number of years or months. In certain industries, such as car manufacturing, a firm may be able to upgrade or expand its production line (capital) in six months: hence the short run would be up to six months. In other industries, such as gas, the construction of new larger pipelines may take up to three years: hence the short run in the gas industry would be a period up to three years.

Short run: That period of time for which at least one of the factors of production, usually land or capital, is fixed.

- The **long run** is that period of time for which all factors of production are variable, so that firms wishing to produce more can consider increasing labour and/or capital and produce on a much larger scale. In our examples, the long run in the car industry would be six months or more, whereas in the gas industry the long run would be three years or more.

We begin this chapter by focusing on the short run and examining short-run costs where firms are operating with a fixed stock of capital. As labour alone can be varied in the short run, a number of implications arise for the costs faced by firms. In order to understand the pattern of short-run costs we first need to examine the production function.

4.2 The production function and the law of diminishing marginal returns

The **production function** illustrates the relationship between the total quantity of goods or services produced and the quantity of factors of production used in the production process. As noted, in the short run we assume that capital is fixed so that the only factor that can be varied is labour.

Now, let us assume that an entrepreneur opens a small factory making shirts. The factory and machinery within represent the entrepreneur's capital stock. In the short run this factory cannot be expanded in size, nor can the machinery be upgraded or improved. Initially, assume that there are no workers. In this case the factory will lie idle and no shirts will be produced. But what if one worker is employed? Shirt production will now take place. Of course, one person alone cannot produce many shirts; nevertheless production will increase from zero. Assume that the first worker produces ten shirts per period: hence the worker raises production from no shirts to ten shirts. We can say that the **marginal product of labour** $(MPL) = 10$. If one worker produces ten shirts then the **average product of labour** $(APL) = 10$. What if a second worker is employed? Two workers can specialize and work together; one perhaps concentrating on cutting the material, the other on operating the sewing machinery. Two workers are more efficient than one, and together they can produce 30 shirts. The second worker has added an additional 20 shirts to total production, so that $MPL = 20$. On average, each worker produces 15 shirts $(30 \div 2)$ so that $APL = 15$. If a third worker is added, production becomes more efficient still and 60 shirts can be produced. In this case $MPL = 30$ (the third worker having raised total production from 30 to 60 shirts) and $APL = 20$ (the three workers produce, on average, 20 shirts each). We can see that both the MPL and APL rise as the production process becomes more efficient with the addition of more workers.

But what if we continue to add extra workers so that there are four, five, six, seven workers etc.? The factory is limited in size. Eventually it will become cramped, workers will start to get into each others' way, start to duplicate work and so on, so that eventually inefficiency sets in. Table 4.1 illustrates this process. The number of workers is shown in the column headed L (labour). Note that total production of shirts can also be termed 'total product of labour' or TPL. We have placed an asterisk when the number of workers is five. Notice that when the fifth worker is added the marginal product of labour starts to fall for the first time. Of course, the total product of labour – or number of shirts produced – continues to rise, but starts to do so at a

Long run: That period of time for which all factors of production are variable.

Production function: Illustrates the relationship between the total quantity of goods or services produced and the quantity of factors of production used in the production process.

Marginal product of labour: The increase in total production as a result of employing one more worker.

Average product of labour: The total output produced per worker employed.

Table 4.1 The total, marginal and average product of labour in the short run

L	Shirts produced (TPL)	MPL	APL
0	0		0
1	10	10	10
2	30	20	15
3	60	30	20
4	100	40	25
5*	135	35	27
6	162	27	27
7	175	13	25
8	184	9	23
9	189	5	21
10	190	1	19

Diminishing marginal returns: Occur when more and more of the variable factor of production is added to the fixed factor of production in the short run.

diminishing rate. As more and more workers are added the marginal product of labour continues to fall. This is because we are adding more and more of the variable factor (labour) to the fixed factor (capital). When the fifth worker is added we can say that the law of **diminishing marginal returns** starts to set in. Diminishing marginal returns will inevitably prevail as more and more of a variable factor is added to a fixed factor in the short run. Of course, in different industries, diminishing marginal returns set in at different times.

We can use the figures presented in Table 4.1 to plot the *TPL*, *MPL* and *APL* curves. The graph of *TPL*, which is more commonly known as the *production function*, is shown in Fig. 4.1(a). The *MPL* and *APL* curves are shown in Fig. 4.1(b). Note how *MPL* rises initially, but when five workers are employed it starts to fall. Notice also that when *MPL* is above *APL* then *APL* rises. This can also be seen in Table 4.1. When *MPL* is below *APL* then *APL* falls. Finally, when *MPL* is equal to *APL* then *APL* is at a maximum.

The slope of the production function, or *TPL*, is worthy of explanation. As the number of workers employed is raised from zero to four, workers become increasingly productive so that each additional worker leads to successively higher increases in total shirts produced. The slope of the production function therefore steepens as the number of workers approaches four. When the fifth worker is added, diminishing marginal returns set in so that the fifth worker adds less to total output than the fourth. The slope of the production function starts to flatten. As more and more workers are added beyond the fifth, it becomes progressively flatter as each additional worker adds successively less to total output.

4.3 Short-run costs

The analysis of the production function and diminishing marginal returns is the key to understanding the firm's short-run cost curves. The firm's costs are determined

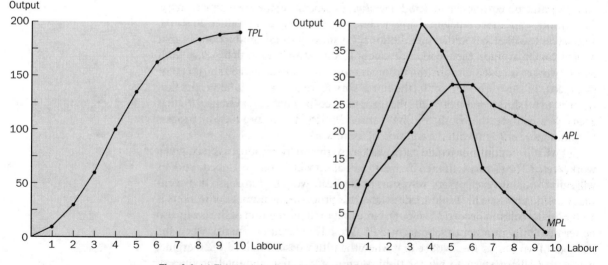

(a)

Fig. 4.1 (a) The total product of labour, more commonly known as the production function; (b) the average product of labour and the marginal product of labour.

by the quantities of labour and capital used in production. You will recall that we defined the short run as that period where labour is the only factor that can be varied. Capital is fixed. Given this assumption, we can distinguish between **fixed costs** and **variable costs**. Fixed costs are those costs that do not vary with the quantity of output produced. In our example these are the capital costs – the costs of renting or leasing the factory and machinery costs. Variable costs are those costs that *do* vary with the quantity produced. These will be made up of wage costs, as well as heating and lighting expenses, which will tend to be higher the more is produced. A firm's **total cost** (TC) is therefore its total fixed costs (TFC) plus its total variable costs (TVC):

$$TC = TFC + TVC \qquad (4.1)$$

In our example we shall assume that the firm pays each worker the same amount. When the marginal product of labour rises then the actual cost of producing each successive unit, more commonly known as **marginal cost**, falls. The marginal cost is in fact the change in total costs as a result of a change in quantity produced. We have so far defined the quantity produced as the total product of labour. More commonly this is known simply as 'quantity' or 'output' This can be expressed as

$$MC = \frac{\Delta TC}{\Delta Q} \qquad (4.2)$$

where Δ denotes a change, and Q = quantity or output.

As soon as diminishing marginal returns set in, the marginal product of labour starts to fall and the short-run marginal cost starts to rise. It is therefore the effect of diminishing marginal returns to the variable factor (labour) that determines the shape of the marginal cost curve. This will also affect the average variable costs. The average variable costs (AVC) are the total variable costs (TVC) per unit of output (Q): that is, $AVC = TVC/Q$. Short-run average variable costs will fall initially, as the first few workers are highly productive and output of shirts rises. However, average variable costs will start to rise as a result of diminishing marginal returns.

In order to illustrate these costs let us continue with our earlier example and assume that each worker is paid £50 per period. To produce more shirts more workers will be employed. As this happens wage costs will obviously rise. Any cost that increases as production increases is known as a *variable cost*. Of course, certain costs will not vary as production rises. For example, the annual building lease or rental will be the same however many shirts the firm produces. If we make the assumption that capital is fixed in the short run then capital costs will not rise with increased production. Let us assume, for illustration, that such fixed capital costs are £250.

Table 4.2 illustrates the relationship between TPL, MPL and APL and short-run costs. In examining the table recall that TPL is the same as the quantity of output produced. From now on we refer to this as Q. Columns 1–4 reproduce the information presented in Table 4.1. Columns 5 and 6 contain data on total fixed costs (TFC) and total variable costs (TVC) respectively, which, when added together, give the total cost (TC) of producing in the short run, shown in column 7. In column 8, short-run marginal costs are shown. In order to see how these are calculated consider the increase in production from 0 to 10 shirts. The increase in total costs associated with this increase in shirt production is 50 (from 250 to 300). Thus the marginal cost is 50 (ΔTC) divided by 10 (ΔQ), which is equal to 5. Now consider the increase in production from 10 to 30 shirts. The increase in shirts produced is 20. The

Fixed costs: Costs that do not change with the output level; also referred to as overhead costs or unavoidable costs.

Variable costs: Costs that vary with the output level; also referred to as direct costs or avoidable costs.

Total cost: The sum of the costs of all inputs used in producing a firm's output; can be divided into fixed and variable costs.

Marginal cost: The change in total cost resulting from increasing production by one unit.

Table 4.2 The relationship between the total, marginal and average product of labour and a firm's costs in the short run

1 L	2 Q	3 MPL	4 APL	5 TFC	6 TVC	7 TC	8 MC	9 AFC	10 AVC	11 ATC
0	0		0	250	0	250		–	–	–
		10					5			
1	10		10	250	50	300		25	5	30
		20					2.5			
2	30		15	250	100	350		8.3	3.3	11.6
		30					1.7			
3	60		20	250	150	400		4.2	2.5	6.7
		40					1.3			
4	100		25	250	200	450		2.5	2	4.5
		35					1.4			
5*	135		27	250	250	500		1.8	1.8	3.6
		27					1.9			
6	162		27	250	300	550		1.5	1.9	3.4
		13					3.8			
7	175		25	250	350	600		1.4	2	3.4
		9					5.6			
8	184		23	250	400	650		1.3	2.2	3.5
		5					10			
9	189		21	250	450	700		1.3	2.4	3.7
		1					50			
10	190		19	250	500	750		1.3	2.6	3.9

increase in total costs associated with this increase is 50 (from 300 to 350). Thus the marginal cost is 50 divided by 20, which is equal to 2.5. Note how marginal costs fall until the point of diminishing marginal returns is reached when the fifth worker is added. Beyond this point marginal costs start to rise. Columns 9–11 show the breakdown of short-run average costs. For example, average variable cost (AVC) is calculated by dividing TVC by the number of shirts produced (Q).

We can now use these figures to plot the short-run cost curves. Short-run total cost, total variable costs and total fixed cost are shown in Fig. 4.2(a), and short-run average total cost, average variable cost and marginal cost are shown in Fig. 4.2(b). Fig. 4.2(a) shows the total cost curve (TC) – that is, total fixed costs (TFC), which do not vary with output – plus total variable costs (TVC), which increase with output. The total cost curve has exactly the same shape as the total variable cost curve. This shape is determined by the principle of diminishing marginal returns. Notice that as output initially increases, total variable costs (and total costs) rise only slowly. This is because the first few workers are highly productive. As more workers are employed output continues to rise. After the addition of the fifth worker, diminishing marginal returns set in so that total variable costs start to increase more rapidly. This is shown as point A on the total variable cost curve and point B on the total cost curve.

The principle of diminishing marginal returns is most clearly illustrated by the shape of the marginal cost curve (MC). As the first four workers are added to the production process marginal costs fall. Once the fifth worker is added, and diminishing marginal returns set in, marginal costs start to rise sharply. The **average total cost** curve (ATC) is the total of average fixed costs (AFC) and average variable costs (AVC). Note from Table 4.2 (column 9) how average fixed costs fall as total fixed costs are spread over an increasingly larger range of output. Average variable costs fall initially as workers are increasingly productive, but start to rise as diminishing marginal returns set in. The ATC curve has a shallow U shape. This is because it combines the effect of falling average fixed costs, as output increases, with rising average variable costs beyond the point of diminishing marginal returns.

The relationship between short-run average total costs and marginal costs is

Average total cost: The total cost of producing any given output divided by the number of units produced. Average cost can be divided into average fixed and average variable costs.

(a)

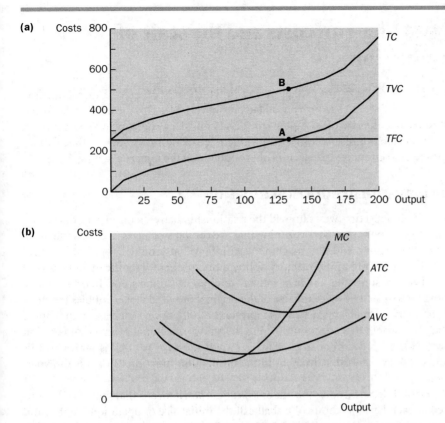

(b)

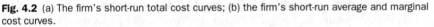

Fig. 4.2 (a) The firm's short-run total cost curves; (b) the firm's short-run average and marginal cost curves.

worth explaining in a little more detail. Reference to Table 4.2 (columns 8 and 11) and Fig. 4.2(b) reveals that, when marginal cost is below average total cost, average total cost falls. Similarly, when marginal cost is above average total cost, then average total cost rises. Finally, when marginal cost is equal to average total cost (this is not obvious from the table) average total cost is constant (that is, is at a minimum).

The following additional simple example may help you to conceptualize the relationship between marginal and average values. Suppose you are in a tutorial class where the average age is 20 years. Someone, who is younger than average, arrives late to join the class. What happens to the average age of the marginally enlarged class? Clearly the average age will fall. Alternatively, if the late arrival is older than average, then the average age of the class will rise. Only where the extra (marginal) person has exactly the same age as the average will the average age of the class remain unchanged.

We have now completed our discussion of the firm's short-run cost curves. The most important point to remember is that the shapes of these curves are determined by the principle of diminishing marginal returns. Of course, a discussion of a firm's cost curves will not tell us about the quantity produced or the price at which the goods are sold. The quantity and price are in part determined by the objectives of the firm. We assume that firms are interested in the maximization of profit. Profit is the difference between revenues and costs. We shall turn to the issue of revenues in section 4.5. We now examine the firm's costs in the long run.

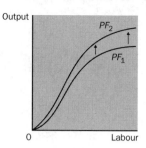

Fig. 4.3 The effect of an increase in the capital stock on the production function.

Table 4.3 How output changes following an increase in the capital stock

Plant 1		Plant 2	
L	**Q**	**L**	**Q**
0	0	0	0
1	10	1	15
2	30	2	35
3	60	3	70
4	100	4	110
5*	135	5	152
6	162	6	198
7	175	7*	230
8	184	8	246
9	189	9	260
10	190	10	265

Returns to scale: The percentage increase in output as a result of a percentage increase in both factors of production.

4.4 Long-run costs and the scale of production

We defined the short run as that period in which only one factor of production, labour, is variable. In the long run, all factors are variable. This means that the firm is able to change the size of its capital stock and consider producing on a larger scale. Let us return to our discussion of the production function and examine the relationship between output and the factors of production in the long run.

The long-run production function

In the previous section we examined the relationship between output produced and quantity of labour employed assuming that the capital stock was fixed. Capital is, of course, the factory and the machinery within. What would happen if the firm decided to move into a larger factory or buy more machinery for the manufacture of shirts? Let us assume that the firm actually doubles its capital stock. In other words, it moves into a factory twice the size of the original one, and it also doubles the stock of machinery for making shirts. This represents a 100 per cent increase in the capital stock. How would this affect output? Fig. 4.3 shows our initial production function drawn with a fixed capital stock. This is PF_1. If the capital stock is increased this would cause an upward movement in the production function to PF_2, as shown in Fig. 4.3.

As Fig. 4.3 demonstrates, the increased capital stock means that more can be produced at each level of labour. We shall call the initial size of operation Plant 1, and the new higher capital stock Plant 2. Table 4.3 compares output in the two plants. Not surprisingly, with a higher capital stock, the firm is able to produce more shirts with a given quantity of labour. Note that, even at the new higher capital stock, the production function will still exhibit diminishing marginal returns. However, given that the factory is now larger, this will occur at a higher quantity of labour (where $L = 7$) than in the smaller plant.

Returns to scale

In the long run a firm can consider increasing the quantities of both labour and capital in the production process. When a firm increases both factors by an equal amount a *change in scale* is said to take place. If the firm were to increase both the number of workers employed and the capital stock by 100 per cent (that is, move into a factory with 100 per cent more space and increase the number of machines by 100 per cent) then output would be expected to increase. The amount by which output increases determines the **returns to scale**.

In our example, if output increases by exactly 100 per cent, the firm is said to exhibit *constant returns to scale*. If output were to increase by less than 100 per cent, the firm would exhibit *decreasing returns to scale*. Decreasing returns to scale often arise because of the need to increase administrative spending and to develop a more complex management structure as a firm grows in size. Finally, if output were to increase by more than 100 per cent, the firm would exhibit *increasing returns to scale*. For example, a small firm may need only a single one-ton truck for transportation. If it were to increase the size of its operations then it might wish to sell the one-ton truck and buy a two-ton truck. One two-ton truck can transport more than twice the volume of goods of a one-ton truck. This is because of the 'container principle', whereby large containers have a bigger volume relative to surface area than do smaller containers.

If we refer back to Table 4.3 we can examine the returns to scale of the shirt-making enterprise in our example. In the smaller plant, Plant 1, if one worker is employed then ten shirts are produced. Now, if both the capital stock and labour force are doubled, the firm is operating in Plant 2 with two workers. The total number of shirts produced is 35. Thus a doubling of all inputs has led to a more than doubling of output. The firm experiences increasing returns to scale. However, what if five workers had been employed in Plant 1 and then the firm had doubled the size of all inputs? The firm would then be operating in Plant 2 with ten workers. Shirt production would increase from 135 shirts to 265 shirts. This is a less than doubling of output. The firm starts to experience decreasing returns to scale. Ultimately, whether the firm experiences increasing, decreasing or constant returns to scale determines the nature of the long-run cost curves. We shall now consider long-run average and long-run marginal costs.

Long-run average costs

In the long run, if firms increase the size of their operations and labour force by 100 per cent and output increases by more than 100 per cent, costs as a proportion of output (that is, average costs) will fall. This effect is known as securing **economies of scale**. Similarly, if output increases by less than 100 per cent, average costs will rise. Such an outcome would imply the existence of **diseconomies of scale**. Finally, where a 100 per cent increase in all inputs results in a 100 per cent increase in output, average costs will be constant.

In the case of economies of scale, long-run average costs $(LRAC)$ will fall over the range of output, as shown in Fig. 4.4. Where a firm experiences diseconomies of scale, average costs will rise over the range of output, as shown in Fig. 4.5. The long-run average cost curve will be horizontal where a firm experiences neither economies nor diseconomies of scale.

It is most commonly assumed that in the initial stages of production and expansion a firm will experience economies of scale. During this phase, long-run average costs will fall. Once a certain level of output is reached, these economies are exhausted, and long-run average costs are constant. If the firm continues to grow it will eventually experience diseconomies of scale, and long-run average costs will start to rise. This means that the long-run average cost curve will look like the one depicted in Fig. 4.6. Long-run average costs are, of course, closely related to short-run average costs. Consider again our shirt-making enterprise. In the short run it operated from a small factory, and we depicted the short-run average cost curve of this plant size in Fig. 4.2(b). In the long run, the firm could move into a larger factory with more machinery. We saw that, initially, it would benefit from increasing returns to scale and thus average costs would be reduced. Fig. 4.7 illustrates the short-run average cost curve ATC_1 associated with the smaller Plant 1, and the short-run average cost curve ATC_2 for Plant 2. Given the smaller Plant 1, the firm will produce output level Q_1, where average total costs are minimized. If the firm produces beyond Q_1 with the same plant, average costs will start to rise. Beyond Q_1 the firm will wish to expand its operations to plant size 2, and will produce to the point where average total costs are

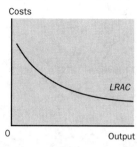

Fig. 4.4 Economies of scale and the long-run average cost curve.

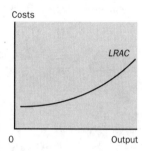

Fig. 4.5 Diseconomies of scale and the long-run average cost curve.

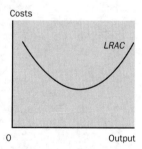

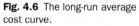

Fig. 4.6 The long-run average cost curve.

Economies of scale: Occur when long-run average costs fall as output increases.

Diseconomies of scale: Occur when long-run average costs rise as output increases.

Costs

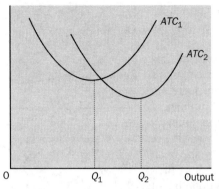

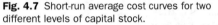

Fig. 4.7 Short-run average cost curves for two different levels of capital stock.

Costs

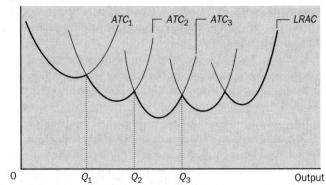

Fig. 4.8 Constructing the long-run average cost curve from short-run average cost curves.

Box 4.1

Long-run average cost and the minimum efficient scale

There have been a number of studies of long-run average costs conducted both in the United Kingdom and abroad. Many of these studies have attempted to discover exactly what happens to a firm's long-run average costs. You may recall that if a firm's long-run average costs are falling as output increases then this is known as economies of scale. For many firms, long-run average costs will fall but will eventually reach a minimum point below which they fall no further. Once minimum average costs have been achieved then the level of output associated with these average costs is known as *minimum efficient scale* (MES).

The MES is the point where long-run average cost is minimized.

Empirical work has often attempted to estimate the MES as a percentage of the total industry size. If, for example, MES as a percentage of total industry size is very low, then this would imply that many firms could exist within the industry, and that each could achieve the minimum efficient scale. Such an industry would be highly competitive. Conversely if MES was very high as a percentage of total industry size, this would imply that very few firms could exist within the industry as very few would be able to minimize long-run average costs. Such an industry would be dominated by perhaps one or two large firms and would be relatively uncompetitive.

Two of the most famous studies are that of F.M. Scherer *et al.*[1] and C.F. Pratten.[2] These are useful for comparisons, as Scherer's work was carried out in the USA while Pratten's work uses UK data. The table below summarizes the results for five common industries.

Industry	MES as % of industry size	
	UK	USA
Ball bearings	20	1.4
Cigarettes	24	6.5
Refrigerators	85	14.1
Shoes	0.3	0.2
Steel	72	2.6

The table suggests that in the UK in general the industries shown are less competitive with MES being a much higher percentage of total industry size. The most notable comparison is in the refrigerator industry. The figure of 85 per cent would suggest that only one firm could achieve minimum long-run average costs in the UK. In the USA the figure is much lower, suggesting that the industry is more competitive. This result should not be surprising. The USA is a far larger market than the UK so that each industry will be bigger than its UK counterpart. In simple terms this means that there is more 'room' for many firms in each industry.

[1] F.M.Scherer, A.Beckenstein, E.Kaufer and R.D. Murphy, *The Economics of Multiplant Operation: An International Comparisons Study* (Cambridge : Harvard University Press, 1975) pp. 80 and 94.
[2] C.F.Pratten, 'A survey of the economies of scale', in *Research on the Costs of Non-Europe*, Vol 2 (Office for Official Publications of the European Communities, 1988)

minimized. This is output level Q_2. For output levels beyond Q_2 the firm will minimize costs by moving to a larger plant size. If the firm continually expanded its operations we could draw a short-run average cost curve for each size of plant, as shown in Fig. 4.8.

The long-run average cost curve is illustrated in Fig. 4.8 as the bold line connecting the outer border of all the short-run average cost curves. For example, if the firm is producing only in the output range $0-Q_1$ then plant size 1 is the most efficient scale. If it is producing in the range Q_1-Q_2 then plant size 2 is more efficient. Plant size 3 is most efficient for producing in the range Q_2-Q_3 and so on. The long-run average cost curve shows the lowest cost of producing any output given that all factors of production can be adjusted to their optimal level.

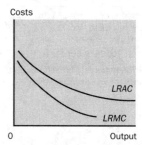
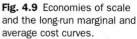

Fig. 4.9 Economies of scale and the long-run marginal and average cost curves.

Long-run marginal costs

The relationship between long-run marginal costs and long-run average costs is the same as in the short run (see section 4.3). If we consider the case of a firm experiencing economies of scale, each successive unit of output adds less to costs than the average. The long-run marginal cost curve (*LRMC*) is thus below the long-run average cost curve (*LRAC*), as shown in Fig. 4.9. For a firm experiencing diseconomies of scale, each successive unit of output adds more to costs than the average so that the long-run marginal cost curve is above the long-run average cost curve, as shown in Fig. 4.10. For a firm experiencing economies of scale, in the early stages of expansion long-run marginal costs will fall and will be below long-run average costs. As diseconomies of scale start to set in, long-run marginal cost will start to rise and will eventually rise above long-run average costs. This is illustrated in Fig. 4.11. Box 4.1 considers some evidence of firms' long-run costs in different industries.

We have now completed our examination of a firm's costs; in the next section we examine firms' revenues.

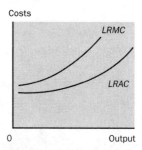

Fig. 4.10 Diseconomies of scale and the long-run marginal and average cost curves.

4.5 Firms' revenues

A firm seeking to maximize profit will attempt to determine that level of output at which the difference between revenue and costs is maximized. In order to understand revenues clearly we shall distinguish between total revenue, average revenue and marginal revenue.

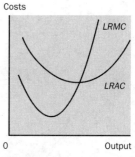
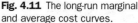

Fig. 4.11 The long-run marginal and average cost curves.

- **Total revenue** (*TR*) is the total amount earned by a firm from selling its output in a given period. If a firm sells 10 units of a good at £6 each, total revenue is £60 (10 × £6). In short, $TR = P \times Q$, where P = price and Q = quantity.

- **Average revenue** (*AR*) is the amount earned in a period per unit sold. For example, if the firm earns £60 from the sale of 10 units, average revenue is equal to £60 ÷ 10 = £6. In fact, average revenue is exactly the same as the price. In short, $AR = TR/Q$.

- **Marginal revenue** (*MR*) is the revenue earned from the sale of each successive unit of the good. In other words, *MR* measures the increase in total revenue as the firm sells one more unit of the good. So, if the firm sells one extra unit at a price of £6, marginal revenue = £6. More generally, marginal revenue can be calculated as a change in total revenue divided by the change in quantity leading to that change in total revenue. If an increase in sales of 5 units leads to an increase in

Total revenue: The amount of money that a firm receives from the sale of its output; equals the price of output multiplied by the number of units sold.

Average revenue: Total revenue divided by the number of units sold; also equals price.

Marginal revenue: The amount of money that a firm receives from an additional unit of output.

total revenue of £30, marginal revenue will be equal to £30/5 = £6. In short, $MR = \Delta TR/\Delta Q$.

We now turn to a closer examination of how revenues change according to output. We shall look at just two cases. First, we shall examine how revenues vary for a firm with no market power. Such firms are unable to set their own prices and instead simply adopt the price determined by the market forces of supply and demand. These are known as **price takers**. We then examine revenues for firms that are able to determine their own price. Such firms, known as **price makers** or **price setters**, invariably have some degree of market power.

Revenues and price takers

A firm that is a price taker cannot set its own price. We shall study such firms in more detail in Chapter 5, section 5.5, when we examine the perfectly competitive market structure. Briefly, such firms are very small relative to the total size of the market, and each produces an identical product. This means that a firm cannot independently raise its price as customers will simply buy from the other firms with a lower price. It also means that a firm cannot independently lower its price as this would lead to an infinitely large increase in the demand for its product, which the firm would be simply unable to satisfy. Instead, firms merely adopt the price determined by the forces of supply and demand in the market. Fig. 4.12 illustrates the relationship between the market determined price and the price-taking firm.

On the left of the diagram we see industry supply and demand. These determine a price level of £6 and quantity of 100 000. The right-hand side of the diagram shows the individual firm. Because the firm is so small relative to the market size, it cannot affect the market price by changing its output. The horizontal price line shown is effectively the demand curve for the individual firm. Note that we have labelled this demand curve $D = AR = MR$. If the firm sells one unit, it does so at a price of £6, so that $AR = TR/Q = £6/1 = £6$. If it sells 1000 units each at a price of £6 then $AR = TR/Q = £6000/1000 = £6$. Average revenue is thus constant at £6 (and is the same as the price!). Marginal revenue will also be equal to £6. Each successive unit is sold at this price as the firm is unable to sell at any other price: thus $P = AR = MR$.

What about total revenue? If each unit is sold for £6, total revenue will simply be

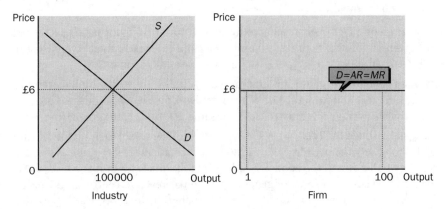

Fig. 4.12 The perfectly competitive market and the price-taking firm.

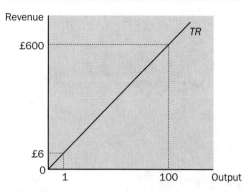

Fig. 4.13 The total revenue curve for the price taker.

£6 multiplied by the quantity sold. Fig. 4.13 illustrates the total revenue curve for a price-taking firm. Note that total revenue is simply a straight line through the origin. Total revenue rises at a constant rate as more of the good is sold.

Revenues and price makers

If a firm is able to set its own price it has a degree of market power and faces a downward-sloping demand curve. In the most extreme case just one firm exists in the industry, and this is known as a *monopoly*. We shall look at this market structure in more detail in Chapter 5, section 5.6. Because such firms face a downward-sloping demand curve, to sell more of a good they must set a lower price. Here then, unlike the case of the price taker, price will fall as more and more units are sold. This means that the revenues for a price maker are somewhat different from those of a price taker. A representation of the revenue schedules of a price-making firm are presented in Table 4.4.

Table 4.4 shows that if the price-making firm wishes to sell 100 units of its output it must set a price of £10. If it wishes to increase sales to 200 units price must be reduced to £9 and so on. Let us examine total revenue first. Total revenue rises as the firm increases sales (and lowers the price) up to the point where the price is £6 and sales are 500. Beyond this point, total revenue stops rising. A further reduction in price to £5 increases sales to 600 units, but total revenue is constant at £3000. Further attempts to boost sales through lower prices do so at the cost of lower total revenue. The total revenue curve is illustrated in Fig. 4.14. Average revenue, as we have seen, is the total revenue per unit sold. As is evident from Table 4.4, average revenue is the same as the price.

Marginal revenue, the change in total revenue from the sale of each successive unit, falls as the price is reduced. The marginal revenue is calculated as the change in total revenue (ΔTR) divided by the change in output (ΔQ). For example, when output is 100 units, total revenue is £1000. However, when output is raised to 200 units, total revenue is £1800. Therefore marginal revenue is £8 (£800 ÷ 100). Note how the fall in marginal revenue is more marked than the fall in average revenue. This is because, in order to sell more units of the good, the firm lowers the price not just on the extra units sold but on all other units as well. Once 600 units are sold, marginal revenue is zero. This is the point at which total revenue is maximized. You will recall from our discussion in Chapter 3, section 3.5, where we examined the principal–

Table 4.4 The total, marginal and average revenue for a price maker

Q	P	TR	MR	AR
0				
			10	
100	10	1000		10
			8	
200	9	1800		9
			6	
300	8	2400		8
			4	
400	7	2800		7
			2	
500	6	3000		6
			0	
600	5	3000		5
			−2	
700	4	2800		4
			−4	
800	3	2400		3

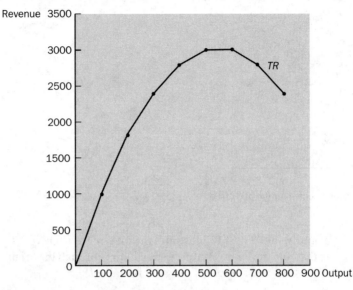

Fig. 4.14 The total revenue curve for the price maker.

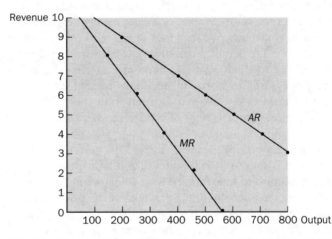

Fig. 4.15 The average and marginal revenue curves for the price maker.

agent problem and its bearing on profit maximization, that some firms will seek to maximize revenue rather than profit. If, in our example, the firm was a revenue maximizer, it would produce to that point where marginal revenue was equal to zero – that is, where total revenue was maximized.

Fig. 4.15 illustrates the firm's average and marginal revenue curves. Note how the average revenue curve illustrates the price at which each quantity of output is sold. Thus when sales are 100 price is £10; when sales are 200 price is £9, etc. It is therefore the firm's demand curve!

Having completed our examination of revenues and costs, we now have all the tools necessary to determine how firms maximize profit.

4.6 Profit maximization

In order to maximize profit any firm will need to maximize the difference between total revenue and total cost. We have looked at revenues for firms that are price takers and for firms that are price makers. In fact both types of firm will use the same decision rule in order to maximize profit.

A firm will maximize profit by producing that level of output where marginal revenue is equal to marginal cost. In other words, firms will produce a level of output such that the revenue received from the sale of the last unit of output is exactly equal to the cost of producing the last unit of output. Fig. 4.16 illustrates profit maximization for a firm that is a price taker.

Fig. 4.16 shows the horizontal demand curve for the price-taking firm. This is drawn at the price set by the industry forces of supply and demand, P^*. You should check back to the previous section to ensure that you understand that this is also the marginal revenue curve. The marginal cost curve is also shown. The two curves intersect at the profit-maximizing level of output Q^*. Let us consider why a lower level of output Q_1 is not the profit-maximizing level of output. At the output level Q_1, the marginal revenue is given by point A. The marginal cost is given by point B. Clearly, marginal revenue is greater than marginal cost at this level of output. Notice too that marginal revenue is greater than marginal cost at output levels between Q_1 and Q^*. Therefore the firm should raise production from Q_1 to Q^* because each unit sold between Q_1 and Q^* would be adding to profits. What about output level Q_2? At Q_2 marginal revenue is given by point C and marginal cost is given by point D. Clearly marginal revenue is less than marginal cost at this level of output. Therefore the firm should reduce output. If it continued to produce output level Q_2, each unit beyond Q^* would be adding more to costs than to revenues and thus reducing profit. When marginal cost and marginal revenue are not equal, profits are less than they could be. Only when the firm produces Q^* is profit maximized.

One further point of clarification in respect of Fig. 4.16 should be made here. The $MC = MR$ rule applies only when the marginal cost curve is *rising*: that is, where the marginal cost curve cuts the marginal revenue curve from below. Although we have not shown the MC curve in its entirety, it actually cuts MR twice – the first time when it is falling at a low level of output.

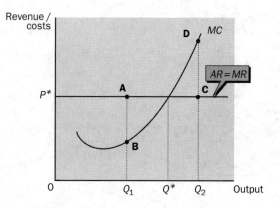

Fig. 4.16 The profit-maximizing output decision for the price taker.

(a)   **(b)**

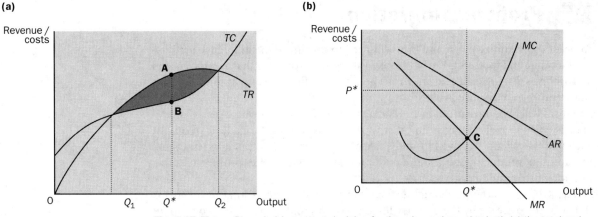

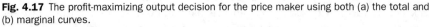

Fig. 4.17 The profit-maximizing output decision for the price maker using both (a) the total and (b) marginal curves.

Now let us examine the profit-maximizing situation for a firm that is able to determine its own price. Although the revenue curves for a price maker are somewhat different, the same rule applies. The firm will maximize profit where marginal revenue is equal to marginal cost. In order to illustrate we shall use two approaches. First we will use the 'total' curves, total revenue (TR) and total cost (TC), and then we shall use the 'marginal curves' as we did for the price taker.

Fig. 4.17(a) illustrates the firm's total revenue and total cost curves. We have seen these curves before. The total cost curve was introduced in Fig. 4.2(a), while the total revenue curve is the same as in Fig. 4.14. The shaded area indicates the level of profit. This lies between output levels Q_1 and Q_2. Note that at Q_1 and Q_2 the two curves intersect, so that total revenue and total cost are equal. Profit is therefore zero. The level of output that maximizes profit is that where the 'gap' between total revenue and total cost is at its greatest – that is, between points A and B at output level Q^*. Geometrically, the two curves are furthest apart where the slopes of the two curves are the same. The slope of the total cost curve is the marginal cost. The slope of the total revenue curve is the marginal revenue. In other words, profit is maximized where marginal revenue is equal to marginal cost.

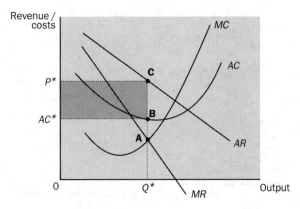

Fig. 4.18 The profit-maximizing output decision for the price maker.

Fig. 4.17(b) illustrates the marginal curves. The level of output, Q^*, is the same as in Fig. 4.17(a). In Fig. 4.17(b) this is determined at point C, where the marginal revenue and marginal cost curves intersect. Now that we have determined the level of output for the price maker, what about the price? For the price maker, this is determined in Fig. 4.17(b). From output level Q^* we simply read off the price from the average revenue curve. The profit-maximizing price is therefore P^*. Note that for a price maker, price is greater than the marginal revenue. How much profit is actually made at this point? In order to answer this question we need to introduce the average cost curve. Fig. 4.18 reproduces Fig. 4.17(b) with the addition of an average cost curve. We assume that the firm has a U-shaped average cost curve. Profits are maximized where marginal revenue and marginal cost are equal at point A. This is the output level Q^*. The profit-maximizing price is P^*. At this level of output, reading off from the average cost curve from point B we can see that the level of average cost is AC^*. The difference between price and average cost represents the profit per unit sold. The total profit made is the shaded area $P^* AC^* BC$. Box 4.2 provides an example that illustrates how the analysis covered in this section can be applied to the case study of rail pricing.

Having discussed firms' costs, revenues and profits, we turn in the next chapter to issues of market structures and market power.

Rail pricing

We can use the concepts of marginal cost and marginal revenue in order to analyse a large number of business decisions. One such decision is that of pricing. In the wake of the privatization of British Rail, a number of the newly created regional railways raised their fares sharply at certain times of the day, most notably during rush hour when demand was at its peak. Not unnaturally such decisions caused outrage among some rail users. Many of the companies stated publicly that in the absence of price increases, given the large demand for rail services, extra carriages costing up to £100 000 per year would need to be hired, and that this cost could not be justified. Higher prices were the only way that demand pressure could be eased.

We can use our framework to examine the rationale for this decision to raise prices. The first thing to note is that the costs associated with operating a train service are complex. Given an existing number of carriages, then, provided that there is some spare seating, extra passengers can be carried at a marginal cost of virtually zero. However, once existing capacity is maximized so that all carriages are full, then a large expenditure is necessary in order to carry more passengers.

Fig. 4.19 illustrates the problem. A demand curve (AR) and a marginal revenue curve (MR) are shown. The marginal cost curve (MC) deserves a little explanation. Note that marginal cost is very low until existing capacity is reached at Q_0. At this point, extra carriages will need to be hired in order to carry more passengers. The marginal cost is therefore extremely high at this level of demand. The MC curve becomes vertical. If a price of P_1 were to be set then the level of demand would be Q_1. We can

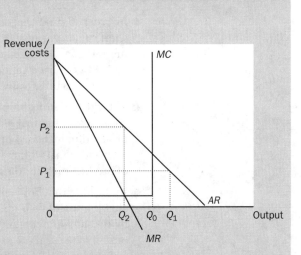

Fig. 4.19 Rail pricing: example 1.

see that not all of these passengers could be carried in safety and comfort. Profits would be maximized by setting marginal revenue equal to marginal cost. This would mean setting a price of P_2, which would reduce demand, and hence carriage congestion, to Q_2. The point we are trying to make here is that the railway companies were simply doing what any business would do.

What about expanding capacity to meet the extra demand? This is not an issue in Fig. 4.19 as profit can be maximized with the existing capacity. However, demand conditions might be slightly

Box 4.2 continued

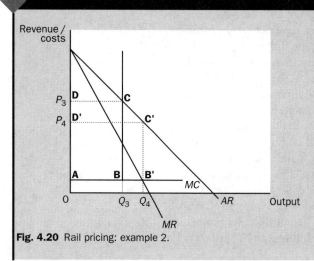

Fig. 4.20 Rail pricing: example 2.

different. Fig. 4.20 shows the marginal cost curve once again. Note that once the additional expenditure on extra carriages has been incurred then the marginal cost of accommodating extra passengers becomes negligible once again. There are now two price–quantity combinations that satisfy the profit maximization condition: P_3, Q_3 and P_4, Q_4. Which is the correct price–quantity combination? In order to answer this question we would need to know the level of profit at each price–quantity combination. At the combination P_3, Q_3 the total variable profit (that is, revenue less variable costs) is given by the rectangle ABCD. At the combination P_4, Q_4, associated with increased capacity, variable profit is the rectangle AB'C'D', from which the cost of the extra carriage should be deducted. If the carriage cost is large relative to the revenue obtained from carrying the extra passengers then it would be better to stick with existing capacity and raise fares.

◼ Summary

◆ In order to produce goods and services, the firm uses labour and capital. In the short run, capital is fixed so that the firm can expand production only by increasing the quantity of labour employed. Eventually, as more and more labour is added to the fixed capital stock, diminishing marginal returns set in where each worker adds progressively less to total output than the previous worker.

◆ The existence of diminishing marginal returns dominates the firm's short-run costs. Assuming that all workers are paid the same wage, in the initial stages of production increased productivity ensures that production costs fall; however, as each additional worker becomes progressively less productive the short-run costs of production start to rise.

◆ In the long run, both labour and capital are variable so that firms can completely alter the size of their operations. When the firm increases both labour and capital by the same proportion a change in scale is said to take place. In such instances, output may rise more or less than proportionately. The response of output to such a change in scale dominates the nature of the firm's long-run costs. In general it is assumed that a firm's output rises more than proportionately in the initial stages of expansion but that as production continues to increase then output rises less than proportionately. This gives rise to a U-shaped long-run average cost curve, with costs falling initially before starting to rise.

◆ The revenues of the firm depend on whether the firm has the ability to determine its own price. Firms that cannot set prices independently are known as price takers. Such firms sell as much as they can at the prevailing market price. These firms face a horizontal, perfectly elastic demand curve. Firms that have the ability to set prices are known as price makers. Such firms have to lower price in order to increase sales, as the demand curve they face slopes downwards from left to right.

◆ Firms maximize profit where the cost of producing the last unit of output (that is, the marginal cost) is equal to the revenue generated from the sale of the last unit of output (that is, the marginal revenue). The actual level of profit achieved is determined by the difference between the price at which output is sold and the average cost per unit of output.

Key terms

◆ Short run
◆ Long run
◆ Marginal product of labour
◆ Average product of labour
◆ Diminishing marginal returns
◆ Marginal cost
◆ Average total cost
◆ Average variable cost
◆ Returns to scale
◆ Total revenue
◆ Marginal revenue
◆ Average revenue
◆ Price taker
◆ Price maker
◆ Profit maximization

Self-test questions

True (t) or false (f)

1. In the short run labour is the only variable factor of production.

2. Diminishing marginal returns occur when more and more of the variable factor of production is added to the fixed factor of production in the short run.

3. Marginal cost is the cost per unit of output produced.

4. Total variable costs rise as output increases.

5. Average fixed cost is constant as output increases.

6. If a doubling of both labour and capital results in a doubling of output, this is known as increasing returns to scale.

7. Economies of scale occur when costs per unit of output fall as output increases in the long run.

8. For a price taker, price is equal to both average revenue and marginal revenue.

9. Price makers face a perfectly elastic demand curve.

10. If marginal cost is greater than marginal revenue then, in order to maximize profit, a firm should increase output.

Complete the following sentences by inserting the missing word(s)

1. The ____ illustrates the relationship between total quantity of goods or services produced and the quantity of factors of production used in the production process.

2. Diminishing marginal returns will inevitably set in as more and more of a ____ is added to a fixed factor in the short run.

3. ____ are those costs that do not vary with the quantity of output produced.

4. As soon as diminishing marginal returns set in then the ____ starts to fall and the short-run marginal cost starts to rise.

5. If a firm increases both factors by an equal amount then this is known as a ____

6. Diseconomies of scale occur when ____ rise as output increases.

7. Marginal revenue measures the increase in ____ as the firm sells one more unit of the good.

8. In order to maximize profit, any firm will need to maximize the difference between ____ and total cost.

9. A firm will ____ by producing that level of output where marginal revenue is equal to marginal cost.

10. The difference between price and ____ represents the profit per unit sold.

▮ Questions for discussion

◆ Consider a local bus company. How does the marginal cost of providing transport for each passenger tend to vary according to the time of day?

◆ What specific economies of scale might a larger firm benefit from?

◆ Why should the profit-maximizing firm always produce at that output which equates marginal cost with marginal revenue?

▮ Further reading

Koutsoyiannis, A. *Modern Microeconomics* (2nd ed.) (Basingstoke: Macmillan, 1979). Chapters 3 and 4 present a very detailed, though slightly technical, study of the firm's costs and production decisions.

Shepherd, W.G. *The Economics of Industrial Organization* (Englewood Cliffs: Prentice Hall, 1990). Contains a complementary mix of theory and well-presented industry case studies.

Ferguson, C.E. *The Neoclassical Theory of Production and Distribution* (Cambridge: Cambridge University Press, 1969). Chapter 6 presents a very clear graphical analysis of the firm's cost curves.

Market Concentration and Power

CHAPTER 5

Key issues

▶ What are the main sources of market power?

▶ What are the major market structures in the modern economy?

▶ What implications do different market structures have for competition?

▶ How does game theory help us to analyse firms' strategic behaviour?

▶ Do competitive or uncompetitive market structures dominate in the real world?

Contents

5.1 Introduction

In the previous chapter we discussed the different costs that arise in production, in both the short run and the long run, and how firms' revenues are affected by a change in the quantity of output produced. In the present chapter we discuss the main sources of market power, and introduce the different *market structures* in which firms operate, reflecting on the implications of each of these structures for the firm, the consumer and wider society. As we shall see, despite the outlined claims of mainstream economic theory in favour of firms as effective organizers of production, certain real-world market structures place clear limits on their ability to allocate scarce resources efficiently. Firms, it appears, may not always 'get it right' as far as the consumer and wider society is concerned. Moreover, because firms in some market structures can misallocate resources, governments may choose to regulate their activities and curtail their freedoms in various respects. This gives rise to specific relationships between business and government, the general form of which we first introduced in Chapter 1, section 1.2.

5.2 Sources of market power

A firm that has **market power** has the ability to set its price without risking the loss of its entire market share. Recall our analysis of the revenues of firms in Chapter 4,

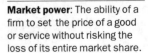

Market power: The ability of a firm to set the price of a good or service without risking the loss of its entire market share.

section 4.5, where we made a simple distinction between price-taking and price-making firms. Price takers must adopt the ruling market price. If they set a higher price, demand for their product evaporates entirely because consumers switch to other firms supplying the good or service at the market price. Price makers, on the other hand, enjoy a *degree* of independence. They can set a higher price without putting demand at risk in its entirety: hence they enjoy a form of market power denied to price takers. What then makes a firm a price maker? What, in other words, are the main sources of market power? Several are readily identifiable:

- the lack of rival firms
- customer preferences
- location
- product differentiation.

The lack of rival firms

The South African firm De Beers is responsible for about 90 per cent of the world's diamond supply. De Beers clearly has considerable market power. It can set diamond prices according to its own preferences, secure in the knowledge that buyers have few alternative sources of supply. Of course, this does not mean De Beers can set *any* price it chooses. Like any other price-making firm, De Beers still faces a downward-sloping demand or average revenue curve (refer back to Fig. 4.15 for a reminder). This means that if it sets a price above the range of its demand curve, demand will evaporate. As we emphasized in Chapter 2, section 2.10, when discussing the OPEC oil price increases of the 1970s, even the most powerful producers are constrained by the market context in which they operate.

Customer preferences

Some firms enjoy degrees of customer preference or loyalty that others struggle to develop. Consider the following example. In 1999 *Ride Magazine* conducted a motorcycle owners' survey amongst its readership. One of the issues researched was the quality of service provided by motorbike dealers. The 12 000 survey respondents reported a preference for single-franchise dealers with only one branch above the big so-called 'bike superstore' chains that sell models made by several manufacturers. One reason why the small single-franchise dealers were rated more highly was simply the individual care and attention that they paid to their customers, especially in after-sales service. In terms of market power, this means that the favoured single-franchise dealers may set prices independently, with reduced risk that their customers will buy their next new bike elsewhere.

Location

The location of a firm can also be a source of market power. Most people who shop in supermarkets will tend to use the one that is most convenient for them – usually the one closest to their place of work or to their home. If you live a few yards away from Tesco, you are unlikely to shop at the Asda store on the other side of town. Even if Asda offered demonstrably lower prices this might not be sufficient to compensate for the cost in time and money of getting there. Thus, by virtue of an accessible location, firms can set prices that are different from those of their competitors without risking substantial market share.

Product differentiation

By differentiating its product from that of a rival, a firm can derive a degree of market power. This is because the product becomes more refined and hence, for some consumers, more desirable than close substitutes. For example, the producers of branded sports and leisure wear may vary the prices they set on the assumption that many of their customers will pay a little extra for the privilege of showing off their brand. If some rugged outdoor type dresses from head to foot in smart Timberland gear, it's a safe bet that he or she is not going to stop because of a modest price increase.

5.3 Measures of market concentration

Our list of sources of market power also suggests that there will be *degrees* of market power. Because it controls most of the world's supply of diamonds, De Beers will be in a stronger position in its market than say a motorbike dealer is in the congested market for motorbikes. This means that De Beers can increase the price of diamonds more freely than the motorbike dealer can raise his or her new bike prices without the attendant risk of a collapse in demand. Simply, in the market for diamonds, De Beers has few competitors; in the market for motorbikes, dealers have many.

This might suggest that a critical general influence upon the strength of market power of firms in a market is the *number* of firms present in that market. Yet this actually tells us little about the degree of market power of those firms; it does not, for example, tell us anything about their size. There may be as many as 20 firms in a given market, yet just two of them could have a market share of 99 per cent. In cases like this, the market would clearly be dominated by the two biggest firms, and each would have a considerable degree of market power. Such a market or industry would be said to be highly *concentrated*. The degree of concentration will tell us far more about market power in an industry than will the number of firms. How do we measure the degree of concentration? The two most commonly used methods are the *concentration ratio* and the *Herfindahl–Hirschmann index.*

Concentration ratios measure the total market share of the largest firms in an industry. For example, the two-firm concentration ratio measures the market share of the two largest firms in the industry. Table 5.1 shows the five-firm concentration ratio for a sample of different industries in the UK. We can see that the tobacco industry is highly concentrated, in that the five largest firms have a collective market

Concentration ratios:
Measure the total market share of the largest firms in an industry.

Table 5.1 The five-firm concentration ratio for selected UK industries

Industry	Five-firm concentration ratio (%)
Tobacco	99.5
Motor vehicles	83.0
Footwear	48.2
Clothing	20.7
Plastics processing	8.8

Herfindahl–Hirschmann Index:
Measures the degree of
market power by summing the
square of the market shares of
each firm in an industry.

share of 99.5 per cent. The smaller firms within that industry, with a market share of just 0.5 per cent, will therefore have very little market power. By contrast, the plastics processing industry has a five-firm concentration ratio of just 8.8 per cent. If the largest five firms control just 8.8 per cent of the total market share, there will clearly be a very large number of firms within the industry. Such an industry will be very competitive, and the firms in it will have relatively little room for independent price setting because they have little market power.

The **Herfindahl–Hirschmann index (HHI)** is an alternative measure of the degree of market power, which sums the square of the market shares of each firm in an industry. This is done in order to weight the values for the larger firms more heavily. If accurate data are unavailable for very small firms within the industry the resulting errors will not be large. The general formulation for an industry with N firms is as follows:

$$\text{HHI} = S_1^2 + S_2^2 + S_3^2 + S_4^2 + \ldots S_N^2 \tag{5.1}$$

where S_i = market share of the ith firm.

In order to illustrate, consider an industry with four firms. The market share of each firm is as follows:

- Firm 1: 40%
- Firm 2: 35%
- Firm 3: 15%
- Firm 4: 10%

The HHI is therefore calculated as

$$0.4^2 + 0.35^2 + 0.15^2 + 0.10^2 = 0.16 + 0.1225 + 0.0225 + 0.01 = 0.315$$

What does this tell us? In order to answer this question, consider the case where just one firm existed in the industry, with a market share of 100 per cent. The HHI would be equal to 1. The industry would be highly concentrated, and dominated by one firm with an extremely high degree of market power. Now, consider the case of say 1000 firms existing in an industry, each with a tiny market share. The HHI would be very close to 0. The industry would have a very low degree of concentration, and each firm would have negligible market power. The industry would be highly competitive. Hence the closer the value of the HHI to 1, then the more highly concentrated the industry and the lower the degree of competition in that industry.

How useful are our measures of industrial concentration? Both measures give an insight into how the degree of competition within an industry is affected by the size of firms as well as by the number of firms in that industry. However, these measures do not present a clear-cut picture. For example, consider the brewing industry. The concentration ratio and/or Herfindahl–Hirschmann index will only tell us about the degree of concentration at the national level. However, the brewing industry tends to be highly localized, with different brands of beer generally being available only in certain regions. Such an industry would be more concentrated at the local level than at the national level.

5.4 Market structures

A market structure is a means of characterizing a market by reference to the *level and intensity of competition* that prevails between firms in it. Think about the kinds of competition that exist between firms in the markets for the following goods and services:

- haircuts
- groceries
- new cars
- train travel.

Competition actually varies quite considerably in intensity and form across these markets. Let us briefly consider each in turn.

Haircuts

Barber shops and hairdressing salons are numerous, and they offer a fairly uniform service. True, customers may elect to patronize one establishment regularly, but if it closes, there are many others to choose from. Because they are plentiful and generally small (which means that the industry is not highly concentrated), barber shops are in fairly intense competition. This may manifest itself in several ways: for example in the form of investment in furniture and fittings to improve the appearance of the shop. Most obviously, however, barber shops have to be competitive in terms of the price they charge. In any given city or district there will be a 'going rate' for a haircut, which few barbers will exceed by more than a modest amount. To do so would entail the risk of losing customers to rivals. Note that the main connection we have established here is between, on the one hand, the large number of small firms competing in the market and, on the other, the wide range of consumer choice and consequent need for all firms to remain price competitive. This, of course, is another way of saying that barbers have very little market power.

Groceries

What about the market for groceries? Here too there appears to be extensive consumer choice and fairly strong competition based on the relatively large number of retail outlets in most towns and cities. However, in some countries, such as the UK and France, grocery retailing is increasingly the preserve of a smaller number of very large supermarket chains – the likes of Tesco, Asda and Sainsbury's in the UK, and Leclerc and Mammouth in France. It is in fact becoming concentrated in such chains. This development has not eliminated smaller 'corner shop' grocery retailers, but their numbers have certainly declined over the last 20 years or so. What then can we say about the level of competition in grocery retailing? Is it becoming less intense than formerly because of the declining numbers of firms and growing market concentration? We can certainly say that competition is changing in form. In the UK at least, while the major grocery retailers assert their commitment to price competitiveness, most also offer 'loyalty cards' and other similar inducements to entice regular patronage, novelties that traditional grocers tended not to indulge in. Here it appears that price competition has been partly superseded by forms of *non-price competition*. In this case, then, it is possible to link falling numbers of firms and greater concentration with an increase in non-price competition.

New cars

Cars are produced on a *world* scale by a small number of very large firms: Ford, BMW, Toyota, Renault and so on. Clearly, these firms are in competition with one another, but because there are only about a dozen of them in total the market is highly concentrated. This means that the ways in which they compete may be different and less intense than if there were one or two thousand car makers. So how does competition between car makers manifest itself? Unlike groceries, cars are highly differentiated products with a host of particular design features and optional 'extras'. Typically, because they are few in number and because they make highly 'branded' products, car makers tend to compete *less* on price and much more on the intrinsic merits of the product. BMW do not suggest that their cars are cheaper than Toyota's or Renault's. Their advertising asserts that BMWs are *better* cars. Here then there is relatively little price competition but more *persuasion* of consumers through the medium of advertising. Again the prevalence of non-price competition appears to be based in part on the restricted number of firms and high concentration in the industry, and it is again possible to identify a causal link between constrained consumer choice and limited price competition.

It is important to stress here that we are *not* arguing that car makers think that competitive pricing is unimportant. Indeed, in certain segments of the car market – those of the family saloon or the economy hatchback for instance – manufacturers do sometimes compare their models favourably in price terms with those of their rivals. What we would stress, however, is that even here there are more pronounced emphases on reliability, versatility, exhilaration, gender, sexual assertiveness, environmental protection, safety and so on. You can probably even 'pin the car' on such a list. This general approach tends to suppress price as *the* factor of choice in the competitive process amongst car makers.

Train travel

Finally, the example of train travel. Usually, suppliers of train travel have no immediate competitors in the shape of rival train firms. Of course, train firms *are* in competition in the wider travel market: alternative forms of transport are offered by coach firms, airlines and private motoring. However, it is the absence of *immediate* rivals that permits train operators relative freedom from the imperatives of price competition. Train operators tend to advertise standards of service and comfort rather than fare comparisons with other transport providers. Thus, in a market where there are very few firms, price competition is at its lowest relative intensity and non-price competition appears to dominate.

Now, to what use can we put this discussion of different market types? Economic theory *also* recognizes four major market structures. These are differentiated by the intensity of price and non-price competition. Now, as we shall see, although the examples we have just given are *not* literal illustrations of each theoretical market structure, there are some parallels between them. The four major market structures identified by theory are:

- *Perfect competition*: This is a benchmark or 'ideal type' with which other market structures may be compared. It is characterized by an infinitely intense level of *price* competition – to the extent that all firms in the market are forced to charge the *same* price. The number of firms in a perfectly competitive market is large, and – as suggested by our examples – this has an important bearing on the form and intensity of competition that prevails.

- *Imperfect competition*: Here, although the number of firms is still high, the relative intensity of price competition is somewhat moderated by the presence of slightly differentiated products. As noted, differentiated products enable firms to charge different prices from those of their competitors. Firms that elect to charge higher prices may do so in the knowledge that consumer preferences for their particular product will, to some extent, safeguard the level of demand.

- *Oligopoly*: An oligopolistic market is dominated by a small number of firms, each large in relation to the market. Oligopolistic firms tend not to engage in intensive price competition, focusing instead on non-price competition.

- *Monopoly*: A pure monopoly exists where there is one firm in a market selling a good or service for which there are no close substitutes. Here, as might be anticipated, competition both in price and non-price forms is relatively weak.

For ease of analysis, we shall confine *detailed* discussion of market structures in this chapter to a contrast between perfect competition and monopoly. Although we also consider imperfect competition and oligopoly, the essential understanding of firms that we wish to elaborate here can be made by reference simply to the most and least competitive market structures.

5.5 Perfect competition

A **perfectly competitive market** is defined by a series of assumptions, a brief glance at which will convince the reader that this is indeed an 'ideal type' rather than an attempt to depict any real-world market structure. The assumptions run as follows:

- A perfectly competitive market is composed of a large number of independent profit-maximizing firms, each of which is small in relation to the market. As such, none is in a position to influence market conditions. There are also many consumers, each small in relation to the market.

- Any firm may leave the market if it chooses to do so, and other firms are free to enter it.

- Factors of production enjoy perfect mobility. This means that land, labour, capital and enterprise can move with ease between uses.

- There is perfect knowledge in the market. All firms and consumers are constantly aware of all prevailing economic conditions.

- Firms in the perfectly competitive market produce a homogeneous product: that is, one with no identifiable brand. This assumption means that loyalties to particular firms cannot be developed.

These assumptions are not reproduced in their entirety in any typical market. While the first two might be observable in the real world, the possibility of the simultaneous existence of perfect mobility and perfect knowledge is clearly remote. The final assumption is, moreover, probably the antithesis of concrete business practice. Virtually every firm tries to persuade the consumer that its product or service is in some way superior to that of its competitors. Consider the following anecdotal example. While engaged in some research a few years ago, the authors interviewed a director of a major UK biscuit and confectionery firm. In his industry, the director claimed,

Perfect competition: A market structure characterized most notably by a situation in which all firms in the industry are price takers and there is freedom of entry into and exit from the industry.

the ambition of every firm was to invent the equivalent of the *Mars bar*, such was the brand loyalty and high level of demand enjoyed by this product.

The perfectly competitive firm as a price taker

While perfect competition does not exist, it is useful as a means to assess the performance of actual market structures. What then are the implications of the restrictive assumptions that we have just outlined? The most important of these is that firms in a perfectly competitive market are *price takers*. We introduced the concept of firms as price takers in Chapter 4, section 4.5. All perfectly competitive firms must observe the single equilibrium price set by the market. Any one firm that imposed a higher price for its output would quickly cease to trade because it would immediately lose all demand. This is because consumers in the market would immediately be aware (given the assumption of perfect knowledge) that they could buy exactly the same (homogeneous) product elsewhere at a lower price. Nor would it be in the interest of any one firm to try to raise demand for its output by charging a price below the ruling market price given that it can sell all it wants at the ruling market price.

The revenue and cost curves of the perfectly competitive firm

You will recall from our discussion in Chapter 4, section 4.5, that, as a price taker, the perfectly competitive firm will face a perfectly elastic demand curve. This is because, by assumption, every firm must take the prevailing equilibrium market price as given. Demand for the firm is then perfectly responsive to a change in price. As we saw in Chapter 4, the firm's demand curve is the equivalent of its average revenue curve. Average revenue simply indicates the amount that a firm receives per unit of output sold. The average revenue curve for a firm in perfect competition is also its marginal revenue curve. Recall from Chapter 4 that the marginal revenue curve indicates the extra revenue associated with each additional unit of output produced. Fig. 5.1 reproduces the revenue curves for a perfectly competitive firm. You should check back to Chapter 4, section 4.5, in order to confirm why the average

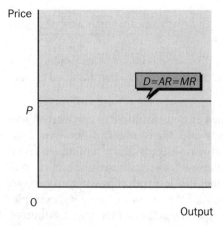

Fig. 5.1 The revenue curves for a firm in a perfectly competitive market.

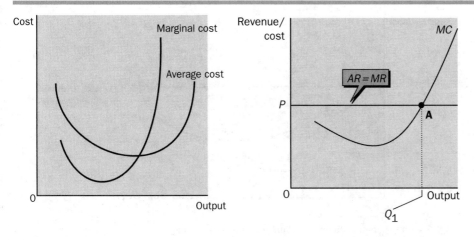

Fig. 5.2 Cost curves for the firm in a perfectly competitive market.

Fig. 5.3 The profit-maximizing output decision.

revenue curve and the marginal revenue curve are also, in fact, the demand curve for the firm.

If we assume that the firm's objective is to maximize profits, it will produce up to the point where marginal revenue and marginal cost are equal. Fig. 5.2 depicts the average cost curve and marginal cost curve faced by a representative firm in a perfectly competitive market. Once again you should check back to Chapter 4, sections 4.2–4.3, in order to make sure you understand how these curves are derived. You will recall that average cost falls at first because, as the firm begins to produce, although its total costs will rise, fixed costs are shared over (that is, divided by) an increasingly large output. Eventually, average costs begin to rise despite further increases in the output total because of the law of diminishing returns. Diminishing returns imply that, after a certain point, as more variable factors are added to a given set of fixed factors, the marginal and average costs of production begin to increase.

Fig. 5.3 reproduces Fig. 4.16 in order to show exactly where the firm will maximize profit. Fig. 5.3 illustrates the firm's marginal revenue and marginal cost curves. Profit is maximized at the output level Q_1 (point A), where marginal cost (MC) and marginal revenue (MR) intersect.

The short-run position of the perfectly competitive firm

In Fig. 5.4 we consider the short-run position of the perfectly competitive firm. The firm's output decision reflects its assumed desire to maximize profits and, accordingly, it produces at Q_1, where $MC = MR$. Reference to the vertical axis reveals that the average cost of this level of output is at point A, while the average revenue associated with it is at P_1. Total cost is indicated by the rectangle $0ABQ_1$ (average cost multiplied by the number of units produced), while the rectangle $0P_1CQ_1$ indicates total revenue (average revenue times the number of units produced). Thus the shaded area AP_1CB – total revenue less total cost – represents the (maximum) profit earned at Q_1. For reasons that we shall explain shortly, this level of profit is also known as **supernormal profit**.

As noted, this is a short-run position for the firm. Remember that the short run is that period in which only variable factors of production, such as labour, can be altered.

Supernormal profits: Profits that exceed the minimum amount a firm must earn to induce it to remain in the industry.

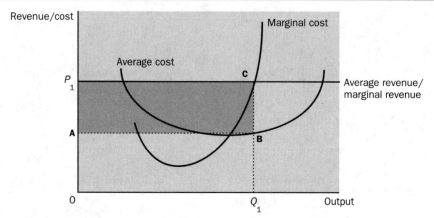

Fig. 5.4 The short-run position of a firm in perfect competition.

In the long run all factors are variable, which also means that, should they wish to, firms can enter (or leave) the market. The question is: why would they choose to enter? The answer, of course, is the existence of supernormal profit. Given our assumption of perfect knowledge, others will be aware of the level of profit in the market; they can enter it, by securing the requisite factors of production. As new entrants come into the market, conditions change and the short run gives way to the long run.

The long-run position of the perfectly competitive firm

Some of the details of the movement from the short to the long run are sketched out in Fig. 5.5. In Fig. 5.5(a) we see the effect of the new entrants on the market. The supply curve shifts to the right from S_1 to S_2. This results in a fall in the market-clearing equilibrium price from P_1 to P_2 and an increase in the equilibrium quantity demanded and supplied from Q_1 to Q_2. For the representative firm, the implications of this change in market conditions are clear. As a *price taker* the firm must observe the new equilibrium market price. Accordingly, in Fig. 5.5(b), its demand curve (which, remember, is also its average revenue and marginal revenue curve) shifts downwards from AR_1, MR_1 to AR_2, MR_2.

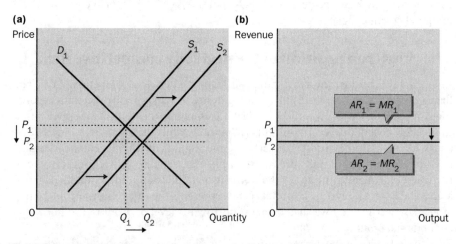

Fig. 5.5 The short and the long run in (a) the perfectly competitive market and (b) the price-taking firm.

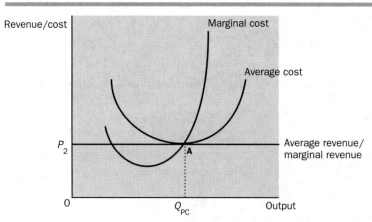

Fig. 5.6 The long-run position of a firm in perfect competition.

The remaining question is, of course, what effect this has on the supernormal profit that the firm was earning in the short run. In Fig. 5.6 the representative firm's AR/MR schedule has fallen in line with Fig. 5.5(b). The firm still seeks maximum profit, and therefore output is fixed at Q_{PC}, where $MC = MR$. Here, however, we can see that the rectangles of total revenue and total cost are one and the same: $0P_2AQ_{PC}$. This means that the firm is now *covering its costs* but is no longer earning supernormal profit. In fact, economists refer to this as a position where **normal profit** is being earned. Normal profit is the return required to keep the firm in the market, and includes requisite payments to all factors of production. In the long run, then, the perfectly competitive firm earns only normal profit, but this *is* sufficient to keep it in business. Notice also that should *too many* firms enter the market, to the extent that each firm's AR/MR schedule falls below the average cost curve, all firms will incur losses. This will provide an incentive for firms to leave the market until normal profit positions for those that remain are achieved.

The perfectly competitive firm and allocative efficiency

Finally, it is important to note that, in both the short run and the long run, the representative firm is producing at a point at which price equals marginal cost. This means that the firm is efficiently allocating resources as far as *wider society* is concerned. In other words, the firm is producing exactly the amount of output that society as a whole would like it to. This is a big claim, which we need to explain and justify.

In Fig. 5.7 we present the marginal revenue and marginal cost curves of a perfectly competitive firm. The firm produces at Q_2, the output that equates MC and MR and at which price (P_2) equals marginal cost (P_2). Notice that at output Q_1, price (P_2) is greater than marginal cost (P_1). Our contention is that, socially, Q_1 would be an undesirable output; it would be preferable if the firm produced at Q_2 (which it will anyway in order to maximize profits). Consider the *single unit* of output at Q_1. How does society value this unit? If we assume that the firm's MC curve is a good representation of society's view of the marginal costs of production,[1] we can say that

Normal profits: The minimum amount that a firm must earn to induce it to remain in the industry.

[1] This is on the assumption that there are no externalities associated with the firm's activities. We explain the concept of an externality in Chapter 7, section 7.4. Briefly, externalities refer to costs or benefits arising from a firm's activities that impact upon 'third parties': that is, any individual not directly engaged in transactions with the firm.

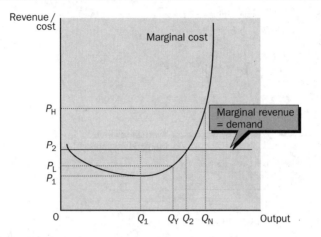

Fig. 5.7 The perfectly competitive firm and allocative efficiency.

society's estimate of the cost of the unit at Q_1 is P_1. What of the value that society places on the unit at Q_1? Given that the MR/demand curve of the firm indicates the price that consumers are willing to pay for this unit (P_2), we can say that P_2 is a good approximation of society's valuation of it. We now know society's estimate of the cost of the unit (P_1) and its valuation of it (P_2). Since the value placed on the unit is greater than its cost, the unit is deemed to be socially desirable. Notice that other units beyond Q_1, such as Q_Y, are similarly desirable (value P_2, cost P_L). In fact, above Q_1 all units are socially desirable up to and including Q_2. However, units beyond Q_2, such as Q_N, are socially undesirable because, socially, their costs of production exceed the valuation placed on them (Q_N costs P_H but is only valued at P_2). The general conclusion is the anticipated one: the socially desirable output for the firm is at that output where price = marginal cost. As we shall see, this rule applies to *all* firms in *all* forms of market structure.

Perfect competition: a summary

The perfectly competitive market produces some highly desirable outcomes. In the long run it provides sufficient incentive in the form of normal profit to retain firms in the market. At the same time, the output that firms produce can be seen to be set at a socially desirable level. We assume that the perfectly competitive firm in the free market is an effective means of allocating scarce resources. Yet perfect competition is only a *model*; its assumptions are not validated, in their entirety, in any real markets. Its usefulness, therefore, lies in the establishment of standards against which to judge market reality. Let us now compare perfect competition with the *least competitive* market structure: monopoly.

5.6 Monopoly

The word 'monopoly' conjures up images of gigantic firms that dominate markets and consumers. For economists, this is not an appropriate way to conceptualize monopoly. Monopoly is defined by *market exclusion*. Whenever a firm can prevent others from entering the market, it is in a position to exploit *monopoly power* in that market. This means that the scale of the firm has no necessary bearing on whether or not it is a monopoly; what counts is its ability to keep potential rivals out.

Exclusion can happen in a variety of ways. Buffet cars on trains possess monopoly power because, for the duration of a journey, passengers have no other place to go for refreshment. Motorway service stations have monopoly power because they are the most readily available source of fuel for those driving long distances. In cases such as these, monopoly power arises because of a lack of close substitutes. The train passenger could make some sandwiches and a flask of coffee before leaving for the station; and the driver could leave the motorway to find cheaper petrol. But these options involve delays, or work the consumer would rather not do: thus he or she patronizes the supplier with monopoly power.

The question now arises: what does the monopolist *do* with monopoly power? One possibility is that because, by definition, monopoly power involves some *absence of competition*, the monopolist is able to charge higher prices than would otherwise be the case. Hence one would normally expect to pay more for food and drink on trains and motorway service station fuel.

Before examining the economic implications of monopoly in detail, let us complete our review of the forms it can take.

"The spell check doesn't recognise Monopoly"

Microsoft: a firm with monopoly power.

- **Pure monopoly**: A pure monopoly exists where there is a sole supplier of a good or service in a market for which there are no close substitutes. The qualification concerning substitutes is an important one. There is, for example, only one tunnel under the English Channel. However, *Eurotunnel*, its operator, does not have a pure monopoly on cross-Channel travel because of the presence of a number of rival ferry operators. By contrast, in the UK the postal service does enjoy the status of a pure monopoly as the state forbids any other operator to carry mail for less than £1 per item. This means that all mainstream letter business is reserved for the Royal Mail. Note, however, that recently emerging close substitutes threaten even this monopoly: fax and email are the most obvious examples.

- **Legal monopoly**: In the UK, a monopoly is defined in law as a market share of 25 per cent or more. Monopolies and potential monopolies are liable to investigation by a government body, the Competition Commission. The Competition Commission seeks to establish whether or not particular monopolies operate against the public interest, in particular by limiting competition. Its recommendations are forwarded to a government minister, who decides whether or not to act on them.

- **Natural monopoly**: Some industries, because of their technical characteristics, tend to be most efficiently organized under the mandate of a single firm. The most common examples of natural monopoly are the electricity, water, gas and telecommunications industries. Clearly, it would be wasteful if an economy had several rival firms in, say, the supply of gas. Each firm would have its own separate infrastructural supply network, running pipelines to customers or potential customers – a pointless duplication when one would suffice. In the UK, until the 1980s, in order to protect consumers from the abuse of monopoly power, these industries were publicly owned. Now they are all in private ownership but subject to forms of public regulation and accountability. We examine the issues surrounding privatization in Chapter 7, section 7.7.

Pure monopoly: A market structure in which there is a sole supplier of a good or service that has no close substitutes and for which there are barriers to entry into the industry.

Legal monopoly: As defined in the UK, a legal monopoly arises when a firm enjoys a market share of 25 per cent or more.

Natural monopoly: Arises when a single firm is the most efficient structure for the production of a particular good or service.

Sources of monopoly power

We have seen that the existence of monopoly power requires exclusivity in a market for goods or services with no close substitutes. As in the case of the Royal Mail, such exclusivity can be granted by the state. There are a number of other instances of state-sanctioned monopoly. For example, monopolies may be created where this encourages artistic or technological innovation. Thus musicians and authors are granted copyrights on their work, and new inventions are similarly protected by patents. The assumption here is that, without the right to exploit their work exclusively for a period, innovators would not have the incentive to commit scarce resources to the processes of research and development. This implies that, though monopoly might be associated with certain problems, it is acceptable for (say) the duration of a patent because of the wider long-term benefits it brings.

The economic implications of monopoly

On the familiar assumption of profit maximization, we begin here by reviewing the cost and revenue curves of the monopolist in order that the profit-maximizing output might be determined. Note that, as for perfect competition and all other market structures, the profit-maximizing output for monopoly is where the marginal cost and marginal revenue curves intersect.

We have seen that, in perfect competition, the firm is a *price taker*: it *must* take the ruling market price as given. For the monopolist, no such restriction applies. In the case of pure monopoly, the firm is the industry. The monopoly firm can determine its own price. In Chapter 4 we discussed why such a firm is known as a price maker. The monopolist faces a demand curve that slopes downwards from left to right, as in Fig. 5.8. The demand curve is also the monopolist's average revenue curve, as it indicates the revenue received per unit of output (and this must be the selling price).

Fig. 5.8 also depicts the *MR* curve for the monopolist. As the demand (average revenue) curve that the monopolist faces is downward sloping, in order to sell an extra (marginal) unit the price on *all* units must fall. Hence the marginal revenue curve has a much steeper slope than that of the average revenue curve. Check back to Chapter 4, section 4.5, if you are unsure why this is the case.

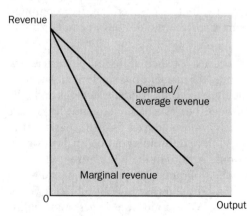

Fig. 5.8 Revenue curves for the monopolist.

The monopolist's output decision

In order to maximize profits, the monopolist will produce at an output that equates MC and MR. Fig. 5.9 illustrates the monopolist's output decision. Fig. 5.9 is remarkably similar to Fig. 4.18. The profit-maximizing output is at Q_M. At Q_M the monopolist will set price at P_1, which will also be the average revenue associated with this output. The average cost is at point A. We are now in a position to determine the level of *supernormal profit* earned by the monopolist. The total revenue associated with Q_M is the price of this output times the output itself. Thus total revenue is represented by the rectangle $0Q_MCP_1$. Total cost, however, is given by the rectangle $0Q_MBA$. Taking total cost from total revenue leaves the shaded area $ABCP_1$, which represents profit. Significantly, because monopoly is defined by barriers to entry, this position (and the supernormal profits that go with it) is a *permanent one*. Unlike the case of the perfectly competitive market, here there will be no new entrants, and therefore supernormal profits will not be competed away by other firms.

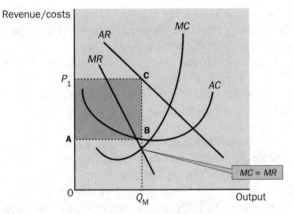

Fig. 5.9 The long-run position of the monopolist.

Monopoly and allocative efficiency

In perfect competition we saw that the output generated by each firm maximized profits at a point where price equals marginal cost. You will recall that the price of a good can be taken to represent society's marginal valuation of it, while its marginal cost approximates society's view of the costs of its production. Thus, where price is above marginal cost, the output concerned is deemed to be socially desirable, but when marginal cost exceeds price that unit of output should not be produced. It follows that the output at which price and marginal cost are equal is *the* socially efficient one, as it marks the boundary between socially desirable and socially undesirable output.

In Fig. 5.10 we can see that the output for profit maximization, which the monopolist will select, is Q_M (where $MC = MR$). However, a socially efficient allocation of resources demands that output be set at a higher level: Q_2 (where price = MC). This means that the economic implication of monopoly is that it *misallocates resources*: the social preference would be for more resources to be committed to the industry and a greater output produced (Q_2) at a lower price (P_2).

We must stress here that the problem with monopoly is that, compared with the

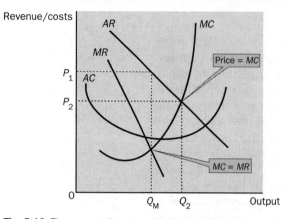

Fig. 5.10 The monopolist as a misallocator of resources.

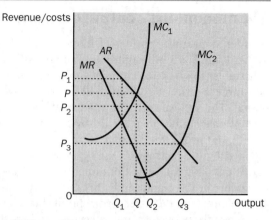

Fig. 5.11 From perfect competition to natural monopoly: lower prices and greater output but a misallocation of resources.

perfectly competitive market structure, it *misallocates resources*. If a monopolist took over a perfectly competitive industry, it might be expected to restrict output and raise prices, but this is not necessarily so. Take, for example, the case of an industry that is a natural monopoly but which is organized along perfectly competitive lines. Recall that the single supplier is the most effective form of organization for a natural monopoly. In perfect competition, with output divided between a large number of small firms, costs are unnecessarily high as each firm maintains its own (say) infrastructure of gas pipelines. With the emergence of the monopolist only one set of pipelines is retained, and the cost basis of the industry falls sharply. This possibility is illustrated in Fig. 5.11. In a perfectly competitive industry, equilibrium occurs where supply (the summation of individual firm's marginal cost curves, MC_1) equals demand (AR). A perfectly competitive output Q and price P are established where $P = MC_1$. If the industry is monopolized, with the monopolist facing the *same* cost and demand conditions as previously prevailed when the industry was perfectly competitive, output would fall to Q_1 and price would increase to P_1. If, however, costs were reduced following monopolization, say from MC_1 to MC_2, it is possible for the price to fall below, and output increase above, that which would prevail under a perfectly competitive industry: that is, P_2 compared with P and Q_2 compared with Q. This of course means that the economic effect of monopoly is *not*, as is sometimes claimed, *always* to lower output and increase price. Monopoly does, however, *consistently misallocate resources*. Notice in Fig. 5.11 that a socially efficient allocation of resources for the monopolized industry would require an output of Q_3 (where price $= MC_2$) and price set at P_3.

Reflections on monopoly

Although allocative inefficiency is a major problem of monopoly, it is not the only one. By definition, monopoly involves some restriction of competition. This has wider significance because competition is the ultimate guarantor of consumer sovereignty. In a competitive market, no one producer will be able to set excessively high prices or offer substandard goods or services because others will always be prepared to meet the perceived demands of consumers better. Now, as the whole canon of conventional economic theory rests on the certainty that free markets are indeed created and conditioned by the demands of consumers, the impairment of consumer sovereignty raises some serious questions concerning the validity of economic theory itself. So, just how serious are these questions?

For many economists, there is actually little cause for alarm here. Even where there is an absence of competition and monopoly exists, wider interests usually, at some level, prevail. Consider the following two examples.

First, the outcome of the pricing policies of the oil **cartel**, the Organization of Petroleum Exporting Countries (OPEC) in 1973–74 and 1979.[2] OPEC, which controls a large proportion of the oil consumed by the advanced Western economies is, without doubt, a very strong monopoly. For industrialized societies, oil is an important fuel with no readily available substitute. Knowledge of this fact permitted OPEC to reap the rewards of a *fourfold* increase in the price of oil in 1973–74, followed by a further *twofold* increase in 1979. The *initial* response in the oil-importing nations was stoicism: the oil was vital and nothing could replace it, so the higher prices simply had to be met. OPEC's monopoly seemed then to have placed it in an extremely powerful position, and further price increases might have been expected. However, although OPEC was not threatened by any serious competition, its ability to control events in the market was sharply curtailed in the first half of the 1980s, and the price of oil actually *fell* over this period. Why? The answer lies in the response of the oil-importing nations to the price rises: they scaled back their demand for oil as, for instance, people began to run cars with smaller engines. This example reveals the *limits to monopoly*. Even where something close to a pure monopoly exists, the monopolist is not free to set *any* price he or she likes without suffering the consequences. The basic law of demand – that at higher prices less will be demanded (and vice versa) – will assert itself *through the actions of consumers*. Yet even if consumers are the ultimate source of authority in the face of monopoly, this does *not* mean that monopoly can simply be ignored as an economic issue. In the OPEC case, the oil price increases caused major problems of adjustment for the oil-importing nations. Many countries experienced difficulties in adapting to the changed relative price of oil. Indeed, the continuing debt problems of some less-developed countries can be directly traced to the so called 'oil shock'. Monopolies may cause significant *disruption* to markets for a time, which would be less likely to occur in more competitive environments. Thus the oil shock could not have happened had the members of OPEC been in competition rather than collusion.

Second, what of the noted encouragement of monopolies by the state? How does this policy – implemented through the granting of patents and copyrights – square with the notion that monopolists dominate markets and act contrary to social preferences on resource allocation? The suggestion here is not that governments favour the creation of monopolies, rather that they recognize monopoly as an important potential source of *innovation* in the economy. Innovation is a challenging process. It may require years of effort and heavy investment to develop a new marketable product or piece of technology. There would be little point in a firm spending decades and large sums of money in, say, coming up with a cure for the common cold if, as soon as it was put on the market, rival manufacturers simply copied it and sold it themselves. However, an incentive to undertake the necessary research and development would be created if the firm was granted a patent on its invention for a period of time. This argument was first advanced by Joseph Schumpeter (1883–1950). Schumpeter also suggested that the greater size of the typical monopolist would

Cartel: A group of firms or producers that agree to act as if they were a single firm or producer, for example with regard to pricing and output decisions.

[2] This example was considered in more detail in Chapter 2, section 2.10.

enable it to finance research and development on a scale beyond most smaller competitive firms. In this view then, while monopoly might indeed restrict output, raise price and misallocate resources, these are not the only criteria by which it should be judged. Monopoly may also an important source of innovation in the modern economy.

Government control of monopoly

Market failure: Arises when the market either fails to provide certain goods, or fails to provide them at their optimal or most desirable level.

We now turn to the question of whether or not monopoly should be controlled or regulated by the state. If monopolies can disrupt markets, if they can set high prices secure in the knowledge that competitors are absent, or, indeed, if they are able to offer poor-quality goods or services because the consumer has little other choice available, should the state – recognizing a case of **market failure** – step in and do something to rectify matters? In practice, most governments in Western economies

---

Box 5.1

Wall's angry at sales restrictions – ice cream wars company warns of legal action

Birds Eye Wall's, the frozen food division of Unilever, is considering legal action against the government over measures to improve competition in the ice cream industry.

A Competition Commission report recommended banning several practices including exclusive deals with retailers to sell only one make of ice cream.

It also said Wall's, the market leader with two-thirds of the market for wrapped ice creams, should allow shopkeepers to stock other makes in the freezer cabinets it lent them.

But Unilever persuaded Stephen Byers, Trade Secretary, to reject the recommendation that Wall's be forced to stop supplying ice cream directly to retailers.

The Commission said the in-house distribution operation was undermining the independent wholesalers that distributed rival products. But Mr Byers said: 'It is a drastic step to stop a company from distributing its own products and I am not convinced the Commission's remedy is necessary.'

He added he would consult on other ways of helping wholesalers such as capping at 20–25 per cent the share of the market Wall's could distribute directly.

Meanwhile he will force Wall's to raise the commission it pays to independent wholesalers to at least 22.5 per cent, enough to be viable.

Iain Ferguson, Birds Eye Wall's chairman, said the recommendations were 'discriminatory, unworkable, unprecedented and disproportionate'. The group was consulting its lawyers on a judicial review of the findings and recommendations.

Many leisure attractions have signed exclusive deals with manufacturers in return for cash and other support. And existing deals such as that of Wall's with the Millennium Dome for £3m will not be affected.

But Wall's will not be able to reserve more than half the space in the freezer cabinets it supplies to retailers. Competitors have accused Wall's of pre-empting the space in small shops by excluding rival products.

Yesterday's Competition Commission report is the fourth in 21 years on an industry worth barely £500m a year in sales. But it is the first to win the unqualified support of the competition.

Nestlé, the Swiss company that is a distant second in the market, said it was 'enthusiastic'. Mars, the US confectionery group whose voice has been raised loudest in complaint since it launched its ice cream bars in Europe in 1989, said it was 'a victory for the consumer and common sense'. Treats, the smallest of the big four, gave 'full support'.

Walls Magnum: everybody's favourite ice cream?

The report said that Wall's, which produces all the UK's most popular brands including Magnum, Cornetto and Solero, operated a monopoly against the public interest.

It had raised its market share for wrapped, impulse-purchase ice cream from about 45 per cent of the impulse market in 1979 to 65 per cent in 1998.

Wall's said it had achieved its number one position by the strength of its brands, its spending on marketing and its supplying outlets promptly in hot weather.

Source: Financial Times 29 January 2000

do, though – as we shall see in Chapter 7 – some economists of the *liberal school* think that state intervention to control monopoly may actually create bigger problems than monopoly itself.

As noted, in the UK, issues of monopoly are investigated by the Competition Commission (formerly known as the Monopolies and Mergers Commission (MMC)). This agency decides whether or not a monopoly – or potential monopoly in the case of a proposed merger between firms – is likely to be against the public interest. A government minister, the president of the Board of Trade, at his or her discretion, then acts upon the Competition Commission's recommendation. A second government agency, the Office of Fair Trading, has the job of initially recommending to the president of the Board of Trade that particular monopolies or mergers should be investigated. This rather convoluted process is designed to prevent the Competition Commission from becoming 'judge and jury' in a case. Box 5.1 summarizes a recent interesting instance of monopoly regulation in the UK market for ice cream.

The main issue in Box 5.1 is the extent to which one ice cream manufacturer – Wall's – is able to use its dominant position in the market to exclude the products of its rivals. It had been Wall's practice to lend freezer cabinets to shopkeepers from which to sell its wrapped ice creams. Wall's clearly thinks this is reasonable. It's paying for the freezers; why should it allow them to be used to subsidize the marketing of rival products? The Competition Commission sees things differently. Because Wall's enjoys market dominance, its freezer strategy is a good way of trying to 'saturate' the market, making it difficult for competitors even to get their products into the shops. The Competition Commission has recommended and the Trade Secretary has endorsed a ruling that requires non-freezer exclusivity. In this case, then, the government is seeking to restrict the monopoly position of one firm in the interests of greater competition and, above all, in the interests of consumer choice.

5.7 Imperfect competition

Imperfect competition[3] and oligopoly (see section 5.8 below) are the two intermediate market structures that lie between the *extremes* of perfect competition and monopoly. Both exhibit a greater degree of competition than monopoly. Like monopolies, imperfectly competitive firms and oligopolies are *price makers*. They are, in other words, able to set prices independently of their competitors. Recall that *price-taking* firms in perfect competition must all take the market price as given.

Imperfectly competitive firms are price makers because they sell *differentiated products*. As noted, differentiated products are similar to each other, but they do possess some distinguishing features. City centre pubs and bars, for example, might be thought to be in imperfect competition. There are plenty of them and they mostly sell the same beers, wines and spirits. The market is also relatively easy to enter and leave. The distinguishing features here might be the ambiance of any particular establishment, or the quality of its beer.

As price makers, imperfectly competitive firms face a normal downward-sloping demand/average revenue curve, such as that depicted in Fig. 5.8. They also have a marginal revenue curve of the same general form as the *MR* curve in the figure. Moreover, we know that the average and marginal cost curves of all firms are similar

---

[3] Sometimes imperfect competition is referred to as monopolistic competition, as it blends elements of monopoly with competition.

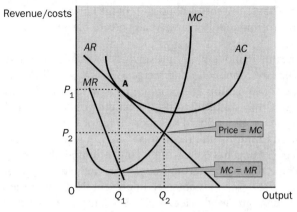

Fig. 5.12 The long-run position of the imperfectly competitive firm.

to those in Fig. 5.2. Putting all this information together, and assuming profit maximization, we arrive at a supernormal profit position for the imperfectly competitive firm that is identical to that of the long-run position of the monopolist (as depicted in Fig. 5.9). However, for the imperfectly competitive firm, this is a *short-run* position only. An imperfectly competitive market allows firms freedom of entry and exit. Thus, because supernormal profits attract new entrants, the demand/*AR* curves of all firms in the market shift to the left as the level of demand is 'shared out' between more firms. This means that imperfectly competitive firms will, in the long run, earn only *normal profits*. New firms continue to enter the market until all supernormal profit is eroded. The long-run position of the representative imperfectly competitive firm is depicted in Fig. 5.12. As always, the profit-maximizing output, at Q_1, is determined by the $MC = MR$ rule. That only normal profits are earned here is evident because total revenue and total cost are equal (both are represented by the rectangle $0P_1AQ_1$). Notice also that, unlike the firm in a perfectly competitive industry, the firm is not producing at the lowest point of its average cost curve.

5.8 Oligopoly

Oligopoly is typified by the presence of a small number of firms each large in relation to the market. Market entry here is more difficult than in imperfect competition, and hence profits earned by oligopolists tend to be less easily 'competed away'. The obstacles to entry into an oligopolistic market may be significant, but they are not – as in the case of monopoly – insurmountable. Consider the following three examples.

- Oligopoly can be protected by *industrial scale*. As discussed in Chapter 3, the car industry is composed of firms that produce very large volumes of output as a means of keeping down the average cost of each car. This has the incidental effect of dissuading new entrants to the industry. To compete effectively in the 'mass production' car market, it is necessary to produce in large quantities at the outset. This means that any potential entrant has to risk a huge volume of capital to break into the industry. For many potential rivals, such risks are prohibitive.

- A second means of preserving oligopoly involves the development of an extensive *product range*. If a market can be segmented by subtle variations on a single

Oligopoly: A market structure in which a small number of firms compete with each other.

product, entry can be deterred. The most infamous example of this source of oligopoly is the soap powder industry. In the UK, two firms – Lever Brothers and Procter and Gamble – produce between them an extensive range of soap powders. Any third market entrant, manufacturing and selling one new powder, would gain only a small proportion of the market rather than one third of it.

- Finally, *brand loyalties* offer firms the possibility of creating exclusive market space for *their* goods and services. We noted the example of the *Mars bar* earlier in this chapter. It might be argued that firms such as *Coca Cola* and the fast food chain *McDonald's* have achieved a place in popular consciousness that accords their output an even greater degree of brand loyalty. Branding this successfully decisively establishes the oligopolistic position of these firms.

A noted feature of the oligopolistic market is the degree of *price stability* that it is sometimes thought to exhibit. Although oligopolists in the same market are clearly in competition with each other, this can be restricted to *non-price forms*. For example, in petrol retailing, competition has traditionally been of the 'free gift' or 'bonus points' variety, where customers are given drinking glasses, mugs and other assorted items according to the volume of petrol they buy. For a long time, petrol prices did not vary greatly between different garages, and price rises – when they occurred – tended to happen everywhere simultaneously. However, in the UK in recent years the petrol market has become more price competitive, chiefly as a result of the *entry into the market* of the large supermarkets, such as Tesco and Sainsbury's, and their practice of selling cheaper petrol than the established garage chains.

Fig. 5.13 illustrates a possible reason for price stability under oligopoly. Notice that the oligopolist's AR or demand curve is assumed to be '*kinked*'. This is because the oligopolistic firm thinks that any increase in price above P_1 will be ignored by its rivals, and that they will accordingly rapidly gain market share at its expense. However, the firm also supposes that, should it cut price below P_1, all its rivals will follow suit. In these circumstances, its market share will be unchanged. The net result of these deliberations is that the firm will tend not to indulge in price competition, and – because they follow the same reasoning – nor will its rivals. Fig. 5.13 demonstrates a second reason for price stability amongst oligopolists. The kink in the demand curve produces a discontinuity in the firm's marginal revenue curve. This means that the same profit-maximizing output Q_1 (where $MC = MR$) will apply, irrespective

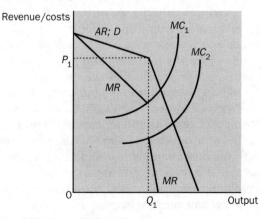

Fig. 5.13 Price stability under oligopoly.

of shifts in the marginal cost curve between MC_1 and MC_2. Thus the oligopolist can absorb some limited shifts in cost without a change in output or price.

Oligopoly is, to some extent, unique amongst market structures in the sense that firms act *interdependently*. That is, each time the firm makes a price or output decision then it must take into account the likely reaction of other firms in the industry. This interdependence gives rise to the kinked demand curve that we have just discussed. To see why interdependence exists only under oligopoly, consider first the case of monopoly. A monopolist is the sole firm in the industry, and thus by definition does not have any rivals to consider. What about the perfectly competitive firm? In perfect competition there are a large number of small price-taking firms. They need not consider what other firms are doing, as each faces exactly the same price-taking situation. Finally, in imperfect competition, because of the possibility of product differentiation, each firm faces a downward-sloping demand curve and has a degree of market power. However, although this permits some independence in pricing and output decisions, imperfectly competitive firms are too small to have any significant impact upon the market as a whole. This again means that the decisions of individual firms in this market structure will not be a major concern for their competitors. Yet, in oligopoly, because there are so few firms, and because each is so large relative to market size, the price or output decisions of one firm *must* directly impact upon the revenue and profit of the other firms. As noted, the soap powder industry is a classic example of an oligopolistic industry in the UK. Brand names such as Bold, Daz, Ariel, Lux and Persil are all produced by just two firms: Lever Brothers and Procter and Gamble. Should Lever Brothers suddenly decide to reduce the price of all of its brands, it would expect Procter and Gamble to respond in a similar manner. Thus all prices would be reduced, and no firm would have increased sales. As it is aware of this possibility, Lever Brothers would probably opt not to reduce price in the first instance. Instead, it might decide to embark upon an extensive advertising campaign, or perhaps improve the quality of its product. If these moves were successful they would directly impact upon the market share and profitability of Procter and Gamble, encouraging this firm to formulate a response of some sort.

Because there is so much uncertainty associated with the need to consider the reactions of a rival firm, oligopolistic firms sometimes choose not to compete with each other at all. Instead they may form a cartel, whereby the firms act together as one sole producer. The firms agree to coordinate the quantity produced by each in order to achieve a certain level of industry output. They also agree a price that all 'members' will charge. In other words, they *collude* and act like a monopolist. As noted, one of the most famous cartels is the Organization for Petroleum Exporting Countries (OPEC). OPEC was formed when a number of oil-producing nations decided to collectively reduce the world supply of oil and thereby raise the world price of oil. In order to achieve this, it was essential that each of the individual countries agreed to reduce its oil production. In fact, each country was allocated a production 'quota'. By acting in this manner OPEC was able to engineer a massive increase in the world price of oil in the early 1970s, with serious economic consequences for most of the world's industrialized economies, which were heavily dependent on imported oil. However, after a period of time, the OPEC cartel broke down, partly because different countries began to exceed their production quotas so that the price of oil began to fall.

The OPEC example illustrates a problem inherent in cartels: the problem of instability. Cartels tend to work for a period of time and then fracture. Why should this be the case? Let us assume that there are two firms considering forming a cartel. For

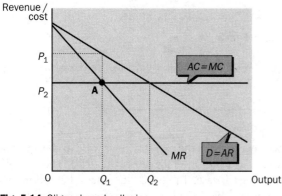

Fig. 5.14 Oligopoly and collusion.

simplicity we shall call them Firm 1 and Firm 2. Fig. 5.14 illustrates the revenue and cost curves for one of these firms. We assume that these curves are identical for each firm. Notice that average and marginal cost are assumed to be constant for all levels of output. If the two firms collude and form a cartel, they will each produce at point A, where marginal cost and marginal revenue are equal. The price will be P_1 and the quantity produced by each firm will be Q_1. The cartel is effectively acting like a single monopolist. The problem is that both firms have an incentive to 'cheat' on this agreement. Each firm could increase output beyond Q_1 and raise its own profits, because each extra unit of output would add more to revenue than to costs. Note that beyond Q_1 the demand curve (AR) lies above the average cost curve, so that a small increase in output would raise the profits of the 'cheat'. The cheat could add to its own profits by producing up to the output level Q_2. Once Q_2 was reached, any further increase in output would add more to costs than to revenue. If just one firm were to raise output then total *industry* output would increase so that the price would start to fall. The cheating firm would make more profits at the expense of the firm that stuck to the cartel agreement.

Let us assume that the cartel produces 1000 units in total, and that the cartel price is £10 per unit. Each individual firm will produce 500 units, and will gain revenue of £5000 (500 × 10). Now what if Firm 1 decides to cheat? Firm 1 decides to raise output to 1000 units so that the industry output is now 1500 units. This reduces the industry price to, say, £6 per unit. The revenue of Firm 1 is now £6000 (1000 × £6), and Firm 2, which sticks to the cartel agreement, now receives just £3000 in revenue (500 × £6). Firm 1 has made more revenue at the expense of Firm 2. Firm 2 now has two choices. It could stick to the cartel, but this means it would have to accept the reduction in revenue. Alternatively, it could also cheat and increase its own output to 1000 units. This would lower the industry price to, say, £4. The total revenue for both firms would now be just £4000. This is £1000 less than they would have earned had they stuck to the agreement. It is this incentive to cheat that often results in the breakdown of a cartel. In the next section we shall look more closely at this issue.

5.9 Game theory

Game theory is a method of analysing the behaviour of oligopoly firms where one firm has to take into account the reactions of a rival firm. Each 'game' has alternative

Table 5.2

		Firm 2	
		Stick	**Cheat**
Firm 1	**Stick**	5000, *5000*	3000, *6000*
	Cheat	6000, *3000*	4000, *4000*

strategies and pay-offs. In our cartel example, the two strategies were to cheat on the cartel agreement ('cheat') or to stick to the cartel agreement ('stick'). The pay-offs were the total revenues resulting in each case. Table 5.2 illustrates a pay-off matrix for our example. Each square shows the pay-off for each firm, for each possible pair of strategies. The pay-off on the left is that for Firm 1 and the pay-off on the right (in italic type) is for Firm 2. If both firms stick to the cartel, then the pay-off is that in the top left corner. Both firms' total revenue is £5000. If Firm 1 cheats but Firm 2 sticks to the agreement then the pay-offs are in the bottom left corner. The revenue for Firm 1 is £6000 and the revenue for Firm 2 is £3000, etc.

Let us now analyse the situation again from the point of view of each firm. Each firm can only observe what the other is doing with a long lag. This means that if Firm 1 were to cheat, Firm 2 would not realize until some time afterwards. During this time, its revenues would have been falling. Firm 2 would obviously want to avoid this happening. Consider Firm 1. It does not know what Firm 2 will do. It does know, however, the pay-offs in each case. So Firm 1 knows that if Firm 2 sticks to the cartel agreement then it (Firm 1) can *either* cheat and gain revenue of £6000 *or* stick to the agreement and gain revenue of £5000. Clearly it would be better to cheat. On the other hand, if Firm 2 were to cheat on the agreement then Firm 1 knows that it could *either* also choose to cheat and gain revenue of £4000, *or* it could stick to the agreement and gain revenue of £3000. Once again, it would be better to cheat. We can say therefore that whatever Firm 2 decides to do, Firm 1 will always decide to cheat. In other words, we say that Firm 1 has a **dominant strategy** to cheat.

We can now look at the problem from the perspective of Firm 2. Remember the pay-off for Firm 2 is that on the right in each square. Firm 2 knows that if Firm 1 sticks to the cartel agreement then it (Firm 2) can cheat and gain revenue of £6000 or stick to the agreement and gain revenue of £5000. Clearly it would be better to cheat. On the other hand, if Firm 1 were to cheat on the agreement then Firm 2 could also choose to cheat and gain revenue of £4000, or it could stick to the agreement and gain revenue of £3000. Once again, it would be better to cheat. Therefore Firm 2 will also always choose to cheat on the agreement. Its decision is the same as for Firm 1. Both firms have a dominant strategy to cheat on the cartel agreement. The resulting equilibrium is known as a *dominant strategy equilibrium*.

In the dominant strategy equilibrium for our example the cartel will break down, and each firm will gain total revenue of £4000. For each firm this is less than they would gain if they both honoured the agreement. It is an optimal outcome for neither firm. However, because neither firm is prepared to trust the other both will gain lower revenue. This is a classic case of the *prisoners' dilemma*. Originally, the situation was analysed in terms of two prisoners arrested for a crime and detained separately. Each can either confess or deny the crime. If both confess they receive a modest prison sentence. If both deny they are set free. However, if one confesses and the

Dominant strategy: A strategy that is best for one firm whatever the other firm chooses to do.

Table 5.3

		Firm 2	
		Cut price 3%	No change
Firm 1	Cut price 3%	−180, −160	+120, −200
	No change	−160, +120	0, 0

other denies then the 'confessor' gets a light sentence while the other prisoner receives a very long sentence. If each could trust the other to deny then they would go free. Each is concerned, however, that the other will confess, leaving him or her to face a long sentence. Both therefore confess and accept the modest sentence. This is not the best outcome for either of them.

Game theory can be used to analyse any strategy where a firm's or individual's return depends on the actions of another firm or individual. Consider the pay-off matrix in Table 5.3. In this example there are two firms in an industry. Each firm has two strategies: to reduce prices by 3 per cent, or to make no price change. Both firms know the pay-offs to each strategy but they do not know what the other firm will do. Once again, the pay-offs for Firm 1 are shown on the left and those for Firm 2 on the right of each square. Let us consider Firm 1. It knows that if Firm 2 chooses to reduce price by 3 per cent then it (Firm 1) can *either* follow suit and reduce price by 3 per cent, in which case it will receive a pay-off of −180 (that is, a loss of £180), *or* it can keep its own price constant and receive a pay-off of −160 (that is, a loss of £160). So, if Firm 1 believes that Firm 2 will reduce price then it should keep its own price constant. What if Firm 2 were to keep its own price constant? Firm 1 could *either* reduce price by 3 per cent, in which case it would make a pay-off of 120 (that is, a profit of £120), *or* it could also keep its own price constant and receive a pay-off of 0. So, if Firm 1 believes that Firm 2 will keep its price constant, it should reduce its own price. Firm 1 does not have a dominant strategy. If Firm 2 reduces price, Firm 1 is better off keeping its own price constant. If Firm 2 keeps its price constant, Firm 1 is better off cutting its own price. The decision of Firm 1 will obviously depend upon what Firm 2 chooses to do.

Now let us consider the decision of Firm 2. If Firm 1 were to reduce price by 3 per cent then Firm 2 could follow suit and reduce price by 3 per cent, in which case it would make a pay-off of −160 (that is, a loss of £160), or it could keep its own price constant and receive a pay-off of −200 (that is, a loss of £200). If Firm 2 believes that Firm 1 will reduce price it should also reduce price by 3 per cent. What if Firm 1 were to keep its own price constant? Firm 2 could reduce price by 3 per cent, in which case it would make a pay-off of 120 (that is, a profit of £120), or it could also keep its own price constant and receive a pay-off of 0. So, if Firm 2 believes that Firm 1 will keep its price constant, it should reduce price by 3 per cent. Clearly Firm 2 *does* have a dominant strategy. Whatever Firm 1 chooses to do, Firm 2 will always achieve a higher pay-off by reducing price by 3 per cent.

What will be the equilibrium of this game? Firm 2 will always choose to reduce price by 3 per cent. In this case, the best option for Firm 1 will be to keep its own price constant. The equilibrium pay-off will therefore be (−160, +120). This equilibrium is not a dominant strategy equilibrium because only one firm has a dominant strategy. Such an equilibrium is known as a **Nash equilibrium** (after American

Nash equilibrium: A situation in which both firms are doing the best they can, given what the other firm is doing.

mathematician John Nash). A Nash equilibrium describes a situation where both firms are doing the best they can, given what the other firm is doing.

5.10 Price discrimination

Any firm with a degree of market power is able to engage in **price discrimination**. Price discrimination occurs when a firm sells the same good to different consumers at different prices. In order to price discriminate, a firm must be able to identify two different markets for the good. As an example, consider a bus company that has just opened a new bus route from the suburbs to the city centre. The company believes that the bus service will be used both by commuters who have to rely on the bus service to get to work by 9am, and by students who use the service to get into college. Students need only arrive at the college for classes, which may be timetabled throughout the day. Assume that the cost of providing the bus service is a flat fee of £5000 per year. In order to set the fare, the firm will need to estimate the likely demand for the bus service. Extensive market research reveals that 10 000 bus trips per year would be made by commuters to work, who would pay a fare of £1. However, the research also reveals that the students, on much lower incomes, would be prepared to pay a maximum fare of only 40p. At this fare, 10 000 student trips per year would be made. If the fare was higher than 40p, no student would be prepared to use the bus service. Which fare would maximize profits? If the firm charged a price of £1 to *all* passengers, then only commuters would use the service. Total revenue would be £10 000 (10 000 × £1). Hence total profit would be £5000 (£10 000 − £5000). If the firm charged a fare of 40p to *all* passengers, then both commuters and students would use the service, and total revenue would be £8000 (20 000 × 40p). Total profit would be £3000 (£8000 − £5000). What if the company decides to follow a 'two-tier' pricing policy? It charges commuters £1 per trip and charges students 40p per trip. Total revenue will now be £14 000 ([10 000 × £1] + [10 000 × 40p]), and total profit will be £9000 (£14 000 − £5000). Clearly, in order to maximize profit, the firm needs to charge two different prices to two different consumer groups: in other words, it needs to practice price discrimination.

Fig. 5.15 illustrates how price discrimination can raise total revenue and profit. The figure shows a demand curve. At a price P_2, the quantity demanded would be Q_2

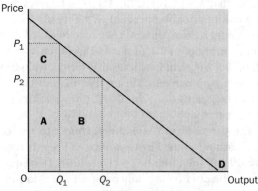

Fig. 5.15 The effects of price discrimination.

and the total revenue would be the area under the demand curve A + B. However, if the market were to be split, with $0-Q_1$ customers being charged a price of P_1, and Q_1-Q_2 customers being charged a price of P_2, total revenue would be higher. The revenue from selling to $0-Q_1$ customers at P_1 would be the area A + C. The revenue from selling to Q_1-Q_2 customers at P_2 would be the area B. So total revenue from this pricing strategy is equal to the area A + B + C, which is greater than total revenue earned from selling to all customers at P_2 (area A + B).

Our example suggests that price discrimination is a rational strategy for any firm seeking to maximize profits. However, there are a number of points to consider. First, how can the bus company identify which passengers are commuters and which are students? If it cannot 'separate' the two, then the discrimination policy will fail. Commuters could masquerade as students and avoid the higher fare. The company must therefore ensure that it can identify each type of passenger. One way of doing this would be to ask passengers to produce a student identity card in order to prove that they are a student. Successful price discrimination requires both the *identification of* and *separation of* different markets or types of customer. Moreover, as in our example, it is essential that each different market has different demand characteristics, or – more specifically – different demand elasticities. In our example, commuters rely on the bus service to get to work on time. They are prepared to pay a higher fare to use the service. Their demand is relatively inelastic. Students, on the other hand, who can travel at various times throughout the day, and who have much lower incomes, will consider other means of transport if the bus fare is too high. They may walk, or use a bicycle to save money. Therefore, student demand for bus travel will be relatively price elastic. Any firm wishing to price discriminate successfully will charge the higher price in that market where demand is more price inelastic and the lower price where demand is more price elastic.

Examples of price discrimination

Price discrimination occurs in many industries. The example we have looked at is highly realistic, as many local bus companies offer student discounts.

Price discrimination is also used in the rail industry. It is much cheaper to travel between 9am and 4pm than it is to travel between 4pm and 6pm. This is because those travelling between 4pm and 6pm are usually commuters, whose demand for the rail service is relatively price inelastic. Those travelling at other times are more likely to be 'leisure' travellers with alternatives sources of transport at their disposal. Their demand will be relatively price elastic.

Airlines too engage in price discrimination. Aeroplane seats are sold at many different prices, even within the same class of compartment. Round trips between any two cities tend to be far cheaper if the traveller is staying over on a Saturday night. This pricing policy enables the airline to separate business travellers (who will not wish to stay over on a Saturday night) from other travellers. Business travellers' demand will be more price inelastic than for other types of traveller.

One final example of price discrimination is telephone pricing. The cost of a call is more expensive between 9am and 6pm on weekdays than at other times of the week. This is known as **peak load pricing**, which is also practised in the electricity industry and in some cinemas and restaurants, where prices will tend to be higher in the evenings.

Peak load pricing: A situation in which a firm charges higher prices during times of peak demand and lower prices at other times.

5.11 Market structures: an institutionalist view

Having reviewed the four major market structures identified by economic theory – perfect competition, imperfect competition, oligopoly and monopoly – an obvious question now arises as to the relative importance of each in the real economy. Although perfect competition has been presented as an ideal, its near neighbour – imperfect competition – appears to possess some important attributes, which might be thought to recommend it over both oligopoly and monopoly. In particular, the imperfectly competitive market retains a high degree of openness and intensity of competition, and firms operating within such a market structure have few powers of market exclusion. The key to their survival must therefore be their ability to remain competitive, one against the other, in the way that they satisfy consumer demands. It follows that, if an economy is characterized by the presence of many imperfect markets, the pre-eminence of consumer sovereignty is still firmly established. Such an economy will be close to, if not quite at, the Adam Smith ideal. So what do modern advanced economies actually look like? Do they approximate to imperfect competition or do they tend to be dominated by oligopoly and monopoly?

Of the various schools of economic analysis, *institutionalism* has the most decisive perspective on such questions, particularly in the writings of John Kenneth Galbraith. Galbraith's work has concentrated on the American economy, but its generalities are applicable to the other advanced capitalist nations in Europe and the Far East. Galbraith's primary claim is that, in many respects, the advanced economies are in fact *increasingly* dominated by relatively small numbers of extremely large and therefore *powerful* firms. Power here means the ability to manipulate and control one's own environment. Thus, Galbraith argues, the largest firms are able to organize the markets in which they are situated to the exclusion of other interests, such as those of smaller firms and – especially – the consumer.

This situation is a relatively new one. The capitalism of the eighteenth and nineteenth centuries was not of this form; it was typified by the kind of imperfectly competitive markets characterized above. *Then*, the tenet of consumer sovereignty *did* generally apply. But in the interim, and especially since 1945, the key *institutions* of capitalism – including the firm – have undergone profound change. The period after the Second World War witnessed not only the emergence of giant firms but also the development of 'big' government and very large trade unions. Galbraith argues that the reshaping of these key institutions of capitalism has important implications for the way the system actually works and, moreover, in *whose interests* it works. Here we concentrate on his analysis of firms.

The emergence of significant numbers of large firms across a variety of industries in the advanced capitalist economies since 1945 is, in the institutionalist view, the result of rapid *technological development* over this period. We noted in Chapter 3 (section 3.3) that Henry Ford's adoption of the flow-line method of car assembly, while making cars cheaper and easier to produce, required the overall scale of production to be much higher than it had ever been before. As elements of 'Fordism' were taken up by other industries, they too increased their scales of production. In industries unsuited to the flow-line, other forms of technological change with associated high investment costs also tended to make the efficient scale of production higher such that, again, the size of firms tended to increase.

THE DIRECTORS

DREDGE/RIGG

Consumer sovereignty or producer sovereignty?

So how far has this process gone? In Galbraith's view, approximately *half* of private sector production in the United States[4] now rests in the hands of large firms that are either monopolies or oligopolies. The other half can be attributed to firms that broadly conform to the rules of imperfect competition. In this latter segment, then, the principle of consumer sovereignty still applies: in attempting to maximize profits, firms must prioritize the interests of consumers, and the course of production is strongly conditioned by consumer demand. Galbraith calls the uncompetitive part of the economy the *planning system* and the competitive part the *market system*. The term 'planning' is appropriate because firms in this sector are able to *plan and direct the development of their own markets*. This is clearly a very strong assertion and, moreover, one that flies in the face of the orthodoxy of consumer sovereignty: how is it justified?

As noted, the institutionalist approach suggests a link between the *size* and *power* of a firm. Now, there can be no doubt that the leading firms in the advanced economies are indeed extremely large. For example, the total annual sales of the American car maker General Motors has in recent years been consistently greater than the national incomes of countries such as Denmark and Norway. But how *precisely* does scale translate into power? The Galbraithian claim is that the largest firms enjoy a measure of influence over consumers, costs and prices that escapes smaller firms. Let us think about each of these 'spheres of influence' in a little more detail.

Consumers

Consumers, to take the first case, are clearly receptive to advertising, otherwise firms – large and small – would not bother to do it. The largest and best-resourced firms will be able to afford the heaviest advertising – this is also clear. But what does advertising do? In the conventional view, it allows the *individual* firm to provide information about *its* product in the hope of persuading people of its *particular* merit. Ford promotes the *Mondeo* in the hope that car buyers will prefer it to a Rover or a Renault. For Galbraith, however, the picture is complicated when one considers the *combined and cumulative* effect of advertising by the car industry as a whole. This amounts to continuous persuasion not that this car or that car is better but that *private motoring per se* is desirable. While this might indeed be the case, private motoring is only one

[4] Galbraith claims that his argument applies equally well to most other modern industrial economies.

way of getting from place to place. An obvious alternative would be to use buses, an environmentally friendlier option in these congested times. But are bus services promoted as extravagantly as new cars? Of course, the answer is 'no', because bus firms are generally smaller and not so well off as carmakers. The *combined* effect of car advertising is then to affirm a *psychological desire* for private motoring above other forms of transport when, in fact, the *material need* is only for mobility. Now, although virtually all firms can and do advertise, the superior resources of the planning sector mean that only its members are likely to be able to generate persuasion on a scale sufficient for general product affirmation, such as that achieved by the giant car firms. None of this means that consumers become mere dupes of the planning system, but it does suggest that firms in the planning system can fix the interests and generate the allegiance of consumers in ways denied to the smaller firms in the market system.

Costs and prices

Their scale also permits firms in the planning system to exert unusually strong influence over costs and prices. A good example of this is the power that the major UK supermarkets have over the producers of food and other goods that they sell. Because the largest supermarkets now account for the vast proportion of retail sales their suppliers are forced into a subordinate business relationship for want of alternative outlets for the goods they produce. Turning now to prices, we have already characterized imperfectly competitive firms, oligopolies and monopolies as *price makers*, but there is an important difference between the first of these and the other two in the extent to which the prices they set have significance in the wider market. The ability of the imperfectly competitive firm to establish a unique price is conditioned by the degree of product differentiation that it can achieve in a crowded and fairly competitive market. Even when substantial product differentiation permits relatively high prices to be set compared with the market 'norm', these have no general market relevance: consumers can elect to buy the product in question or choose a readily available and cheaper alternative. In markets dominated by oligopoly and monopoly the situation is rather different. Here, because most production is (at best) shared amongst a small number of large firms, whatever prices are set *are* significant for the market as a whole because consumer choice is relatively limited. This is most apparent in the case of pure monopoly, but it is also a familiar trait in oligopoly where, as noted, there tends to be a degree of price stability amongst firms, with competition – such as it is – restricted to non-price forms. Once again, then, firms in the planning system enjoy a measure of market control far beyond that available to their counterparts in the market system.

The implications of this analysis are profound. Galbraith refers to the notion of consumer sovereignty as the *accepted sequence*, meaning that the chain of command in a market economy flows from the consumer to the producer. As we have seen, Galbraith's work contends that, in the market system at least, the accepted sequence works largely as anticipated, and the firm is subordinate to the consumer. However, given the conditions outlined above, in the planning system there is a dramatic reversal of influence. Here, the firm has the *power* to shape and control the market, and to impose its priorities and preferences on the consumer: in Galbraith's phrase there is then a *revised sequence* as consumer sovereignty is replaced by *producer sovereignty*. While conventional economics does not wholly ignore the concept of power – independent price making and market exclusion are clearly forms of power

– in the institutionalist view it fails to recognize the extent of the power of the planning sector and its negative implications for the trumpeted ideals of competitive capitalism.

Summary

◆ Firms that are able to set their price independently are said to posses a degree of market power. Market concentration is often used to indicate the degree of market power within an industry.

◆ Economic theory recognizes four market structures: perfect competition, imperfect competition, oligopoly and monopoly. Perfect competition provides an idealized view of how markets should work given the highest possible level of competition between their constituent firms. Its principal attributes are absolute consumer sovereignty and the socially efficient allocation of resources. Although the assumptions of perfect competition are not all met in the real economy, it provides a useful benchmark against which the relative merits of actual market structures may be assessed.

◆ In contrast to perfect competition, pure monopoly is characterized by an absence of competition. This inevitably entails a misallocation of resources. However, it is not the case that monopolies always restrict output and raise prices to the detriment of the consumer. In the case of natural monopoly, a single supplier may raise output and lower prices to levels that could not be achieved in a competitive environment. Nor need monopolies be especially large. Monopoly power is defined by barriers to entry, not size. Finally, monopolies necessarily impinge upon the sovereignty of the consumer.

◆ Firms in the two remaining market structures are, like monopoly, price makers. Arguably, oligopoly is characterized by lower levels of competition and weak consumer sovereignty, while imperfect competition, because it retains competitiveness, necessarily prioritizes consumer interests.

◆ Finally, the work of J.K. Galbraith contends that large parts of modern capitalist economies tend towards oligopolistic and monopoly organization. This poses serious questions as to the ultimate *raison d'être* of the contemporary capitalist system: whose interests does it primarily serve, those of the consumer or the producer?

Key terms

◆ Market power
◆ Market concentration
◆ Market structure
◆ Perfect competition
◆ Monopoly
◆ Imperfect competition
◆ Oligopoly
◆ Game theory

◆ Price taker
◆ Price maker
◆ Normal and supernormal profit
◆ Resource misallocation
◆ Price discrimination
◆ Institutionalism
◆ Planning system
◆ Market system
◆ Accepted sequence
◆ Revised sequence

■ Self-test questions

True (t) or false (f)

1. If a market is dominated by a very small number of firms then that market is said to be highly concentrated.

2. Perfectly competitive firms are price takers.

3. Firms in perfect competition can earn supernormal profits only in the short run.

4. Firms maximize profits by selling goods at the highest possible price.

5. Allocative efficiency for society as a whole occurs where firms produce an output that equates price and marginal cost.

6. When an industry is monopolized the outcome is always a higher price and reduced output.

7. In the long run monopolists can earn supernormal profits.

8. Imperfectly competitive firms are price takers.

9. Imperfectly competitive firms enjoy powers of market exclusion.

10. Firms with a degree of market power can engage in price discrimination.

11. Oligopolists enjoy powers of market exclusion.

12. For institutionalists, capitalism is an increasingly uncompetitive system.

Complete the following sentences by inserting the missing word(s)

1. _____ measure the total market share of the largest firms in an industry.

2. The demand or average revenue curve of a firm in perfect competition is _____.

3. Perfectly competitive firms produce _____ goods and services.

4. Supernormal profits are profits that _____ the minimum amount a firm must earn to induce it to remain in the industry.

5. Normal profit is the _____ amount a firm must earn to induce it to remain in the industry.

6. Monopoly is sustained by _____.

7. For any firm, the maximum profit output occurs where _____.

8. Imperfectly competitive firms, oligopolists and monopolists are all _____.

9. Price stability under oligopoly has been explained by the _____ demand curve faced by the oligopolist.

10. Oligopoly is, to some extent, unique amongst market structures in the sense that firms act ____.

11. ____ occurs when a firm sells the same good to different consumers at different prices.

12. Galbraith calls the less competitive part of the private sector in the modern economy the ____.

13. Where consumer sovereignty is subverted by less competitive firms, there exists a ____.

Questions for discussion

◆ Why should the profit-maximizing firm always produce at that output which equates marginal cost with marginal revenue?

◆ To what extent might the following exert monopoly power: a late-night corner shop; a 'local' pub; the *Financial Times* newspaper; British Gas; the Channel Tunnel?

◆ Do monopolies tend always to raise price and lower output?

◆ What is the significance of Galbraith's notion of the 'revised sequence'?

Reflective questions on 'boxed' material

◆ Read Box 5.1 on the Competition Commission's investigation into the UK market for wrapped ice cream. What arguments might you offer as a spokesperson for Wall's in trying to deflect criticism that your behaviour is uncompetitive?

Further reading

George, K.D., C. Joll and E.L. Lynk *Industrial Organization* (4th ed.) (London: Routledge, 1992). A comprehensive examination of the economics of the firm.

Atkinson, B., F. Livesey and B. Milward, eds. *Applied Economics* (Basingstoke: Macmillan, 1998). Chapters 1–5 provide an overview of the firm in applied UK and European contexts.

Shepherd, W.G. *The Economics of Industrial Organization* (Englewood Cliffs: Prentice Hall, 1990). Contains a complementary mix of theory and well-presented industry case studies.

Pindyck, R. and D.L. Rubinfield *Microeconomics* (4th ed.) (Englewood Cliffs: Prentice Hall, 1998). Contains a comprehensive but elementary section on game theory and strategy.

Galbraith, J.K. *Economics and the Public Purpose* (Harmondsworth: Penguin, 1973). Offers a summary of Galbraith's views, including those on the structure and influence of large firms.

Internet links

The *Financial Times'* s website offers a global business news archive, most of which – in our experience – can be accessed without charge. You can search for companies, industries, particular business issues, and so on. A great site: **http://www.ft.com/**

Investment Policy and Appraisal

Contents

Key issues

▶ How do firms generate funds for investment?

▶ How do firms appraise investment projects?

▶ What is the importance of the 'time value of money'?

▶ How is investment appraisal affected by a restriction of investment funds?

6.1 Introduction

In Chapter 3, section 3.5, we looked at the different objectives of firms. We noted, for example, that some firms will seek to maximize profits while others may wish to maximize sales revenue. We saw that, for many firms, the objective is to maximize the wealth of their owners or shareholders. In order to achieve this, firms will need to maximize profits. The level of profits earned will ultimately determine the amount of dividends available for shareholders. However, whatever their objectives, all firms will, at times, have to make important investment decisions. Investment inevitably involves an initial cash outlay made in the expectation of receiving future returns, and each firm will want to ensure that any investment project is consistent with that firm's overall objective, such as profit maximization. In order to ensure that this is the case, firms will need a method of *appraising* all possible investment projects.

This chapter, then, is concerned with the different methods of **investment appraisal**. Throughout the chapter we shall be assuming that the objective of firms is to maximize profits, so that any investment proposal is appraised with this objective in mind. At the outset it should be emphasized that no method of investment appraisal can give a definitive decision as to whether the firm should invest or not; it can only act as a guide in decision-making. This is largely because any investment appraisal will necessarily involve the estimation or forecasting of future cash inflows that arise as a result of the investment itself. As the future is inherently uncertain, any investment appraisal method can only give advice on the basis of such forecasts. Ultimately, investment decisions will be taken on the basis of managerial judgement; however, in making a judgement, any rational manager will be influenced by the results of investment appraisal.

Investment appraisal: The use of techniques to ensure that all projects are consistent with the objective of the firm.

6.2 Sources of investment finance

In order to undertake capital investment, firms will often need access to large sources of funds. Broadly speaking, firms have three alternatives sources of investment finance:

- retained earnings
- debt finance
- equity finance.

Retained earnings

By far the biggest source of investment finance is **retained earnings**, whereby firms use internally generated funds in order to invest. One of the major advantages of using such funds is that firms do not have to pay the transactions costs associated with debt or equity finance. For example, there are no brokerage costs or loan arrangement fees. Nevertheless, such funds do not represent a free source of finance. Firms must always consider the opportunity costs of using such funds – the cost of the best alternative use of the funds forgone. One example of an alternative use would be to offer dividend payments to shareholders. The firm will obviously have to balance the need to satisfy shareholders, who demand a *current* return on their investment, with the need to use funds in profitable investment projects that guarantee the future profitability of the firm and provide *future* returns for shareholders.

Debt finance

If the firm chooses not to use retained earnings as a source of finance then an alternative is to obtain **debt finance**. Or, put simply, to borrow. One of the most common ways of doing this, especially in the short term, is by bank overdraft. This is a particularly useful source of finance for firms that need to borrow regularly. The amount of money that can be borrowed is generally restricted according to the bank's willingness to extend the overdraft facility. Generally, rates of interest on overdrafts are variable and therefore potentially costly for a firm. Furthermore, overdrafts are repayable on demand, which means that the firm cannot always plan accurately ahead and must always ensure that it has sufficient funds to repay the overdraft at any time.

Bank loans are a longer-term source of debt finance. Loans tend to have a fixed rate of interest, and are made over a specified period of time. Often banks charge a loan 'arrangement fee' in addition to the interest rate.

There is one other source of long-term debt finance open to the firm, and that is to issue some form of long-term instrument of debt. For private sector firms, the most common form of debt stock is **debentures**. Debentures are usually purchased by institutional or private investors, and are basically loan documents issued by a company that pay a rate of interest. These are issued over a period between 5 and 30 years. At the end of this period, the loan is paid back. The amount of debentures that a firm can issue is restricted by the value of the firm's assets. Hence smaller firms will not be able to raise as much debenture finance as larger firms. As with most debt, the liabilities on the debentures must be repaid regardless of whether or not the firm makes a profit.

Retained earnings: Funds generated internally by the firm, such as profits from previous investment projects.

Debt finance: Arises when a firm borrows in order to obtain the necessary funds for investment.

Debentures: Documents that are issued by a firm in order to borrow funds. The document entitles the lender of funds to an annual interest payment during the period of the loan.

Equity finance: Arises when a firm obtains investment funds by issuing shares.

Dividends: Sums of money paid by a firm to shareholders. Each shareholder receives a dividend for each share held.

Capital gains: Arise when the value of an asset, such as a share, rises above the price at which it was purchased. The owner can then sell the asset at a profit.

Rights issues: Occur where a firm issues shares to the market but gives existing shareholders the option to buy the shares first.

Payback: The length of time that it takes for the cash inflows from an investment project to equal the initial cash outlay.

Equity finance

Equity finance now accounts for almost 60 per cent of total capital issues in the UK. Firms obtain funds by issuing shares. Those buying the shares, commonly known as *shareholders*, are the owners of the firm. In buying the shares they provide the firm with funds for investment. Naturally, shareholders will demand a return on their investment, which may arise in the form of **dividends** or **capital gains** as the market value of shares rises. Share prices in public companies are quoted on the stock market.

Firms wishing to issue shares for the first time must comply with stock market regulations, such as the provision of financial statements and full details of trading history. All firms must have a minimum amount of capital. Furthermore, firms will need to advertise the share issue in advance and issue a prospectus with full details of the issue. They will also need to pay an underwriting fee. Underwriters guarantee to buy any shares not purchased by investors. In the event of weak demand for the shares this will prevent the market price from falling too low, and will guarantee that the firm can raise the required capital. Underwriting firms charge a fee for their service. This means that share issues can be an expensive way to raise funds, and they are therefore not suitable for smaller firms.

Shares will, of course, also be issued by those firms already listed on the Stock Exchange, with shares already outstanding. Issues by such firms are known as **rights issues**. Existing shareholders are given first opportunity to buy the shares, usually at a discount. After a period of time, the remaining shares are offered to the market. Once again the issue will be underwritten. The rights issue price will depend largely on market perception of the firm's financial health. So, for example, if the firm is believed to be raising funds to finance profitable investment then the price will be higher than if the firm is thought to be raising funds to ease financial problems. The rights issue will tend to lower the overall market price of the firm's shares as it represents an increase in the supply of shares to the market.

Whichever method of raising finance is chosen, and of course the firm may choose a combination of these methods, costs are incurred. If the firm borrows from a financial institution or borrows by issuing debentures then it must pay interest. If firms issue shares then shareholders will demand a return in the form of dividends. These costs are known as the *cost of capital*, and we return to this issue when we discuss discount rates later in the chapter.

6.3 Payback and accounting rate of return

The payback method

The payback method is one of the most widely used of all investment appraisal methods. **Payback** can be defined as the length of time that it takes for the cash inflows from an investment project to equal the initial cash outlay. Payback can be used to compare alternative investment projects whereby the preferred project is that with the shorter payback period. Additionally, payback can be used to appraise projects in terms of a *decision rule*. For example, a firm may decide to accept only those projects that have a payback period of 5 years or less. This decision rule may be based on the average chosen in the industry. Alternatively, it may be based on past experience, if, for example, the firm has found that successful investments are those that have achieved payback within this time period.

In order to illustrate how the payback method can be used, we consider two alternative projects X and Y. For project X the relevant cash flows are

Year	Cash flow
0	−£10 000
1	£6 000
2	£3 000
3	£1 000
4	£1 000

and for project Y the relevant cash flows are

Year	Cash flow
0	−£50 000
1	£30 000
2	£20 000
3	£15 000
4	£10 000

The figures show that project X has an initial outlay of £10 000 (where year 0 is defined as the initial year), and generates cash flows in the following four years as shown. An examination of the figures will show that after 3 years the investment has recouped the initial outlay. Thus the payback period for project X is 3 years. Project Y has a much greater initial outlay of £50 000. However, we can see that the cash outflow is fully recouped after just 2 years, meaning that the payback period for project Y is just 2 years. If the firm could choose to invest in only one of these projects (that is, the projects were mutually exclusive) then project Y would be preferred as it pays back one year quicker than project X.

The two projects may be mutually exclusive simply because the firm in question has a maximum of £50 000 to invest. If investment funds were unlimited the firm might be able to invest in both projects. If we assume that the firm has a decision rule to accept only those projects that pay back in 3 years or less then both projects would be acceptable. If the decision rule was to accept only those projects that pay back within 2 years then only project Y would be acceptable.

Advantages of payback

The main advantage of the payback method is that, once all cash forecasts have been made, it is quick and simple to calculate. Furthermore, firms using this method need not concern themselves with forecasting cash flows beyond the payback period. In other words, they are concerned only with how long it takes for the project to pay back the initial cash outlay, and not with cash flows that occur after payback. Given the uncertainty associated with any cash flows arising in the future, and assuming that cash flows forecast in, say, 50 years are likely to be more uncertain than those forecast to arise in 2 years, the payback method favours the selection of low-risk projects. Finally, payback is a useful way of appraising projects when firms have limited funds for capital investment. It may be, for example, that a firm with a 3 year payback acceptance decision rule has several potential projects that meet this criterion, but that it has insufficient capital to invest in all of those projects. In order to 'ration' its capital effectively, it could simply change its decision rule to 2 years, which might reduce the number of desirable projects and ease the pressure on investment funds.

Disadvantages of payback

Though payback has a number of attractions as a method of appraising investment projects, there are associated disadvantages that mean that it is probably inadequate as an investment appraisal technique unless used in conjunction with a more sophisticated technique.

One of the major problems of payback is that it cannot distinguish between projects with the same payback period. Furthermore, it may encourage excessive investment in short-term projects. This problem can be illustrated with reference to the following example. There are two projects for consideration, projects A and B. For project A the relevant cash flows are

Year	Cash flow
0	−£50 000
1	£5000
2	£10 000
3	£15 000
4	£20 000
5	£100 000
6	£200 000

and for project B the relevant cash flows are

Year	Cash flow
0	−£50 000
1	£25 000
2	£25 000
3	£15 000
4	£0
5	£0

An examination of the figures will show that both projects have the same initial cash outlay. Project B has a payback period of 2 years, while project A has a longer period to payback of 4 years. According to the basic criterion, project B would be chosen in preference to project A. However, if we examine for each project the returns arising after the payback period, we can see that project A is far superior. Payback is unique amongst investment appraisal techniques in that it emphasizes cash flow and not profit. Clearly, therefore, exclusive reliance on payback as a means of investment appraisal may not lead to the selection of the most profitable projects. Finally, and perhaps most importantly, payback ignores a concept known as the **time value of money**.

The time value of money refers to the fact that a given sum of money has a different value depending on when that sum arises. For example £1000 received today is worth more than £1000 received in one year's time. This is because money can be invested in order to earn a rate of interest over time. Returning to our example, if we assume a rate of interest of 5 per cent then £1000 invested for one year will be worth £1050 at the end of the year. So assuming that the investment takes place, £1000 received today is worth more than £1000 received in one year (because today's £1000 can be invested and must be worth more than £1000 in one year hence). Now consider the implications for payback.

Time value of money: Arises because cash flows received today are worth more than equivalent cash flows received at a later date. Hence future cash flows have to be discounted in order to calculate their value today, i.e. their present value.

Take a simple investment project with an initial cash outlay of £1000, which generates a return of £1000. At first glance we may think that the payback period is one year. This would only be true if the time value of money were zero. In fact, the payback period will be greater than one year because, strictly speaking, given that the time value of money is positive, then £1000 received in one year is not worth as much as the initial £1000 outlay, and thus the project has not fully paid back after one year. The time value of money is discussed in more detail in section 6.4.

The accounting rate of return method

The accounting rate of return method (ARR) is sometimes referred to as the return on capital employed (ROCE). This method of investment appraisal is widely used in practice. The ARR method estimates the accounting rate of return that an investment project should yield. The firm will have some target rate of return for all projects, known as a *hurdle* rate, and those projects that are acceptable are those yielding a return equal to, or exceeding, the hurdle rate. The hurdle rate may be based on the industry average or on the returns available on other types of investment, for example in government stock. ARR is a measure of accounting profit, and in Box 6.1 we examine the relationship between accounting profit and economic profit.

Accounting profit and economic profit

The accounting rate of return (ARR) is a common measure of accounting profit, which is defined as the surplus over accounting cost. Accounting cost is a different concept from that of opportunity cost, which we first introduced in Chapter 1, section 1.3.

In order to clarify the distinction consider the following example. An engineer currently earning £20 000 per annum is contemplating setting up her own company. She would need to spend all of her £5000 savings (currently earning 5 per cent interest per annum) on equipment, and her net income would be £25 000 per annum. This £25 000 represents her accounting profit. However, her economic profit is somewhat different. In order to calculate economic profit we need to deduct

opportunity cost. This opportunity cost would be the income forgone from going independent (that is, lost salary of £20 000) plus lost interest per annum on her savings (5 per cent × £5000 = £250 per annum). Economic profit would be £25 000 − £20 000 − £250 = £4750.

The difference between economic and accounting profit stems from the different purposes of the accountant and the economist. The accountant is concerned only with the precise recording of a firm's receipts and payments. The economist, however, is concerned with the measurement of profits for decision-making purposes. This will inevitably involve opportunity cost – that is, a consideration of what the firm chooses *not* to do, as well as what it chooses to do.

Rather confusingly, there are a number of ways of defining ARR, all of which may not generate the same result. In Box 6.2, each of these methods is illustrated. However, what is important is that, whichever definition is chosen, it is used consistently. The definition used here to illustrate the method is

$$\text{ARR} = \frac{\text{Estimated total profit}}{\text{Estimated initial investment}} \times 100\% \tag{6.1}$$

Let us assume that a project consists of the purchase of a piece of capital machinery that costs £40 000 and generates returns over a period of 3 years. The cash flows are illustrated below

Year	Cash flow
0	−£40 000
1	£15 000
2	£20 000
3	£25 000

With initial investment of £40 000, we need to calculate estimated total profit in order to solve for the ARR. In order to do this we need to calculate profit each year, then sum the total. At the start of the project, the asset has a value of £40 000. At the

---

Box 6.2

Defining the accounting rate of return

The accounting rate of return can be calculated in a number of ways. The most commonly used definitions are as follows:

$$ARR = \frac{\text{Estimated total profit}}{\text{Estimated initial investment}} \times 100\% \quad (6.1)$$

$$ARR = \frac{\text{Estimated average profit}}{\text{Estimated average investment}} \times 100\% \quad (6.2)$$

$$ARR = \frac{\text{Estimated average profit}}{\text{Estimated initial investment}} \times 100\% \quad (6.3)$$

where

$$\text{Estimated average profit} = \frac{\text{Estimated total profit}}{\text{Number of periods}}$$

$$\text{Average investment} = \frac{\text{Initial investment} + \text{Scrap}}{2}$$

In order to illustrate each of these methods, assume a capital project with a 3 year life. We shall take different values from those used in the text. Suppose, for example that the initial cost of the capital equipment is £300 000 and profits each year after depreciation are £60 000, £80 000 and £100 000 respectively. Finally, the project has a scrap value of £50 000. We can now calculate ARR, according to each of our definitions.

(6.1):

$$ARR = \frac{£240\,000}{£300\,000} \times 100\% = 80\%$$

(6.2):

Estimated average profit = £80 000
(i.e. £240 000 ÷ 3)
Estimated average investment

$$= \frac{£350\,000}{2} = £175\,000$$

Hence $ARR = \dfrac{£80\,000}{£175\,000} \times 100\% = 45.7\%$

(6.3):

$$ARR = \frac{£80\,000}{£300\,000} \times 100\% = 26.7\%$$

Each definition gives a quite different value for the accounting rate of return. It is vital therefore that a firm chooses one definition and uses it consistently.

---

end of the project it is worth just £4000 in 'scrap value'. In other words, it depreciates by £36 000 over the 3 years. Hence annual depreciation is £12 000 (£36 000 ÷ 3). Annual profit per year is calculated as the annual return minus the annual depreciation figure of £12 000:

Year
1	£15 000 − £12 000	= £3000
2	£20 000 − £12 000	= £8000
3	£25 000 − £12 000	= £13 000
	Total profit	= £24 000

Using our definition above we can calculate ARR as follows:

$$ARR = \frac{£24\,000}{£40\,000} \times 100\% = 60\%$$

If we assume that the firm's hurdle rate for all projects is 10 per cent, then clearly this project would be acceptable. Note that if we had used a different method of calculating ARR, such as method (6.3) in Box 6.1, the calculated ARR would be different. Using definition (6.3):

$$ARR = \frac{\text{Estimated average profit}}{\text{Estimated initial investment}} \times 100\%$$

Estimated average profit is quite simple to calculate. Total profit was calculated to be £24 000. Hence average profit per year is simply £24 000 ÷ 3 = £8000. So now we can calculate:

$$ARR = \frac{£8000}{£40\,000} \times 100\% = 20\%$$

Once again, given the hurdle rate, this is acceptable. Clearly, different definitions of ARR yield quite different results. This means it is essential that firms use one definition consistently, otherwise comparisons over a period of time or between different projects would be meaningless.

Advantages of ARR

The main advantage of ARR is that it emphasizes the importance of profitability. It is therefore consistent with the firm's objective of profit maximization. Furthermore, ARR is expressed as a percentage figure, which means that it can be easily understood and interpreted.

Disadvantages of ARR

Though it has been widely used in investment appraisal, ARR is, in fact, declining in popularity. To a large extent this may be explained by the ambiguity of the technique. There exists no consensus on which of the definitions is most appropriate. Furthermore, the ambiguity of the method means that it can be manipulated by firms in investment appraisal; firms can use whichever definition produces the desired investment decision. Additionally, because ARR generates a percentage result, then – unless adjusted – it cannot distinguish between different sizes of project. Put simply, a 10 per cent return on an investment of £100 million would yield far more profit than a 20 per cent return on £1 million.

We have now examined payback and the accounting rate of return as techniques of investment appraisal. Both techniques have their advantages and disadvantages and, as a result, firms may often use them as complementary techniques in appraising projects. For example, firms may adopt a two-stage method of appraisal. In the first stage they appraise projects according to payback. They may decide to consider only those projects that pay back within, say, 5 years. Once these projects have been identified, firms embark on the second stage of the appraisal by setting a hurdle rate and appraising the projects using the ARR technique. Thus payback is used as an initial 'screening device'. In fact the evidence suggests that payback is widely used in this way, with a more sophisticated technique being used in the second stage of the appraisal process. We now consider why more sophisticated techniques are necessary.

6.4 The time value of money and discounting

The time value of money

In the introduction to this chapter, we said that the objective of many firms is ultimately to maximize the wealth of their shareholders. The income of shareholders arises from the receipt of dividends. The greater the profit generated by a firm, the greater the potential dividend. However, rather than pay dividends *now*, firms may decide to invest profits in investment projects that involve a cash outlay made in the expectation of receiving *future* returns. These returns will lead to increased dividend payments to shareholders in the future. Therefore the investment decision involves trading off the payment of dividends now against the payment of dividends in the future. We saw in the previous section that, because money has a time value, a sum of money received in the future will be worth less than an equivalent sum received now. Hence, in undertaking investment appraisal, a firm will want to use a technique that will allow it to calculate whether future dividend payments to shareholders are sufficient to compensate them for forgoing dividends now. Increasingly, therefore, firms are using investment appraisal techniques that incorporate the time value of money. We shall look at these techniques in more detail in section 6.5.

Discounting

Those investment appraisal techniques that incorporate the time value of money are known as *discounted cash flow techniques*. This is because they *discount* any cash flows that arise in the future. This discounting process enables the firm to calculate the value now, of a sum of income received in the future. In other words, it is possible to calculate the *present value* of a future sum.

Firms, and indeed individuals, will each have their own discount rates, which vary from firm to firm and person to person. Consider this simple illustration. If an individual is given the choice of receiving £100 now or £115 in one year's time, that person's decision will reveal something about their own discount rate. If the person prefers the £100 now, this means that their discount rate is *higher* than 15 per cent. If they prefer £115 in one year their discount rate is *lower* than 15 per cent. If they are totally indifferent, in other words they consider the two choices to be exactly equivalent, the person's discount rate is exactly 15 per cent.

We can calculate the present value of any future value as follows:

$$PV = \frac{FV}{(1 + r)^n} \qquad (6.4)$$

where PV = present value; FV = future value; r = discount rate (expressed as a decimal); and n = number of years.

Given a discount rate of 20 per cent, the present value of £300 received in 2 year's time can be calculated as

$$PV = \frac{£300}{(1 + 0.20)^2} = \frac{£300}{(1.44)} = £208.33$$

Assuming a discount rate of 20 per cent, the present value of £300 received in 2 year's time is £208.33. An individual, or firm, with a discount rate of 20 per cent would be indifferent between receiving £300 in 2 year's time or £208.33 now.

Notice that the longer the period, then the lower the present value of a future sum of income. If the sum of £300 were to be received in 3 year's time the present value would be

$$PV = \frac{£300}{(1 + 0.20)^3} = \frac{£300}{1.728} = £173.61$$

This tends to lead to the acceptance of investment projects that give high returns in the short term in preference to those with longer lives, but may lead to excessive investment in short-term projects.

Our discussion begs the question of how the discount rate is chosen. Each firm will choose a discount rate that reflects the cost of raising the funds for investment –

that is, the cost of capital. If, for example, the funds are raised via a loan charging 10 per cent interest, then this may be used as the discount rate. If funds are raised by a share issue, the discount rate will be determined by the rate of return demanded by the shareholders on their investment in the shares. In addition, firms might adjust their discount rates in order to account for an element of risk inherent in the project. Because all returns are in the future they are based on forecasts. If there is a risk that the forecasts are wrong this will mean that firms raise the discount rate to reflect such a risk. Effectively, the appraisal of the project becomes more rigorous.

Now that we have seen how discounting works we can turn to discounted cash flow techniques of investment appraisal.

6.5 Net present value and internal rate of return

Net present value

The **net present value** (NPV) technique of investment appraisal calculates whether the present value of future returns to an investment is greater than the present value of the cost of the investment. If it is, the project is profitable and should be undertaken.

Consider the following investment in a labour-saving piece of capital machinery:

Cost of capital machinery: £300 000 with no scrap value.
Life of capital machinery: 5 years
Labour savings: £50 000 in year 1
                  £150 000 in year 2
                  £200 000 in year 3
                  £100 000 in year 4
                  £50 000 in year 5

The discount rate is 10 per cent.

$$\text{NPV} = \frac{£50\,000}{(1.1)} + \frac{£150\,000}{(1.1)^2} + \frac{£200\,000}{(1.1)^3} + \frac{£100\,000}{(1.1)^4} + \frac{£50\,000}{(1.1)^5} - £300\,000$$

$$= £45\,455 + £123\,967 + £150\,263 + £68\,301 + £31\,046 - £300\,000$$

$$= £119\,032$$

The positive NPV indicates a profitable project that should be accepted. Obviously, at a higher discount rate, the NPV would be reduced, and at very high rates would become negative, meaning that the project would be unprofitable. This underlines the importance of choosing the discount rate carefully. If a situation arose whereby the firm selected a discount rate that was too low then an unprofitable project might be accepted. Of course, the whole method of appraising investments in this way also relies on accurate forecasts of all future returns.

Internal rate of return

Like the NPV, the **internal rate of return** (IRR) is a discounted cash flow technique incorporating the time value of money. The IRR technique calculates the discount rate that gives a net present value of zero: that is, that discount rate that ensures that the present value of all future returns to an investment is exactly equal to the present

Net present value technique of investment appraisal: Calculates whether the present value of future returns from a project is at least equal to the cost of that project.

Internal rate of return: The discount rate that generates a net present value equal to zero.

value of the cost of the investment. This provides a yardstick by which the project can be appraised. If, for example, the company has a cost of capital of 12 per cent and the investment project has an internal rate of return of 15 per cent, the project is profitable and should be accepted. If the project had an internal rate of return of less than 12 per cent it would not be profitable and should therefore be rejected.

In the discussion of NPV, we considered a project with an NPV of £119 032 at a discount rate of 10 per cent. The IRR for this project is therefore greater than 10 per cent. If we appraise the same project with a much higher discount rate, the NPV will become negative. For example, using a discount rate of 25 per cent the NPV would be −£4256 (that is, £40 000 + £96 000 + £102 400 + £40 960 + £16 384 − £300 000). This means that the IRR is somewhere between 10 per cent and 25 per cent.

It would be extremely time consuming to find the IRR by process of trial and error. Instead the IRR can be calculated by appraising the project using two discount rates: a low rate (r_L) and a high rate (r_H). The NPV at each rate is calculated and the following formula is used:

$$\text{IRR} = r_L + (r_H - r_L)\left(\frac{\text{NPV}_L}{\text{NPV}_L - \text{NPV}_H}\right) \tag{6.5}$$

where NPV_L = NPV at the lower discount rate; NPV_H = NPV at the higher discount rate.

Using the same project as an example then the IRR can be calculated:

$$\text{IRR} = 10 + (25 - 10)\left(\frac{119\,032}{119\,032 - (-4256)}\right) = 24.48\%$$

Thus for our project the internal rate of return is 24.48 per cent. However, what we have done by using this formula is generate a *linear approximation'* to the 'true' IRR. By using the formula we implicitly assume that the relationship between the NPV and the discount rate is linear when the relationship is, in fact, non-linear.

Fig. 6.1 illustrates the relationship. The NPV is shown on the vertical axis, and the discount rate (r) on the horizontal axis. The curved line AB illustrates the actual relationship between the discount rate and the NPV. The 'true' IRR is indicated on Fig. 6.1. By using the formula above, we have in fact calculated an approximation to the IRR using line AC. This approximation to IRR is indicated on the figure. Note that if we had chosen a higher discount rate in calculating the IRR, say 30 per cent,

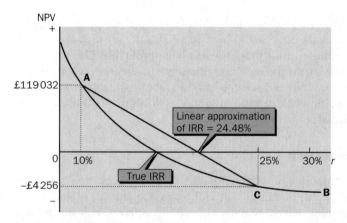

Fig. 6.1 Estimation of the internal rate of return using linear interpolation.

the line AC would be a flatter line and we would have calculated a slightly different approximation to the IRR.

Advantages and disadvantages of discounted cash flow techniques

Both of the methods that we have just discussed are quite sophisticated techniques of investment appraisal, and their major advantage over other methods is the fact that they incorporate the time value of money.

The IRR is especially useful in investment appraisal, as firms can very quickly compare the return on each project with the cost of raising finance. Generally, therefore, the IRR is far more easily understood at management level than NPV. However, the IRR is often confused with the accounting rate of return (ARR) we considered earlier. Furthermore, like the ARR, as a percentage measure the IRR cannot distinguish between the relative sizes of investments. Finally, for certain types of investment, it may even be possible to identify two discount rates that generate an NPV of zero! This begs the question of which IRR is correct.

The NPV method has none of these disadvantages, and can be easily adapted to situations where the discount rate may differ over the life of the project. It would be very difficult to incorporate such changes into an IRR calculation. The NPV is also simpler and quicker to calculate than the IRR. Finally, the NPV can be easily adapted to consider investment appraisal when capital for investment projects is restricted – that is, where the firm is *capital rationed*.

Before we turn to the issue of capital rationing, it is worth examining the popularity of all our investment appraisal methods amongst the 100 largest firms in Britain. The figures in Table 6.1 show the percentage of firms using each method and how use of each technique has changed over time.

The results suggest that the more sophisticated discounted cash flow techniques are increasingly used in conjunction with, rather than instead of, techniques such as payback and ARR. Payback is clearly a very popular method, though many firms use it as an initial 'screening' device before using more rigorous techniques. Interestingly, IRR is more popular than NPV. This may be due to the ease of interpreting and ranking percentage returns on different projects. Box 6.3 illustrates how a project such as the Channel Tunnel can be appraised using some of the techniques discussed in this section.

Table 6.1 Relative popularity of investment appraisal methods

	1975	1980	1986	1992
Payback	73	81	92	95
ARR	51	49	56	50
IRR	44	57	75	81
NPV	32	39	68	74

Sources: Pike, R.H. (1988) 'An empirical study of the adoption of sophisticated capital budgeting practices and decision-making effectiveness', *Accounting and Business Research*, Vol. 18, No. 72, pp. 341–51; and Pike, R.H. (1996) 'A longitudinal survey of capital budgeting practices', *Journal of Business Finance and Accounting*, Vol. 23, No. 1, pp.79–92.

Appraising the Channel Tunnel

We can use some of the techniques developed in this chapter to appraise any one of a number of investments. In this case study we consider the Channel Tunnel, which was approved by the Anglo-French Treaty of 1986 and opened in mid 1994. The two governments established a holding company, Eurotunnel, to manage the project and raise the necessary finance. The finance was obtained primarily via debt and equity capital. Approximately £8 billion was raised from a series of loans provided by a consortium of 60 international banks, and approximately £2 billion was raised in equity capital. Eurotunnel employed a consortium of British and French construction companies, TML, to build the tunnel, and signed an agreement with the British and French governments giving it the right to operate the tunnel

for 50 years, after which time it would come under the joint control of the two governments. The project was therefore funded entirely by the private sector.

The rate of return that could be earned by the tunnel depended on a number of factors. These included the rate of growth of cross-Channel traffic, the pricing structure adopted, the response of rival carriers (such as ferry companies), the type of regulation in the market, and, of course, the appropriate discount rate.

An independent body, Traffic and Revenue Consultant (TRC), provided the initial estimates for annual revenue. The TRC estimated that revenue for 1994 would be £465 million rising to £971 million by the year 2003 and rising further to £1213 million by the year 2013. We can

use these figures as a basis for an appraisal of the total project. Obviously our figures will be only an approximation; nevertheless it is a useful way of demonstrating the usefulness of our appraisal techniques.

If we take the TRC figures as a starting point so that revenue for 1994 was assumed to be £465 million, we then assume that it increases pro rata to a level of £971 million by 2003 (that is, by £56.2 million per year). We then assume another pro rata increase to £1213 million by 2013 (that is, by £24.2 million per year). We then assume

This would imply the following revenues (in millions):

1994	£465
1995	£521.2
1996	£577.4

increasing by £56.2 million per year until

2003	£971	(rounded up to a whole number)
2004	£995.2	
2005	£1019.4	

increasing by £24.2 million per year until

2013	£1213

Although, of course, revenue will continue to grow beyond this point we can use our figures to give us some indication of the total profitability of the project.

Using payback, the most simple technique, then by the end of the year 2004 the project would have paid back £8.2 billion. In other words, the project has a payback period of approximately

6.6   Investment appraisal and capital rationing

Capital rationing: A situation whereby a firm does not have sufficient capital available to invest in all the profitable projects in which it is interested.

Capital rationing can be best defined as a situation where the finance available for new investment is limited to an amount that prevents acceptance of all positive NPV projects. Firms may have identified a number of projects in which they would like to invest but simply do not have the capital available to invest in all of these projects. Capital rationing may be imposed on the firm via external sources. For example, banks may refuse to loan money to the firm, perhaps because the bank considers the

Box 6.3 continued

11 years. This tells us only about the cash flows associated with the project and nothing about its profitability. We also need to bear in mind that we have ignored the interest costs payable on the loans, which would almost certainly increase the length of time to payback.

The accounting rate of return is more difficult to calculate given that we have no idea of the ongoing costs of maintaining the tunnel. Obviously the tunnel will suffer from 'wear and tear', which will involve remedial work. However, as a rough approximation we shall assume, in this example, that there are no repair costs until after the year 2013. As we are also ignoring interest costs then we can assume that annual revenue is, in fact, annual profit. Though this is unrealistic it is still a useful illustration. You will recall that one of the formulae for calculating the ARR was

$$\frac{\text{Estimated average profit}}{\text{Estimated initial investment}} \times 100\%$$

Over the period 1994–2013, the average profit can be calculated as total profit earned divided by the number of years. This gives an average annual profit of £911.26 million (£18 225.2 million ÷ 20).

Therefore the ARR would be

$$\frac{£911.26\,\text{m}}{£8\,\text{bn}} \times 100\% = 11.39\%$$

Remember once again that, given that we have ignored certain costs, this figure is likely to be lower in reality. Furthermore the figure of 11.39 per cent tells us nothing unless we have some 'yardstick' against which to measure it.

Finally let us appraise the project using one of the more rigorous techniques of appraisal. Specifically we shall use the net present value method (NPV). In order to do this we need an appropriate discount rate. Because of the hazards of using estimates of revenue many years into the future, it is likely that a discount rate would be chosen to reflect this risk. For the purpose of illustration we shall use 10 per cent.

Hence

$$\text{NPV} = \frac{£465}{(1.1)} + \frac{£521.2}{(1.1)^2} + \frac{£577.4}{(1.1)^3} + \ldots$$
$$+ \frac{£1213}{(1.1)^{20}} - £8000$$

$$= £422.73 + £430.74 + £433.81 + \ldots$$
$$+ £180.30 - £8000$$

(all figures in millions and correct to two decimal places)

$$= -£1285 \text{ million} \quad \text{(correct to the nearest whole number.)}$$

This negative figure means that, given the chosen discount rate, the tunnel will take more than 20 years to become profitable. It is worth pointing out just once more that our figures will actually understate the loss by the year 2013, as we have ignored repair costs and interest payments. Of course, the project will continue to generate revenues well beyond the year 2013, and will eventually become profitable. Given the discount rate that we have chosen, this would occur before the end of the 50 year period for which Eurotunnel manages the project.

What our techniques demonstrate is the long-term nature of such building projects. The Channel Tunnel will take 11 years (at the very least) to pay back the initial investment cost. If we use an appropriate discounting technique then it will be more than 20 years before the project actually breaks even.

proposed project to be too risky. Alternatively, the firm may seek to raise capital via a share issue but be unable to raise sufficient funds because the stock market is performing badly. Examples such as this, where rationing is imposed externally, are known as *hard capital rationing*.

Firms may, however, decide internally to limit the amount of funds available for capital investment. This may be because they do not wish to borrow further funds for investment, perhaps because of the interest burden. Or it may be that management is reluctant to issue additional shares in case outsiders gain a controlling interest in the firm. Examples such as this, where the rationing is imposed internally, are known as *soft capital rationing*.

Where capital rationing exists, then the NPV method of investment appraisal requires slight, though simple, modification. As capital is limited, it becomes a scarce resource. What firms need to do, therefore, is maximize net present value per unit of scarce resource, rather than simply maximize net present value. In short, the firm maximizes NPV per unit of investment. This is calculated as:

$$\frac{\text{NPV}}{\text{Investment}} = \text{NPV index (NPVI)} \tag{6.6}$$

Consider the following example. A firm contemplating four projects is capital rationed for the next period. It has only £60 000 of capital available for investment. The appropriate discount rate is 10 per cent.

The cash flows, and NPV, of each project are as follows:

	Year			
Project	**0**	**1**	**2**	**NPV (10%)**
W	−10 000	6 000	7 000	1240
X	−20 000	14 000	10 000	991
Y	−30 000	10 000	28 000	2231
Z	−40 000	30 000	20 000	3802

Which projects should the firm accept in order to maximize shareholder wealth? The temptation may be to select project Z, which has the highest NPV, and then invest the remainder of the £60 000 (that is, £60 000 − £40 000 = £20 000) in project Y. This would not, however, maximize profit.

In such a case the return would be

$$3802 + \left(\frac{20\,000}{30\,000}\right) 2231 = £5289$$

Note that the firm is able to invest only £20 000 in project Y, of a total of £30 000, which means that it only achieves a return in proportion to the investment. If we now calculate the NPVI for each project as follows:

$$\text{NPVI(W)} = \frac{1240}{10} = 124$$

$$\text{NPVI(X)} = \frac{991}{20} = 49.6$$

$$\text{NPVI(Y)} = \frac{2231}{30} = 74.4$$

$$\text{NPVI(Z)} = \frac{3802}{40} = 95.1$$

The firm should select each project in decreasing order of NPVI until all capital is consumed. Therefore the firm should select project W (using £10 000), project Z (using £40 000), and invest the remaining £10 000 in project Y, which would represent an investment of one third of that project.

The overall return would be

$$\text{NPV(W)} + \text{NPV(Z)} + \left(\frac{1}{3}\right) \text{NPV(Y)}$$

$$= 1240 + 3802 + \left(\frac{1}{3}\right) 2231 = £5786$$

Note that this represents a higher profit than £5289, the profit that would have resulted had the firm invested according to the simple NPV.

Capital rationing: empirical evidence

In a survey of British industrial companies, R.H. Pike (1983) looked at the issue of capital rationing, and found that, in most cases, capital rationing is imposed internally by the firms themselves. Many of the firms surveyed felt that market demand was not sufficient to justify higher investment. Other firms felt that insufficient profitable opportunities existed, owing to general economic uncertainty. A number of the firms were reluctant to increase borrowing levels in order to raise investment funds. Pike found that, when firms were capital rationed, they tended to rely on payback techniques to appraise investment projects, thereby minimizing the problems of insufficient cash flows and enabling them to quickly reinvest the returns in other profitable projects.

6.7 Concluding remarks

The methods of investment appraisal discussed in this model are essential tools of management decision-making. Each method has its own advantages and disadvantages. Management will use one or perhaps two techniques such as these in order to enable it to pursue the objectives of the firm. Broadly we can generalize our methods into two categories:

- *Sophisticated techniques* are those that discount cash flows to ensure that the time value of money is incorporated into investment appraisal. NPV and IRR are the most widely used sophisticated techniques.

- *Unsophisticated techniques* are those that do not take into account the timing of cash flows. Such techniques, like payback and ARR, while still useful and widely adopted should therefore be used only as a 'rule of thumb' and in conjunction with one of the more sophisticated techniques.

One final point, which is worth emphasizing, is that such methods of investment appraisal do not replace management judgement. Ultimately, the methods are only a guide, and managers must decide whether the project, profitable or not, fits in with the company's plans. For example, if a firm has two profitable projects under consideration, should it choose the short-term project or the long-term project? Should it invest in one industry or another? The techniques we have discussed cannot answer these questions.

Summary

◆ Firms need to ensure that any project undertaken is consistent with their overall objectives. For most firms, this will be the maximization of profit. The methods used are known as investment appraisal techniques.

◆ In order to raise finance for investment firms may use retained earnings. Alternatively, they may seek to borrow from a financial institution or borrow by issuing debentures. Firms might also consider raising funds by issuing shares. No source of funds is costless. For example, banks will demand interest; shareholders will require some form of return. These are known as the cost of capital.

◆ Payback and accounting rate of return are two techniques of investment appraisal that are widely used and relatively easy to apply. Neither, however, takes into account the timing of cash flows.

◆ Discounted cash flow techniques, such as net present value and internal rate of return, incorporate the time value of money and are therefore more sophisticated techniques of investment appraisal.

◆ Capital rationing arises when firms have insufficient capital to invest in all desired projects. In such cases firms will need to modify investment appraisal techniques to ensure that they are maximizing NPV per unit of investment.

Key terms

◆ Investment appraisal
◆ Payback
◆ Accounting rate of return
◆ Discounted cash flow
◆ Net present value
◆ Internal rate of return
◆ Capital rationing

Self-test questions

True (t) or false (f)

1. Payback can be defined as the length of time that it takes for the cash inflows from an investment project to equal the initial cash outlay.

2. Payback tends to encourage excessive investment in long-term projects.

3. Payback emphasizes cash flow, rather than profit.

4. The accounting rate of return technique takes into account the time value of money.

5. The main advantage of the accounting rate of return is that it emphasizes the importance of profitability.

6. The internal rate of return technique calculates that discount rate which ensures that the present value of all future returns to an investment is exactly equal to the present value of the cost of the investment.

7. Capital rationing may be imposed on the firm via external sources. This is known as soft capital rationing.

Complete the following sentences by inserting the missing word(s)

1. _____ is the use of techniques to ensure that all projects are consistent with the objective of the firm.

2. Payback can be defined as the length of time that it takes for the cash inflows from an investment project to equal the _____.

3. One of the major problems of payback is that it cannot distinguish between projects with the same _____.

4. The _____ method estimates the accounting rate of return that an investment project should yield.

5. The time value of money arises because cash flows received today are worth more than _____ received at a later date.

6. The investment decision involves trading off the payment of dividends now with _____.

7. Those investment appraisal techniques that incorporate the time value of money are known as _____.

8. The _____ calculates the discount rate that gives a net present value of zero.

9. The _____ technique of investment appraisal calculates whether the present value of future returns to an investment is greater than the present value of the cost of the investment.

10. Capital rationing can be best defined as a situation where the finance available for new investment is limited to an amount that prevents _____.

Questions for discussion

◆ What are the advantages and disadvantages of payback ?

◆ Why might accounting rate of return be a more useful technique of investment appraisal than payback?

◆ Explain the concept of 'time value of money'

◆ What is an internal rate of return?

◆ A firm is considering investing in a project that costs £10 000. The 3 year project has the following cash flows:

Year 1: £6000, Year 2: £4000, Year 3: £3000.

The project has no scrap value and the firm's discount rate is 10 per cent.

Calculate the payback period

Calculate the ARR

Calculate the NPV

Calculate the IRR.

Further reading

Brealey, R.A., S.C. Myers and A.J. Marcus *Fundamentals of Corporate Finance* (2nd ed.) (McGraw-Hill, 1998). Has a very detailed discussion of discounted cash flow techniques, with useful examples.

Damodaran, A. *Applied Corporate Finance: A Users Manual* (John Wiley and Sons, 1999). Contains a thorough section on all of the investment appraisal techniques discussed in this chapter.

Lumby, S. *Investment Appraisal and Financial Decisions* (5th ed.)(Chapman & Hall, 1994). A very readable text, a large section of which is devoted to the issue of investment appraisal.

CHAPTER 7

Business and Government

Contents

Key issues

▶ Do markets sometimes fail to produce desirable outcomes in coordinating the demand for and supply of some goods and services?

▶ If markets do 'fail', can the state intervene to correct the problem?

▶ Can the state itself similarly fail when it intervenes in markets?

▶ What kinds of relationship between business and government are implied by market failure?

▶ What kinds of policy might governments pursue to help business perform better?

7.1 Introduction

Chapters 1 and 2 of this book elaborated the perspective that the free and competitive market can be an effective means of resolving the basic economic questions surrounding the use and allocation of scarce resources. However, in Chapter 5 we saw that once the implicit assumption that free markets are necessarily competitive is relaxed, established certainties as to the inherent strengths of *laissez-faire* begin to melt away. In *real* markets, the existence of monopoly and oligopoly directly undermines consumer sovereignty, and may be inimical to general consumer interests. From a business perspective, such apparent shortcomings in market-based resource allocation are highly important because they provide a rationale for government intervention in markets. Business must therefore accept that it will have various forms of relationship with government.

In the present chapter, we begin to examine the nature of the relationship between government and business by introducing the notion of **market failure**. Conventional economic theory recognizes three *main* forms of market failure:

- monopoly
- public goods
- externalities.

Market failure: Arises when the market either fails to provide certain goods, or fails to provide them at their optimum or most desirable level.

We saw in Chapter 5, sections 5.4–5.5, that the existence of monopoly, because it is perceived to distort the proper functioning of the market, may give rise to various forms of state intervention in the market. For example, the government may take steps to limit the commercial freedom of monopolists (see Chapter 5, Box 5.1, for a case study), or it may choose to assume the ownership of a monopoly by nationalizing it. Now, because they too are forms of market failure, the existence of public goods and externalities provides *an additional rationale for state intervention*, and adds new dimensions to the relationship between business and government.

Yet some *liberal* economists claim that market failure is a relatively rare occurrence, and that the problems associated with its particular forms can be overstated. The liberal school also raises the issue of *state or government failure*. Its argument is simply that, in intervening to 'solve' a particular case of market failure, the government itself often gets things wrong, and the economic problem becomes worse rather than better. This suggests that market failure, such as it is, should be tolerated because in many instances it is preferable to state failure. In effect the liberals argue that the government intervenes far *too much* in markets. Their preference is to let business get on with its role in resource allocation unhindered. The present chapter also considers these views.

In the UK especially, but also in many other economies, the belief that the market – regardless of certain shortcomings – is the *best* means by which to allocate scarce resources has informed the policy of *privatization*. Privatization involves the surrender of some aspects of state influence over economic activity and the consequent reassertion of market priorities. We use an overview of the privatization process in the UK as a means to further illustrate issues around the relationship between business and government, which is the core theme of this chapter.

> **Concept**
>
> **Competition policy**
>
> Competition policy involves attempts by government to promote competitive practices between firms in markets.

Finally, we also consider attempts by government to improve business performance. This kind of state activity has two contexts. First, primarily as safeguard for consumer interests, governments may attempt to establish rules for the preservation of competition in markets. In Chapter 5, we reviewed government policy in respect of monopoly: in most instances monopolies are perceived as economically undesirable, and their formation is resisted. A more general form of such **competition policy** is practised alongside government attempts to control monopoly. Here, one emphasis is on promoting competition to ensure that consumers are treated properly and fairly. In a competitive environment – the argument runs – firms cannot afford to do otherwise. Second, as well as improving the performance of firms in a 'consumer protection' sense, governments may also be minded to address the issue of business performance in the sense of *achievement*. Thus the UK government may have concerns about the vitality of UK firms in comparison (say) with their rivals in Europe, the United States or Japan. What the UK government can do about such concerns is the preserve of its **industrial policy**.

> **Concept**
>
> **Industrial policy**
>
> Industrial policy involves attempts by government to enhance the performance of firms in markets.

7.2 Market failure

What does market failure mean? A successfully functioning free market is based on the tenets first identified by Adam Smith in *The Wealth of Nations* (1776). These have undergone remarkably little modification in the intervening 200 years. Smith supposed that free markets were composed of many independent producers and consumers. This makes markets *competitive* and *individualistic*. Producers compete against one another to try to secure the business of each individual consumer. When a transaction takes place, it assumes the form of a *discrete* contract between the producer and the consumer in which a *clearly identifiable* volume of goods or services changes hands. These are not trite observations; they closely define the necessary elements without which the market would not work as anticipated. *It would indeed then exhibit signs of failure.*

We have already seen that competition is an important source of dynamism in the market. Without competition, the incentive for producers to be entrepreneurial and innovative is reduced; they can churn out the same old goods and services and earn a profit unconcerned that their lethargy will be exposed by the dynamism of rivals simply because there are no current rivals. If it becomes established, such stagnation certainly merits the charge of market failure, and its most obvious source is *monopoly*.

Similarly, free markets must be *individualistic* in the sense that the goods and services bought and sold pass privately from producer to consumer. It would not be possible for a market to exist in cases where the nature of particular goods and services prevented individuals from exclusively owning or consuming them. As we will see, such **public goods** do exist, and the market fails because it is unable to coordinate their production and consumption.

Finally, Smith's notion of the successfully functioning market rests on its *discretion*. When individual producers and consumers participate in market transactions, they do so willingly and voluntarily because they expect to gain from such transactions. Smith supposed that as the millions of individual economic agents present in society worked away, undertaking more and more transactions, the overall volume of gain would increase. The general effect would therefore be a more productive and contented society. There is, however, a crucial and implicit assumption here that each and every transaction affects *only* those who directly participate in it. But what if there are, as it were, 'innocent bystanders' at the edge of a transaction who are in some way harmed or advantaged by it? When such *external effects* (externalities for short) arise, the free market, with its working assumption of discrete individualism, fails to recognize them.

These then are the senses in which free markets can fail: where the underlying *necessary* assumptions of competition, individualism and discretion – which are at the heart of the Smithian framework – break down. We have already (in Chapter 5) reviewed aspects of market failure that can be attributed to monopoly. Although we return to this issue in our discussion of privatization and competition policy, for the present we concentrate on the remaining two forms of market failure: *public goods* and *externalities*.

7.3 Public goods

Public good: One that, once produced, can be consumed by everyone.

Private good (or service): One that is wholly consumed by an individual.

Many kinds of goods and services are consumed privately and exclusively. If I drink a pint of beer no one else can drink the same pint. If you visit the cinema to watch a film I cannot sit in the same seat as you at the same screening. In each case, the good and service are comprehensively and exclusively 'used up'. In fact, as we shall see, these **private good** characteristics are essential if the market is to be employed as the framework for their delivery.

However, some goods and services do not have such private attributes. Take, for example, street lighting. If I take a walk at night I consume street lighting, but my consumption does not diminish the supply available to anyone else: thus street lighting is said to be *non-rival in consumption*. At the same time, once street lighting is provided, it is difficult to imagine how individuals could be prevented from consuming it if they wished to: they would simply have to step outside on a dark evening. Street lighting is therefore also *non-excludable*. These two *public good* characteristics make it very difficult to see how a street lighting service could be made available via the market mechanism.

The central obstacle is what is known as the **free rider problem**. If a private firm elected to supply street lighting who would buy it? Every potential consumer would know that if just *one* person agreed to pay for the service everyone else could consume it for free: its supply would not be eroded with consumption (it is non-rival), nor could the provider or the paying consumer prevent free consumption by others (it is non-excludable). Thus the *public* characteristics of the service mean that no-one has an incentive to buy it; everyone is content to be a free rider. Hence there is no private demand and – as a consequence – no private supply. Now, because public goods are not available through the market, if they are judged to be intrinsically desirable, we have an economic rationale for their provision in some way by government. Effectively, the government *forces* society to pay collectively through taxation for something it will not pay for privately. Of course, in democratic societies, governments have an electoral mandate for such action.

Other examples of public goods include national defence, the justice system, and roads. Let us consider this list a little more closely in the context of the noted public good characteristics of non-rivalness in consumption and non-excludability. National defence, to take the first case, effectively 'blankets' any society for which it is provided. Whether they like it or not, all UK residents are *equally* safeguarded by the UK's defence system. Even those who are pacifists or members of the Campaign for Nuclear Disarmament 'consume' the services of the armed forces, and they do so just as intensively as any general or admiral. National defence is therefore a *pure* public good because it exhibits *perfect* non-rivalness and non-excludability.

Similarly, the justice system is administered on behalf of all citizens equally. Every individual is protected by the police and the courts from criminal activity. However, notice here that it is possible for the private sector to become independently involved in *some* aspects of this service. Private security firms, for example, offer protection to individuals, shops and businesses in exactly the same way as, say, cleaning firms offer their services. This means that *part* of the security element of the justice system – effectively the 'criminal dissuasion' work of the police – has *limited* non-rivalness and non-excludability. In this respect, then, the police service may be thought to lie somewhere between a pure public good and a private good. Overall, however, its responsibilities for the administration of justice and the maintenance of public order elevate its essential public good characteristics.

Roads are a rather different matter. Non-rivalness applies here only up to a point. On a road where traffic is flowing freely, additional vehicles may join without undue hindrance to other road users. However, on a motorway such as the M25, which orbits London, there is a notorious congestion problem, which means, by definition, that consumption has become rival. As more and more vehicles join the M25, traffic flow slows down, ultimately to a stop. It is also possible to exclude traffic from roads. Large parts of the French motorway network are tolled; only those who pay are able to use it. So neither non-rivalness nor excludability applies with any degree of completeness here.

Conventionally, though, roads are still classed as public goods despite the fact that their form is less pure than both national defence and the justice system. The main reasons for their 'public good status' are the practical and political difficulties that would be associated with systematic exclusion and wholly private provision. Thus, while tolling systems might be appropriate for motorways, they could hardly be installed on most roads. Moreover, given the cultural significance of private motoring in Western societies – typically embodied in notions of the 'freedom of the open road' – systematic exclusion would hardly be likely to command a popular mandate. The implication is that, for the most part, governments must indeed assume responsibility for road provision.

However, there are signs of change even here. There is a basic problem with public road provision: roads are *free at the point of use* for car owners. This means that there is no price constraint on consumption, and motorists can consume as much of the road network as they choose at no extra charge. They have to pay for petrol and the other costs of car ownership, but these are not direct charges for road use. Motorists also have to pay a road tax, but this is levied on a lump-sum basis and not according to intensity of road use. Now, when we couple the 'free' use of roads with rising car ownership, there can be only one outcome: traffic congestion. In many towns and cities and on many motorways, congestion is now reaching crisis proportions. In London, the average speed of traffic is 8 miles per hour, matching the speed of horse-drawn vehicles in the nineteenth century. On the M25 there is queuing for up to 5 hours on most days. On present trends, it is estimated by the Transport Research Laboratory that a quarter of Britain's motorway network will be just as congested by 2010.

What can be done about traffic congestion? An obvious solution would be to build more roads. In a market sense, this would mean increasing supply to try to meet demand. The difficulty here, however, would be that demand too would continue to rise. As the economy continues to grow, so too will car ownership. Congestion cannot be tackled only in this simplistic way. An alternative approach would be to try to make the market for road use behave more like a 'normal' market. This would involve charging motorists for road use in the same way that consumers are charged for lots of other goods and services. For example, if we take the issue of urban congestion, it might be appropriate to charge motorists who wish to drive into city centres on weekday mornings during peak hours. The aim here would be to dissuade some people from driving to work. Electronic 'tagging' technology makes this kind of policy a practical proposition. The dissuaded motorists would then be obliged to walk, cycle, or use trains or buses to get to work. Whatever their preferences, car-based urban congestion would be eased. This policy becomes even more attractive if the revenue derived from charging for road use is used to subsidize alternative forms of transport, making them more attractive to those displaced from the car. Box 7.1 provides details of recent experiments with road pricing in two British cities.

An immediate objection to road pricing is that it might be considered to be unfair. Those who can afford to pay road charges do so, and benefit from easier journeys, while poorer motorists are forced off the road. Equity considerations such as this are recognized by economists. However, whether or not the equity 'costs' of a particular policy are outweighed by its other benefits is a judgement that must be made through the political process.

The government wants to charge drivers electronically to use city roads

By Charles Batchelor

British motorists will have their first serious experience of electronic road tolling towards the end of next year when trials start in Leeds and Edinburgh.

After 40 years of research around the world, six years of preparation in the UK, including tests on a route into Leicester, and the spread of electronic road tolling schemes in Singapore, Norway and the US, Britain is about to apply the technology to its congested road network.

The trials form part of the Government's efforts to reduce car use by charging drivers for individual road journeys, making motorists more aware of the cost at the point of use. The aim is to raise funds to finance public transport while reducing congestion and pollution.

The most common systems around the world rely on roadside gantries that register an electronic tag or transponder on a vehicle's windscreen by short-range microwave or infra-

red transmission. The system then debits the appropriate amount from the driver's account – which has either been pre-paid or will be billed subsequently.

Cars that fail to transmit the appropriate signal, because they do not have a tag or transponder fitted or because their owners have not paid their road charge bills, will have their number plates recorded on camera for action by the tolling authority.

Greater flexibility can be achieved by installing a transponder into which the driver inserts his own smart card. This allows different drivers to use the same car and to be billed individually, while they can also use their cards to pay for services such as parking or public transport. The transponder can also provide details of the balance remaining on the driver's account.

Source: Financial Times 6 July 1999

7.4 Externalities

The third form of market failure arises because many ostensibly market-based and private transactions between individuals affect other third parties or 'innocent by-standers'. The result may be a good or a bad one, but in either case the market is unable to comprehend what is happening. Generally, the market produces too many transactions that have **negative externalities** and too few that have **positive externalities**. As for public goods, the appearance of externalities provides a rationale for state intervention in the market. It is the state's purpose here to reduce negative externalities and promote positive ones.

> **Externalities**: Also known as third-party effects. Costs incurred or benefits received by other members of society not taken into account by producers and consumers.

Negative externalities

Environmental pollution is a notorious form of negative externality. If a firm uses a river as a sink into which it releases waste products this clearly impacts upon those who use and value the river. Ornithologists, anglers and those who simply like to take a riverside walk will all be adversely affected by the firm's decision to pollute. Now the firm's interests clearly lie in producing an output as efficiently as possible, so, from its own standpoint, polluting the river is sensible if cleaner methods of waste disposal are more expensive. Similarly, for those who consume the firm's products the decision to pollute is also preferred as they will wish to pay lower product prices rather than higher ones. The key point here is that both the firm and the consumer are acting rationally in the *individualistic world of the market*. Their focus is entirely upon the cost of the *private transaction* to which they are party: the interests of river users simply do not register economically.

Now this is clearly a problem, because a clean river *does* have value to those who use it or who might use it in the future. If the firm could be made to recognize this it would presumably take steps to dispose of its waste in an environmentally friendly, if more expensive, manner. This would mean that the firm appreciated both the *private* and *wider social costs* of its activities. In such circumstances, the firm's output would become dearer – higher prices reflecting higher production costs – but only because the pollution externality had been *internalized*. So how can the firm be made to take account of the externalities it generates? This is where the state comes in. If river pollution carried a financial penalty of sufficient weight, then all potential polluters would have an incentive to find clean methods of waste disposal even where these carried higher costs – better to meet the higher cost than the even higher fine. In the UK, river pollution is discouraged in precisely this way. Box 7.2 provides an example.

Box 7.2

Record fine for polluting river

By Nicholas Schoon

Britain's second largest water company was yesterday fined a record £175 000 for poisoning a river and killing thousands of fish. It was the largest pollution fine a water company has ever received. Severn Trent Water Authority admitted leaking ferric sulphate – used to treat drinking water – into one of the best stretches of salmon river in Wales, killing all but 2 per cent of the stock.

It was the company's 34th conviction since privatization seven years ago, Cardiff Crown Court heard. Judge John Prosser told company executives that the leak was due to a combination of design defects, gross mismanagement and inferior maintenance. 'To be convicted so many times shows that the management of the company is very slack indeed,' he said.

Prosecutor Mark Bailey, acting for the government's new Environment Agency, said the pollution from Severn Trent's Elan Valley water treatment works at Rhayader, Powys, flowed down the small river Elan and into the

Wye, where it killed 33 000 young salmon in June last year. 'The sheer number of fish killed is higher than (in) any other incident,' he said. The chemical had turned the river acid, causing large quantities of aluminium to be released from sediments. This metal is highly toxic to fish.

The company, which pleaded guilty to polluting the river, was also ordered to pay costs and compensation of almost £44 000, including £8500 towards restocking with fish.

Severn Trent's barrister, Benjamin Nichols, told the court that the chemicals leaked through a hairline crack in a pipe, which was repaired as soon as it was spotted.

After the verdict, Peter Gough, of the Environment Agency, said it showed that 'thorough investigations into incidents such as this pay off. Companies must realize the seriousness of their actions.' Severn Trent said it was distressed by the size of the fine but had no plans to appeal.

Source: *The Independent* 6 August 1996

There are of course other forms of negative externality and consequently other forms of preventive state intervention. Building and construction, for example, are subject to *development control and planning legislation*. For instance, if you own a house with a garden, the local authority would not permit you to build a second house in the garden because your private decision involving your own property would impact negatively upon your neighbours. Box 7.3 offers a second example of the externality issues associated with a more substantial construction project. Here, the government has approved an application by Manchester Airport to build a new

Box 7.3

Second runway approved for Manchester Airport

Manchester Airport won government approval yesterday to build a second runway but faces bitter opposition from environmentalists who pledged to continue their fight against the £172m project.

Business leaders in the north-west welcomed the runway as a substantial boost to the regional economy. The airport's expansion is forecast to create about 7000 jobs on site and more than 43 000 in the region as passenger numbers double to 30m over the next decade.

The airport won planning permission after a nine-month public inquiry in 1995 which focused on the scheme's environmental impact. Construction of the 3050m runway – the first to be built in the UK for 20 years – will begin in the spring and is due to be completed in three years.

Mr Graham Stringer, chairman of Manchester Airport, said: 'The second runway is the biggest postwar economic boost to the region. It will create 50 000 new jobs – the equivalent employment potential of 10 Nissan car plants.' However, environmentalists promised to seek a

judicial review of the government's decision. They warned that the construction would be fought along similar lines to the campaign against the Newbury bypass, the scene of clashes between security guards and protesters.

Mr Chris Maile, of the Green Party in the north-west, said the airport would draw campaigners from anti road protests. He added: 'This will destroy three woods and part of the Cheshire countryside which is as scenic as anything in Kent . . .'

The airport argues that the impact of the runway has been overstated. It has agreed to more than 100 measures to protect the environment, including no night flights from the second runway and noise limits.

Sir George Young, Transport Secretary, praised the environmental measures as he announced planning approval. He said the second runway would also help to relieve the capacity constraints at airports in the south-east . . .'

Source: Financial Times 16 January 1997

runway, but on the understanding that the airport authorities will take steps to protect the environment. The chief concerns mentioned in the box are the disturbances (that is, externalities) caused by night flights and noise. Notice, however, that protesters have also raised concerns over woodland that, the government accepts, will be destroyed by the development. This particular externality (the lost woodland) is therefore deemed to be tolerable given the substantial economic benefits associated with the new runway.

Positive externalities

A positive externality arises when a private transaction produces *unintended benefits* for economic agents who are not party to it. Because the market does not recognize anything beyond the immediacies of the transaction itself, it is unable to appreciate its true (higher) value. For society as a whole, private transactions that generate positive externalities are clearly a good thing. However, the problem is that, because they are *only* private transactions, they occur entirely at the discretion of individuals. Now, as *some* individuals may choose not to undertake the transactions in question, some wider social benefit will inevitably be lost: in other words, the market *under-provides* transactions that carry positive externalities. Again, this creates a rationale for the state to intervene in the market to ensure that the extra transactions do take place so that their associated external benefits can be realized.

An example is in order here. Before 1958, many people in the world faced the threat of contracting smallpox: a fatal disease. In 1977 the disease disappeared entirely: now no one will ever die of smallpox again. The worldwide eradication of smallpox was achieved by a vaccination programme sponsored by the *World Health Organization* (WHO). This is a supranational health promotion body, which is funded by most of the world's governments.

The smallpox eradication is in fact a majestic example of the externality principle. Vaccination for smallpox, or indeed any other contractable disease, could be left to the market. Individuals would then subjectively balance the costs and benefits of vaccination. The costs would include the price, the discomfort of consumption (own up – who's scared of needles?) and, of course, the risk of catching the disease. The benefit to the individual would be *personal* immunity from infection. Given such costs, *some* individuals would choose not to be vaccinated, or – more to the point in less developed parts of the world especially – would not be able to afford vaccination. They would not therefore gain the benefit of personal immunity. But there is also a wider benefit here, which the individual (and hence the market) fails to take into account. This is that everyone who is vaccinated achieves both a personal safeguard against disease and the status of a *non-carrier* – that is, someone from whom disease cannot be caught. The point, of course, is that non-carriers benefit everyone; they reduce the risk of disease being passed on. In this sense, the private vaccination decision has clear potential social benefits, and the more people who are vaccinated the better – from *society's* point of view. Here then is the rationale for state intervention of the form undertaken by the WHO. If the state provides free vaccination, the level of consumption may rise to the point at which the risk of contracting disease is very small or even, as in the case of smallpox, eliminated entirely.

7.5 Public goods, externalities and business

The public goods and externality principles we have outlined so far imply a pronounced role for the state in certain kinds of market. While, as a corollary, this might suggest restrictions on business freedom, it is important to recognize that there are no hard and fast rules here. In this section we examine two instances of established forms of public service delivery where the British government has elected to surrender ground to business but, in the light of changing circumstances, may well choose to reassert its right to intervene.

The two cases we have in mind are *railways* and *air traffic control*. The common thread that joins them is the issue of public safety. Both services have in the recent past been deemed by government to be suitable for delivery by the private sector. In the case of railways, privatization occurred in the period 1995–7. At the time of writing, air traffic control is scheduled to be sold to the private sector in 2000.

Let us begin by briefly reviewing the economic case for the *state* delivery of these services. The externality principle applies in both instances, the public goods argument in one. In a modern economy, both services clearly have a great deal of merit. Mobility is important; we want a reliable and safe rail system that connects our towns and cities, and we also wish to fly safely. The proposition is that if we wish to *guarantee* the provision of a good and safe railway network and adequate air traffic control these services should be organized and underwritten by the state. To rely on the market is to risk underprovision to the extent that the services become *less safe*; and if the railways and skies become more prone to accidents they clearly may have negative impacts on both their direct users and third parties.

There is also the possibility that private sector delivery may mean that important external *benefits* carried by the railways will be unrealized. Here, the external benefit is the reduction of congestion on the roads as some people and firms use trains instead of cars and lorries. Air traffic control, by contrast, has a public goods dimension associated with it. If *one* individual or firm elected to finance a system of air traffic control, all other users of airspace, and for that matter people on the ground, could use it as well: it is non-rival in consumption and non-excludable.

But if these are valid claims, and both services may be justifiably retained in the public sector because of the externality and public goods principles, why have they been privatized or – in the case of air traffic control – lined up for privatization? In fact, the assumption is that privatization will lead to an improvement in the delivery of rail and air traffic control services *beyond* a level attainable by the public sector. In the case of railways, the government argued that public ownership had been associated with long-term under-investment in most forms of rail infrastructure. The result was a poor service with declining passenger numbers. The government's view was that private rail operators would be in a position to revive investment in the network. They would have a strong motive (profit) to provide a standard of service that attracted people back to the railways. For air traffic control, similar arguments apply. Box 7.4 sums up the nature of the debate here. The government's position, as

Box 7.4

Air traffic control sale set for next year

By Keith Harper

Legislation to complete the partial sell-off of Britain's air traffic control service, which could raise between £350m and £500m, will almost certainly be introduced in the Queen's speech, government sources claimed last night.

This controversial sale, which staff and a growing number in Labour's own ranks will strongly oppose, could be completed next year.

The partial privatization, in which 51 per cent of the business will be offered in a trade sale to a domestic buyer or consortium, was announced by the deputy Prime Minister, John Prescott, yesterday. The government will retain 49 per cent of the shares and will be able to exercise outright control where national security is involved.

Foreign buyers will be excluded because of the delicacy of the operation. The most likely buyers are National Grid and the business operations company Serco, which has the backing of Japanese banks.

Mr Prescott said the sell-off would be to a 'strategic partner' which would need to be a 'robust company or consortium'. A total of 5 per cent of the shares would be held by staff in what Mr Prescott described as a 'new partnership company', but they would not be able to prevent the private company from exerting overall operational control.

National air traffic control is in a state of flux,

with a new £600m site at Swanick, Hampshire, still unready. It should have been opened in 1996, but this has been delayed until the winter of 2002. It still faces teething problems.

But Mr Prescott said the government 'could not wait for Godot'. Decisions had to be made on ensuring the best possible air traffic service for the 21st century.

The service will be hived off from the Civil Aviation Authority, which is responsible for air safety regulation. The strategic partner will provide air traffic services but will not be responsible for air safety regulation. Mr Prescott insisted that the money raised from the sale would not go to the Treasury but would be recouped by his department for spending on specific public transport projects.

Doubts about the need to sell the business were expressed by two key staff groups, the air traffic controllers and the pilots. With growing numbers of aircraft in the skies, their primary concern is safety. Chris Darke, general secretary of the British Airline Pilots' Association, said: 'There is no guarantee that the government's proposal will improve aviation safety or secure long-term investment. Pilots are the front-line interface and by making this change in ownership we could end up with a service which is worse . . .'

Source: Guardian 28 July 1999

expressed in the box, appears to be that public sector management of air traffic control has been sluggish. The noted £600 million project at Swanick has experienced a six-year delay, and the implication is that this kind of outcome would be less likely were properly motivated private sector managers in charge. At the same time, greater commercial freedom for air traffic control will provide the long-term investment necessary to secure 'the best possible . . . service for the 21st century'.

These *were* the government's plans up until the autumn of 1999; however, the Paddington rail disaster appears to have changed matters somewhat. This accident, in which many people lost their lives and many others were seriously injured, has had the effect of refocusing attention on the issue of public safety. In the post-Paddington climate, there appears to be an emerging consensus that the public sector still has an important role to play in providing acceptable guarantees of *safe* service delivery. In effect, the externality principle (the suppression of negative externalities) – underpinning state intervention – has been reasserted. Although the privatization of air traffic control is still to go ahead, the Queen's speech of November 1999 (which sets out the government's legislative programme) made it clear that public safety regulation would remain in public hands, and that the (public) Civil Aviation Authority would retain its responsibility for the development of airspace policy. In the case of the railways, we have the remarkable spectacle of a recently created private railway company requesting partial 'renationalization' in order to 'improve the safety and quality of Britain's antiquated rail network'. Box 7.5 provides further details of this request. Again, the implication is that adequate service delivery in the presence of potential negative externalities may require significant forms of state intervention.

Box 7.5

Renationalize us, Railtrack tells Prescott

By Patrick Wintour, Will Hutton and Oliver Morgan

Railtrack bosses have asked the government to renationalize part of the company in an attempt to free more cash to improve the safety and quality of Britain's rail network.

In a sign of Railtrack's desperation over its inability to fund the safety and track improvements required during the next decade, the company has suggested the government take a 15 per cent shareholding. In return, Railtrack would be given a stake in London Underground,

or the franchise to run trains on the East Coast main line.

Railtrack is due to finance a £28 billion renewal and investment programme over the next 10 years but its Chief Executive, Gerald Corbett, fears the Paddington crash 'has changed everything'. The company faces an intense squeeze with demands for lower margins, more efficiency and investment in safety just as its share price has fallen sharply.

Railtrack feels it has been made the

scapegoat for Paddington. Among the options it is exploring is the Government taking a stake – a partial renationalization – so that if it has to sell more shares in the City to raise cash in a rights issue at least it can be certain that one shareholder, the Government, will buy. At present, the Government gives an annual £1.3bn subsidy to fund the industry but this figure is due to fall.

Source: Observer 24 October 1999

7.6 The liberal view: market failure and state failure

Despite the existence of an established case for forms of state intervention in the modern economy, a mixture of private and public resource allocation is not the preference of every group of economists. The *liberal school*, for example, contends that economies that adhere as closely as possible to free market principles are inherently superior to those that permit the state to encroach substantially on questions of resource allocation. This view rests on three propositions:

- that the state too 'fails'
- that state failures may be worse than those of free markets
- that the failures of the free market are, in any case, invariably overstated.

Let us examine each of these propositions in turn.

State failure

The notion of state failure has one central theme: that the presence of the state in resource allocation ruptures the vital *individualist* connection between consumer and producer. Markets we know are organized on *voluntarist* principles. Every consumer who enters a market does so because he or she wants to, because there is a good or service in that market for which he or she is willing to pay. Liberals argue that voluntarism is extremely important. It is in fact the *only* way we can be sure that markets are delivering goods and services that people actually want. When the state involves itself in a market – such as transport or housing – it may, for example, tax individuals in order to provide them with the transport or housing *it* thinks that they should have. In the liberal view, the individual's perceptions of his or her own needs are replaced by bureaucratic interpretations of those same needs. This, the liberals claim, is an insurmountable problem. The state seems to be asking 'Who knows best what *you* should spend *your* money on?', and replying '*We do*'.

There are three particular aspects of state failure that flow from this analysis.

First, it seems quite obvious that the state's interpretation of the needs of the individual can be mistaken. Indeed, how can a bureaucracy assess with any accuracy the highly nuanced desires in an entire society? The liberals argue that only the market can do this because – through Smith's invisible hand – it does actually respond to each and every individual's expressed demand. But is the corollary true: does the state actually provide things that people do *not* want? Consider the following example. In the field of housing, it is not unreasonable to point to the 1960s and 1970s government preoccupation with the construction of tower blocks as the solution to a perceived housing problem. Now widely viewed as a mistake, tower blocks are no longer built and many have been demolished because people simply do not want to live in them. Tower blocks are, literally, a monumental example of state failure.

The second aspect of the liberal interpretation of state failure is *coercion*. The market, we know, is voluntarist in nature: economic agents engage in market transactions because they want to. For liberals, this means that markets underscore both economic and personal freedom. However, as the state involves itself in various ways in the provision of goods and services, it necessarily impinges upon the freedom of individuals to dispose of their own resources in ways that they themselves choose. Individuals find themselves taxed by the state so that it can service what the leading liberal Hayek has called 'abstractions' such as 'the good of the community'. Yet although taxpayers may vehemently resent what is done with *their* money (recall our earlier example of taxes levied on members of the Campaign for Nuclear Disarmament helping to finance nuclear weaponry, regardless of their evident disapproval) they have no choice in the matter. Those who evade taxation are liable to be fined or even imprisoned. In the liberal view, this is coercion pure and simple, and it betokens a wider constraint on economic and personal freedom in proportion to the amount of state intervention in what would otherwise be free markets.

The third and last particular aspect of state failure is that state intervention in part of a market can have the effect of subverting the efficient operation of the whole of that market. For example, as noted, local authorities in the UK have been active in the provision of public housing for more than 100 years. The liberal claim is that this has had a devastating affect upon the general functioning of the UK housing market. The problem here is one of *crowding out*. There are three generally recognized types of housing tenure: owner occupied, privately rented and rented from the state. However, for a long time, the housing market in the UK has been dominated by owner occupation and state-rented accommodation, with only a relatively small private rented sector. How has this situation come about? Partly, the answer lies in the determination of the state that there should be more collective housing provision. As more public housing has been built and let at relatively low rents subsidized by the taxpayer, the effect has been to reduce the level of demand for private rented accommodation; consequently less private rented accommodation has been supplied. Moreover, at the same time, the state has also seen fit to give tax relief to owner occupiers on their mortgage interest payments. This has had the effect of simultaneously raising the demand for owner occupied property. The private rented sector has been caught in the middle of these two broadening avenues of intervention and (hence the phrase) *crowded out*. This state-inspired distortion of the housing market has also had consequences for the effective functioning of other parts of the UK economy. For example, the liberals claim that unemployment could be reduced if the unemployed were more easily able to move around in search of work. At present this is difficult because the most flexible element of the housing market – the private rented sector – is too small.

State failure versus market failure

Liberalism accepts aspects of the conventional economic argument that markets can fail: monopoly, public goods and externalities are all valid concepts that may legitimate state intervention. However, we are also aware of the liberal notion of state failure. This creates an interesting dilemma: if a market is not able to function effectively, should we use this as justification for state intervention, with its attendant risk of state failure; or should we simply tolerate market failure itself? Effectively, what we have here is a competition between two inferior options. The preferred situation is a properly functioning free market. Thereafter it becomes a choice between state intervention and possible failure and the failing market: which is worse? The liberal position is that each case should be judged on its merits. This may be contrasted with the conventional view, which, liberals imply, seems to proceed on the intrinsic assumption that when the state intervenes to 'correct' a market failure, it is usually effective in doing so.

Market failure in the liberal view

Liberal economists do not deny that markets can fail. They concede that, because of their innate indivisibility, pure public goods such as national defence and the greater part of the public road network must be provided by the state; markets that operate on an *individualist* basis cannot deliver goods and services that must be consumed *collectively*. However, beyond this, the liberal view is that market failure can be overstated. Consider, for example, the externality issue. Here the liberal school argues that, while certain externalities clearly demand government intervention, many others are merely conveniences which permit the state to involve itself in markets that would be better served by *laissez-faire*. The leading liberal Milton Friedman has, for example, argued that while the provision of city parks is an appropriate 'externality justified' activity for government, the maintenance of national parks is not. Urban public parks are an unlikely private sector interest. They certainly provide benefits to many city dwellers. Some will use them directly; others might simply walk past or live nearby and enjoy the view. The problem for the potential operator of the private city park is that he or she will not be paid for benefits accruing to the latter group. Even direct users may not be prepared to pay if their intention is simply to take a brief stroll past some greenery on their way to another destination. So although most citizens will gain from a city park, it is unlikely to be profitable. This, Friedman concedes, means that the state may usefully provide such amenities in order that their external benefits may be realized. He thinks, however, that national parks are different. Generally, people do not walk past them or live overlooking them. Nor do they use them as pleasant short-cuts. Thus users of national parks are usually purposeful visitors who could be charged – via an entrance fee – for the benefits they derive from such use. For Friedman, this is the decisive point. As individuals can be made to pay for the benefits of consumption, if there is a demand for a national park the market will have an incentive to provide it and there is no need for state involvement at all. If, however, there is insufficient demand then why should the state tax individuals to provide them with something they do not wish to have? Here then the externality justification for state intervention has been stretched too far. Friedman argues that this has happened in a range of markets to erroneously justify *inter alia* public housing, price support in agriculture (see discussion of the EU's Common Agricultural Policy in Chapter 2, section 2.5) and legislation imposing minimum wage levels (see Chapter 8, section 8.5).

Liberalism: a summary

Conventional economics supposes that the main areas of market failure readily justify state intervention. The state should control or regulate monopoly, arrange for the provision of public goods, and attempt to control negative externalities while simultaneously promoting positive ones. The liberal position is that this interpretation of state competences is too simple. Liberals dispute the presence of many externalities that are used to justify intervention in the real economy. They also harbour doubts about the ability of the state to correct actual instances of market failure. For liberals the state too can fail, and its failures may be more serious than those of the market. Ultimately, then, state intervention should always be both a matter of careful judgement and, because of its potentially adverse consequences, one of last resort. In the liberal view, the restriction of state activity gives the freest reign to the superior allocative mechanism of the market.

7.7 Privatization

Privatization entails the surrender of some aspect of state influence over economic activity and the consequent reassertion of market priorities. There are many examples.

Since the early 1980s, in countries such as the UK and New Zealand, governments have adopted policies intended to return most nationalized industries to the private sector. Table 7.1 lists the major UK privatizations that have occurred since 1979. In the formerly planned economies of Eastern Europe and the Far East, where economic activity was under very extensive state control until 1989, an even more decisive privatization programme of this sort is currently under way.

Privatization can also assume more subtle forms. For example, during the 1990s, a system of GP 'fundholding' was operated in the British National Health Service (NHS). This allowed family doctors a much greater degree of choice than hitherto in the referral of patients to hospitals and clinics. Effectively, fundholding doctors could choose which hospital they thought would provide the best service. Although the system remained wholly in the public domain, the change was intended to instil a degree of *consumer sovereignty* into the NHS. Hospitals could no longer simply provide surgical and other procedures that GPs then had to consume on behalf of their patients; they had instead to compete against one another in order to attract the

Table 7.1 Major privatizations in the UK

Organization	Year of sale	Industry
British Petroleum	1979	Oil
National Enterprise Board Investments	1980	Various
British Aerospace	1981	Aerospace
Cable & Wireless	1981	Telecoms
Amersham International	1982	Scientific goods
National Freight Corporation	1982	Road transport
Britoil	1982	Oil
British Rail Hotels	1983	Hotels
Associated British Ports	1983	Ports
British Leyland	1984	Cars
British Telecom	1984	Telecoms
Enterprise Oil	1984	Oil
Sealink	1984	Sea transport
British shipbuilders and naval dockyards	1985	Shipbuilding
National Bus Company	1986	Transport
British Gas	1986	Gas
Rolls-Royce	1987	Aero-engines
British Airports Authority	1987	Airports
British Airways	1987	Airlines
Royal Ordnance Factories	1987	Armaments
British Steel	1988	Steel
Water	1989	Water
Electricity distribution	1990	Electricity
Electricity generation	1991	Electricity
Trust ports	1992	Ports
Coal industry	1995	Coal
Railways	1995–97	Railways
Nuclear energy	1996	Electricity

Source: Martin, S. and D. Parker *The Impact of Privatization* (Table 1.2 p. 2) (London: Routledge, 1997)

'custom' of GPs. Here, then, privatization involved the incorporation of market principles into the public sector. The British experiment with fundholding ended in April 1999.

In the UK, also in the 1990s, many of the services provided by local government were made subject to a process of *compulsory competitive tendering* (CCT). This required local authorities to allow bids from private firms for work that was formerly done by the authorities themselves. If a private firm could do the job cheaper than the local authority then it obtained the contract for a given period. As a result of CCT, services such as refuse collection, street cleaning and the provision of school meals in many towns and cities are now undertaken by private firms. Again, as the state still finances and has ultimate responsibility for such services, this falls short of local 'denationalization' but, again, it does admit private sector influences into what had been a wholly public domain. In 1997, a new Labour government announced plans to move from the CCT system to one of *best value*. It is interesting to note that although this new scheme removes some of the prescriptive elements of CCT, the essential message to local government has arguably not been substantially changed. It is now expected to pursue 'best value' in providing services to local taxpayers. The expectation is that best value will involve service delivery partnerships between the public and private sectors: in other words there will *continue* to be private sector involvement in what were 20 years ago wholly public forms of activity.

The rationale for privatization

Why privatize? The answer to this question lies in the purported advantages of the free market, which were sketched out in Chapters 1–3 of this book. The market empowers the consumer, it promotes the division of labour, and it sparks the entrepreneurial zeal of the profit-motivated producer. The case for privatization is that it extends these features into new areas of economic activity and, at the same time, necessarily compresses the boundaries of undesirable state-determined resource allocation.

But on what *necessary* basis are forms of state-determined resource allocation rejected? The proponents of privatization argue that, historically, when the state assumes responsibility for *industrial activity* in particular, chronic poor performance and decay are the inevitable results. Nationalized industries, it is argued, tend to suffer from general deficiencies that arise as a result of the insulation of the (state) producer from the 'realities' of the market. Private firms, on the other hand, *must* respond to consumer demands; they *must* introduce new technologies and new working practices in order to remain competitive; they *cannot* pay workers more than their competitive position allows; they *cannot* tolerate indolent or incompetent management. The suggestion is that these and other strictures do not apply with anything like the same force in industries that are nationalized. In the public sector, the state is always able to excuse poor commercial practice because the ultimate market sanction of bankruptcy is removed.

While state ownership might protect industry at one level, it can also dangerously frustrate its development at another. Nationalized industries such as the former British Telecom, privatized in 1984, had their ability to raise investment capital strictly controlled. This is because governments wish to constrain the rate of growth of public expenditure. At the same time, the capacity of nationalized industries to enter foreign markets is limited: in the British Telecom case it was clearly not politically acceptable for the British government (in its British Telecom guise) to start to compete with, say, Deutsche Telecom for its domestic market. Now, in an extremely dynamic internationalizing industry such as telecommunications, the ability to innovate and achieve economies of scale is crucially important. Therefore it was argued that, if it was to become a 'leading edge' telecommunications provider, British Telecom had to be freed from the constraints imposed by nationalization: it needed to raise adequate amounts of investment capital and gain access to bigger markets. Privatization enabled both of these imperatives to be realized.

So far we have concentrated on the *microeconomic* benefits of privatization: the stimulus it gives to firms as they are forced to compete in the market and the opportunities for better-resourced growth it also provides for them. However, privatization has also been defended on macroeconomic grounds. Since 1979 the privatization programme in the UK has yielded over £60 billion. As this sum is regarded as negative government spending, its effect has been to reduce government borrowing substantially – sometimes thought to be a desirable outcome for *macroeconomic* management reasons.

The case against privatization

The central weakness of the privatization view is that a change of ownership in itself confers no obvious benefits. Where the privatized firm is a monopoly, the normal rules of competitive practice remain suspended. Because it lacks competitors, a private monopoly is just as insulated from the 'realities' of the market as the nationalized industry; indeed, given the freedom to exploit its exclusive position more assiduously, a private monopoly might be considered to pose more problems than a public one. This means that the acid test for the success of privatization must be the extent to which it *promotes competition*.

In the UK, the privatization process has been attended by the creation of a number of regulatory 'watchdogs', such as the Office of Telecommunications (Oftel) for the

---

Box 7.6

More than 1.5 million switch gas supplier

More than 1.5 million people have chosen to switch to a different gas supplier in the newly competitive gas market, Ofgas revealed today.

As gas competition comes on stream today to an extra 3.2 million homes in an area that includes the West Midlands, Wiltshire and Wales, Director General of Gas Supply Clare Spottiswood revealed that another 2 million people across the country have signed contracts and are waiting to change to a new supplier.

Clare Spottiswood said, 'This total of more than 3.5 million represents around 17.5 per cent of the whole market, and easily makes gas the most popular of the privatized utilities. Britain has the most competitive gas market in the world.

'People are switching for two reasons: first, it's easy – it's the same gas; it comes through the same pipes, and the only change is which company sends you the bill. Second, competitive suppliers are offering real savings – up to £60 or £70 a year off the average annual gas bill.

'There have been reports that gas competition is suffering because some people have experienced difficulties [in changing supplier]. Today's high switching figures give the true picture. Whilst a minority have legitimately complained . . . the vast majority are rapidly exercising their right to choose a new gas company, and hence lower prices.'

Source: Office of Gas Supply press release 24 April 1998

telecommunications industry and the Office of Gas and Electricity Markets (Ofgem) for the gas and electricity industries. The purpose of these and other similar bodies has been to prevent the newly privatized monopolies from exploiting their monopoly positions, and to oversee the introduction of more competitive environments in each industry. Yet progress on the latter front has been slow. For example, although British Gas was privatized in 1986 a competitive market in industrial gas supplies emerged only in 1992, and supplies to households remained exclusive to British Gas until 1998. However, wherever competition *has* been introduced, it is significant that prices to consumers have fallen (see Box 7.6).[1] This has led disinterested researchers to suggest that UK government privatization policy would have been improved had it put the promotion of competition above the simple transfer of ownership from the public to the private sector. Adam Smith would surely have agreed.

7.8 Competition policy

Competition in markets is important. It underwrites the sovereignty of consumers and it is the process through which 'good' firms (in the sense that they are good at serving the interests of consumers) drive out bad ones. We saw in Chapter 5 how governments may seek to control monopolies because of the threat that these firms pose to the competitive process. Many governments actually go much further than this: they try to ensure that there are satisfactory levels of competition in *all* markets, not just those where there may be problems posed by monopoly.

The *Competition Commission* is one of two main government bodies charged with safeguarding competition in the UK. The other is the *Office of Fair Trading* with, at its head, the *Director General of Fair Trading* (DGFT). The activities of both the Competition Commission and the DGFT are guided by the most recent piece of government competition legislation: the *Competition Act 1998*.

Competition Commission

The Competition Commission was in fact created by the Competition Act 1998. The Competition Commission replaced the old Monopolies and Mergers Commission (MMC) on 1 April 1999.

The Competition Commission's work is divided into two parts: a *reporting* side and an *appeals* side. Its reporting role, inherited from the MMC, involves the investigation of matters referred to it concerning:

- mergers
- monopolies
- anti-competitive practices
- the regulation of public utilities
- the performance of government bodies.

The Commission cannot initiate its own investigations into any of these areas. This is to avoid any possibility that it has prejudged a particular issue by selecting it for review in the first place. Accordingly, the Commission must wait for matters to be

---

[1] Box 7.6 makes reference to Ofgas, the former gas regulator that was merged with Offer (the Office of Electricity Regulation) in 1999 to form the new single regulatory body for gas and electricity: Ofgem (The Office of Gas and Electricity Markets).

drawn to its attention. Most referrals come from the DGFT, the Secretary of State for Trade and Industry, and the government-appointed regulators of the utilities. In each particular case, the Competition Commission is required to report on whether the particular market development under scrutiny is against the public interest. It is then up to the government to act upon the report as it sees fit.

The appeals side of the Commission's work relates to the 'prohibition provisions' of the Competition Act 1998. Essentially, the prohibition provisions ban agreements or concerted practices between firms that 'prevent, restrict or distort competition in the UK'. The intention is to deter any form of collusion between firms that might help them to further their interests at the expense of either consumers or other firms. The prohibition provisions came into effect on 1 March 2000. They are enforced by the DGFT and the utility regulators. Again, to address the issue of prejudgement, firms that find themselves falling foul of (say) the DGFT in respect of the prohibition provisions can appeal to the Competition Commission. Its job is to uphold or deny the appeal. Appeals can be made against both decisions by the DGFT that firms have been involved in a banned practice, and the financial penalties that might be imposed following such decisions.

Competition Act 1998

Box 7.7 provides a government summary of the Competition Act 1998. The summary was written with a business audience in mind. Notice the flavour of the language.

Box 7.7

The Competition Act 1998: introduction to the new law

Why is the Act so important?

- Because your business may be in danger of being fined up to 10% of its UK turnover
- Because your business may be a victim of others' anti-competitive behaviour and if you don't know the rules you won't be able to protect yourself

The Act is introducing new competition rules which prohibit agreements, business practices and conduct that damage competition in the UK.

The new rules are designed to ensure that UK businesses remain competitive. Complying with them will help to ensure that your business is as competitive as it can be – which is good for you and good for consumers. Make sure that your employees know about the new rules.

Who does the Act apply to?

Businesses of all types – even sole traders.

What does the Act prohibit?

Anti-competitive **agreements** and the **abuse of a dominant position** in a market.

The Act prohibits **agreements** and **practices** that prevent, restrict or distort competition – or are intended to do so. These can be formal agreements or informal, written or not.

How will the Act be enforced?

The Director General [of Fair Trading] has wide-ranging powers to investigate suspected breaches. His officials can enter premises and demand relevant documents, and may even get a warrant to make a search. Offending agreements or conduct can be ordered to be terminated.

What if my business is a victim?

The OFT welcomes complaints from anyone who suspects the rules are being broken. You can complain in writing or by telephone and your identity can be protected. However, you will be asked for evidence to support your complaint. We may launch a formal investigation if there are reasonable grounds for suspecting that the rules are being or have been broken.

What if my business is involved in a cartel?

You can be fined up to 10% of your UK turnover. Prohibited agreements will be void and unenforceable, and any third party harmed by an unlawful agreement or conduct may be able to sue you for damages.

The OFT's top priority is to detect and act against cartel activity, such as price fixing and market sharing. If your business is involved in a cartel, and you blow the whistle, you can receive a significant reduction in any fine. You can get complete immunity from any financial penalties if you are the first to come forward.

When does it all start?

In order to give . . . time to prepare for the new legislation, the prohibitions will not come into force until 1 March 2000 . . .

Source: OFT website **(http://www.oft.gov.uk/html/comp-act/introduction/index.html)** 3/11/99

The Act is acknowledged to be about consumer protection, but the government is also keen to demonstrate that it is also intended to help business: 'The new rules are designed to ensure that UK businesses remain competitive.' The summary also describes the *broad* financial penalties that are imposed on offenders – up to 10 per cent of UK turnover.

Yet, in clarifying elements of the Act, the government has indicated that its interpretation of the '10 per cent of turnover' threshold is fairly draconian. As Box 7.8 reveals, this threshold may apply for up to *three* years, making the new regime much more stringent than anything in previous competition law.

Box 7.8

Penalty regime is last piece in minister's puzzle

Kevin Brown and David Wighton report

The maximum fines for price-fixing set out yesterday by Stephen Byers, the Trade and Industry Secretary, would allow the UK competition authorities to impose some of the world's biggest financial penalties on members of cartels.

Competition experts were surprised by his decision to allow fines of up to 10 per cent of UK turnover for a maximum of three years – a more stringent regime than the European Union's, which limits penalties to 10 per cent of turnover for a year.

'I think this is tough,' said Martin Coleman, head of competition at Norton Rose, the London law firm. 'They want to scare the hell out of people to get them to comply. There will be a few cases where the maximum fine will be paid, but it is going to push up the tariff so that even on less severe infringements the fine is going to be higher.'

Department of Trade and Industry officials see the penalty regime as the last piece in a jigsaw of competition initiatives designed to attack the perception of 'rip-off Britain' in which consumers are persistently exploited.

The targets are companies that fix prices through illegal agreements or abuse of market dominance. Comparatively few of these have come to light in the past, but some competition experts think that if the UK has a generally high level of prices, secret cartels might provide some of the explanation.

However, the Competition Act is not likely to be used against targets of government rhetoric such as supermarkets and car companies, whose prices are high for other reasons, such as a lack of competition.

The Act, which takes full effect in March, brings the UK into line with other EU member states, which all have domestic competition legislation based on the broad competition provisions of . . . the Treaty of Rome. . .

Source: Financial Times 10 August 1999

The Director General of Fair Trading

The DGFT has competition powers that allow him to:

... act indirectly on behalf of consumers by ensuring that market structures are in place which allow for competition and respond to competitive pressures. These in turn produce powerful incentives for businesses to be as efficient as possible, to compete with each other on price and service, to invest in innovation, and to strive for market share by offering greater choice, better quality, or greater convenience related to consumer needs.

Source: Office of Fair Trading Annual Report 1998

An example of the kind of consumer protection and advocacy practised by the DGFT can be found in a 1997 Office of Fair Trading (OFT) report: *Selling Second-hand Cars*. In this document the OFT noted that used car purchases are the chief source of consumer complaints to local authority trading standards departments and Citizens Advice Bureaux. Many people who buy second-hand cars clearly feel they do not get a satisfactory deal. The OFT conducted a review of the market and reported its findings in a consultation paper published in 1996. The 1997 report was intended to follow up on the consultation process by producing a set of recommendations that would improve the functioning of the market and thereby promote consumer interests.

'Clocking' – adjusting the mileage of second-hand cars to enhance their value – is one of the more infamous practices of unscrupulous car dealers. Amongst its recommendations, the OFT report included several measures intended to tackle this problem. For example, it suggested that the voluntary arrangements for entering vehicle mileages on registration documents should become mandatory, and that MOT records should be computerized. All information from these sources could then be made available to car database compilers. Such changes would make clocking much more detectable because of the existence of reliable and widely available mileage records for every car.

This consumer protection function of the DGFT is evident in a range of markets. Box 7.9 provides an instance of intervention in the banking sector. Here, the DGFT responded to customer complaints that their bank had changed their accounts unfairly by promising enforcement action, should it be required, in this case and in the industry generally. He also encouraged bank customers to realize and take advantage of their existing rights.

Both these examples might appear to portray the state as a *constraint* on business and the custodian of consumer interests. While it is true that the DGFT is charged

---

Box 7.9

Bridgeman warns banks about unfair contract terms

Banks have been warned, by the Director of Fair Trading, John Bridgeman, to ensure fairness in their contracts with consumers or else risk enforcement action.

The OFT is currently investigating complaints by account holders that Northern Rock plc restructured accounts without warning and denied them the freedom to move them elsewhere without notice. He has asked the bank for information about the terms and conditions of its customer accounts.

Mr Bridgeman said: 'The complaints about Northern Rock's restructuring of accounts raises questions about what appears to be a cavalier attitude to savers. The nature of the market is that interest rates will fluctuate but it cannot be acceptable for consumers to be "sold" a high interest account and then find that the product has turned to something rather less advantageous and that they are locked into it.

'Customers do not expect banks to change arbitrarily the nature of a product, lock them into less favourable terms and conditions, fail to give adequate warning of any changes and treat some account holders differently from others.

'The Unfair Contract Terms in Consumer Contracts Regulations enable me to examine contracts for unfairness and take companies to court if they fail to amend or remove terms which I believe cause detriment to consumers. A term is unfair if it unduly weights the contract against the consumer and in favour of the business. The regulations define as potentially unfair those terms which enable a supplier to alter unilaterally the terms of a contract or any characteristic of a product or service.

'Finding unfair terms in the contract used by one bank will allow me to look at similar terms in other contracts, and I am prepared to do this if any bank fails to put its own house in order. Unfair contract terms have no place in modern banking and should be removed without delay. They are, in any case, unenforceable in law. Consumers do not need a ruling on fairness from the OFT to challenge such terms or seek redress if they feel they have suffered loss.'

Source: OFT press release, 15 May 1998

with consumer protection, we should emphasize that economics would also understand that duty necessarily involves the protection of the competitive firm. Anti-
competitive action on the part of one or more firms will certainly be injurious to
consumers, but it will also undermine the efforts of other firms to meet consumer
needs in terms of service and price. The dodgy car dealer and shady banker both
survive by abstracting from the competitive process. In doing so they hoodwink
consumers and deny legitimate businesses the opportunity to provide these same
consumers with a decent service.

7.9 Industrial policy

This chapter has so far reflected upon a number of different kinds of relationship
between business and government. The existence of public goods, externalities and
anti-competitive practices all give rise to state action in a market context, the
primary purpose of which is either to replace business or to regulate it. Here, we
introduce a form of state intervention that is concerned not to supplant business or
moderate its behaviour but to *boost* it – to improve business performance. As we
have just seen, competition policy does this to some extent but only by focusing
upon the more reprehensible elements in the business world. In contrast, industrial
policy involves government working *positively* with business: offering it guidance,
acting as its advocate and providing it with resources.

Many kinds of government action fall under the heading of industrial policy, and
in a book of this sort we cannot do justice to them all. Rather than try to summarize
here everything the government tries to do for business, we instead concentrate on
two important dimensions of industrial policy in the UK. These are:

- the *1998 Competitiveness White Paper*: the most recent articulation of industrial
  policy
- the *Department of Trade and Industry* (DTI): the government department with
  most responsibility for actually implementing industrial policy.

The 1998 Competitiveness White Paper

White Papers are broad policy statements by the UK government. The 1998 Competitiveness White Paper sets out a framework for improving the performance of
British business relative to its competitors in other countries. The government hopes
to help firms improve both their productivity (the amount they produce relative
to resource inputs) and their ability to innovate. However, the White Paper also
recognizes that business must take the lead in entrepreneurial activity: it is not for
government itself to take business decisions; rather, the government's role is to act

as a catalyst investor and regulator to strengthen the supply side of the economy.

The *supply side* refers to that part of the economy that actually produces goods and
services. We have already seen how by regulating the supply side – with measures
such as the Competition Act 1998 – governments can help to raise the performance
of the economy (to some extent blurring the distinction between competition policy
and industrial policy). However, the notion of government as a 'catalyst investor' is
not something we have met before. This refers to the resourcing by government of

key sectors of the economy in the anticipation that firms will follow up with their own more substantial investments later on. For example, the White Paper commits the government to spend £1.4 billion to modernize the British science and engineering base. At the same time, the state is to

vigorously promote the commercialization of university research, [and it will] help one million small businesses harness information and communication technologies (ICTs) to compete more effectively in the digital marketplace.

Britain also needs:

entrepreneurial individuals with the vision to turn new ideas into winning products and processes. Entrepreneurship is the lifeblood of the new British economy, in large companies as well as small. To encourage a new generation of entrepreneurs, who will create the business on which our future prosperity will depend, the Government will:

- create a new Enterprise Fund to support the financing of small businesses with growth potential . . .
- improve the help given to start-ups – providing a new high-quality advice service targeting 10 000 growth start-ups a year in England . . .
- look at ways of removing the stigma associated with business failure.

This list of intentions is not exhaustive. Our purpose here is to give a flavour of the kind of industrial policy the government is currently pursuing. Notice that the consistent themes in each of the initiatives mentioned above are indeed government as a *supporter* of business and government as a *facilitator* of entrepreneurship. Intervention may involve the provision of finance, as in the £1.4 billion subsidy of science and engineering and the new enterprise fund; or it may involve other kinds of resource commitment such as the development of the small business advice service. The wish to deal with the stigma of business failure is interesting. In the highly entrepreneurial US economy, business failure is often said to be viewed positively. Business involves risk, the argument runs, and *some* unfortunate outcomes are inevitable. But people in business learn from their mistakes and perhaps make better decisions next time. The point is there *is* a next time: entrepreneurship is not dulled by failure. The government would like to stimulate the same spirit of purpose in Britain.

The Department of Trade and Industry

As noted, the DTI is the government department with primary responsibility for the implementation of industrial policy. Accordingly, its agenda will closely mirror the priorities established in the 1998 Competitiveness White Paper. The DTI's most recent declaration of objectives is revealed in Box 7.10. Many of these are already familiar – the focus on science and engineering and business start-ups, for example. However, there are some pronouncements on policy that we have not yet covered. Objective 3 in Box 7.10 is to create strong and competitive markets. In the domestic economy this will be done by agencies such as the Competition Commission in ways we have described. But the objective has European and international dimensions too. As we saw in Chapter 2, section 2.5, the European single market programme is an attempt by member states of the European Union to revitalize the European economy by establishing a coherent integrated market across all their territories. The DTI wishes to speed progress on the development of the single market in areas that

Department of Trade and Industry aim and objectives

Aim

To increase competitiveness and scientific excellence in order to generate higher levels of sustainable growth and productivity in a modern economy.

Objectives

1. Promote enterprise, innovation and increased productivity

in particular by encouraging successful business start-ups, and by increasing the capacity of business, including SMEs, to grow, to invest, to develop skills, to adopt best practice, and to exploit opportunities abroad, recognizing the development of the knowledge economy and taking account of regional differences.

2. Make the most of the UK's science, engineering and technology

in particular by achieving standards of international excellence and maximizing the contribution of its outputs to economic development and the quality of life.

3. Create strong and competitive markets

in particular by taking action to improve the openness, efficiency and effectiveness of markets at home, in Europe and across the world, and to ensure the provision of secure, diverse and sustainable supplies of energy at competitive prices.

4. Develop a fair and effective legal and regulatory framework

in particular by improving and enforcing a framework for commercial activity which encourages enterprise and avoids unnecessary burdens on business, while providing a fair deal for consumers, and by developing a framework for employers and employees which promotes a skilled and flexible labour market founded on the principles of partnership.

Source: DTI Strategic Framework 1999–2000

have hitherto been slow to change. Although it is not mentioned in the box, a key priority for the new millennium is to enhance the single market in financial services. As we noted in Chapter 2, section 2.5, this is an industry in which there is room for a greater degree of integration at the European level. At the international level, the DTI commits itself to securing agreement to a new 'round' of trade and investment negotiations. This is a reference to the World Trade Organization (WTO) talks launched in Seattle in December 1999. The WTO is an international agency with a membership that encompasses the majority of the world's nations. Its basic purpose is to promote openness and fair competition in international markets. The DTI's premise in supporting the WTO's work is that competition *works*; the level of abstraction is unimportant – at the national, European and international levels, open and competitive markets are generally the best means of promoting efficient resource allocation. We consider the work of the WTO in more detail in Chapter 13, section 13.5.

Reflecting on industrial policy

A final note of caution is appropriate before we leave the issue of industrial policy. The general strategy we have discussed is that preferred by the Labour administration elected in May 1997. Though the general approach is currently echoed in other European countries and by the European Union, it is important to be aware that alternative perspectives to industrial policy do exist. Indeed, this should not surprise us. For example, we have seen in the present chapter (section 7.6) how the liberal school harbours deep suspicions about state intervention in most of its forms. In the liberal view, many of the DTI's objectives as outlined in Box 7.10 are highly questionable, the subsidies to science and technology in particular. If there is a market-based demand that can be profitably met by scientific innivation then *firms* will discern it and respond appropriately. The liberal position is that it is not the state's responsibility to take the lead here. The liberals would ask: What do government ministers and career civil servants know about the *fine detail* of this or that market or of the technologies therein? A less interventionist industrial policy might then emphasize the regulation of markets in order to promote competition, but it would not extend to government involvement *in* markets; restrict monopolies and prevent cartels by all means, but do not proceed to more grandiose schemes in which governments tax firms and consumers in order to provide them, ultimately, with the opportunity to buy things it thinks they want.

◼ Summary

◆ The existence of clear forms of market failure provides a rationale for state intervention in free markets.

◆ Not all economists share this orthodox view. One branch of dissent comes from the liberal school. Liberals raise doubts about the real extent of market failure, and introduce the issue of state failure. On the other hand, we saw in Chapter 5 that the institutionalist school raises a different set of questions about monopoly in particular. In the institutionalist view, orthodox approaches understate both the extent and the dangers of concentrations of monopoly power in modern economies.

◆ Privatization appears to sympathize with a *laissez-faire* perspective. However, the important conclusion is that the extent of competition in a market matters more than the distribution of ownership between the public and private sectors.

◆ Competition policy is used by the government to improve the effectiveness of markets. Its main emphasis is on the prevention of cartels and other market 'distortions' that are inimical to consumer interests.

◆ Industrial policy involves attempts by governments to improve the performance of the supply side of the economy. Industrial policy may encompass wide forms of intervention and spending by government. This is not welcomed by some groups of economists.

◼ Key terms

◆ Market failure
◆ Monopoly
◆ Public goods
◆ Free rider problem
◆ Negative externalities
◆ Positive externalities
◆ State failure
◆ Freedom

◆ Crowding out
◆ Privatization
◆ Competition
◆ Competition policy
◆ Industrial policy

▊ Questions for discussion

◆ Explain the significance of the 'free rider' problem.

◆ In most economies, taxis are licensed by the state for externality reasons. What externalities might unlicensed taxis generate?

◆ What is state failure? Give some examples.

◆ What are the implications of state failure for orthodox economics?

◆ Why is the privatization of a nationalized industry, such as the railway network, no guarantee in itself of improved economic performance?

◆ What is competition policy?

◆ Why would virtually all economists agree that competition policy is a good idea but disagree about the usefulness and validity of industrial policy?

Reflective questions on boxed material

◆ Boxes 7.7, 7.8 and 7.9 describe various aspects of UK competition policy. Effective competition policy is something that clearly benefits consumers. What arguments might you use if you had to convince a business audience that it is in their interests too?

▊ Further reading

Alt, J.E. and K.A. Chrystal *Political Economics* (Brighton: Wheatsheaf Books, 1983). Provides an excellent overview of the debate in economics over the role of the state.

Friedman, M. *Capitalism and Freedom* (Chicago: University of Chicago Press, 1962). Provides a brief and very readable exposition of the liberal view of market failure and market competence.

Jackson, P.M. and C.M. Price (eds) *Privatization and Regulation* (Harlow: Longman, 1994). Offers a useful overview of privatization issues in the UK and the wider international context.

Le Grand, J., C. Propper and R. Robinson, *The Economics of Social Problems* (3rd ed.) (Basingstoke: Macmillan, 1992). Provides excellent applied discussions of social problems such as the environment and transport, and considers how they can be tackled.

▊ Internet links

The *Department of Trade and Industry's* website is at: **http://www.dti.gov.uk/**
The *Office of Fair Trading's* website is at: **http://www.oft.gov.uk/index.htm**
The *Competition Commission's* website is at: **http://www.competition-commission. gov.uk/**

The *Adam Smith Institute* is an independent body that promotes market-based reform, following a broadly liberal ethos. Its website is at: **http://www.adamsmith.org.uk/** The *Institute for Public Policy Research* does the same kind of job as the *Adam Smith Institute* but from a left-leaning perspective. It was created specifically as an alternative to free market think tanks. Its website is at: **http://www.ippr.org.uk/**

Factor Markets

CHAPTER 8

Key issues

▶ Do factor markets work in the same way as markets for goods and services?

▶ In the labour market, which factors determine demand and supply?

▶ How is skill in the labour market rewarded?

▶ Does minimum wage legislation destroy jobs?

Contents

8.1 Introduction

In previous chapters much of our discussion tended to concentrate on markets in goods and services. In the present chapter, we extend some of the concepts we have already introduced to the analysis of **factor markets**. Recall that there are four factors of production, the services of which are combined by firms in order to produce an output. They are:

- labour
- capital (factories, machines and so on)
- land (all natural resources used in production)
- entrepreneurial skill.

Factor markets are clearly of interest in themselves. It is important, for example, to understand the operation of the labour market. If the labour market fails to clear, unemployment may result. In such circumstances we need to consider what, if anything, can be done about it (see Chapter 10, sections 10.2–10.3). An analysis of factor markets also allows us to understand how the income a society generates is distributed amongst the groups that comprise it. In other words, such an analysis will tell us why particular social groups – workers, entrepreneurs, the owners of capital and land – earn what they do. However, as we considered entrepreneurship in conjunction with the theory of the firm in Chapter 3, we shall concentrate here on the markets for capital, land and, especially, labour. We begin with an analysis of the labour market.

Factor market: A market for a factor of production.

8.2 The labour market

Essentially, factor markets and goods markets work in the same way. The principles underlying the interaction of demand and supply are as applicable to labour markets as they are to the markets for office furniture, cinema tickets or any other good or service. A useful way to start to look at the labour market would therefore be to examine it as a *perfectly functioning abstraction*. We began our analysis of market structures and firms in precisely the same way with a model of perfect competition. The purpose behind this kind of approach is to allow us to see how a market might work under 'ideal' conditions and to contrast this with the much greater – and more problematic – complexity of the real world.

One of the by now familiar tenets of conventional economics is that free markets *clear*. In other words, markets are possessed of forces that push them towards situations in which the quantities demanded and supplied are perfectly matched. At such points in every market, because there is no tendency for further change to take place, each prevailing price is by definition an equilibrium price. Given certain assumptions, we can reproduce exactly same kind of analysis in the context of the labour market. Thus, if we assume:

- that work is not qualitatively different between occupations
- that labour is (like a good in perfect competition) homogeneous
- that there exist perfect mobility and perfect knowledge in the labour market
- and, finally, that there exist large numbers of independent buyers (firms) and sellers (individual men and women)

then *the* labour market in an economy – our assumptions mean that there would be only one – can be represented as in Fig. 8.1. Here, the wage rate – the *factor price* firms must pay to hire the services of labour – is depicted on the vertical axis, while the quantity of labour demanded and supplied is depicted on the horizontal axis. The market is in equilibrium at wage rate W_e, with the quantity demanded and supplied at Q_e. From our discussion in Chapter 2, the reader should be able to verify that at all possible wage rates below W_e, there will exist an excess demand for labour. This will be eroded as firms begin to offer higher wage rates in an attempt to overcome labour

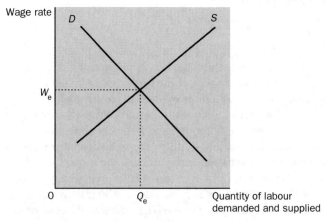

Fig. 8.1 The interaction of demand and supply in the labour market.

shortages. Higher wages encourage more workers to enter the market and supply extends. However, at the same time, higher wages also cause the demand for labour to contract. Eventually, a point will be reached where the quantities demanded and supplied are equal: this will be at wage rate W_e. Conversely, at all possible wage rates above W_e there will be an excess supply of labour. In other words, some workers who are willing to work at the prevailing wage rate will not be able to do so because the requisite demand is not there. Recognizing such conditions, firms will begin to offer lower wages secure in the knowledge that they will still be able to recruit all the labour they need. Wages will continue to fall until W_e is again reached and the quantities demanded and supplied are equal. We consider the influences on the *positions* of the demand and supply curves for labour in later sections.

For the moment, consider the familiar implicit message that this analysis delivers. The suggestion is that if markets are left alone and are competitive then they will tend to clear. In the case of the labour market, this means that labour is in neither excess demand or excess supply. 'Competitiveness' in the labour market entails both the capacity for individual workers to freely enter and leave the market and flexibility in wage rates. As we shall see, some economists claim that many problems in labour markets can be overcome if they are characterized by openness and if wages are sufficiently flexible (see Chapter 10, section 10.2).

Let us now examine the effects of relaxing some of our highly restrictive assumptions. To begin with the first assumption, there are plainly significant differences in the quality of work between occupations. For example, miners and people who work on oil rigs are exposed to more unpleasant and dangerous working environments than teachers, librarians and others in what we might term the 'indoor professions'. This means that, if all jobs were rewarded with the same generally determined equilibrium wage, many miners, oil rig workers and others would choose to take up less arduous and less hazardous jobs instead. So, because occupations vary greatly in quality, wage rates must differ to compensate those who undertake the less pleasant tasks. The level of compensation is conditioned by something called the *principle of net advantages*. This requires that the pecuniary (money) and non-pecuniary advantages of different jobs should, when taken together, tend to be equal. When the principle of net advantages applies, workers will not be collectively repelled from the least attractive jobs. The implication of this first concession to the real world is that we have not one uniform labour market but a *series* of labour markets across which differences in occupational quality are perceived and in which different wage rates are paid.

Yet some very pleasant jobs are extremely well paid. This suggests that differences in the quality of work should not be our only concession to reality. In professional football, for example, the most successful players are amply rewarded for doing what many people would joyfully do for nothing. Unfortunately, however, Everton are not going to sign you (probably) or us (definitely) for the simple reason that, in the real world, our second assumption does not apply. Labour is not homogeneous. To be a professional footballer requires a *natural talent* that most people do not possess. This means that the supply of top-class footballers is extremely limited and, as we know, when restrictions on supply are coupled with strong demand, higher market prices result. For the purposes of comparison, let us also consider the ability requirements of a second occupation: a bus driver. Here the 'natural talent' element of the job is relatively modest: many if not most people of working age could be trained to drive a bus competently. Even if labour is not homogeneous it would seem that the

Labour market segmentation:
Arises when labour faces
barriers to entry to a particular
labour market.

Collective bargaining: Involves
negotiations between a trade
union and one or more
employers over pay or
workplace conditions.

potential supply of drivers is very large. Now, when plentiful supply is coupled with relatively low demand, lower market prices result. However, there is an additional issue here. Most bus operators tend to recruit trainee drivers not from the general labour force but from only the male half of it. Why? Although women are clearly not physically incapable of this kind of work, it appears that reciprocally confirming *social and institutional barriers* prevent them from participating in it to any significant extent. Driving a bus is socially regarded as 'men's work'. Accordingly, bus operators have a tradition of recruiting and training men. There are many such examples of *gendered* work, and most similarly incline against employment opportunities for women. Our point is that these further separate or **segment** the labour market into discrete elements. Indeed, the greater the degree of natural, social and institutional *heterogeneity* of labour, the greater the degree of labour market segmentation. Of course, social and institutional heterogeneity in the labour market is *socially constructed* and includes all forms of discrimination whether on the basis of ethnic origin, religious belief, disability, sexual orientation or gender; it has no independent objective existence.

Our third initial simplifying assumption was that there is perfect mobility of labour and perfect knowledge in the market. We have just discounted one element of the first part of this assumption: that labour is able to move freely between occupations. But, in addition to natural talent and the kinds of social and institutional barriers to work mentioned above, many jobs require specialist qualifications. For example, to obtain a licence to drive a hackney cab in London it is first necessary to 'do the knowledge'. This entails learning, usually over a period of years and in great detail, the layout of London's major roads and principal destinations. Similarly, people are not permitted to fly aircraft, pilot ships, or practise medicine, law or accountancy without the appropriate training.

It is also important to recognize the existence of *geographical* barriers to mobility in the labour market. An excess demand for labour and excess supply can coexist in different parts of an economy simply because unemployed workers cannot (perhaps because of a lack of affordable housing) or do not want to move to where the jobs are. The degree of labour mobility in the European single market is an interesting case in point. All citizens of the European Union (EU) are now free to live and work in any EU country, but how many actually choose to search for work abroad is a very open question (for a discussion of the single market see Chapter 2, section 2.5). The implication here is that labour markets can also be geographically segmented as individuals restrict their search for work to familiar localities. Finally, the segmentation of markets may be compounded by *poor information flows*. Our initial simplifying assumption was perfect knowledge, but workers cannot compete for jobs that they do not know exist.

The final assumption in our specification of a perfectly competitive labour market was the presence of many independent workers (the suppliers of labour) and firms (the institutions that demand it). But, in the UK for example, roughly 40 per cent of workers belong to trade unions whose aim is to provide a **collective** presence in labour markets for their members. In so far as trade unions are successful in **bargaining** higher wage rates than the market would bear in more competitive circumstances (say above W_e in Fig. 8.1), the effect of their action is to reduce the numbers employed while securing more favourable returns for those who remain in work. Of course, collectivity can be attractive to firms too. It is not uncommon for employers' organizations to negotiate with trade unions on behalf of their member firms. For example, in the UK engineering industry, the Engineering Employers' Federation undertakes such a task. However, perhaps the most marked form of labour market distortion comes under the guise of the *closed shop*. Here, in order to secure or continue in employment, workers are required to join a designated trade union. This arrangement is thought to be attractive to both unions and firms, because it may provide for 'some stability' in the workplace. Its economic effect is, of course, to constrain labour supply by throwing up yet another barrier to independent activity and freedom of movement in the labour market.

Real-world labour markets are then far removed from our idealized model. What we appear to have is a complex set of labour markets with a range of uneven barriers between them. The barriers include: natural talent or skill, training, qualifications, age, gender (and other forms of discrimination), distance, information and trade union membership. Now, recall our definition of monopoly power from Chapter 5, section 5.6. Monopoly power can arise wherever there are barriers to entry in a market. This means that, in reality, many labour markets are characterized by the presence of monopoly power. Of course, in those cases where there are the most stringent and daunting barriers to entry, labour will enjoy the highest levels of monopoly power and may find its rewards magnified accordingly. But what does all this mean for our opening remarks about the governance of the labour market by the familiar laws of demand and supply? Are the propositions concerning excess demand and supply, and notions of the equilibrium market clearing wage depicted in Fig. 8.1 now irrelevant? Fortunately, they are not. What we must recognize, however, is the changed context in which they operate. Within each segmented labour market, *particular* demand and supply conditions will determine the *particular* equilibrium wage rate for that market. In the next two sections of this chapter we consider the determinants of labour demand and supply in more detail. This analysis then allows us to conclude our discussion of labour as a factor of production by reviewing the operation of some real world labour markets.

8.3 The demand for labour

The firm's demand for labour – and, indeed, for any factor of production – is a **derived demand**. This means that firms do not hire labour for itself but for the services it can perform in the production process. Labour is demanded because it helps to produce goods and services that can then be sold, yielding the firm revenue: the source of profit. Let us now examine how it is possible to derive the individual firm's demand curve for labour.

Recall (see Chapter 4, section 4.6) that a firm maximizes profit by producing an output at which the marginal or extra cost (*MC*) associated with the last unit produced equals the marginal or extra revenue (*MR*) derived from the last unit sold (the *MC* = *MR* rule). Let us apply this principle to the individual firm's demand for labour. We begin with an analysis of the firm's *short-run* demand for labour. In the short run, we assume that the quantities of some factors of production are fixed (capital, for example) while others can be varied. Thus a firm can increase output relatively easily by hiring more labour, but it takes time to buy and install new machinery. On the basis of this assumption, labour is often referred to as a *variable* factor of production in the short run, while capital is a *fixed* factor, again in the short run. In the long run all factors of production are variable.

Derived demand: Arises for a factor of production because of the demand for the output that the factor helps to produce. The factor in itself does not generate demand.

Marginal physical product:
The change in total output
resulting from a unit change in
the variable factor.

Marginal revenue product: The
change in a firm's total
revenue resulting from the sale
of output produced by one
more unit of the variable factor.

The firm's demand for labour in the short run

In the short run, the question of how much labour the individual firm demands turns on the contribution that each extra worker makes to profit. In other words, for every extra worker, the firm asks itself: Is this person adding more to revenue than he or she is costing to employ? If the answer is yes, then the person is employed; if no, then he or she is not. The contribution an extra worker makes to the firm's profit depends on three things:

1. how much additional output he or she produces

2. the price the extra output sells at

3. his or her wage.

The first of these – the additional output he or she produces – is called the **marginal physical product** (*MPP*). Now, recall from Chapter 4, section 4.2, that the law of diminishing returns states that, as additional units of a variable factor are used by a firm in the context of a given volume of fixed factors, the marginal product of the variable factor will eventually begin to fall. Here, the implication of the law of diminishing returns is that, as extra workers are employed, MPP falls. The second issue is the price at which the extra worker's additional output is sold. If we assume the firm to be perfectly competitive, this price will be given: the perfectly competitive firm can sell as much as it likes at the prevailing market price. Putting 1 and 2 above together, we can now say that the extra revenue associated with each additional worker hired by a perfectly competitive firm will be given by his or her MPP multiplied by the market price of the product in question. This extra revenue is called the **marginal revenue product** of labour (*MRP*).

Fig. 8.2 depicts the individual perfectly competitive firm's marginal revenue product schedule, *MRP*. At a market wage *W*, for example, its demand for labour will be set at Q_1. At this point, the contribution made by the last worker to the firm's revenue is identical to his or her wage (*W*). This means that earlier workers over the range of the schedule *MRP* will be contributing more to revenue than cost. For example, for the worker at Q_2 the cost/wage is still the market rate *W* but the *MRP* is 0B. The 'profit' on this worker is therefore 0B – 0W. On the other hand, for workers beyond the point Q_1, *MRP* is below the market wage rate. It is clearly not in the firm's interest to extend employment beyond Q_1 because workers in this range add more to cost

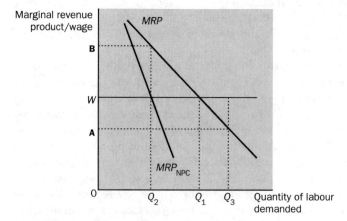

Fig. 8.2 The individual firm's demand for labour.

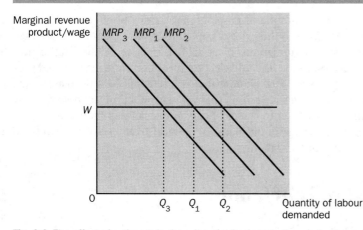
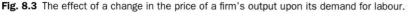

Fig. 8.3 The effect of a change in the price of a firm's output upon its demand for labour.

than to revenue. For example, at Q_3, the wage W exceeds the MRP by $0W - 0A$. The MRP schedule is the individual firm's demand curve for labour. A fall in the wage rate will *ceteris paribus* engineer an extension in the quantity of labour demanded, while an increase in the wage rate will be associated with a contraction in the quantity of labour demanded by the firm.

For a perfectly competitive firm, when the market price increases the marginal revenue product of labour also increases. Simply, the goods produced by each worker bring in more revenue. This causes the MRP schedule to shift to the right and leads to an increase in the firm's demand for labour. In Fig. 8.3, the MRP schedule shifts from MRP_1 to MRP_2. At a market wage W, for example, the quantity of labour demanded would increase from Q_1 to Q_2. Conversely a reduction in the market price of the perfectly competitive firm's output will cause the MRP schedule to shift to the left (from MRP_1 to MRP_3 in Fig. 8.3), resulting in a decrease in its demand for labour. At a market wage W, the quantity of labour demanded would fall from Q_1 to Q_3.

What happens to the individual firm's demand for labour when we relax our assumption that it is perfectly competitive? The essential difference concerns point 2 above – the selling price of the firm's output. As discussed in Chapter 5, a *non-perfectly competitive* firm faces a downward-sloping demand curve. Unlike the perfectly competitive firm, it cannot sell as much as it likes at a given market price. For the non-perfectly competitive firm, higher output means a *lower* selling price. The implication here is that the additional output produced by an extra worker will reduce the price of all the firm's output and thus *steepen* the slope of its MRP curve as the $MRPs$ of all employed workers fall. In Fig. 8.2 the non-perfectly competitive firm's MRP curve is labelled MRP_{NPC}. At the market wage W, the quantity of labour demanded by the non-perfectly competitive firm will be Q_2. Note that, assuming the non-perfectly competitive firm and the perfectly competitive firm have the same technology, this is less than the quantity of labour demanded by the perfectly competitive firm at the same wage rate.

The firm's demand for labour in the long run

As noted, the difference between the short and the long run is that in the long run *all* factors of production become variable. This means it is possible for the firm to increase (say) the amount of capital it employs. Two kinds of effect upon labour demand can then occur. First, if the price of capital relative to labour changes then the firm will alter its demand for labour. If capital falls in price, relative to the price of labour, then *ceteris paribus* the firm will elect to introduce more mechanized production methods at the expense of labour (that is, there will be a decrease in the demand for labour) and vice versa. Second, changes in production technologies may also cause the demand for labour to change. For example, an improvement in technology that results in an increase in the marginal physical product of labour will lead to an increase in the demand for labour.

8.4 The supply of labour

The supply of labour in an economy

The total supply of labour in an economy is strongly conditioned by changes in population. For example, according to the Organization for Economic Cooperation and Development (OECD), over the 1980s five-sixths of the increase in the labour force in its member countries was attributable to population growth. However, the population of working age in the OECD area is now growing much more slowly (half of 1 per cent per year in the early 1990s) than it did in the 1970s (more than 1 per cent per year), and the OECD suggests that the expected continuation of this trend will lead to an increase in the proportion of older workers in the labour force. Labour supply is also influenced by international migration. Increased migration into Western Europe has been particularly marked since the liberalization of the formerly planned economies of Eastern Europe, which began in 1989. Moreover, greater freedom of movement in the East has been mirrored by the abolition of border and passport controls between mainland EU and other European countries following the *Schengen Agreement*, which is part of the EU's single market programme.

Inside the general constraint of population growth, institutional and social factors will also influence the supply of labour in an economy. For example, an increase in the school leaving age or a lowering of the retirement age will compress the population of working age. Similarly, longer holidays and a shorter working week will also reduce labour supply. While these factors have traditionally been decided at the national level, it is interesting to note that, for EU member countries, they are now increasingly determined collectively through the EU itself. The length of the working week is a case in point. Under the Social Chapter of the Maastricht Treaty (1991) it was agreed that the length of the working week in most EU countries should be restricted to a maximum of 48 hours.

While what we might term the 'boundaries' of the working population are conditioned by the socially acceptable and institutionally determined ages of entry and exit, the duration of the working week and holiday entitlement, these factors do not wholly determine actual labour supply. To be of working age is one thing; to be **economically active** in the labour market is another. The economically active are those people of working age who are either in some kind of paid employment or who are seeking it. Table 8.1 describes economic activity for women and men in Great Britain (the UK excluding Northern Ireland) in 1988 and 1998. Notice from the table that the economic activity rate for women over this period has increased from 69.9 to 71.5 per cent, whereas for men the rate has fallen from 88.2 to 83.9 per cent.

Economically active individuals: People of working age who are either in work or actively seeking it. People of working age not in employment and not seeking it are deemed to be economically inactive.

Table 8.1 Economic activity in Great Britain: women and men of working age (16–59/64) 1988 and 1998; spring of each year (not seasonally adjusted)

	1988 ('000)	1998 ('000)	% change 1988–98
Women (16–65)			
All	16 602	17 068	3
Economically active	11 600	12 206	5
Economic activity rate (%)	*69.9*	*71.5*	
In employment	10 613	11 542	9
Full-time	6159	6519	6
Part-time	4434	5020	13
Employment rate	*63.9*	*67.6*	
ILO Unemployed	987	664	–33
ILO Unemployment rate (%)	*8.5*	*5.4*	
Economically inactive	5002	4862	–3
Men (16–64)			
All	18 169	18 738	3
Economically active	16 020	15 715	–2
Economic activity rate (%)	*88.2*	*83.9*	
In employment	14 561	14 633	0
Full-time	13 856	13 471	–3
Part-time	675	1159	72
Employment rate	*80.1*	*78.1*	
ILO Unemployed	1458	1082	–26
ILO Unemployment rate (%)	*9.1*	*6.9*	
Economically inactive	2150	3024	41

Source: Labour Market Trends (March 1999), National Statistics, © Crown Copyright 2000

This means that the **participation** of women in the labour market has increased, while that of men has decreased. The net effect has been an increase in overall labour supply. Considering those in employment, the table allows us to calculate that there has been an overall shift from full-time to part-time work, with an increase of just over 1 million part-time jobs over the period, compared with a *decrease* of 25 000 in full-time jobs. Of the additional part-time jobs, 55 per cent have been taken by women. Although there are 25 000 fewer full-time jobs, the number of women in full-time employment has increased by 360 000. The number of men in full-time employment has accordingly decreased by 385 000. The general pattern of rising participation rates for women is replicated across most of the OECD area, as indicated in Fig. 8.4 (exceptions include Denmark, Sweden and Finland).

Participation rate: The proportion of economically active workers in a particular group of the population.

The individual's supply of labour

The general law of supply, introduced in Chapter 2, section 2.3, states that supply varies positively with price. At first sight, we might expect the same relationship to hold in the labour market: the greater the reward in terms of the wage rate, the more hours we would expect an individual to be willing to work. However, we must also recognize that the opportunity cost of work is the leisure time that the individual must surrender in order to work. The issue of the individual's supply of labour now becomes the more complex one of balancing the rewards gained from work against

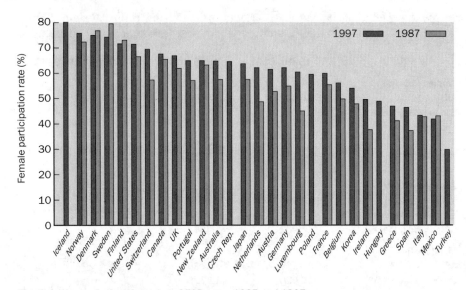

Fig. 8.4 Women in the job market: OECD area, 1987 and 1997.
Source: OECD website. Reproduced by permission of the OECD.

the subjective value that he or she places on the leisure that must be given up. Consider the position of someone who is unemployed. Such a person clearly has a lot of free time but a relatively low income comprising (say) some form of welfare benefit. This means that he or she would be likely to value some extra income gained from work (of which he or she currently has little) more than a few hours of leisure forgone (he or she has leisure in abundance). Thus, if a wage rate in excess of benefit is offered, the rational decision is to begin to work. Of course, the difference between the benefit rate and the wage rate must be sufficient to convince the individual that work is worthwhile.

Reservation wage: The minimum rate required to induce an individual to accept a job.

Fig. 8.5 represents the individual's supply of labour. Notice that the supply curve here intersects with the vertical axis at £3 per hour. This is the **reservation wage**: that is, the rate required to induce this person to begin to work. A rate of £2 per hour would not be enough. It might be too close to the benefit rate, such that the oppor-

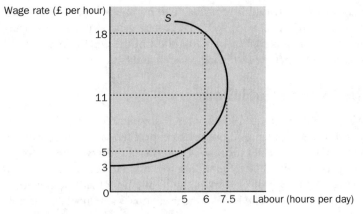

Fig. 8.5 The individual's supply of labour.

tunity cost of work (lost leisure) is valued more highly than £2 per hour. If the wage rate is £5 per hour, the individual wishes to work 5 hours per day. The £25 he or she earns (5 × £5) is of greater subjective value than the 5 hours of leisure per day forgone. So far then, the relationship between the wage rate and labour supply is of the expected positive form: the higher the wage rate, the more hours worked. It is important to understand that there are *two* effects taking place here. As the wage rate increases, there is a positive incentive to work more hours as the marginal benefit of work compared with leisure increases: the so-called *substitution effect*. At the same time, an increase in the wage rate will also generate a disincentive to work more hours because a higher wage rate reduces the number of hours required to obtain a given income: the so-called *income effect*. When the substitution effect dominates, a higher wage rate increases the number of hours for which the individual is willing to work. At a wage rate of £11 per hour, the 7.5 hours worked represents the maximum length of the working day desired by our subject (who earns £11 × 7.5 = £82.50 per day). Thereafter, despite higher wages, he or she wishes to work *fewer* hours, and the supply curve takes on a negative or backward-sloping form. In this situation, the income effect dominates the substitution effect. Quite simply, the individual has reached a point where his or her dwindling leisure time now has a very high subjective value, and further improvements in the wage rate afford the opportunity to maintain a satisfactory income while reducing the number of hours worked. Another way of putting it is to say that the relatively high income associated with the high wage rate stimulates the individual's demand for all goods and services, including leisure: effectively he or she now has the money to 'buy' more leisure by working less. In Fig. 8.5, when the individual is paid £18 per hour, he or she wishes to work 6 hours per day. Notice that, at this rate, the daily wage of £108 (£18 × 6) does allow our subject to take more leisure while more than preserving his or her income.

The supply of labour to a particular occupation

Having discussed both the supply of labour to the economy as a whole and an individual's supply of labour, we now turn to consider the supply of labour to a particular occupation. Here we need to be aware of two issues.

First, different occupations will offer qualitatively different forms of work. As noted, work on an oil rig is likely to be more dangerous and unpleasant than a 9 to 5 'desk' job. Thus, in order to retain workers, occupations that offer low-quality work must offer higher monetary compensation. This implies some degree of segmentation between different occupations, with *ceteris paribus* higher wages being paid in the more dangerous ones. Clearly, then, different occupations will have different labour supply curves. Supply conditions between occupations may also differ for other reasons. We have already seen, for example, that variations in natural talent, training and trade union membership may act as constraints on labour supply.

Second, the supply curve for an occupation is likely to be positively sloped such as *S* in Fig. 8.1. In order to induce an increase in the quantity of labour supplied to particular occupation, the wage rate will need to be increased.

The elasticity of labour supply

The **elasticity of labour supply** measures how responsive the quantity of labour supplied is to a change in the wage rate. The elasticity of supply in a particular

Elasticity of labour supply: Measures the responsiveness of the quantity of labour supplied to changes in the wage rate.

occupation will vary according to the degree of skill and training involved and the time period under consideration. For certain highly skilled occupations, such as those in medical practice, it would be difficult or impossible for the quantity supplied to *immediately* extend following an increase in the wage rate. In these occupations the supply curve will be relatively inelastic. By contrast, for relatively low skilled occupations such as petrol pump attendants, the quantity supplied will be much more responsive to an increase in the wage rate. However, over time, labour supply will become more elastic as people acquire the necessary skills to undertake certain occupations.

8.5 Issues in the labour market: bringing demand and supply together

Skilled and unskilled labour

In Fig. 8.6, the supply curve S_1 represents the supply of unskilled labour. Notice that it has a positive slope, indicating that the supply of labour is not perfectly elastic. At a wage rate W_1, the quantity of unskilled labour supplied is Q_1. A modest proportionate increase in the wage rate from W_1 to W_2 induces a relatively large proportionate increase in the quantity of labour supplied from Q_1 to Q_2. Thus, over this wage rate range, supply is elastic (recall from Chapter 2, section 2.11, that price elasticity of supply – P_{es} – is given by the proportionate change in quantity supplied divided by the proportionate change in price or, in this case, wage). Next consider the supply curve S_2. This represents the supply of skilled workers. It has a slope slightly steeper than S_1, and lies above it. Why? The *position* of S_2 reflects the higher wage rate required by skilled workers. If they were paid at the same rate as unskilled workers there would be less incentive to skill acquisition. In order to encourage workers to spend time and money obtaining a skill (which can often necessitate leaving the labour market and paid employment for a period), there have to be adequate rewards. Thus, to induce the supply of Q_1 skilled workers requires a wage rate of W_3. The slightly steeper *slope* of S_2 *suggests* that the elasticity of supply for skilled workers may not be much different from the elasticity of supply of unskilled

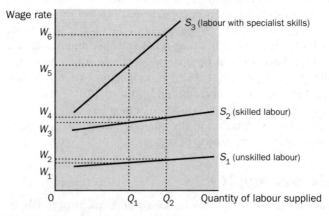

Fig. 8.6 The supply of skilled and unskilled labour.

workers.[1] Finally, the supply curve S_3 represents the supply curve for highly special-ized labour. It lies above both S_1 and S_2 because specialist skills are still more diffi-cult and costly to obtain and therefore require even higher wage rates to make skill acquisition worthwhile. In order to induce the quantity of Q_1 specialists, the wage rate W_5 must be paid. The much steeper slope of S_3 *suggests* that the elasticity of supply of specialist labour may be not be quite as high over the same period when compared with the other two categories – though in our diagrammatic presentation it is still elastic.

Let us now introduce demand into the analysis. In section 8.3 we saw how the demand for labour reflects labour's marginal revenue product (MRP). The profit-maximizing firm will recruit additional workers up to the point at which the MRP equals the wage rate. The MRP curve is in effect the firm's demand curve for labour. It follows that if we sum all of the quantities of labour demanded at each wage rate by all firms active in a particular labour market, we arrive at the *demand curve for that market*. We can also distinguish between the market demand for skilled and unskilled labour. Remember that the demand for labour is a derived demand. Firms value labour for its contribution to the production process. It is the case, therefore, that skilled labour will be more valued than unskilled labour because of its greater capa-bilities as manifested by its marginal revenue product. Accountants sell specialist services that command a high price, and this justifies the relatively high wage rates they are paid. On the other hand, dry-cleaners sell services that command a relatively low price: accordingly, because workers in this occupation are less productive, their wage rates will be lower. *Generally then, the demand curves for skilled workers will be above those of unskilled workers.* Fig. 8.7 illustrates the point. The curve D_1 represents the demand for unskilled labour. At a wage rate W_1, Q_1 workers are demanded. The demand for skilled labour is represented by the curve D_2. The higher marginal prod-uct of skilled labour justifies the payment of a higher wage rate W_2, at which the demand for labour is also Q_1. Thus the wage premium for skilled labour is the distance $0W_2-0W_1$.

Let us now combine our analyses of supply and demand. In Fig. 8.8 we reproduce

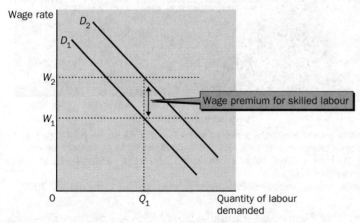

Fig. 8.7 The demand for skilled and unskilled workers.

[1] Note, however, that the response of labour supply to changes in wage rates cannot be simply 'read' from the slope of the supply curve. In every case it is a question of the *particular* change in the wage rate and the *particular* change in supply that follows.

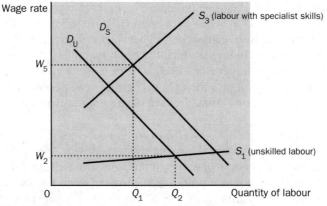

Fig. 8.8 The markets for skilled and unskilled labour.

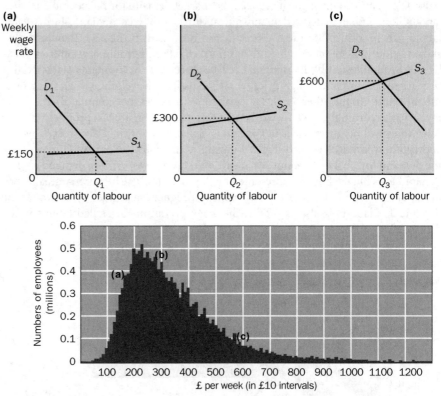

Fig. 8.9 Stylized labour market conditions and the distribution of gross weekly rearnings, full-time employees on adult rates, Great Britain, April 1997. (a) Market type 1: relatively weak demand and supply. (b) Market type 2: intermediate demand and supply. (c) Market type 3: relatively strong demand and supply.
Source: *Labour Market Trends*, November 1997, National Statistics, © Crown Copyright 2000.

the supply curves from Figure 8.6 for unskilled and highly skilled labour, and add two demand curves that correspond to the demand in a market for unskilled (D_U) and highly skilled labour (D_S). For unskilled labour, lower productivity and elastic supply conditions combine to produce an equilibrium wage rate W_2 and quantity Q_2. The higher productivity of highly skilled labour coupled with the wage premium

Table 8.2 Highest and lowest paid occupations, Great Britain, April 1998

Full-time employees on adult rates whose pay for the survey period was unaffected by absence	Average gross weekly pay (£)
Highest paid	
1. General administrators; national government	1116.9
2. Treasurers and company financial managers	976.5
3. Medical practitioners	901.2
4. Management consultants, business analysts	794.3
5. Underwriters, claims assessors, brokers, investment analysts	743.4
6. Organization and methods and work study managers	720.1
7. Police officers (inspector and above)	716.6
8. Solicitors	686.9
9. Education officers, school inspectors	685.6
10. Advertising and public relations managers	683.2
Lowest paid	
1. Kitchen porters, hands	166.8
2. Hairdressers, barbers	175.7
3. Waiters, waitresses	175.9
4. Bar staff	176.2
5. Childcare and related occupations	178.9
6. Counterhands, catering assistants	182.0
7. Petrol pump forecourt attendants	185.0
8. Launderers, dry-cleaners, pressers	187.1
9. Retail cash desk and check-out operators	190.9
10. Sewing machinists, menders, darners and embroiderers	195.2

Source: *Labour Market Trends* (December 1998), National Statistics, © Crown Copyright 2000.

for skill and a much less elastic supply yields a much higher equilibrium wage W_5. Table 8.2 provides some evidence on the wage rates paid in a variety of occupations, which tends to support this theoretical analysis. From the table we can see that amongst the highest-paid jobs are those in the medical, legal and financial professions. The rewards here reflect *both* the high prices charged for the services of doctors, solicitors and accountants – the high marginal revenue products of these people – and the fact that there are relatively few of them in the labour market (because their training is very demanding and lengthy). The poorest-paid jobs – kitchen work, waiting, bar work and so on – have much less robust demand and supply conditions. Low marginal revenue products, low skills and relatively elastic supply all combine here to depress wage rates.

Consider, finally, Fig. 8.9. This brings together the theoretical precepts we have built up on the workings of labour markets and some evidence on the numbers of workers in the UK earning particular wage rates. It is then a representation of some *stylized forms* of labour market conditions that prevail in the UK and a rough estimate of their relative importance. Market type 1 is intended to typify the demand and supply conditions for unskilled labour. The equilibrium wage we illustrate in this market is an arbitrary £150 per week. From the frequency distribution of UK wage rates, we can see that about 1 million full-time workers earn between £140 and

£160 per week. This, of course, does not mean that our stylized labour market is 1 million workers strong. These people will be spread across a *variety* of industries and regions in what are, therefore, *different* labour markets. These markets will, however, be of the same general form. We could, of course, choose to further disaggregate market type 1 into a number of subsets that covered a wider wage range, say from £100 to £200 per week. The stylized 'weak demand and supply' markets would now encompass almost 3 million workers (out of a total of about 19 million in full-time work). For market type 2, where demand and supply conditions are more robust, the equilibrium wage is £300 per week. The frequency distribution shows that roughly 1.2 million workers are within £10 of this wage rate. Again, if we disaggregate this market into subsets that cover the wage range, say, £210 to £400 per week, then the number of workers in our stylized intermediate markets is about 9 million – roughly half of the UK's full time workforce. Finally, for market type 3, where demand and supply conditions are the strongest (of those markets considered: we have ignored markets in which the highest wage rates are generated), the equilibrium wage is £600 per week. The frequency distribution shows that about 200 000 people earn between £590 and £610 per week. Disaggregating the market to cover a wider wage range, £500 to £700 per week, raises the number of workers included to about 2.5 million. In each of our stylized market diagrams we have given the equilibrium quantity of labour demanded and supplied as Q_n. Given the data in the frequency distribution, these should not be taken as ordinal quantities (Q_1 the smallest etc.) as easily the greatest numbers of workers are employed in our stylized intermediate market(s).

Human capital

Human capital is the reserve of skill and knowledge that a worker can gather. Our discussion so far suggests that it can boost the wage-earning potential of the worker from both the demand and the supply side. On the demand side it raises the worker's marginal revenue product as he or she becomes capable of more challenging tasks. On the supply side it provides the means of entry into a select group of workers, whose relatively small numbers cannot be easily increased. For those who fail to invest in their own human capital or who have in the past invested in what has become the wrong sort of human capital, both earning and employment prospects are relatively poor.

The point is exemplified in Box 8.1. The argument here is that labour market demand and supply conditions in the UK and most other developed countries have moved in favour of those who have invested not just in human capital but in what has turned out to be the *right sort* of human capital. Two important factors underpin this view. First, rapid technological change across all sectors of the economy continues to raise the demand for those with what we might broadly term transferable computing and information technology skills. Second, the chronic decline in industrial and manual work, which itself is partly fuelled by technological change, has rendered traditional craft and 'factory skills' increasingly redundant. In terms of Fig. 8.8, labour markets in the developed world may be dividing into those that are moving towards a situation typified by the curves D_S and S_3 and, unfortunately, those that more readily approximate D_U and S_1.

While the educational and career choices of individual workers are central to the accumulation of human capital, firms too have an important role to play here. When

Human capital: The skill and knowledge that a worker can gather. Note that some forms of human capital will be more valuable than others. The crucial factors are again demand and supply: is what you can do strongly demanded, and how many others can do the same thing?

Box 8.1

Employment opportunity in a changing labour market

Throughout the OECD the employment rate of low skilled and poorly educated workers has been falling since at least the early 1980s; while in the UK and the US there is clear evidence that relative wages of unskilled workers have also been falling. These increases in the relative demand for skilled labour have been accompanied by, and may have directly caused, an increase in the supply of skilled labour. The proportion of people in lower skilled groups has been falling throughout the developed world. The situation is sometimes described as a race between the supply of and the demand for skilled labour. Where the increase in the supply of skilled workers has not been rapid enough to meet the demand for skills, the relative position of skilled workers has been maintained. But in many countries, including the UK over the last twenty years, the increase in the supply of skilled workers has not been rapid enough to meet the increased demand. The relative wages of skilled workers have been bid up – leaving those without skills, and particularly manual workers, in a deteriorating labour market position.

The dramatic decline in employment rates of people with relatively low skills [should also be noted]. The widening gap in job prospects between skilled and unskilled men aged 25 to 49 has been particularly dramatic. Only 5 per cent of prime-age men with a degree are not in work, compared to 33 per cent of those with no qualifications . . .

Another long-run trend, intertwined with the decline in the demand for lower skilled workers, has been the shift away from industrial and manual work. Typically, full-time male workers with few educational qualifications, but craft skills specific to their industry, have found their skills made obsolete by structural change. Since the 1960s employment in manufacturing has fallen from around a third of overall employment to around 15 per cent.

There are two main explanations of the deterioration of the labour market prospects of low skilled and manual workers:

- the rapid development and diffusion of new technology, and new forms of work organization, may be biased against those with poor skills; and

- the increase in international trade with countries with a relatively abundant supply of low skilled labour may be putting downward pressure on the demand for low skilled labour in the developed countries.

A wide and expanding academic literature on both these phenomena has highlighted a role for both, but with technological change the more significant.

There is strong evidence that the growth in demand for skilled workers has been associated with the spread of microcomputers and computer-based technologies over the last couple of decades. Although the pace of technological change is certainly not new, it may be that there are particular features of the current wave of technical progress that leave poorly educated workers at a disadvantage relative to those with skills. The tasks which computers currently perform well are routine tasks involving judgement and face to face communication. We would, then, expect to see new technology shifting the relative demand for labour in favour of skilled workers, while increasing the overall levels of growth and productivity.

The best evidence in support of this view is that the increasing demand for skills is very broad-based, occurring within industries and within establishments, rather than just between industrial sectors. Those industries relatively sheltered from international competition have seen changes in the demand for skill, as well as those that are not. Industries with larger investments in research and development, innovation and use of computers have shown the strongest changes in relative demand for skills. There is also evidence that utilization of more skilled workers is complementary with investment in physical capital and the introduction of new technology. The central point here is the evidence suggests the IT revolution, in particular, may be making many traditional unskilled jobs redundant, while increasing the employability of those with skills to make the best use of it.

Source: HM Treasury *Employment Opportunity in a Changing Labour Market* (27 November 1997). Crown Copyright: reproduced with the permission of the Controller of Her Majesty's Stationery Office.

Box 8.2

A strong link between companies' investment in workers and stock market performance is revealed

By Linda Blimes, Konrad Wetzker and Pascal Xhonneux

It is almost a management truism that companies gain a competitive edge by valuing their workers and investing in them. Yet there is little hard evidence to back this up. In one of the first studies of its kind, our analysis of more than 100 German companies reveals a strong link between investing in employees and stock market performance. Companies which place workers at the core of their strategies produce higher long-term returns to shareholders than their industry peers.

Not every successful company invests a great deal in its employees. However, we found that the shares of companies which focus on their workforce outperform competitors who make human resources a low priority.

The research examined companies in 10 industrial sectors, including car manufacturing, banking and pharmaceuticals, over a seven-year period from 1987 to 1994. 'Employee focus' was divided into two components: traditional human-resource policies and opportunities for 'intrapreneurship' within the company. Both of these are

necessary to produce exceptional shareholder value: employee benefits alone will not do the trick.

The first traditional type of employee focus was measured in four ways:

- expenditure per employee on training, and continuing levels of training
- number of lay-offs relative to the industry average and efforts to help relocate redundant employees
- extent to which the corporate philosophy recognizes the contribution of employees as reflected in mission statements and publications
- general human resources policies, including recruitment, performance evaluation and feedback, and promotion opportunities.

'Intrapreneurship' means giving an employee the freedom to take decisions and to maximize the scope for individual initiative within a given job. Four criteria were used to measure the extent to which companies encouraged intrapreneurship:

- flexible work hours

- project organization, including the prevalence of teams, number of levels of hierarchy, and independence of working units
- opportunities for employees to learn skills in new areas, and speed with which a firm can transfer staff to new fields
- extent to which employees share in company performance through profit-sharing, performance pay and bonuses.

The results are striking. In every industry, those companies which scored most highly on these criteria produced a greater 'total shareholder return' (TSR) than their competitors. TSR is the sum of share price increases and dividends over a given period. The companies receiving the lowest scores also produced the lowest TSR in their sector.

We also looked at the data over a shorter four-year period. Even then, the degree to which a company invests in human resources is still a good predictor of stock market success, with those investing most performing best and vice versa.

Source: *Financial Times* 10 February 1997
Reproduced courtesy The Boston Consultancy Group

firms train workers they both enhance the earning potential of those whose skills are upgraded and improve their contribution to the production of goods and services. Recent research in Germany appears to suggest this is the case (see Box 8.2). Firms that add to the human capital of their employees *ceteris paribus* tend to perform better than those that do not.

Minimum wages

In virtually all developed countries, governments choose to intervene in labour markets to set legally enforceable minimum wage rates. In March 1999 the UK government set a new national minimum wage at £3.60 per hour for workers over the age of 21 and a rate of £3.00 per hour for those aged 18–21. In 1983, a Conservative administration had abolished a number of wages councils that set minimum rates in several industries where wage rates are typically low. Why did the Conservatives abolish wage protection, and why was the Labour government so keen to see it restored in this new form? The debate about minimum wages clearly has some *normative* aspects to it. Many people think it is *unfair* of employers to pay workers relatively low wages: low wage rates exploit those who do not have the skills to move up in the labour market. Others argue that governments are wrong to interfere in employment arrangements freely entered into by workers and firms. The *positive* dimension is, however, rather different. The key questions here are:

- Will the establishment of a national minimum wage rate raise the incomes of low-paid workers?
- What will be the effect of a minimum wage on the level of employment; will it create jobs or destroy them?

These questions are closely related. Let us see why by first examining the economic case against the imposition of a national minimum wage. We should begin by putting this issue into context. Remember that we are dealing with not one labour market but many, variously segmented by occupation, geography, industry, gender and so on. Recall also, from the frequency distribution in Fig. 8.9, that the majority of Britain's full-time workers are not in markets where relatively low pay dominates. This means that, on the reasonable assumption that the national minimum wage is intended to raise the pay of those at the bottom of the wage range, *the minimum wage will be an irrelevance in many labour markets*. That said, its opponents argue that where it has an impact, its effect will be to raise the wages of some low-paid workers at the expense of the jobs of other low-paid workers. This conclusion derives from simple market analysis. If, in a given labour market, there is a relatively low *equilibrium* wage rate, any attempt to raise wages will cause the quantity of labour demanded to contract and the quantity supplied to extend. The inevitable cost of the improvement in the wage rate is job loss. Referring back to Fig. 8.1, the reader should be able to verify that any wage rate above W_e will produce an excess supply of labour. Moreover, the higher the minimum wage is above W_e, the greater the resultant excess supply of labour. So, the central conclusions of its critics are that, in markets where it has an impact, the minimum wage will destroy jobs, improve the wages of those still in work, and lower the incomes of those made unemployed. Finally, we should note the claims of some employers that the minimum wage may spill over into labour markets where it has no formal influence. We have seen how skilled workers require compensation in the form of higher wages for the costs of acquiring those skills. This creates a **pay differential** between skilled and unskilled work. If unskilled workers have their wages boosted by a minimum wage the differential that skilled workers enjoy will be partially eroded. In these circumstances skilled workers may press employers to restore lost differentials. To the extent that they are successful, the impact of the minimum wage may ripple through to labour markets where low pay is not an issue.

There are, however, problems with the basic argument that the main economic effect of minimum wage legislation is to destroy jobs. In the first place, it assumes that labour is paid according to the value of its marginal revenue product. This may not always be the case. In Fig. 8.10, the firm's *MRP* curve does not slope smoothly down from left to right in the expected fashion but follows a path with abrupt changes in it. This reflects *indivisibilities* in the employment of labour. Indivisibilities arise when it is not possible to add relatively small amounts of labour to that already employed. According to Shaw (see source of Fig. 8.10 for reference), this limitation may apply particularly to small firms. Take, for example, a firm that employs only two people, both of whom have many years of work experience. This sets their marginal revenue product contributions to the firm at a given level. If the firm were to recruit a third worker who is inexperienced, his or her *MRP* will be at a *level* below

Pay differentials: Exist where there are wage rate premiums attached to particular kinds of work. The most common pay differentials are between skilled and unskilled work.

that of the first two and not, as we have previously assumed, merely on a downward-sloping MRP curve. In terms of Fig. 8.10, the MRP of the first two workers is at W_3, while that of the third is at W_1. Now, if the wage level set in the market is W_2, the firm will set demand at Q_2 and not employ the third worker because his or her MRP is below the wage: this individual's cost of employment would be above the revenue he or she brought in. Notice, however, that the MRP of the first two workers is *above* the market wage level. The point here is that a minimum wage could be set at any level above the market wage and up to W_3, *without causing the firm to reduce its demand for labour.* That government-led changes in wage rates might not have any pronounced impact on the demand for labour is also borne out by experiences in the UK and elsewhere. Thus the noted Conservative abolition of wages councils in 1983 has produced no evidence that new jobs have been created in the affected industries as a result. Moreover, minimum wage legislation in the United States appears not to be a drag on what is generally acknowledged to be one of the most dynamic labour markets in the world.

One point of agreement between those who anticipated that the national minimum

---

Box 8.3

Workers still losing out on minimum wage

By Paul Kelso

Six months after the introduction of national minimum wage legislation, illegal employment practices, insufficient enforcement and a climate of fear among low-paid workers mean that thousands are still not receiving the minimum hourly rate of £3 or £3.60.

Women, particularly those for whom English is not a first language, and younger workers are among those most likely to be underpaid and the problem is particularly acute in the north-west of England, which has a high concentration of low-paid workers . . .

A conference in Manchester to mark the first six months of the national minimum wage . . . heard yesterday that employers had adopted various sharp practices, as well as overt non-payment, and that workers were often too frightened of losing their jobs to make a formal complaint. A TUC submission to the government's low pay commission . . . includes employers understating hours worked on pay slips to make it appear as if the minimum had been paid, and wrongly telling workers they were not eligible for the minimum because they were self-employed, part-time or on piece rates.

The low pay commission reported that a 'significant number' of workers had been dismissed as a result of demanding the rate, while 23% of callers to its minimum wage advice line had either been refused the rate or suffered some reduction in terms and conditions as a result.

A sewing machinist working 60 to 70 hours a week for £1.60, although her pay slip said she was on £3.60 an hour, was dismissed for asking about the minimum wage, as was a cleaner working 72 hours a week for £2.50 an hour. A catering worker paid £3.20 an hour was told the industry was exempt from the rate, and a woman who worked 15 hours a week at £3 per hour was told that only those who work 16 hours a week were eligible . . .

The conference heard that the greatest problem regarding enforcement was the workers' fear of being sacked. 'Low-paid workers who we speak to often say £2.50 an hour and a job is better than no job at all,' said Paul Fairweather of the National Citizens Advice Bureaux . . .

. . . The employers' group, the Confederation of British Industry (CBI), said the minimum wage had not had a significantly adverse impact on the economy, despite predictions of increased unemployment and wage inflation.

In a written assessment to the low pay commission, the CBI said it found little evidence of an impact on employment or average earnings, an insignificant impact on inflation, and 'high' compliance with the legislation. The CBI believes the success is due to the 'prudent' level of £3.60 . . .

Source: *Guardian* 2 October 1999

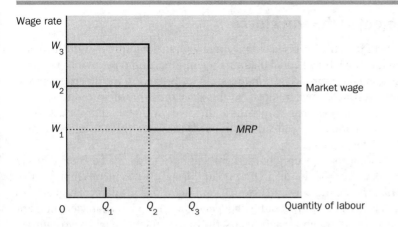

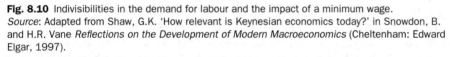

Fig. 8.10 Indivisibilities in the demand for labour and the impact of a minimum wage.
Source: Adapted from Shaw, G.K. 'How relevant is Keynesian economics today?' in Snowdon, B. and H.R. Vane *Reflections on the Development of Modern Macroeconomics* (Cheltenham: Edward Elgar, 1997).

wage in the UK would destroy significant numbers of jobs and those who thought that relatively few jobs would be lost concerned the *level* at which the minimum was to be set: the higher the level, the greater the danger that firms would reduce their demand for labour. In the event, the £3.60 hourly rate has been adjudged 'prudent' even by the previously hostile Confederation of British Industry (CBI), the main employers' organization in the UK. The CBI concedes that the minimum wage has not so far had the negative impact that its critics had predicted. Box 8.3 discusses this and other attitudes to the minimum wage. The box also suggests that unscrupulous employers are finding ways to get around the legislation.

8.6 Human resource management

In Chapter 3, section 3.5, we discussed the objectives of firms. Although the conventional assumption is that firms seek to maximize profits, we also considered alternative objectives such as growth maximization and sales revenue maximization. Human resource management is a key part of the process that helps the firm to achieve its chosen objective. Regardless of what the firm seeks to do, it will require a range of necessary resource inputs such as capital, raw materials and, of course, labour. There are important decisions to be made here. For example, the firm must find workers with the right skills and knowledge and ensure that they are well motivated. This is the role of **human resource management** (HRM). In short, HRM helps firms to determine which people are required and how, as employees, they should be trained and managed.

In what follows we provide a brief overview of the three stages in the HRM process. The first stage is the *recruitment* of the workforce; the second stage is the *management* of the workforce; and the final stage is the *disposal* of the workforce. Note that the precise HRM methods that a firm adopts may vary in line with particular industrial practices or the stage of development of the firm itself.

Human resource management: The employment, training and management of the workforce in order to ensure that the firm is able to achieve its overall objective.

Recruitment of the workforce

The first stage of the HRM process is concerned with making sure that the firm employs the right people. It will entail planning the number and types of jobs required as well as deciding the appropriate remuneration for these jobs. Job descriptions and responsibilities must also be developed. At this stage the firm will introduce a selection process that ensures that it recruits individuals with the appropriate skills, knowledge and experience. Finally, the firm needs to ensure that the selection process is carried out equitably.

When recruiting for a given job, the firm will have to decide whether that job is best *internalised* within the firm (that is, by hiring a permanent employee) or whether to *contract out* the job to an external contractor or consultant. The extent to which a firm chooses to contract out will depend on certain job characteristics. For example, the more infrequently a job occurs, the more attractive it will be to contract out. If the job is internalized there will be a risk of the relevant workers being under-utilized. The greater the frequency of a job or task, the lower is the risk of under-utilization, and hence the greater the likelihood that the job will be internalized. The complexity of a job or task is also important. For simple tasks, where the output is easy to measure, it will usually pay to contract out. However, for more complex tasks, in particular those where quality is crucial, it is often better to internalize. Finally, those tasks that require firm-specific skills (as opposed to job-specific skills) will tend to be internalized. A prime example of a job-specific skill that is often contracted out is information technology. For example, a firm wishing to install a new computer system will tend to use external specialists. Very recently, a large number of firms relied on such specialists and consultants in order to ensure that their information systems were 'millennium bug compatible'.

Management of the workforce

Once the firm has recruited a workforce, it is vital that it is managed effectively. This may entail the development of performance appraisal systems. It will also involve the design of training programmes to ensure that employee skills are up to date, and the introduction of development programmes to enable employees to undertake more responsible jobs. Conventional theory suggests that firms will invest only in the training of non-transferable, or firm-specific, skills. Once the training is complete, both the firm and the employee have a degree of bargaining power. The firm could threaten to dismiss the employee, whose skills would then be of minimal value elsewhere, while the employee could threaten to go on strike. This would impose a cost on the firm, who would need to train another employee. Those skills that are transferable (that is, job specific) would not be provided by the firm. This is because, once training is complete, the firm would need to pay a skilled wage sufficient to prevent the employee from leaving to join a different employer. In such cases the firm would not recoup the training cost. Therefore, whenever such skills are required, the firm will hire skilled workers from outside. Those permanent employees wishing to acquire such job-specific skills would need to fund the training costs themselves. In practice, however, many firms do provide transferable skills. For example, many firms provide financial support for their employees to study on MBA programmes. Such programmes are examples of *benefits in kind*, many of which are not subject to taxation. Offering these packages can be beneficial to both the firm and the employee. Furthermore, by funding training in qualifications such as an MBA, firms can 'screen out' less able candidates. This is because such candidates, who know they may fail the relevant examinations, would not apply in the first instance.

The issue of remuneration is an important one. In section 8.3 we saw that, in a competitive market, workers will be paid at the market-clearing wage rate. However, there is some evidence that firms will often pay a wage rate higher than this. These higher wages are known as **efficiency wages.** Efficiency wages may be paid for a number of reasons. Higher wages can act as a motivational device for employees. The assumption here is that better-paid employees will perform well at work in order to avoid the risk of losing their jobs and having to accept lower wages in a different job. High pay can also raise the quality and quantity of applicants for a particular job, which should result in a higher-quality workforce. Higher pay will also tend to reduce employee turnover, which imposes costs on firms such as the need to advertise posts and train new workers. The theory of efficiency wages is explored in more detail in Chapter 10, section 10.2.

Efficiency wage: A wage rate paid that is above the market-clearing wage rate.

Finally the firm will need to formulate a disciplinary and grievance procedure and consult with the appropriate trade unions on conditions and terms of employment. The management of the workforce would also entail advising employees on health and safety issues.

Disposal of the workforce

The last element of the HRM process is concerned with the termination of employment. Employees may leave a firm for a number of reasons, such as retirement, redundancy, expiry of a fixed-term contract, or dismissal. This stage may involve a number of provisions, including: the design of a redundancy and severance policy; provision of advice for gaining alternative employment; organization of pre-retirement courses; and the development of procedures for dismissal and/or appeals against dismissal.

In summary, HRM is concerned with the effective management of employees in a way that will enable the firm to meet its chosen objective. It is crucial that the firm is able to get the best out of its workforce. Each individual firm will need to develop an HRM framework that is appropriate for its own needs.

8.7 Factor incomes and economic rent

Having discussed the labour market in some detail, we now finally and briefly consider the operation of capital and land markets. As noted at the beginning of this chapter, a number of key principles are common to all factor markets. Thus the demand for capital and land is, like that for labour, a *derived demand*. This means that the notion of marginal revenue product – the change in a firm's total revenue from employing an additional unit of a factor – is again relevant when studying the individual firm's demand for capital and land. It follows that the quantity of capital or land demanded by a profit-maximizing firm will be that which equates the *MRP* of the relevant factor with its price (interest for capital and rent for land). If, for example, the return from the installation of one more machine by a firm exceeds the rate of interest that the firm must pay on the funds it borrows to make this investment, then the investment should proceed. In other words, the firm's *MRP* of capital

Economic rent: Payment to a factor of production above that necessary to retain it in its present use.

Transfer earnings: Payments to a factor necessary to retain it in its present use.

is currently above the price of capital, and the firm can therefore make additional profit by raising its demand for capital. On the other hand, a farmer who rents an extra field on which to grow more crops will break the rental agreement if he or she finds that the price the crop can be sold for is less than the season's rent on the field. Because the *MRP* of land is below its price the demand for land will fall.

While we used basic demand and supply analysis to analyse the labour market, all factor markets can also be studied using the concept of **economic rent**. This is not the same as rent, the reward to land. Economic rent can be earned by *any* factor of production. It is defined as payment to a factor over and above the **transfer earnings** of that factor. Transfer earnings are the payments that the factor requires to remain in its present use. For example, although the best professional footballers are very well paid, because most join a football club straight from school few are qualified to do much else except play football. This means that most of their income is economic rent. Most alternative jobs that they could do will be relatively very poorly paid. The transfer earnings of footballers will therefore be generally low.

Fig. 8.11 depicts three factor markets: for unskilled labour, finance capital and land. Consider first the market for unskilled labour. Supply here is perfectly elastic because the pool of workers is extremely large. At very high levels of supply, it is conceivable that the curve will turn upwards, but for our purposes it remains flat over the relevant range. In this case, the total value of wages paid to labour (the wage rate W_1 multiplied by the number of hours worked) is represented by the rectangle $0W_1AQ_1$. The earnings of labour here are all required transfer earnings: there is no element of economic rent. This is because, for Q_1 hours labour to be supplied, the volume of wages paid must be *exactly* $0W_1AQ_1$. Given that supply is perfectly elastic, if a lower wage was paid no labour would be forthcoming.

The market for finance capital on the other hand has normally sloped demand and supply curves: S and D respectively. At the equilibrium interest rate r_e, the demand and supply of capital is Q_1. The volume of revenue generated for the providers of this amount of capital is the return on it (at the rate r_e). However, notice that the rate r_e is necessary to induce the supply only of the *very last* unit of capital advanced. All the preceding units of capital would still be supplied at rates between r_e and r_1. This means that, except for the last unit, all capital advanced earns economic rent in the form of unnecessarily high rates of return. The transfer earnings, in this case the combination of interest rates that would be *just* sufficient to bring forth a supply of

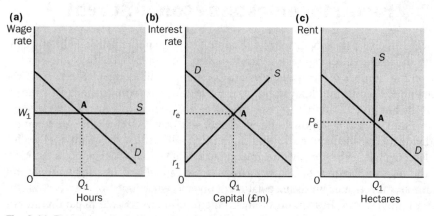

Fig. 8.11 Economic rents in the markets for (a) unskilled labour, (b) capital and (c) land.

Q_1, are given by the quadrilateral r_1AQ_10. Economic rent on the other hand is represented by the triangle r_1Ar_e.

Finally, consider the supply of land. A given piece of land is in fixed supply, which does not vary regardless of the rent paid for it: the land is always supplied. This means the value of the land is *wholly* dependent upon demand, and all of its earnings take the form of economic rent. This explains why land values are exceptionally high in central London relative to places like central Liverpool. In London, intensive demand is forthcoming from business, government and relatively affluent residents; in Liverpool, the levels of demand from the equivalent sources are much lower. In Fig. 8.11, the market for a given piece of land is in equilibrium at rent P_e, with supply at Q_1. Thus the rectangle $0P_eAQ_1$ is pure economic rent. If rent was halved or even set at zero, the land would still be in supply; there are no minimum transfer earnings necessary to induce its supply.

The significance of economic rent lies in its influence on the potential earnings of factors of production. Where no economic rent is earned, as in our unskilled labour market example, factor returns are effectively fixed by *supply considerations* at the level of transfer earnings. There is no scope for improvement unless supply conditions change. At the other extreme, where earnings are all economic rent, returns are wholly *demand driven*. If demand increases then so, commensurably, does economic rent. As modern Premiership footballers know from their own experience, this can be hugely advantageous. Even a moderately talented Premiership footballer can now enjoy millionaire status. How is this possible when only a few years ago such rewards were unthinkable? The answer is that, as noted, footballers' wages are mostly economic rent, and therefore demand driven. The last and most crucial piece in the jigsaw is that the demand for footballers has suddenly ballooned because of the amounts that television companies are willing to pay for the right to screen top football matches. Should programme commissioners grow lukewarm about football, the rewards for footballers will fall back again.

■ Summary

◆ Factor markets, like the markets for goods and services, are governed by the laws of supply and demand. Demand in factor markets is a derived demand: it is dependent upon the demand for the output that factors produce.

◆ The labour market is segmented because of barriers to labour mobility. Labour may be prevented from moving freely between different market segments by the presence of *inter alia* skill or training requirements, the need for natural ability, trade unions, distance, poor information and discrimination.

◆ In the short run, the firm's demand for labour is regulated by the level of the wage. The firm will employ labour up to the point at which the marginal revenue product (*MRP*) of labour and the wage are equal. In the long run, changes in the price of capital and technological advances can affect the *MRP*, which is also the firm's demand curve for labour.

◆ The supply of labour in an economy is governed overall by the rate of population growth. It is also conditioned by a range of social and institutional factors affecting participation rates. In most industrialized countries, the participation rates of women have been rising, while those of men have fallen.

◆ The supply of labour to a market will be positively sloped. The elasticity of labour supply is dependent upon time and the possibility of new workers acquiring the skills or aptitudes necessary to join the market.

◆ The highest market wage rates will be paid to workers in occupations for which there is a strong demand and relatively inelastic supply.

◆ Investing in the right sort of human capital gives workers the best chance of earning a relatively high wage, though it makes sense for firms too to invest in their workers.

◆ In industrial countries such as the UK, minimum wage legislation has no relevance in many labour markets. While, theoretically, minimum wages may help the low paid at the expense of job destruction, the case is not incontrovertible. There is little evidence that they significantly impede the functioning of market processes.

◆ The concept of economic rent helps us to understand why factors in inelastic supply can earn relatively high returns.

■ Key terms

◆ Net advantages
◆ Natural ability
◆ Barriers to labour mobility
◆ Segmented labour markets
◆ Bargaining power
◆ Derived demand
◆ Marginal revenue product
◆ Economically active
◆ Participation rates
◆ Reservation wage
◆ Substitution and income effects
◆ Elasticity of labour supply
◆ Human capital
◆ Minimum wage
◆ Economic rent
◆ Transfer earnings

■ Self-test questions

True (t) or false (f)

1. Generally, wage levels are determined by the interaction of demand and supply.

2. Labour is a fixed factor of production.

3. The marginal revenue product curve is the firm's demand curve for labour.

4. An increase in the price of its output will cause the marginal revenue product curve of a firm to shift to the left.

5. In the advanced economies over the last 30 years, the participation rates of women in the labour market have increased while those for men have decreased.

6. The reservation wage is the wage at which people decide to move between jobs.

7. When the income effect dominates, the individual's supply of labour will fall as the wage rate increases.

8. Accountants, solicitors and other professionals are highly paid because they are relatively few in number *and* because of the high prices paid for the services that they offer.

9. The economic case is clear: minimum wages legislation destroys jobs.

10. Economic rent is payment to a factor of production above that necessary to retain it in its present use.

Complete the following sentences by inserting the missing word(s)

1. The demand for labour is a _____ demand.

2. The additional output produced by a worker is called the _____.

3. The quantity of labour demanded by a firm equates the marginal revenue product of labour with the _____.

4. The individual's supply of labour is subject to _____ and _____ effects.

5. The minimum rate required to induce an individual to accept a job is called the _____.

6. The elasticity of labour supply measures the responsiveness of the quantity of labour supplied to changes in the _____.

7. The reserve of skill and knowledge that a worker can gather is called _____.

8. The argument that wage levels in a particular occupation are too low is a _____ argument.

9. The payments necessary to retain a factor in its present use are called _____.

10. When the earnings of a factor are composed entirely of economic rent, they are entirely driven by _____.

◼ Questions for discussion

◆ Why is the concept of labour market segmentation useful in explaining wage rate variation between occupations?

◆ Why is the demand for labour a derived demand, and how does this influence our analysis of the demand for labour by a firm?

◆ Which factors govern the supply of labour in an economy?

◆ Which factors govern the supply of labour to the German building industry? (Hint: labour migration may be important here.)

◆ Your ability to read this book is in part a reflection of the skills of the primary school teachers who taught you to read. Why should a job as socially, culturally and economically important as teaching young children be so poorly rewarded relative to the jobs done by Alan Shearer, 'Sting' and Jeffrey Archer?

◾ Further reading

Penn, R., M. Rose and J. Rubery *Skill and Occupational Change* (Oxford: Oxford University Press, 1994). Presents the findings of detailed research on the nature of job change in the UK in the 1980s.

Ferner, A. and R. Hyman (eds) *Changing Industrial Relations in Europe* (Oxford: Basil Blackwell, 1998). Provides a contemporary overview of European industrial relations and labour market issues.

Adnett, N. *The European Labour Market* (2nd ed.) (Harlow: Addison Wesley Longman). Reviews employment and employment policy issues in a European context.

Jacobsen, J.P. *The Economics of Gender* (2nd ed.) (Oxford: Basil Blackwell, 1998). Considers the differences between women's and men's economic opportunities, activities and rewards

◾ Internet links

The *Policy Studies Institute* (PSI) is an independent organization that undertakes research into public policy. One of the PSI's research groups looks at employment issues. All of the PSI's work can be accessed via its website at: **http://www.psi.org. uk/index.htm**

The *International Labour Organization*, founded upon the basis of humanitarian concerns for the rights of workers and now also concerned to promote full employment and the raising of living standards, has a website with some online information and a wealth of sources of further reading on labour market issues. The site is at: **http:// www.ilo.org/**

The Macroeconomy, Macroeconomic Policy and Business

CHAPTER 9

Key issues

► What are the main objectives of macroeconomic policy?

► What is the nature of each of these objectives, and how can they be measured?

► What are the costs of failing to achieve each objective?

► What potential conflicts exist between the main objectives of macroeconomic policy?

Contents

9.1 Introduction: the macroeconomic context of business

The first half of this book dealt with **microeconomics**. It will be recalled that this involves the study of the behaviour and performance of individual units within the economy, such as the individual market, consumer, firm and worker. **Macro-economics**, the subject matter of the second half of the book, is concerned with the study of the behaviour and performance of the economy as a whole. Thus, for example, the microeconomic focus upon the level of output in particular markets is generalized at the macro level into an analysis of the overall or *aggregate* level of output produced in the economy. Similarly, micro analyses of the number of people employed in particular markets are, in macro terms, transformed into concerns about the total levels of employment and unemployment in the economy.

While macroeconomics takes in the complete picture of the way in which the economy works, it is important to recognize at the outset that such a broad approach is also associated with the loss of some detail. An analysis of the general trend in the level of unemployment, for example, inevitably glosses over possible unevenness in its distribution. Thus, in both the UK and the EU as a whole, there are long-established concerns over sharp differences in regional unemployment rates. This kind of problem is not immediately apparent from an inspection of aggregate data on unemployment. Similarly, while an increase in national output is usually to be applauded, we

Macroeconomics: The study of the economy as a whole.

Macroeconomic policies:
Policies used by governments
to try to influence overall
economic performance.

might also have a legitimate interest in how the extra output is shared out. The macro focus tends to neglect this in its preoccupation with the output total.

The profitability of business is critically affected by the macroeconomic environment in which firms operate. By way of illustration, imagine, for example, a situation in which an economy is experiencing an upturn in the level of domestic economic activity. During an upturn, output improves and unemployment falls, and the potential for firms to raise their profits increases. However, as demand increases, upward pressure on wage costs and prices may have a damaging effect on sales performance and hence on business profitability. As the price of domestic goods increases, domestic customers may switch their expenditure towards buying more imported foreign goods. Domestic firms may also lose custom from declining export sales as their goods become less competitive abroad. Such changes in the macroeconomic environment may have further consequences. Long-term investment decisions may be adversely affected as greater uncertainty (over both future income flow and the rate of interest) diminishes firms' incentive to invest.

Given the importance of the macroeconomic environment to business it is *crucial* that students taking degree course in subject areas such as business studies and management studies understand what causes changes in the macroeconomy and what influence government policy has on the macroeconomic environment. **Macroeconomic policy** is concerned with the attempts of policy-makers to influence the behaviour of macroeconomic aggregates in order to improve the overall performance of the economy. As subsequent chapters will make clear, there is much debate and controversy surrounding the appropriate mix of policies required to improve economic performance.

The remainder of this book is organized as follows. In Chapter 10 we examine the debate over the cause of, and cure for, unemployment and inflation. In Chapter 11 we consider what factors determine economic growth over time, and the different theories that economists have put forward to explain short-term fluctuations in aggregate economic activity. In Chapter 12 we discuss the continuing debate amongst economists over the issue of whether the authorities need to, can and should stabilize the macroeconomy. In the final four chapters we turn to a more detailed consideration of the international macroeconomic environment. In Chapter 13 we consider such key issues as the gains from international trade, the changing patterns of international trade in the post-war period, and how international trade policy has unfolded since 1945. In Chapter 14 we explain what factors affect exports and imports, how exchange rates are determined, and the main forms of exchange rate policy. In Chapter 15 we examine the activities of multinational firms, including patterns of multinational activity, why multinationals exist, and government policy towards multinational firms. Finally in Chapter 16 we consider the globalization debate and reflect on whether or not it is appropriate to make reference to a global economy.

The purpose of this present chapter is to provide a background context to the more detailed discussion of macroeconomics that follows in Chapters 10–16. In particular we shall examine the four *main* objectives of government macroeconomic policy: namely, the pursuit of

- a stable and satisfactory rate of economic growth
- a high and stable level of employment
- a low and stable rate of inflation
- medium-term balance of payments equilibrium.

In each case we describe the nature of the objective and indicate why it is thought to be desirable. We also briefly consider the extent to which these policy goals can be achieved simultaneously. The chapter concludes with a brief historical overview of the changing policy priorities that have operated at the macro level since the end of the Second World War.

9.2 Economic growth

Economic well-being or *welfare* is a decisively materialist concept. In a micro context, we have seen that the amount of goods and services that an individual is able to consume is the exclusive criterion of satisfaction: 'more is better'. At the macroeconomic level a similar logic applies: the greater the level of output produced and consumed in an economy, the higher will be its living standards in relation to a given population. One way of measuring overall economic performance is to aggregate – just add up – the value of goods and services produced in a country over a given time period, usually a year. The total that results is known as the **gross domestic product** or **GDP**.

GDP, which is the total value of goods and services produced in a country by the factors of production located in that country – regardless of who owns these factors – can be measured in *three* different ways:

- First, it can be measured by aggregating the value of **final output** of new goods and services (cars, video recorders, food, haircuts, etc.) produced within an economy over a given time period (usually a year). The output method involves summing the *net* output of all industries in the economy by estimating the *value added* by each industry to the final output of goods and services produced. For example, the value added by the car industry can be defined as the value of cars produced minus the value of its inputs (iron and steel, glass, etc.) from other industries. For the economy as a whole, imports are inputs and are therefore excluded from GDP, while exports are included in GDP.

- Second, GDP can also be measured by summing the incomes paid to the factors of production (that is, the wages of labour, profits of capital and rent of land and property) used to produce the total output of goods and services. The income method involves measuring GDP at factor cost: that is, what it costs to pay the factors of production that are used to produce the total output of goods and services.

- Finally, GDP can be measured by adding together the expenditure made on final goods and services, including expenditure by foreigners on exported goods and services, and excluding purchases of imported goods and services from abroad by domestic residents. The expenditure method initially measures GDP at market prices: that is, the prices at which final goods and services are purchased. Subtracting indirect taxes on expenditure and adding subsidies provides a measure of GDP at factor cost in line with those obtained from the output and income methods.

Before turning to discuss the relationship between the three methods of measuring GDP it is worth pointing out that one further adjustment is required to GDP to provide a measure known as **gross national product (GNP)**, the main measure of national income or national output in a country. As noted, GDP measures the total value of goods and services produced in a country by the factors of production

Gross domestic product: The total value of goods and services produced in a country by the factors of production located in that country.

Final output: Goods and services that are sold to their ultimate users.

Gross national product: The value of final goods and services produced by domestically owned factors of production.

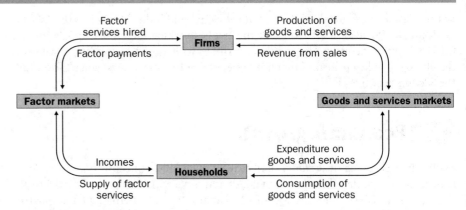

Fig. 9.1 The circular flow of income.

located in that country *regardless* of who owns them. If net property income (that is, receipts of income from assets and property owned and held abroad, minus corresponding payments made to overseas residents) is added to GDP it provides the measure known as gross national product.

The relationship between the three methods of measuring GDP can be visualized using a circular flow of income diagram (see Fig. 9.1). For ease of exposition, we assume initially that there is no government sector or foreign trade sector. In our highly simplified economy there are only two sectors that contribute to the flow of goods and services: firms and households. Households consume a range of goods and services produced by firms. In order to produce these goods and services, firms hire the services of factors of production (labour, capital and land) in factor markets from households. Payments made by firms to the factors of production (wages, profits and rent) flow as incomes to households. Households then spend their incomes on the goods and services produced by firms in goods and services markets. Household expenditure flows back to firms in the form of revenue that firms receive from the sales of final goods and services to households. In Fig. 9.1 a real flow of factor services, and of goods and services, repeatedly circulates around the economy in a clockwise direction between households and firms. This real flow is matched by repeated corresponding money flows of incomes and expenditure from firms to households in an anticlockwise direction. If households spent *all* their incomes on firms' final output of goods and services, and firms used *all* the revenue they received from such sales to buy factor services from households, then income would continuously flow around the economy at an unchanged level.

We now drop our initial simplifying assumptions and consider how this circular flow of income is affected when an economy has both a government sector and a foreign trade sector. In doing so we find that there are three main injections of income into the circular flow depicted in Fig. 9.1. First, firms sell some of their output abroad to foreigners. Clearly the revenue from such export sales (X) enters into the circular flow as an injection of income. Second, government expenditure (G) on the purchase of goods and services is an injection of income into the circular flow. Such expenditure includes both current expenditure on goods and services (for example, expenditure on the incomes paid to public sector employees) and capital expenditure (for example, expenditure on hospital building). Transfer payments (such as expenditure on unemployment benefits), which are transfers between different sections of the community, are excluded as they are not paid out in return for the production of goods and services. Third, private-sector investment expenditure (I) enters the circular flow as an injection of income. Such expenditure includes purchases of *fixed investment* (as in plant and machinery, for example), *inventory investment* (for example, increases in stocks of finished goods that have not yet been sold) and *residential investment* (that is, purchases of new houses). Total injections of income into the circular flow therefore consist of private-sector investment expenditure (I), government expenditure (G) and exports (X).

Just as there are three main injections of income into the circular flow so too there are three main withdrawals from the circular income flow depicted in Fig. 9.1. First, both households and firms purchase imported goods and services (M) from abroad. Such expenditure is a withdrawal from the circular flow of income. Second, households and firms are unable to spend all the income they receive via the circular flow since they have to pay taxes (T) to the government. Third, some income is taken out of the circular flow through savings (S). Total withdrawals from the circular income flow consist of savings (S), taxes (T) and imports (M). If injections are greater than withdrawals, the level of income will rise, and vice versa. Income will circulate at an unchanged level only when total injections are exactly matched by total withdrawals. The importance of this equilibrium condition will be discussed more fully in Chapter 10, section 10.2. In summary, the sum total of value added by all industries in the economy is equal to the sum total of all incomes derived from producing the total output of goods and services by factors of production and the sum total of expenditure made on the final output of goods and services produced in the economy. The output, income and expenditure methods are merely different ways of measuring the same circular flow illustrated in Fig. 9.1 after allowing for injections and withdrawals.

It is important to stress that, while economists use data on GDP to measure economic growth, economic growth refers to an increase in **real GDP**. The money or nominal value of GDP may change from one year to the next because of a change in the quantity of goods and services actually being produced and/or a change in the price of goods and services. **Nominal GDP** measures GDP at the prices prevailing at the time. Real GDP measures GDP at the prices prevailing in some particular *base* year. GDP at constant prices (real GDP) will change only if there has been a change in the quantity of goods and services actually produced.

Fig. 9.2 depicts the movement of real GDP (at 1995 prices) for the UK economy since 1948 showing the change in the actual *volume* of goods and services produced. We can make two observations concerning the way in which real GDP has changed over this period. First, the established trajectory of real GDP is clearly upwards. This means that, over the long term, domestic output and income in the UK have tended to increase incrementally. **Economic growth** refers to an increase in real GDP, while the annual percentage change in real GDP is known as the *rate* of economic growth. As we shall see, *long-term* growth in output can be observed in most economies (Table 9.1 describes the growth performances of the **G7** economies since 1970) and reflects changes in factors such as the form and use of technology in new capital equipment, refinements in the organization of production and increases in the supply of labour. Second, however, it is evident from Fig. 9.2 that there are a number of periods when the real GDP growth path moves decisively away from its long-term trend. In some cases real GDP actually falls, indicating a reduction in the output total in comparison with earlier achievements. Reference to Table 9.1 reveals that,

Real GDP: The value of gross domestic product measured in terms of the prices that prevailed in some particular base year; also known as GDP in constant prices.

Nominal GDP: The value of gross domestic product measured in terms of the prices prevailing at the time; also known as GDP in current prices.

Economic growth: An increase in real GDP over time.

G7: The group of seven main industrial economies in the world: the USA, Japan, Germany, France, Italy, UK and Canada.

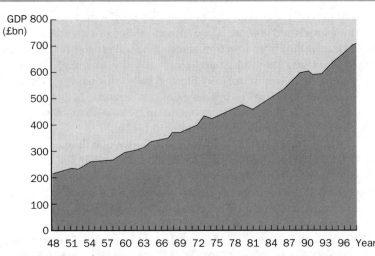

Fig. 9.2 UK real GDP 1948–98, 1995 prices (£bn).
Source: Economic Trends Annual Supplement 1999.

Recession: Entails a decline in real GDP that lasts for at least two consecutive quarters of a year.

for the UK, periods of negative growth can be observed in 1974–75 and 1980–81, following the quadrupling of oil prices by the Organization of Petroleum Exporting Countries (OPEC) in 1973–74 and the second OPEC oil price increase in 1979, together with the introduction of the Conservative Government's anti-inflation strategy at the start of the 1980s. The most recent period of **recession** in the UK occurred in 1991–92. In 1991 real GDP fell by 1.5 per cent. By contrast, there are also several instances of relatively rapid economic growth, or boom, when real GDP moves sharply above its trend. In the period 1985–88, for example, real GDP in the UK grew at an annual average rate of 4.4 per cent.

The presence of a long-term growth trend mixed with such short-term fluctuations gives rise to the question of *what is a desirable or appropriate rate of economic growth*. If rapid growth generally equates with strongly rising living standards, should government policy not have as one of its prime objectives the pursuit of as fast a rate of growth as is possible? Similarly, given that severe recessions are associated with falling output and a drop in the standard of living as fewer goods and services are produced and consumed, should governments not seek to avoid such episodes at all costs? In answering these questions it is important to be clear about certain constraints under which government policy operates in both the long and the short term. As noted, the long-term growth path reflects, amongst other things, the technological and organizational sophistication of production, together with the volume of inputs – such as labour – that it is able to command (see Chapter 11, section 11.2). Because of their very nature, governments can influence these so-called *supply-side* factors only gradually over time. This means that the established trend in economic growth can be conditioned upwards only very slowly.

However, *short-term* growth is much more open to the influence of government policy (see Chapter 11, section 11.6). Thus governments may try to engineer faster growth in periods before elections in order to curry favour with voters. Why then can they not sustain the rate of expansion over a longer period? One answer is that they are *constrained by other macroeconomic policy objectives*. A high rate of growth, for example, results in higher incomes, some of the increases in which people may

Table 9.1 Growth in real GDP for the G7, 1970–98

	United States	Canada	Japan	France	Germany	Italy	United Kingdom
1970	0.1	2.6	9.4	7.2	4.9	5.3	2.4
1971	3.3	5.8	4.2	4.8	3.0	1.9	2.0
1972	5.5	5.7	8.4	4.4	4.3	2.9	3.6
1973	5.8	7.7	7.9	5.4	4.8	6.5	7.3
1974	−0.6	4.4	−1.2	3.1	0.3	4.7	−1.7
1975	−0.4	2.6	2.6	−0.3	−1.3	−2.1	−0.7
1976	5.4	6.2	4.8	4.2	4.9	6.5	2.8
1977	4.7	3.6	5.3	3.2	3.0	2.9	2.4
1978	5.4	4.6	5.1	3.3	3.1	3.7	3.4
1979	2.8	3.9	5.2	3.2	4.3	5.7	2.8
1980	−0.3	1.5	3.6	1.6	1.0	3.5	−2.2
1981	2.3	3.7	3.6	1.2	0.1	0.5	−1.3
1982	−2.1	−3.2	3.2	2.5	−1.0	0.5	1.8
1983	4.0	3.2	2.7	0.7	1.7	1.2	3.7
1984	7.0	6.3	4.3	1.3	2.8	2.6	2.4
1985	3.6	4.8	5.0	1.9	2.3	2.8	3.8
1986	3.1	3.3	2.6	2.5	2.3	2.8	4.2
1987	2.9	4.3	4.1	2.3	1.4	3.1	4.4
1988	3.8	4.9	6.2	4.5	3.6	3.9	5.2
1989	3.4	2.4	4.7	4.3	3.7	2.9	2.1
1990	1.2	−0.2	4.8	2.5	5.7	2.2	0.6
1991	−0.9	−1.8	3.8	0.8	13.2	1.1	−1.5
1992	2.7	0.8	1.0	1.2	2.2	0.6	0.1
1993	2.3	2.3	0.3	−1.3	−1.2	−1.2	2.3
1994	3.5	4.7	0.6	2.8	2.9	2.2	4.4
1995	2.3	2.8	1.5	2.1	1.9	2.9	2.8
1996	3.4	1.7	3.9	1.1	1.3	0.7	2.6
1997	3.9	4.0	0.9	2.0	2.0	1.5	3.5
1998	3.9	3.1	–	3.2	1.9	1.4	2.1

Source: International Monetary Fund *International Financial Statistics Yearbook* (1999)

choose to spend on imported goods and services from abroad. If the higher import bill is not matched by increased export earnings, a balance of payments deficit problem may emerge. As we shall see, balance of payments deficits must ultimately be corrected, and therefore a more moderate rate of economic growth may have to be actively sought. Periods of rapid expansion can also be associated with higher rates of inflation and, again, policy to trim the rate of economic expansion might be necessary in order to help bring inflation down towards more tolerable levels. It is interesting to note that the historically high rates of growth experienced in the UK in the late 1980s were associated with both balance of payments and inflationary problems, and that these were subsequently addressed by the 1991–92 recession.

Though governments are constrained from operating the economy at short-term growth rates far above the long-run growth trend, it will be equally evident that there is no advantage in accepting meagre expansion below this trend. Slower short-term growth will entail only marginal increases in output and income for the economy as a whole and – in consequence – minimal improvements in living standards. Moreover, if growth becomes negative it is likely to be associated with higher levels of unemployment as falling output prompts firms to reduce the number of people they employ.

If there are constraints on the extent to which the rate of economic growth can be raised in the short term, and it is also recognized that slow growth may possess some serious disadvantages, what can be said about the objective of macroeconomic policy in respect of growth? Generally it is accepted that governments should aspire to a *satisfactory* rate of economic growth. As a policy target, 'satisfactory growth' may appear a little vague or imprecise, but let us briefly consider its meaning in the context of our earlier discussion. A wildly variable rate of economic expansion, oscillating between rapid growth, which has to be curtailed because of its adverse inflationary and/or balance of payments implications, and severe recession, which is associated with rising unemployment and falling living standards, would clearly not be desirable. This suggests that a satisfactory rate is one that is *economically sustainable in the light of the broader framework of macroeconomic objectives.*

The comparative performance of similarly advanced industrial economies might also be considered to be important when attempting to assess the adequacy of a given growth rate. Table 9.1 compares real GDP growth rates since 1970 for the so-called *G7* group of the world's largest industrial economies: the United States, Japan, Germany, France, Italy, the United Kingdom and Canada. It is apparent from the data contained in the table that the Japanese economy has the best record of real output growth amongst these countries over the period concerned. The United Kingdom's performance is the poorest of the seven, and as such may be considered to be unsatisfactory in relative terms.

Finally in this section we note some qualifications regarding the use of real GDP as a proxy measure or indicator of living standards. As we have seen, real GDP provides a simple measure of the overall economic performance of a country in terms of its material output of goods and services. However, a more reliable indicator of average personal living standards is provided by data on real GDP *per capita*. Real GDP per capita is real GDP divided by the total population of the country. For any given level of real GDP the smaller the population the more goods and services are available for each person in the economy. Real GDP per head will remain constant only if real GDP is growing at exactly the same rate as the population of the country. If the real GDP of a country is growing at a slower rate than its population, then real GDP per head will fall, and vice versa. As we shall discuss in Chapter 11, section 11.3, the rate at which a country's population grows can help to explain its standard of living.

Furthermore, while real GDP per capita figures provide a rough indicator of average living standards they don't tell us anything about the *distribution* of income in a country or how that distribution changes over time. This is an important consideration that needs to be borne in mind when using real GDP per capita figures as an indicator of average personal living standards. Real GDP per capita would only provide a reliable measure of what each person in the economy actually received if income was equally distributed among the total population of a country. Aside from these qualifications it is also important to reflect briefly on whether data on real

GDP, and real GDP per capita, provide a complete picture of economic welfare and quality of life in a country. Here we note two main problems. First, data on real GDP do not include non-market activities, such as leisure. People's happiness depends not only on the consumption of material goods and services but also on the amount of time spent at leisure. Second, data on real GDP do not include the output of negative **externalities** (see Chapter 7, section 7.4) such as pollution, traffic congestion and noise, all of which have an adverse effect on happiness and the welfare of people living in a country. In summary, given these two most fundamental omissions, it is important to remember that figures on real GDP provide only a *crude* measure of national economic welfare.

9.3 Unemployment

An internationally recognized definition of unemployment considers the **unemployed** to be people of working age who are jobless but who are both available for work and actively seeking employment. Note that the definition requires *active* participation in the labour market on the part of the unemployed: the unemployed person's situation must impact upon overall market processes. The **unemployment rate** is the proportion of the total labour force (the total of those employed and unemployed) whose members are currently out of work. Unemployment is measured at a point in time. Whether or not the level of unemployment changes over time depends on flows into and out of a pool of unemployed labour. As illustrated in Fig. 9.3 there are six main inflows. Four of these inflows involve people previously employed who become unemployed because they are made redundant, are fired or sacked,

Unemployed people: Those available for work and actively seeking jobs but unable to find them.

Unemployment rate: The percentage of the labour force unemployed.

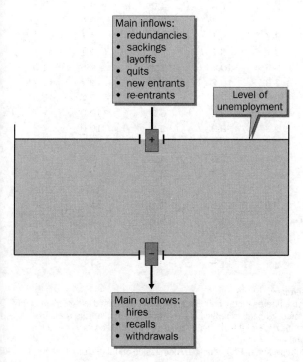

Fig. 9.3 The main inflows into and outflows from a pool of unemployed labour.

temporarily laid off, or voluntarily quit their existing job. Two further inflows into the pool of unemployed labour involve people not previously in the labour force who are now looking for work, namely new entrants (such as school leavers) and re-entrants (for example, people who have raised a family and are now returning to the labour force). There are three main outflows from the pool of unemployed labour. Some people previously unemployed find new jobs, some who have been temporarily laid off are recalled, while others withdraw from the labour force (perhaps upon retirement, or because, disheartened at the prospect of ever finding work, they stop actively seeking employment).

Table 9.2 Standardized unemployment rates for the G7, 1970–98 (per cent of civilian labour force)

	United States	Canada	Japan	France	Germany[a]	Italy	United Kingdom
1970	4.8	5.6	1.1	2.5	0.8	5.3	3.0
1971	5.8	6.1	1.2	2.7	0.9	5.3	3.6
1972	5.5	6.2	1.4	2.8	0.8	6.3	4.0
1973	4.8	5.5	1.3	2.7	0.8	6.2	3.0
1974	5.5	5.3	1.4	2.8	1.6	2.9	5.3
1975	8.3	6.9	1.9	4.0	3.6	5.8	4.3
1976	7.6	7.1	2.0	4.4	3.7	6.6	5.6
1977	6.9	8.1	2.0	4.9	3.6	7.0	6.0
1978	6.1	8.4	2.2	4.7	3.0	5.3	5.7
1979	5.8	7.5	2.1	5.3	2.7	5.8	4.7
1980	7.2	7.5	2.0	5.8	2.6	5.6	6.2
1981	7.6	7.6	2.2	7.0	4.0	6.2	9.7
1982	9.7	11.1	2.4	7.7	5.7	6.8	11.1
1983	9.6	11.9	2.7	8.1	6.9	7.7	11.1
1984	7.5	11.3	2.7	9.7	7.1	8.1	11.1
1985	7.2	10.5	2.6	10.1	7.2	8.5	11.5
1986	7.0	9.6	2.8	10.2	6.5	9.2	11.5
1987	6.2	8.8	2.8	10.4	6.3	9.9	10.6
1988	5.5	7.8	2.5	9.8	6.2	10.0	8.7
1989	5.3	7.5	2.3	9.3	5.6	10.0	7.3
1990	5.6	8.2	2.1	9.0	4.8	9.1	7.1
1991	6.8	10.4	2.1	9.5	4.2	8.8	8.8
1992	7.5	11.3	2.2	10.4	4.5	9.0	10.1
1993	6.9	11.2	2.5	11.7	7.9	10.3	10.5
1994	6.1	10.4	2.9	12.3	8.4	11.4	9.6
1995	5.6	9.5	3.2	11.7	8.2	11.9	8.7
1996	5.4	9.7	3.4	12.4	8.9	12.0	8.2
1997	4.9	9.2	3.4	12.3	9.9	12.0	7.0
1998	4.5	8.3	4.1	11.7	9.4	11.9	6.3

[a] Prior to 1993 data refers to West Germany.
[b] The data for standardized unemployment rates for the period 1970–77 are expressed as a percent of the total (rather than the civilian) labour force. With the exception of Italy there is no marked change in the recorded unemployment rates so that the data for the other six economies can be read as if they are a consistent series over the entire period.
Source: OECD Economic Outlook (various issues). Reproduced by permission of the OECD.

Table 9.2 summarizes the recent experience of unemployment in the G7 economies. Four points emerge from the trends evident in the table. First, the best and most consistent record is that of Japan. The Japanese unemployment rate over the whole period (with the exception of 1998) remains below 3.5 per cent. Second, amongst the European countries, though all rates increased during the 1980s in particular, unemployment in Germany on average has been lower than the general levels experienced in the UK, France and Italy. Third, in the post-1993 period, when the former East Germany is assimilated into the data, unemployment rates in Germany have increased markedly. Finally, unemployment in the USA has also been relatively stable but at a higher average rate than in Japan. We should also emphasize that the data in the table convey only the broadest picture of the course of unemployment in each country. The more detailed nuances of its distribution by age, gender, social class and locale must be left to finer, more disaggregate analyses.

Unemployment is a serious policy problem for both economic and social reasons. Economics, as we know from Chapter 1, is concerned with resource allocation: how are the resources a society has being used; are they being used as well as they might be? Unemployment means that a proportion of one particular resource, perhaps the most important one, labour, is not put to any use whatsoever. This waste is compounded by the need to devote still more resources, such as the money tied up in the benefits system, to alleviate the plight of the unemployed; and by the loss of tax revenue to the state that unemployed people would contribute if they had jobs. Far better, from an economic perspective, to have a situation in which all who are willing to work have the opportunity to do so. In such circumstances, the welfare or well-being – defined by higher incomes and consumption levels – of individuals who might otherwise be unemployed is raised.

For society as a whole, greater employment means more people producing more output, thereby adding to real GDP. As is evident from Tables 9.1 and 9.2 the spectacular contemporary growth performance of the Japanese economy and the low Japanese unemployment rate is not a coincidence. By contrast, lower employment means fewer people producing less output, thereby reducing real GDP. For example, for the US economy it has been estimated that every 1 per cent increase in unemployment reduces the level of real output by 2.25 per cent.

The social and economic problems associated with unemployment fall into two main categories: those that impact directly upon the unemployed themselves, and those that are borne by society as a whole. The first and most obvious burden of unemployment for the individual is financial hardship. Though there is relatively wide variation in the benefit levels set in, for example, the major European countries, in most cases the benefits paid to the unemployed are substantially below the average level of wages. Low incomes may be the precursor of a further set of difficulties for the unemployed and their families: poor standards of health and educational underachievement, for example. Long-term unemployment in particular is also recognized to have significant psychological consequences, such as increased stress and low self-esteem, for those it afflicts. The wider social costs of unemployment arise because a proportion of the population is, or may perceive itself to be, economically and socially disenfranchised from the mainstream. If some people feel excluded from society and the kinds of material welfare that it appears to offer to the majority, then a range of consequences may emerge: increases in political and racial tension and rising crime and delinquency have all been associated with higher levels of unemployment.

Unemployment is clearly a serious macroeconomic problem, and the objective of

Full employment: A situation in which all unemployment is frictional and structural, and cannot be reduced by increasing aggregate demand.

Structural unemployment: Unemployment that arises from a mismatch between the skills or location of existing job vacancies and the present skills or location of the unemployed; also known as mismatch unemployment.

Frictional unemployment: Unemployment that arises because it takes time for workers to search for suitable jobs; also known as search unemployment.

Inflation: A situation in which the overall or general level of prices rises over time.

Inflation rate: The rate at which the general level of prices increases; expressed as a percentage on an annual basis.

Price index: A measure of the average level of prices of a set of goods and services relative to the prices of the same goods and services in a particular base year.

policy in this area, noted at the beginning of the chapter, is to maintain a high and stable level of employment. However, the notion of **full employment** does not mean that every member of the working population will always be in a job. Clearly, in a dynamic and changing economy, as new industries emerge and older ones mature, there will be a periodic refocusing of employment opportunity. This is likely to give rise to **structural unemployment** (see Chapter 10, section 10.2) as some workers, newly released from declining industries, may not have the skills and aptitudes demanded by employers in industries that are growing and offering new employment opportunities. Over time the required skills can be learned, and people can then move back into work. In this sense, structural unemployment may be considered to be a consequence of changes that inevitably occur in a dynamic economy. Similarly, it might be expected that, even in the absence of any structural economic shifts, a competitive labour market will embrace a fair degree of fluidity as people move from job to job, seeking promotion, new challenges or new working environments. In the midst of the many job changes that are constantly taking place in the economy, some people will find themselves temporarily unemployed or *between* jobs for a short period: this is known as **frictional unemployment** (see Chapter 10, section 10.2).

In a competitive and ever-changing economy some unemployment is inevitable: the question is, how much? In the UK, for example, full employment in the 1950s and 1960s was associated with an achieved level of unemployment of around 2.5 to 3 per cent. However, since the mid-1970s the UK, along with most of the G7 economies, has experienced a significant rise in the level of unemployment. As is evident from Table 9.2, this is particularly the case for the (cited) European economies in the 1980s. In Chapter 10, sections 10.2–10.3, we consider possible reasons why unemployment has risen, what level is now believed to be consistent with full employment, and the range of policies open to governments to reduce unemployment.

9.4 Inflation

Inflation is a process of continually rising prices. The **inflation rate** in an economy thus denotes the pace at which the price of goods and services on average has risen over a given period of time. Though negative inflation (deflation) is possible, the experience in most economies since 1945 is that of positive inflation. As for other macroeconomic variables, inflation is calculated on an annual basis. Inflation is measured by reference to movements in an **index** of prices. A wide range of price indices may be used, including the Retail Price Index (which seeks to measure movements in the cost of a 'basket' of goods and services bought by a typical household), the Index of Producer Prices, and the implicit GDP deflator (which seeks to measure movements in the prices of all goods and services produced by dividing GDP valued at current prices by GDP at constant prices). All index numbers relate to a particular base year: for example, 1995 = 100. Once an index has been constructed the *rate* of inflation can be measured by calculating the percentage change in the index from one year to the next. For example, if an index stood at a value of 120 in 1997 and at a value of 135 in 1998, then between 1997 and 1998, prices on average would have risen at a rate of 12.5 per cent. The rate of inflation between 1997 and 1998 is calculated as follows: $((135-120)/120) \times 100 = 12.5$ per cent. If the index stood at 148.5 in 1999, then although the average level of prices would have risen, the rate of inflation would have fallen to 10 per cent, that is $((148.5-135)/135) \times 100 = 10$ per cent.

Table 9.3 Consumer prices for selected economies, 1970–98 (per cent)

	United States	Canada	Japan	France	Germany	Italy	Mexico	Iceland	United Kingdom
1970	5.8	3.4	7.7	5.2	3.4	5.0	na	13.6	6.4
1971	4.3	2.8	6.1	5.5	5.3	4.8	na	6.6	9.4
1972	3.3	4.8	4.5	6.2	5.5	5.7	na	9.7	7.1
1973	6.2	7.6	11.7	7.3	6.9	10.8	na	20.6	9.2
1974	11.1	10.9	24.5	13.7	7.0	19.1	na	42.9	16.0
1975	9.1	10.8	11.8	11.8	6.0	17.0	na	49.1	24.2
1976	5.7	7.5	9.4	9.6	4.6	16.7	15.8	28.9	16.5
1977	6.5	8.0	8.2	9.4	3.7	19.3	29.1	30.3	15.8
1978	7.6	8.9	4.2	9.1	2.7	12.4	17.5	43.8	8.3
1979	11.3	9.1	3.7	10.8	4.0	15.7	18.2	44.4	13.4
1980	13.5	10.2	7.8	13.6	5.4	21.2	25.8	58.8	18.0
1981	10.3	12.4	4.9	13.3	6.3	19.3	28.2	50.6	11.9
1982	6.1	10.8	2.7	12.0	5.2	16.4	58.7	50.0	8.6
1983	3.2	5.9	1.9	9.5	3.3	14.9	102.3	85.2	4.6
1984	4.3	4.3	2.3	7.7	2.4	10.6	65.3	28.9	5.0
1985	3.5	4.0	2.0	5.8	2.1	8.6	57.8	32.5	6.1
1986	1.9	4.2	0.6	2.5	−0.1	6.1	86.2	21.2	3.4
1987	3.7	4.3	0.1	3.3	0.2	4.6	131.8	17.8	4.1
1988	4.1	4.0	0.7	2.7	1.3	5.0	114.2	25.8	4.9
1989	4.8	5.0	2.3	3.5	2.8	6.6	20.0	20.8	7.8
1990	5.4	4.8	3.1	3.6	2.7	6.1	26.7	15.9	9.5
1991	4.2	5.6	3.3	3.2	3.6	6.5	22.7	6.8	5.9
1992	3.0	1.5	1.7	2.4	5.1	5.3	15.5	3.7	3.7
1993	3.0	1.9	1.2	2.1	4.4	4.2	9.8	4.1	1.6
1994	2.6	0.2	0.7	1.7	2.8	3.9	7.0	1.5	2.5
1995	2.8	2.2	−0.1	1.8	1.7	5.4	35.0	1.7	3.4
1996	2.9	1.6	0.1	2.0	1.4	3.8	34.4	2.3	2.4
1997	2.3	1.6	1.7	1.2	1.9	1.8	20.6	1.8	3.1
1998	1.6	1.0	0.6	0.8	0.9	1.7	15.9	1.7	3.4

Source: OECD Economic Outlook (various issues). Reproduced by permission of the OECD.

Table 9.3 describes the inflation performances of the G7 economies since 1970, together with, for comparative purposes, those of Iceland and Mexico. From the table, it is evident that the lowest and most stable inflation rates have been achieved by Germany and Japan. Indeed, in 1986, the general price level in Germany actually fell, if only by the smallest of margins. The rates quoted in the table are averages for each economy as a whole. Thus the inflation rate for a given economy in a particular year cannot be taken as a literal record of the pace of price change for every, or indeed any, good or service: it is simply a reasonably accurate approximation of what is going on. This is another example of the loss of detail associated with analysis at the macro level.

The experience of inflation amongst the G7 since 1970, as depicted in Table 9.3, is quite varied. In contrast to the noted capacity for inflation control in Germany and

Perfectly anticipated inflation: A situation in which the actual rate of inflation is equal to the anticipated or expected rate of inflation.

Imperfectly anticipated inflation: A situation in which the actual rate of inflation differs from the anticipated or expected rate of inflation.

Hyperinflation: A situation in which the rate of inflation is extremely high for more than a year.

Japan, the performance of the UK and Italy, for example, with rates close to or above 20 per cent in 1980 is quite poor. However, even the worst G7 experience pales beside those of Iceland and Mexico. The inflation rates of these two countries in the 1980s are noteworthy in respect of the absolute size of the figures involved – a rate of 131.8 per cent for Mexico in 1987, for example – and, in addition, for their *variability*. This is a characteristic feature of very high inflation: it appears to be more prone to substantial oscillation.

We now turn to consider the significance of inflation: why and at what rates might it be considered a problem? Take first a hypothetical situation in which the agents in an economy – consumers, employers, workers, government and others – are aware of the future course of prices. In this case, the rate of inflation could be said to be **perfectly anticipated**, and it would be possible to effect movements in other nominal variables such that real economic circumstances remained unchanged. Thus, if the rate of price inflation turned out to be as expected, say, 15 per cent over a future period, equivalent increases in the money value of wages, benefit levels and other incomes would leave the real purchasing power of people receiving such incomes unchanged. The inflation, even though relatively high, would not appear to have any 'concrete' impact. In fact, economists identify two problems, which can still occur even if inflation can be perfectly anticipated in this way: so-called 'shoe leather' and 'menu' costs.

Shoe leather costs arise because, in the presence of inflation, cash is continually losing its real purchasing power. This provides people with an incentive to hold as little cash as possible, and to put their money instead into a bank or some other financial institution where it will earn interest. However, because they need cash for everyday purchases, people will be continually withdrawing small amounts from their accounts, wearing out shoe leather on each visit to the bank or cashpoint. Of course, shoe leather is a metaphor for the general costs of inconvenience and administration associated with many cash withdrawals. *Menu costs* reflect the time and resources used in continually repricing goods and services in shops, vending machines, parking meters and so on, in line with the prevailing inflation rate. Given the relatively moderate inflation rates experienced in most Western industrial economies since the Second World War, there is general agreement that such shoe leather and menu costs are relatively small. However, such costs become more significant as economies begin to experience more rapid rates of inflation. While shoe leather and menu costs would arise even in the hypothetical case of inflation being perfectly anticipated, in reality inflation is **imperfectly anticipated** – for example, the actual rate of inflation turns out to be higher than expected – and, as a result, an additional more important set of costs arises.

As suggested from the experiences of Mexico and Iceland recorded in Table 9.3, inflationary surges, unless checked, can develop a momentum of their own, and may eventually lead to extremely rapid rates known as **hyperinflation**. The most widely known instance of hyperinflation occurred in Weimar Germany in the 1920s, where, at its height, the annual rate climbed to 1 billion per cent. Now, given that the market is perhaps *the* central institution of competitive capitalism, and that markets are coordinated by price signals, it follows that the extreme distortion of prices by cumulatively higher rates of inflation is a direct challenge to the integrity of the capitalist system itself. To put this another way, consider a situation in which money is constantly and quickly drained of its value. As soon as income is earned the imperative will be to spend it before its purchasing power is diminished. At the same time, there will be frantic pressures on all social groups to negotiate and struggle for higher money incomes in order to try to offset imploding real incomes. The apocalyptic consequences for economy and society of the intensification of this kind of process, as inflation surges ever higher, are not difficult to imagine: ultimately, the payments system would collapse, leaving exchange to be coordinated by the process of barter.

Inflation does not need to reach 'hyper' proportions for it to be sufficient to distort and weaken the way in which markets work. The famous American economist, Milton Friedman, has argued that as the rate of inflation increases, so too does its variability. Greater variability of inflation generates more *uncertainty* as to what the actual rate will be at any given time. This makes it more difficult for economic agents to distinguish between changes in the general price level and changes in the **relative prices** of different goods and services. Accordingly, economic agents will make mistakes. For example, imagine a situation where the price of a particular good, good X, is £30 and the price of another good, good Y, is £10. The relative price of good X to good Y is 3:1. Now if prices increase across the economy by 10 per cent, the price of good X will increase to £30.30 and that of good Y to £10.10, but relative prices will remain unchanged. However, higher prices in the market for good X might prompt firms to enter in the anticipation of higher profits. The overall level of output in the market increases accordingly but if price rises are occurring right across the economy and there is no new or extra demand present, unsold stocks of good X will pile up. The possibility of errors of this sort breeds distrust as to the reliability of price signals and encourages economic agents to spend time and resources unproductively trying to discern what is really going on. Ultimately then, markets become less efficient than they would otherwise be in the absence of high and rising inflation, and Friedman argues that lower output and higher unemployment are the inevitable result. Friedman also suggests that similar consequences follow when increased uncertainty induced by higher rates of inflation makes economic agents more cautious: they become more reluctant to take the consumption and investment decisions that would occur in periods of greater price stability.

A second major problem associated with a high rate of inflation concerns the damage visited upon international competitiveness. An economy that experiences rapid increases in prices will find it more difficult to trade successfully in an environment where its trading partners enjoy more moderate rates of inflation. Very simply, the price of its exports will be rising faster than the price of substitutes in foreign markets; and, at home, the price of domestic goods will be rising faster than the price of imports. *Ceteris paribus*, this means that the balance of trade in goods and services for the more inflationary economy will deteriorate and, as we explain in the next section of this chapter, trade deficits, where imports surge ahead of exports, cannot be sustained in the medium term. What is crucial here then is not the rate of inflation *per se* but the rate of inflation experienced in one country relative to that experienced elsewhere.

When inflation is imperfectly anticipated it raises a further set of redistributive problems because of its differing impacts upon different groups of people in society. In financial markets, for example, inflation helps borrowers but penalizes lenders. Just as inflation drains money of its value, so it reduces the real value of debt. A sum borrowed at the beginning of a period of high inflation will, in real terms, be worth much less when the debt comes to be subsequently repaid. For those in debt this is clearly a substantial boon: they can borrow and spend now, but the real value of the

Relative price: The ratio of the price of one good to the price of another good; expressed as the number of units of one good that one unit of another good will buy.

sum they have to repay in future will be diminished in direct proportion to the inflation rate. Similarly, the expected real value of the interest paid on a debt will be eroded when inflation turns out to be higher than anticipated. For lenders, the implications are reversed: inflation reduces the real value of their capital tied up in loans, and it similarly erodes the real value of interest earnings when inflation is imperfectly anticipated. Overall, then, inflation has the effect of redistributing income from lenders to borrowers.

Unanticipated inflation has similar redistributive effects among other groups in society. For example, it disadvantages those with incomes that were fixed in less inflationary times. Thus people who are retired may have saved capital to provide for their old age. If inflation diminishes the real value of their savings, and of any income stream that they derive from such savings, they will be severely disadvantaged because they have no further access to other sources of income, such as wages, which may be easier to adjust for inflation. At the same time, wage earners, if they are in a strong enough bargaining position, may actually increase the real value of their incomes if they can negotiate an increase in their money wages above the rate of inflation. Here, redistribution would be from the non-waged to the waged. Generally, in distributive terms, we may conclude that inflation injures those who are unable to defend or raise their real incomes and advantages those in debt or who have the capacity to revise their real income levels.

Given the range of real economic problems associated with inflation, what kind of inflationary target should governments adopt? Zero inflation or price stability would be the most ambitious target, and some governments do have aspirations in this direction. The German central bank (the Bundesbank), for example, reflecting the experiences of the Weimar period, was constitutionally charged with protecting the value of the deutschmark.[1] However, more realistically, governments tend to have as an objective a low and stable rate of inflation. This confronts both the dangers of spiralling price increases and the uncertainty that arises from high and variable rates of inflation. In the UK, for example, Gordon Brown – the Chancellor of the Labour government elected to office in May 1997 – has given the Bank of England's Monetary Policy Committee the task of achieving an inflation target. This target is currently set at 2.5 per cent, plus or minus 1 per cent.

9.5 The balance of payments

The **balance of payments** is a record of the transactions that take place between the residents of one country and the rest of the world over a given period. As for other macroeconomic variables, the balance of payments is usually measured on an annual basis. Balance of payments transactions come in a variety of forms. The most obvious category is trade in goods and services. Imports and exports of goods are known as *visible* trade, while service transactions are called *invisible* trade. Other balance of payments transactions include: foreign borrowing and lending; buying and selling financial assets such as shares abroad; and buying and selling real assets such as firms in international markets. A full discussion of the various components of the balance of payments accounts can be found in Chapter 14, section 14.2.

Balance of payments: A record of a country's international transactions.

[1] Following the introduction of the euro, the Bundesbank lost its responsibility for monetary policy in Germany. Monetary policy for the euro area as a whole is now controlled by the European Central Bank, whose main aim is to achieve low inflation, in the range 0–2 per cent.

Table 9.4 Openness for the G7, 1950–92 (exports + imports/nominal GDP, per cent)

	1950	1955	1960	1965	1970	1975	1980	1985	1992
United States	8.5	9.0	9.4	9.5	11.4	16.4	21.1	18.0	21.9
Canada	41.2	39.7	36.0	38.4	42.9	47.2	55.1	54.5	54.0
Japan	18.2	20.3	21.1	19.7	20.3	25.6	28.3	25.6	18.0
France	28.2	26.5	27.0	25.8	31.1	37.0	44.3	47.2	44.9
W. Germany	19.7	29.0	35.2	35.6	40.4	46.5	53.3	61.5	60.0
Italy	18.6	20.2	25.8	27.2	32.8	41.1	46.5	46.1	39.6
United Kingdom	46.6	44.9	43.5	39.5	45.3	53.6	52.3	56.9	48.9

Source: Penn World Tables

Why are balance of payments considerations an important element of macro-economics? To help answer this question, think about the range of goods you will use or consume today. Many of the clothes you are wearing, for example, will have been manufactured abroad, probably in the Far East as well as in other parts of the EU. The television you watch tonight might be Japanese and the bed you sleep in Swedish. This kind of exercise gives us some idea of how interdependent most of the world actually is. We live in an international economy, which is characterized by increasing openness (we prefer 'international economy' rather than 'global economy' for reasons we explain in Chapter 16). This means that more and more of the output that individual economies produce is being sold in other countries. For the most part, such openness, because it is associated with increasing market accessibility, faster economic growth and wider consumer choice, is viewed very positively.

Table 9.4 illustrates the increasing openness of the world's major industrial economies over the postwar period. The data express the combined money value of exports and imports as a percentage of *nominal GDP*: that is, GDP valued in the prices ruling in each year. Though some economies, the USA and Japan for example, have a lower relative dependence on trade, all except Japan have seen a growth in openness over the period in question. For the European nations of Germany, France and Italy, the increase is particularly marked. This probably reflects their collective participation in the long process of economic integration that began in the 1950s.

We can identify two main reasons why such openness is likely to increase still further over the next decade and beyond. First, economic integration is gaining momentum. In particular parts of the world, formerly separate economies or groups of economies are coalescing to form unified or single markets and free trade areas. The single market in Europe, for example, provides for the free movement of both goods and services and factors of production amongst all European Union member states. Prior to the establishment of the European Economic Community (EEC) in 1957, the countries of Europe were much more fragmented, with a host of restrictions on both the range and form of cross-border transactions that their citizens were permitted to engage in. Now, for economic purposes at least, we are all citizens of the single market rather than of our respective economies. Similarly, the North American Free Trade Area (NAFTA), created in 1993, binds together the economies of the United States, Canada and Mexico into a unified market, which has no internal barriers to trade, although separate markets in factors of production, such as labour, continue to exist.

The second factor promoting accelerated openness in world markets is the liberalization of many of the former centrally planned economies such as China, Vietnam and those in eastern Europe. Markets in these economies are increasingly open to Western investment and goods, and the West itself is available as a potentially lucrative market for the outputs that the reforming economies produce. Indeed, for the more dynamic of the eastern European states such as Hungary, the Czech Republic and Poland, there is the very real prospect of complete integration with the European single market in the not too distant future.

Because of the high and increasing degree of openness in world markets, balance of payments problems are clearly a significant macroeconomic issue. What then are the policy objectives that arise in this area? In order to simplify the discussion we shall concentrate here on the balance of payments as represented by trade in goods and services. Initially, three possibilities arise for the balance of payments position of an economy:

- *deficit*, where the total value of imports exceeds the value of exports
- *surplus*, where export revenues are greater than the total import bill
- *balance*, where the values of exports and imports are roughly equal.

In the case of a deficit, it follows that domestic residents have an appetite for imports that is not matched by their ability to sell goods and services abroad: they are, in other words, net importers. At this point, the fact that different currencies are involved in international trade becomes significant. Exports are a means of generating the reserves of foreign currency or foreign exchange necessary to pay for imports. If the residents of a country are – collectively – net importers, it follows that they have a need to acquire foreign currency to pay for imports that is not matched by the level of foreign currency earnings that their exports currently generate: they have, in other words, a foreign currency 'gap'. This gap can be filled in two ways. Either residents can draw on currency reserves that they have accumulated in previous periods, or they can borrow the foreign currency that they require. Now, while both courses of action are possible in the short term neither is sustainable indefinitely: foreign currency reserves and the goodwill of lenders are both finite. This means that balance of payments deficits cannot be sustained in the medium term because of the exhaustion of the supplies of foreign currency necessary to finance them; *a persistent balance of payments deficit is, therefore, a policy problem.*

A surplus on the balance of payments, on the other hand, has the effect of augmenting the reserves of foreign currency held in the domestic economy. Because domestic residents are net exporters, it follows that they will be more than meeting the foreign currency requirements of their current level of imports. The extra foreign currency their net exports generate, because it is not immediately needed, is simply added to any existing reserves. A balance of payments surplus might thus appear to be relatively attractive, particularly when the positive knock-on effects of strong export demand on economic growth and domestic employment levels are also taken into consideration. However, this is not the whole story. A consistent surplus and the piling up of foreign currency reserves also represents missed consumption opportunities: it would be possible for domestic residents to finance more imports comfortably – and thereby raise their welfare – from the revenues generated by current export performance. Alternatively, they could increase investment abroad and/or raise overseas aid. A balance of payments surplus, therefore, even though it might represent export dynamism is, in itself, no real achievement. A surplus can also be a sign of considerable economic weakness. In a recessionary period when real GDP grows more slowly, the capacity to import is constrained by a slowdown in the growth of income. At the same time, assuming export markets are unaffected – their strength is in part a function of foreign incomes – the balance of payments may improve sharply – that is, move away from deficit – but, clearly, this is far from any kind of achievement. Further caveats concerning the desirability of balance of payments surplus are considered in Chapter 14.

Given that a deficit is a problem and a surplus is hardly laudable, it follows that the objective of policy in respect of the balance of payments is *balance in the medium term*. Balance equates the import-derived foreign currency demands of domestic residents with their export-derived foreign currency earnings. This means that there is no foreign currency 'gap' to be closed, nor any potential consumption or investment forgone. The emphasis is on balance over the medium term, rather than every year, because individual years' deficits and surpluses have the effect of cancelling each other out.

Finally, in this section, we briefly consider the relationship between the balance of payments and the other objectives of macroeconomic policy. To some extent this has been anticipated by earlier discussion. We have already indicated, for example, that improvements in the balance of payments can be achieved from the implementation of domestic austerity measures: if domestic residents are made poorer by the onset of recession they cannot afford to buy as many imports as in previous periods. We also noted, in our discussion of growth, that a rapidly expanding economy with rising income levels will usually be associated with a deterioration in the balance of payments: in other words a movement towards or into deficit. Such links between the balance of payments and other macroeconomic targets give rise to a wider definition of the notion of balance of payments balance or *equilibrium*. We may consider the balance of payments to be in a desired equilibrium over a period of years if a balance is achieved without the need for slower growth, with all its attendant disadvantages, to make this happen. In Chapter 14 we offer further revisions of this definition.

9.6 A brief overview of macroeconomic policy since 1945

It is a commonplace that economic ideas are *reactive* in that they change and develop to confront new or emergent economic problems. If the macroeconomic objectives we have discussed are, broadly speaking, met for many economies over a sustained period, then there will be little pressure to search for new forms of understanding and policy: economists and governments will seemingly have 'got it right'. However, when targets are missed, perhaps disastrously so, there will be an obvious need to revise the thought behind and conduct of macro policy.

The first major instance of this kind of shift in macroeconomic thinking and action occurred as a result of the **Great Depression** of the early 1930s. During this period, output and employment in most of the world's major industrial economies fell dramatically. For example, in the US, real GDP fell by 35 per cent between 1929 and 1933, with unemployment reaching a peak of 25 per cent in 1933. Previously,

Depression: A very severe and prolonged recession.

although cycles of fast and slower growth had been experienced, economic progress had proceeded relatively smoothly on a generally uninterrupted upward path. This meant that the prevailing economic orthodoxy of **classical economics**, seemingly having 'got it right', was not open to serious challenge. The Great Depression offered hugely changed circumstances and the opportunity for the advancement of radically different theory and policy.

As a response to the 'new' economic problems posed in the 1930s, the British economist John Maynard Keynes wrote *The General Theory of Employment, Interest and Money*. This book, published in 1936, contained the seeds of a revolution in macroeconomics; indeed, it is often credited as the first work to be framed in a conscious macro dimension. Keynes argued that governments, through managing the total or **aggregate demand** for the output of an economy, could vanquish depression and produce full employment (see Chapter 10, section 10.2, for a much more detailed explanation of this approach). Keynes's work proved to be exceptionally influential in both academic and government circles, to the extent that during the 1950s and 1960s both macroeconomic thought and policy came to reflect the broad thrust of his views. Moreover, his influence was not confined to Britain; rather it assumed the proportions of a new ruling orthodoxy in all of the advanced Western economies. **Keynesian economics** or **Keynesianism** – as the new approach became known – set its sights firmly on maintaining a high and stable level of employment in order to avoid the social, economic and political costs of unemployment. Accordingly, as governments absorbed and put into practice Keynesian ideas, the major short-term policy objective of the early postwar period became full employment. As we have seen, there is a correlation between higher levels of employment and faster short-term economic growth, and so growth too became an objective associated with Keynesianism. However, recall our earlier qualification that growth over the longer term is much less open to the influence of government policy.

What of the other macroeconomic objectives under Keynesianism? We have noted that the balance of payments can act as a constraint upon the successful attainment of both employment and growth objectives. When more people are employed and incomes are rising quickly there will be a consequent increase in imports without any necessary compensatory movement in exports. In this situation, the balance of payments will worsen. Because balance of payments deficits cannot be tolerated beyond the medium term, it may prove necessary to trim the growth rate and accept higher levels of unemployment. The final policy objective – inflation – tended to remain comfortably low in most economies for the period of the 1950s through to the mid-to-late 1960s when Keynesianism was dominant, and therefore, following the problem–response notion introduced at the beginning of this section, the issue of inflation was not the focus of a great deal of attention. Where slightly faster inflation did provoke mild concern, it tended to be addressed as a constraint on employment and growth in a similar manner to the balance of payments.

Keynesianism was coincident with an era known as the *postwar boom*. This lasted from the end of World War Two until about 1970. The postwar boom was characterized by the general experience in most economies of historically rapid rates of economic growth, full employment and low inflation. Whether or not Keynesianism can be credited with some or all of these achievements is, however, a matter of some dispute. The period since 1970 has been one in which economic progress has faltered somewhat. Growth rates have been lower, unemployment higher on average and, in particular, inflation has been higher and more variable. Furthermore, the inflationary surge experienced in major Western economies at the end of the 1960s and beginning of the 1970s was so radically different from the gradual rates that prevailed during the postwar boom that it served to undermine the Keynesian orthodoxy, clearing the ground for a second comprehensive revision of macro thought and policy.

The changed economic circumstances after 1970 served to expose two major weaknesses in Keynesian theory. First, in its understandable preoccupation with unemployment, Keynesianism had tended to neglect inflation both as a phenomenon, which needed explanation, and as a problem for policy. Second, in its limited theorization of inflation, Keynesianism posed it as an 'alternative' to unemployment: in other words, economies could suffer from high unemployment or high inflation but not both at the same time. The new 1970s phenomenon of **stagflation** thus provided a set of circumstances for which Keynesianism had no ready analysis or answers.

It should be clear that a theoretical approach, which could explain the emergence of virulent inflation rates and higher unemployment, would challenge Keynesianism for the economic high ground. This is what the revived doctrine of **monetarism**, associated with the work of Milton Friedman, actually did. As we shall discuss in Chapter 10, section 10.4, Friedman has argued that inflation is essentially determined by the rate of monetary growth relative to the rate of real output growth, and has stressed the need for monetary control to combat inflation. Moreover, if inflation is kept low and stable by government policy, then it is suggested that markets can be relied upon to produce favourable outcomes in respect of the other three macroeconomic variables introduced in this chapter. To a great extent, the view that many governments have distilled from this approach over more recent years is that inflation should be accorded priority in respect of the conduct of macroeconomic policy.

In summary, then, the postwar period up to the 1970s was successively dominated by two different macroeconomic perspectives, which gave rise to two sets of policy imperatives. During the postwar boom, the work of Keynes inspired an approach that emphasized the policy problem of unemployment; while, since the 1970s, the work of Friedman has shifted the policy consensus firmly towards the control of inflation. This refocusing of policy has been paralleled by a move away from the Keynesian management of aggregate demand in favour of inflation targets and the management of the supply side of the economy – areas we shall explore more fully in subsequent chapters.

Stagflation: A situation where high unemployment and high inflation occur simultaneously; a combination of stagnation and inflation.

■ Summary

◆ Macroeconomics involves the study of the economy as a whole. Macroeconomic policy is concerned with the efforts of policy-makers to influence the behaviour of four key variables: the rate of economic growth, the level of unemployment, the rate of inflation, and the balance of payments position. We must recognize that macroeconomic policy objectives in respect of each of these variables cannot be pursued independently. For example, efforts to raise the rate of economic growth in the short term must be tempered with an acknowledgement of its potentially negative effects upon inflation and the balance of payments.

◆ Failure to achieve macroeconomic objectives carries a variety of consequences. Attaining slower rates of economic growth than desirable will entail only modest increases in general living standards, and may be associated with rising unemployment.

In turn, unemployment carries economic and social costs. It wastes scarce human resources and it inflicts poverty and a sense of hopelessness on the unemployed. Inflation is economically undesirable as it can distort and undermine a central feature of capitalist resource allocation: the price mechanism. It also disadvantages those on fixed incomes, and may threaten the trading position of the economy as a whole. Finally, adverse balance of payments positions may necessitate actions that undermine other objectives. For example, balance of payments deficits usually require some moderation in the rate of economic growth.

◆ There is a strong correlation between the emergence of new macroeconomic problems and the development of macroeconomic thought and policy. Since 1945, macroeconomic policy has been dominated successively by the development and application of first Keynesianism and then monetarism. Keynesianism promoted the widespread involvement of the state in many aspects of the economy. Monetarism, on the other hand, demands much more circumspect forms of state intervention.

■ Key terms

◆ Macroeconomics
◆ Macroeconomic policy
◆ Economic growth
◆ Unemployment
◆ Full employment
◆ Inflation
◆ Hyperinflation
◆ Balance of payments surplus and deficit
◆ Balance of payments balance
◆ Keynesianism
◆ Postwar boom
◆ Stagflation
◆ Monetarism

■ Self-test questions

True (t) or false (f)

1. Macroeconomics is concerned with the study of the behaviour and performance of the economy as a whole.

2. Economists use nominal GDP data to measure economic growth.

3. Whether or not the level of unemployment rises or falls over time depends on the extent to which flows into a pool of unemployed labour are counterbalanced by flows out of it.

4. Full employment is a situation in which all unemployment is frictional and structural.

5. Inflation is a process whereby the price of all goods and services increases at the same rate over time.

6. In the hypothetical case of inflation being perfectly anticipated, there are no costs of inflation.

7. The main costs of inflation arise when inflation is imperfectly anticipated.

8. The balance of invisible trade measures the difference between the value of goods exported and imported.

9. A persistent balance of payments deficit will act as a constraint on the achievement of other macroeconomic objectives and is a policy problem.

10. Stagflation involves a situation in which high unemployment and high inflation occur simultaneously.

Complete the following sentences by inserting the missing word(s)

1. Economic growth entails an increase in ____ GDP over time.

2. The ____ is the name given to the seven main industrial countries in the world.

3. Unemployed people are those who are available for work and are ____ seeking jobs but cannot find them.

4. When the actual rate of inflation is equal to the anticipated or expected rate of inflation, inflation is said to be ____.

5. When the rate of inflation turns out to be higher than anticipated it ____ borrowers and ____ lenders.

6. A situation in which a country experiences an extremely high rate of inflation for over a year or more is referred to as ____.

7. The balance of payments is a record of a country's ____.

8. When a country exports more goods and services than it imports, its balance of payments on such transactions will be in ____.

9. The birth of modern macroeconomics can be traced back to the publication in 1936 of *The General Theory of Employment, Interest and Money* written by ____.

10. The two schools that dominated macroeconomics in the postwar period up to the 1970s were ____ and ____.

Exercises

1. Using the data contained in Tables 9.1–9.3 calculate the average rate of growth (Table 9.1), unemployment (Table 9.2) and inflation (Table 9.3) experienced in each of the G7 economies since 1970. Which economies have the best, and worst, records with respect to these three key indicators of macroeconomic performance?

2. Using data presented in Table 9.1, plot a graph of the rate of economic growth (vertical axis) experienced over the period 1970–98 (horizontal axis) for any one of the countries listed.

3. Taking the same country as that chosen in completing exercise 1, use data presented in Table 9.2 to plot a graph of the rate of unemployment (vertical axis) over the period 1970–98 (horizontal axis).

4. Again taking the same country, use data from Table 9.3 to plot a graph of the rate of inflation (vertical axis) over the period 1970–98 (horizontal axis).

5. From inspection of the three graphs you have drawn, does there appear to be any evidence to suggest that there exists a relationship between any of these three key indicators of macroeconomic performance?

■ Questions for discussion

◆ What are the main objectives of macroeconomic policy?

◆ Why are fast rates of economic growth not necessarily desirable?

◆ What are the main costs of unemployment? Are there any circumstances in which firms might benefit from a rise in the level of unemployment in the economy?

◆ How important is it to control inflation?

◆ In what ways will an increase in the rate of inflation adversely affect firms?

◆ Why is a surplus on the balance of payments undesirable?

◆ What potential conflicts exist between the main objectives of macroeconomic policy?

◆ What is the link between economic performance and the development of economic thought and policy?

■ Further reading

Artis, M.J. *The UK Economy: A Manual of Applied Economics* (Oxford: Oxford University Press, 1996). Provides an up-to-date, systematic and balanced assessment of the problems and performance of the UK economy.

Johnson, C. and S. Briscoe *Measuring the Economy* (Hardmondsworth: Penguin, 1995). Provides a well-written guide to understanding British official statistics on the macroeconomy.

■ Internet links

The *UK Treasury* has an excellent website, which offers lots of information and discussion about the performance of the UK economy. The site also provides reviews of wider economic issues such as European economic integration. The site can be found at: **http://www.hm-treasury.gov.uk/**

Information on the macroeconomic policies and performances of the major economies can be found at the *OECD*'s website: **http://www.oecd.org/**

Unemployment and Inflation

CHAPTER 10

Key issues

▶ Is the cause of, and cure for, unemployment to be found inside or outside the labour market?

▶ What are the main theories that economists have put forward to explain unemployment?

▶ How can governments reduce unemployment?

▶ How have economists sought to explain the substantial rise in unemployment that has taken place in the EU since the 1970s?

▶ What causes inflation?

▶ How can the authorities reduce the rate of inflation?

▶ Is it necessary to increase unemployment in order to reduce the rate of inflation?

Contents

10.1 Introduction

In section 9.1 of the previous chapter we emphasized that the profitability of business is critically affected by the macroeconomic environment in which firms operate. Changes in unemployment and inflation can have a substantial effect on the success of firms. The purpose of this chapter is to examine the debate over the causes of, and cures for, unemployment, and inflation. In the first half of the chapter we look at the main theories put forward by economists to explain unemployment, and consider the policy implications that derive from these competing theories (sections 10.2–10.3). In the second half of the chapter we turn our attention to the issue of inflation. We consider what causes inflation, and what governments can do to reduce the rate of inflation (section 10.4). Inevitably, given the subject matter under consideration, this is a relatively long chapter, and whenever necessary you should be prepared to retrace your tracks and re-read earlier sections that build into, and help your understanding of, the analysis being discussed.

10.2 The debate over the cause of, and cure for, unemployment

In Chapter 9, section 9.3, we discussed the nature and measurement of unemployment, together with its economic, social and political costs. While there is a general consensus that the maintenance of a high and stable level of employment is an important objective of macroeconomic policy, there is considerable debate over why unemployment exists and what governments can do to reduce it. At the outset it is worth emphasizing that the central question that underlies this continuing debate is whether the cause of unemployment is largely to be found *inside* or *outside* the labour market. If unemployment is essentially due to imperfections in the labour market, then government policy to reduce unemployment needs to be directed to alleviate such imperfections. However, if the cause of unemployment is largely to be found outside the labour market – because of insufficient spending in the goods market – then government policy needs to be directed to stimulate aggregate demand in the economy.

Historically, economists have applied many adjectives to the term unemployment. These include: voluntary, involuntary, classical/real wage, frictional/search, structural/mismatch and demand-deficient/cyclical, to name but a few. In addition, some economists refer to a natural rate of unemployment, while others prefer to speak of a non-accelerating inflation rate of unemployment. It is hardly surprising, given such a plethora of terms and concepts, that students often find the issue of unemployment one that is particularly difficult to get to grips with. In attempting to shed light on the controversy over the causes of – and appropriate cures for – unemployment, we shall trace how economists from the nineteenth century through to the present day have put forward new and often controversial theories to explain unemployment. In sketching out the history of unemployment theory in this way it is possible to identify the development of *five* main approaches within mainstream economics:

- the classical approach
- the orthodox Keynesian approach
- the monetarist approach
- the new classical approach
- the new Keynesian approach.

The classical approach

In the nineteenth century, economists adhering to the so-called classical approach maintained that so long as money wages and prices were flexible, and free to adjust, the labour market would always tend to clear at full employment equilibrium. Given a perfectly competitive labour market, anyone able and willing to work could do so at the ruling market-clearing equilibrium real wage rate. This situation is illustrated in Fig. 10.1, where the aggregate demand for labour (D_L) equals the aggregate supply of labour (S_L) at the market-clearing equilibrium real wage rate ($W/P)_e$, and employment (N) is at its full employment level (N_F). Now, if the real wage rate is initially set at ($W/P)_1$, above its market-clearing level, the supply of labour (N_2) exceeds the

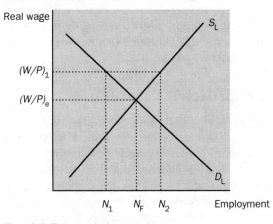

Fig. 10.1 The classical approach.

demand for labour (N_1). Competition among the excess supply of unemployed workers ($N_2 - N_1$) to find work would then lead to a reduction in money wages and hence a reduction in the real wage rate (assuming prices remain unchanged) until such time as full employment was restored.

In classical analysis, **Say's law** (named after the French economist Jean-Baptiste Say) guaranteed that aggregate demand would be sufficient to absorb the full employment level of output produced. According to this law 'supply creates its own demand' in that the act of production yields income that will be sufficient to purchase *whatever* level of output is produced. Given a competitive labour market, in which full employment was the normal state of affairs, Say's law ruled out the possibility of any deficiency of aggregate demand: demand would always be sufficient to purchase the full employment level of output produced. Aside from some short-term temporary unemployment, which may occur as the real wage rate adjusts to its new market-clearing level following a change in demand or supply conditions in the labour market, the *only* source of unemployment in this classical approach is *voluntary unemployment*, which arises because there are people who, while they are capable of working, for various reasons choose not to work.

How then did classical economists explain the mass unemployment experienced in Western economies in the 1930s? Classical economists attributed the persistence of such mass unemployment to the downward inflexibility of money (and real) wages due to the actions of trade unions, and argued that full employment would be restored only if money (and real) wages were cut to their market-clearing level. In Fig. 10.1, *classical unemployment*, or what is sometimes referred to as *real wage unemployment*, occurs when the real wage rate is kept too high, resulting in an excess supply of labour equal to $N_2 - N_1$ at $(W/P)_1$. In this situation unemployment exceeds the level that would prevail at the market-clearing real wage rate $(W/P)_e$.

Keynes attacked the classical explanation of the cause of unemployment and also the solution that classical economists put forward to solve the problem. In his *General Theory of Employment, Interest and Money*, published in 1936, he put forward a new, and at the time revolutionary, theory that provided a very different explanation of, and remedy for, the then-prevailing severe unemployment. In contrast to classical economists, Keynes placed the cause of the mass unemployment of the 1930s *outside* the labour market: he argued that it was, in fact, essentially rooted in a deficiency of

Say's law: States that supply creates its own demand.

aggregate demand in the goods market. In Keynes's view, the cure for unemployment required government intervention to increase aggregate demand in order to restore the economy to its full employment level of output. We now turn to discuss the Keynesian approach to unemployment in more detail.

The orthodox Keynesian approach

Keynesians have traditionally identified three *main* types or categories of unemployment: *frictional*, *structural*, and *demand-deficient* unemployment. **Frictional unemployment** occurs because it will take time for a newly unemployed person to obtain information on job vacancies and find a new job. Because frictional unemployment occurs when individuals are changing jobs and searching for new employment, it is also sometimes referred to as **search unemployment**. Even though there will be search costs involved (for example, loss of earnings, or expenditure on postage and telephone calls), such behaviour is entirely rational as newly unemployed individuals will need to spend time familiarizing themselves with both the pecuniary and the non-pecuniary features of available jobs. What can the government do to reduce this type of unemployment? Measures that reduce the search time moving between jobs will reduce the amount of frictional unemployment. One way to reduce search time is to improve the provision of information about employment opportunities via official job centres. In the UK, for example, the continued existence and growth of private employment agencies suggests that there is considerable scope to improve information on the availability of job opportunities in the official system.

Structural unemployment occurs, as the name implies, because of structural changes that take place in the economy. These changes involve underlying shifts in *both* demand (for example, changing patterns of demand for goods produced by different industries) and supply (for example, changes in the state of technology). Because of such changes some industries and regions will contract, while others expand. As labour is not perfectly mobile (see Chapter 8), some industries and regions will experience unemployment, while others face labour shortages. In the contracting sectors, more individuals will be looking for jobs than there are job opportunities available: in these sectors an excess supply of labour will exist. In contrast, in the expanding sectors of the economy, new job opportunities will outstrip the supply of individuals looking for jobs: in these industries an excess demand for labour will prevail. Because structural unemployment arises from a mismatch of skills and geographical job opportunities, following underlying changes in demand and supply, it is also sometimes referred to as **mismatch unemployment**. What can the government do to reduce this type of unemployment? One way to reduce both the extent and the duration of structural unemployment is to design policies aimed at improving the occupational mobility of labour (such as retraining programmes) and geographical mobility of labour (for example, providing financial assistance to help cover the costs of moving from one area to another). In addition, policy measures that encourage new/old firms to locate/relocate in areas of high unemployment (via grants, for example) will help to reduce the amount of structural unemployment.

We now turn to consider the third main type or category of unemployment, namely **demand-deficient unemployment** or what is sometimes referred to as **cyclical unemployment**. In the Keynesian approach, the level of real national income/output and hence employment is *largely* determined by the level of aggregate expenditure or

Frictional unemployment: Unemployment that arises because it takes time for workers to search for suitable jobs; also known as search unemployment.

Structural unemployment: Unemployment that arises from a mismatch between the skills or location of existing job vacancies and the present skills or location of the unemployed; also known as mismatch unemployment.

Demand-deficient unemployment: Unemployment that arises because aggregate demand is insufficient to provide employment for everyone who wants to work at the prevailing real wage; also known as cyclical unemployment.

demand in the economy. As such, the economy may come to rest at less than full employment equilibrium, owing to a deficiency of aggregate expenditure. In contrast to the classical model, the Keynesian view is that less than full employment equilibrium is the *normal* state of affairs. Let us now examine why this is the case.

In Chapter 9, section 9.2, we discussed the three ways in which national income can be measured; each of these can be conceptualized using the circular flow of income. You will recall that aggregate expenditure or **aggregate demand** (*AD*) is the sum of the following major categories of expenditure: consumer expenditure (*C*), investment expenditure (*I*), government expenditure (*G*) and expenditure on net exports (*X–M*). More formally, we can express this in the following way:

$$AD = C + I + G + X - M \tag{10.1}$$

In order to explain why – in the simple Keynesian model – the level of real output and employment is essentially determined by aggregate demand, and why the economy may come to rest at less than full employment equilibrium, we first need to consider briefly what determines each of these components of aggregate demand.

> **Aggregate demand:** The total planned expenditures of all buyers of final goods and services.
>
> **Autonomous expenditure:** Expenditure that does not depend on the level of national income.

Consumer expenditure

In the Keynesian model the main determinant of aggregate consumer expenditure is held to be the level of national income: the higher the level of national income, the higher the level of total consumer expenditure undertaken. This relationship between aggregate consumption and aggregate income, which is known technically as the *consumption function*, is depicted in Fig. 10.2.

In Fig. 10.2 consumer expenditure (*C*) and national income (*Y*) are shown on the vertical and horizontal axes respectively. The 45° line shows points of equality between the two axes. In consequence, where the consumption function crosses the 45° line at point E, consumption equals income (*C = Y*). The reader may have spotted that, in order to further simplify our discussion, we have drawn a linear consumption function. This allows us to express the relationship between aggregate consumer expenditure and national income in the form of an equation of a straight line:

$$C = \alpha + \beta Y \tag{10.2}$$

In this equation the intercept (α) shows the level of aggregate consumer expenditure undertaken independently of the level of national income. Such expenditure is said to be **exogenous** or **autonomous** consumer **expenditure**, and depends on factors

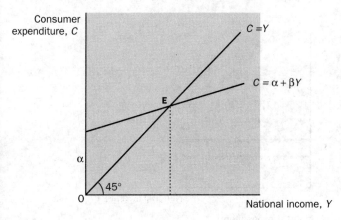

Fig. 10.2 The consumption function.

Marginal propensity to consume: The change in consumption expenditure resulting from an additional unit of income.

such as the level of wealth. The important point to note about autonomous consumer expenditure is that it is *not* determined by the level of national income. Returning to the equation of a straight line, the slope of the consumption function (β) indicates the extent to which consumer expenditure changes when national income changes. Economists refer to this coefficient as the **marginal propensity to consume**. This is an important coefficient, as you will come to see when we discuss the Keynesian approach to business cycles in Chapter 11, section 11.6.

Investment expenditure

What determines the level of investment expenditure undertaken in the economy? The main determinants of investment expenditure include: the rate of change of current sales; expectations about future sales and factor prices; the cost of capital equipment; and the rate of interest. *Ceteris paribus*, investment expenditure will tend to rise following: an increase in the rate of change of current sales; an upward revision of business expectations about the future profitability of investment; a fall in the cost of capital equipment; or a fall in the cost of borrowing funds to finance such expenditure, and *vice versa*. In the simple Keynesian model, investment expenditure is assumed to be autonomously or exogenously determined. Because, in Fig. 10.3, it is assumed to be independent of the level of national income, investment expenditure is depicted as a horizontal line.

Government expenditure

Having considered briefly the main determinants of consumer expenditure and investment expenditure, we now need to comment on government expenditure. For the purposes of constructing the Keynesian model it is sufficient to note that government expenditure, like investment expenditure, is assumed to be independent of the level of national income. Such expenditure depends on government policy. In consequence, government expenditure is also depicted as a horizontal line in Fig. 10.3.

Net export expenditure

Finally, we need to consider what determines net export expenditure. The three main determinants of the level of export and import expenditure are income, relative prices, and non-price factors such as tastes. These determinants are discussed more fully in Chapter 14, section 14.2. At this point in our discussion we shall focus on how income affects expenditure on imports and exports. The income variable

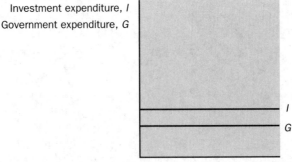

Investment expenditure, *I*
Government expenditure, *G*

I

G

National income, *Y*

Fig. 10.3 Investment and government expenditure.

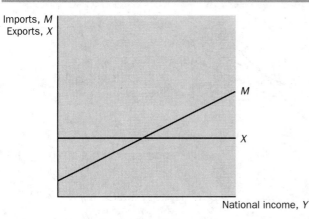

Fig. 10.4 Import and export expenditure.

relevant to imports is domestic national income. As national income rises, some part of this increase will be spent on buying more imports from abroad. This positive relationship between imports and national income is illustrated in Fig. 10.4. The slope of the import function depicts the **marginal propensity to import**, and indicates the extent to which import expenditure changes when national income changes. In contrast, the income variable relevant to exports is not domestic national income but rather income in the rest of the world. *Ceteris paribus*, as world income increases, the demand for a country's exports will increase. Because exports are determined independently of the level of domestic national income, the export schedule in Fig. 10.4 is depicted – as it is for investment and government expenditure – as a horizontal line.

Marginal propensity to import: The change in import expenditure resulting from an additional unit of income.

The equilibrium level of national income in the Keynesian model

Having briefly discussed what determines each component of aggregate demand, we are now in a position to consider what determines the equilibrium level of national income in the Keynesian model, and why the economy may come to rest at less than full employment equilibrium. This analysis is illustrated in Fig. 10.5.

The 45° line in the top panel of Fig. 10.5 shows points of equality between aggregate demand (vertical axis) and aggregate output or national income (horizontal axis). Where aggregate demand and aggregate output are equal ($AD = Y$), firms will be selling all the goods they produce, and in such circumstances there will be no tendency for income to change. We encountered this equilibrium condition in a slightly different form in Chapter 9, section 9.2, where we explained how the level of income will remain unchanged only when injections ($G + I + X$) are matched by leakages ($T + S + M$). The three main injections of investment expenditure, government expenditure and gross export expenditure are assumed to be determined independently of national income, while consumer expenditure increases as national income increases. In consequence, the aggregate demand schedule shown in Fig. 10.5 slopes upwards to the right. The equilibrium level of national income is established where the aggregate demand schedule crosses the 45° line: that is, where aggregate demand (AD) equals aggregate supply (Y).

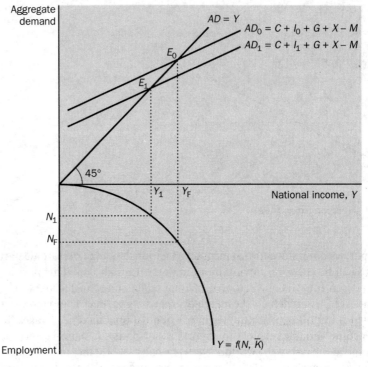

Fig. 10.5 The Keynesian model.

Let us assume that the economy is initially operating at its full employment equilibrium level of national income (Y_F) with aggregate demand equal to AD_0: that is, where AD_0 crosses the 45° line at point E_0. By referring to the bottom panel of Fig. 10.5, which shows the short-run aggregate production function, we can trace the implications of the level of income (determined by aggregate demand) in terms of the level of employment – in this case full employment (N_F). Now suppose that investment expenditure decreases from I_0 to I_1, causing the aggregate demand schedule to shift downwards from AD_0 to AD_1. Investment expenditure might decrease owing to a downward revision of business expectations of the future profitability of investment. In his *General Theory* (1936), Keynes suggested that investment could be influenced by tides of irrational pessimism and optimism, which he referred to as a change in investors' 'animal spirits', causing large swings in the state of business confidence. Following the fall in investment and associated fall in aggregate demand, a new equilibrium level of national income (Y_1) would be established where AD_1 crosses the 45° line at point E_1. Reference to the bottom panel of Fig. 10.5 reveals that the level of employment (N_1) required to produce the new equilibrium level of national income (Y_1) is now below its full employment level. In other words, at Y_1, aggregate demand is insufficient to provide employment for everyone who wants a job, resulting in so-called *involuntary unemployment*. The reader should note that income and employment will be affected in the same manner, *ceteris paribus*, following an autonomous decrease in consumer expenditure, government expenditure or net export expenditure.

How could the government intervene to eliminate the resultant demand-deficient unemployment and restore the economy to its full employment income level (Y_F,

N_F)? The solution lies in **aggregate demand management**: the government needs to change its stance with respect to its fiscal and/or monetary policy. Traditionally, orthodox Keynesians have emphasized **fiscal policy** measures involving changes in government expenditure and/or tax payments. Such changes act *directly* on the level of aggregate demand, and are believed by orthodox Keynesians to be both more predictable and faster acting on the level of economic activity than monetary policy measures. For example, increased government expenditure or reduced direct taxation (stimulating increased consumers' expenditure as households' disposable income increases) is held to have a strong and predictable effect on the level of income and employment as the initial increase in spending leads to successive rounds of further increases in expenditure. Following such expansionary fiscal policy, income will rise by more than the initial increase in spending, to a new equilibrium level where aggregate demand and aggregate supply are again equal. This phenomenon, known as the **multiplier** process, is discussed more fully in Chapter 11, section 11.5. In contrast, **monetary policy** changes are held to operate indirectly, mainly through changes in the rate of interest, which affect aggregate demand by causing a change in investment expenditure. In a recession, when firms' expectations about profitable investment opportunities are depressed, the response of investment expenditure to a fall in the cost of borrowing funds may be small. In such circumstances, the power of monetary policy will be limited. In consequence, orthodox Keynesians express a preference for fiscal policy, rather than monetary policy measures, to restore full employment.

At this stage it would be useful to draw together our discussion of the Keynesian approach to unemployment and consider the three main types of unemployment within the context of the labour market. The demand for labour (D_L) comprises the level of employment (N) plus the level of vacancies (V), while the supply of labour (S_L) comprises the level of employment (N) plus the level of unemployment (U):

$$D_L = N + V \qquad\qquad (10.3)$$

$$S_L = N + U \qquad\qquad (10.4)$$

It follows that when the labour market clears and the demand for labour (D_L) equals the supply of labour (S_L), then vacancies (V) will equal unemployment (U). In this situation all unemployment will fall in the category of frictional and structural unemployment (that is, non-demand-deficient unemployment), and demand-deficient unemployment will equal zero. As illustrated in Fig. 10.6, this occurs at a real wage

Aggregate demand management: The use of fiscal and monetary policies to influence the level of aggregate demand.

Fiscal policy: Entails measures that alter the level and composition of government expenditure and taxation.

Monetary policy: Entails measures that alter the money supply and/or interest rates.

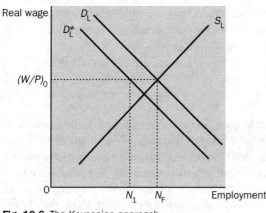

Fig. 10.6 The Keynesian approach.

rate $(W/P)_0$ at the intersection of D_L and S_L. Now, suppose as before that investment expenditure decreases, causing output and employment to fall. As the aggregate demand for goods and services within the economy falls, the demand curve for labour will shift to the left from D_L to D_L^*, resulting in demand-deficient unemployment at the prevailing real wage rate $(W/P)_0$. This would be an *additional* source of unemployment on top of any existing frictional or structural unemployment. Note that in Fig. 10.6 there are N_F workers willing to work at the prevailing real wage rate $(W/P)_0$ but demand from firms (which in our example have collectively cut investment) that would produce a level of employment of only N_1. This demonstrates that Keynesian demand-deficient unemployment occurs when there is an excess supply of labour at the ruling wage rate: in other words, when the real wage rate is above the market-clearing wage rate. Now, the important point to make about demand-deficient unemployment is that its cause lies *outside* the labour market: people who want to work cannot find jobs not because they are in a search process (which would involve frictional unemployment), nor because they need retraining to take jobs in new industries (which would involve structural unemployment), but because *there are not enough jobs to go around*: the demand is not there to sustain them. Finally, we should again emphasize that, in the Keynesian view, it is of course possible for all three types of unemployment to exist simultaneously.

The Keynesian approach to unemployment stands in bold contrast to the classical approach discussed earlier. In the classical approach full employment is determined within the labour market, with Say's law ruling out the possibility of any deficiency of aggregate demand. Classical economists argued that as long as money wages and prices were free to adjust, the labour market would clear, with any excess supply of labour being eliminated by downward pressure on the real wage rate. Why then does the labour market fail to clear in the Keynesian approach? The answer to this question lies in the assumption made by Keynes that workers would not be prepared to accept a cut in money wages when there is unemployment. The reason he advanced for this is that workers are concerned to maintain their real wage *relativities*. Workers would strongly resist a cut in money wages that affected only their section of the workforce because such a cut would adversely affect their real wage relative to other workers. Given the assumption that money (and hence real) wages tend to be sticky in a downward direction, the labour market will fail to clear. Furthermore, cutting everybody's wages would fail to restore labour market equilibrium. According to Keynes a generalized cut in wages would merely reduce aggregate 'effective' demand in the economy and result in a further fall in output and still higher unemployment. In the orthodox Keynesian approach both the cause of, and cure for, unemployment are largely to be found outside the labour market.

The monetarist approach

The monetarist approach to unemployment derives from the highly influential work of the famous American economist Milton Friedman who, in his Presidential Address to the American Economic Association in 1967, coined the term the **natural rate of unemployment**. According to Friedman, the natural rate – or what can alternatively be thought of as the long-run *equilibrium* rate – of unemployment depends on both the structure of the economy and the institutions within it. He specifically highlights as determinants of the natural rate of unemployment such factors as

Natural rate of unemployment:
The rate of unemployment that exists when the labour market is in equilibrium; composed of frictional and structural unemployment.

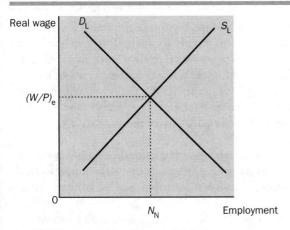

Fig. 10.7 The monetarist and new classical approaches.

market imperfections in the labour and goods markets, the cost of gathering information on job vacancies and labour availabilities, and the costs of mobility.

The natural rate of unemployment is associated with equilibrium in the labour market at the market-clearing real wage rate. This situation is illustrated in Fig. 10.7, where the equilibrium or natural level of employment (N_N) is established at the market-clearing real wage rate $(W/P)_e$. The natural rate of unemployment corresponds to the amount of unemployment that would exist where the aggregate supply of, and demand for labour, were equal. Although monetarists do not approach unemployment in terms of the sum of various types or categories, it is possible to define the natural rate as a situation in which there is no demand-deficient unemployment. As such, the natural rate can be conceptualized as embracing the two main types of non-demand-deficient unemployment, namely frictional and structural unemployment

How can the government reduce the natural rate of unemployment in order to achieve higher output and employment levels? Rather than the macroeconomic (demand-management) policies favoured by orthodox Keynesians, monetarists advocate that governments should pursue *microeconomic* (supply management) policies designed to improve the structure and functioning of the labour market. Within the labour market any policy that leads to either an increase in the supply of labour (shifting the supply curve to the right) or the demand for labour (shifting the demand curve to the right) will increase the equilibrium level of employment and reduce the natural rate of unemployment. Among the wide range of policy measures that have been advocated are policies designed to increase:

- the incentive to work, for example through tax and social security reforms
- the flexibility of wages and working practices, and to reduce distortions that prevent the labour market from working efficiently, for example through trade union reform
- the geographical and occupational mobility of labour
- the efficiency of markets for goods and services (for example by privatization – see Chapter 7, section 7.7) and for capital (for example through the abolition of various controls on activity in financial markets).

Many of these proposed measures are, of course, highly controversial. For example, the reform of social security or welfare payments to unemployed people entails cutting such benefits. The purpose here is to lessen the relative 'attractiveness' of unemployment in comparison with low-paid work. While this measure might increase the supply of labour (shifting S_L in Fig. 10.7 to the right), raise the equilibrium level of employment and thereby reduce unemployment, it would also raise equity or fairness questions about low pay and the impartiality of the state *vis-à-vis* the unemployed and less scrupulous employers.

In summary, given that in the monetarist view the natural or long-run equilibrium rate of unemployment derives essentially from labour market imperfections, reducing the natural rate necessitates measures designed to increase competitiveness in the labour market.

Before turning to discuss the new classical approach to unemployment it is important to note that, while monetarists argue that the labour market will clear in the long run with a corresponding equilibrium or natural rate of unemployment, in the short run actual unemployment may be above or below the natural rate. In other words, for monetarists, the labour market may be in disequilibrium in the short run. In section 10.4, when we come to discuss the relationship between inflation and unemployment, commonly referred to as the Phillips curve, you will see how in the short run unemployment may be temporarily reduced below or raised above its natural rate following expansionary or contractionary aggregate demand policies. However, in the long run, monetarists argue that there is no trade-off between inflation and unemployment. As such the natural or equilibrium level of employment and unemployment is held to be independent of the level of aggregate demand, and is associated with a stable rate of inflation (see section 10.4).

The new classical approach

During the 1970s, a new and highly controversial new classical approach to unemployment emerged. In the United States, the most prominent new classical economist is Robert Lucas Jr (University of Chicago), the 1995 Nobel Laureate in Economics; while in the UK the new classical approach is mainly associated with the work of Patrick Minford (Cardiff Business School). In contrast to both Keynesian and monetarist approaches, the assumption underlying the new classical approach to unemployment is that the labour market *continuously* clears. In other words, in line with the classical approach discussed earlier, new classical economists assume that anyone wishing to find work can do so at the market-clearing equilibrium real wage rate: that is, at $(W/P)_e$ in Fig. 10.7. As we shall discuss in Chapter 11, section 11.6, in the new classical approach fluctuations in employment are held to reflect voluntary changes in the amount that people want to work. Unemployment is treated entirely as a *voluntary* phenomenon, with those who are unemployed voluntarily choosing not to work at the current market-clearing real wage rate. Moreover, any unemployment that results from trade union bargaining and higher real wages in a particular sector is also considered to be voluntary in that workers have chosen unions to represent them. Viewed in this way, new classical economists argue that those who are unemployed could find jobs if only they were prepared to lower their sights and accept inferior or less well paid jobs.

If all unemployment is regarded as being voluntary as new classical economists argue, is there anything governments can do to reduce unemployment? In the new classical view, any policy measure that increases the *microeconomic incentive* for workers to supply more labour will reduce unemployment. For example, it is claimed that by reducing the real value of unemployment benefits unemployment will fall as unemployed workers spend less time looking for the 'right' job, and certain low-paid jobs become more attractive, compared with the reduced benefits that can be obtained when out of work, ensuring that fewer job vacancies remain unfilled.

The new Keynesian approach

During the 1980s, a new Keynesian approach to unemployment was developed to challenge the new classical view that unemployment is entirely a voluntary phenomenon. Within the extensive new Keynesian literature a number of models have been put forward to explain why an 'equilibrium' real wage rate can emerge that is above the market-clearing real wage rate. Such models are therefore capable of generating involuntary unemployment in long-run equilibrium. In what follows we shall outline two such new Keynesian explanations of real wage rigidity in the labour market: efficiency wage and insider–outsider theories.

Efficiency wage model

The essence of efficiency wage theories is that the productivity (effort or efficiency) of workers depends positively on the real wage rate that workers are paid. In consequence, it is both profitable and rational for firms to pay a so-called efficiency wage that is above the market-clearing real wage rate. Efficiency wage theories suggest that, even in the face of an excess supply of labour, it will not be in firms' interests to lower the real wage rate, as to do so would lower productivity and raise costs. Before we outline the main reasons why firms may pay an efficiency wage above the market-clearing real wage rate, it is useful to consider the implications of this analysis by reference to Fig. 10.8.

In Fig. 10.8 full employment (N_F), where the aggregate demand for labour (D_L) is equal to and matched by the aggregate supply of labour (S_L), would occur at a market-clearing real wage rate $(W/P)_e$. If, however, firms pay an efficiency wage $(W/P)^*$ above this market-clearing real wage rate, there will be an excess supply of labour ($N_2 - N_1$), and involuntary unemployment will result. Suppose now that a shock occurs that shifts the aggregate demand for labour to the left from D_L to D_L^*.

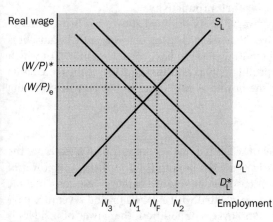

Fig. 10.8 The new Keynesian approach.

In this situation, if the efficiency wage remains at $(W/P)^*$, the excess supply of labour will increase from $N_2 - N_1$ to $N_2 - N_3$, and the amount of involuntary unemployment will increase.

Let us now outline the four versions of efficiency wage theory that have been put forward in the literature. First, the *labour turnover model* suggests that quit rates are a decreasing function of the real wage rate paid to workers. In consequence, firms have an incentive to pay an efficiency wage in order to deter workers from quitting and reduce costly labour turnover: for example the costs involved with hiring and training new employees. At the same time, the existence of involuntary unemployment that results from the payment of an efficiency wage above the market-clearing real wage rate also acts as a disincentive to workers to quit their job.

Second, the *adverse selection model* suggests that workers' abilities and reservation or minimum wage, which would induce them to take a job, are closely connected. In consequence, by paying an efficiency wage, firms will not only attract the best or most productive applicants but will also deter the most productive workers from quitting.

Third, the *shirking model* suggests that, in many jobs, workers can exercise considerable discretion with respect to how well they perform their job, and that there is a real possibility that some workers will shirk their work effort. Such behaviour may be difficult to detect and/or costly to monitor, especially where teamwork predominates. In a fully employed economy where firms pay the market-clearing real wage rate, the threat of dismissal for workers caught shirking will fail to act as an effective deterrent since they can easily find alternative employment at the same real wage rate. If, however, firms pay an efficiency wage above the market-clearing real wage rate (as depicted in Fig. 10.8) then there will be a disincentive for workers to shirk, since if they are caught and are subsequently dismissed they will not readily find employment elsewhere but will join those who are already involuntarily unemployed. In other words, by paying an efficiency wage, firms discourage shirking and raise worker productivity or effort. In addition to acting as a disciplinary device, an efficiency wage also allows firms to reduce costs in monitoring workers' performance.

Finally, the *fairness model* suggests that workers' productivity or effort is closely connected to their morale, which is in turn linked to the notion of being treated fairly with respect to pay. By paying an efficiency wage above the market-clearing real wage rate the morale and loyalty of workers will increase and workers will respond by working harder, increasing their productivity.

In the four versions of efficiency wage theory outlined above, it is firms who decide to pay an efficiency wage above the market-clearing real wage rate because it is both profitable and rational for them to do so. We next consider a model in which no positive effect of real wages on productivity is assumed, and where the focus shifts away from firms as employers to the power of employees in partially determining wage and employment outcomes.

Insider–outsider model

Within the insider–outsider model of real wage rigidity the so-called *insiders* are the incumbent employees and the *outsiders* are the unemployed workers. The power of insiders arises from labour turnover costs. As mentioned earlier, these costs include hiring and firing costs (such as those associated with advertising and severance pay) and also the costs of training new employees. In addition, the power of insiders is reinforced by the fact that they can refuse to cooperate with or can even harass new employees. As a result, insiders can affect the productivity of new employees. In these circumstances, it is argued that insiders have sufficient bargaining power to raise real wages above the market-clearing rate without the fear of losing their jobs and being undercut by outsiders. Unemployed outsiders are unable to price themselves back into work by offering to work for a lower real wage than incumbent employees, because of the power of insiders. In consequence, the insider–outsider model is able to explain why real wages are set that result in involuntary unemployment. One policy implication to reduce unemployment that derives from this model is to increase the market power of unemployed outsiders. For example, measures targeted at the long-term unemployed (those people who have been out of work for a year or more) such as government retraining programmes would help to increase the power of unemployed outsiders.

Hysteresis effects and unemployment

So far in discussing the new Keynesian approach to unemployment we have focused our attention on various theoretical models that can help to account for the existence of involuntary unemployment as an *equilibrium* phenomenon. In this context equilibrium is defined as a situation where there is no incentive for economic agents to change their behaviour. In other words, as illustrated in Fig. 10.8, equilibrium can occur in the labour market where there is an excess supply of labour and involuntary unemployment persists. We now turn to consider new Keynesian hysteresis theories in which the resultant long-run equilibrium level of unemployment is affected by the path taken by the actual level of unemployment.

Earlier, in discussing the monetarist approach to unemployment, we introduced Friedman's concept of a natural rate of unemployment to describe the long-run equilibrium rate of unemployment. We also noted that the natural rate of unemployment is associated with a stable rate of inflation (see section 10.5). While aggregate demand shocks can influence the actual rate of unemployment in the short run, in the long run the natural rate is determined by supply-side influences independently of aggregate demand. Rather than refer to the natural rate, many Keynesians prefer to speak of the **non-accelerating inflation rate of unemployment (NAIRU)** to describe the long-run equilibrium rate of unemployment that is consistent with stable inflation. However, in marked contrast to monetarists, new Keynesians argue that the natural rate (or NAIRU) *is* affected by the path taken by the actual rate of unemployment. In other words the natural rate (or NAIRU) is affected by the level of aggregate demand.

Why do new Keynesians believe that the natural rate (or NAIRU) is affected by the path taken by the actual rate of unemployment? In order to explain why this is the case, suppose the economy is initially operating at its natural rate of unemployment. If the economy experiences, for example, a contractionary aggregate demand shock it may then undergo a prolonged recession. In circumstances where the actual rate of unemployment remains above the natural rate for a prolonged period the natural rate (or NAIRU) will tend to increase owing to so-called **hysteresis effects**. Such effects act like a magnet pulling the natural rate in the same direction. Not only will those who are unemployed suffer a deterioration of their human capital (skills) exacerbating the problem of structural unemployment, but also the number of long-run unemployed, who exercise little influence on the wage bargaining process, is likely to increase. Both forces will raise the natural rate (or NAIRU). Following our

NAIRU: The rate of unemployment at which inflation is stable.

Hysteresis: The proposition that the equilibrium value of a variable depends on the history of that variable.

discussion based on the insider–outsider model, outsiders will be unable to price themselves back into work in the face of high and rising unemployment. As such, hysteresis effects provide a strong case for the authorities to stimulate aggregate demand during a protracted recession.

10.3 A case study: unemployment in Europe

While estimates of the natural rate (or NAIRU) diverge and are themselves fraught with difficulties, most economists agree that the natural rate of unemployment in Europe increased from around 3 per cent in the 1960s to over 9 per cent in the early 1990s. Some indication of this phenomenon is provided by Fig. 10.9 and Table 10.1. Figure 10.9 depicts the average standardized unemployment rate in the European Union (EU), the United States and Japan over the period 1970–98. Table 10.1 shows

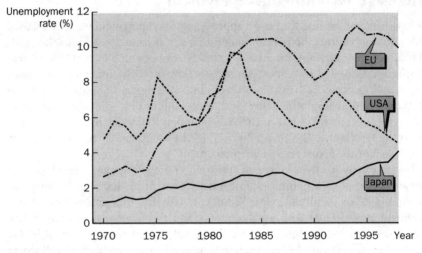

Fig. 10.9 Standardized unemployment rates for the EU, USA and Japan.
Source: *OECD Economic Outlook.*

Table 10.1 Quinquennial average unemployment rates (standardized) in the EU, selected European countries, United States and Japan

	EU	Germany[a]	France	Italy	UK	USA	Japan
1970–74	2.9	1.0	2.7	5.2	3.8	5.3	1.3
1975–79	5.2	3.3	4.7	6.1	5.3	6.9	2.0
1980–84	8.9	5.3	7.7	6.9	9.8	8.3	2.4
1985–89	9.9	6.4	10.0	9.5	9.9	6.2	2.6
1990–94	9.6	6.0	10.6	9.7	9.2	6.6	2.4
1995–98	10.5	9.1	12.0	12.0	7.6	5.1	3.5

[a] Prior to 1993 Germany data refer to West Germany.
Note: The data for standardized unemployment rates for the period 1970–77 are expressed as a percentage of the total (rather than the civilian) labour force. With the exception of Italy there is no marked change in the recorded unemployment rates so that the data for the other economies can be read as if they are a consistent series over the entire period. Data are correct to one decimal point.
Source: *OECD Economic Outlook*

5 year (quinquennial) averages for unemployment in the EU, together with those for selected European countries, the United States and Japan for the five quinquennia (and most recent 4 year span) over the period 1970–98. Reference to Fig. 10.9 reveals that, during the 1970s, unemployment in the EU rose steadily and by 1979 had roughly caught up with that experienced in the United States. At the start of the 1980s unemployment rose sharply in both the EU and the United States. However, while unemployment fell steadily in the United States after 1983, in the EU it has remained high, and since the early-to-mid-1980s has been significantly above that experienced in the United States. We now turn to consider how economists have sought to account for the substantial rise in unemployment that has taken place in the EU since the 1970s.

Two main theories have been put forward to explain the rise in European unemployment. One theory explains high European unemployment in terms of labour market rigidities. Among the specific changes that it is alleged have reduced the flexibility of the labour market and resulted in higher unemployment are:

- more powerful trade unions, who by obtaining real wage increases above the increase in the value of output produced per worker, and by imposing restrictions on working practices limiting firms' ability to adjust to changes in economic circumstances, have raised firms' costs

- higher unemployment benefits, which have acted as a deterrent for the unemployed to find a job, especially for unemployed unskilled workers to take up low paid jobs

- minimum wage laws that have made it unprofitable for firms to hire unskilled workers.

Changes in technology, it is argued, have further reduced the demand for unskilled relative to skilled workers. The term **Eurosclerosis** has been applied to describe such developments. In other words, labour market rigidities are it is suggested leading to the *sclerosis* (a term applied to describe a hardening of the tissues) of the economic system in Europe, resulting in high unemployment. While some of these factors may explain part of the rise in European unemployment in the 1970s, many economists doubt that they offer a plausible explanation of European unemployment experience since the 1980s, when many of these rigidities were reduced. For example, trade union density (the percentage of the labour force that is unionized), which can be used to proxy trade union power, has declined in most European countries since the early 1980s.

The second main theory explains high European unemployment in terms of hysteresis effects in that following prolonged periods when actual unemployment has been high the natural rate (or NAIRU) has itself increased. Two episodes are highlighted. First, in the 1970s, unemployment in most European countries rose sharply following the OPEC oil price increases that occurred in 1973–74 and 1979 (see for example the experience of Germany, France and Italy recorded in Table 9.2). Second, in the early 1980s, following the lead given by the Thatcher government in the UK, most European countries sought to reduce inflation via monetary contraction, resulting in recession and rising unemployment (see section 10.4). For example, reference to Table 9.2 reveals that actual unemployment in the UK rose from 4.7 per cent in 1979 to 11.1 per cent in 1982. In particular, adherents of this second main theory argue that periods of prolonged recession in Europe have led to an increase in

Eurosclerosis: A term used to describe the belief that Europe suffers from excessive labour market rigidities.

the number of long-term unemployed who have not only lost skills/work habits but who also exercise little influence on the process of wage determination (in line with the insider–outsider model). According to this theory, prolonged unemployment has led to an increase in long-term unemployment, which has in turn caused an increase in the natural rate of unemployment (or NAIRU).

What tentative conclusions can be drawn from our overview of unemployment in Europe? Most economists tend to take an *eclectic* position between the two main views we have outlined. As such they recognize that the substantial rise in European unemployment can be attributed in part to changes in the labour market on the *supply side*, and in part to two major adverse (OPEC) supply shocks and deflationary policies on the *demand side*. In the latter case, the evidence suggests that there are significant output/employment costs involved in reducing inflation (see section 10.4), and that such costs can be sustained by hysteresis effects. A major problem facing policy-makers in Europe is to reduce persistent unemployment. While some economists argue that this may require some reform of the unemployment benefit system with respect to the level and duration of benefits that are paid, it is especially important that *active* labour market policies are pursued that are targeted at the long-term unemployed, such as retraining programmes, or the payment of recruit-

---

Box 10.1

Jobless back-to-work initiatives: Brown proposes 'hit squads' to tackle unemployment pockets

Hit squads of employment advisers, who will encourage jobless people into work, have been proposed by Gordon Brown, the Chancellor, to tackle local pockets of high unemployment. In a speech yesterday, Mr Brown said his Budget later this month would give details of the action teams. They are part of a package that will include payments to those who get jobs of up to £400 to help with the costs of travelling to work. The unemployed will also receive free mobile phones and pagers.

However, some businesses and economists suggested continuing to drive unemployment lower might become increasingly difficult. Yesterday the Treasury published figures that, it said, showed there were tens of thousands of vacancies even in areas of relatively high unemployment. Although some analysts dispute the precise figures, there is no denying that the labour market is healthy. The north–south divide is less significant than some of the recent publicity might suggest. The Bank of England's new measure of regional variations in unemployment show the gap is much narrower than it was during the late 1980s. But pockets of high unemployment persist, scattered throughout the country. Even in booming

"Hello! I'm on the dole..."

London, there are 10 000 people unemployed in the borough of Haringey, which, at more than 13 per cent, has the highest unemployment rate in the country. It is these pockets that the Chancellor now hopes to crack. The problem is that there are many good reasons why people remain out of work. Unemployed people are less willing than counterparts abroad to travel to find work. Often, too, they have low skills, the wrong skills, or no skills at all.

The standard of employees coming through the government's New Deal has been criticized by some employers. Stephen Alambritis of the Federation of

Small Business said: 'The quality of people sent by the Employment Service under the New Deal is very poor. They are sending candidates who are unemployable, and who lack basic numeracy skills.' For some unemployed people, despite a series of reforms designed to 'make work pay', there is still not sufficient incentive to take a job. Paul Convery of the Unemployment Unit, the campaigning group, said: 'For a lot of people, if they are going to be only £10 a week better off in a job, they will say, is it really worth working really hard for 37 or 40 hours a week?' The action teams, modelled on US policies using direct persuasion to get people off welfare, may be of only limited effectiveness while the other problems remain. 'The US evidence, based on very carefully controlled experiments, suggests putting pressure on people to take jobs is not very effective', said Andrew Oswald of Warwick University.

There is broad support for Mr Brown's strategy of trying to cut unemployment by reducing the mismatch between job vacancies and unemployed people. But a lot must be done before that mismatch can be reduced to 1960s levels.

Source: Financial Times 1 March 2000

ment subsidies to employers who take on long-term unemployed workers. Furthermore, in a prolonged recession where actual unemployment has risen significantly above the natural rate (or NAIRU), governments should seek to stimulate aggregate demand. But the main lesson to learn above all else is not to let unemployment increase in the first place. Once unemployment has been allowed to rise, as it has in the EU, it is extremely difficult to bring down again.

To conclude our discussion of unemployment, in Box 10.1 we reproduce an extract from the *Financial Times* that outlines some specific initiatives introduced by Gordon Brown, the Chancellor of the Labour government, to reduce pockets of high unemployment in the UK. Once you have carefully read this extract you should consider the following three questions:

- Are the measures outlined in Box 10.1 aimed inside or outside the labour market?
- Advocates of which of the main approaches to unemployment would you anticipate would support these measures?
- Given that some people doubt whether these initiatives will be sufficient to tackle the problem, what additional measures would you put forward to reduce pockets of high unemployment?

Let us now turn to consider the debate over the cause of, and cure for, inflation.

10.4 The debate over the cause of, and cure for, inflation

In Chapter 9, section 9.4, we defined inflation as a process of continually rising prices and outlined how it can be measured. In addition we discussed the economic, social and political costs associated with inflation. You will recall that the main costs of inflation arise when inflation is imperfectly anticipated. We now turn to the debate over the cause of, and cure for, inflation. This debate can be conveniently divided between two main explanations of inflation involving monetarist and non-monetarist views. We begin our discussion with the monetarist explanation, which embodies two of the most famous relationships that exist in macroeconomics: the quantity theory of money, and the (expectations-augmented) Phillips curve.

The monetarist view

The quantity theory of money: old and modern

The monetarist view of inflation is best summarized by Milton Friedman's pronouncement that 'inflation is always and everywhere a monetary phenomenon in the sense that it can be produced only by a more rapid increase in the quantity of money than in output.' This belief is embodied in the *quantity theory of money*, a body of doctrine concerned with the relationship between the money supply and the general price level.

The traditional quantity theory, which has taken a variety of forms, has a long history dating back to before the seventeenth century. Rather than discuss any one particular formulation of the theory, in what follows we present a stylized version of the old (classical) quantity theory. This stylized version of the old quantity theory of money can be described by the equation

$$MV = PY \tag{10.5}$$

where M = the nominal money supply; V = the income velocity of circulation of money during a given time period (the average number of times money circulates throughout the economy in exchange for final output); P = the average price of final output; and Y = the real quantity of final output produced during a given time period.

By definition, the nominal money supply multiplied by the average number of times it circulates in exchange for final output *must* be equal to the average price of the final output multiplied by the real quantity of final output produced during a given time period (see Box 10.2). To turn the quantity equation $MV = PY$ into a theory we must discuss what determines each of the four variables M, V, P and Y. Classical economists argued that the authorities controlled the nominal supply of money in the economy. Hence M was determined independently of V, P and Y in the quantity theory relationship. The income velocity of money was thought to depend on institutional factors, such as the length of the payments period, and was also treated as being independent of the other variables. As institutional factors were held to change slowly over time, V was assumed, for practical purposes, to be constant. Turning to the right-hand side of the quantity theory relationship, classical economists believed that the level of real output was determined by real forces, such as the supply of factors of production. Furthermore, they believed that output would always return to full employment in the long run. In consequence, Y was assumed to be constant at the full employment level of output. Given these assumptions, classical economists argued that in the *long run P*, the average price of final output, would be determined solely by the supply of money, and that any change in the money supply would lead to a proportionate change in the general price level. For example, with V and Y assumed to be constant, a 10 per cent rise in the money supply would lead to a 10 per cent rise in the general price level (see Box 10.2). Classical economists thereby postulated a purely monetary explanation of the determination of the general price level and its rate of change: inflation. In the latter case the old quantity theory relationship can be rewritten and expressed in terms of percentage rates of change. Maintaining the assumption that V and Y are constant we obtain the old quantity

---

Box 10.2

The quantity theory of money: a numerical example

To illustrate the postulated relationship between the money supply and the general price level suppose the values of M, V, P and Y are as follows:

  M, the nominal money supply = £90 000
  V, the income velocity of circulation of money = 4
  P, the average price of final output = £3
  Y, the real quantity of final output produced = 120 000 units.

Within our stylized version of the quantity theory:

  $MV = PY$
  £90 000 × 4 = £3 × 120 000

Now suppose that the authorities decide to increase the nominal money supply by 10 per cent, from £90 000 to £99 000. With V and Y held constant then a 10 per cent increase in the money supply will lead to a 10 per cent increase in the average price of final output to maintain the quantity theory relationship.

In other words:

  $MV = PY$
  £99 000 × 4 = £3.30 × 120 000

theory prediction that, in the long run, the rate of inflation ($\dot{P}$) is determined by, and equal to, the rate of growth of the money supply ($\dot{M}$):

$$\dot{P} = \dot{M} \tag{10.6}$$

In the mid 1950s Friedman reformulated the old quantity theory of money relationship. Although his restatement of the theory was, in the first instance, a theory of the demand for money, the modern quantity theory of money provides the basis for the monetarist explanation of inflation. In contrast to the old quantity theory, in which V and Y were assumed to be approximately constant over time, in the modern quantity theory V and Y are held to be *stable* and *predictable* in the long run. Once the assumption that Y is constant is relaxed, then, in the long run, the rate of inflation is determined by, and equal to, the rate of growth of the money supply minus the rate of growth of real output:

$$\dot{P} = \dot{M} - \dot{Y} \tag{10.7}$$

The policy proposal that follows from this modern quantity theory approach is that the authorities should seek to control the rate of growth of the money supply, in line with the underlying rate of growth of real output, in order to ensure long-term price stability.

Our discussion so far has focused on how, according to the monetarist view, the rate of monetary expansion essentially determines the rate of inflation in the long run. We now turn to consider how, in the short run, the effects of a change in the rate of monetary expansion are divided between changes in output and inflation. This involves an examination of the relationship between unemployment and inflation, commonly referred to as the *Phillips curve*.

The original Phillips curve

In 1958 the results of a *statistical* investigation undertaken by A.W. Phillips into the relationship between unemployment (U) and the rate of change of money wages ($\dot{W}$) in the United Kingdom, over the period 1861–1957, were published in *Economica*. Phillips found evidence of a *stable* relationship between these two variables that appeared to have existed for almost a century. The negative (non-linear) relationship between unemployment and wage inflation is depicted in Fig. 10.10. The estimated average relationship indicated that, when the level of unemployment was

Phillips curve: The relationship between the inflation rate and the unemployment rate.

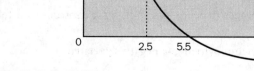

Fig. 10.10 The Phillips curve.

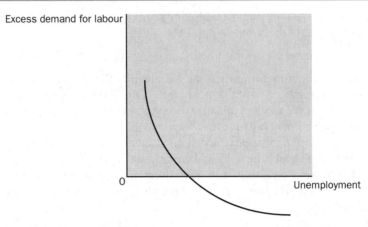

Fig. 10.11 The relationship between excess demand for labour and unemployment.

approximately 5.5 per cent, the rate of change of money wages was zero. Furthermore, at an unemployment level of approximately 2.5 per cent, the rate of change of money wages was approximately 2 per cent, which was roughly equal to the then-average growth of productivity (output per worker). In consequence a 2.5 per cent level of unemployment was compatible with price stability. For this reason the Phillips curve is presented in some textbooks with price (rather than wage) inflation on the vertical axis, with the curve cutting the horizontal axis at an unemployment level of 2.5 per cent.

Now, as noted, Phillips's study was a statistical investigation, and the economic rationale for the curve was provided by Lipsey in an article subsequently published in *Economica* in 1960. Utilizing standard demand and supply analysis that we first encountered in Chapter 2, Lipsey argued that money wages will rise when there is an excess demand for labour. Moreover, the greater the extent of excess demand for labour the faster the rate or speed at which money wages will increase. While it is straightforward to illustrate a state of excess demand diagrammatically, it is more problematic to actually measure excess demand for labour. To get round the problem that excess demand for labour is not directly observable, Lipsey used the level of unemployment as a proxy or surrogate measure for excess demand in the labour market. He postulated that a negative (non-linear) relationship exists between excess demand and unemployment, as shown in Fig. 10.11. Reference to Fig. 10.11 reveals that when the demand for and supply of labour are equal (that is, excess demand is zero) there will still be, as discussed earlier in section 10.2, some positive amount of unemployment. As excess demand for labour increases unemployment will fall (for example as vacancies increase and jobs become easier to find) but by increasingly smaller amounts. Unemployment will never actually fall to zero because of various factors such as those individuals who change their jobs and who will be unemployed while they are searching for new employment.

A combination of two hypotheses, namely that

- the rate of increase in money wages depends positively on excess demand for labour, and
- excess demand for labour and unemployment are negatively related,

provided the economic rationale for the Phillips curve shown in Fig. 10.10.

The Phillips curve can also be described by the equation:

$$\dot{W} = f(U)$$

where $\dot{W}$ = rate of change of money wages, and U = unemployment (a proxy measure for excess demand for labour).

During the 1960s the Phillips curve was quickly adopted as part of the then-prevailing Keynesian economic orthodoxy, not least because it provided the authorities with a menu of possible inflation–unemployment combinations for policy choice. Given the apparent *stable trade-off* between inflation and unemployment, policy-makers were faced with a clear-cut choice. If they decided to run the economy at a lower level of unemployment they would have to accept a cost in terms of a higher rate of inflation. Alternatively, reducing the rate of inflation would involve a cost in terms of higher unemployment. Although some Keynesians argued that inflation was caused by rising costs (a cost-push theory), most Keynesians adhered to a **demand-pull** theory of **inflation**. In this view, inflation was caused by an excess demand for goods and services when the economy was at, or above, full employment.

By the late 1960s the original Phillips curve had broken down. Fig. 10.12 illustrates the breakdown of any stable relationship between inflation and unemployment with data for the UK economy over the period 1970–98. Reference to Fig. 10.12 reveals that the UK economy (as has been the case in other Western economies) has experienced at various times a simultaneous increase in both the rate of inflation and unemployment (so-called *stagflation*). Broadly speaking, economists reacted to the breakdown of the original Phillips curve in one of two main ways. Some Keynesian economists abandoned the demand-pull theory of inflation and turned to a **cost-push** theory of **inflation** (see below). Other economists sought to modify the demand-pull theory by arguing that inflation is caused by both excess demand *and* expectations of future rates of inflation. We first turn to discuss the expectations-augmented Phillips curve and how this fits into the monetarist view of inflation.

The expectations-augmented Phillips curve

In Chapter 8 we discussed how within orthodox microeconomic analysis of the labour market the demand for, and supply of, labour are specified in real, not money,

Demand-pull inflation: Inflation caused by an excess demand for goods and services when the economy is at, or above, full employment.

Cost-push inflation: Inflation caused by cost increases even though there are no shortages of goods and services and the economy is below full employment.

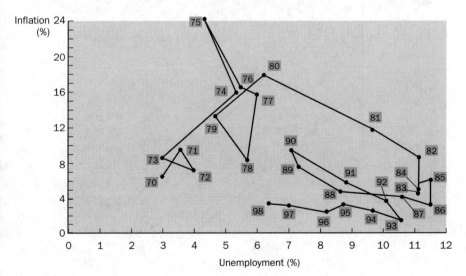

Fig. 10.12 Inflation and unemployment in the UK, 1970—98.

Real wage: The money wage divided (or deflated) by a price index: the amount of goods and services that a money wage can buy.

Short-run Phillips curve: Depicts the relationship between inflation and unemployment that exists for a given expected rate of inflation.

terms. In other words, although money wages are set in wage negotiations, what really matters to both firms as employers and workers as employees is the **real wage** that is negotiated. In addition, given that wage bargains are struck for an advance period (for example, lasting for one year), the rate of inflation expected throughout the period of the contract has a crucial bearing on the real wage negotiated. In the light of these considerations, Friedman augmented the original Phillips curve with the expected rate of inflation as an additional variable determining the rate of change of money wages.

The introduction of the expected rate of inflation as an additional variable that determines the rate of change of money wages modifies the original Phillips curve. As we shall now discuss, the expectations-augmented Phillips curves implies that there is no longer a single unique Phillips curve; rather there exist a whole family of **short-run Phillips curves**. Each short-run Phillips curve is associated with a different expected rate of inflation. As the expected rate of inflation increases, the short-run Phillips curve will shift upwards. In other words, each level of unemployment corresponds to a unique rate of change of real wages. This analysis is illustrated in Fig. 10.13, where both to simplify the analysis and for ease of diagrammatic presentation two assumptions are made:

- Productivity growth remains constant at zero, with the result that firms will pass on any wage increases in the form of price increases, in order to maintain their profit margins.
- The short-run Phillips curves are linear.

Fig. 10.13 maintains the same axes as the original Philips curve of Fig. 10.10 and shows three short-run Phillips curves, each associated with a different expected rate of inflation, and a *vertical long-run Phillips curve (LRPC)* at the natural rate of unemployment (U_N). Suppose the labour market is initially in equilibrium (that is,

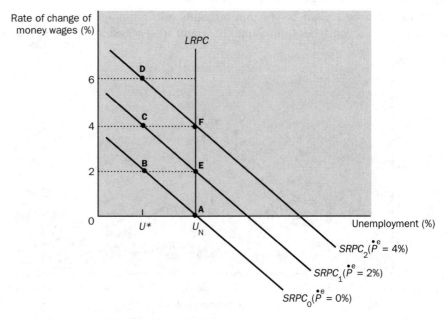

Fig. 10.13 The expectations-augmented Phillips curve.

there is zero excess demand) at the natural rate of unemployment (see section 10.2) with a zero rate of increase in money wages. Assuming productivity growth is zero, a zero rate of increase in money wages ($\dot{W}$) will be matched by a zero rate of increase in prices ($\dot{P}$) and the expected rate of increase in prices ($\dot{P}^e$) will also be zero. In this situation the real wage is constant as the rate of increase in money wages is exactly equal to the rate of increase in prices. Furthermore, inflation is perfectly anticipated, with the actual and expected rates of inflation equal at zero. In Fig. 10.13 this initial situation is indicated by the short-run Phillips curve $SRPC_0$ which cuts the horizontal axis at point A, at the natural rate of unemployment.

Now, suppose that the government decided to increase aggregate demand in the economy by embarking on a policy of monetary expansion in an attempt to *maintain* unemployment below U_N at U^*. As firms increased their production to meet the increase in aggregate demand for goods, the demand for labour would increase, and money wages would start to rise at a rate of 2 per cent. Given recent experience of zero actual and expected inflation rates workers would interpret the 2 per cent increase in their money wages as a 2 per cent increase in their real wages, and respond by increasing the supply of labour. As the demand for and supply of labour increased, unemployment would fall from U_N to U^*, a movement along the short-run Phillips curve ($SRPC_0$) from point A to point B. Assuming productivity growth was zero, a 2 per cent rate of increase in money wages would lead to a 2 per cent rate of increase in prices. Sooner or later workers would start to adapt their expectations of future inflation in the light of such changed circumstances and take their revised expectations into consideration when negotiating money wage increases. As individuals fully revised their expectations of inflation upwards from zero to 2 per cent the short-run Phillips curve would shift upwards from $SRPC_0$ to $SRPC_1$. In other words, once the 2 per cent rate of actual inflation was fully anticipated ($\dot{P} = \dot{P}^e = 2$ per cent), money wages would have to increase at a rate of 4 per cent in order to achieve the 2 per cent increase in real wages necessary to maintain unemployment at U^*: that is, point C on $SRPC_1$. In this situation the authorities would have to increase further the rate of monetary expansion in order to finance the 4 per cent rate of wage and price inflation. As individuals revised their expectations of inflation upwards the short-run Phillips curve would again shift upwards, this time from $SRPC_1$ to $SRPC_2$. At an expected inflation of 4 per cent money wages would have to increase at a rate of 6 per cent, in order to achieve the 2 per cent rise in real wages required by the continued existence of excess demand in the labour market at U^*: that is, point D on $SRPC_2$. In this situation the authorities would have to increase the rate of monetary expansion still further in order to finance the 6 per cent rate of wage and prices inflation, and so on.

To sum up: in the monetarist view, inflation is *initiated* by excessive monetary expansion, which leads to excess demand in the labour market. This causes a rise in money wages, which firms then pass on to consumers in the form of higher prices. Expectations of further price increases lead to increased wage claims resulting in an inflationary 'wage–price' spiral. For monetarists, the chain of causation runs from changes in the money supply (and its rate of expansion) to changes in prices (and their rate of increase, namely inflation). As we shall shortly come to discuss, in the non-monetarist view this chain of causation is reversed.

Policy implications

One of the main policy implications of this analysis is that any attempt to *maintain* unemployment below the natural rate will result in an accelerating rate of inflation, which can be financed only by accelerating monetary growth. If, however, the authorities refuse to increase continuously the rate of monetary expansion unemployment will return to U_N and, in line with the quantity theory of money, in equilibrium in the long run the rate of monetary expansion will equal the rate of inflation ($\dot{P} = \dot{M}$). At U_N the real wage will be restored to its original level and there will be no disturbance in the labour market. Joining together all such points of equilibrium (points A, E, F etc.) a vertical long-run Phillips curve (*LRPC*) is obtained at the natural rate of unemployment. In summary, monetarists argue that while an inflation–unemployment trade-off exists in the short run along a given short-run Phillips curve, once economic agents have fully adjusted their inflationary expectations the trade-off disappears, resulting in a vertical long-run Phillips curve at the natural rate of unemployment. The natural or equilibrium level of unemployment is associated with a stable (or non-accelerating) rate of inflation, which is itself determined by the rate of monetary expansion.

Before we consider the policy implications of reducing inflation it is useful to note that the expectations-augmented Phillips curve can be described by the equation

$$\dot{W} = f(U) + \dot{P}^e \tag{10.9}$$

where $\dot{W}$ = rate of change of money wages, U = unemployment, and $\dot{P}^e$ = the expected rate of inflation. When the economy is in equilibrium at the natural rate of unemployment and there is no excess demand for labour, the rate of increase in money wages ($\dot{W}$) will equal the rate of increase in prices ($\dot{P}$) and the expected rate of increase in prices ($\dot{P}^e$). In this situation the real wage will be constant. The vertical long-run Phillips curve traces a locus of possible points where inflation is perfectly anticipated (that is, $\dot{W} = \dot{P} = \dot{P}^e$) at the natural rate of unemployment. The intersection of the short-run Phillips curve (*SRPC*$_0$) with the vertical long-run Phillips curve at point A represents our initial starting point where the rate of wage and price inflation, and the expected rate of inflation, are all equal to zero. Points E and F represent other potential long-run equilibrium situations.

Let us now turn to consider the output–employment costs of reducing inflation. As we have seen, in the monetarist view inflation is essentially a monetary phenomenon propagated by excessive monetary growth. It follows from this analysis that inflation can be reduced only by slowing down the rate of monetary expansion. Reducing the rate of growth of the money supply will, in the short run, result in an increase in the level of unemployment above the natural rate. The extent and duration of the rise in unemployment depends on two main factors: whether the authorities pursue a policy of rapid or gradual monetary contraction, and the speed at which economic agents revise their expectations of inflation downwards in the light of changed circumstances. We illustrate why this is the case in Fig. 10.14.

In Fig. 10.14 we assume that the economy is initially operating at point A, with a 6 per cent (stable) rate of wage and price inflation (determined by a 6 per cent rate of monetary expansion), and unemployment is at its natural level (U_N). At point A, which is both a short-run and a long-run equilibrium position, inflation is perfectly anticipated, with the actual and expected rates of inflation equal at 6 per cent. Now suppose the authorities decide that they want to reduce the rate of wage and price inflation to 2 per cent and move to point B on the long-run Phillips curve (*LRPC*). One option open to the authorities would be to rapidly reduce the rate of monetary

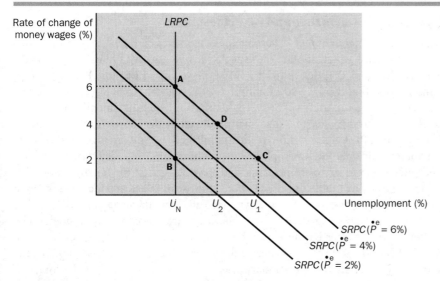

Fig. 10.14 The unemployment costs of reducing inflation.

expansion from 6 per cent to 2 per cent in order to attain their new inflation target of 2 per cent. Such a policy stance would initially result in a relatively large increase in unemployment from U_N to U_1: that is, an initial movement along the short-run Phillips curve associated with an expected rate of inflation of 6 per cent, from point A to point C. As the rate of wage and price inflation fell individuals would revise downwards their expectations of inflation and the short-run Phillips curve would shift downwards. Eventually unemployment would return to U_N, and a new short-run and long-run equilibrium would be established at point B. Alternatively the authorities might choose to reduce the rate of monetary expansion gradually from 6 per cent to 4 per cent and thereafter from 4 per cent to 2 per cent. Such a policy stance would involve a smaller initial increase in unemployment above the natural rate from U_N to U_2: that is, an initial movement along the short-run Phillips curve, associated with an expected rate of inflation of 6 per cent, from point A to point D. The short-run Phillips curve would, as before, shift downwards as individuals revised their expectations of inflation downwards in line with the fall in the actual rate of wage and price inflation. As the authorities gradually reduced the rate of monetary expansion further from 4 per cent to 2 per cent, they would reduce inflation to their target of 2 per cent, and eventually unemployment would return to U_N. In contrast to the policy option of rapid **disinflation**, sometimes referred to as **cold turkey**, reducing inflation by **gradual** monetary contraction would take longer. Recognition of this has led some economists to advocate the use of supplementary policy measures, such as prices and incomes policy (see below), to accompany gradual monetary contraction. Such supplementary policy measures would speed the adjustment process to a lower rate of inflation *if* they succeeded in reducing individuals' expectations of inflation. The faster individuals revise their expectations of inflation downwards, the shorter the period of time for which unemployment will remain above the natural rate following a decrease in the rate of monetary expansion. Of particular importance in this context is the *credibility* of any anti-inflation strategy pursued by the authorities.

Disinflation: A decrease in the rate of inflation.

Cold turkey: A rapid and permanent reduction in the rate of monetary growth, aimed at reducing the rate of inflation.

Gradualism: An approach to disinflation that involves a slow and gradual reduction in the rate of monetary growth.

Prices and incomes policy: Measures that establish guidelines or controls for wage and/or price increases.

Credibility: The degree to which people believe the authorities' announcements about future policy.

Keynesians, monetarists and new classicists

We now turn to highlight *four important differences* between Keynesians, monetarists and new classicists with respect to the expectations-augmented Phillips curve and the policy implications that derive from it. First, *nowadays* while most Keynesian economists accept that the long-run Phillips curve is vertical, some Keynesians believe that there is a long-run trade-off between inflation and unemployment, although one that is less favourable (steeper) than that predicted by the short-run Phillips curve. They argue that the long-run (non-vertical) Phillips curve still offers the authorities a menu of possible inflation–unemployment combinations for policy choice.

Second, in contrast to monetarists and new classicists, Keynesian economists tend to be more favourably disposed towards the use of **prices and incomes policy** as an anti-inflationary weapon. Some Keynesians advocate the *temporary* use of prices and incomes policy as a supplementary policy measure to accompany gradual monetary contraction. Other Keynesians, who assign a role to wage increases made independently of the state of excess demand, advocate the *permanent* use of prices and incomes policy as an anti-inflationary weapon. In the latter case, if the long-run (non-vertical) Phillips curve could be shifted downwards by the adoption of a prices and incomes policy, the trade-off between inflation and unemployment could be improved, allowing the authorities to achieve a lower rate of inflation at any given target level of unemployment.

Third, in marked contrast to monetarists and new classicists, new Keynesians argue that the natural rate of unemployment (or, as discussed above in section 10.2, what they would prefer to refer to as NAIRU) is affected by the path taken by the actual rate of unemployment. In other words new Keynesians argue that the natural rate (NAIRU) is affected by the level of aggregate demand. If, following monetary disinflation, the economy experiences a prolonged recession, the natural rate or NAIRU will tend to increase as hysteresis effects pull the long-run Phillips curve to the right.

Fourth, in contrast to the views held by most Keynesians and monetarists, new classicists do not see the need to follow a policy of gradual monetary contraction in order to reduce inflation. According to the new classical view, the unemployment costs associated with monetary disinflation will be non-existent or negligible provided policy is **credible.** If the authorities announce a reduction in the rate of monetary growth and the policy announcement is believed to be credible, rational economic agents will immediately revise downwards their expectations of inflation in line with the anticipated effects of monetary contraction on the rate of inflation. In terms of Fig. 10.14, inflation would be reduced from 6 per cent to 2 per cent without any increase in unemployment. The short-run Phillips curve associated with a 6 per cent expected inflation would therefore immediately shift downwards to that associated with a 2 per cent expected inflation: that is, the economy would immediately adjust from point A to point B on the long-run Phillips curve. In such circumstances, the authorities might just as well announce a rapid reduction in the rate of growth of the money supply in order to reduce inflation to their new target rate. If, however, there is widespread scepticism that the authorities are not fully committed to disinflation through monetary contraction, individuals will not adjust their inflation expectations downwards. In such a situation, the unemployment costs involved with the adjustment process will be more severe than the case where the authorities have no such credibility problem.

The monetarist view that inflation can be reduced only by slowing down the rate of monetary expansion had an important bearing on the course of anti-inflation policy pursued in many countries during the 1980s. For example, in the UK the Conservative government elected into office in 1979 sought to reduce the rate of monetary growth progressively in order to achieve its overriding economic policy objective of reducing the rate of inflation. As part of its medium-term financial strategy (see Box 10.3), first introduced in the March 1980 Budget, the Thatcher government announced declining targets for monetary growth. Such targets reflected an *explicit* acceptance of the monetarist view that a reduction in monetary growth is both necessary and sufficient to reduce the rate of inflation. At the same time the pre-announcement of declining monetary growth targets reflected an *implicit* acceptance of the view that economic agents form their expectations of inflation rationally and would quickly revise their inflationary expectations downwards, thereby minimizing the unemployment costs associated with monetary disinflation. Table 9.3 reveals that the Thatcher government achieved some measure of success in reducing inflation in the UK in the early 1980s. Between 1979 and 1983 inflation fell from 13.4 per cent to 4.6 per cent, and most economists agree that the domestic monetary (and fiscal) policies pursued contributed

Box 10.3

The medium-term financial strategy of the Thatcher government

In May 1979 a Conservative government under the leadership of Mrs Margaret Thatcher was elected to office in the UK. The new administration made reducing inflation the overriding objective of its economic policy. This objective was conditioned by its belief that a high rate of inflation increases uncertainty, impedes economic efficiency, discourages investment, and adversely affects international competitiveness (see Chapter 9, section 9.4). In order to reduce inflation, the government in 1980 introduced its so-called medium-term financial strategy (MTFS), which embraced both monetary and fiscal policy. The strategy involved the pre-announcement of declining targets for both the rate of growth of the money supply and the public sector borrowing requirements (**PSBR**) for a number of years ahead. In the former case, as noted in the text of the chapter, the targets set for the rate of growth of the money supply reflected both an explicit acceptance of the monetarist view that inflation can *only* be reduced by slowing down the rate of monetary expansion, and an implicit acceptance of the view that economic agents form their expectations of future rates of inflation rationally (a view largely associated with new classical macroeconomics – see Chapter 12, section 12.3). From the mid 1980s onwards, the government gradually changed its strategy towards setting monetary growth targets, in that they no longer occupied the centre stage in the implementation of

monetary policy, and with entry into the exchange rate mechanism of the European Monetary System in October 1990 (see Chapter 14, section 14.6), the UK economy witnessed the formal end of what the media at the time dubbed 'Thatcher's monetarist experiment'.

The targets set for the PSBR within the MTFS reflected a number of views held by the Conservative government:

- an implicit acceptance of the (controversial) view that there exists a stable and predictable relationship between the size of the PSBR and monetary growth
- that the long-term credibility of its anti-inflation strategy by monetary targeting depended on its reducing the PSBR
- a desire to avoid excessive upward pressure on interest rates through sales of government bonds for fear of crowding out private-sector investment in the economy (see Chapter 12, section 12.3)
- a desire to reduce the size of the public sector and provide scope for cuts in income tax to increase the incentive to work.

For more detailed and highly accessible accounts of the Thatcher monetarist experiment in the UK the reader is referred to Keegan, W. *Mrs Thatcher's Economic Experiment* (Harmondsworth: Penguin, 1984) and Smith, D. *The Rise and Fall of Monetarism* (Harmondsworth: Penguin, 1987).

PSBR: The amount of money the public sector (central government, local authorities and nationalized industries) has to borrow after taking into consideration its total expenditure and revenue.

substantially to reducing the rate of inflation in the UK. However, most economists also agree that the restrictive domestic policies pursued made a significant contribution to the rise in unemployment experienced in the early 1980s. Table 9.2 reveals that between 1979 and 1983 unemployment rose from 4.7 per cent to 11.1 per cent. *Prima facie* evidence from other economies also suggests that the unemployment costs of reducing inflation are not insignificant. For example, the pursuit of restrictive monetary policy in the US economy in the early 1980s was also associated with deep recession. Tables 9.2 and 9.3 reveal that, while inflation fell from 11.3 per cent to 3.2 per cent in the US economy between 1979 and 1983, over the same period unemployment rose from 5.8 per cent to 9.6 per cent. Most economists agree that the restrictive domestic policies pursued contributed significantly to the rise in US unemployment, along with other contributory factors including the second oil price shock.

Box 10.4

Re-think at the Fed: Greenspan is adjusting his policies in a world where inflation seems dead

says Gerald Baker

In its unprecedented growth spurt over the past three years, the US economy has broken several rules: first, history says sustained growth above the economy's long-term trend will inevitably end in higher inflation. For three years, the US has grown at an annual rate of just under 4 per cent – 1.5 percentage points above the long-term trend. Yet overall inflation has fallen steadily – to an annual rate of 0.8 per cent in the last three months of 1998, its lowest in more than 20 years. Second, theory suggests that a fall in unemployment below a certain level will lead to a spiral of accelerating wage and price inflation as demand for workers forces employers to pay higher wages, without a corresponding increase in output. In the past few months, the unemployment rate has fallen to 4.2 per cent, its lowest level in 30 years and well below what even the most sceptical economists regard as the lowest rate consistent with stable inflation. Yet average annual earnings growth has been little changed in the past year and is now 3.6 per cent; consumer price inflation is 1.7 per cent per year, half what it was three years ago. Third, experience indicates that low unemployment leads also to declining productivity, or output per hour. As employers hunt for workers in increasingly tight labour markets, the quality of the people they are able to hire diminishes. But even as unemployment has declined, the rate of productivity growth has doubled in the past two years, from its sluggish rate in the early 1990s, to over 2 per cent now.

The Fed has resisted pulling the interest-rate trigger for most of the past two years, even as inflation warning lights have been flashing. One reason is an unusual divergence between conditions in labour and product markets. Labour markets have grown tighter in the past few years, reducing excess capacity in the form of workers looking for jobs. Yet productive capacity use has actually fallen. Industrial capacity utilization – at around 80 per cent – is now down to near recession levels. While employers will have difficulty in drawing down much further from the remaining pool of unemployed labour, it is equally clear that they could in principle expand output without experiencing potentially inflationary production bottlenecks. Big investments – especially in information-technology-related equipment – have raised the output per hour produced by each worker. This improvement is a key factor in the benign inflationary environment. Higher productivity enables companies – and the economy as a whole – to produce more without raising prices. In addition to this phenomenon, some economists argue that US companies have changed their behaviour in response to the intensification of global competition in recent years. Because of fierce competition at home and abroad, companies are increasingly unable to raise prices for fear of losing market share. Instead, they have had to find different ways of dealing with the cost pressures they face. Ms Rivlin (Vice Chair of the US central bank) last week offered

one possible explanation that links these two phenomena. She argued that increased global competition to hold down prices may have induced a radical change in companies' behaviour. Instead of pushing up wage inflation, tight labour markets may actually have reduced it by encouraging companies to invest more in plant and technology and in the training of their workers. That may have raised productivity, and held inflationary pressures in check.

If that is what is happening, then it suggests a possible alternative to the new paradigm. The new paradigm implies that the US is moving from the old world of hard choices and policy trade-offs to a nirvana of inflation-free growth. Under the alternative view, the old rules may not work for now. But this nirvana will prove simply to be a transition, and the US economy will eventually settle down at a new period in which it will again face trade-offs between price stability and growth. In other words, the economy will not go on for ever functioning as benignly as it has done in the past three years. At some point the old rules will reassert themselves, but simply at a higher rate of growth. That implies that Fed officials should not throw away all the old analytical appliances yet. They may need to be tweaked and adjusted to reflect the way the world has changed. But eventually, their day will come again.

Source: Financial Times 15 April 1999

Box 10.4 presents comment and analysis on the remarkably low combination of inflation and unemployment (see also Tables 9.1–9.3) experienced in the US economy over recent years. While some commentators have suggested that this experience provides prima facie evidence that policy-makers should abandon such analytical tools as the expectations-augmented Phillips curve, others are far from convinced that policy-makers should jettison such instruments in guiding their policy decision-making. One aspect drawn out in Box 10.4 is the importance of the international economic environment. Let us now turn to consider inflation as an international monetary phenomenon.

Inflation as an international monetary phenomenon

So far we have discussed the monetarist view of inflation implicitly in the context of a closed economy in which no international trade takes place. In a closed economy (or an open economy operating under flexible exchange rates – see Chapter 14, section 14.5), the domestic rate of inflation is held to be determined by the domestic rate of monetary expansion relative to the rate of growth of domestic real output. However, in a regime of **fixed exchange rates** such as the **Bretton Woods system** (see Chapter 14, sections 14.5–14.6), which operated from the mid 1940s until the early 1970s, inflation is viewed as an international monetary phenomenon. Under a regime of fixed exchange rates, monetarists argue that nations are linked together in a world economy in which the aggregate world money supply (and its rate of change) determines world prices (and their rates of change). Domestic monetary expansion will influence the domestic rate of inflation only to the extent that it influences the rate of growth of the world money supply and in consequence the rate of growth of world prices. An increase in the world rate of monetary expansion (due to the rapid monetary expansion by either a large country relative to the rest of the world, or a number of small countries simultaneously) would create excess demand and result in inflationary pressure throughout the world economy. On the basis of this analysis, monetarists have argued that the acceleration of inflation that occurred in Western economies in the late 1960s was primarily the consequence of an increase in the rate of monetary expansion in the USA to finance increased expenditure on the Vietnam War. Inflationary pressure initiated in the USA was then transmitted to other Western economies via the US balance of payments deficit.

For an economy operating under a regime of **flexible exchange rates** monetarists argue that a country's domestic rate of inflation will be determined, as in the case of a closed economy, by its domestic rate of monetary expansion (relative to the rate of growth of domestic real output). If the domestic rate of monetary expansion in an economy is greater than that in the rest of the world, then it will experience a faster domestic rate of inflation compared with that prevailing in other countries, and its currency will depreciate.

Having discussed the monetarist view of inflation in some detail we now turn to discuss the second main conflicting explanation of inflation, the non-monetarist view.

The non-monetarist view

In contrast to the monetarist view, in the non-monetarist view (also sometimes referred to as the cost-push or sociological explanation of inflation) wage increases are regarded as the initiating force of inflation. Furthermore, such wage increases can occur *independently* of the state of demand and supply conditions in the labour market. Adherents to this view argue that there exist various social pressures that lead to largely *exogenous* wage increases. Given these social pressures, the common theme in the non-monetarist approach is that, because wages are such an important component of firms' costs of production, if money wages continually rise at a faster rate than the growth of productivity, then an inflationary wage–price spiral will result in a similar manner to that analysed in the monetarist view. In the absence of monetary expansion, unemployment will increase as inflation reduces the real value of the money supply. Proponents of the non-monetarist view argue that, in the past, governments have increased the money supply in order to prevent unemployment from rising. This response by the government explains, in this view, the strong correlation between changes in the money supply and changes in prices. In contrast to the monetarist view, in the non-monetarist view causation runs from changes in prices to changes in the money supply, rather than the other way round.

In what follows we outline some of the social pressures that, it is alleged, lead to wage increases and initiate the inflationary process. Two examples will suffice. First, some writers argue that class conflict is inevitable in a capitalist society and that inflation results from the struggle between workers and capitalists as each group strives to achieve a bigger share of national income for themselves. If workers succeed in securing wage increases above productivity growth, capitalists' profit margins will be reduced. In order to maintain the share of profits in national income, capitalists will react by increasing their prices. Workers then react by pressing for wages increases, resulting in the familiar inflationary wage–price spiral. The more workers' aspirations for real income growth exceed productivity growth the faster will be the ensuring inflation. Second, some writers suggest that inflation results from the attempts of unions to improve or maintain their members' position in the league table of wages. If one union succeeds in improving its *relative* wage position, other unions seeking to restore or improve on the previous order of wage differentials will react by pushing for wage increases. Such a process will lead to leapfrogging as each union tries to improve its relative wage position, resulting in an inflationary wage–price spiral.

In the two examples of the non-monetarist view cited above, the common theme is that trade unions continually push for increases in money wages above the growth of productivity. Such wage increases feed into price increases, which in turn leads to further wage increases and so on. If this is the case then it is important to ask why firms are willing to accede to such inflationary wage claims. The usual answer given to this question by adherents of the non-monetarist view is that the balance of power in negotiating wage increases has tended to move away from firms in favour of unions. Among the reasons put forward to explain this is that increased welfare benefits have enabled workers to resort to longer periods of strike action if their wage claims are not met. Furthermore, given the changing nature of the production process, firms are more willing to accede to claims for wage increases rather than resist and face 'costly' strike action. As production has become more capital-intensive in many industries, firms have become more vulnerable to their whole production process being disrupted by a small number of workers threatening strike action. In addition, greater foreign competition has meant that, in the event of strike action, output may be lost as customers turn to foreign markets. In these circumstances, it is argued, it is less costly for firms to give in to wage claims than to face the severe costs that result from strike action that disrupts the production process.

The non-monetarist view of inflation outlined above emphasizes rising wage costs as the initiating force of the inflationary process. Before considering the policy implications of this view mention should also be made of the role of increases in other production costs in triggering higher prices. Some writers have drawn attention to rising costs of imported raw materials and fuels, which firms pass on to consumers in the form of higher prices. As domestic prices rise, unions demand money wage increases in order to maintain their members real wages. As a result an inflationary wage–price spiral develops, which is then accommodated by monetary expansion in order to prevent a rise in unemployment. In particular the two oil price hikes that occurred in 1973–74 and 1979 are highlighted as triggering the high rates of inflation experienced in many Western economies in the mid 1970s and early 1980s (see Table 9.3).

Policy implications

Let us now turn to examine the policy implications of this non-monetarist view of inflation. Given the belief that money wage increases, or other increased costs of production, initiate inflation, the introduction of a *permanent* prices and incomes policy is seen as the best way to control the inflationary spiral. Such a policy involves implementing a series of *direct controls* or rules that govern the extent to which wages and prices can increase. For example, for wage increases not to be inflationary, money wage increases need to be controlled to ensure that they do not exceed the average increase in productivity. Of interest is that past policy has traditionally focused on *wage control*, rather than income control, in part because other forms of income, such as dividends and interest, are much more difficult to influence.

Despite the simple logic behind the introduction of prices and incomes policy, such a policy involves a number of potentially important problems and is not without its critics. There are four main difficulties associated with prices and incomes policy:

- There are a number of problems involved with the implementation of both a wages and a prices policy. For example, both workers and firms may find ways of evading wage and price controls respectively.

- A wages policy operates *outside* the market mechanism and in consequence may result in a misallocation of resources. For example, firms in growth industries may find it difficult to expand production if they are not allowed to offer wage increases that are necessary to attract additional workers required.

- If a prices and incomes policy is accompanied by excessive monetary expansion the policy will ultimately be doomed to failure. Unless the extreme view is taken that excess demand never affects wages and prices, excessive monetary expansion must result in inflationary pressures, which will inevitably lead to the breakdown of a policy seeking to control wage and price increases.

- While a prices and incomes policy may succeed in moderating the rate of wage and price increase during the period in which it is operated, once the policy is relaxed, or breaks down, wages and prices may subsequently 'catch up' by increasing at a faster pace.

10.5 Concluding remarks

In this chapter we have considered the debate over the cause of, and cure for, unemployment and inflation. In tracing the history of unemployment theory in the first half of the chapter we were able to identify five main approaches to the controversy over unemployment. In discussing these competing explanations we sought to show that the central question that underlies the continuing controversy is whether the cause of, and cure for, unemployment is largely found *inside* or *outside* the labour market. In the second half of the chapter we presented two competing explanations of the cause of, and cure for, inflation. In the monetarist view the cause of inflation is excessive monetary expansion – a case of 'too much money chasing too few goods'. Since governments cause inflation they also have it within their power to reduce inflation through monetary contraction. In contrast, in the non-monetarist view, inflation is caused primarily by largely exogenous wage increases, which arise from various social pressures. In this view the best way to control inflation is through the introduction of prices and incomes policy. While our presentation has highlighted the difference between these two competing explanations it is important to note that some economists take an eclectic or compromise stance, suggesting that inflation can be caused by both excessive monetary expansion and various cost-push pressures. Indeed, the consensus view is that while *sustained* inflation is not possible without excessive monetary expansion, *temporary* bouts of inflation can be attributed to non-monetary causes arising from the supply side of the economy.

◾ Summary

◆ The central question that underlies the debate over unemployment is whether the cause of, and consequently cure for, unemployment is essentially to be found inside or outside the labour market.

◆ Orthodox Keynesians identify three main types or categories of unemployment: frictional, structural and demand-deficient unemployment. Each type of unemployment requires a different policy solution. In the Keynesian approach, the level of employment is largely determined outside the labour market by the level of aggregate demand in the economy. Because aggregate demand may be too low to guarantee full employment, governments need to stimulate aggregate demand to maintain high and stable levels of employment.

◆ Monetarists refer to a natural or long-run equilibrium rate of unemployment that is independent of the level of aggregate demand and is consistent with a stable rate of inflation. The natural rate depends on a number of factors, and can be reduced by measures that improve the flexibility of the labour market.

◆ In the new classical approach the labour market is assumed to be cleared continuously. Unemployment is treated entirely as a voluntary phenomenon.

◆ New Keynesian economists have put forward efficiency wage and insider–outsider theories to explain the existence of involuntary unemployment as an equilibrium phenomenon. The long-run equilibrium rate of unemployment or NAIRU that is consistent with stable inflation is affected by the level of aggregate demand. Where the actual rate of unemployment remains above NAIRU for a prolonged period, NAIRU will increase owing to hysteresis effects.

◆ Two main theories have been put forward to explain the rise in European unemployment. One view focuses on labour market rigidities, which have led to an increase in the natural rate (or NAIRU); the other focuses on hysteresis effects pulling NAIRU up following periods when actual unemployment has been high.

What is needed to reduce the present high level of unemployment in the EU is a set of solutions that involve both aggregate supply and aggregate demand policies.

◆ The debate over the causes of, and cures for, inflation can be divided between two main competing explanations involving monetarist and non-monetarist views.

◆ In the monetarist view the rate of inflation, in the long run, is determined by the rate of monetary expansion relative to the rate of growth of real output. While an inflation–unemployment trade-off exists in the short run, in the long run the Phillips curve is vertical at the natural rate of unemployment. The natural rate of unemployment is associated with a stable rate of inflation, which is itself determined by the rate of monetary expansion.

◆ In the short run monetary disinflation results in an increase in the level of unemployment above the natural rate. How much unemployment increases depends on whether the authorities pursue a policy of rapid or gradual monetary contraction and how quickly inflation expectations are revised downwards. *Prima facie* evidence from the UK and US economies in the early 1980s suggests that the unemployment costs of monetary disinflation are significant.

◆ Under a regime of fixed exchange rates inflation can be regarded as an international monetary phenomenon.

◆ In the non-monetarist view of inflation wage increases, which can occur independently of labour market conditions, are seen as the initiating force of an inflationary wage–price spiral. As the balance of power in negotiating wage increases has changed in favour of trade unions, firms have become more willing to accede to claims for wage increases. Prices and incomes policy is seen as the best way to control the inflationary spiral, according to proponents of the non-monetarist view.

◆ Some economists take an eclectic stance between the monetarist and non-monetarist views, and argue that inflation can be caused by both excessive monetary expansion and various cost-push pressures.

■ Key terms

◆ Classical/real wage unemployment
◆ Frictional/search unemployment
◆ Structural/mismatch unemployment
◆ Demand-deficient/cyclical unemployment
◆ Natural rate of unemployment/NAIRU
◆ Efficiency wages
◆ Insiders versus outsiders
◆ Hysteresis
◆ Eurosclerosis
◆ Quantity theory of money
◆ Phillips curve
◆ Inflation–unemployment trade-off
◆ Expectations-augmented Phillips curve

◆ Monetary disinflation
◆ Gradualism versus cold turkey
◆ Credibility
◆ Cost-push inflation
◆ Prices and incomes policy
◆ Eclecticism

Self-test questions

True (t) or false (f)

1. Classical unemployment occurs when the real wage is maintained above the level at which the aggregate demand for labour equals the aggregate supply of labour.

2. Frictional unemployment is also known as search unemployment.

3. Measures that increase the search time moving between jobs will reduce the amount of frictional unemployment.

4. Structural unemployment is also known as cyclical unemployment.

5. Policies that improve the mobility of labour will reduce the amount of structural unemployment.

6. Demand-deficient unemployment is also known as mismatch unemployment.

7. The cause of demand-deficient unemployment lies inside the labour market.

8. The natural rate of unemployment is the rate of unemployment that exists when the labour market is in equilibrium.

9. Governments can reduce the natural rate of unemployment by pursuing macroeconomic policies that stimulate aggregate demand.

10. New classical economists treat unemployment as an entirely voluntary phenomenon.

11. According to new Keynesian economists, it is neither profitable nor rational for firms to pay an efficiency wage that is above the market-clearing real wage rate.

12. New Keynesians argue that NAIRU is affected by the path taken by the actual rate of unemployment.

13. The quantity theory of money is a doctrine concerned with the relationship between the money supply and the price level.

14. Classical economists believed that, in the long run, a change in the money supply would lead to a proportionate change in output.

15. The Phillips curve depicts the relationship between inflation and unemployment.

16. Phillips found no evidence of a stable relationship between inflation and unemployment.

17. Friedman augmented the original Phillips curve with the expected rate of inflation as an additional variable determining the rate of change of money wages.

18. The short-run Phillips curve will shift upwards as individuals revise their expectations of inflation downwards.

19. Attempts to maintain unemployment below the natural rate of unemployment will result in a stable rate of inflation.

20. Gradualism is an approach to disinflation that involves a rapid and permanent reduction in the rate of monetary growth.

21. The output/employment costs of reducing inflation will be lower the faster economic agents revise their expectations of inflation downwards in the light of changed circumstances.

22. According to the new classical view, the unemployment costs associated with disinflation will be non-existent or negligible provided the policy of announced monetary contraction is credible.

23. In the non-monetarist view of inflation, rising wage costs are regarded as the initiating force of the inflationary process.

24. In the non-monetarist view of inflation, the chain of causation runs from changes in the money supply (and its rate of expansion) to changes in prices (and their rate of increase).

25. In the non-monetarist view of inflation, the introduction of a permanent prices and incomes policy is seen as the best way to control inflation.

26. Some economists argue that inflation can be caused by both excessive monetary expansion and various cost-push pressures.

Complete the following sentences by inserting the missing word(s)

1. Classical unemployment is also known as _____ unemployment.

2. The three main types of unemployment identified by Keynesians are _____, _____ and _____ unemployment.

3. Expenditure that does not depend on the level of national income is referred to as _____ expenditure.

4. When the labour market clears and the aggregate demand for labour equals the aggregate supply of labour all unemployment will fall in the category of _____ and _____ unemployment.

5. In the Keynesian approach the level of unemployment is largely determined outside the labour market by the level of _____ in the economy.

6. The term 'the natural rate of unemployment' was coined by the famous American economist _____.

7. Governments can reduce the natural rate of unemployment by pursuing _____ policies that improve the structure and functioning of the labour market.

8. The four versions of the efficiency wage theory are the _____ model, the _____ model, the _____ model and the _____ model.

9. New Keynesians refer to _____ to describe the long-run equilibrium rate of unemployment that is consistent with stable inflation.

10. The proposition that the equilibrium value of a variable depends on the history of that variable is known as _____.

11. 'Inflation is always and everywhere a _____ phenomenon' (Friedman).

12. In the modern quantity theory of money, V and Y are held to be _____ and _____ in the long run.

13. The trade-off between inflation and unemployment is depicted by the _____ .

14. In providing a theoretical rationale for the Phillips curve, Lipsey argued that money wages will rise when there is an _____ .

15. Inflation, if caused by an excess demand for goods and services when the economy is at or above full employment, is referred to as _____ .

16. The expectations-augmented Phillips curve analysis implies that there are a whole family of short-run Phillips curves, each associated with a different _____ .

17. Monetarists argue that in the long run the Phillips curve is _____ at the _____ rate of unemployment.

18. In the non-monetarist view of inflation, wage increases can occur _____ of the state of demand and supply conditions in the labour market.

19. The non-monetarist view of inflation is also sometimes referred to as the _____ or _____ explanation of inflation.

20. In the non-monetarist view of inflation, the best way to control inflation is to introduce measures that establish guidelines or controls for wage and/or price increases. Such measures are referred to as _____ .

21. Wages policy operates _____ the market mechanism and may result in a misallocation of resources.

Exercise

1. Fig. 10.12 illustrates the breakdown of any stable relationship between inflation and unemployment for the UK economy over the period 1970–98. In a similar fashion, using data presented in Tables 9.2 and 9.3, plot the relationship between inflation and unemployment for the US economy over the same period.

▮ Questions for discussion

◆ What is the difference between frictional and structural unemployment? What policies can help to reduce each type of unemployment?

◆ What is demand-deficient unemployment? How can the government reduce this type of unemployment?

◆ What is meant by the term the 'natural' rate of unemployment? What policies might be used to reduce the natural rate?

◆ Why may firms find it profitable and rational to pay a so-called efficiency wage that is above the market-clearing real wage rate?

◆ How might hysteresis effects cause a rise in the natural rate of unemployment?

◆ How have economists sought to explain the rise in unemployment that has taken place in the EU since the 1970s? What can governments do to reduce unemployment?

◆ What are the main differences between the monetarist and non-monetarist views of inflation?

◆ Do governments or trade unions cause inflation?

◆ Is there a permanent trade-off between inflation and unemployment?

◆ What factors determine the unemployment costs of reducing inflation?

◆ In recent years the Bank of England's Monetary Policy Committee has, on a number of occasions, increased interest rates in order to dampen inflationary pressures in the UK economy. How might increased interest rates adversely affect firms?

◆ Does the remarkably low combination of inflation and unemployment experienced in the US economy over recent years (see Box 10.4) imply that the natural rate of unemployment has fallen in the USA?

◆ What initiates inflation in the non-monetarist view? What are the main problems that may arise in implementing prices and incomes policy?

Further reading

Dawson, G. *Inflation and Unemployment: Causes, Consequences and Cures* (Aldershot: Edward Elgar, 1992). A thoughtful, lucid and comprehensive guide to the issues of both unemployment and inflation.

Layard, R., S. Nickell and R. Jackman *The Unemployment Crisis* (Oxford: Oxford University Press, 1994). An accessible and comprehensive explanation of the causes of, and sources of fluctuations in, unemployment, citing the recent experience of OECD countries.

Vane, H.R. and J.L. Thompson *An Introduction to Macroeconomic Policy* (4th ed.) (Hemel Hempstead: Harvester Wheatsheaf, 1993). Chapters 11 and 12 provide more detailed discussion of fiscal and monetary policy respectively.

Friedman, M. *Unemployment versus Inflation?* (London: Institute of Economic Affairs, 1975). A very clear and accessible evaluation of the Phillips curve, written by the most famous living economist in the world.

Internet links

The *Office for National Statistics* has a website that offers micro and macro time series data online, including data on employment and unemployment. The site is at: **http://www.statistics.gov.uk/**

The *Department for Education and Employment* has responsibility for employment issues in the UK. Its website offers a series of press releases that describe the changing patterns of employment and unemployment in the UK. The site is at: **http://www.dfee.gov.uk/index.htm**

The Bank of England *Inflation Report* offers an assessment of inflation pressures and prospects for the UK economy. Summaries of the Inflation Report are available from: **http://www.bankofengland.co.uk/**

For other economies, inflation issues will also be subject to a watching brief by *their* central banks. Links to a large number of the world's central banks are provided by the *Bank for International Settlements* at: **http://www.bis.org/cbanks.htm**

Economic Growth and Business Cycles

Contents

Key issues

▶ What factors determine economic growth over time?

▶ What role can the government play in promoting growth?

▶ What are business cycles?

▶ What are the main theories that economists have put forward to explain business cycles?

▶ Can the authorities control business cycles?

11.1 Introduction

In Chapter 9, section 9.2, we discussed the nature and measurement of economic growth. You will recall that economic growth, the source of *sustained* increases in material living standards over time, refers to an increase in real GDP. Not only is economic growth important for raising living standards but so too is the rate of growth actually achieved in an economy. Even small differences in growth rates can make a tremendous difference to the growth of living standards and the level of **potential output** over the course of a few decades. As a rough rule of thumb the number of years it takes for an economy to double its productive capacity can be found by dividing 72 by its rate of growth. For example, an economy will take approximately 36 years to double its output of goods and services if its growth rate is 2 per cent, but only 18 years if its growth rate is 4 per cent.

In Chapter 9, section 9.2, we also discussed how an economy will experience short-term fluctuations of output (real GDP) around its secular or long-term trend path, a phenomenon referred to as the *business cycle*. During an upturn in economic activity output increases, unemployment falls, and the potential for firms to raise their profits increases. During a downturn in economic activity, output decreases, unemployment rises, and profits may fall. Because, over long periods of time, short-term fluctuations in output are dominated by the growth of potential output as the productive capacity of the economy increases, we begin this chapter with a discussion of those factors that determine an economy's rate of economic growth over

Potential output: The maximum output that can be produced in an economy, given its factor endowments, without generating inflation; also known as full employment output.

time. In the second half of the chapter we consider the main theories put forward by economists to explain periodic fluctuations in economic activity and the question of whether or not the authorities can control business cycles.

Depending upon the nature and level of the course you are studying you now have a choice to make as to which sections to read on the subject of economic growth. For most readers section 11.2 provides a brief, but adequate, overview of the factors that determine economic growth over time, and what role the government can play in promoting growth. Other student readers, for example those on MBA programmes, should read sections 11.3–11.4, which by the nature of their content are more technically demanding, before proceeding to read sections 11.5–11.6 on business cycles.

11.2 Economic growth: an overview

Our starting point in discussing the causes of economic growth is consideration of the **aggregate production function** (see Chapter 4, section 4.2). The aggregate production function is a function that relates the quantity of aggregate output that can be produced to a *given* quantity of factor inputs. This relationship can be written as

$$Y = A(t)\, F(K,N) \tag{11.1}$$

where Y is real output; $A(t)$ represents technological know-how at time t; and F is a function that relates real output to K, the quantity of capital inputs, and N, the quantity of labour inputs. Real output will increase over time if there is an increase in the quantity of factor inputs (capital and/or labour) and/or there is an increase in the productivity of capital and labour inputs (that is, an increase in output per unit of factor input) due to an increase in technological know-how.

This analysis can be illustrated graphically using either the short-run aggregate production function (Fig. 11.1) or the production possibility frontier (Fig. 11.2). The short-run aggregate production function depicted in Fig. 11.1 relates real output (Y) to the quantity of labour inputs (N) for *given* technological know-how (A) and quantity of capital inputs (K). The decreasing slope of the aggregate production

Aggregate production function: A functional relationship between the quantity of aggregate output produced and the quantities of inputs used in production.

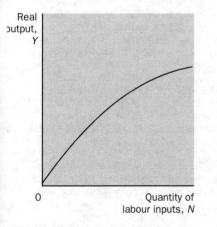

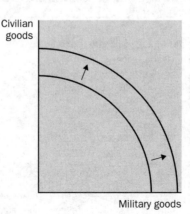

Fig. 11.1 The short-run aggregate production function.

Fig. 11.2 The production possibility frontier.

function reflects diminishing returns to the factor input, N (see Chapter 4). Over time as economic growth occurs the function will shift upwards following an increase in the quantity of capital inputs and/or an increase in the productivity of factor inputs K and N due to an increase in the value of A: for example, following an improvement in the state of technology.

Economic growth, which involves an increase in real output over time, can also be conceptualized using the production possibility frontier shown in Fig. 11.2. Fig. 11.2 illustrates two production possibility frontiers, before and after economic growth has taken place. Each frontier shows production possibilities involving various combinations of civilian and military goods when an economy's resources are efficiently employed. Economic growth involves an outward movement of the production possibility frontier, thereby increasing the economy's capacity to produce goods. Such a movement in the frontier results from either an increase in the quantity of factor inputs available or an improvement in the quality of those factor inputs.

What the above analysis illustrates is that economic growth depends on increases in the quantity *and* quality of both capital and labour inputs. Box 11.1 summarizes the results of a study by Edward Denison of *Trends in American Economic Growth* over the period 1929–82, and gives some indication of the relative importance of various sources of economic growth.

We now turn to consider what role the government can play in promoting increases in the quantity and quality of K and N. At the outset it is important to stress that this issue is the subject of considerable controversy, and economists disagree in their views over what role the government can play in promoting economic growth.

Let us consider the quantity of capital inputs. The physical stock of capital in the form of plant, machinery and infrastructure can only be increased by investment. One option that is open to the government is to stimulate private-sector investment by increasing the rate of return on, or reducing the cost of, capital by changing company taxation. For example, the cost of capital can be reduced by changing investment and depreciation allowances. However, whether or not tax changes

---

Box 11.1

Sources of US economic growth 1929–82 (per cent)

Annual growth rate of output	2.9
Percentage of growth due to:	
Growth in labour input	32
Growth in labour productivity	
Education per worker	14
Capital	19
Technological change	28
Economies of scale	9
Other factors	−2

Source: Denison, E.F. *Trends in American Economic Growth* (Washington, DC: The Brookings Institution, 1985)

Some indication of the relative importance of various sources of economic growth is contained in a study by Edward Denison of *Trends in American Economic Growth* over the period 1929–82. Denison's findings concerning the sources of US economic growth over this period are summarized opposite. Between 1929 and 1982 real output grew at an annual rate of 2.9 per cent. Denison estimated that 32 per cent of US economic growth over this period was due to growth in the quantity of labour input, while 68 per cent came from growth in labour productivity, itself due to four main factors. According to Denison's estimates 28 per cent of US economic growth was due to technological change (the most important influence on labour productivity), 19 per cent resulted from capital formation, 14 per cent was due to increased education per worker, and 9 per cent resulted from economies of scale.

would succeed in stimulating private-sector investment requires detailed knowledge of a country's tax system, in order to establish how different firms would be affected, and is beyond the scope of this text. Another option open to the government is to increase public-sector investment by infrastructure provision such as road and rail networks. While noting this option it is important to remember that economists differ in their views over the degree to which the private and public sectors should be involved in the provision of infrastructure. In addition to increasing the quantity of capital, investment in research and development is required in order to increase the *quality* of capital by discovering, developing and diffusing new technical knowledge. As noted earlier, improvements in technological know-how increase the productivity of both capital and labour, generating an increase in output per unit of factor input. The government can seek to influence the supply of technology either *directly* by, for example, financing research and development itself, or *indirectly* by, for example, encouraging the private sector to engage in research and development through such initiatives as research grants, tax incentives and patent rights. For example, patent rights allow monopoly profits to accrue to their inventors and thereby provide an incentive for individuals and firms to engage in research and development.

> **Human capital**: The knowledge and skills of workers in an economy.

So far we have outlined the importance of physical capital to the growth process. Some recent theories of economic growth have stressed the accumulation of **human capital** – the knowledge and skills of a country's workers – as the key to achieving economic growth. As human capital is acquired through education, training and experience one option open to the government is to encourage investment in human capital by, for example, the provision of subsidized university education. Investment in human capital may also have wider social benefits by generating 'ideas' for the development of new goods. Such theories, in part, help to explain the lack of convergence of per capita income levels and growth rates between poor nations (as in Africa, for example) and industrial nations. Poor nations with little human capital cannot hope to catch up industrial nations simply by accumulating physical capital. These theories also point to another reason why poor nations may fail to catch up industrial nations, namely because of 'idea gaps'.

Having discussed, albeit briefly, the factors that determine economic growth over time you should now turn to sections 11.5–11.6, where we consider the business cycle. Before considering the main approaches to the cause and control of business cycles in section 11.6, we first describe the main features of business cycles in section 11.5.

11.3 The Solow growth model

The best framework to start studying economic growth is provided by a model that was developed in the 1950s and 1960s by Robert Solow, Professor of Economics at Massachusetts Institute of Technology. For his important and influential work on the theory of economic growth Solow was awarded the Nobel Prize in Economics in 1987. As we shall discuss, the Solow growth model identifies which factors determine growth in output over time and also sheds light on some of the reasons why standards of living (real GDP per person) vary so widely between countries. Our starting point is consideration of the aggregate production function, which forms the bedrock of the model.

The aggregate production function

The **aggregate production function** (see also Chapter 4, section 4.2) is a function that relates the quantity of aggregate output that can be produced to a *given* quantity of factor inputs. This relationship can be written as

$$Y = A(t) \, F(K, N) \tag{11.1}$$

where Y is real output; $A(t)$ represents technological know-how at time t; and F is a function that relates real output to K, the quantity of capital inputs, and N, the quantity of labour inputs. Real output will increase over time if there is an increase in the quantity of factor inputs (capital and/or labour) and/or there is an increase in the productivity of capital and labour inputs (that is, an increase in output per unit of factor input) due to an increase in technological know-how.

At the outset it is important to highlight three key properties exhibited by the neoclassical production function used by Solow in his analysis:

- Factor inputs of labour and capital can be smoothly *substituted* for each other in the production process. In other words, firms can use more capital inputs and fewer labour inputs, or vice versa, to produce the same quantity of output.

- Factor inputs experience **diminishing returns**. For example, as first discussed in Chapter 4, while an increase in the quantity of labour inputs with the quantity of capital inputs held constant will result in an increase in real output, output will increase at an ever-declining rate. Similarly diminishing returns will result from an increase in the capital stock to a fixed labour force.

- It is assumed that the aggregate production function exhibits **constant returns to scale**. Constant returns to scale mean that when all factor inputs increase in some proportion, real output will increase in that same proportion. For example, if both the quantity of labour and capital inputs were doubled, the amount of real output produced would also be doubled.

Given the assumption of constant returns to scale, then for a given technology we can express the aggregate production function in per capita terms. As such, output per worker (Y/N) will depend on the amount of capital input per worker (K/N), or what is sometimes referred to as the **capital–labour ratio**. This relationship is depicted in Fig. 11.3, and can be written as

$$Y/N = A(t) \, f(K/N) \tag{11.2}$$

The astute reader will have noticed that in order to highlight that the aggregate production function is expressed in terms of output and capital input *per worker* we use a small letter f in equation (11.2) rather than the capital letter F used in equation (11.1).

The aggregate production function depicted in Fig. 11.3 relates output per worker (Y/N) to the amount of capital input per worker (K/N) for a given technology at a point in time t. For example, with a given technology at time t_0, y_0 output per worker ($Y/N = y$) can be produced with k_0 capital input per worker ($K/N = k$). The decreasing slope of the aggregate production function reflects diminishing returns to increases in the amount of capital input per worker. In other words, increases in capital input per worker result in increases in output per worker, but at an ever-declining rate. Finally, it is important to note that technological change over time (for example, from t_0 to t_1) would shift the aggregate production function upwards, increasing

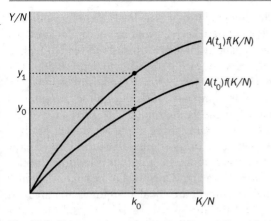

Fig. 11.3 An aggregate production function relating output per worker to capital input per worker.

output per worker for a *given* amount of capital input per worker. For example, as illustrated in Fig. 11.3, technological change would allow a higher level of output per worker (y_1) to be produced with k_0 capital input per worker.

The steady state

We now turn to consider the long-run *equilibrium* or steady-state growth rate within the neoclassical model developed by Solow. From equation (11.1) it can be seen that growth in output over time depends on both the rate of technological change and the rate at which factor inputs (the capital stock and the labour force) grow over time. One of the most important implications of the Solow growth model is that the economy reaches a steady state in the long run. A long-run equilibrium or **steady state** occurs when output per worker and capital input per worker are constant or unchanging over time. In the simplest case, when there is no change in the state of technology, output (Y), capital input (K) and labour input (N) all grow at the same rate.

In Fig. 11.4 a steady state in the long run is achieved at point X with a constant level of output per worker (y_0) and a constant amount of capital input per worker (k_0). Steady state is achieved at the intersection of the steady-state investment line (I)

> **Steady state**: A situation in which output per worker and capital input per worker are no longer changing.

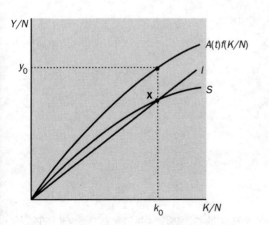

Fig. 11.4 Steady state in the Solow growth model.

and the saving curve (S). Each point along the steady-state investment line indicates how much investment per worker is *required* to keep the amount of capital input per worker *constant* after taking account of labour force growth and the need to replace the fraction of the capital stock that wears out each year owing to depreciation. The line slopes upwards because the faster is labour force growth (and depreciation), the more investment per worker is needed to equip new workers with the current level of capital input per worker and replace depreciating capital. The saving curve (S), which represents saving per worker, has the same shape as the per worker production function because saving is assumed to be proportional to income in the Solow model. As capital input per worker increases so too does output per worker, resulting in an increase in saving per worker. All saving is assumed to be channelled into investment so that saving and actual investment are equal at all times, maintaining goods market equilibrium. In Fig. 11.4 the steady-state level of capital input per worker (k_0) is achieved at point X, the intersection of the steady-state investment line (*I*) and the saving curve (S). Reference to Fig. 11.4 reveals that if capital input per worker is below k_0, saving per worker is greater than investment per worker necessary to maintain capital input per worker constant. As the extra savings are invested and converted into capital, capital input per worker will rise towards k_0. Conversely, if capital input per worker is above k_0, then saving per worker is less than the amount of investment per worker required to maintain capital input per worker constant, and capital input per worker will fall towards k_0. In the steady state the positive effect of investment (determined by saving) on the amount of capital input per worker balances the negative effects of labour force growth and depreciation. When capital input per worker is constant at k_0, output per worker is also constant at y_0 over time. In this simple case, output (*Y*), capital input (*K*) and labour input (*N*) all grow at the same rate, and all ratios are constant: that is, the steady state.

The model we have outlined allows us to examine the relationship between a nation's output per worker and factors such as its saving rate, labour force growth and rate of technological progress. We first consider what the Solow growth model predicts will happen following an increase in the nation's saving rate. Suppose the economy is initially in steady state with capital and labour inputs growing at the same rate with a steady-state capital input per worker established where the steady-state investment line (*I*) and saving curve (S_0) intersect. In Fig. 11.5 this initial situation

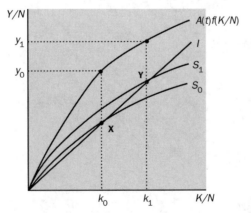

Fig. 11.5 The effects of an increase in the saving rate on capital input per worker and output per worker.

is achieved at point X with k_0 capital input per worker and y_0 output per worker. Assuming that saving is channelled into actual investment, an increase in the saving rate will *initially* increase the rate of capital formation. In the absence of any change in the rate of growth of the labour force or in technological progress, an increase in the rate of capital formation will result in an increase in the amount of capital input per worker. In terms of Fig. 11.5, an increase in the saving rate will raise the saving curve from S_0 to S_1 and capital input per worker will rise from k_0 to k_1 until the economy reaches a new steady state at point Y. Once the economy has made the adjustment from point X to point Y there will be no further increases in either capital input per worker or output per worker. In the new steady state both capital input per worker and output per worker will be stable. The Solow model predicts that countries with higher saving rates will have higher steady-state levels of capital input per worker and therefore higher levels of output per worker, giving a higher standard of living. However, the model predicts that, while an increase in the saving rate will lead to a *temporary* period of faster growth (when output per worker is increasing from y_0 to y_1), it will not affect the long-run equilibrium or steady-state growth rate. Once the new equilibrium has been reached the rate of capital formation and growth rate in output will have returned to their initial levels equal to the rate of growth of the labour force.

We finally turn to briefly consider the effects of a change in the rate of growth of the labour force (Fig. 11.6) and technological change (Fig. 11.7) in the Solow growth model. In Fig. 11.6 the economy is initially in steady state at point X with a steady-state capital input per worker k_0 established where the saving curve (S) and steady-state investment line (I_0) intersect. If the rate of growth of the labour force increases, the amount of investment per current member of the labour force will have to rise to maintain a given capital input per worker. In other words, an increase in the labour force growth rate will cause the steady-state investment line to pivot up to the left from I_0 to I_1. In the new steady state, point Y, the level of capital input per worker is lower (k_1) generating a lower level of output per worker (y_1). The Solow model consequently predicts that countries with higher rates of growth in their labour force will have lower steady-state levels of capital input per worker and therefore lower levels of output per worker.

Fig. 11.7 illustrates the effects of an improvement in technology on capital input

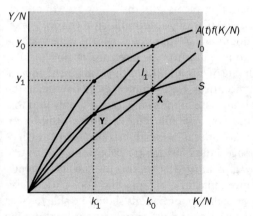

Fig. 11.6 The effects of an increase in the rate of growth of the labour force on capital input per worker and output per worker.

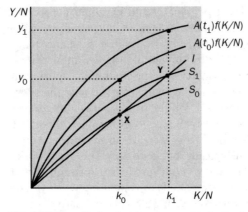

Fig. 11.7 The effects of an improvement in technology on capital input per worker and output per worker.

per worker and output per worker. In Fig. 11.7 the economy is initially in steady state at point X with a steady-state capital input per worker k_0 established where the saving curve (S_0) and steady-state investment line (I) intersect. As discussed, an improvement in technology shifts the aggregate production function upwards from $A(t_0) f(K/N)$ to $A (t_1) f(K/N)$, increasing output per worker for any given amount of capital input per worker. Since saving per worker is assumed to be proportional to output per worker, the saving curve also shifts upwards from S_0 to S_1 at any given amount of capital input per worker. A new steady state will eventually be reached at point Y where the new saving curve (S_1) intersects the steady-state investment line (I) with a higher level of capital input per worker (k_1) and output per worker (y_1). In the Solow model, *sustained* growth of output per worker can only be explained by technological progress. The model predicts that in the steady state both capital input per worker and output per worker grow at the rate of technological progress.

11.4 The new endogenous growth models

During the 1970s economists' interest in the theory of long-run economic growth waned, in large part owing to a number of problems with the Solow growth model. Here we highlight two such problems. The first is that technological change is **exogenous**. As the Solow growth model does not explain or consider the determinants of technological change, it provides no insight into how government policy could raise the long-run equilibrium growth rate of output. Although government policies can influence the saving rate (via tax incentives, for example), as we have seen, the model predicts that a (policy-induced) increase in the saving rate will only lead to a *temporary* period of faster growth and will not affect the long-run equilibrium growth rate. The long-run equilibrium growth rate depends on the rate of growth of the labour force and technological change, both of which are exogenous.

The second problem with the Solow growth model concerns the **non-convergence** of levels of per capita income of advanced industrial nations and poor nations *over time*. If technological change is freely available, poor nations should be able to close the gap in living standards between themselves and industrial nations by using the technology developed in industrial nations. Moreover, poor nations have less capital

Exogenous variable: A variable that is not explained within a particular model; its value is taken as given.

Convergence: The tendency for output per worker in different countries to converge over time.

input per worker and in consequence their marginal product of capital is higher than in advanced industrial nations. Higher returns to capital in poor nations should attract foreign investment and cause their capital stock to grow more quickly than in industrial nations. As a result, output per worker in industrial and poor nations should converge over time. However, rather than converging, the difference in living standards between advanced industrial nations and the poorest nations (as in Africa, for example) has widened.

The late 1980s witnessed a resurgence of interest by economists in the theory of long-run economic growth. The leading architects of what is commonly referred to as the *new endogenous growth theory* are Paul Romer of Stanford University and Robert Lucas Jr of the University of Chicago. While the new endogenous growth models are highly technical, and are beyond the scope of this text, it is useful to briefly outline some of the main ideas involved. Endogenous growth models have extended the basic Solow growth model by making the rate of technological change **endogenous**. In addition, they have abandoned the assumption that all nations have the same access to technological opportunities. Some models of endogenous growth, for example, stress the accumulation of **human capital** – the knowledge and skills of a nation's workers – as a key to achieving economic growth. In these models the level of output per worker depends on *both* the amount of physical capital input per worker *and* human capital input per worker. Poor nations with little human capital cannot hope to catch up industrial nations simply by accumulating physical capital. So different levels of investment in human capital – through training and education – help to explain the lack of convergence of per capita income levels and growth rates over time. Other models of endogenous growth stress endogenous innovation, in which the development of 'ideas' for new goods is seen as the key to achieving economic growth. Poor nations may therefore fail to catch up industrial nations because of 'idea gaps'. Overall, the new endogenous growth literature has helped to explain differences in living standards among nations and given insights into how government policy can influence long-term growth rates by, for example, encouraging education, training, capital formation and research and development.

Having discussed the factors that determine economic growth over time, we now turn to consider the business cycle. Before considering the main approaches to the cause and control of business cycles we first describe the main features of business cycles.

11.5 Main features of business cycles

The **business cycle** (or trade cycle as it is sometimes called) can be defined as periodic fluctuations in the pattern of economic activity. While recurrent cycles in a number of aggregate economic series such as employment, consumption and investment can be observed, the business cycle is usually defined as deviations of output (real GDP) from its secular or long-term trend path. Fig. 11.8, which depicts a stylized business cycle using this definition, can be used to describe the main features of business cycles.

The *period* of the cycle, or length of time it takes to complete a full cycle, can be measured by the time gap between any two points at the same stage of the cycle. Reference to Fig. 11.8 reveals that it may be measured by the time between successive

- troughs, e.g. A and E
- peaks, e.g. C and G

Endogenous variable: A variable that is explained within a particular model.

Human capital: The knowledge and skills of workers in an economy.

Business cycle: Fluctuations in aggregate economic activity; in particular movements in output around its trend.

- upcrosses (of the trend), e.g. B and F
- downcrosses (of the trend), e.g. D and H.

Only in the hypothetical case of a *perfectly* regular cycle depicted in Fig. 11.8 will these alternative measures of the period of the cycle coincide. The *amplitude* of the cycle, which gives an indication of the severity of the cycle, may be measured by the total difference of successive peaks and troughs from the trend path of output: for example $c + e$ or $e + g$. Note that the amplitude of the cycle will remain constant only where the deviations of output above and below the trend are perfectly regular from one time period to the next, as depicted in Fig. 11.8. In practice, cycles will vary in both their timing and their amplitude.

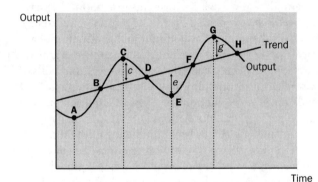

Fig. 11.8 A stylized business cycle.

Fig. 11.8 can also be used to distinguish between the different phases of the cycle. The *expansionary phase* refers to the movement from a trough or lower turning point (such as point A) to a successive peak or upper turning point (such as point C) in the cycle; while the *contractionary phase* refers to the movement from a peak (such as point C) to a successive trough (such as point E). The terms *boom* and *slump* are also often used in connection with the business cycle. These terms refer to the periods of rapid expansion (boom) and contraction (slump) before the movement of output from the trend begins to flatten out near the top and bottom of the cycle respectively. Note also that with respect to the contractionary phase of the cycle, the term *recession* is generally used to describe a slowdown in the growth rate of output below the trend growth rate, while the term *depression* is usually reserved for the most severe recessions.

Having described the main features of business cycles we are now in a position to consider alternative explanations of the cause of the cycle. Before considering the five main approaches to the cause and control of cycles it is important to stress that, unlike the stylized cycle depicted in Fig. 11.8, in practice business cycles are characterized by recurrent fluctuations in output/real GDP from its trend, of varying length and amplitude. Furthermore, this pattern of behaviour is also observed in a number of other aggregate economic series. While controversy exists over the duration of cycles, economists usually have in mind short cycles of approximately 3–10 years in length when they refer to the business cycle.

11.6 The debate over the cause and control of business cycles

At the centre of the debate over the cause and control of business cycles lie a number of fundamental questions, most notably:

- Is the economy inherently stable?
- What is the main source of shocks that affect the economy?
- How long does it take for the economy to self-equilibrate once subjected to a shock?
- Can the authorities intervene to reduce fluctuations in economic activity?

In attempting to answer these questions it is possible to identify the development of *five* main approaches within mainstream economics:

- the Keynesian approach
- the monetarist approach
- the new classical approach
- the real business cycle approach
- the political business cycle approach.

The Keynesian approach

Keynesians believe that the economy is *inherently unstable* and is subject to erratic shocks, which cause it to fluctuate between periods of rapid expansion and contraction. The erratic shocks that cause these fluctuations in economic activity are attributed primarily to a change in autonomous expenditures, most notably investment. Furthermore, Keynesians contend that, after being subjected to some disturbance, the economy can take a long time to return to the neighbourhood of full employment/potential output.

In the Keynesian approach the expansionary and contractionary phases of the business cycle are explained by the interaction of the multiplier process and the accelerator. Let us now examine why periods of economic expansion and contraction, once begun, tend to develop their own momentum. Starting from a position of less than full employment, suppose there occurs an increase in the amount of autonomous investment expenditure undertaken in the economy. An increase in investment expenditure will result in an increase in employment in firms that produce capital goods. Newly employed workers in capital-goods industries will spend some of their income on consumption goods. The rise in demand for consumer goods will lead to increased employment in consumer-goods industries and result in further rounds of expenditure. In consequence, an initial rise in autonomous investment produces a *more than proportionate* rise in income, a process known as the **multiplier** (see Box 11.2). The rise in income will *induce* a further increase in investment as new capital equipment is needed to meet the increased demand for output. Since the cost of capital equipment is usually greater than the value of its annual output, new investment will be *greater than* the increase in output that brought it about. This latter phenomenon is referred to as the **accelerator** (see Box 11.3). The *interaction* of the multiplier process and the accelerator explains why periods of economic expansion

Multiplier: The ratio of the change in income to a change in autonomous expenditure.

Accelerator principle: The theory that the level of net investment depends on the change in output.

Box 11.2

The multiplier: an algebraic derivation and numerical example

Consider first a hypothetical economy in which there is no government sector or international trade undertaken. The output (Y) of such an economy would be split between the production of consumption (C) and investment (I) goods:

$$Y = C + I \qquad (11.1)$$

Let us further assume that investment expenditure is autonomously determined, while consumer expenditure depends positively upon income. As discussed in Chapter 10, section 10.2, the form of the consumption function can be represented by a simple linear equation:

$$C = \alpha + \beta Y \qquad (11.2)$$

If we substitute equation (11.2) into equation (11.1) we obtain

$$Y = \alpha + \beta Y + I \qquad (11.3)$$

Rearranging equation (11.3) and factorizing we obtain

$$Y(1 - \beta) = \alpha + I \qquad (11.4)$$

Finally, dividing both sides of equation (11.4) by $(1 - \beta)$ we obtain

$$Y = \frac{1}{1 - \beta}(\alpha + I) \qquad (11.5)$$

Equation (11.5) determines the equilibrium level of income. The multiplier is given by

$$\frac{1}{1 - \beta}$$

and is equal to the reciprocal of 1 minus the marginal propensity to consume (β). Alternatively, in this hypothetical economy,

with no government or foreign trade, the multiplier is equal to the reciprocal of the marginal propensity to save. For example, with a marginal propensity to consume of 0.8 (and by definition a marginal propensity to save of 0.2) the multiplier would be equal to 5. Following a change in investment, income will change (ΔY) by some multiple of the original change in investment expenditure (ΔI). For example, if investment expenditure increased by £2 million, income would increase by £10 million, i.e. $\Delta Y = \Delta I \times 5$.

The above analysis needs to be modified if we consider an economy with a government sector that engages in international trade. While an initial increase in investment spending will lead in exactly the same way to successive rounds of increased expenditure, some part of the *extra* income will be withdrawn, not only in the form of savings (marginal propensity to save), but also as import spending (marginal propensity to import) and taxes paid to the government (marginal tax rate). The multiplier will in consequence depend on the fraction of income withdrawn from the circular flow (see Chapter 10, Section 10.2) via savings, imports and taxes, and can be generalized as

$$\frac{1}{w}$$

For example, if the fraction of income withdrawn (w) from the circular flow is 0.5, then the multiplier will be equal to 2. Finally, it is interesting to note that the same multiplier process will apply following a change in exports or government expenditure.

or contraction will tend to develop their own momentum. Following an initial increase in autonomous investment, the rise in income due to the multiplier process will be reinforced by an increase in new investment, via the accelerator, which will in turn have a further multiplier effect on income and so on.

Although the interaction of the multiplier process and the accelerator can explain both the expansionary and contractionary phases of the cycle, the Keynesian approach requires the addition of *ceilings* and *floors* to account for turning points in the cycle. Periods of rapid expansion cannot continue indefinitely. As the economy approaches its full employment or potential output 'ceiling', the rate at which income/output increases will slow down as a result of resource constraints. As the rate of increase in income slows down, this leads to a reduction in new investment through the operation of the accelerator (see Box 11.3), which in turn leads to a fall in income through the multiplier process, and so on. The cycle now passes into its contractionary phase

The simple accelerator theory of investment: a numerical example

The relationship between output (Y) and the amount of capital (K) required to produce it can be described by the equation

$$K = \alpha Y \qquad (11.6)$$

The **capital–output ratio**, α, is also referred to as the accelerator coefficient. New investment (I) will be required to increase the capital stock (ΔK) to meet an increase in output/sales (ΔY):

$$I = \Delta K = \alpha \, \Delta Y \qquad (11.7)$$

The following numerical example illustrates the 'simple' accelerator theory of investment.

1 Year	2 Output, Y (£)	3 Required capital stock, K (£)	4 Change in output, ΔY (£)	5 Change in required capital stock, ΔK (£)
1	50	150	0	0
2	51	153	1	3
3	53	159	2	6
4	56	168	3	9
5	61	183	5	15
6	63	189	2	6
7	64	192	1	3
8	64	192	0	0

Columns 2 and 3 show that the value of capital equipment is three times the value of annual output produced and sold. The capital–output ratio is fixed at 3:1. An increase in the production and sales of annual output requires new investment to increase the required capital stock. Columns 4 and 5 show that new investment is proportional to the *change* in output sales. For example, as sales of annual output increase by £5 from year 4 to year 5, new investment of £15 is required. Reference to columns 4 and 5 also reveals that as the increase in sales of annual output slows down in years 6 and 7, new investment falls.

as it moves from an upper turning point to a lower turning point. The movement of output from trend will eventually flatten out near the bottom of the cycle. The contractionary phase of the cycle will be reversed when the economy hits a 'floor'. Sooner or later, as the existing capital equipment wears out, it will fall to a level where it needs replacing in order to produce the current sales/production of annual output. New investment for replacement orders will, through the interaction of the multiplier and accelerator, start the expansionary phase of the cycle again and so on.

What are the implications of the Keynesian approach for **stabilization policy** and the control of business cycles? Given the belief that the economy is inherently unstable and is not rapidly self-equilibrating, Keynesians stress the *need* to stabilize the economy. Furthermore, in their view, governments *can* and therefore *should* use **discretionary** aggregate demand (especially fiscal) **policies** to offset fluctuations in autonomous expenditures (such as private sector investment) and stabilize the economy (see Chapter 10, section 10.2, and Chapter 12, section 12.3).

Capital–output ratio: The ratio of the amount of capital to the amount of output produced by it.

Stabilization policies: Policies aimed at stabilizing output and employment at, or near, their full employment or natural levels by influencing the level of aggregate demand.

Discretionary policy: A situation in which the authorities are free to vary the strength of fiscal and/or monetary policy, in any way they see fit, in order to achieve their desired objectives.

The monetarist approach

In contrast to Keynesians, monetarists believe that the economy is *inherently stable*, unless disturbed by erratic monetary growth. Most of the actually observed instability is attributed to fluctuations in the money supply induced by the authorities. Furthermore, monetarists contend that, when subjected to some disturbance, the economy will return fairly rapidly to the neighbourhood of the natural level of output and employment. The dominant position assigned to monetary shocks in determining the course of economic activity is embodied in the quantity theory approach to macroeconomic analysis. In Chapter 10, section 10.4, we discussed how the effects of a change in the rate of monetary expansion are divided between real and nominal variables in the monetarist view. You will recall that this involves a distinction between short-run and long-run effects. While an inflation–unemployment trade-off exists in the short run, in the long run the trade-off disappears. In the monetarist view, changes in the rate of monetary growth result in short-run fluctuations in output and employment around their natural levels. However, in the long run, the trend rate of monetary growth only influences movements in the price level and other nominal variables.

The monetarist view that monetary shocks are the dominant cause of business cycles is based on two kinds of empirical evidence. The first kind of evidence is the empirically observed tendency for monetary changes to *precede* changes in economic activity. One of the earliest studies concerning the timing of monetary changes was undertaken by Milton Friedman in the late 1950s. In his study, Friedman compared rates of monetary growth with turning points in the level of economic activity. On the average of 18 non-war cycles in the United States since 1870, he found that

- peaks in the rate of change of the money supply had preceded peaks in the level of economic activity by an average of 16 months; and
- troughs in the rate of change of the money supply had preceded troughs in the level of economic activity by an average of 12 months.

While accepting that timing evidence, such as this, is by no means decisive, monetarists argue that it is *suggestive* of an influence running from monetary changes to changes in economic activity.

The second kind of evidence to support the monetarist belief that monetary shocks are the dominant cause of business cycles was presented by Milton Friedman and Anna Schwartz in their influential study of the *Monetary History of the United States, 1867–1960*, published in 1963. In this work they found that the *rate of growth* of the money supply had been slower during cyclical contractions than during cyclical expansions in the level of economic activity. Indeed, the only times when there was an appreciable *absolute* fall in the money stock coincided with the six *major* US recessions identified over the period examined. Examining the specific historical circumstances surrounding events, Friedman and Schwartz concluded that the factors producing the absolute fall in the money supply during these major recessions were mainly independent of contemporary or prior changes in nominal income and prices. In other words, monetary changes were the *cause*, rather than the consequence, of all major American recessions. For example, Friedman and Schwartz argue that the severity of the Great Depression, 1929–33, was due to a dramatic decline in the money stock. Between October 1929 and June 1933 the money stock in the USA fell by about a third. An initial mild decline in the money stock from 1929 to 1930 was, they argue, converted into a sharp decline by a wave of bank failures beginning late in 1930. Those bank failures produced a loss of faith on the part of both the public, in the banks' ability to redeem their deposits, and banks, in the public's willingness to maintain their deposits with them. In Friedman and Schwartz's interpretation of events, the Federal Reserve System could, by adopting alternative policies, have prevented the banking collapse and the dramatic fall in the money stock that coincided with the period of severe economic contraction.

Given the belief that the main cause of economic fluctuations is policy-induced changes in the rate of monetary growth, monetarists advocate that the authorities should pursue a monetary **rule**, rather than attempt to use monetary policy in a discretionary manner. Several rules have been suggested, the best known of which is Friedman's rule that the authorities should pursue a *fixed* rate of monetary growth in line with the long-run growth potential of the economy. Note that a monetary growth rule is not submitted as a panacea to fluctuations in the level of economic activity. While instability may arise from sources other than the mismanagement of the money supply, monetarists believe that by avoiding sharp swings in monetary policy the authorities can remove the main source of economic disturbances. Even when the economy is subjected to shocks that can be identified as arising from other sources, monetarists argue against the use of discretionary monetary policy to stabilize the economy. Their fear that discretionary monetary policy could turn out to be destabilizing is based on a number of arguments including the length and variability of time lags associated with monetary policy, and the inflationary consequences of maintaining unemployment below the natural rate, a problem compounded by uncertainty over what precise value to attribute to the natural rate (see Chapter 10, sections 10.2 and 10.4). In the former case, monetarists argue that stabilization policy could in reality make economic fluctuations more severe because, by the time monetary policy changes affect economic activity, the underlying state of the economy may have changed, making the measures adopted inappropriate (see Chapter 12, section 12.3). In summary, given their belief that the economy is inherently stable and is rapidly self-equilibrating, monetarists question the need to stabilize the economy via discretionary aggregate demand policies. Furthermore, even if there were a need they tend to argue that discretionary aggregate demand policies cannot, and therefore should not, be used to stabilize the economy.

Rules: Pre-specified guidelines that determine the conduct of policy.

The new classical approach

During the 1970s a new classical approach to explaining business cycles was developed. This approach derives largely from the influential work of Robert Lucas Jr of the University of Chicago, who was awarded the Nobel Prize in Economics in 1995. The theory developed by Lucas and other leading new classical economists is similar to the monetarist explanation in that business cycles are viewed as being primarily caused by monetary shocks. However, in the new classical approach it is *unanticipated monetary shocks* that are the dominant cause of business cycles. As we shall now discuss, in the new classical *equilibrium theory* economic agents respond optimally to the prices they perceive, and markets continuously clear.

Consider an economy that is initially in a position where output and employment are at their natural levels. Suppose the authorities *announce* that they intend to increase the money supply. According to the new classical approach rational economic agents would take this information into account in forming their expectations and fully anticipate the effects of the announced increase in the money supply on the general price level. In this situation, output and employment would remain unchanged at their natural levels. Now suppose that the authorities *surprise* economic agents by increasing the money supply without announcing their intentions. In this situation firms and workers with *incomplete information* would *misperceive* the resultant increase in the general price level as an increase in relative prices and respond by increasing the supply of output and labour respectively. A central element of this approach is the structure of information available to economic agents. To illustrate the role that incomplete information plays in the new classical approach we focus on the supply decisions of firms.

A firm's production plans are made on the basis of information on the price of its output. When a firm experiences a rise in the current 'market-clearing' price of its output it must decide how to react to the rise. Where the price rise reflects a *real* increase in demand for its product the firm should respond to the increase in the current price of its output *relative* to the price of other goods, by increasing production. In contrast, where the change in price merely reflects a *nominal* increase in demand across all markets, producing a *general* increase in prices, no supply response is required. In other words, a firm is faced by what is referred to as a *signal extraction problem* in which its supply response depends on its distinguishing between relative as opposed to absolute price changes. In the new classical approach it is assumed that a firm has information both on the current price of its own goods and on prices in the limited number of markets in which it trades. However, information on the general price level for other markets becomes known only after a time lag. Suppose an unanticipated monetary shock occurs that leads to an increase in the general price level and therefore in prices in all markets throughout the economy. In this situation, individual firms with incomplete information will, it is argued, misperceive the increase in the current price of their goods as an increase in the relative price of their output and respond by increasing their output.

Why will output and employment remain above (or below) their natural levels for a succession of time periods? The fact that output and employment levels in any one time period are correlated with their preceding values can be explained by the inclusion of an accelerator mechanism in the analysis. As before, consider an economy that is initially in a position where output and employment are at their natural levels. Following an unanticipated monetary shock, which causes an unexpected rise in prices, firms will respond by increasing output. In a situation where no spare capacity exists, new investment will be required to increase the capital stock in order to produce extra output following the perceived real increase in demand for firms' output. Given the durability of capital goods, errors made in one time period will, in consequence, continue to affect output in subsequent time periods.

What are the implications of the new classical approach for stabilization policy and the control of business cycles? The new classical approach suggests that changes in monetary or fiscal policy can affect output and employment only if they are unanticipated. For example, suppose the money supply is determined by the authorities according to some rule, and the public *knows* the rule and bases its behaviour and decision-making on the anticipated growth of the money supply. In this situation the authorities will be unable to influence output and employment even in the short run by pursuing a systematic monetary policy. Only departures from a known monetary rule, resulting from policy errors made by the monetary authorities or unforeseen changes in policy, will have real effects because they are unanticipated. Any attempt to influence output and employment by random or non-systematic aggregate demand policies would, it is argued, only increase the variation of output and employment around their natural levels and increase uncertainty in the economy. Stabilization policy would only be beneficial in two situations. First, if the authorities had superior information, compared with the private sector, then they could exploit this information to influence the economy. Second, if the authorities were able to react to shocks more quickly than the private sector, there would be scope for discretionary intervention to stabilize the economy. Nevertheless, having noted these two possible situations, it is the case that the new classical approach, in line with the monetarist approach, maintains a non-intervention position with respect to macroeconomic policy.

The early 1980s witnessed the demise of the 'monetary surprise' version of the new classical approach to business cycles. A number of criticisms were raised against the new classical approach involving both theoretical and empirical failings. In the former case, for example, critics of the approach drew attention to the fact that both aggregate price level and money supply data are published within a short time lag and are readily available to economic agents. Given the availability of such data, they questioned how business cycles could be caused by supposed information gaps. In the latter case, the results of a number of empirical tests suggested that both unanticipated *and* anticipated money supply shocks have real output and employment effects. The depth of the recessions in both the USA and the UK in the early 1980s (see Table 9.2 and Chapter 10, section 10.4), following announced monetary disinflation policies, provided further ammunition to the critics that systematic monetary policy has real effects. Criticisms of the monetary surprise version of the new classical approach led a number of economists who were sympathetic to the 'equilibrium' approach to develop a new version in which business cycles are predominantly caused by persistent *real* (supply-side) shocks, rather than unanticipated monetary (demand-side) shocks, to the economy. This approach, which is largely associated with the work of American economists, most notably Finn Kydland of Carnegie Mellon University and Edward Prescott of the University of Chicago, is commonly referred to as the *real business cycle approach*.

The real business cycle approach

According to proponents of the real business cycle approach business cycles are driven by persistent *supply-side shocks* to the economy. These *random* supply-side shocks can originate from such sources as changes in raw material or energy prices, natural disasters, the development of new products and the introduction of new techniques of production. Despite the wide variety of potential supply-side shocks most real business cycle models are based on the premise that these shocks result mainly from *large* random fluctuations in the rate of technological progress. In the real business cycle approach, observed fluctuations in output and employment are *equilibrium* phenomena and are the outcome of rational economic agents responding *optimally* to unavoidable changes in the economic environment. Furthermore, observed fluctuations in output are viewed as fluctuations in potential output, not as deviations of actual output from the trend. In the real business cycle approach the distinction between actual and potential output is abandoned. Given the belief that the economy is subjected to large random fluctuations in the rate of technological progress, the fluctuating path of output over time follows a so-called **random walk** and is nothing more than a continuously fluctuating full employment/potential output equilibrium. As such, the approach integrates business cycle theory with the theory of economic growth.

What are the implications of the real business cycle approach for stabilizing

Random walk: The path of a variable whose changes over time are unpredictable.

Pareto efficiency: A situation in which it is impossible to make someone better off without making someone else worse off; also known as Pareto optimality.

Political business cycle: Fluctuations in the level of output and employment caused by the manipulation of the economy for electoral gains or due to partisan differences.

economic fluctuations? As fluctuations in output and employment are held to reflect the **Pareto-efficient** responses to a succession of supply-side shocks hitting the economy, the approach provides no role for monetary and fiscal policies for stabilization purposes. On the one hand, monetary factors are regarded as being irrelevant in explaining such fluctuations, with monetary policy having no influence on real variables. On the other hand, attempts to stabilize fluctuations in output and employment through fiscal policy would, it is claimed, reduce welfare because government taxation and spending policies would distort output and employment from the optimal amounts chosen by firms and workers.

The real business cycle approach to business cycles and the implication that stabilization policy has no role to play is *highly* controversial, and has been subjected to a number of criticisms. Two examples will suffice. First, most economists question whether supply shocks are large enough or frequent enough to explain observed aggregate fluctuations in output and employment. With the exception of the two OPEC oil price shocks that occurred in 1973–74 and 1979, it is difficult to identify adverse supply shocks that are powerful enough to explain major recessions, especially episodes such as the Great Depression in the 1930s. The idea that major recessions are caused by technological *regress* strikes many critics as being particularly implausible. Second, real business cycle models assume wage and price flexibility so that markets continuously clear and equilibrium always prevails. Critics of the new classical approach have put forward a variety of reasons to explain wage and price stickiness that prevent continuous market clearing. For example, as discussed in Chapter 10, section 10.2, new Keynesians have put forward various explanations of real wage rigidity in the labour market that can account for the existence of involuntary unemployment as an equilibrium phenomenon. Indeed, most economists believe that demand shocks, arising from changes in monetary policy, can have significant real effects in the short run, because of the nominal price and wage rigidities that characterize actual economies.

The political business cycle approach

In the **political business cycle** approach, business cycles are policy induced and reflect the objectives of politicians either in terms of getting re-elected or in terms of ideological/partisan differences.

Consider first the possibility of a political business cycle resulting from a government manipulating the state of the economy just before an election, in order to improve its chances of being re-elected. This particular approach, which is associated with the work of William Nordhaus in the mid 1970s, is based on the beliefs that (a) the main goal of political parties is winning the next election, and (b) the state of the economy has a strong influence on voters. As an election approaches, the government pursues expansionary policies (for example by increasing its expenditure and/or reducing taxes) in order to reduce unemployment and gain votes. Once they are re-elected, contractionary policies will be required to dampen down the inflationary pressures that arise as output rises above its full employment/potential level. As inflation subsides and unemployment increases, the stage is set once again for the government to engineer expansionary policies to reduce unemployment and gain popularity before the next election. Changes in macroeconomic policy produce a political business cycle. Although this approach is intuitively appealing, it suffers from a number of weaknesses. Three examples will suffice. First, the approach would seem to be more appropriate for countries with fixed election dates, such as the USA, rather than countries where election dates are variable, such as the UK. Second, the approach implies that in a two-party system political parties will offer similar policies to attract voters at the centre of the political spectrum (so-called median voters), and ignores the fact that political parties are likely to have ideological or partisan aims in addition to that of obtaining power. Third, the approach implies that voters are myopic or short-sighted, and do not learn from past experience that politicians generate a pre-election boom, followed by a post-election slump.

Since the mid 1980s interest in the political business cycle approach has been rekindled, most notably by the work of Alberto Alesina of Harvard University. Alesina has put forward a partisan model in which political parties do not pursue a simple vote-maximizing strategy and differ in their priorities and preferences. In particular, right-wing parties are assumed to attach more importance to keeping inflation in check than left-wing parties, who care more about unemployment. Voters know that given such priorities parties will pursue different policies when they are in office. In this model, what drives the cycle is the fact that election results are unknown before they occur. Wage contracts set before an election will be determined by the rate of inflation expected after the election. The expected rate of inflation will depend on which party is expected to form the next government. For example, if wage negotiators expect that a left-wing government currently in office will be re-elected, they will form contracts that have a high expected rate of inflation built into them. If a right-wing party then gains office it will tighten monetary policy in order to reduce inflation. In a situation where contracts cannot be instantly renegotiated, unemployment will rise. The opposite sequence of events would follow if a right-wing government in office was replaced by a left-wing party. In this case, after the election a left-wing government would expand the economy and reduce unemployment. In both cases, once inflation expectations had adjusted to the new situation, at a later stage in the government's term of office output and employment would return to their natural levels (see the discussion of the expectations-augmented Phillips curve in Chapter 10, section 10.4). Unlike Nordhaus's political business cycle model, which predicts a pre-election boom and a post-election slump, Alesina's partisan model predicts a slump after a change in policy regime to a right-wing government and a boom after a change of regime to a left-wing government.

The political business cycle approach provides another reason for those economists who favour giving central banks greater independence, enabling monetary policy to be conducted free from consideration of electoral gain and partisan influences (see Chapter 12, Box 12.1).

11.7 Concluding remarks

In this chapter we have considered what factors determine economic growth over time and the debate over the cause and control of business cycles. Clearly, economic growth is the result of extremely complex processes involving economic, political and institutional considerations. As a starting point only, in section 11.3 we examined a model that identifies *some* of the main determinants of economic growth over time. Like all economic models the Solow growth model simplifies reality and omits many important considerations. Nevertheless, as we have seen, the model sheds light on *some* of the reasons why standards of living vary so widely between countries. The recent resurgence of interest in the theory of long-run growth has produced more sophisticated models in which the rate of technological change is endogenous. These models provide a rationale for governments to adopt policies that encourage education, training, capital formation and research and development in order to increase the economy's productive capacity. Despite these further insights, exactly what role the government can and should play in encouraging growth remains the subject of intense controversy.

As to the main theories of business cycles, four theories suggest that cycles are primarily caused by demand shocks. In the Keynesian approach, the main cause of cycles is changes in autonomous expenditures. Monetarists emphasize changes in the rate of monetary growth as the main source of cycles, while the new classical approach highlights unanticipated monetary shocks as the dominant cause of cycles. The political business cycle approach ascribes the existence of cycles to government macroeconomic policy. In contrast to these approaches, proponents of the real business cycle approach suggest that business cycles are primarily caused by supply shocks. While our presentation has highlighted the differences between these competing explanations, it is important to remember that many economists take an eclectic stance recognizing that no one key causal factor can account for all business cycles. Some cycles will be triggered by demand shocks, others by supply shocks. On some occasions demand and supply shocks will *both* be important. Whether governments cause cycles and what policies they should pursue to reduce fluctuations in economic activity remain highly controversial issues. In the next chapter we turn to consider the issue of stabilizing the economy more fully.

◼ Summary

◆ Economic growth can be defined as an increase in real GDP. The annual percentage increase in real GDP measures the rate of economic growth.

◆ Real output will increase over time if there is an increase in the quantity of factor inputs and/or in the productivity of inputs.

◆ In the Solow growth model, a long-run equilibrium or steady-state growth rate occurs where output, capital input and labour input all grow at the same rate. The model allows us to examine the relationship between a nation's output per worker and its saving rate, labour force growth and rate of technological progress. *Ceteris paribus*, an increase in the saving rate, a decrease in the rate of growth of the labour force or an improvement in technology increases the level of capital input and output per worker. The long-run equilibrium growth rate depends on the rate of growth of the labour force and technological change, and is not affected by a change in the saving rate. As both the rate of growth of the labour force and technological change are exogenous, the Solow model provides no insight into how government policy could raise the long-run equilibrium growth rate of output.

◆ New endogenous growth models help to explain the lack of convergence of per capita income levels and growth rates over time, and provide a number of insights into how government policy can influence the long-run growth rate.

◆ The business cycle can be defined as deviations in output from trend. Cycles that vary in both their timing and amplitude involve expansionary and contractionary phases, and upper and lower turning points.

◆ In the Keynesian approach, the main cause of business cycles is fluctuations in autonomous expenditures. Expansionary and contractionary phases are explained through the interaction of the multiplier process and the accelerator, while ceilings and floors account for turning points in the cycle. Keynesians believe that governments need to, can and therefore should stabilize the economy.

◆ In the monetarist approach, the main cause of business cycles is held to be monetary actions that result in changes in the rate of growth of the money supply. By pursuing a monetary growth rate rule, monetarists argue that the authorities can remove the major source of economic disturbances.

◆ In the new classical approach, unanticipated monetary shocks are the dominant cause of business cycles. Surprised by such shocks, economic agents, with incomplete information, mistake general price changes for relative price changes and react by changing the supply of output and labour. Governments can influence output and employment only by pursuing random or non-systematic monetary policy. New classicists claim that such policy will, however, only increase the variation of output and employment around their natural levels, and increase uncertainty in the economy. In line with the monetarist approach, the new classical approach maintains a non-interventionist position with respect to macroeconomic policy.

◆ In the real business cycle approach, business cycles are primarily caused by persistent real supply shocks to the economy, mainly large random fluctuations in the rate of technological progress. Fluctuations in output and employment are held to reflect the optimal response of economic agents to such shocks. Because cycles are due to a succession of supply shocks hitting the economy, there is no role for the government to stabilize fluctuations in output and employment through aggregate demand policies.

◆ The political business cycle approach suggests that cycles are policy induced and reflect the objectives of politicians either in terms of getting re-elected or in terms of partisan differences.

◆ No one key factor can account for all business cycles. On some occasions demand and supply shocks will both be important.

Key terms

◆ Aggregate production function
◆ Production possibility frontier
◆ Quantity and quality of factor inputs
◆ Solow growth model
◆ Steady-state growth
◆ Convergence
◆ Endogenous growth models
◆ Human capital
◆ The period of the cycle
◆ The amplitude of the cycle

◆ Expansionary and contractionary phases

◆ Multiplier process

◆ Accelerator

◆ Multiplier–accelerator interaction

◆ Ceilings and floors

◆ Monetary shocks

◆ Monetary rule

◆ Unanticipated monetary shocks

◆ Signal extraction problem

◆ Real shocks

◆ Politically induced cycles

◆ Partisan priorities and preferences

■ Self-test questions

True (t) or false (f)
(Questions 6–10 are only for students who have read sections 11.3–11.4)

1. It will take approximately 24 years for an economy to double its productive capacity if its growth rate is 3 per cent.

2. Real GDP per capita will fall when the real GDP of a country is growing at a faster rate than its population.

3. The economy's capacity to produce goods can only increase if there is an increase in the quantity of factor inputs available.

4. Economic growth involves an inward movement of the production possibility frontier.

5. Economists are unified in their views over what role the government can play in promoting economic growth.

6. The Solow growth model predicts that countries with higher rates of growth in their labour force will have higher levels of output per worker.

7. According to the Solow growth model the long-run equilibrium or steady-state growth rate depends on the saving rate.

8. In the Solow growth model sustained growth of output per worker depends on technological progress.

9. Endogenous growth models have extended the basic Solow growth model by making the rate of technological change endogenous.

10. According to endogenous growth models differences in the level of investment in human capital can help to explain the lack of convergence of output per worker in different countries.

11. The business cycle entails recurrent cycles in a number of aggregate economic series.

12. Business cycles will vary in both their timing and their amplitude.

13. In the Keynesian approach monetary shocks are the dominant cause of business cycles.

14. Keynesians contend that the economy will rapidly self-equilibrate after being subjected to some disturbance.

15. In the monetarist approach the main cause of business cycles is fluctuations in autonomous expenditures.

16. Monetarists argue against the use of discretionary monetary policy to control the business cycle.

17. In the new classical approach supply-side shocks are the dominant cause of business cycles.

18. The new classical approach maintains a non-interventionist position with respect to macro-economic policy.

19. Proponents of the real business cycle approach make a distinction between actual and potential output, acknowledging that output fluctuates around its long-term trend.

20. According to the real business cycle approach business cycles are primarily caused by demand shocks.

21. According to the political business cycle approach business cycles are caused by government manipulation of the economy for electoral gains or due to partisan differences.

Complete the following sentences by inserting the missing word(s)
(Questions 3–6 are only for students who have read sections 11.3–11.4)

1. The decreasing slope of the short-run aggregate production function reflects _____ returns to the quantity of labour inputs.

2. Economic growth depends on increases in the quantity and _____ of both capital and labour inputs.

3. As a result of _____ increases in capital input per worker result in increases in output per worker, but at an ever-declining rate.

4. A situation in which output per worker and capital input per worker are constant or unchanging over time is known as _____.

5. In the Solow growth model both the rate of growth of the labour force and technological change are _____.

6. The leading architects of the new endogenous growth theory are _____ and _____.

7. Economists refer to the knowledge and skills of workers in an economy as _____.

8. The business cycle can be defined as deviations of output (real GDP) from its _____.

9. The movement from a trough to a successive peak is referred to as the _____ of the cycle, while the movement from a peak to a successive trough is referred to as the _____ of the cycle.

10. In the Keynesian approach the expansionary and contractionary phases of the business cycle are explained by the interaction of the _____ and the _____.

11. The process whereby an increase in autonomous expenditure produces a more than pro-portionate increase in income is known as the _____.

12. In the monetarist approach _____ are the dominant cause of business cycles.

13. Friedman has advocated that the authorities pursue a _____ rate of monetary growth in line with the long-run growth potential of the economy.

14. The new classical approach to explaining business cycles derives largely from the influential work of _____.

15. In the new classical approach _____ monetary shocks are the main cause of business cycles.

16. Proponents of the real business cycle approach argue that business cycles are driven by persistent _____ to the economy.

17. The real business cycle approach is largely associated with the work of two American economists, namely _____ and _____ .

18. Nordhaus's political business cycle model predicts a pre-election _____ and a post-election _____ .

▊ Questions for discussion

(Questions 3–7 are only for students who have read sections 11.3–11.4)

◆ What factors determine economic growth over time?

◆ What role can the government play in promoting growth?

◆ According to the Solow model what effect will each of the following have on the level of output per worker:

an increase in the saving rate
an increase in labour force growth
a technological improvement?

◆ Explain why the saving rate does not affect the steady-state growth rate in the Solow model.

◆ What determines the long-run equilibrium growth rate in the Solow model?

◆ Explain why according to the Solow model sustained growth of output per worker depends on technological progress.

◆ What are the main problems with the Solow growth model?

◆ What is the main cause of business cycles in the Keynesian approach? How are the expansionary and contractionary phases of the business cycle explained in the Keynesian approach?

◆ What is the main cause of business cycles in the monetarist approach?

◆ Compare and contrast the main policy implications of the Keynesian and monetarist approaches for the control of business cycles.

◆ What is the main cause of business cycles in the new classical and real business cycle approaches?

◆ What role is there for stabilization policy in the new classical and real business cycle approaches?

◆ What is the main cause of business cycles in the political business cycle approach?

▊ Further reading

Crafts, N. and G. Toniolo (eds) *Economic Growth in Europe Since 1945* (Cambridge: Cambridge University Press, 1996). Provides a fascinating re-examination of the topic of economic growth in Europe after the Second World War.

Morgan, B. and J.R. Shackleton 'The ups and downs of business cycle theory' in Shackleton, J.R. (ed.) *New Thinking in Economics* (Aldershot: Edward Elgar, 1990). Provides a deftly written survey of business cycle theory.

Friedman, M. *The Counter-Revolution in Monetary Theory* (London: Institute of Economic Affairs, 1970). An accessible non-technical discussion that places the monetarist counter-revolution in historical perspective and describes the central propositions of monetarism.

Internet links

The *Institute for Fiscal Studies* and *Biz/Ed* jointly sponsor a virtual economy website that allows visitors to investigate how the British economy works. The site offers data, case studies and overviews of macro theory. It can be found at: **http://ve.ifs.org.uk/**

Stabilizing the Economy

Contents

Key issues

▶ Why do economists disagree over the issue of whether the authorities need to, can and should stabilize the economy?

▶ Should macroeconomic policy be operated at the discretion of the authorities or on the basis of rules?

▶ What are the main problems encountered by policymakers in implementing stabilization policy?

12.1 Introduction

In the preceding two chapters we have examined the debate over the causes of and appropriate responses to unemployment, inflation, economic growth, and the business cycle. Given the nature of our discussion, it should be evident that there is much controversy between macroeconomists over these important issues. The purpose of this present chapter is to draw together a number of themes addressed in Chapters 10 and 11 and consider the continuing debate over stabilization policy aimed at keeping output and employment at, or near, their full employment or natural levels by influencing the level of aggregate demand. In particular, we shall focus on the controversy of whether, in their conduct of macroeconomic policy, the authorities should be given discretion to change the strength of fiscal and monetary policy in the light of particular economic circumstances, or whether monetary and fiscal policy should be conducted by rules.

12.2 Discretionary policy and policy rules

Before proceeding to discuss alternative views on stabilization policy we need first to highlight the difference between discretionary policy and policy rules.

Discretionary policy takes place when the authorities are given the *freedom* to vary the strength of fiscal and/or monetary policy in any way they see fit in order to achieve their desired objectives. In monitoring the course of the economy, policy may be changed either: (a) frequently in an attempt to maintain output and employment at, or near, their full employment or natural levels – so-called *fine tuning*; or (b) occasionally in response to a large divergence in output and employment from their full employment or natural levels – so-called *rough tuning*. In contrast, where policy is conducted by rules, the authorities are *committed* to follow a *pre-specified* rule that determines the conduct of fiscal and/or monetary policy. Rules themselves may, or may not, be linked to changes in economic conditions. With a **passive policy rule** the pre-specified rule for the policy instrument is not linked to prevailing economic circumstances. An example of a passive monetary policy rule is one where the authorities are committed to pursue a *constant* rate of monetary growth. Whatever the state of the economy the authorities would pursue a given fixed rate of monetary growth of say 3 per cent per annum. An **activist policy rule**, however, involves **feedback** from the state of the economy to the policy instrument. An example of an activist monetary policy rule would be one where the money supply is targeted to grow at a rate of say 3 per cent per annum if unemployment is 6 per cent, but monetary growth is automatically increased (decreased) by 1 per cent per annum for every 1 per cent by which unemployment rises above (falls below) 6 per cent. If unemployment rose to 8 per cent, monetary growth would be increased to 5 per cent. Conversely, if unemployment fell to 4 per cent, monetary growth would be reduced to 1 per cent. Both active and passive policy rules tie the hands of the authorities to pursue pre-specified rules without leaving them any discretion to change the strength of fiscal and/or monetary policy.

As we shall now discuss, the debate over stabilization policy critically depends on whether one views the economy as inherently unstable, subject to frequent shocks that lead to inefficient fluctuations in output, employment and inflation; or whether one views the economy as naturally stable. Broadly speaking, those economists who subscribe to the former view emphasize the need for stabilization policy, and argue that the authorities should be given discretion to use fiscal and monetary policy to offset shocks and keep output and employment close to their full employment or natural levels. Other economists, who subscribe to the latter view, tend to question the need for stabilization policy, and favour rules over discretion, blaming ill-conceived policies for inefficient departures of output and employment from their natural levels experienced from time to time.

Passive policy rule: A pre-specified rule for the conduct of policy not linked to prevailing economic circumstances.

Activist policy rule: A pre-specified rule for the conduct of policy that is linked to the state of the economy; also known as a feedback rule.

12.3 The rules versus discretion debate: problems of stabilization policy

The Keynesian view

In the *orthodox* Keynesian view, the economy is *inherently unstable*, experiencing frequent shocks that lead to inefficient fluctuations in output, employment and inflation. The main sources of instability that cause these fluctuations in economic activity are aggregate demand shocks. Furthermore, orthodox Keynesians contend that, after being subjected to such disturbances, the economy will not rapidly self-equilibrate, and will take a long time to return to the neighbourhood of full employment output. Given these beliefs, orthodox Keynesians stress the *need* for stabilization policy and argue that the authorities *can* and therefore *should* use discretionary fiscal and monetary policies to stabilize the economy.

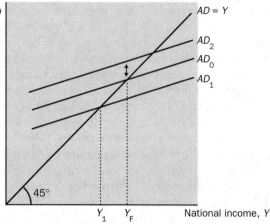

Fig. 12.1 Stabilization policy in the orthodox Keynesian model.

Using the Keynesian model first introduced in Chapter 10, section 10.2, we can illustrate how the authorities would, via discretionary policy activism, seek to stimulate the economy after it had been subjected to some contractionary aggregate demand shock, and deflate the economy when it was overheating. In Fig. 12.1 we assume that the economy is initially operating at its full employment level of output (Y_F). Following some contractionary aggregate demand shock, which shifts the aggregate demand curve from AD_0 to AD_1, the economy could, if left to its own devices, come to rest below full employment at Y_1 for a prolonged period of time. Orthodox Keynesians argue that, by taking appropriate corrective action (that is, expansionary fiscal and/or monetary policy) that offsets the contractionary shock and shifts the aggregate demand curve back from AD_1 to AD_0, the authorities can stabilize the economy at, or close to, its full employment level. Alternatively, the economy might be subjected to an expansionary aggregate demand shock, which shifts the aggregate demand curve from AD_0 to AD_2, causing the economy to overheat as aggregate demand exceeds national income at the full employment level of output. The resulting *inflationary gap*, indicated by the arrows in Fig. 12.1, would require deflationary fiscal and/or monetary policy to close the gap and offset the expansionary shock, shifting the aggregate demand curve back from AD_2 to AD_0.

In both situations analysed above, it is clearly important that the authorities exert the *correct dosage* of stimulus or restraint. Consider, for example, the former case of the economy experiencing a contractionary aggregate demand shock. If the authorities fail to stimulate aggregate demand sufficiently the economy will come to rest below its full employment equilibrium. In contrast, if the authorities overstimulate aggregate demand beyond that required to establish full employment, then an inflationary gap will ensue. While acknowledging this potential problem, orthodox Keynesians believe that the authorities can and therefore should use discretionary fiscal and monetary policies to stabilize the economy at, or close to, their full employment levels. Indeed, in the 1950s and 1960s, when Keynesian economics was the conventional wisdom, many Western governments attempted to fine tune their economies using discretionary aggregate demand policies. However, by the late 1960s/early 1970s, many Western governments began to experience a steady rise in unemployment and inflation (see Tables 9.2 and 9.3), leading some economists to question the ability of conventional Keynesian economics to deal with the problem of so-called stagflation.

Before discussing subsequent developments associated with monetarist and new classical views, which provide a critique of discretionary policy activism involving fine tuning, we need to mention the views of *new* Keynesians. New Keynesians accept that the economy is not as unstable as once believed. Nevertheless, they argue that the economy does experience shocks, from both the demand side *and* the supply side, which cause undesirable and inefficient economic fluctuations. As such, in line with orthodox Keynesians, they recognize the need for stabilization policy, and believe that the authorities can and therefore should use discretionary aggregate demand policies to stabilize the economy. However, unlike orthodox Keynesians, new Keynesians do not support what they regard as over-ambitious attempts to fine tune the macroeconomy, and have instead championed the case for rough tuning. In particular, as discussed in Chapter 10, section 10.2, hysteresis effects provide new Keynesians with a strong case that the authorities should stimulate aggregate demand during a prolonged recession.

The monetarist view

During the late 1960s and early 1970s, a monetarist counter-revolution took place (most notably in the USA), which led to a continuing debate over stabilization policy. As outlined in Chapter 11, section 11.6, monetarists, in stark contrast to Keynesians, believe that the economy is *inherently stable*, unless disturbed by erratic monetary growth. Furthermore, they contend that, when subjected to some disturbance, the economy is rapidly self-equilibrating and will return fairly quickly to the neighbourhood of the natural level of output and employment. Given these beliefs, monetarists question the need for stabilization policy involving the management of aggregate demand. Even if there were a need, they argue that discretionary fiscal and monetary policies cannot, and therefore should not, be used to stabilize the economy. We now consider more fully the monetarist case against discretionary policy activism.

While monetarists accept that fiscal policy can be used to influence the level of output and employment in the short run, they argue that in the long run fiscal expansion (such as an increase in government expenditure) will replace or crowd out components of private sector expenditure so that real income remains unchanged at its natural level. **Crowding out** will be complete where private sector expenditure is reduced by the same amount by which government expenditure is increased, so that the long-run government expenditure multiplier is zero. The monetarist view contrasts with the Keynesian view in which an increase in government expenditure will, through the multiplier process (see Box 11.2), lead to an increase in income by some multiple of the original change in government expenditure.

A number of reasons have been put forward to explain why crowding out may occur. Two examples will suffice. First, crowding out may arise as a direct result of the way in which an increase in government expenditure is financed – a so-called financing effect. Consider the case where an increase in government expenditure is financed by increased sales of government bonds. In order to induce the public to buy more government bonds, the rate of interest on new bond issues will have to increase. When the cost of borrowing funds rises, the level of private sector investment will be reduced as firms cancel investment projects they had planned to finance by borrowing before interest rates increased. Second, crowding out may occur in an

Crowding out: The reduction in private sector expenditure that results following an increase in government expenditure.

open economy operating under a regime of **fixed exchange rates** (see Chapter 14, section 14.5) owing to a price level effect. If the domestic price level increases following an increase in government expenditure and the exchange rate is fixed, exports will become less competitive with foreign-produced goods, while imports will become more competitive with domestically produced goods (see Chapter 14, section 14.2). In other words, an increase in government expenditure will result in a fall in exports and an increase in imports.

In discussing fiscal policy we have so far considered only why monetarists typically argue that an increase in government expenditure will, in the long run, replace or crowd out some components of private-sector expenditure. We next need to consider why monetarists question the likely impact of tax changes as a stabilization instrument. In contrast to the Keynesian view, in which consumption expenditure depends on current income, Milton Friedman has argued that consumption spending depends on **permanent** (long-run average) **income** that people expect to receive. Tax changes that people believe will be in effect for only a year or two will have only a negligible effect on permanent income. In consequence, temporary tax changes will have only a small effect on consumption, and are useless for stabilization purposes. Finally, turning to monetary policy, as discussed in Chapter 10, section 10.4, monetarists argue that discretionary monetary policy can also influence output and employment, but again only in the short run. In the long run, monetary policy can determine only nominal variables and their rates of change.

If both fiscal and monetary policy can influence output and employment in the short run, why are monetarists against discretionary policy activism? In summary, monetarists argue that, owing to numerous problems associated with stabilization policy (including time lags, forecasting errors and uncertainty), the authorities should refrain from attempting to stabilize the economy in the short run, by discretionary aggregate demand management policies, for fear they do more harm than good. We first examine how, given the existence of time lags, it is possible for discretionary policy activism to be destabilizing. In discussing time lags in the conduct of stabilization policy, it is customary to divide the lags into an inside lag and an outside lag. The *inside lag* is the period of time it takes to initiate a policy change, such as a tax cut or an increase in the money supply. The *outside lag* is the time between an initiated policy change and its influence on the economy.

The inside lag can be divided into two components: a recognition lag, and an administrative lag. The *recognition lag* is the time lag between a disturbance or shock affecting the economy and the authorities recognizing that some kind of corrective action is needed. This lag will be the same for both fiscal and monetary policy. The *administrative lag* is the time lag between recognizing that action is required and actually planning, and implementing, the corrective policies. Unlike the recognition lag, the administrative lag will not be the same for fiscal and monetary policy. In the United States the administrative lag associated with fiscal policy is longer than that for monetary policy. While monetary policy actions can be implemented fairly swiftly by the Federal Reserve System, most fiscal policy changes require the approval of both Houses of Congress, and the legislative process involved can sometimes be painfully slow. For example, in the 1960s an income tax cut first proposed in 1962 by President Kennedy, in order to stimulate the American economy, was not actually implemented until 1964. In contrast, in the United Kingdom, the legislative process required to implement fiscal policy changes is much quicker as long as the government in office enjoys a parliamentary majority.

Permanent income: The average income that people expect to receive over a period of years in the future; also known as normal income and average expected income.

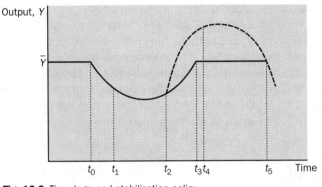

Fig. 12.2 Time lags and stabilization policy.

Once a policy change has been implemented we move on to the outside lag. Unlike the inside lag, the outside lag is a *distributed* lag in that the effects of a policy change on the economy will be spread out over time. A policy change, such as a tax cut or a change in the money supply, will not lead to an immediate increase in spending and employment in the economy, and its effects are likely to continue over several periods. The length of the outside lag will vary depending on a number of factors including: the state of the economy at the time when the policy change is implemented; the way the private sector responds to the policy change; and whether fiscal or monetary policy changes are implemented. In the latter case, for example, it is generally accepted that monetary policy has a relatively long outside lag. Monetary policy works through interest rate changes, which in turn influence investment spending in the economy. Given that many firms will plan new investment far in advance, their response to interest rate changes is likely to be slow, and may take many months. Owing to the length of the inside lag associated with fiscal policy (especially in the USA) and the length and variability of the outside lag associated with monetary policy (see Chapter 11, section 11.6), monetarists argue that any attempt to use discretionary fiscal and/or monetary policy to stabilize the economy could do more harm than good. This possibility is illustrated in Fig. 12.2.

Figure 12.2 depicts a situation where output is initially at its full employment or natural level ($\bar{Y}$). At time t_0 a disturbance affects the economy that reduces output below $\bar{Y}$. However, given the inside lag, it is not until time t_1 that the authorities actually implement an expansionary policy. There then follows a further outside time lag before the initiated policy change starts to affect the economy at time t_2 and thereafter. Without discretionary stabilization policy output would return to $\bar{Y}$ by time t_3. With discretionary stabilization policy output rises above its full employment/natural level. At time t_4, the authorities initiate contractionary policy, which again begins to affect the economy only after a further period of time has elapsed. With stabilization policy output now falls below its full employment/natural level at time t_5 and thereafter. It can be seen that, in this example, owing to time lags stabilization policy has actually destabilized the economy, resulting in more severe fluctuations in output than would otherwise have occurred if the authorities had not engaged in activist discretionary policy intervention.

In addition to the problems raised by time lags, uncertainty over both the size of policy multipliers associated with fiscal and monetary policy in the short run and what precise value to attribute to the natural rate of unemployment make it possible for discretionary policy activism to be destabilizing. In the latter case, given the belief that the long-run Phillips curve is vertical, any attempt to *maintain* unemployment below the natural rate by discretionary aggregate demand policies will result in accelerating inflation (see Chapter 10, section 10.4). In consequence, monetarists advocate that discretionary aggregate demand policies should be replaced by some form of monetary rule. Finally, it is interesting to note that, in addition, some monetarists justify their position that policy is best conducted by rules rather than discretion for fear that opportunistic politicians cannot be trusted not to use activist discretionary policy to manipulate the economy for political gain.

The new classical view

The 1970s witnessed the development of the new classical approach to macroeconomics, an approach that cast further doubt on whether traditional Keynesian aggregate demand policies can be used to improve overall economic performance and stabilize the economy.

Underlying the new classical model of the macroeconomy is the joint acceptance of three main tenets:

- rational expectations
- the assumption that all markets in the economy continuously clear
- the Lucas surprise supply function.

Rational expectations assumes that agents make the best use of all available information – including information on current and prospective policies – to form their forecasts or expectations of the future value of a variable. For example, if economic agents believe that the rate of inflation is determined by the rate of monetary expansion then they will make the best use of all publicly available information on rates of monetary expansion in forming their expectations of future rates of inflation. The Lucas surprise supply function states that output only deviates from its natural level in response to deviations of the actual price level from its expected value. As discussed in Chapter 11, section 11.6, in the absence of price surprises, which arise from incomplete information, output will remain at its natural level. The combination of the rational expectations hypothesis, the assumption of continuous market clearing and the Lucas surprise function produces a number of important implications for macroeconomic policy. In what follows we outline three insights associated with the new classical approach that are relevant to the debate over stabilization policy:

- the policy ineffectiveness proposition
- the time inconsistency of discretionary policy
- the Lucas critique of traditional methods of policy evaluation.

Policy ineffectiveness proposition

In line with monetarists, new classicists believe that the economy is inherently stable and that when subjected to some disturbance will quickly return to its natural level of output and employment. While the main source of disturbances is attributed to monetary shocks in both approaches, according to the new classical view only *unanticipated* monetary shocks affect output and employment, and then only in the short run (see Chapter 11, section 11.6). Furthermore, rational economic agents will

Rational expectations: An approach that assumes that people make the best use of all available information to forecast the future.

react *very* quickly to aggregate demand shocks, returning the economy to its long-run equilibrium in a very short period of time. Not only is stabilization policy totally unnecessary but the authorities will also be unable to influence output and employment, even in the short run, by pursuing systematic aggregate demand policies. According to the so-called **policy ineffectiveness proposition**, which was first put forward in the mid 1970s by Thomas Sargent and Neil Wallace, anticipated monetary policy will be completely ineffective. The proposition implies that only random or arbitrary policy actions undertaken by the authorities have real effects, because they cannot be anticipated by rational economic agents. However, given that such actions would only increase the variation of output and employment around their natural levels and increase uncertainty in the economy, the policy ineffectiveness proposition provides new classicists with a strong argument against discretionary policy activism and in favour of rules.

Policy ineffectiveness: The proposition that anticipated changes in monetary policy have no effect on output and employment.

Time inconsistency: The temptation for policy-makers to deviate from a previously announced policy once private decision-makers have adjusted their behaviour to the announced policy.

Time inconsistency

In the mid 1970s, the influential work of Finn Kydland and Edward Prescott on the problem of time inconsistency of policy provided another argument in the case for fixed rules over discretion. In some situations, in order to influence the expectations of private decision-makers, the authorities may announce that they intend to pursue a particular policy or course of action. However, once private decision-makers have reacted to the announced policy, the authorities may then be tempted to renege on their previous announcement. **Time inconsistency** describes a situation where an announced policy that is optimal today may not remain optimal in subsequent periods once private decision-makers have adjusted their behaviour accordingly. The problem of time inconsistency can be illustrated with a simple example. To encourage students to work hard a lecturer announces that his course will end with a hard exam. After students have responded by studying hard and learning the course material, the lecturer may then be tempted to cancel the exam in order to avoid marking the exam scripts.

In macroeconomics one of the best examples of the problem of time inconsistency concerns the Phillips curve trade-off between inflation and unemployment. In Chapter 10, section 10.4, we discussed how the expectations-augmented Phillips curve implies that while the long-run Phillips curve is vertical at the natural rate of unemployment, there exists a whole family of short-run Phillips curves, each associated with a different expected rate of inflation. For example, as the expected rate of inflation decreases, the short-run Phillips curve will shift downwards so that, for any given rate of unemployment, inflation will be lower the lower are expectations of inflation. In Fig. 12.3 we assume that the economy is initially operating at point A with a 4 per cent rate of inflation and unemployment at its natural rate (U_N). Now suppose that the authorities want to reduce inflation to zero per cent and move to point B on the long-run Phillips curve ($LRPC$). The authorities announce a policy of monetary contraction in order to reduce expectations of inflation held by workers and firms. However, once workers and firms have reduced their inflation expectations, shifting the short-run Phillips curve downwards form $SRPC_0$ to $SPRC_1$, the authorities will have an incentive to renege or cheat on their previously announced policy and implement expansionary monetary policy in order to reduce unemployment. By exercising their discretionary powers and engaging in monetary stimulus, the authorities can create an 'inflation surprise' and move to point C on $SRPC_1$. Point C is however unsustainable since unemployment (U^*) is below its natural rate

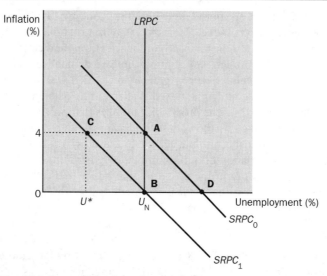

Fig. 12.3 The problem of time inconsistency.

(U_N) and the actual rate of inflation is greater than expected. As rational economic agents revise their inflation expectations upwards, shifting the short-run Phillips curve back from $SRPC_1$ to $SRPC_0$, the economy will return to point A on the $LRPC$ with an *inflationary bias*. In situations where the authorities have such discretionary

---

Box 12.1

Central bank independence and inflation performance

A number of economists have undertaken research that has examined the relationship between central bank independence and macroeconomic performance in advanced industrial countries for the period from the 1950s to the late 1980s. These studies have uncovered two main results. First, there appears to be no relationship between central bank independence and real macroeconomic performance, such as average unemployment and real output growth. Second, there is a striking *inverse* relationship between central bank independence and inflation performance. More central bank independence is strongly associated with lower, and more stable, inflation. Countries with more independent central banks – such as the USA, Switzerland, and Germany – have experienced the lowest average inflation. In contrast, countries with less central bank independence – such as Spain, Italy and New Zealand – have experienced higher average inflation. No doubt with these findings in mind, and also to help establish the *credibility* of monetary policy, a number of countries over recent years have given a higher *degree* of independence to their central banks. For example, in the early 1990s the central bank of New Zealand was given greater independence *and* accountability for its actions. In the latter case, if the head of the central bank of New Zealand fails to fulfil pre-agreed low inflation targets, he/she is fired. Interestingly, since being given greater central bank independence (and accountability), New Zealand has achieved lower inflation performance. More recently Gordon Brown, the Chancellor of the Labour Government in the UK, announced in May 1997 that the Bank of England would be given responsibility for setting interest rates. Although the Chancellor would set the inflation target, the Bank of England would have 'operational independence' in deciding interest rates to meet the inflation target*. In short, giving central banks more independence acts as a pre-commitment to policies favouring lower average rates of inflation.

*You can access the minutes of meetings of the Bank of England's Monetary Policy Committee, which has responsibility for setting UK interest rates, at the Bank's website. See Internet links at the end of this chapter.

powers and have in consequence an incentive to cheat, the credibility of announced policies will be significantly weakened. Aware that the authorities may be inconsistent over time, workers and firms are likely to distrust policy announcements. In circumstances where the announced policy of monetary contraction lacks credibility, agents will not revise their inflation expectations downwards. If the authorities actually carry out their announced policy, unemployment will rise above the natural rate: that is, a movement along $SRPC_0$ from point A to D.

The implication of the analysis we have discussed is that economic performance may be improved if discretionary powers are taken away from the authorities, and the authorities make a commitment to pursue a fixed monetary growth rate rule. In this case, policy will be seen to be credible and agents will reduce their inflation expectations downwards, making possible a policy of lower inflation without higher unemployment. The inflationary bias present when the authorities are given discretion in the way they conduct monetary policy has led some economists to advocate giving the responsibility for anti-inflation policy to a central bank that is *independent* of the government. In Box 12.1 we discuss the relationship between central bank independence and inflation performance.

Lucas critique

In 1976, the leading new classical economist Robert Lucas Jr put forward a further criticism of traditional policy evaluation that is popularly known as the **Lucas critique**. In order to understand the significance of this critique we must first explain briefly the role of a macroeconometric model in providing forecasts and simulations of the effects of policy changes. A macroeconometric model consists of a set of equations that describe the behaviour of the economy as a whole. The estimated numerical values for the parameters of the model, such as the marginal propensity to consume, are themselves based on past behaviour. Once constructed, macroeconometric models can be used not only to provide forecasts of the future course of key macroeconomic variables, such as output, unemployment and inflation, but also to study the effects of various policy changes on these variables. Lucas, however, argues that traditional macroeconometric models should not be used to predict the consequences of alternative policy changes, since the parameters of such models may change as economic agents adjust their expectations and behaviour in response to the policy change.

One example of the Lucas critique concerns the role of rational expectations in determining the output/employment costs of reducing inflation. According to the new classical view, the output/employment costs of monetary disinflation will be non-existent or negligible provided a policy change is credible. If the authorities announce a reduction in the rate of monetary expansion and the policy announcement is believed to be credible, rational economic agents will immediately revise their expectations of inflation downwards, in line with the anticipated effects of monetary contraction on the rate of inflation (see Chapter 10, section 10.4). New classicists claim that traditional estimates of the output/employment costs of reducing inflation are unreliable because they do not take into account how agents adjust their expectations and behaviour to a policy change. The traditional approach incorporates **adaptive expectations**, where economic agents form their expectations of the future value of a variable solely on the basis of recent past values of the variable. For example, agents' expectations of inflation will depend solely on past inflation, and will not change following a policy change. In consequence, new classicists argue

Lucas critique: The argument that traditional policy evaluation may be misleading as it fails to take into account that people may change their expectations and behaviour when policy changes.

Adaptive expectations: An approach that assumes that people's expectations of the future value of a variable are based solely on recently observed values of that variable.

that traditional policy evaluation overestimates the output/employment costs of reducing inflation because it is subject to the Lucas critique. In summary, the Lucas critique has cast doubt on the reliability of traditional estimates of the impact of various policy changes on key macroeconomic variables.

The real business cycle view

While both monetarists and new classicists question not only the need for stabilization policy but also whether the authorities can stabilize output and employment by discretionary policy intervention, a much more radical view emerged in the 1980s associated with the real business cycle approach to economic fluctuations. As discussed in Chapter 11, section 11.6, according to this approach economic fluctuations are the optimal response of the economy to supply shocks. In consequence, there is no role for the authorities to stabilize fluctuations in output and employment through conventional aggregate demand policies.

12.4 Concluding remarks

In this chapter we have outlined various views concerning the debate over stabilization policy. Two main views can be identified. One view, held by orthodox Keynesians and new Keynesians, is that the authorities need to, can and therefore should stabilize the economy using aggregate demand policies. Even though nowadays most Keynesian economists accept that the long-run Phillips curve is vertical, they justify discretionary policy intervention to stabilize the economy on the following grounds: (a) the period of time required for the economy to return to the natural rate of unemployment after having been subjected to some shock or disturbance; and (b) the potential to identify and respond to major shocks that periodically hit the economy. The other main view, held by monetarists and new classicists, is that there is no need for stabilization policy involving the management of aggregate demand and that, in any case, discretionary fiscal and monetary policies cannot and therefore should not be used to stabilize the economy. Given the divide between these two broad groupings of economists, the debate over stabilization policy is likely to continue and remain a controversial area in macroeconomics.

Summary

◆ One of the key questions that divide macroeconomists is whether the authorities need to, can and therefore should stabilize the economy at, or near, the full employment or natural level of output by influencing the level of aggregate demand.

◆ Discretionary policy takes place in circumstances where the authorities are free to vary the strength of fiscal and/or monetary policy in any way they see fit at the time. In contrast, the authorities may be committed to follow a pre-specified rule that determines the conduct of fiscal and/or monetary policy. Rules may or may not be linked to prevailing economic circumstances.

◆ The debate over stabilization policy critically depends on whether one views the economy as being inherently unstable or naturally stable. While both orthodox

Keynesians and new Keynesians subscribe to the former view, arguing that there is a need for stabilization policy, new Keynesians regard attempts to fine tune the macroeconomy as being overambitious, and instead advocate rough tuning.

◆ Both monetarists and new classicists, believing the economy to be inherently stable, question the need for stabilization policy involving the management of aggregate demand. Highlighting a number of problems associated with stabilization policy, most notably those associated with time lags, monetarists argue that discretionary policy activism may make matters worse, and advocate that discretionary aggregate demand policies should be replaced by some form of monetary rule. New classicists' support for rules over discretion is based on the insights provided by policy ineffectiveness, the problem of time inconsistency and the Lucas critique.

◆ In the real business cycle approach there is no role for stabilization policy.

▉ Key terms

◆ Discretionary policy
◆ Fine tuning and rough tuning
◆ Policy rule: active and passive
◆ Inflationary gap
◆ Crowding out
◆ Inside and outside lags
◆ Rational expectations
◆ Policy ineffectiveness
◆ Time inconsistency
◆ Macroeconometric model
◆ Lucas critique

▉ Self-test questions

True (t) or false (f)

1. An example of discretionary policy occurs where the authorities are given the freedom to increase government expenditure during a recession.

2. Policy rules tie the hands of the authorities to pursue pre-specified rules for fiscal and/or monetary policy.

3. Keynesians stress the need for stabilization policy, and argue that the authorities can and should use discretionary fiscal and monetary policies to stabilize the economy.

4. New Keynesians suggest that shocks, from both the demand side and the supply side of the economy, can cause undesirable and inefficient economic fluctuations.

5. Monetarists argue that discretionary fiscal and monetary policies can be used to stabilize the economy.

6. According to monetarists an increase in government expenditure will, in the long run, crowd out some components of private sector expenditure so that real income remains unchanged at its natural level.

7. According to the new classical policy-ineffectiveness proposition, anticipated monetary policy changes will have no effect on output and employment.

8. In the new classical view economic agents form their expectations in line with the adaptive expectations approach.

9. The problem of time inconsistency of policy has provided another argument in support of fixed rules over discretion.

10. According to the real business cycle view the authorities can stabilize fluctuations in output and employment using discretionary fiscal and monetary policies.

Complete the following sentences by inserting the missing word(s)

1. Frequent intervention by the authorities to maintain output and employment at, or near, their full employment or natural levels is known as ____.

2. A ____ policy rule is one where the pre-specified rule is not linked to the state of the economy.

3. Keynesians contend that the economy is inherently ____.

4. Orthodox Keynesians stress the need for discretionary ____ policies to stabilize the economy.

5. The period of time it takes to initiate a policy change is referred to as the ____ lag.

6. The time lapse between an initiated policy change and its influence on the economy is referred to as the ____ lag.

7. Monetarists contend that the economy is inherently ____ .

8. According to the new classical view only ____ monetary shocks affect output and employment and then only in the ____.

9. New classical economics is an approach based on the three assumptions of continuous market clearing, incomplete information and ____ .

10. The argument that traditional policy evaluation may be misleading as it fails to take into account that people may change their expectations and behaviour when policy changes is known as the ____ .

◼ Questions for discussion

◆ What is the difference between 'fine tuning' and 'rough tuning'? Which is the more realistic option?

◆ Why do economists disagree over the issue of whether the authorities need to, can and should stabilize the economy?

◆ What are the main problems encountered by policy-makers in implementing stabilization policy?

◆ What are the main time lags associated with fiscal and monetary policy? Why does the existence of these lags make it possible for policy intervention to have a destabilizing effect on the level of economic activity?

◆ Why do monetarists question the use of changes in government expenditure and taxes as instruments to influence the level of economic activity in the long run?

◆ In what ways will a change in interest rates affect firms?

◆ What is meant by the term 'time inconsistency'? Why does time inconsistency imply that economic performance may be improved if discretionary powers are taken away from the authorities?

◆ Should macroeconomic policy be operated at the discretion of the authorities or on the basis of rules?

Further reading

Stewart, M. *Keynes and After* (3rd ed.) (Hardmondsworth: Penguin, 1986). An excellent non-technical introduction to Keynesian economics and monetarism.

Marin, A. *Macroeconomic Policy* (London: Routledge, 1992). Examines the central tenets of the Keynesian and monetarist schools in a clear and non-technical manner.

Shaw, G.K. *Rational Expectations* (Brighton: Wheatsheaf Books, 1984). A concise, lucid and analytical introduction to rational expectations and its implications.

Internet links

The minutes of the monthly meetings of the *Bank of England's Monetary Policy Committee* can be accessed via the Bank's website at: **http://www.bankofengland.co.uk/** Information on the macroeconomic policies and performances of the major economies can be found at the *OECD*'s website: **http://www.oecd.org/**

International Trade

Contents

Key issues

▶ Why do countries trade?

▶ Can all countries gain from trade?

▶ How have patterns of trade changed since 1945?

▶ How has trade policy unfolded since 1945?

13.1 Introduction

International trade is simply the extension of the market process across international boundaries: the buying and selling of goods and services in foreign markets rather than in the domestic economy. To begin our discussion of international trade it is useful to consider the following three basic questions:

- What *advantages* does trade offer over and above the confinement of economic activity to the domestic market alone?
- What is the economic basis for trade?
- Is trade always a mutually advantageous process or are some economic agents potentially *disadvantaged* by it?

The advantages of trade

The most obvious advantage of international trade is that it provides mutual access to a range of goods and services that might otherwise be denied to domestic populations. The residents of Germany, for example, cannot easily produce and consume tropical fruits or lie on a tropical beach on holiday except through trade: the German economy and German factors of production are not suited to the production of either of these things, so demand for them must be met from abroad. More significantly, many economies have no means whatsoever of meeting certain basic material consumption needs out of domestic resources. Ireland, for example, has no independent recourse to oil or even coal; both of these important fuels have to be

Swedish design around the world.

imported. This, the *consumption* motive for trade, is not restricted solely to items that are beyond the powers of the domestic economy to produce. A growing number of countries have industries that sell their outputs into the markets of rival foreign producers. For example, French cars are sold in Britain and British-made cars are bought in France. Some British residents clearly prefer French cars to those produced at home and vice versa. Such preferences for foreign goods over their domestically produced counterparts may simply reflect differences in taste but can also be based on price or quality factors. Whatever the motivation, trade makes much wider consumption choices possible in comparison to those available under *autarky* (meaning self-sufficiency).

If trade opens up new opportunities for consumption, what of its effects upon *production*? It should be clear that goods and services sold abroad provide incomes and employment for those who produce them. As we shall see, the relatively rapid rates of economic growth enjoyed by the advanced industrial countries in the two decades after the Second World War, together with the more recent exceptional growth performances of the newly industrializing countries of the Pacific Rim, such as South Korea, have their basis – at least in part – in the growth of international trade. There is a close affinity between success in foreign markets and domestic economic progress, which is perhaps best expressed by the phrase *export-led growth*. Of course, trade also gives access to the global range of raw materials upon which production rests. As few countries, if any, are completely self-sufficient in raw materials, trade provides the vital conduit through which the earth's resources can be put to productive use.

The economic basis for trade

Having briefly reviewed the advantages of international trade, we now introduce the fundamental economic principle upon which it is rests. This, the notion of *specialization and exchange*, is associated with the work of the British (classical) economists Adam Smith and David Ricardo.

In his book *An Inquiry into the Nature and Causes of the Wealth of Nations*, published in 1776, Smith argued that labour can be made more productive by allocating it *specialist* tasks. He famously used the example of pin-making to demonstrate that a group of workers, each with a particular and complementary skill in which they are well versed, will collectively be much more productive than they would be if each alone tried to master the full repertoire of pin-making skills. In other words, it is better to be adept at a small range of tasks than to undertake many with questionable competence. As for individuals, Smith declared, so for nations. It is appropriate for countries to limit the range of economic activities to those to which they are *best*

Free trade

Free trade implies an absence of government regulation in the international markets for goods and services.

◆ **Concept**

International division of labour

The international division of labour describes patterns of specialization in the production of goods and services between nations.

Comparative advantage: The ability of a country to produce a commodity at a lower opportunity cost, in terms of other commodities forgone, than another country.

◆ **Concept**

Protectionism

Protectionism occurs where the principle of free trade is compromised. Usually, protectionist policies are implemented by governments concerned to promote domestic industries over their foreign rivals.

suited and to engage in trade (exchange) to obtain those goods and services that they desire but cannot or choose not to produce. Smith also provided a rationale for **free trade**, unregulated and unchecked by government interference. The argument here is that individuals will freely enter into transactions that benefit them: hence the greater the number of transactions, the greater the benefit. At the international level the same reasoning applies: the greater the volume of trade, the greater the benefit derived by those engaging in it. Thus trade should be allowed to flourish unconstrained. Note the mutually supportive link here between the notion of an **international division of labour** (nations specializing in what they are best at) and the argument for free trade. In a free and open international economy, countries will be motivated to push their productive specialisms as far as they are able, utilizing to the full factors of production in the most appropriate ways.

Ricardo's contribution to this analysis, published in his book *On The Principles of Political Economy and Taxation* in 1817, was to demonstrate that *all* countries can gain from specialization and exchange, and not just those that have reached a certain level of economic development. In such circumstances, there are no sustainable arguments to confound the general case for free trade. We review the Ricardian concept of **comparative advantage**, which is at the heart of this thesis, in section 13.2 below.

Some negative consequences of trade

The free trade arguments advanced by Smith and Ricardo have become a cornerstone of modern economic orthodoxy, but this is not to say that international trade is not without its problems or that the case for *managed* trade can find no advocates. Later in this chapter we shall provide some examples of instances in which the international division of labour has shifted over time between nations. In such circumstances, countries with long-standing specialisms in the production of particular goods can find themselves 'outcompeted' in those specialisms by emergent rivals. This situation requires that the newly uncompetitive nations shift factors of production out of their threatened specialisms and reallocate them to uses in which they retain or can develop a competitive edge. However, while in theory the reallocation of resources can proceed in a smooth and timely manner, the reality is usually rather different and may involve bankruptcies and unemployment in industries with deteriorating competitiveness. This is because opportunities for the reinvestment of capital and re-employment of labour in new sectors usually emerge slowly and not at a pace sufficient to offset the original industrial decline. This kind of *adjustment problem* may give rise to calls for domestic industries to be **protected** by governments from the full force of international competition that completely free trade would unleash. We examine the contemporary validity of this position in section 13.5 of this chapter.

13.2 The theory of comparative advantage

Ricardo's theory of comparative advantage suggests that all countries will have some particular efficiency in the production of a good or service *relative to another country*. This means that every country can gain from specialization and trade. It does not matter if a given national economy is economically advanced or backward in comparison with its neighbours: it can still find an appropriate avenue of production upon which to concentrate.

At the time of its publication, Ricardo's work, together with that of Smith, constituted a radical attack on the prevailing philosophy of international trade, namely **mercantilism**. Mercantilists thought that the key to national prosperity was the accumulation of gold and silver bullion. Bullion was, of itself, manifest wealth but it could also be used to finance wars with other foreign powers. The key to the accumulation of bullion was strong export performance – in order to maximize the inflow of gold and silver arising from payments for goods sold abroad – together with import restraint to minimize bullion outflow. The mercantilists argued that the state had a duty to implement policies to promote exports and protect domestic industry from import penetration: both were a means of furthering national prosperity. Note that this establishes mercantilism as a profoundly interventionist philosophy. Finally, in the mercantilist view, international trade could only ever be attractive to one group of nations: those consistent net exporters who followed an aggressive trade policy, accumulated bullion and were prosperous. Other nations, less successful in the drive for exports, tended to lose bullion and were economically enfeebled.

Ricardo thought that this conceptualization of strong nations carving out overseas markets at the expense of the weak was wholly mistaken. Indeed, he argued that there were no economically strong or weak nations in the mercantilist sense: all were possessed of a comparative advantage in the production of some good or service. The truly striking element in his approach, compared with what had gone before, was its demonstration that, as a consequence of the existence of comparative advantage, international trade could no longer be considered to be a 'zero sum game' in which the strong nations elbowed aside the weak. Instead, trade was a 'positive sum' process that actually raised the production and consumption possibilities of participant nations, leaving them *all* better off.

The theory of comparative advantage is best explained with the help of a simple example. We begin by identifying two countries: Germany and Ukraine, each of which, fully using the resources available to it, can produce some combination of two goods: cameras and beer. Let us assume that the *production possibilities* in Table 13.1 apply: Germany, in other words can produce either 20 million cameras or 20 million units of beer (in a given time period) if all its resources are allocated to either camera or beer production respectively, or some combination of both products in between these two values. Similarly, Ukraine can produce either 5 million cameras or 15 million units of beer or some combination in between. Fig. 13.1 graphs the possible production combinations for both countries, assuming, for ease of exposition, constant returns to scale. For each country we can now express the opportunity cost of one good in terms of the other. Recall that opportunity cost refers to the amount of one good that must be given up in order to obtain a given increase in the

◆ Concept

Mercantilism

Mercantilism was an economic philosophy advanced by merchants and politicians prior to the rise of industrial capitalism. Mercantilism emphasized the importance of accumulating bullion from balance of trade surpluses, and advocated tariffs and other protectionist measures to achieve that end.

Table 13.1 Hypothetical production possibilities

	Cameras		Beer
Germany	20 million units	*or*	20 million units
Ukraine	5 million units	*or*	15 million units

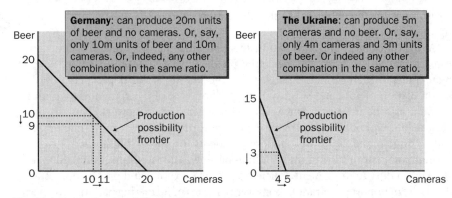

Fig. 13.1 Production possibility frontiers.

output of the other good. In the case of Germany it can be seen, for example, that the opportunity cost of producing 1 camera is 1 unit of beer (20 million cameras would 'cost' 20 million units of beer; 20m ÷ 20m = 1). Therefore, to produce *one* million more cameras (for example, from 10 million to 11 million cameras), *one* million units of beer must be sacrificed (that is, from 10 million to 9 million units). In Ukraine, however, the opportunity cost of the amount of beer that must be forgone to produce one more camera is higher. Here, the maximum of 5 million cameras that can be produced would cost the forgone production of 15 million units of beer. Thus the opportunity cost of a camera in Ukraine is 3 units of beer (15m ÷ 5m = 3). To produce *one* million more cameras (for example, from 4 million to 5 million cameras), *three* million units of beer must be sacrificed (that is, from 3 million units to zero).

This means that Germany can produce cameras at a lower opportunity cost in terms of beer production that must be forgone than Ukraine. Germany, in other words, has a *comparative advantage in camera production* over Ukraine. On the other hand, it is apparent that Ukraine has a comparative advantage in beer production over Germany. In Germany, each extra unit of beer produced involves the loss of 1 camera; but in Ukraine it is possible to produce 3 extra units of beer for the loss of a camera (that is, the opportunity cost of producing one unit of beer is the loss of a third of a camera). *In opportunity cost terms, Ukraine can produce beer at a lower opportunity cost compared with Germany*: in other words, it has a comparative advantage in beer production over Germany.

The different opportunity costs suggest that there is scope for specialization in the two countries. Germany could produce only cameras, at which it appears adept, and no beer, while Ukraine could do the reverse. Each country would be producing the commodity in which it has a comparative advantage (that is, producing at the lowest opportunity cost) in comparison with the other country. We now need to demonstrate that, in this situation, there is scope for trade between Germany and Ukraine that is mutually advantageous. Consider Germany first. Suppose the German economy produced *only* cameras: 20 million of them, some of which it wished to exchange for beer from Ukraine. The crucial issue is the exchange ratio that needs to be agreed. We know that to obtain one unit of beer in Germany there is a 'price' to be paid of one camera. If Germany could persuade Ukraine to let it have, say, 2 units of beer per camera, then this would represent a huge improvement on what was available domestically. The obvious question now concerns the receptiveness of Ukraine

Table 13.2 Germany and Ukraine in autarky

	Production and consumption	
	Cameras (millions)	Beer (millions of units)
Germany	15	5
Ukraine	4	3
'World' output in autarky	19	8

Table 13.3 Specialization and trade

	Produces	Exports	Imports	Consumes
Germany	20m cameras	5m cameras ← → 10m beers		15m cameras; 10m beers
Ukraine	15m beers	10m beers ← → 5m cameras		5m cameras; 5m beers
'World' output and consumption after trade	⟶			20m cameras; 15m beers

to this offer. In Ukraine, the opportunity cost of producing a camera is 3 units of beer. If Germany offers to exchange its cameras for only 2 units of beer this is a very acceptable arrangement for Ukraine. It would be advantageous for Ukraine to produce only beer (that is, 15 million units) and to exchange some of its beer production for German cameras. The important point to notice is that there is a different international exchange ratio (or price) for cameras and beer compared with that prevailing in the two domestic economies.

Table 13.2 summarizes the position of both countries in autarky (no trade) with an arbitrary division of production between the two goods. Note the *total* output levels for cameras and beer in this situation: 19 million cameras and 8 million units of beer. We shall now consider complete specialization in both countries, where some of the output of each is traded at an exchange ratio of 2 units of beer per camera. Again, the volumes traded are selected arbitrarily simply for illustrative purposes. The results are summarized in Table 13.3. Here it can be seen that both countries have gained from the process. In Germany, camera consumption has remained at the same level as in autarky but the consumption of beer has doubled from 5 to 10 million units. In Ukraine, camera consumption has increased by 1 million units and beer consumption by 2 million units. World production and consumption has increased by 1 and 7 million units of cameras and beer respectively.

It is evident then that specialization and exchange has indeed improved the consumption positions of both countries, and Ricardo's critique of the mercantilist view – that countries can gain through trade only at the expense of their rivals – appears vindicated. Similarly, the Ricardian case for free trade is equally well founded. Note that in our example Germany is capable of producing more of *both* commodities than is Ukraine. It is said to possess an **absolute advantage** in the production of both. Adam Smith had originally supposed that trade could take place only between countries that had an absolute advantage in the production of particular goods. Ricardo's great contribution was to show that the important criterion was the existence of comparative, not absolute, advantage. Now, because all countries have a

Absolute advantage: The ability of a country to produce more of a particular commodity than another country, using an equal quantity of factor inputs.

comparative advantage in something, all may gain from the trade process. *This means that free trade is in the interest of all countries*, and that, as a corollary, its inverse – the kind of protectionism recommended by the mercantilists – is inimical to the general economic good.

13.3 Reflecting on comparative advantage: further developments in trade theory

The basic message that emerges from the theory of comparative advantage is very clear: the best way to organize the international economy is to allow specialization and trade to flourish. Yet there are still some questions that our description of the principle so far has left unanswered. These are:

- Are there really *no* problems whatsoever with the trade process in the Ricardian view?
- What kind of factors determine a country's comparative advantage?
- How are we to reconcile Ricardo's expectation of specialization with the fact that, as noted, many countries produce the *same* commodity (the car was the example used earlier) and sell it in each others' markets?

To begin with the first of these questions, it is the Ricardian case that, for each country *as a whole*, trade offers no threats, only opportunities. However, Ricardo himself acknowledged that, for some groups inside the national economy, problems could arise as a result of free trade. His specific reference was to the losses that free trade might visit upon British landowners at the end of the Napoleonic wars in 1815 (recall that Ricardo's book was published in 1817). War had raised British food prices, to the benefit of the landowners on whose property the food was produced. Because free trade threatened to open the British market to imports of cheaper foreign food, landowners were in favour of the protection, by government, of the domestic food market. However, a second British interest group – the newly emerging manufacturing class – wanted a liberal trading environment that would allow them to profit from open overseas markets. Ricardo's suggested compromise was that the free-trade-enriched manufacturers should compensate the disadvantaged landowners. In this way, internal objections to the effects of trade could be overcome and its larger benefits secured. We consider the modern parallels to this situation in section 13.5 on trade policy.

What of the *source* of comparative advantage? In his original formulation, Ricardo highlighted the importance of *labour productivity* as the key determinant of a country's specialization decision. The more productive its labour becomes in the fashioning of one particular commodity as against an alternative, the lower the opportunity cost of the commodity. Returning to our earlier example (summarized in Table 13.1 and Fig. 13.1), consider the impact of a five-fold increase in productivity in the German camera industry. Instead of 20 million cameras in a given time period, it is now able to produce 100 million cameras. We assume conditions in the German beer industry are unchanged. Formerly, the opportunity cost of a camera was one unit of beer. Now, given the improvement in camera industry productivity, one camera costs only a fifth of a unit of beer (20m ÷ 100m = 1/5). If Ukraine is still happy to trade at the existing international ratio of 1 camera for 2 units of beer, then the leap in German camera productivity provides the basis for an even better deal for the Germans. Domestically, they can now get only 1/5 of a unit of beer for every camera they sacrifice (instead of one unit as previously) but internationally they can still obtain 2 beers per camera; and they're producing many more cameras.

Although the concept of comparative advantage still survives as the underlying essence of modern international trade theory, Ricardo's emphasis on labour productivity as its (sole) source has fared less well. In particular, given the existence of a number of factors of production, it seems reasonable to question the validity of elevating only *one* factor as a means of explaining patterns of trade. This concern eventually prompted a further important step in the development of trade theory with the emergence, in the 1920s, of the **Heckscher–Ohlin** model of international trade, named after its Swedish originators. The Heckscher–Ohlin model supposes that a country's comparative advantage will reflect its particular *endowments* of factors of production. Because, globally, factors are not evenly spread, the basis for specialization and exchange is established. For example, those countries that are richly endowed with fertile land will find it beneficial to devote resources to the production of agricultural output. For countries with a relative abundance of labour, specialization in the production of labour-intensive goods and services will be preferable. The advantage of this kind of approach is that it has expectations that appear to conform to some very obvious real-world general trading patterns. 'Land-rich' countries such as New Zealand and Brazil do tend to specialize in outputs that exploit their natural resource endowments, while a country such as Japan, which has fewer natural resources but a relative abundance of capital (in the shape of technologically advanced factories and machines), specializes in manufactured goods. Unfortunately, despite the stamp of realism that the Heckscher–Ohlin model appears to possess, its formal construction required that only *two* factors of production could be considered, rather than the four that microeconomic theory identifies. The preferred two factors were labour and capital. Despite such simplification, the model was still regarded as an advance upon the foundations provided by Ricardo.

In 1947 the central hypothesis of the Heckscher–Ohlin model was famously subjected to an empirical test by an economist named Leontief. Using a model of the American economy, Leontief expected to be able to demonstrate specialization by the USA in capital-intensive goods and, therefore, that US exports were similarly capital intensive. Given that America was by far the most technologically advanced nation in the world at that time, this was a reasonable hypothesis. However, Leontief's results were the reverse of those anticipated. His work suggested that the USA was an exporter of labour-intensive goods and an importer of capital-intensive goods: in other words, the USA was *not* specializing in the production of goods that required the use of its most abundant factor. Yet because the Heckscher–Ohlin model was supported by an apparent wealth of casual empirical evidence concerning the kind of international division of labour noted above, economists – including Leontief himself – were reluctant to dismiss it, and his findings subsequently became known as the **Leontief paradox**.

This impasse between an intuitively defensible model and apparently contradictory empirical evidence subsequently resulted in a number of analyses that attempted to reconcile the two. The most widely accepted of these have usually involved some acknowledgement that comparative advantage must have its roots in something a little more complex than two simple categories of labour and capital. For example, Leontief thought that his results might be explained by the higher quality of labour

Concept

Heckscher–Ohlin model

The Heckscher-Ohlin approach to international trade holds that a country's production and trade specialisms will reflect its particular factor endowments.

Concept

Leontief paradox

The Leontief paradox refers to the finding by the economist Leontief that, for the United States, the predictions of the Heckscher–Ohlin model did not appear empirically verifiable.

Inter-industry trade: The tendency for countries to trade the same kinds of goods and services.

in the USA. This subsequently became known as the *human capital* argument, and rests upon the proposition that the relatively heavy investment in education and training that takes place in the advanced economies makes labour there much more productive than elsewhere. The specialization of the USA in labour-intensive industries, as discovered by Leontief, can therefore be explained by the abundance of high-quality labour in the USA. In this sense, there is no paradox: it is just that the basis of comparative advantage is indeed more complex than the formalities of the Heckscher–Ohlin model can allow. The model itself, with due deference to its Ricardian foundations, remains the central element of orthodox trade theory in modern economics.

In our third question reflecting upon comparative advantage, we raised a further facet of real-world trade complexity. In his original formulation, Ricardo argued that countries specialize in *particular* goods, which they then trade for *different* goods that the domestic economy either cannot or chooses not to produce. The Heckscher–Ohlin model was a slightly more sophisticated endorsement of this same view. But, of course, the world is not that simple. A large proportion of trade takes place between countries in the *same* product lines. As noted, the car industry is an obvious case in point. There is little sign of specialization and exchange of the kind Ricardo expected here: an increasing number of countries make cars and sell them to each other. Trade between nations in the same goods is known as **inter-industry trade**, and the rapid increase in this kind of activity in the period after the Second World War has prompted the most recent developments in trade theory.

Although it might at first appear that the growth of inter-industry trade serves to undermine the traditional Ricardian approach, with its emphasis on the development of patterns of specialization, this is not the case. Contemporary trade theory recognizes that Ricardo's rather rigid demarcation between 'country A producing good X and country B producing good Y, with trade between them' is increasingly outdated, but it continues to respect the essence of comparative advantage: *that different forms of production will be more efficiently conducted in different places*. Because everywhere is not the same in terms of economic attributes, it makes sense to use some places for one (suitable) form of production and other places for other (suitable) forms.

This kind of approach has provided the basis for a number of new advances in international trade theory. One of these, **product life cycle theory**, describes the relationship between, on the one hand, the initial launch of a new good and its subsequent path to the status of a mature and recognized product and, on the other, its evolving *geography of production*. Let us take the car as an example of the application of this theory. When the car was first invented, the location of its production was constrained by a number of factors. First, as a new and expensive good, its market was initially small, and prospective customers needed to be affluent. Second, its technical complexity demanded a skilled labour force. Finally, new car makers may have gained from close proximity to one another: perhaps from sharing information or resources, or simply by 'keeping an eye on the competition'. Taken together, these factors tended to mean that car production was *restricted to certain economically advanced locations*. Eventually, the car became a mature commodity. Its form was no longer experimental and changing but established and stable. The way in which it was produced changed too. Skilled labour was no longer pre-eminent, as the introduction of the assembly line allowed cars to be produced in vast numbers by semi-skilled or even unskilled labour. Such efficient production – taking advantage of

Concept

Product life cycle theory

Product life cycle theory understands patterns of international trade by referencing the development of commodities over time. As they move from a stage of innovation through to maturity, products have different international geographies of production and therefore varying trade patterns.

scale economies – lowered the price of cars even to within reach of the pockets of the people who made them. Finally, in a large and established market, car manufacturers began to compete much more heavily on price than they had done in the earliest stages of production. These new circumstances meant that the location of production became much more flexible; the old imperatives restricting it to economically advanced locations disappeared and, indeed, there were positive benefits to be reaped from seeking out places where costs could be minimized.

The above stylized analysis permits us to grasp the notion of a **shifting comparative advantage**, which favours different locations as a product moves from a stage of innovation to one of maturity. At first, because certain factors – such as skilled labour inputs – are crucial, production must be retained in the innovating areas; for car making these are the advanced industrial nations. Later, when other factors become more important upon the maturing of the product, a wider distribution of production is favoured and may encompass, for example, less developed country locations. More generally, this kind of approach enables us to understand some of the reasons for the growth of inter-industry trade. If product life cycle theory is applicable to many 'durable' consumer goods then it is possible to conceive of a highly complex patterning of trade (such as actually exists in the real world), which reflects the processes of innovation and maturation of many different products as their production migrates to, and they are exported from, newly appropriate locations. Again, however, we should be aware that the essence of 'locational appropriateness' is captured in Ricardian comparative advantage.

Finally, in this section, we should emphasize the potential richness of the theoretical path to which this kind of approach to international trade gives rise. We have concentrated here on product life cycle theory as one explanation of inter-industry trade, but there is, in addition, a range of complementary material that highlights other potentially significant factors. These would include a more systematic review of the interaction between, *inter alia*, national patterns of investment and innovation, economies of scale and government policy (see guide to further reading at the end of this chapter).

13.4 Patterns of trade since 1945

We referred earlier to the rapid growth in international trade that has occurred since the end of the Second World War. In this section we shall briefly describe the scale of this process and demonstrate its economic importance. We shall also describe the striking changes in the patterns of trade that have emerged over the period.

Table 13.4 illustrates the positive nature of the relationship between trade and economic growth: the more rapid the annual rate at which trade expands, the faster the growth in world output. It is evident from the table that in periods in which the growth in trade has been relatively sluggish, such as 1913–50, the rate of growth of output has been similarly poor. By contrast, faster trade growth is usually equated with faster output growth. There is in fact a *causal* link between these two variables: it is the opening up of new and bigger international markets for goods and services that motivates firms to increase output levels.

In Chapter 9, section 9.6, we described the years 1945–70 as the **postwar boom**: a period during which most of the advanced economies experienced unprecedented rates of economic growth, together with full employment and low inflation. Table

---

Concept

Shifting comparative advantage

Shifting comparative advantage implies that patterns of comparative advantage are not stable over time. Countries may lose and gain comparative advantage in different products.

Table 13.4 World output and trade growth, 1820–2000 (annual average % change)

	Output	Trade
1820–1870	2.2	4.0
1870–1913	2.5	3.9
1913–1950	1.9	1.0
1950–1973	4.9	8.6
1971–1980	4.0	5.0
1981–1990	3.4	4.7
1991–2000[a]	3.1	6.1

[a] Data for 1999 and 2000 are IMF estimates.
Source: Adapted from P. Armstrong, A. Glyn and J. Harrison, *Capitalism Since 1945* (Oxford: Basil Blackwell, 1991); GATT (1987); and IMF (1999).

Table 13.5 Regional shares in total world merchandise exports[a] (per cent)

	1980	1990	1997	1998[a]
Developed economies	63.13	73.57	68.35	69.85
Developing economies	29.13	23.31	27.52	26.08
Transition economies	7.77	3.11	4.15	4.06
World	**100**	**100**	**100**	**100**
North America	14.43	15.18	16.34	16.55
Western Europe	40.10	47.62	41.26	43.30
Central and Eastern Europe/Baltic States/CIS	7.74	3.07	4.03	3.95
Africa	5.91	2.98	2.28	1.97
Asia	15.63	21.83	25.69	24.53
Latin America	5.39	4.24	5.06	5.08
Middle East	10.55	3.90	3.19	2.53
World	**100**	**100**	**100**	**100**

[a] Figures for 1998 are provisional; other caveats apply – see Technical Notes in WTO, Annual Report, 1998, International Trade Statistics
Source: World Trade Organization website: statistics, accessed 22 November 1999

13.4 indicates the central contribution made by the growth in world trade to this 'golden era'. Between 1950 and 1973 trade grew at an annual average rate of 8.6 per cent, more than double that in any previous period; while output expanded at 4.9 per cent, again about twice the best previous rate. However, it is also evident from the table that the more modest expansion of trade since the beginning of the 1970s has, not unexpectedly, been associated with slower growth in world output.

If world trade has expanded at a rapid if uneven rate over the postwar period, which countries have been the biggest participants in this process? Table 13.5 summarizes the distribution of *world merchandise exports* since 1980. A country's export performance is the ultimate indicator of its competitive strength in international markets. From the top portion of the table we can see, first, that the overall export share of the developed economies has remained reasonably stable over the period as a whole – at roughly two-thirds. This suggests that despite the purported success of many less developed countries in the trade process, the international economy is still overwhelmingly the preserve of the advanced nations. The developing economies' share of world exports is also relatively stable – at around 25 per cent. Finally, the transition economies have seen their small share of merchandise exports fall over the last 20 years. This undoubtedly reflects their exposure to more competitive world markets after the collapse of central planning from 1989 onwards.

The bottom portion of Table 13.5 describes the export performance of different *regional groups* in the international economy. Here some of the patterns described above are broadly replicated. North America and western Europe (consisting only of developed economies) have seen their export shares hold steady. The transition countries in central and eastern Europe, by contrast, have lost ground in export markets relative to other regions. There are other clear differences in long-term export performance between the remaining regional groups. Let us concentrate first on the more successful participants in the trade process. The Asian nations, for example, have managed to increase their collective share of world exports from 15.63 per cent in 1980 to about 25 per cent by the end of the century. Given that the relative slowdown in the growth of trade overall during the last three decades of the century (compared with the postwar boom) has meant that overseas markets have become more keenly contested, this is a remarkable achievement. Of the Asian group of economies, Japan consistently assumes the largest export share. Its individual share of the world merchandise export market in 1997 was 7.6 per cent; in the same year it accounted for over a quarter of all merchandise exports from Asia. However, the prize for the *rate* of export growth must be awarded to a select number of other Asian economies: China, Hong Kong, South Korea, Malaysia, Singapore and Taiwan. Since 1980, the collective share of world exports of these economies has increased *threefold*. In fact, the achievements of the so-called Asian 'tiger' economies in opening up foreign markets have resulted in rates of economic growth consistently above those of any of the established advanced industrial nations. Between 1981 and 2000, for example, the real annual average GDP growth rate of the Asian economies was 7.1 per cent. Over the same period, the comparable figures for the United States and the EU were 2.7 and 2.1 per cent respectively.

How can the unparalleled expansion in export trade shares enjoyed by the 'tiger' economies be explained? The answer, in fact, lies in the Ricardian notion of shifting comparative advantage. These nations have managed to cast off long-established patterns of specialization in favour of others that have allowed them to enter new and growing world markets. In particular, they have shifted resources away from the production of primary commodities (foodstuffs and raw materials) and towards the production of *manufactures*. This has been possible because these *newly industrializing countries* (NICs) are able to fashion certain kinds of manufactured items more efficiently than the advanced countries. By taking advantage of lower labour costs, for example, the NICs have begun to produce a range of labour-intensive manufactures that they can price extremely competitively in world markets. However, as we shall see, this has posed certain problems for newly *un*competitive industries in the advanced nations.

Of the other regions in the bottom portion of Table 13.5, only Latin America has managed to preserve its share of world exports over the period since 1980. For Africa and the Middle East the decline in export share has been quite dramatic. The fortunes of countries in the Middle East are closely tied to the price of oil. To a great extent, the 1980 export share figure of 10.55 per cent reflected the very sharp oil price increases of 1973–74 and 1979. The subsequent fall in oil prices over the 1980s had the effect of trimming back the share of the Middle East in world exports from its 1980 high point. The other notably poor performance revealed in the table is that of Africa, which has seen its share of world merchandise exports fall by about two-thirds over the period in question.

We have spent some time considering merchandise export performance, as trade in goods accounts for 80 per cent of total international trade; trade in services accounts for the remaining 20 per cent. Table 13.6 describes the service export shares of the world's major regions. Notice from the table that both North America and Asia have increased their shares in service trade since 1980, while the shares of western Europe and Africa have fallen. However, in 1998 western Europe was still responsible for almost half of all service exports.

We are now aware of the distribution of international trade: we know which countries and regions enjoy most of it and which are enjoying the fastest growth in

Table 13.6 Regional shares in world exports of commercial services (per cent)

	1980	1990	1997	1998[a]
North America	12.37	19.22	20.03	20.05
Western Europe	58.12	53.27	45.52	48.25
Central and Eastern Europe/Baltic States/CIS	na	na	na	na
Africa	3.48	2.37	2.08	2.03
Asia	13.71	16.78	22.67	19.38
Latin America	4.76	na	na	na
Middle East	na	na	na	na
World	**100**	**100**	**100**	**100**

[a] Figures for 1998 are provisional; other caveats apply – see Technical Notes in WTO, Annual Report, 1998, International Trade Statistics
Source: World Trade Organization website: statistics, accessed 22 November 1999

Table 13.7 Intra-regional export shares, 1990–98 (per cent)

	1990	1991	1992	1993	1994	1995	1996	1997	1998
NAFTA[a]	41.4	42.2	43.7	45.8	48.0	46.2	47.6	49.1	51.0
EU	59.0	58.7	59.5	56.2	56.8	63.5	62.8	62.1	62.5
MERCOSUR[b]	8.9	11.1	14.0	18.5	19.2	20.3	22.7	24.8	24.8
ASEAN[c]	18.7	19.3	19.1	20.0	22.7	23.0	22.9	22.1	20.6
Andean Community[d]	3.8	5.8	7.8	9.8	10.5	11.8	10.4	10.0	10.0

[a] The North American Free Trade Agreement; cements together the economies of Canada, Mexico and the USA into a free trade zone.
[b] Mercado Comun del Sur, another regional trade bloc, comprises Argentina, Brazil, Paraguay and Uruguay.
[c] Association of Southeast Asian Nations; comprises Brunei, Indonesia, Laos, Malaysia, Myanmar, Philippines, Singapore, Thailand and Vietnam.
[d] Comprises Bolivia, Columbia, Ecuador, Peru and Venezuela.
Source: IMF *World Economic Outlook*, October 1999 (Table 5.1).

trade shares. But what of the *pattern* of trade: who trades mostly with whom? Some answers to this question can be found in Table 13.7. The evidence here is that already heavy *intra-regional* and, by implication, *inter-industry* trade processes are increasing. In the EU in 1990, for example, 59 per cent of exports were retained; by 1998 this figure had increased to 62.5 per cent. This means that EU countries are trading more intensively with each other, rather than with nations in other parts of the world. Now, given that the EU nations have similarly advanced industrial structures, this also suggests that inter-industry trade is becoming ever more dominant. More dramatic increases in intra-regional trade are evident in other parts of the world. In MERCOSUR and the Andean Community, for example, intra-regional export shares roughly trebled between 1990 and 1998. Evidence of this sort – revealing more trade between equivalent economies in the same kinds of goods and services – explains the development of the new and more complex forms of Ricardian trade theory described in section 13.4: modern trade processes appear to bear little similarity to the simple binary-specialism model that Ricardo originally advanced.

Tariff: A tax on traded goods. When levied on imports, the assumption is that importers will pass the tax on to domestic customers in the form of higher prices, thus reducing the quantity of imports demanded.

13.5 International trade policy

On the basis of the theory and evidence offered in this chapter so far the issue of trade policy should, for all nations, be an uncontentious one. Because it permits the deployment of resources in their most productive uses together with the mutually advantageous exchange of the resulting maximized output, free and unrestricted trade should always be the preferred option. This is one of the cast iron certainties of orthodox economics. Yet *all* nations *do* engage in many forms of protectionism. Indeed, the post-1970 period has been one in which protectionism has become more widespread than at any time since the years between the two world wars. The obvious question arises: if free trade is so mutually advantageous, why protect?

Understanding protectionism

One of the most instructive ways to think about the development of trade policy involves use of the framework provided by *institutionalist economics*. The work of this school was first introduced in Chapter 5 in the context of a discussion of the theory of the firm. In Chapter 5, section 5.11, we described the institutionalist emphasis – exemplified in the writings of J.K. Galbraith – on the evolutionary development of capitalist economies. Very simply, this approach suggests that because the world's economies are not all at the same stage of development they require different kinds of policy to help them flourish. In terms of trade policy, this means that for some nations, at particular stages, elements of protectionism are indeed appropriate.

In advancing this view, Galbraith draws on the work of an early institutionalist and critic of Smith and Ricardo: the German economist Friedrich List (1789–1846). List was an advocate of German protectionism in the first half of the nineteenth century. His concern, reflecting the idea of different stages of national economic development, was that the strong industrial base of the then more advanced British economy would suppress the growth of new German industries. The development of the German economy as a whole would therefore be constrained unless its industries could be insulated from their superior British competitors. Such insulation was available through the imposition of **tariff**-based protection, which would raise the prices of imports from Britain. However, once German industrialization had attained a level of maturity that would permit it to compete on a more equal basis with Britain, then a liberal German trading regime would be appropriate. The important point here is that the form of trade policy that an economy adopts must be in keeping with the particular stage of development of that economy, and as the economy matures so the choice of trade policy will change. This conclusion is clearly at odds with the free trade recommendations of Smith and Ricardo.

As Galbraith notes, such views made List an early advocate of the **infant-industry** argument for protection. This supposes that protection is legitimate in cases where industrial development in an economy might be denied because of the presence of superior foreign competition. In these circumstances, protection offers a respite to infant domestic industries until they achieve a degree of maturity and self-sufficiency that allows them to survive and grow independently. Box 13.1 contains an example of

Concept

The infant-industry argument

The infant-industry argument suggests that nascent domestic industries may need to be protected from mature foreign competitors until such time as they have acquired the necessary scale or expertise to compete openly with them.

Quotas: Quantitative limits on goods. They may be applied on a volume basis (i.e. number of goods) or according to value. Quotas are usually placed on imported goods. However, in the case reported in Box 13.1, they apply to production by foreign firms in the Chinese economy.

trade policy in China that is based on the infant-industry argument. China is one of the world's fastest-growing economies and, as the box points out, an important market for American and European mobile phone manufacturers. However, the Chinese government has ambitions to develop its own domestic mobile phone industry, and to this end it intends to impose **quotas** on mobile phones production in China by foreign firms. The slack will be taken up by Chinese firms. Although it is not currently acknowledged by the Chinese government, the presumption may be that, once Chinese manufacturers have established themselves in the marketplace, the quotas will be lifted.

Though the infant-industry argument gained wide currency in the nineteenth century when many economies were industrializing in the wake of the British lead, it is by no means absent from contemporary economic debate. Indeed, it is a curious irony that it is now interest groups in the *advanced nations* that have adopted the idea that temporary protection for acutely threatened domestic industries is a sensible form of trade policy. The notion of shifting comparative advantage is again relevant here.

Earlier we noted that the basis of the economic success of the newly industrializing countries (NICs) has been the development of new manufacturing industries that are able to compete in world markets against the formerly dominant industries

---

Box 13.1

Cell phone groups face big cut in China sales: quota plan designed to give local manufacturers 50 per cent of the market

Foreign companies selling mobile phones in China are set to lose significant market share to nine local companies under government plans to promote the country's fledgling producers.

Zhou Deqiang, a vice-minister of information industry, yesterday said Beijing would 'strive' to ensure that domestic companies had about a 50 per cent share of the local handset market in three years, up from less than 5 per cent at the moment.

China is the world's fastest growing market for mobile phones. Mr Zhou's comment tallies with an estimate in the official Beijing Daily newspaper, which said that China's government had allocated 1.4bn renminbi ($167m) in state funds for the development of mobile phone handsets this year. More would be available from now on, it added.

Mr Zhou's remark follows a government announcement that China planned to impose production quotas on foreign mobile phone manufacturers, including Motorola of the US, Ericsson of Sweden and Nokia of Finland, which control around 85 per cent of China's market.

The quotas will be allocated to foreign and local manufacturers after negotiation. Each company will then be entitled to as many government-issued seals of approval as their quota allows,

and each mobile phone sold will have to bear an official seal, an MII official said.

The approval last month of nine local companies to sell mobile phones in the domestic market has raised concerns that Beijing may try to create space for them by imposing quotas that cramp the expansion of foreign companies.

The number of mobile phone subscribers in China climbed by 12.3m to 37.6m in the first nine months of this year, Mr Zhou said. China is the second most important telecoms equipment market after the US for Nokia and Ericsson. Nokia's sales in China last year were $1.9bn, or 32 per cent of total sales, up 66 per cent from 1997.

There has been no indication of the size of the quotas to be imposed on foreign multinationals next year, but there is no doubt about the ambitions of their fledgling rivals – all of which are highly regarded Chinese corporations with strong state or quasi-state backing.

Zhang Ruimin, president of the Haier Group, one of China's most respected companies, said it aimed to control 20 per cent of the mobile handset market in five years . . .

Source: Financial Times 10 November 1999

of the advanced nations. The concern in the advanced countries is the loss of jobs, incomes and profits that this more intense competitive environment brings. As an illustration, consider the contents of the *Guardian* newspaper report reproduced in Box 13.2. This example reveals the particular source of shifting comparative advantage as it affects the British textile, clothing and footwear industries: differences in wage rates between the UK and other locations, such as Morocco, where production is now undertaken. Because the textile, clothing and footwear industries are based on relatively low-skill and labour-intensive production techniques, production becomes more efficient if it migrates to lower-wage locations. Though the *Guardian* report concentrates on the worries of the unions about job losses, British firms too may be concerned if output from less developing countries threatens their markets at home or abroad. While some firms may relocate some production overseas as a means of increasing competitiveness, this may not be possible for all firms or for all production. This means that shifting comparative advantage is a problem for both British workers *and* British firms.

The final paragraph of the report indicates the kind of solution that the unions see as a way forward. On the one hand, there is the possibility of using investment in new technology and training to re-establish domestic competitiveness. High-technology production, which demands the utilization of more skilled labour, might be a means of carving out markets for 'quality' output that low-cost production could not

---

Box 13.2

50 000 jobs in textiles could go overseas

Fifty-thousand jobs could be lost in the textile and footwear industry by the end of the decade as manufacturers accelerate the transfer of production to the developing world, union leaders warned yesterday.

New job cuts by leading companies have particularly affected the North-West, the Midlands and Scotland. Unions defending 400 000 jobs in Britain's fifth largest manufacturing industry are calling for a long-term commercial strategy.

. . . The unions said recent announcements by industry leaders like Coats Viyella, Claremont, Dewhirsts, Baird and Peter Black's footwear linked job losses with plans to transfer production to areas like North Africa.

In a joint statement, three unions with a combined membership of 150 000 in textiles and footwear said: 'The current stream of announcements is threatening the existence of a major strategic industry.

'We lost hundreds of thousands of jobs in the clothing industry in the 1980s, and

the UK economy cannot afford to lose a further tranche in the 1990s.'

The unions – the general workers' union GMB, the transport union TGWU and footwear employees' union NUKFAT – called on government and the employers 'to stop this flow of job losses becoming a flood.'

They said: 'For our part we are desperate to cooperate in such a plan. Our industry will disappear if action is not taken.' The unions said that British companies could not compete 'with the appallingly low wages, low skill markets of developing countries without some backing from government.'

British industry pay rates were based on a guaranteed minimum of around £3 an hour. Gross pay of around £4 an hour was achieved with productivity pay. Pay for clothing workers in Morocco – now one of the chief recipients of British orders – was 62p an hour.

The unions named companies planning to move 'significant proportions' of production overseas in the next few years as including Coats Viyella, which is

planning to close 12 UK factories, with the loss of 7750 jobs by the year 2000, as its non-UK production doubles to 40 per cent.

Courtaulds was planning to increase overseas production from 20 to 30 per cent, and Claremonts, which is making 700 Glasgow workers redundant, is increasing production abroad from 15 to 20 per cent. Dewhirsts is also doubling its overseas output from 25 to 50 per cent, said the unions.

'We are talking about exporting even more jobs to countries such as Morocco, Mauritius and the Philippines,' said Des Farrell, national secretary of the GMB. 'This is a very worrying trend.'

. . . The unions are seeking government support both to protect British jobs in international trade negotiations and to increase investment in new technology and training to keep British fashion at the forefront of international quality markets. All sections of the industry should be involved in survival strategy talks.

Source: *Guardian* 13 September 1996

threaten. On the other hand, there is the possibility of relying on 'international trade negotiations': in other words, protectionism. Textile trade is, in fact, an already heavily protected process. Since 1961, textile exports from developing countries to many of the advanced nations, including the whole of the European Union, have been restricted by the operation of a protocol known as the *Multi-Fibre Arrangement* (MFA). The main objective of the MFA has been to prevent the sudden disruption of the established patterns of trade in textiles so that the textile industry in places like Britain could adjust more slowly to the presence of new and vibrant sources of competition: effectively, the infant-industry argument in reverse. The MFA has always been viewed as a *temporary* form of trade policy, and it is currently due to expire in 2004.

We appear now to have a fairly robust rationale for protection. It appears defensible in cases where new infant industries require less than full exposure to open competition for a period in order that they might mature; and it is also demanded by already mature industries, again temporarily, so that they can become acclimatized to more intense competitive pressures. But where does this leave the 'cast iron' case for free trade? The crucial issue here appears to be the *stability* of comparative advantage. When patterns of international specialization are firmly established and settled, factors of production are reasonably secure: labour, capital, land and enterprise are each valued in their current uses and are rewarded accordingly. There is then no pressure from factors of production for protection. However, when there is the possibility of a significant shift in comparative advantage in a particular industry, such security evaporates. In the case of the infant industry, those with resources committed to a new venture will wish to see their investment safeguarded from aggressive foreign competition; governments too may have an interest in nurturing what may be a strategically important form of production. In older established industries, threatened by new and dynamic forms of foreign competition, the emerging insecurity may be even more fevered. The example of the British textile unions quoted above is a case in point. What emerges from this discussion is an appreciation that openness in international trade will be championed by those who are in *unchallenged* forms of production and, therefore, in a position to gain from trade. For others, coping with shifts in comparative advantage, some resort to protection may be preferred. We can explore this view further by reflecting upon the history of the main vehicle for the development of world trade policy over the postwar period: the *General Agreement on Tariffs and Trade* (GATT) (1947–94), and its successor body, the *World Trade Organization* (WTO) (1995–).

The institutions of international trade policy: from GATT to the WTO

The GATT originated in the early years after the Second World War as a means of securing tariff reductions and preventing new tariffs emerging amongst its then 23 signatory countries. The period between the two world wars had witnessed a huge escalation in retaliatory tariff protection involving many nations, causing a *two-thirds* fall in the value of world trade in the early 1930s. As international markets were closed off and world demand fell, producers cut back on the output of goods they could no longer sell, and unemployment rose everywhere: the world economy entered its deepest ever *slump*. It was the connection between the slump and high tariffs that motivated the advent of the GATT so soon after the end of the Second

World War: nations were determined that they would not repeat the protectionist mistakes of the 1930s.[1] Initially, the GATT was intended solely as an interim measure that would begin the process of cutting the vast array of tariffs accumulated in the 1930s; it was soon to have been superseded by the creation of a new international trade body. In the event, plans for this organization collapsed, and instead the GATT matured from a mere treaty into an organization in its own right. In 1995, the GATT's permanent secretariat in Geneva and its membership in excess of 125 countries or so-called 'contracting parties' were inherited by the WTO.

The GATT can be seen to have had three main objectives. These were:

- to prevent an immediate postwar resumption of the kind of protectionism that had done so much damage in the 1930s
- to dismantle the tariff structures built up during this period
- to provide a protocol that would ensure that international trade relations were conducted on an *open* and *multilateral* basis.

In the 1930s too many nations had begun to act unilaterally and bilaterally: segmenting and preserving 'their' markets for themselves and their preferred partners. It was thought that the promotion of a multilateral environment was the natural way to prevent the same thing from happening again. The work of the GATT over the postwar period as a whole has largely been conducted in a series of negotiating 'rounds', each of which has attempted to address an agenda of tariff reduction. The rounds have also provided a forum for the refinement of rules and codes that the GATT nations agree will govern trading relations between them. We do not need here to go into the detail of each of the *eight* rounds that took place during the life of the GATT, but it is useful to give a brief overview of the general course of their development.

The first half of the life of the GATT coincided with the postwar boom. As noted, during this period growth rates for the advanced nations were at an historic high, and full employment targets were consistently met. These conditions provided a fertile background for the GATT Rounds – six in all – that took place before 1970. Countries are more likely to lower trade barriers and expose domestic industries to international competition if the level of economic activity is generally high. In such circumstances, factors of production released from declining industries will be more quickly absorbed by new and expanding ones.

The longest and most notable of the pre-1970 rounds was the 1964–67 *Kennedy Round*. Although earlier meetings had succeeded in implementing significant tariff reductions, the Kennedy Round is credited with finally dismantling the tariff structures erected during the 1930s. This was clearly an important milestone in the development of the GATT, as it meant that two out of three of its objectives had been achieved: there had been no resumption of the kind of protectionism that typified trade policy in the 1930s, and the barriers to multilateral trade that had emerged during that decade had now gone. Unfortunately, the Kennedy Round also marked the high point of GATT's achievements. Since 1970, new problems of protectionism have emerged onto the world stage, and it is as yet unclear whether these are resolvable. We emphasize the word 'new' here to distinguish post-1970 protectionism from the '*old*' tariff structures of the 1930s. But where has the **new protectionism** come from? Part of the answer lies in the ending of the postwar boom. The benign

[1]Although a detailed analysis of the 1930s slump is beyond the scope of this book, some suggestions for further reading are given at the end of the chapter.

Concept

New protectionism

The new protectionism refers to the non-tariff-based protectionism that has emerged in the world economy over the postwar period. It is usually contrasted with the 'old' tariff-based protectionism of the interwar period.

economic climate associated with strong growth and full employment was replaced after 1970 by a much more sombre one conditioned, in the advanced nations in particular, by much slower growth rates and rising unemployment. Now, whereas the boom period made tariff concessions easier to justify, the new recession-seeded era made nations much more reluctant to expose their economies to more intense international competition when lower levels of economic activity meant that alternative sources of employment would be harder to find for factors released from uncompetitive industries.

The end of the boom was not the only issue affecting trade policy from the early 1970s: important shifts in comparative advantage were also evident at this time. In particular, the noted tendency of *industrialization* amongst formerly 'less developed' nations was decisively under way. We described earlier how the NICs were able to begin to compete with the advanced nations in certain labour-intensive branches of manufacturing – textiles, clothing, footwear and sports goods are amongst the most typical examples – by using the relatively low-paid labour available to them. This process posed clear difficulties for the equivalent industries in the advanced nations, and at a time when the advanced economies as a whole were experiencing an economic slowdown. How then did threatened interests in the advanced nations react? The simple answer is that they lobbied governments for protection from the NICs, but because of the presence and authority of GATT this had to be implemented in a *non-tariff form*. Recall again the difference between the old and the new protectionism. The old protectionism of the 1930s was tariff based; the new protectionism post-1970 is not. In fact the new protectionism assumes a variety of guises. Its object, at root, is to enhance the competitive position of domestic industry *vis-à-vis* its rivals. This means that protection can include measures such as: state subsidy (which reduces the costs of production to industry and allows it to lower prices); preferential state procurement (where governments make *their* purchases from domestic industry alone); discriminatory administrative action (where imports are discouraged by the imposition of arduous bureaucratic procedures); quota restrictions on imports (such as the Multi-Fibre Arrangement discussed earlier); and, finally, 'persuading' exporters to voluntarily limit their exports.

The latter form of new protection – the so-called '*voluntary export restraint*' (VER) – is particularly insidious. The GATT/WTO trade rules explicitly commit member nations to a multilateral philosophy. This makes it very difficult for individual nations to be selected as the targets of protection. For example, the EU (which acts collectively in trade policy matters) cannot legally place restrictions on footwear imports from Indonesia; if it wants to protect its domestic market from Indonesian competition, it must discourage footwear imports as a whole. This, of course, might cause a number of countries to invoke retaliatory measures against the EU. However, if the EU can persuade Indonesia to *voluntarily* limit its exports then this potential problem is solved. A bilateral agreement on the *export* side allows the EU to discriminate against Indonesian imports alone without formally breaking GATT/WTO principles. Indonesia might be amenable to this course of action because it presents it with a securely open export market (albeit a smaller one) and for fear of more draconian EU protection should this option fail. The discriminatory potential of the VER has made it an increasingly popular measure with the advanced nations in the context of shifting comparative advantage. Because they are selectively threatened by particular NICs in particular industries, they require the kind of finely tuned protection the VER offers. Conversely, the more widespread its use, the greater the threat the VER poses to the multilateral trade framework bequeathed by GATT. Moreover, the VER has increasingly become a tool for the management of trade *between* the advanced nations. For example, Japanese car exports to both the EU and the United States have been periodically limited by VER agreements since the 1980s.

That many countries have resorted to the use of VERs does not mean that discriminatory action in trade policy is forbidden under the GATT/WTO institutional framework. It is possible for contracting parties to protect their markets in the face of illegal or destabilizing competition from particular sources. This means that *in certain circumstances*, if (say) Canada thinks that electrical goods from Poland are endangering its own electrical goods firms in the Canadian market, it can take action against the offending Polish exporters. The main justification for such discriminatory retaliation is the issue of **dumping**. Here, dumping refers to the sale of goods in foreign markets at or below their costs of production in the country of origin. The reasons for dumping might include market predation, where the intention is to drive rival producers out; or a simple need to sell accumulated stocks of goods. Anti-dumping petitions are raised by WTO members and investigated by the WTO itself. Where dumping is identified, the offended country may impose anti-dumping duties on the goods in question in order to raise their prices in the domestic market and thus 'level the playing field'. Box 13.3 provides a recent example of anti-dumping action by the USA in the market for steel. Interestingly, although the USA imposed anti-dumping duties on steel imports from Brazil, the concluding paragraph in the box reveals that Brazil hopes to negotiate a VER in steel with the USA in order to give it (Brazil) 'a guaranteed market share'. This means that the USA and Brazil may be

> **Dumping**: The export of goods to foreign markets with prices set at or below the costs of production.

Box 13.3

US imposes steep duties to curb imports of cheap steel

The [US] commerce department yesterday imposed steep anti-dumping duties on steel imports from Japan and Brazil, as the US industry prepared to file a second round of complaints next week.

In response to an initial round of complaints, the department found that hot-rolled steel, the industry's basic commodity, was being sold by Japanese companies as much as 68 per cent below market prices. Brazilian companies sold the same product for as much as 71 per cent below market levels.

Duties will correspond to the amount each company undercuts the market.

Anti-dumping measures are also being considered against Russian hot-rolled steel imports. The US and Russian governments are in talks aimed at establishing quotas for all Russian steel imports.

The second round of complaints will focus on surging imports of cut-to-length steel plate, used in shipbuilding and construction. Possible targets are companies in Japan, South Korea, India, Indonesia, France, Italy, the Czech Republic and Macedonia.

The complaints are part of a campaign against imports by the US steel industry and the steelworkers' union. In addition to the anti-dumping duties, they are seeking the imposition by congress of quotas on steel imports from the main producing countries. This follows the failure to persuade the White House to impose quotas.

Without congressional action, the industry is forced to counter imports through existing US anti-dumping laws, product by product and country by country.

William Daley, commerce secretary, said the administration had been trying to warn Japan for two years that it could not export its way out of its economic difficulties.

Brazil, which was also found to have subsidized its steel production, is hoping to enter talks with the US on a voluntary restraint agreement that would give it a guaranteed market share.

Source: Financial Times 13 February 1999

prepared to move from a trading arrangement covered by international agreement to one that currently lies outside the international trade policy framework. Economic expediency has a major bearing on issues of international trade.

The Uruguay Round

There is a further twist here. Recognizing the threat to openness in international markets posed by VERs, the most recently completed *Uruguay GATT Round* (1986–94) agreed that they should be phased out over a 10-year period: like the MFA, VERs will be officially illegal after 2004. However, similar intentions have been declared in the past. The MFA itself, for example, is actually the result of a series of temporary deals, but as each expiry date has approached a new 'temporary' accommodation has been reached: the end result is effectively a *permanent* policy. If protectionist lobbying pressures are intense enough, perhaps similar 'temporary' extensions will be made to the VER framework. Certainly, current developments in the international steel market would suggest that VERs are not yet merely a matter of historical curiosity.

The Uruguay Round was also notable for two other features. First, it provided for the replacement of the GATT as an organization by the World Trade Organization (WTO), the new body that will oversee the implementation of the agreements of the round and the establishment of a new system for the settlement of trade disputes. Essentially, the WTO now presides over a *framework of agreements* for the continuing liberalization of the international trading environment. Fig. 13.2 sketches out this framework. Note that the GATT itself continues as an *agreement* alongside the newer parts of the liberalization agenda such as the *General Agreement on Trade in Services* (GATS). The emergence of GATS reflects the increasing importance of service trade in the world economy. This now accounts for about one fifth of total trade. The IMF estimates that, during the 1990s, service trade grew at an average rate of about 7 per cent per year, slightly faster than merchandise trade (trade in goods). The agreement on *Trade Related Aspects of Intellectual Property Rights* (TRIPS) is intended to provide international safeguards for copyrights, patents and trademarks.

Second, the Uruguay Round, for all the popular adulation given to its successful completion, very nearly ended in crisis and collapse. The uncertainty was the result of a long-running dispute between, on the one hand, the European Union and, on the other, the United States and a disparate group of food-producing countries known as the Cairns Group.[2] The European Union, which heavily subsidizes agricultural production, was reluctant to concede the principle of completely free trade in agri-

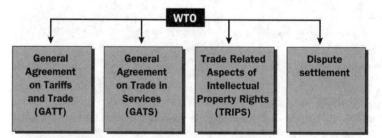

Fig. 13.2 The World Trade Organization's agreements.

[2] The Cairns Group comprises: Argentina, Australia, Brazil, Canada, Chile, Columbia, Fiji, Hungary, Indonesia, Malaysia, Philippines, New Zealand, Thailand and Uruguay.

culture that the US/Cairns Group preferred. Ultimately, a compromise position acceptable to both sides *did* emerge, but not before the Uruguay Round had been brought to the brink of disaster. The significance of this dispute lies less in its own seismic proportions, though these were considerable, than in its general form. Both the EU and the US/Cairns Group are collective representations of very powerful trading interests, of which there are an increasing number in the international economy. The previously mentioned North American Free Trade Agreement (NAFTA), for example, which came into force in 1994, binds together the markets of the USA, Canada and Mexico; while the Asia-Pacific Economic Co-operation (APEC) forum plans a similar arrangement for an even larger number of countries, including the USA and Japan, by 2010. Now although such groupings are organized on the basis of *internal* free trade, they offer no similar external commitments, and there is a natural concern – reflecting the experiences of the Uruguay Round – that the segmentation of the international economy into *trading blocs* of this type might provide an environment in which large-scale (inter-bloc) protectionism becomes a distinct possibility. The last time the world economy witnessed equivalent segmentation was in the 1930s, when rampant protectionism did severely threaten the integrity of the world economy.

What implications has this discussion for the debate over free trade? At one level we have the arguments of Smith and Ricardo, who were convinced of its universal merits and whose work still forms the kernel of modern trade theory. Yet at a slightly lower and 'messier' level we have the institutionalist views of those like List and Galbraith, who find that the tidy framework of comparative advantage can become blurred when real economies, with shifting hierarchies of competitiveness, are considered. Here, pressures for protection from vulnerable factors of production are to be expected. Indeed, as in the infant-industry case, protection may even be rationalized as a means to stabilize production temporarily until its competitive promise is realized. Similarly, in the case of established but weakening industries, such as British textiles (see Box 13.2), temporary protection may allow new sources of competitiveness to be developed or alternative sources of factor employment to emerge. One way to reconcile the differences between the two approaches might be to suggest that, while open international markets do not imperil the security of factors of production in their strategically established uses, free trade is indeed a preferable arrangement. However, when shifting comparative advantage demands large-scale changes in global patterns of production, then the management of this process, through active trade policy, is required. This seems, broadly, to be a philosophy embodied in the new World Trade Organization. Although its most basic presumption favours openness in trading relations, the WTO explicitly recognizes the principle of *fair competition*. This acknowledges that when the effects of shifting comparative advantage are unexpected, or too abruptly or too intensely felt, countries may legitimately take measures to soften such effects. At the same time, the WTO retains significant powers to mediate – read compromise – in trade disputes. As such it appears at this early stage in its life to be well positioned to oversee the legitimate and temporary use of protection on its own terms.

Issues in WTO's Millennium Round

However, whether or not the WTO will live up to the expectations of its architects is for the moment an open question. A new *Millennium Round* was to have been launched in Seattle in December 1999. However, the WTO's Seattle conference was the focus of vociferous and disruptive lobbying by direct action groups. Even more significantly, stark differences between the developed and less developed countries over the nature and purpose of the Millennium Round meant that little progress was made.

Essentially, the developing countries harbour understandable resentments that the Uruguay Round mostly addressed – at developing country expense – the concerns of the rich nations. For example, the GATS and TRIPS agreements might be said to mostly benefit the developed countries. It is they who have the sophisticated economic infrastructures capable of producing service exports, and they who might require their intellectual property to be defended. Countries in the poorest parts of the world have other more modest trade aspirations. The developing countries would have been more impressed by Uruguay had it, for example, promoted greater liberalization of *agricultural trade*. It is through agricultural exports that many poor countries pay their way in the international economy: such exports are, for many, the only source of the foreign currencies necessary to buy vital foreign goods. Unfortunately, as noted, agricultural issues appeared to be resolved in the Uruguay Round by an agreement primarily between the EU and the United States; the less developed country agenda was sidelined. That the developed countries failed to realize a much more liberal trading environment in agriculture is hardly surprising. The rich OECD countries currently spend an average of 1.5 per cent of GDP on subsidies to their farmers; such subsidies help to keep the produce of farmers from the developing countries out of the developed world's markets (see Chapter 2, section 2.5, for details of the EU's Common Agricultural Policy).

However, agriculture *is* to be included in the Millennium negotiations, whatever their eventual form. The WTO has a 'built-in agenda' for the round, agreed at the close of the Uruguay meetings, of which agriculture is a part. Other matters that will be reviewed under this heading include the GATS. Although the liberalization of trade in services was hailed as an important achievement of Uruguay, it is also acknowledged that there is room for further progress here. In particular, the Millennium negotiations will try to extend the range of services that the GATS embraces. For example, air transport is for the most part currently beyond the scope of the GATS.

Outside the 'built-in agenda', the Millennium negotiations are expected to address a range of other issues. One of the most contentious is likely to be trade aspects of foreign direct investment. This is in fact yet another hangover from Uruguay (where it was known by the acronym TRIMS – trade-related investment measures; agreed during the round but not implemented). The origins of this issue can be traced to the concerns of some of the world's major firms that they were paying too high a price for the privilege of access to certain of the world's largest developing country markets. Host developing countries have, for example, sometimes demanded that foreign multinationals fulfil certain export and 'local content' requirements before they are given leave to invest. Demands such as these are intended to promote export-led growth in the developing country and to ensure that its domestic firms gain from the presence of their new foreign neighbour – 'local content' translates as a guarantee to use local suppliers in the production process. The TRIMS were intended as a charter for foreign investment that would have ensured a 'level playing field' in such matters. In other words, all foreign investors would have to be treated equally by all host countries. This would have had the effect of lowering export and local content requirements, and it would have opened up markets where 'Western' firms had traditionally found access difficult – Japan and South East Asia, for example.

Though it is widely recognized that the developing countries are set against revisiting TRIMS or variations on this theme, it too is likely to find its way onto the Millennium agenda. Given that GATT/WTO rounds are structured *negotiations* and foreign direct investment rules are attractive to some parties, it may be that their admittance will advance progress in other areas of interest to other parties. Thus progress in TRIMS, which some richer nations want, might prove to be a means of advancing the further liberalization of agricultural trade. Outcomes are difficult to forecast, especially when particular groups of countries bring yet still more 'ballast' to the negotiating table. For example, in the month before the commencement of the initial Millennium meetings, the United States proposed that consideration of *labour rights* should be included on the agenda. The charge the USA is implicitly making here is that competition from developing countries in certain industrial sectors may be unfair because it is underpinned by exploitative employment practices, such as the use of child labour. While few would try to defend the employment of children, there are concerns here that the labour rights issue may be used by the USA and other rich countries as a negotiating ploy or even a pretext for protectionism. This is indicative of the horse-trading that the liberalization process can sometimes involve. However, negotiation – however strained and difficult it may become – is always preferable to the most likely alternative: a renewed lapse into generalized unilateral protection.

◼ Summary

◆ International trade permits economies to push the boundaries of specialization and exchange beyond the confines of their own borders. The Ricardian theory of comparative advantage suggests that all participant economies can gain from trade. This conventional wisdom contrasts strongly with older mercantilist notions that trade is a zero sum game.

◆ The policy implication of comparative advantage is that free trade offers benefits to all trading economies. However, where comparative advantage is shifting, there may be claims for protection arising from threatened interests in particular countries or regions.

◆ Since 1945 international trade policy has been possessed of a broad liberalizing ethos under the auspices of the GATT and latterly the WTO. However, coincidence of the ending of the postwar boom and shifting comparative advantage between the developed and less developed countries have led to the re-emergence of protectionism under a new, non-tariff, guise.

◼ Key terms

◆ International trade
◆ Specialization and exchange
◆ Protection

◆ Mercantilism

◆ Comparative advantage

◆ Shifting comparative advantage

◆ Trade policy

◆ The General Agreement on Tariffs and Trade

◆ Uruguay Round

◆ The World Trade Organization

◆ Millennium Round

■ Self-test questions

True (t) or false (f)

1. The notion of comparative advantage suggests that all countries can gain from international trade.

2. Mercantilism has protectionist policy implications.

3. Ricardo highlighted factor endowments as the basis for a country's specialization decision.

4. Economists generally suppose that there is a causal link between growth in trade and economic growth.

5. The Kennedy GATT Round is generally credited with dismantling the last elements of inter-war tariff protection.

6. The majority of the world's international trade continues to take place between its richest nations.

7. Africa's share of international trade has grown steadily since 1970.

8. The growth of the Asian NICs can be explained by their success in international markets for primary commodities.

9. Despite the arguments for free trade, most countries engage in some form of protectionism.

10. The World Trade Organization was created by the Tokyo GATT Round.

Complete the following sentences by inserting the missing word(s)

1. The prevailing philosophy of international trade, which Smith and Ricardo sought to undermine, was called ____.

2. The fundamental policy implication of comparative advantage is that trade should be ____.

3. Ricardo emphasized ____ as the basis of a country's comparative advantage.

4. The Heckscher–Ohlin approach explains the basis of international trade in terms of countries' ____.

5. The Heckscher–Ohlin approach was challenged by the ____.

6. If foreign competition threatens the development of domestic industry, protection is sometimes justified using the ____ argument.

7. ____ arises where countries trade the same or similar goods and services with one another.

8. World trade in textiles is regulated by the ____.

Questions for discussion

◆ What are the advantages of trade?

◆ Explain the arguments underlying the theory of comparative advantage.

◆ What were the later developments in trade theory that built upon Ricardian notions of comparative advantage?

◆ Describe the major patterns of world trade that have evolved since 1945, and explain the notion of shifting comparative advantage.

◆ Why does protectionism arise and what are its main forms?

◆ What are the main issues in the WTO's Millennium Round?

Further reading

Jepma, C.J. and H. Rohen (eds) *International Trade: A Business Perspective* (Harlow: Longman, 1996). A good international trade text written specifically for a business audience.

Kindleberger, C. *The World in Depression* (Berkley: University of California Press, 1975). This is the standard text on the Great Depression.

Kitson, M. and J. Michie, 'Trade and growth: a historical perspective', in J. Michie and J. Grieve Smith (eds) *Managing the Global Economy* (Oxford: Oxford University Press, 1995). Provides a short and very readable historical overview of the links between international trade and national economic performance.

Gerber, J. *International Economics* (Reading, Massachusetts: Addison-Wesley, 1999). A very accessible textbook, aimed at a diverse audience.

Hoekman, B. and M. Kostecki, *The Political Economy of the World Trading System* (Oxford: Oxford University Press, 1995). Discusses the political economy of the world trading system in the context of the World Trade Organization.

Heidensohn, K., *Europe and World Trade* (London: Pinter, 1995). Provides an accessible survey of Europe's trading relations in an integrating world trading system.

Moon, B.E., *Dilemmas of International Trade* (Boulder, Colorado: Westview Press, 1996). Discusses the theory and practice of protectionism, and makes refreshingly open references to modern-day mercantilism.

Stubbs, R. and G.R.D. Underhill (eds), *Political Economy and the Changing Global Order* (2nd ed.) (Oxford: Oxford University Press, 2000). A collection of 33 short essays that discuss a range of different aspects of the international economy. If you want to know about a particular issue, the chances are there will be an up-to-date overview here.

Internet links

The *World Trade Organization* offers up-to-date information on general trade issues as well as its own activities. The WTO can be found at: **http://www.wto.org/**
The *OECD's Trade Directorate* is another good source of information on trade patterns and trade policy. The site is at: **htttp://www.oecd.org/ech/index.htm**

The *World Bank* maintains an international trade site offering data and papers on trade issues. The website is at: **http://www.worldbank.org/research/trade/index. htm**

Asia-Pacific Economic Cooperation, the organization that promotes open trade and economic cooperation between a number of countries in the Asia-Pacific region, maintains a website at: **http://www.apecsec.org.sg/**

The Balance of Payments and Exchange Rates

CHAPTER 14

14.1 Introduction

Having discussed a number of general issues of international trade, we now turn in this chapter to consider trading relationships of the individual economy. The balance of payments provides both a way of thinking about how a country connects to the wider global environment and a means of measuring that connection. In what follows, we first discuss the nature of the balance of payments accounts and notions of balance of payments equilibria and disequilibria, together with a brief examination of the recent balance of payments performances of some selected economies. Because international markets, like all others, are coordinated by price signals, it is necessary to develop an understanding of the role played in the international economy by the different currencies in which prices are quoted. Accordingly, this chapter also offers some discussion of exchange rates and different exchange rate systems.

Both the balance of payments and exchange rates are important for business. The condition of an economy's balance of payments may give rise to different forms of government policy that have significant implications for domestic firms inside the economy and for foreign ones outside it. Exchange rates have a strong bearing on firms' abilities to sell goods and services in both domestic and foreign markets.

Balance of payments: A record of the transactions that take place between the residents of one country and the rest of the world over a given time period (usually one year).

14.2 The balance of payments accounts

The **balance of payments** accounts record the transactions that take place between the residents of one country and the rest of the world over a given period, usually one year. Such transactions take the form of trade in *goods* and *services*, *capital movements* or *financial flows*. These three forms of transaction give rise to a compartmentalization of the balance of payments accounts.[1] Trade in goods and services is recorded in the *current account*, capital movements are recorded in the *capital account*, and financial flows are recorded in the *financial account*. Table 14.1 summarizes the main components of the UK balance of payments accounts.

Current account

As is evident from the table, the current account has two main components: visible trade in goods and invisible trade in services. Because they are associated with *monetary inflows*, exports of goods produced in the UK are recorded as *positive* visible trade

Table 14.1 Structure of the UK balance of payments

Current account

Visible trade

- Exports of goods (monetary inflow)
- Imports of goods (monetary outflow)

Invisible trade

- Services (financial; transport and travel; military services overseas) (inflow and outflow)
- Investment income (interest, profits and dividends) (inflow and outflow)
- Transfers (non-pecuniary and EC contributions) (inflow and outflow)

Capital account

Transfers (migrants' transfers, EU regional fund etc.)

Financial account

Investment

- Foreign direct investment (FDI) in UK (monetary inflow)
- FDI by UK firms abroad (monetary outflow)
- Portfolio investment by overseas residents in UK (monetary inflow)
- Portfolio investment by UK residents abroad (monetary outflow)

Usually considered as long-term flows

Other investment (borrowing and lending)

- By foreign banks to UK (monetary inflow)
- By UK banks abroad (monetary outflow)
- By foreign non-banking sector to UK (monetary inflow)
- By UK non-banking private sector abroad (monetary outflow)

Use of reserves of foreign currency (inflow and outflow)

Net errors and omissions

---

[1] Periodically the authorities revise the presentation of the balance of payments accounts. However, the main task is to understand the principles underlying the accounts. These do not change.

entries. Imports of goods on the other hand, because they give rise to *monetary out-flows*, are recorded as *negative* entries. Thus, if visible trade is in overall *surplus* (value of exports > value of imports) its value will be *positive* in nature, reflecting a net monetary inflow from trade in goods, and vice versa. Invisible trade includes trade in services, income arising from investments and transfers. Similar positive and negative entry conventions apply here. The cost of a holiday taken in the UK by a resident from another country is the equivalent of a service export and, because it is associated with a *monetary inflow*, is recorded as a *positive* invisible trade entry; while the transport cost of shipping using a foreign carrier is a service import (*monetary out-flow*) and is recorded as a *negative* service trade entry. Again, if the value of service exports exceeds the value of service imports, then the resultant invisibles *surplus* has a *positive* sign, reflecting a net monetary inflow. If the situation is reversed then the resultant *deficit* (net monetary outflow) on invisibles will have a *negative* sign.

Capital account

The capital account formerly recorded several kinds of transaction. Now it contains fewer and less significant capital flows associated, for example, with EU regional fund transfers and transfers by migrants abroad back to the UK, or transfers by foreign migrants in the UK to their home economies.

Financial account

The financial account was previously subsumed into the capital account. The financial account contains two kinds of investment transaction: foreign direct and portfolio investment, and 'other' investment, mostly borrowing and lending.

Consider first *foreign direct investment* (FDI) – the buying or selling of British and foreign firms – and *portfolio investment* – the buying or selling of British and foreign share capital. An increase in the UK's FDI and portfolio asset base is indicated by a negative sign (because it denotes a monetary outflow); while a decrease is indicated by a positive sign (because it denotes a monetary inflow).

The 'other investment' category covers mainly *borrowing* and *lending* by the banking and non-banking private sector. Because it is associated with a monetary inflow, borrowing is usually recorded as a positive item, while lending outflows are usually recorded as negative items. However, very occasionally, the repayment of liabilities can result in these signs being reversed.

The third form of transaction recorded in the financial account concerns changes in the **foreign exchange reserves** of the Bank of England. For reasons that we shall explain shortly, an increase in reserves is recorded as a negative item and a decrease in reserves as a positive one.

How the balance of payments works

There is another way to interpret the structure of the financial account. This entails the identification of two broad elements, which we can distinguish by reference to their long-term or short-term nature. Notice from Table 14.1 that FDI and portfolio investment are usually considered to be *long-term financial flows*; in other words, they are not subject to the same degree of variation as the other recorded financial flows. There is an important reason for this, which is central to a clear understanding of how the balance of payments is made to balance. FDI and portfolio investments are in fact **autonomous transactions** on the balance of payments. 'Autonomous'

Foreign exchange reserves: Stocks of foreign currencies held by central banks.

Autonomous transaction: One undertaken for its own sake.

Accommodating transaction:
One undertaken for balance of
payments purposes.

here refers to transactions undertaken spontaneously *for their own sake*. Both FDI and portfolio investment obviously originate in the profit-related ambitions of those who make them. All transactions on the current account are also autonomous in nature: a UK resident, for example, buys an import because he or she finds some personal benefit in doing so. Similarly, capital account transactions such as migrants' transfers can be considered to be autonomous. Now, the remaining items in the financial account – 'other investment' – are all *short-term* in nature. These are collectively known as **accommodating transactions**, and they are undertaken solely in order to *make international trade possible and to make the balance of payments balance*. Table 14.2 shows how they work.

In Table 14.2 we show a hypothetical deficit of −£1 billion for each of the current account and the long-term (LT) investment element of the financial account. For ease of analysis we assume the capital account to be in balance (that is, it sums to zero). Overall, then, autonomous transactions are in deficit to the tune of −£2 billion. This means that economic agents in the UK have sold goods, services, firms, shares and so on abroad worth £2 *billion less* than foreign agents have managed to sell in the UK over the period in question. The −£2 billion is in effect a collective debt owed by the UK to the rest of the world: a *net monetary claim*, here *on* UK residents. How is this debt settled, bearing in mind that foreign residents will want to be paid in their own currencies rather than in British pounds sterling? The answer is that payment is facilitated by (positive) accommodating transactions of £2 billion. The UK must either borrow the £2 billion equivalent of foreign currency that it requires, draw on the reserves of foreign currency that it already holds, or undertake some combination of both. This action leaves the balance of payments accounts as a whole *in balance* (that is, neither in surplus nor in deficit).

What happens if the situation is reversed and the UK runs a surplus on its autonomous transactions? Here, UK residents have a *net monetary claim on the rest of the world*: foreign residents owe a debt that must be settled in sterling. In this case the UK can conduct (negative) accommodating transactions that involve lending the

Table 14.2 How the balance of payments works

Current balance
All are *autonomous* transactions   Net deficit of −£1bn (outflow)

Capital balance
Autonomous transactions   Zero

Financial balance
of which:
Autonomous transactions (FDI and portfolio investment) Net deficit of −£1bn (outflow)
Accommodating transactions[a]   Borrowing of +£2bn (inflow)

Net errors and omissions   Zero

[a] Because autonomous transactions are in a combined deficit of −£2bn, accommodating transactions must be made to cover the deficit. Here the suggestion is that the UK must borrow to cover the amount it owes to foreign residents. However, the deficit could be alternatively accommodated using currency reserves.

necessary sterling abroad. In addition or alternatively, the Bank of England may supply sterling abroad in exchange for foreign currencies, thus increasing its reserves of foreign currency (but note that, as suggested, the increase must by convention be represented by a negative sign). Regardless of the precise course of action taken, it should be clear that, once again, net autonomous transactions are counterbalanced by equivalent net accommodating transactions. In the situation (and its inverse) depicted in Table 14.2 *net errors and omissions* must be zero. Net errors and omissions, formerly referred to as the 'balancing item', indicate any measurement discrepancies between autonomous and accommodating transactions. In our example there are none, but this is seldom the case in reality. Thus the net errors and omissions entry permits the balance of payments to balance in an 'accounting' sense.

Surplus and deficit on the balance of payments

Table 14.3 describes the actual UK balance of payments position for 1998. Note first that autonomous transactions on the current, capital and financial accounts are indeed counterbalanced by appropriate accommodating transactions, although here the presence of a rather large balancing item complicates matters somewhat. To understand the table, note that panel (a) sums all autonomous transactions: that is, current balance + capital balance + net FDI + net portfolio investment. This gives a figure of −£36 902 million, meaning that, in 1998, the UK had a net monetary liability of this amount. To meet this liability the UK undertook accommodating transactions as described in panel (b). Here, the accommodating transactions total is found by summing net other investment + reserve assets, giving a figure of £28 434 million. In the absence of any errors and omissions, the autonomous total (−£36 902) and the accommodating total (£28 434 million) would balance out at zero. Clearly they don't, and the difference between them is accounted for by net errors and omissions of £8468 million, calculated in panel (c).

The table also allows us to comment on an element of apparent ambiguity in the balance of payments. It is true that, in any given period, the balance of payments must balance as overseas debts or receipts are settled, but how does this square with the notions of balance of payments surplus and deficit introduced in Chapter 9, section 9.5? How can the balance of payments balance and simultaneously be in surplus or deficit? A balance of payments (BP) surplus or deficit in fact refers only to autonomous transactions and then, because FDI and portfolio investment flows tend to be influenced by long-term factors, to autonomous transactions on the current account. Capital account transactions are also longer term or relatively small (see Table 14.3). Thus BP surplus or deficit is usually equated with the current account only.

Finally, we should note that the notions of BP surplus and deficit introduced here rest on the assumption of a prevailing **fixed exchange rate system** or an environment in which exchange rates are managed by the authorities rather then left to market forces. In section 14.6 we demonstrate that a market-determined flexible exchange rate system has the effect, in theory, of automatically eliminating BP disequilibria.

Influences upon the current and financial accounts

What are the main determinants of *autonomous* current and financial account transactions as depicted in Table 14.1? What factors influence imports, exports and longer-term investment flows?

Fixed exchange rate: One that is fixed at a predetermined level by intervention by the country's central bank in the foreign exchange market.

Table 14.3 UK balance of payments 1998 (£m)[a]

Current account

Trade in goods

Exports	164 132
Imports	−184 897
Net visible trade	**−20 765**

Trade in services

Service exports	60 070
Service imports	−47 817
Net invisible trade	**12 253**
Net income from investment	**15 174**
Net current transfers	**−6526**
Current balance	**136**

Capital account

Transfers in	1269
Transfers out	−848
Capital balance	**421**

Financial account

Net FDI	−23 285
Net portfolio investment in UK	−14 174
Net other investment	28 269
Reserve assets	165
Financial balance	**−9025**
Net errors and omissions	**8468**

(a) −£36 902 in autonomous transactions (136 + 421 − 23 285 −14 174 = −36 902)

(b) £28 434 in accommodating transactions (28 269 + 165 = 28 434)

(c) n + 28 434 = −36 902 n = 8468 i.e. the value of net errors and omissions

[a] Some minor accounts have been subsumed into major ones for ease of presentation
Source: Central Statistical Office *UK Economic Accounts*, National Statistics, © Crown Copyright 2000.

To take the *current account* first, the *demand for imports and exports* may be analysed in exactly the same way as the demand for any good or service. In Chapter 2, section 2.2, we demonstrated that a picture of demand – quite literally a picture in the shape of a demand curve – is built up using *price* as a starting point. Other factors, such as *income* and *tastes*, are then admitted for consideration. Following the same process, we can say that the *demand for an import* will be determined, in part, by its price relative to the price of home-produced alternatives, which can act as import substitutes. The obvious complication here is that the relative price of imports is influenced by (a) the price-setting decisions of domestic and foreign producers and (b) changes in the *exchange rate*. In the former case, if the price of imports is increasing at a slower rate than that for home-produced alternatives (that is, the rate of inflation in the rest of the world is below that in the home economy) then imports will become more competitive. In considering the influence of the exchange rate on import demand, it will be sufficient to proceed by means of a simple example. Table 14.4 demonstrates

Table 14.4 The effects of a fall in the exchange rate

On imports:

Initial exchange rate: £1 : $4

A pen imported from the USA at $20 will cost £5 (20 / 4 = 5) in the UK

A *fall* in the value of the pound gives a new exchange rate of £1 : $2

This *raises the sterling price of the imported pen* to £10 (20 / 2 = 10)

On exports:

Initial exchange rate is again £1 : $4

A watch exported from the UK at £20 will cost $80 (20 $\times$ 4 = 80) in the USA

A *fall* in the value of the pound gives a new exchange rate of £1 : $2

This *reduces the dollar price of the exported watch* to $40 (20 $\times$ 2 = 40)

the effect of a fall in the sterling exchange rate upon the price, expressed in pounds, of an import from the USA. Because the fall in the pounds value means that *more* pounds are required to obtain a given amount of dollars, the price of an import from the USA must *increase*. A higher import price will in turn mean a contraction in the quantity of imports demanded. Conversely, an increase in the sterling exchange rate will be associated with a lower import price and an extension in the quantity of imports demanded.

As noted, the level of demand for imports is also affected by changes in domestic incomes. Higher domestic incomes facilitate additional expenditure on goods and services generally, some of which will be on imports. As will be recalled from Chapter 10, section 10.3, this involves the concept of the marginal propensity to import, which generally implies that the demand for imports varies positively with domestic incomes. Finally, the tastes and preferences of domestic consumers will clearly influence the demand for imports. We should be aware that some hard material judgements fall under this heading. For example, the prodigious increase in the worldwide sales of Japanese cars over the last three decades is certainly grounded on perceptions of quality and reliability as well as on the aesthetics of design.

Export demand is similarly governed by the price of exports relative to the prices of goods produced by competitors abroad and by income and tastes. To begin with relative prices, we may say that if inflation in the home economy is greater than that prevailing in the rest of the world, then export demand will contract owing to declining international competitiveness. Conversely, lower domestic inflation will be associated with improving international price competitiveness and an extension in export demand. The exchange rate also remains an important influence, but in the case of export demand it works in the opposite direction to that described earlier. From Table 14.4 it can be seen that a fall in the exchange rate, because it reduces the number of dollars that have to be exchanged to obtain a given number of pounds, has the effect of *lowering* the price of UK exports to the USA. Lower export prices will in turn mean an extension in the quantity of exports demanded. Conversely, an increase in the sterling exchange rate will be associated with higher export prices and a contraction in the quantity of exports demanded. Export demand is also a function of foreign incomes and tastes. If incomes overseas are rising, or foreign consumer preferences favour exports, then clearly demand will increase and vice versa.

Turning to the *financial account*, it is possible to identify three main influences upon autonomous investment flows: expectations of exchange rate changes, nominal interest rate differentials between countries, and differences in the perceived profitability of investments overseas.

- First, where exchange rate changes can be anticipated, it is possible for adroit investors to move out of a currency about to fall in value or into one about to increase in value. In both cases it is possible to reap capital gains. For example, holders of sterling at the time of the European exchange rate mechanism crisis in the autumn of 1992 – which forced down the value of the pound (see section 14.7) – had they transferred into deutschmarks in time, would have been able to realize a sterling profit as their deutschmarks quickly became worth more in sterling terms. This means that expectations of a fall in the value of a currency will lead to a capital outflow, while expectations of an increase in the value of a currency will be likely to prompt a capital inflow.

- Second, because *ceteris paribus* higher domestic nominal interest rates improve the returns on financial assets, it follows that they will be associated with capital inflows. Lower nominal interest rates, presaging poorer returns, will occasion capital outflows.

- Finally, a perceived improvement in the profitability of new overseas investments relative to the anticipated returns on new foreign investments in the domestic economy will be associated with a net capital outflow and vice versa.

Disequilibria in the balance of payments

We know that there are two ways in which the balance of payments (BP) can be out of balance: the current account can be either in surplus or in deficit. Neither eventuality is actually a policy problem unless it becomes *persistent*. If a deficit in one year is counterbalanced by a surplus in the next, then, over a run of several such years, the BP will remain broadly in balance and this, as suggested earlier, is the object of policy (see Chapter 9, section 9.5).

What then is the difficulty posed by a persistent deficit? In such a situation we know that the deficit economy – the UK to continue with our present example – will be piling up net monetary liabilities with the rest of the world for each year that the deficit persists. The UK must be consistently importing a greater value of imports of goods (visibles) and services (invisibles) than it is managing to export. In each year, these liabilities are settled (that is, accommodated) by some combination of borrowing from abroad and drawing upon the UK's reserves of foreign currency. *The crucial point is that neither of these avenues of debt settlement can be kept open indefinitely.* A country that tries to run a persistent BP deficit is, in effect, asking the rest of the world to continually lend it more money, or it is hoping that its foreign currency reserves will never reach the point of exhaustion. In the end, of course, lenders will lose patience and reserves must dwindle away (besides borrowing, the only way to replenish reserves, as we will see, is by running a surplus). A persistent BP deficit is, therefore, a policy problem because it cannot be sustained and it may precipitate a crisis of international confidence in the deficit nation.

A persistent surplus appears at first sight to be much less of a problem, and indeed this is usually considered to be the case, not least by some creditor nations themselves as they enjoy the fruits of export-led growth. However, a policy response to persistent surplus may still be required for two reasons. First, BP surplus is associated with the steady accumulation of net monetary claims on the rest of the world. For the surplus country this can involve the acquisition of more and more foreign currency reserves as its credits are settled. Alternatively, it may continually make accommodating loans abroad to indebted nations. The point here is that both forms of BP accommodation mean that opportunities for *current consumption* are being sacrificed. The accumulating reserves and the foreign loans could be converted into spending on imports: consumption would be higher at home, and BP deficits in other countries would be reduced or eliminated entirely. The second reason that BP surplus requires a policy response arises from the fact that, in balance of payments terms, the world economy is a 'zero-sum game': one nation's surplus necessitates concomitant deficits elsewhere. Now, given that the growth of the world economy since 1945 has been predicated on openness in trading relationships and general international economic cooperation (see Chapter 13, sections 13.4 and 13.5), the appearance of significant surpluses and deficits may prompt some countries to seek refuge in highly damaging introspection and even autarky. The rising tide of protectionist sentiment and the re-emergence of isolationist lobbies in the deficit-ridden United States are adequate testament to such dangers.

Finally, it is important to emphasize that the balance of payments is not something that policy-makers can elevate to the status of an ultimate goal to the exclusion of other macroeconomic considerations. Thus the pursuit of balance of payments balance must be tempered by the competing claims of full employment, price stability and a satisfactory rate of growth. To grow only slowly, for example, encumbered by high unemployment in order to maintain a given balance of payments position is really no achievement at all.

The balance of payments performance of selected economies

As a means of elaborating upon some of the themes introduced above, it will be helpful, in concluding this section, to briefly review the balance of payments performances of some actual economies. Table 14.5 describes the current account positions of the G7 economies, plus that of the Euro Area since 1991. Notice that the table measures the deficit or surplus on current account in each case as a percentage of GDP. This approach is used because it scales each deficit or surplus in terms of the size of the economy that must accommodate it. The USA, for example, has a deficit in 1993 much larger *in absolute terms* than Canada in the same year (see Table 14.6 for verification) but, because the US economy is itself much bigger than the Canadian economy, the *relative* significance of the US deficit in 1993 – as illustrated in Table 14.5 – is not so great.

Table 14.5 shows the major current account debtors amongst the G7 to be the USA and Canada. For the period as a whole, the US deficit averages −1.89 per cent of GDP per annum, while for Canada the equivalent figure is −2.12 percent. The UK and Germany experience some combination of deficit and surplus, but their average performances at −0.47 and −0.54 are closest of all the G7 to balance (that is, zero).

Table 14.5 Current balances as a percentage of GDP for the G7 and Euro Area, 1991–2000

	1991	1992	1993	1994	1995	1996	1997	1998	1999[a]	2000[a]	1991–2000 average
United States	−0.1	−0.8	−1.3	−1.8	−1.6	−1.8	−1.9	−2.7	−3.4	−3.5	−1.89
Japan	2.0	3.0	3.1	2.8	2.1	1.4	2.3	3.2	3.0	3.5	2.64
Euro Area	−1.1	−0.9	0.4	0.4	0.7	1.1	1.6	1.4	1.2	1.4	0.62
Germany	−1.0	−1.0	−0.7	−1.0	−0.9	−0.6	−0.2	−0.2	0.0	0.2	−0.54
France	−0.4	0.4	0.8	0.6	0.7	1.3	2.7	2.8	2.6	2.6	1.41
Italy	−2.1	−2.5	0.9	1.4	2.4	3.3	2.9	2.0	1.9	2.2	1.24
United Kingdom	−1.4	−1.7	−1.7	−0.2	−0.5	−0.1	0.8	0.1	0.1	−0.1	−0.47
Canada	−3.7	−3.6	−3.9	−2.3	−0.8	0.5	−1.5	−2.1	−1.9	−1.9	−2.12

[a] Estimates
Source: *OECD, Economic Outlook*. Reproduced by permission of the OECD.

The Euro Area too is on average within 1 per cent of balance, though it errs on the side of current account surplus. Finally, France and Italy enjoy an average surplus of 1.41 and 1.24 per cent respectively, while Japan's performance is one of consistent strong surplus. Table 14.6 gives *absolute* figures for G7 and Euro Area current account balances, again over the period 1991–2000. Table 14.6 starkly demonstrates the symmetry between the current account performances of the USA, Japan and the Euro Area. Because these are three of the world's largest economies (accounting together for approximately 44 per cent of world GNP in 1998) it is highly improbable that a large absolute current account deficit in one would not be reflected in the counterweight of large surpluses in the others. For example, from 1994 onwards when the US deficit first passes the $100 billion mark and then $200 billion, increasing surpluses are recorded in the Euro Area and, especially, Japan.

We can now relate these real-world balance of payments performances back to our earlier theoretical discussions. There we argued that a persistent balance of payments deficit posed an adjustment problem for the deficit nation. This is certainly the case for the United States, which has in fact been in current account deficit since 1982. Indeed, we might reasonably wonder at the ability of the USA to run a deficit for so long: how has this been possible? Part of the answer lies in the noted size and importance of the US economy. While lesser nations might find their accommodating credit lines running dry in the presence of a persistent balance of payments deficit sooner rather than later, because the USA is responsible for about 21 per cent of world GNP it is deemed to be more creditworthy than most. But this is not to imply that the US deficit is unproblematic. Balance of payments adjustment will be required eventually and, as we have seen, this can have painful economic consequences for the adjusting economy. Moreover, as noted, there is evidence that the deficit has prompted a revival of harmful protectionist sentiment in the USA itself. Under a provision in its 1988 Omnibus Trade Bill, the USA reserves the right to take retaliatory protectionist measures against particular countries it finds to be engaged in unfair trade practices. Japan has been a recent target of this so-called 'Super 301' legislation, which had lapsed but was resurrected in 1999. Japan has been singled out for particular attention precisely because of its growing trade surplus with the USA (the surplus increased by 33 per cent in 1998). The country-specific discrimination

Table 14.6 Current balances for the G7 and Euro Area, 1991–2000 (billions of US$)

	1991	1992	1993	1994	1995	1996	1997	1998	1999[a]	2000[a]
United States	−4.4	−51.4	−86.1	−123.8	−115.3	−134.9	−155.2	−233.4	−303.5	−320.4
Japan	68.2	112.4	131.9	130.5	110.4	65.8	94.5	120.7	124.5	142.4
Euro Area	−61.7	−56.5	23.5	22.1	50.9	80.2	105.0	89.5	81.9	91.8
Germany	−17.8	−19.1	−14.0	−20.3	−22.6	−13.8	−4.0	−3.5	1.0	5.3
France	−5.5	4.8	9.8	7.4	10.9	20.5	37.6	39.8	36.8	38.7
Italy	−24.3	−30.0	8.6	13.8	25.7	40.5	33.5	23.2	22.6	26.8
United Kingdom	−14.8	−17.7	−15.9	−2.2	−5.9	−0.9	10.1	1.1	1.8	−1.5
Canada	−22.4	−21.0	−21.8	−13.0	−4.7	3.3	−9.2	−12.4	−11.5	−12.6

[a] Estimates
Source: OECD, *Economic Outlook*. Reproduced by permission of the OECD.

implied by Super 301 action is clearly at odds with the multilateral spirit of the GATT and the WTO (see Chapter 13, section 13.5), and is of a kind with the pernicious trade policies of the 1930s. The links between strategic balance of payments deficit and surplus in the world economy on the one hand and the re-emergence of protectionism on the other are clear.

14.3 The balance of payments and business

Why does the balance of payments matter to business? For the moment we can only partly answer this question. Later, we shall see that *government balance of payments policy* can have serious consequences for firms of all kinds, regardless of whether or not they are directly involved in international trade. However, on the basis of what we have learned so far we can say that balance of payments issues may impinge upon business if payments *imbalances* in the world economy become large or sustained enough to raise the possibility of protectionism. This is most evident in nations under immediate threat of protectionist sanction. We have just noted the hostile disposition of US trade policy towards Japan. In this case, the Super 301 threat is explicitly linked to Japan's burgeoning trade surplus with the USA, and it has direct implications for the Japanese economy and Japanese business. However, it is possible that a revival of targeted protectionism in one economy can spill over into a more generalized form that affects many economies. The EU, for example, is not currently involved in the dispute between the USA and Japan but it easily could be if it felt that its interests were somehow also at stake. When the Super 301 legislation was originally enacted by the USA in the late 1980s, there were calls inside Europe for the EU to arm itself with similar discriminatory trade policy instruments. *Then* the EU did not in the end pursue the matter, but this does not mean it won't in the future in similar circumstances. We also know from Chapter 13, sections 13.4–13.6, that protectionism is a threat to output and incomes in the *world* economy. More trade means more growth and higher incomes; constraints on trade limit output and income growth. This suggests that payments imbalance, even if it is initially between other apparently remote economies, can still impact upon *your* economy and *your* business.

Exchange rate: The price of one currency expressed in terms of another.

14.4 Exchange rates

An **exchange rate** is simply a *price*: the price of one currency expressed in terms of another. At the time of writing (29 November 1999), one pound sterling is valued at 1.59 euros and 1.60 US dollars. These are two of the wide range of current prices at which sterling is bought and sold. Tomorrow, in all likelihood, different prices will prevail. In the remainder of this chapter we shall explain how exchange rates are determined and why they vary over time. We shall also describe the fundamentals of different *exchange rate systems* and their implications for the balance of payments. During the twentieth century two basic forms of exchange rate system have operated: fixed regimes, which have limited the tendency of exchange rates to change; and flexible regimes, which have been much more tolerant of exchange rate variation. We shall examine the relative arguments for these different kinds of arrangement.

14.5 Exchange rate determination

Because an exchange rate is a price, it is determined – like any other price – by the interaction of supply and demand. What then are the influences upon supply and demand in the *foreign exchange market*?[2] For ease of exposition in what follows we limit our discussion to current account transactions. Let us take the Swiss franc as an example. Why would a foreign demand arise for francs? The most simple answer is, of course, that non-residents of Switzerland wish to purchase goods or services from Swiss residents. Because Swiss residents require payment in francs, foreign buyers must obtain (demand) francs in exchange for their own currencies. The *supply* of francs arises from the purchases of foreign goods and services made by Swiss residents. As foreign suppliers similarly require payment in their own currencies, Swiss residents must obtain these in exchange for (a supply of) francs. In this way, the foreign exchange market can be understood as a mechanism that facilitates the trade process: it allows economic agents resident in different countries holding different currencies to buy and sell goods and services to each other.[3]

A diagrammatic representation of the demand and supply sides of the foreign exchange market for francs is given in Fig. 14.1. Here Fig. 14.1(a) demonstrates the negative relationship between the demand for francs and the value of the franc expressed in terms of other currencies (that is, the franc exchange rate). As the value of the franc falls (from $0a$ to $0c$), so do the prices of Swiss goods in foreign markets. Assuming that the foreign price elasticity of demand for Swiss goods is greater than 1, this leads *ceteris paribus* to a proportionately greater increase in the foreign demand for Swiss goods and an *extension* in the quantity of francs demanded (from $0b$ to $0d$). Alternatively, if the franc's value increases, the prices of Swiss goods in foreign markets rise, leading *ceteris paribus* to a proportionately greater fall in the demand for these goods and a *contraction* in the quantity of francs demanded.

In Fig. 14.1(b), the supply curve for francs is derived in a similar manner. A fall in the value of the franc (again from $0a$ to $0c$) causes the price of foreign goods and services in Swiss markets to rise and, therefore, the demand for them to fall. Assuming

---

[2] There are several major foreign exchange markets in the world, the largest of which are in London, New York, Singapore and Hong Kong.

[3] As the attentive reader will have noted, in fact all **autonomous transactions** on the balance of payments give rise to currency demand and supply in the foreign exchange market.

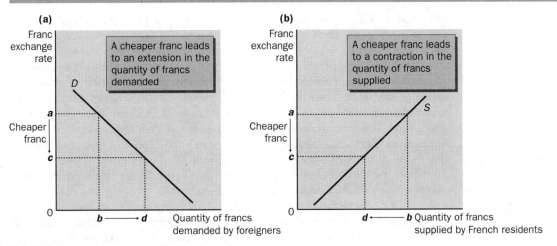

Fig. 14.1 Demand and supply in the foreign exchange market.

that the Swiss price elasticity of demand for foreign goods is greater than 1, this occasions a *contraction* in the quantity of francs supplied on the foreign exchanges (from 0*b* to 0*d*) as Swiss residents require less foreign currency for imports. On the other hand, a rise in the franc's value makes foreign goods in Switzerland cheaper, causing an increase in the demand for them and an *extension* in the quantity of francs supplied.

We can now put the two sides of the foreign exchange market together to see how it works. This is done in Fig. 14.2. The general principles of operation here are identical to those of any normal market. Equilibrium is defined by the intersection of the demand and supply curves. At this point, the exchange rate 0*b* gives rise to a quantity of francs demanded 0*d* and an identical quantity supplied, also 0*d*. Because the exchange rate produces an exact fusion of interest between the two sides of the market – no demand is unmet and no supply is ignored – there are no pressures for it to change: hence the equilibrium.

At *all* other possible exchange rates there can be no such stability. Above the equilibrium exchange rate 0*b*, a stronger franc gives rise to an extension in the quantity supplied as domestic residents increase their demand for cheaper foreign imports. At the same time, however, the quantity of francs demanded contracts as its higher

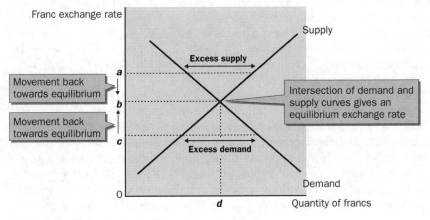

Fig. 14.2 Equilibrium in the foreign exchange market.

value makes Swiss exports more expensive in foreign markets. Thus, at the exchange rate 0a, for example, there is an *excess supply* of francs of the order marked in the diagram. The elimination of excess supply conditions will require a weakening of the franc. As the franc falls in value from 0a, the quantities demanded and supplied come closer together, but they will not be finally harmonized until the equilibrium exchange rate 0b has been reached. It should be clear that exchange rates below 0b, such as 0c, will stimulate conditions of *excess demand*. A cheap franc makes Swiss goods more desirable in foreign markets, and therefore foreign residents demand more francs. But it also reduces Swiss interest in imports and thus causes a contraction in the quantity of francs supplied. The unsatisfied demand for francs that now prevails in the market allows the exchange rate to rise. Again, this pressure is fully dissipated only when the equilibrium rate 0b is attained.

In Fig. 14.2 the demand and supply curves for foreign exchange were derived by reference to the usual market relationships between prices and quantities, with other influences held constant. For the sake of completeness, we should note here that the *positions* of the curves themselves depend on a range of other relevant factors. Some of these were discussed in our introduction to market dynamics in Chapter 2 and include, for example, income and tastes. A fall in incomes in the rest of the world would cause the demand curve for the franc to shift to the left as world demand for all imports fell; whereas a more favourable disposition towards Swiss goods on the part of foreign consumers would shift the franc demand curve to the right as more Swiss goods were sold on world markets. Changes in the domestic interest rate also greatly influence the demand for francs, especially over the shorter run. Because it makes interest-bearing assets denominated in francs more attractive (as returns on them become higher), an increase in the Swiss interest rate, compared with that prevailing in the rest of the world, would be associated with a rightward shift in the demand curve for francs. Conversely, a reduction in the Swiss interest rate, because it lowers the attractiveness of franc-denominated interest-bearing assets, would cause the demand curve for francs to shift to the left. Similar considerations will influence the position of the supply curve.

Having explained the process of exchange rate determination and the notion of equilibrium, we need also to understand why exchange rates *vary*. The underlying connection between trade and the demand and supply of foreign currencies is significant here. If there was no trade, there would be no demand for specifically *foreign* currency; all material needs and desires could be financed using domestic currency. But there *is* trade. The rest of the world does have a taste, for example, for Swiss watches, and this must involve a foreign demand for francs. Now, which of all the world's currencies would we expect to be in the greatest demand? The obvious answer is the currency of the nation that produces the greatest value of exports. Conversely, there would be less demand for the currencies of nations that exported relatively fewer goods and services.

Depreciation: The depreciation of a currency involves a decrease in its value in terms of other currencies. The term depreciation is used when the currency is *not* part of some formal fixed exchange rate system. When a currency decreases in value as a result of government policy inside a fixed system, the term *devaluation* is used.

We are now in a position to understand *secular*[4] movements in exchange rates. These are explained by the long-term trade performances of nations. Countries that gradually lose shares in world export markets will *ceteris paribus* see demand for their currencies fall. If, at the same time, these countries maintain healthy appetites for imports, thereby underwriting a consistent supply of their currencies onto the foreign exchanges, then the inevitable outcome will be *excess* currency supply and **currency depreciation** over the long term. Graphically, this would involve something approximating a steady leftward shift of the demand curve for a typical currency,

[4] A useful word in this context. It means 'slow but persistent'.

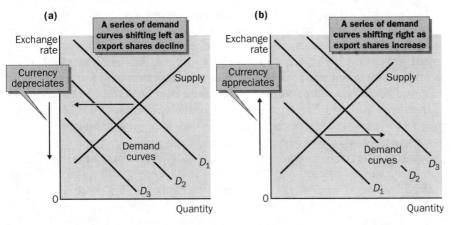

Fig. 14.3 Long-term change in the foreign exchange market.

consistently dragging down the equilibrium exchange rate (see Fig. 14.3(a)). For nations that are able to improve their shares in world export markets, the concomitant strong currency demand would most likely be associated with long-term **currency appreciation**. Graphically, this would involve a steady rightward shift of the demand curve for the typical currency, consistently pulling up the equilibrium exchange rate (see Fig. 14.3(b)). Recall that we have confined our analysis here to the current account only. Clearly, currency supply and demand will also be conditioned by transactions that appear elsewhere in the balance of payments accounts. In particular, FDI and portfolio investment transactions on the financial account will also influence long-term currency movements for the 'typical' advanced economy.

If long-term currency movements can be attributed to trade (and investment) performance, what of short-term movements? The value of currencies changes on a *daily* basis and, on occasion, short-term movements can be very abrupt: how are these to be explained? Short-term currency movements are certainly in part trade-related, but the activities of *currency speculators* can also be an important influence here. Speculation can be a profitable activity for those who are in a position to buy a currency in the anticipation that it will gain in value against other weaker currencies. The increasing size and sophistication of the world's financial markets has facilitated a significant expansion of speculative activity in the last 30 years. Indeed speculation – rather than 'real' trade in goods and services – appears now to be the *primary* focus of transactions on the world's foreign exchanges. We discuss the implications of this remarkable development in more detail in section 14.8 below. Of course, *government* is the other agency that can prompt short-term movements in exchange, particularly through changes in interest rates affecting financial flows. As noted, higher domestic interest rates tend to increase the foreign demand for a currency, thus causing a relatively sharp rise in its value.

Appreciation: The appreciation of a currency involves an increase in its value in terms of other currencies. The term appreciation is used when the currency is *not* part of some formal fixed exchange rate system. When a currency increases in value as a result of government policy inside a fixed system, the term *revaluation* is used.

14.6 Exchange rate systems

Flexible exchange rates

In section 14.4 we characterized two general forms of exchange rate system: those that embrace exchange rate flexibility and those that impose some degree of restriction on exchange rate movements. A flexible system is one that follows free market principles. Exchange rate determination is left entirely to the processes of currency supply and demand described earlier, and governments do not attempt to manipulate the market in order to achieve particular exchange rate outcomes.

A flexible exchange rate system confers a number of advantages upon economies that adopt it. The first and most important of these relates to the balance of payments. We know that one of the central objectives of macroeconomic policy is the achievement of balance of payments balance over the medium term. A flexible exchange rate system *automatically* provides for this objective without the need for any action whatsoever by policy-makers. How? Consider the implications for the foreign exchange market of a balance of payments deficit in, say, the UK. Assuming, for the moment, that all foreign exchange transactions are trade-related, the deficit will necessarily be associated with conditions of *excess supply* of sterling. This is because UK residents will be supplying more sterling to the foreign exchange market than there is demand for. Remember that, here, sterling demand is conditioned by the rest of the world's demand for UK exports. Because the value of imports is greater than the value of exports, there must be a greater volume of sterling supplied than demanded: hence, excess supply. By the familiar market processes identified in Fig. 14.2, a currency in excess supply will depreciate in value. Now, the sterling depreciation has important implications for the relative price competitiveness of exports and imports. Exports become cheaper in foreign markets and, because import prices rise, import substitutes become more attractive to domestic consumers (see Table 14.4 for an example of this process at work). Assuming that the price elasticity of demand for exports *plus* imports is greater than 1 (that is, demand is sufficiently price elastic) there will be an improvement in the UK's trade balance. This is known as the *Marshall–Lerner condition*. We must also presume that there are spare resources so that export industries and import-substituting industries are able to respond to the extra domestic demand stimulus that results from the depreciation.

If depreciation facilitated by a flexible exchange rate system impacts upon a deficit in the way described, at what point does the process end? Given that depreciation itself is prompted by, in our example, an excess supply of sterling on the foreign exchanges, it should be clear that this condition will persist so long as the deficit itself is present. This means that the deficit will continue to exert downward pressure on sterling until balance of payments balance is achieved.

A flexible exchange rate also provides an automatic panacea for balance of payments surplus. An excess of UK exports (to continue with our example) over UK imports in value terms gives rise to an *excess demand* for sterling and an *appreciation* of the sterling exchange rate. This adversely affects the price competitiveness of UK exports and import substitutes and, on the Marshall–Lerner assumption, worsens the trade balance and erodes the surplus. Again, the process continues until balance of payments balance has been achieved and equilibrium in the market for sterling prevents further appreciation of the currency.

The most famous advocate of the case for flexible exchange rates is the economist Milton Friedman. In his view, flexible rates offer nations the opportunity to enjoy *consistent* balance of payments balance. Friedman argues that any early or 'incipient' (the word he uses) deficit or surplus that might arise will be swiftly dissipated by appropriate corrective exchange rate movements. Flexible rates also offer two other advantages in Friedman's view. First, they allow nations to pursue their own *independent* economic goals in respect of the other objectives of macro policy. As we shall see, membership of a *fixed* exchange rate system restricts the ability of participant countries to conduct policy autonomously. Second, flexible rates, because they reflect the free interplay of market forces, offer the most appropriate framework for the international allocation of resources through the trade process. The alternative – rates manipulated by governments – Friedman considers to be inimical to the very desirable objective of free trade.

Fixed exchange rates

There are three sets of issues to be explored in respect of fixed exchange rate systems:

- How can rates be fixed in the first place?
- How can a persistent balance of payments deficit be corrected under a regime of fixed exchange rates?
- If exchange rates can be fixed and if balance of payments deficits can be corrected with fixed rates, what are the *additional* merits of fixed systems that might make them preferable to a flexible system?

On the first of these questions, it is important to realize that fixity cannot be achieved by simple government decree. As we have seen, there are powerful economic forces at work in the foreign exchange markets; restricting the movement of currencies requires equally decisive countervailing action by the authorities. This can take two broad forms: direct intervention in the foreign exchanges using so-called *open market operations*, or the less direct option of *interest rate manipulation*.

The fixing of an exchange rate very rarely involves the establishment of a single point away from which a currency is not permitted to move. The usual approach is to define a *target zone* for the currency. The authorities then respond with appropriate measures when market forces threaten to move the currency above or below the zone. Fig. 14.4 depicts a hypothetical case in which, for the sake of illustration, a target zone has been defined above the market equilibrium. The boundaries of the zone are points *a* and *c* on the vertical axis, while point *b* marks its mid-point and is the *central parity* of the currency. The market equilibrium here is given by point *d*.

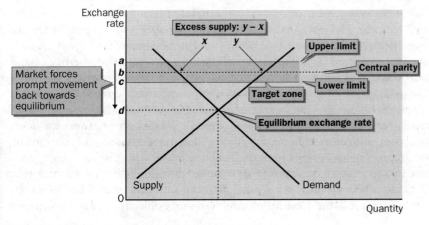

Fig. 14.4 A target zone in the foreign exchange market.

Under free market conditions, should an exchange rate emerge somewhere in the target zone, say because of a sudden surge in import demand in the domestic economy (which, remember, would lead to an excess supply of the currency), market forces would tend to drive the rate back down towards the equilibrium at d. To prevent this from happening and retain an exchange rate above equilibrium, the authorities themselves could buy the excess currency supply that is the driving force of the depreciation process. If, for example, the authorities wished to hold the exchange rate at b, they would need to buy the excess supply of currency xy that arises at this rate. The purchase would, of course, have to be made using reserves of foreign currency. Conversely, should market conditions change such that there are *excess demand* pressures that threaten an appreciation of the currency *above* the upper limit of the target zone at a, then open market operations to *sell* domestic currency in exchange for additional reserves might be undertaken by the authorities. Theoretically, then, it is possible to hold a currency at any given rate, so long as the associated excess demand or supply of the currency at that rate can be met.

The second policy measure that can be used as an alternative or supplement to open market operations involves the noted use of interest rates. If the euro zone[5] authorities, for example, raise interest rates, investments denominated in euros become more attractive to overseas investors. This means that they are more likely to demand euros for investment purposes. The stronger demand for euros leads to a rise in its value against other currencies. In terms of Fig. 14.4, this would involve a shift in the demand curve to the right, such that the demand for euros is higher at every exchange rate and a new higher rate equilibrium is established. Conversely, if the euro zone authorities elected to reduce interest rates, the lower associated demand for euros would shift the demand curve to the left and force down the exchange rate. The interest rate is therefore a potentially powerful weapon that the authorities can use to maintain a currency at a selected level in defiance of the will of the market.

Correcting balance of payments disequilibria under fixed exchange rates

It might well be possible to stabilize exchange rates, but how are balance of payments disequilibria to be corrected under more rigid frameworks of this kind? In answering this question, we concentrate upon the most pressing problem of balance of payments deficit. There are two possible courses of action open to any deficit economy: *expenditure reduction policy* or *expenditure-switching policy* (or, indeed, some combination of both). The aim of **expenditure reduction policy** is to dampen the level of aggregate demand in the domestic economy so that the demand for imported goods and services is reduced. Because the level of exports is unrelated to domestic demand – export demand depends on such factors as foreign incomes, the prices of exports relative to the prices of rival goods produced by competitors abroad, foreign tastes and so on – it follows that the balance of payments position should improve. Moreover, as lower domestic demand may ease domestic inflationary pressures, the international competitiveness of home-produced goods and services should rise, thereby further improving the current account. Domestic demand may be reduced by contractionary monetary or fiscal policy, or some combination of both. Unfortunately, dealing with a balance of payments deficit in this way may have deleterious consequences for some of the other major macroeconomic objectives. Thus a lower level

Expenditure reduction policy: Involves a reduction in the level of aggregate demand in the domestic economy in order to improve the balance of payments position on current account.

[5] The euro zone is that part of the EU where the euro circulates.

of demand is likely to constrain output and effect an increase in unemployment. Recall our caution that balance of payments equilibrium should not be relentlessly pursued at the expense of other goals or objectives.

Turning to **expenditure-switching policies**, the objective here is to encourage overseas residents to buy more exports and to induce domestic residents to purchase home-produced goods and services instead of imports. How are such modifications in consumption behaviour to be achieved? The most obvious method is to *devalue*[6] the domestic currency. This requires the monetary authorities to revise downwards the declared central parity for the currency inside the relevant fixed exchange rate system. Devaluation has the effect of reducing the price of exports in foreign markets as overseas buyers have to part with fewer units of their own currency to obtain a given amount of the devalued currency. The domestic price of imports is simultaneously increased as home consumers must part with more of their currency to obtain a given amount of foreign currency (see Table 14.4 for an illustration). In this way currency devaluation induces relative price changes that favour the products of the devaluing economy. For the devaluation to work – for it to improve the trade balance – two additional conditions must be observed. These were introduced earlier in our discussion of BP adjustment under flexible exchange rates. First, there must be sufficient spare capacity in domestic industries to enable them to respond to greater demand pressures both at home and abroad. Second, the relative price changes themselves must stimulate appropriate behaviour amongst consumers: in other words, there must be a reasonable degree of price elasticity of demand for exports and imports. For a current account deficit to ease following a devaluation, it is generally recognized that the price elasticity of demand for exports plus the price elasticity of demand for imports must be greater than 1 (the noted Marshall–Lerner condition).

It should be clear that the devaluation will also have a positive influence on the levels of output and employment in the domestic economy, in that demand has been raised. However, there may be a potentially adverse affect on inflation. Rising import prices, particularly for strategically important commodities such as fuel, may introduce cost-push pressures into domestic industry. Finally, we should be aware that there are several additional measures available to governments, each of which also has expenditure-switching properties. These include: import controls, export promotion, and the promotion of domestic industry by fiscal or other means.

The advantages of fixed exchange rates

Our analysis so far in this section suggests that exchange rates can be fixed, and that balance of payments deficits can be corrected inside fixed rate regimes. Yet, in themselves, these findings hardly amount to a recommendation of exchange rate fixity; a market-based system also provides for deficit correction. Why then might fixed regimes be actively preferred by policy-makers? There are two arguments for exchange rate fixity: the *integration argument* and the *anchor argument*.

The integration argument proceeds by analogy. An economy is thought to gain certain advantages from its ability to issue a single currency that is uniformly acceptable throughout its territory. In the United States, for example, the dollar serves

Expenditure-switching policies: Policies intended to switch domestic and foreign demand away from foreign goods and towards home-produced goods.

---

[6] To recap, devaluation involves lowering the price of a currency inside a fixed exchange rate system; as such, it is necessarily an action of the monetary authorities. **Depreciation**, on the other hand, is the word used to describe the lowering of the price of a currency inside a flexible regime. This can either be wholly market driven or can be managed by the authorities. The antonyms of devaluation and depreciation are revaluation and appreciation.

equally well in transactions in every state. This means that (say) a New Jersey food processing firm can pay for Californian oranges in dollars, and that a resident of Texas can buy a coffee machine manufactured in Pennsylvania and also pay in dollars. In this way, the dollar provides *monetary coherence* throughout the USA: all transactions are patently transparent. However, if the four US states just mentioned issued *their own individual currencies* then a degree of coherence would immediately be lost. The New Jersey orange buyer would need to obtain the Californian currency, while the Texan would require Pennsylvanian currency to pay for the coffee machine. The inconvenience associated with this more complex situation would clearly be much worse were these separate currencies free to fluctuate in value against each other. In fact, the more complex the monetary arrangement becomes, the greater the potential *fragmentation* of the economy. The danger is that producers and consumers may begin to retreat and confine their activities to their own 'monetary region', thus segmenting and impoverishing the competitive process itself. Consumers may not choose to buy what offers them the best value simply because it comes from another region and the associated transaction might be inconvenient, or the price might be unclear because of currency fluctuations. Economic fragmentation of this sort reduces the exposure of less efficient producers to the full rigours of the competitive process. If greater competition is a desirable objective – and we presume that it is – then the benefit to the US economy of the highest possible degree of monetary coherence is clear. Let us retain the essence of this conclusion and move back to the international level. Different national economies usually have different currencies,[7] which means, in terms of our US example, that there is a choice to be made over the degree of *incoherence* that the prevailing international monetary system should have. On the one hand, fixed exchange rates do not offer the same level of simplicity and transparency that a single currency does; but, on the other, it can be argued that they certainly appear preferable to the more uncertain environment often associated with flexible rates.

The second argument for fixed exchange rates is based on the proposition that membership of a fixed regime restricts the freedom that policy-makers have to pursue expansionary monetary and fiscal policy. This means that participant economies become *anchored* to a policy of disinflation. Consider the implications of a decision by one member of a fixed system to adopt a relatively loose fiscal and monetary stance compared with those of its partners. Such a shift in policy might be motivated by the need to engineer faster growth and lower unemployment in advance of an election. One unwelcome consequence of *reflationary* fiscal and monetary policy is likely to be an increase in the rate of inflation. While this might be viewed *internally* as an acceptable price to pay for the higher level of economic activity expansion generates, participation in a fixed exchange rate system means that, in *external* terms, the policy is impossible to sustain and, indeed, must be reversed. This is because the increase in the rate of inflation has negative implications for the *international competitiveness* of the reflating economy. Faster inflation must mean adverse movements in the relative prices of imports and exports as compared with prices prevailing in the economies of other members of the fixed system. The end result is the likely emergence of a trade deficit for the reflating economy with its fixed system partners. If trade with its partners accounts for a substantial proportion of its overall trade, the reflation will cause an *overall trade deficit* for this economy. Now, we know from earlier discussion that deficits cannot be sustained in the medium term, so the ques-

---

[7] We discuss the exceptional case of the EU's single currency, the euro, below.

tion arises as to what must be done about this newly derived problem. The key point here is that *membership of the fixed system rules out the main form of deficit correction using expenditure-switching policy: currency depreciation.* This leaves expenditure reduction as the only available policy option that can be used to deal with the deficit. Expenditure reduction, of course, involves fiscal and monetary austerity, and thus *must reverse* the original reflation. It is in this way that fixed exchange rate membership necessarily imposes fiscal and monetary discipline upon participant economies.

Managed exchange rate: One that is influenced by intervention of the country's central bank in the foreign exchange market.

Managed rates

Although we have so far framed exchange rate policy in terms of a rather stark choice between market determination and absolute fixity imposed by government, there are several qualifications that must be made here. In the first place, there is the third option of the **management of a floating rate**, sometimes referred to in the literature as a 'dirty' float. It is unlikely that the authorities in any country could remain completely indifferent to the behaviour of the exchange rate, and yet this is what the advocates of completely flexible rates recommend. The continuous depreciation of the currency of a deficit nation, for example, would clearly raise concerns over *how* far it could tolerably sink. Notwithstanding the fact that the strength of a currency is sometimes popularly interpreted as a measure of national economic vitality, a pronounced depreciation would, for example, have extremely serious *inflationary* consequences for the domestic economy as the prices of imports with typically low price elasticities of demand (such as oil) were forced up. Dangers of this kind mean that managed or dirty floating is the more usual alternative to participation in a fixed exchange rate system. In practice, a managed float permits the authorities to intervene in the foreign exchange markets, using direct open market operations, interest rates, or some combination of both, when market imperatives threaten particularly unwelcome currency movements; in all other circumstances the market is the preferred mechanism of control.

If absolute flexibility is not usually a practical option, what of exchange rate fixity; can this tend towards the absolute? We have already noted the common use of intervention zones around a central exchange rate parity, such as that depicted in Fig. 14.4. This means that *some* movement of rates is possible, but what of the parities themselves? Are they immutably fixed? In terms of the history of actual exchange rate systems, the simple answer here is that, in cases where parities have been *fixed but adjustable*, the systems themselves appear more robust than the alternative 'hard' *fixed and not adjustable* parity systems. In order to illustrate this point we now turn to consider some important examples of actual exchange rate systems.

14.7 Exchange rate systems in practice

In this section we shall review the nature and performance of two major *fixed* exchange rate systems:

- the Bretton Woods system (1945–71)
- the European exchange rate mechanism (1979–98).

We shall also examine a flexible exchange rate regime:

- the 'non-system' (1973–date).

The Bretton Woods system

In Chapter 13 we explained how the GATT multilateral trade framework emerged as a response to the chaotic protectionism of the 1930s. Although in *trade policy* terms the protectionism was tariff based, it also had an *exchange rate* dimension. This took the form of a series of *competitive devaluations* in which individual countries lowered the values of their currencies in an attempt to encourage domestic economic recovery. However, as with the tariff, devaluation at this time tended to spawn retaliation rather than recovery, and as more and more countries took part, none was left in a better general economic position than when it started. This kind of background greatly influenced the architects of the postwar international monetary system when they met in Bretton Woods, a small resort town in the US state of New Hampshire, in July 1944.

The Bretton Woods Conference gave rise to an agreement that the postwar world economy would be best served by the adoption of a framework of fixed exchange rates. This, it was believed, would both obviate the dangers of a new round of competitive devaluations and – on the assumption that trade is enhanced by exchange rate stability – stimulate a general environment in which export-led growth could flourish. The new system was to be based on the US dollar, which was fixed in value by the US authorities against gold (at $35 per ounce). All other currencies in the system could then be tied to the dollar – and each other – at fixed values. The British pound, for example, had an initial central parity with the dollar of $4.03. The US dollar was accorded such a pivotal role because of the enormous economic advantage that the USA enjoyed over the rest of the world at the end of the war: at this time fully *half* of the world's output was produced in America, and the US Federal Reserve held *67 per cent* of the world's gold stock. The purpose of fixing the value of the dollar to gold was to limit the ability of the US authorities to indulge in unwarranted monetary expansion. Because the American commitment to gold meant that all other participants in the system could exchange dollar holdings for gold with the Federal Reserve at $35 per ounce, the US authorities could only issue (print) dollars commensurate with their ability to redeem them from other central banks using gold. The general intention here was to ensure inflation control via sober American monetary policy.

The target zone for the Bretton Woods system was set at 1 per cent, which meant that currencies could fluctuate against each other up to a 1 per cent margin above or below the declared parity. To keep currencies inside their target zones it was recognized that active management of the foreign exchange markets through open market operations would be required. Accordingly, the Bretton Woods agreement established the *International Monetary Fund* (IMF), which would lend participant nations intervention currencies in order that they might fulfil their obligations regarding the stability of their own currencies. The IMF was itself resourced by subscriptions from system members. Finally, and most importantly, it was recognized that currencies would need to be *realigned* from time to time, as, for example, new trading patterns and relationships evolved. Accordingly, the rules of the system permitted devaluations by countries in balance of payments deficit of up to 10 per cent of the value of a currency, but larger movements required IMF approval. Note that a clamour for the right to *revalue* was not anticipated. As we have seen, the pressures upon deficit nations are generally more intense than on those in surplus; moreover, surplus nations are often understandably reluctant to allow revaluation to undermine export-led growth.

In summary then, the Bretton Woods system was envisaged as one that would provide a framework of stable exchange rates conducive to trade development. Participant nations, with the help of the IMF, would manage their currencies in this spirit, but periodic realignments were anticipated in order that changes in real economic circumstances – especially the emergence of persistent balance of payments deficits – could be accommodated.

As we shall see, the actual development of the Bretton Woods system during the 1950s and 1960s differed from this agreed blueprint in some important ways, but the most fundamental element – exchange rate stability – remained in place, and was associated with the most sustained and trade-based economic boom in human history.

Given this kind of achievement, why then did the system not last? One answer is that it became an *overly* fixed exchange rate system – something its founders had been concerned to avoid. In part, this reflected a view that emerged from the IMF that, especially for the most important currencies, *any* movement beyond the agreed target zones was undesirable. More generally, it also became apparent that declared parities were widely interpreted as tokens of economic vitality, to the extent that devaluation came to be associated with national weakness and incompetence on the part of policy-makers of the countries experiencing persistent deficits. This had the effect of forestalling those currency realignments that were necessary to the healthy functioning of the system: deficit countries that needed to devalue were reluctant to do so for fear of the consequences of appearing weak, and surplus countries would not revalue because they had no wish to imperil their growth prospects. In this way, the Bretton Woods system *ossified*, unable to make the periodic currency adjustments that would allow the whole currency grid to retain its integrity. Ultimately, something was bound to snap, as indeed the US dollar did in 1971.

This brings us to the second and ultimately fatal weakness of the system: the so-called **dollar dilemma**. We know that the US dollar was selected as the system's pivotal currency at the Bretton Woods conference because of the great strength of the American economy at the time. The overwhelming scale of American production also made the dollar the world's most heavily demanded currency: dollars were necessary to finance the rest of the world's imports of American goods. The imperatives of postwar reconstruction served only to accentuate this situation. In 1948, to begin to meet the huge demand for dollars, the US initiated the *Marshall Plan*, a programme of dollar grants to European countries. However, despite this action, what became known as the period of the *dollar shortage* persisted until the end of the 1950s. Thereafter, the gap between the supply of and demand for dollars began to be closed by other changes in the US economy itself. There was, for example, a significant increase in American foreign direct investment. This raised the flow of dollars abroad as US firms opened foreign production facilities. But herein lay the essence of the problem for the Bretton Woods system. What if the outflow of dollars from the USA became so large that it swamped the American capacity – to which it was committed – to continue to redeem dollars using its gold stock? In such a situation the system would fail because the entire exchange rate framework proceeded from the established gold valuation of the dollar. However, the greater availability of dollars was important as it provided the extra volume of *the* key currency necessary to finance the continued unprecedented growth in world trade. *In effect this meant that the world economy did not want a dollar shortage, but there were great risks should the shortage turn into a glut.* The problem became known as the *Triffin dilemma*, after the economist Robert Triffin who (presciently) identified it in 1960.

Concept

Dollar dilemma

The dollar dilemma referred to the contradictory needs inside the Bretton Woods system for, on the one hand, a sufficient supply of dollars to finance the growth in world trade and, on the other, some constraints on the supply of dollars in order to maintain market confidence in the dollar.

Unfortunately, from the mid 1960s, the shortage *did* give way to glut. The most notable cause was the domestic economic expansion associated both with the escalation of the Vietnam War and with President Johnson's 1964 announcement of the 'Great Society' programme.[8] This served to effect a serious deterioration in the US balance of payments on the current account, resulting in significant increases in dollar holdings by foreign central banks. While confidence in the gold basis of the dollar held, the central banks were happy to accumulate dollar assets; in fact, because they could not obtain sufficient gold for reserve use purposes (as the world supply of gold was growing too slowly) they greatly needed this alternative prime reserve asset. But the threat of a dollar crisis loomed ever larger as these holdings increased. At the beginning of the 1970s a further and even more severe deterioration in the US balance of payments appeared to convince private agents (that is, speculators) in the foreign exchange markets that the dollar would have to be devalued: consequently the dollar was sold heavily in favour of more robust currencies such as the deutschmark and the yen. This meant that the German and Japanese central banks had to buy dollars using their own currencies in order to prevent them from rising in value (they had to meet higher demand with an equivalent increase in supply, in other words). As the following passage illustrates, this very quickly became an impossible task.

On a single day, May 4 1971, the Bundesbank [the German central bank] had to buy $1 billion to hold its dollar exchange rate fixed in the face of the great demand for its currency. On the morning of May 5, the Bundesbank purchased $1 billion during the first hour of foreign exchange trading alone! At that point the Bundesbank gave up and allowed its currency to float.[9]

This tide of speculation against the dollar continued unabated until 15 August 1971, when President Nixon effectively dissolved the Bretton Woods system by announcing that the USA would no longer honour the agreement to exchange dollars for gold. As the fixed gold value of the dollar was at the very heart of the framework of interconnected currency rates the entire structure simply melted away, ultimately to be replaced by the present **non-system** of flexible exchange rates.

The non-system

Although it had been informally operating for some time, the non-system was officially endorsed by the IMF at a meeting in Jamaica in January 1976. That the IMF survived the demise of the system it was designed to oversee is, together with the spirit of international economic cooperation this institution embodies, one of the lasting legacies of Bretton Woods. The Jamaica meeting gave permission for the former Bretton Woods participants to assume any exchange rate policy they found appropriate, subject to the exhortation that they should not seek to manipulate exchange rates for unilateral competitive gain: a clear reference to the regrettable currency dispositions of the 1930s. In fact, as we saw in Chapter 9, section 9.6, the major macroeconomic policy preoccupation of this period was not exchange rates and the balance of payments but *inflation*. Indeed, it is worth pausing for a moment

Non-system: The broad system of flexible exchange rates prevailing in the world economy since 1973.

[8] The Great Society programme involved *inter alia* increases in government spending on education, housing and measures to tackle poverty.

[9] *Source:* Krugman, P.R. and M. Obstfeld, *International Economics* (3rd ed.) p. 549. (New York: Harper Collins, 1994).

here in order to explain how the resurgence in worldwide inflation actually *necessitated* a return to a more flexible exchange rate environment. Table 9.3 illustrates the high and *uneven* incidence of inflation amongst the advanced nations in the 1970s. Compare, for example, the British and German experiences. The average inflation rate in Britain from 1973 to 1979 was 14.8 per cent; in Germany over the same period the rate was 5.0 per cent. As we have seen, differing inflation rates have important effects upon the relative international price competitiveness of nations. The high inflation rate in Britain meant *lost* price competitiveness *vis-à-vis* Germany and other economies with a similar capacity for greater price stability. In a fixed exchange rate system, Britain could regain international price competitiveness only by imposing relatively severe expenditure reduction policies. Domestically, this makes the option of expenditure switching much more attractive. The main form of expenditure-switching policy is currency devaluation or depreciation. Now, under fixed exchange rate conditions, it is simply not possible to engineer the *series* of devaluations required to confront the lost international price competitiveness implications of an inflationary environment. To do so would clearly undermine any pretence of exchange rate stability. This means that a period of high and unevenly experienced inflation will tend to lever countries away from an adherence to exchange rate fixity so that they can use currency depreciation both to protect their international price competitiveness and to stave off the need for severe expenditure-reducing policies.

Although the non-system provides for exchange rate flexibility, this is generally recognized to be a *managed* flexibility. We argued earlier that no country can afford to be entirely indifferent to the behaviour of its exchange rate. Pronounced depreciation can have, for example, severe inflationary consequences for the domestic economy as import prices are forced up, while pronounced appreciation will clearly impinge upon the prospects for exports and growth. It has been a feature of the non-system that exchange rates have, at times, moved to positions that appear to be at variance with conditions prevailing in, and the longer-term interests of, domestic economies. For example, in 1980–81, the sterling exchange rate climbed rapidly to $2.45 on the back of high domestic interest rates and because North Sea oil caused speculators to take a more favourable view of the currency. This can in part help to explain the abrupt contraction in British manufacturing output of some 20 per cent as firms found themselves less able to compete on price in foreign markets and as the relative price of manufactured imports fell. The recessionary impact on the economy as a whole was of an order not seen since the 1930s. Yet in the sterling crisis of 1984–85 the value of the pound plummeted to $1.04 at its lowest point as speculative sentiment turned sour. The central point here is that there was nothing in the 'real' economy that could justify such wild oscillations in the value of the pound over a relatively short period and the damage they caused. It was this kind of experience that helped to prompt the evolution of forms of collective management of the non-system.

While the misalignment of sterling might be a serious problem for the British economy, it has limited impact upon the fortunes of the rest of the world. However, this is not true of the US dollar, which, reflecting the absolute size of the American economy, remains the world's most important currency. In the mid 1980s the dollar was generally recognized to be *overvalued*, given the presence of a large US current account deficit but, contrary to the expectations of currency market theory, there was little sign of the necessary and corrective dollar *depreciation*. This meant, of course, that in the absence of US expenditure reduction policy, the deficit would in all likelihood become even larger. It is at this point that the issue becomes a more generalized one. The intractability of the deficit gave rise to increasingly strident calls for *protection* from American industrial and labour lobbies, and the major economies recognized that the possibility of a retaliatory trade war existed unless some ameliorative action could be taken. Accordingly, the G5[10] group of nations, in the 1985 *Plaza Agreement*, declared their collective intention to orchestrate an appropriate managed depreciation of the dollar. This amounted to a general recognition that the non-system could not be coordinated on the basis of market sentiment alone. In 1987, the G5 plus Canada moved a stage further by recognizing – in the *Louvre Accord* – that a greater degree of stability amongst the world's major currencies would bolster the prospects for trade growth, and therefore for general economic expansion. The Accord established undisclosed target zones for the currencies of its signatories. The zones themselves were informed by an awareness of the basic economic circumstances of each economy such that currency levels would be both stable and appropriate.

The European exchange rate mechanism (ERM)

It would seem from the experiences of Bretton Woods and the non-system that both overly fixed and highly flexible exchange rate regimes have limitations. One of the critical failings of the Bretton Woods system was the absence of any formal mechanism of currency adjustment. It had been envisaged that devaluations would periodically occur in order to dissipate evident balance of payments imbalances, but this simply did not happen on a sufficient scale. Similarly, theoretical predictions that the non-system would be typified by smooth, orderly and appropriate currency movements have not been realized, and substantial intervention has occurred as a result. In practice, what might be required is some kind of compromise between near absolute fixity and limitless flexibility. The ERM, at least for part of its life, can be seen to have been the institutional embodiment of such a compromise. Though it was subsumed by the creation of the euro in 1999, a review of the ERM is still instructive for the wider lessons it carries for exchange rate management.

The ERM was launched in 1979 as a 'zone of monetary stability in Europe'. It was conceived as a fixed but *adjustable* exchange rate system that would do two things. First, it would provide the exchange rate stability conducive to trade growth in an integrating EU (see Chapter 2, section 2.5). Second, by binding their monetary policies to the highly successful policy operated by the German Bundesbank, it would provide a means of *inflation control* for participant nations. Recall the *anchor argument* for fixed exchange rates. This suggests that members of a fixed system cannot permit their inflation rates to diverge significantly from the lowest rate in the system. The lost international price competitiveness that would result cannot be ignored; nor can it be regained by devaluation (fixity forbids regular recourse to this option). In fact the only means by which price competitiveness can be restored is by bearing down on inflation, which *must* involve the setting of an appropriately tight monetary policy. In the ERM, this reduces to mirroring the monetary policy of the Bundesbank.

The parity grid of the ERM was based on a specially created hybrid currency – the European currency unit (ecu). The ecu was a weighted average of the currencies of all member states. Inside the ERM, each central bank declared a parity with the ecu and through it with all other participant currencies. In this way a parity grid for the

[10] The world's five leading industrial nations: the USA, Japan, (the then) West Germany, France and the UK.

entire ERM was formed. The target zone for most currencies was initially set as a 2.25 per cent band (+ or −) around the central parity. In the event of a pair of currencies threatening to move too far apart, *both* central banks were required to intervene in the foreign exchange markets to re-establish the integrity of the target zone. This approach established a degree of *symmetry* in the ERM that had been lacking in Bretton Woods; there, the responsibility for currency defence had fallen primarily upon countries with weaker currencies.

Our main interest here is in the evolution of the ERM. Between 1979 and 1987 the system functioned, as intended, in a fixed but adjustable manner. In other words, the dominant concern was for currency stability within the prescribed limits, but appropriate currency realignments were made from time to time. This meant that the kind of tensions associated with overdue adjustment, which had typified the Bretton Woods system, did not have the chance to build up. However, from 1987, following the advent of the *Basle Nyborg Agreement*, the ERM ossified to produce sets of parities that were in effect *non-adjustable*. This meant that the system had no way to relieve tensions created by exchange rates that became misaligned: they had simply to be defended using the familiar tools of currency management. Ironically, the Basle Nyborg agreement was actually an attempt to strengthen the integrity of the ERM by more forcefully equipping its members to withstand speculative attacks upon their currencies. It established a new protocol of parity defence – facilitating, for example, the coordinated use of interest rate changes – and enhanced the pooled resources available for intervention in the foreign exchange markets. However, the agreement also relegated the option of currency realignment to the status of 'last resort'. Now, in so far as the last resort of realignment fused into a policy of *no* realignment, the ERM became possessed of a fundamental shortcoming as divergent economic performances amongst member states raised inevitable and increasingly stark questions as to the sustainability of established parities.

The integrity of the post Basle Nyborg 'unadjustable' parity grid eventually foundered upon problems associated with the reunification of Germany in 1989. Reunification sparked a huge reconstruction programme in the old East Germany, which was funded by an expansionary fiscal policy in Germany as a whole. Fears that this policy might have inflationary consequences prompted the Bundesbank to operate a tighter – that is, higher interest rate – monetary policy. In turn, higher interest rates had the effect of putting upward pressure on the deutschmark and downward pressure upon other major European currencies such as sterling and the French franc. Eventually, the markets seized first upon sterling, and despite heavy intervention by the Bank of England in its favour and the raising of UK interest rates to emergency levels, the pound left the ERM in October 1992, two years after it had belatedly joined. The lira and the Spanish peseta were floated at the same time. The following summer, renewed tensions in the ERM, which again favoured the deutschmark, were dissipated only by a widening of the margins of fluctuation inside the parity grid from ± 2.25 to ±15 per cent. Fig. 14.5 illustrates the movement to the (very much) wider band.

14.8 Currency speculation and exchange rate systems

The three exchange rate systems discussed in the previous section have all fallen victim to speculative forces. In the case of Bretton Woods, the outcome was terminal;

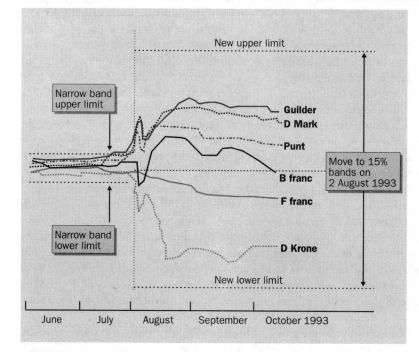

Fig. 14.5 The widening of the ERM band in 1993.
Source: Bank of England Quarterly Bulletin (November 1993).

for the non-system and the ERM, substantial modifications to deter speculation were attempted. In this section we briefly consider the relative scale of speculative transactions on the foreign exchange markets, explain the reasons for the rapid growth in speculation over the last 30 years, and consider the arguments for and against speculation as a defensible form of economic activity.

In section 14.5 we explained that the underlying supply and demand structures of the foreign exchange market were derived from the contours of international trade and investment. A currency is supplied to the market because, for example, its (domestic) holders wish to buy imports for which foreign currencies are required; the demand for the currency arises from the foreign demand for domestic output. To buy this output, foreign residents need the domestic currency in which it is priced. Despite the presence of speculative transactions, it is still reasonable to interpret the basis of the foreign exchange markets in trade and investment terms because such transactions guide the *long-term* movements of currencies. However, the contemporary scale of speculative transactions illustrates their latent and occasionally exercised capacity to engineer substantial shorter-term exchange rate oscillations. It has recently been estimated that trade and investment based transactions on the foreign exchanges now account for only one-fifth of total foreign exchange business, and that most of the rest is given over to speculation. This means that in a typical working week the foreign exchange requirements of *world* trade and investment can be satisfied in one day, leaving the other four free for speculative activity. But where does the money for this – what is sometimes called the world's biggest casino – come from? The answer lies in the spectacular growth of the *Eurocurrency markets* over the last 30 years.

Briefly, the Eurocurrency markets grew out of desire on the part of governments, banks and firms to hold currency deposits beyond the regulatory control of issuing authorities. The first example involved dollar deposits by the old Soviet Union in British banks in London in the 1950s. In the climate of the Cold War, the Soviet Union was anxious to keep its dollar reserve beyond the reach of the American authorities. The banks then lent on these dollars in the normal commercial way. In the 1960s, as American banking regulations were tightened, the attraction of the Euro*dollar* market increased. Dollars from this source could be used in ways denied to banks in the United States. Following the 1973–74 and 1979 oil price rises, OPEC[11] members too made substantial deposits in the Eurodollar market. Indeed 'offshore' banking in order to escape domestic monetary regulation became established for many 'key' currencies and spread to other European centres, such as Paris and Frankfurt, and to financial centres in other parts of the world. In the mid 1990s the size of the Eurocurrency market was estimated to be of the order of $8 trillion. This is the pot from which speculative activity in the foreign exchange markets is financed. When we couple the rapid growth in unregulated offshore banking with the increasing technological sophistication of the financial markets, the basis of the new 'global' casino is clearly apparent.

With its obvious connotations of substantial risk – even recklessness – the word 'casino' is often used pejoratively in the literature. But is this the appropriate way in which to characterize currency speculation? The noted champion of flexible exchange rates, Milton Friedman, thinks not. In his view, speculation is actually a source of *stability* – rather than instability – in the foreign exchange markets. Friedman argues that because speculators are well informed, they will be aware of the long-term exchange rates generally appropriate to the economic performances of countries. Accordingly, they may reasonably be expected to sell a currency for which depreciation is economically warranted *but*, as it *nears* its sustainable level, they will stop selling and perhaps even buy. This means that speculation actually serves to put a higher *floor* under the currency than would be present if the market was wholly trade centred. For a currency that is liable to appreciate, the same kind of analysis puts a lower *ceiling* in place.

Against this argument for speculators as economic social workers, helping currencies to find their appropriate place in the world, there is the view that because currency turbulence is inimical to trade, and as speculation fosters turbulence, speculation is of itself an economic 'bad'. From this perspective, it is far better to manage exchange rate movements so that they both conform to the secular drift of long-term trade performance and retain the kind of short-term stability conducive to trade development and wider economic growth. Whether this is best done through managed flexibility or through a fixed but adjustable exchange rate system is an open question.

14.9 European monetary union

We conclude this chapter with a brief overview of the issue of European monetary union (EMU). What kind of context does the preceding discussion provide for the notion of a *single currency* in Europe? Given the advent of the euro in 1999, there can in fact be no exchange rate fluctuations inside the euro zone region formed by participant

[11] The Organization of Petroleum Exporting Countries, founded in 1960.

Euro symbol

countries and, moreover, the balance of payments relationships that formerly existed between these countries now appear in a wholly different form. Why are such developments thought desirable, and what are the possible costs of a single currency in Europe?

The first thing to say is that we have been part way down this road before. In 1970 the *Werner Plan* anticipated that monetary union for the six original members of the European Economic Community (EEC) would be completed by 1980.[12] However, the resurgence of worldwide inflation over the course of the 1970s prompted differing policy responses amongst the six, and this prevented the kind of monetary policy convergence and gradual tightening of exchange rates that was to presage full monetary union. Present European ambitions for monetary union were revived in the EU's Single European Act (SEA) in 1986. As discussed in Chapter 2, section 2.5, this was the legislation that provided for the European single market. Recognizing that a *fully* integrated market requires as high a degree of monetary coherence as possible, the SEA committed member states to the principle of a single currency. Recall the *integration argument* for fixed exchange rates discussed in section 14.6. This states that a market will operate most efficiently and competitively when it is served by one currency. In section 14.6, we used the hypothetical example of the USA to show that the presence of different regional currencies inside the American economy would be likely to prompt the fragmentation of markets, reducing efficiency and competition to levels below those prevailing when the single national currency – the dollar – is employed. The SEA simply applied the same principle to Europe as a whole: that the evolution of a *single market* in Europe should be mirrored by the emergence of a *single currency* in Europe.

The details of EMU were clarified by the *Delors Report* (1989) and the *Maastricht Treaty* (1991). The Delors Report set the tone for the general form and evolution of monetary union, while the Maastricht Treaty formally endorsed Delors in its key respects and established the timetable and criteria for the introduction of the single currency. The Delors Report laid down three important and interconnected principles. The first concerned the nature of the new European Central Bank (ECB) that would oversee EU monetary policy upon the advent of the single currency. This institution would *replace* the various national central banks that had hitherto been responsible for the conduct of policy in each EU country. Thus it would set the *one* European interest rate and manage the exchange rate of the new single currency against others outside the EU. What we might term the 'general disposition' of the ECB would therefore be of crucial importance. The Delors Report left no room for doubt as to what this should be. The ECB would be modelled on the German Bundesbank; it would, in other words, be committed to *price stability* and would operate *independently*, free of political control as exercised by either national governments or EU authorities. Because the ambition is for the single currency to exhibit a tendency towards low inflation, rectitude in monetary policy (on the part of the ECB) would have to be matched by similar parsimony in the conduct of fiscal policy, which is to remain in the hands of national governments. The second principle of the Delors Report was therefore that national budget deficits in the EU should be reduced and that national fiscal policies should be set on a path of convergence. Finally, the Report recognized that setting an austere tone for the conduct of macroeconomic policy at the European level would have negative implications for employment prospects, particularly in the less economically advanced regions of the EU, such as parts of

[12] The original members of the EEC were: West Germany, France, Italy, Holland, Belgium and Luxembourg.

Portugal, Greece, southern Italy and some northern areas of the British Isles. The third and final principle of Delors was therefore that EU *structural intervention funds* be doubled in size. The purpose of these funds is to assist the economic development of EU regions in chronic decline.

Building upon the Delors Report, the Maastricht Treaty agreed that full monetary union would begin on 1 January 1999 for those EU nations able to meet a series of economic *convergence criteria*. Full EMU would involve the irrevocable fixing of national exchange rates with a view to their replacement by the single currency – the euro – by 2002. The convergence criteria established at Maastricht were:

- that the inflation rate in each national economy should not exceed that of the average of the best three EU national performances by more than 1.5 per cent

- that long-term interest rates in each national economy should not exceed the average of the lowest three rates in the EU by more than 2 per cent

- that the indebtedness of national governments should be limited, expressed as either a 3 per cent ceiling on annual budget deficits, or a ceiling on accumulated debt equivalent to 60 per cent of GDP

- that national currencies must be maintained in the *narrow* (that is, 2.25 per cent) band of the ERM for two years, without undue tensions arising.

The position established at Maastricht was that, for a country to be entitled to participate in monetary union, all four criteria would have to be met. However, developments after 1991, not least the successive crises of the ERM, prompted the emergence of more flexible interpretations. Thus the exchange rate criterion was ultimately based on the post-1993 version of the ERM, with its much wider margins of fluctuation, and there was tacit acceptance of 'creative accounting' on the part of some governments in order to allow them to clear the indebtedness hurdles. It is not unreasonable to conclude, on the basis of these manoeuvres, that the wider *political will* that favoured monetary union in Europe came to override what were perceived as narrower technical objections to this process.

On 1 May 1998, of those countries deemed to have met the Maastricht criteria, 11 elected to proceed to EMU. These were: Austria, Belgium, Finland, France, Germany, Ireland, Italy, Luxembourg, Netherlands, Portugal and Spain. Of the remaining EU member states, the UK, Sweden and Denmark decided against joining in this 'first wave', and Greece failed to meet the convergence criteria. The British government's position is that a *successful* single currency in Europe would be of benefit to those who subscribe to it. Thus, in principle, Britain is committed to the EMU project. However, despite the fact that the UK economy satisfied the Maastricht convergence criteria (except for participation in the ERM), the government considered that the business cycles in the UK and Europe were too far apart to allow British participation at the inception of the euro. At the time the decision had to be made about joining, relatively high interest rates in the UK were deemed necessary to curb inflationary pressures there, while elsewhere in Europe interest rates were generally lower. Participation in EMU in the first wave could have saddled the British economy with an interest rate regime inappropriate to prevailing British economic conditions. Eventually, the government expects that the UK economic cycle will become more closely matched with that generally evident in Europe. Participation in EMU – following a referendum – will *then* be the right thing to do. However, in the government's view, the UK is some distance away from this position.

What then are the great advantages of a single currency in Europe: the bigger prize that has allowed some of the 'technicalities' of Maastricht to be swept aside? We saw in Chapter 2, section 2.5, how the European single market was conceived as the EU's response to the fragmentation of the *customs union* created by the 1957 Treaty of Rome. Recall that the poorer collective performance of the EU economy, relative to the USA and Japan in particular, had prompted concerns in the EU that it had lost something of its competitive edge. This was to be restored by raising the level of economic *integration* in the EU: substituting the customs union for a single market. The addition of the single currency will entail even *further* integration and, its proponents claim, will confer specific benefits on Europe as a whole. The most important of these include, at the 'macro' level, a stronger presence in the international monetary system provided for by the euro than was enjoyed by most national EU currencies. If it begins to eclipse the dollar as the world's key currency, the financial markets may accept lower interest rate premiums as the price of holding the euro: this, of course, means a lower euro zone interest rate than would otherwise prevail and consequent stimuli to investment and consumption in Europe. In micro terms, the single currency has necessarily eliminated the transaction costs associated with exchanging the many different currencies that formerly circulated in the euro zone. Similarly, it has ended the information uncertainties that arise from the denomination of prices in many different currencies in the euro zone market. Because all prices are expressed in euros, producers and consumers are working with clearer price signals, and this will strengthen competitive processes in the euro zone.

The single currency has two main types of cost associated with it. First, there are the obvious once and for all costs of redenomination. The financial and wider economic systems of each euro zone country were tailored to national currencies. The introduction of the euro has required the recalibration of all these systems. The second 'cost' is that potentially associated with the loss of macroeconomic policy independence. Inside the euro zone interest rates are set by the European Central Bank (ECB) in acknowledgement of the prevailing economic conditions of the zone as a whole. What happens if (say) euro zone interest rates appear too low given circumstances in one particular country? Arguably, this was the case in Ireland when the euro was introduced. Irish interest rates fell from 6 to 3 per cent overnight when the Irish central bank's monetary writ passed to the ECB. In the ECB's view, sluggish economic conditions in the euro zone demanded the lower rate, but the Irish authorities had thought that the fast-growing Irish economy needed the higher rate in order to keep inflationary pressures in check. Because the ECB sets euro zone interest rates, Ireland had an interest rate imposed upon it that its policy-makers clearly thought inappropriate.[13]

This example illustrates what is sometimes referred to as the 'one size fits all' problem of euro zone interest rates, and indeed of macro policy more generally. What the advent of the euro appears to demand is that ECB decisions should suit all euro participants. However, that this may not be happening at first – as our Irish example illustrates – is not necessarily a fundamental weakness of the euro. This is because the long-term success of the euro is dependent upon the proper integration of the euro zone nations. They need to behave much more like *one* economy in the future; if they do, a unified macro policy framework will actually be appropriate rather than a potential difficulty.

[13] In normal circumstances, interest rate movements in the advanced economies are usually of the order of a fraction of one per cent. A cut from 6 to 3 per cent was therefore relatively sharp.

This issue is neatly summed up by the question of whether or not the euro zone can become an **optimum currency area**. Briefly, an optimum currency area is a grouping of economies or regions within which goods, capital and labour markets are sufficiently integrated and flexible to allow the effective operation of a single currency across them. Let us return to our example of the Irish economy to illustrate the significance of this concept. In Ireland, already fast economic growth was further stimulated by the lowering of interest rates from 6 to 3 per cent when Ireland joined the euro zone at its inception. On the face of it this appears to be a regrettable development. However, what if the euro zone labour market was flexible to the extent that unemployed people from, say, a hypothetically depressed Spain began to migrate to Ireland attracted by relatively high wages – the product of full employment – and greater job opportunities? Moreover, what if at the same time, encouraged by EU regional policy, firms began to seek out locations in Spain in which to invest because slower growth there had lowered investment costs and because, unlike perhaps in Ireland, there were no labour shortages? In these circumstances, the differences in economic growth between Ireland and Spain would not be a major issue because labour and capital market flexibility would tend to reduce them. Labour would gravitate to Ireland, thus 'cooling' its economy; new investment would tend to focus on low-cost Spain, driving up its economic prospects. This also means that Ireland and any other euro zone economy or region can 'live' with whatever ECB macroeconomic policy framework is set. The euro zone economies should already be reasonably well integrated because of the Maastricht criteria, and even where they are not the euro zone – if indeed it is an optimum currency area – will serve to erode, via market processes and lubricated by the euro itself, the differences between them. This, of course, assumes that the architects of the euro have designed the new currency and its wider framework well. If they have not, and the euro zone is a poorly integrated weak approximation of an optimum currency area, then the experience for participating nations is likely to be an enduringly uneven one. Ultimately, if the euro zone is not something close to an optimum currency area then, economically at least, the euro may be judged a failure.

Finally, a word on the *robustness* of the euro. During its first year of existence, the new currency showed distinct signs of weakness to the extent that, on the eve of its first birthday, the euro fell to parity with the US dollar. One euro was worth only one dollar compared with the 1.19 dollars it had been worth at its launch (see Fig. 14.6). At the time, there was some press comment that the currency might actually disintegrate and, still more, that the euro's weakness would make Britain less likely to adopt it. If we briefly revisit the principles of exchange rate theory introduced earlier in this chapter, we shall see that such observations rather miss the point. The euro's early weakness was probably, at least in part, the result of market nervousness over an entirely new currency. The fact that it combined a formerly strong currency – the deutschmark – with habitually weaker ones naturally made agents in the foreign exchange markets a little hesitant in demanding it. There were also signs that the dip in the euro's value to dollar parity reflected some concerns about an apparent loosening of fiscal policy in Germany. However, as we have demonstrated, the long-term health of a currency is strongly conditioned by the economic and trade performance of the coun-

"See how the Euro falls faster than the stone"

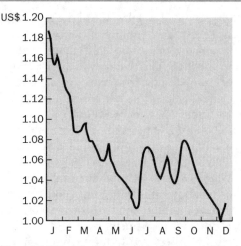

Fig. 14.6 The dollar to euro exchange rate, 1999.
Source: Guardian 7 December 1999.

try that issues it. In the long term it is the economic and export performance of the integrated European economy that underpins the demand for the euro on the foreign exchanges. Though their effects can be destabilizing, short-term adverse movements in currency values are unlikely to turn into secular trends of weakness so long as the issuing economy itself performs reasonably well in an international context. Clearly, long-term considerations are also those that will govern whether or not other economies elect to join the euro zone.

14.10 The balance of payments, exchange rates and business

Let us conclude this chapter with a discussion of the relevance of the balance of payments and exchange rates to business. In section 14.3 we saw how balance of payments imbalance in the world economy, if it foments a rise in protectionist sentiment, has the potential to impact adversely upon other economies, many of which may not themselves be involved in the initial payments problems. Here we consider the more localized problem of the policy reaction to payments imbalance by the authorities in an individual economy. What implications has such *balance of payments policy* for business?

An initial issue here is the nature of the exchange rate regime under which the economy is operating. Consider first balance of payments imbalance under fixed exchange rates.

Fixed exchange rates

Under fixed exchange rates we know that balance of payments imbalance will usually be tackled by some combination of expenditure reduction policy and expenditure-switching policy. In the case of a deficit, this involves slowing down the rate of growth in order to reduce the demand for imports, and currency devaluation to both lower the price of exports in foreign markets and increase the price of imports in the domestic market. Assuming the Marshall–Lerner condition holds and that domestic industry has sufficient capacity to respond to the demand stimulus resulting from the devaluation, the deficit should be eroded.

For some domestic firms, the implications of this policy response will be positive. Those that sell exclusively into foreign markets may find their position improved as the devaluation makes their products cheaper in comparison with goods and services sold by foreign competitors. For firms active in the domestic market, outcomes are more ambiguous. On the one hand, they may find their price competitiveness improves as the devaluation raises the price of imported goods, but, on the other, the domestic market as a whole will come under pressure as economic growth slows and demand slackens. For domestic firms that use imported commodities in their own production processes and sell into the domestic market, matters are even more serious. The devaluation raises the price of imports, putting upward pressure on their own final prices, and they find the size of their market shrinking.

Flexible exchange rates

Under flexible exchange rates remember that all the strain of balance of payments imbalance is borne by the exchange rate. For example, should a deficit begin to emerge, excess supply of the domestic currency on the foreign exchanges will tend to promote a depreciation of the currency in question. In turn, this alters export and import prices in a manner that favours firms in the 'depreciating' country. The main difference between balance of payments deficit correction under fixed and floating exchange rates is thus the absence of any need for expenditure reduction under floating rates. For domestic firms this has the obvious advantage that there will be no depression of demand in the domestic market.

Fixed versus flexible exchange rates in a business context

Our discussion would seem to suggest that, from a business perspective, flexible rates might be the preferred option. However, there is one additional issue that complicates matters. It is a commonplace that many firms prefer stable economic conditions to less stable ones. Business planning – decisions about how much to produce, how much to invest, which markets to target, and so on – is clearly best conducted in an environment of certainty. Now, given that a major source of instability and uncertainty for business has its roots in currency fluctuations, it may be that business interests are best served by the active management of exchange rates. In other words, fixed exchange rates may be preferred by firms because they help foster more stable conditions for business.

Yet it is also the case that firms can protect themselves from the vagaries of currency movements by using forward markets for currencies. Consider the following example. If a German manufacturer of printing machinery contracts to export a machine, priced in euros, to a British printing firm in six months' time, the British firm knows the price it will have to pay in sterling today. However, the British firm cannot know what the euro/pound exchange rate will be in six months' time. Perhaps the euro will weaken against sterling, making the sterling price of the machine lower when it is actually delivered. Alternatively, sterling could weaken, making the sterling price faced by the firm on delivery higher. This kind of uncertainty can be eliminated if the British firm agrees a forward exchange rate with its bank for sterling against the euro at the same time as the contract for the machine itself is signed (there will, of course, be a charge for this service by the bank). So, when the machine arrives, so too do the euros required to pay for it at an exchange rate the printing firm has agreed in advance. It seems then that firms can insulate themselves from some of the uncertainty associated with exchange rate variability under a flexible exchange rate regime. However, this option is not costless, and forward markets usually range only up to 180 days into the future; certainly beyond a year or two they are much more expensive to participate in. This means that, for example, it is difficult to ensure that an income stream earned in a foreign economy will not be vulnerable to depreciation in the long term against the domestic currency.

What are we to make of this process of argument and counter argument? Are fixed or flexible rates better from a business perspective? Possibly the best conclusion is to accept that these are open questions. Currently, the world economy is *generally* organized along flexible lines but many countries choose to manage their currencies either alongside or in partnership with other currencies and countries. We might rationalize this approach as one that recognizes that, while it is highly unlikely that the world's currencies will ossify into a set of permanently stable parities with one another, many countries do find some advantage in a degree of currency management.

◼ Summary

◆ An economy's balance of payments and its exchange rate are inextricably linked. In theory, a floating exchange rate will automatically produce balance of payments balance; policy may then be concentrated on other objectives free of any concern for the external account. However, where exchange rates are fixed or managed, the emergence of balance of payments disequilibria requires active forms of policy correction. Expenditure reduction involves internal deflation, and invokes movement out of deficit by virtue of lower domestic aggregate demand and a reduced demand for imports. In the face of a deficit, the second form of policy, expenditure switching, usually involves currency devaluation or depreciation, which improves the price competitiveness of exports and import substitutes.

◆ Since 1945 the world economy has relied both upon fixed exchange rates (under the Bretton Woods System) and flexible rates (under the 'non-system'). The non-system has, however, not been characterized by freely floating exchange rates. Indeed, at times during the 1980s exchange rates were collectively managed by the major industrialized nations. Moreover, inside the non-system, regional fixed exchange rate regimes, such as the ERM, have been developed. The ERM was succeeded in 1999 by monetary union in Europe.

◆ From a business perspective there is no definitive answer to the question of whether fixed or flexible exchange rate regimes are preferable.

◼ Key terms

◆ Current account
◆ Capital account

◆ Autonomous transactions

◆ Accommodating transactions

◆ Balance of payments disequilibria

◆ Exchange rate

◆ Depreciation

◆ Appreciation

◆ Flexible exchange rates

◆ Fixed exchange rates

◆ Expenditure reduction policy

◆ Expenditure-switching policy

◆ Currency speculation

◆ European monetary union

Self-test questions

True (t) or false (f)

1. Foreign direct investment is recorded in the current account of the balance of payments.

2. Accommodating transactions are those undertaken for their own sake.

3. If a country runs a surplus on autonomous transactions, it has a net monetary claim on foreign residents.

4. Balance of payments disequilibria are usually only a problem when they become persistent.

5. When the dollar falls in value, US exports become more expensive.

6. When the pound sterling increases in value against the euro, holidays in France become cheaper for UK residents.

7. A dirty float occurs when the value of a currency moves wildly up and down.

8. The Bretton Woods system was centred on the US dollar.

9. Some economists think that currency speculators exert a stabilizing influence on foreign currency markets.

10. One 'cost' of EMU is the loss of the option for individual euro zone countries to engage in unilateral devaluation.

Complete the following sentences by inserting the missing word(s)

1. Balance of payments disequilibria are a problem only when they become ____.

2. An exchange rate is the ____ of one currency expressed in terms of another.

3. Balance of payments deficits on current account can be tackled by either ____ or ____.

4. For a devaluation to prompt an improvement in the current account, the ____ must be observed.

5. Exchange rates are determined by the laws of ____ and ____.

6. Short-term movements in exchange rates may be caused by the activities of ____ and the interest rate policies of ____.

7. The two main arguments for fixed exchange rates are the ____ and the ____.

8. The Bretton Woods system was undermined by the manifestation of the _____.

9. The emergence of worldwide _____ in the early 1970s necessitated a more flexible exchange rate environment.

10. The 1985 Plaza Agreement achieved a managed _____ of the dollar.

Questions for discussion

◆ Outline the structure of the balance of payments accounts.

◆ Explain the significance of autonomous and accommodating transactions in the balance of payments.

◆ What is meant by balance of payments surplus and deficit, and which general forms of policy are appropriate to each?

◆ How are exchange rates determined?

◆ Explain the differences between fixed and flexible exchange rate systems and the advantages and disadvantages of each.

◆ What is the economic case for the euro?

Further reading

Jepma, C.J., H. Jager and E. Kamphuis, *Introduction to International Economics* (Harlow: Longman, 1996). Chapter 2 provides a complementary introduction to balance of payments theory.

Internet links

The *European Monetary Institute*, the European Central Bank, has a website that will keep you up to date with the continuing development of the euro and euro zone economies. The site can be found at: **http://www.ecb.int/**

Multinational firms

CHAPTER 15

Key issues

▶ Why are multinationals considered important in the modern economy?

▶ In which of the world's regions and industries are multinationals most active?

▶ Why do firms become multinational?

▶ What forms of policy have emerged in response to the growing significance of multinationals?

Contents

15.1 Introduction

We begin with some issues of definition. This chapter is about **multinational** firms. These are firms that *own and control* production in more than one country. We have already discussed some aspects of multinational activity in earlier parts of this book. For example, in Chapter 14, section 14.2, we learned that the financial account of the UK balance of payments contains two main forms of cross-border investment: *foreign direct investment* and *portfolio investment*.

- *Foreign direct investment* (FDI) entails either buying or selling firms abroad, or the establishment of entirely new production facilities abroad. Thus, when (say) the German electronics manufacturer Siemens buys an American electronics firm, or sets up a new electronics plant in the USA, it is engaging in FDI. Siemens' motive, we may reasonably assume, would be to increase profits.

- *Foreign portfolio investment* involves buying shares in foreign firms. If a British pension fund purchases a shareholding in Siemens, it is adding to its share portfolio. The objective of the pension fund manager is to maximize the income stream from the portfolio in order to pay pensions to members of the pension fund when they retire.

Multinational activity falls into the first of these two categories: it concerns FDI. The central difference between FDI and portfolio investment is that FDI requires the *active* management of production facilities abroad. When it purchases or sets up a foreign plant, Siemens, metaphorically, must 'roll up its sleeves' and engage in the

Multinational: A firm that owns and controls assets in more than one country.

Transnational: A firm that owns and controls assets in more than one country, and which organizes production without regard to any particular nation state.

usual entrepreneurial tasks of production, distribution, marketing and so on that yield profit. Portfolio investment is not like this. Beyond the basic decision to buy or sell shares, it is primarily *passive* in nature. The portfolio investor takes no responsibility for the running of the firms in which he or she has an interest; the only concern is to maintain an investment portfolio that maximizes share income. Recall our opening definition of multinational investment: it arises where there is ownership and *control* of foreign production; portfolio investment implies only ownership.

There is a second issue of definition to be considered here. The term **transnational** is sometimes used instead of multinational. This may be because the two are thought to be interchangeable, or because transnational means something different and it is employed to this effect. In fact these terms do have different meanings, and it is therefore incorrect to use them as synonyms. A transnational firm is one that has no identifiable national base: it organizes the production facilities it owns without regard to national affiliation or interest. A transnational is then a truly *global* firm. Multinational firms, by contrast, maintain national affiliations. Earlier we referred to Siemens as a *German* multinational. This is not just a means of labelling. Siemens has material characteristics that make it identifiably German. For example, in 1997, one-third of Siemens' sales, just over half of its employment and 62 per cent of its assets were in Germany. A visit to the Siemens website (see Internet links at the end of this chapter) will confirm that it is headquartered in Munich and Berlin and that research and development facilities are also maintained in Germany. This makes the German economy central to Siemens' corporate strategy. Siemens does have very significant international interests in other parts of the world, but this firm would almost certainly *not* be in a position to develop these comfortably as alternatives to its 'home' operations were, for instance, the German economy to enter some catastrophic recession, or the German government to implement economic policies by which it felt profoundly threatened.

Siemens: a German multinational
© Siemens

Note that the focus of this chapter is upon multinationals. This is because, in our view, the transnational firm is still a rarity in the international economy. Multinational firms are increasing in scale and number, but it is debatable whether many have yet shaken off the national contexts in which they have long been grounded. We develop this theme further in the course of the chapter.

Why look at multinationals?

The multinational corporation (MNC) is of interest because it is arguably one of the most important and fastest-growing agents in the international economy. MNCs now account for about 25 per cent of world output.[1] In 1998 the *foreign* sales of MNCs (that is, those made outside the 'home' economy) amounted to $11 trillion; in comparison world exports were valued at $7 trillion. As the United Nations Conference on Trade and Development (UNCTAD) *World Investment Report 1999* points out, this means that consumers in foreign markets rely more on MNCs for the delivery of goods and services than they do on international trade.

There are now some 60 000 MNCs that own and control more than 500 000 affiliated enterprises in foreign countries. Most MNCs are headquartered in the developed countries, but they are also present in the developing economies and economies in transition. The largest 100 MNCs have been identified by UNCTAD as particularly significant in terms of their contribution to international production. Taken as a whole, this group sold products worth $2.1 trillion in foreign markets in 1997, accounting for 22 per cent of total MNC overseas sales. In the same year they employed 6 million people in foreign enterprises. The largest of the giant MNCs is the US firm General Electric. In 1997, General Electric had assets worth $304 billion, of which $97.4 billion were invested in foreign economies. In the same year this firm made worldwide sales of $90.8 billion and it employed more than a quarter of a million people. To put this into some kind of context, imagine that General Electric was a country. Taking its total sales as the factor of rank against the GDPs of nation states, it would have been 41st in the list of the world's biggest economies in 1997, above countries such as Ireland, Chile and New Zealand.[2] On the same basis, the MNC with the world's highest sales – General Motors – would have ranked 25th, higher than, for example, Denmark, Norway and Israel.

Having briefly reflected on the sheer scale of MNCs, let us now consider the speed at which they are growing. In Chapter 13, section 13.4, we argued that the primary motor of the postwar boom (1945–70) was the unprecedented growth in international trade. However, as Paul Hirst and Graham Thompson have pointed out (see guide to further reading at the end of this chapter), the rate of trade growth itself has, since the start of the 1980s, been eclipsed by FDI flows. In other words, overseas investment by MNCs is now the most dynamic element in the world economy. From Table 15.1 it can be seen that between 1981 and 1990, while world output and trade grew at annual average rates of 3.4 and 4.7 per cent respectively, FDI outflows increased at a rate of 34 per cent (1983–90). Although the rate of growth of FDI outflows slowed over the 1990s (10.8 per cent between 1991 and 1998), this was still above the rates of growth of world output and trade at 3.1 and 6.1 per cent respectively. The

---

[1] The source for this and much of the evidence presented in this chapter is the United Nations Conference on Trade and Development (UNCTAD) *World Investment Report 1999*.
[2] Comparisons of this kind are not unproblematic. GDP is a measure of *value added*, whereas a firm's sales are not.

Table 15.1 World output, trade and FDI outflows (ten-year averages) per cent

	1981–1990	1991–2000[a]
Output	3.4	3.1
Trade	4.7	6.1
FDI outflows	34.0[b]	10.8[c]

[a] Includes estimates and projections.
[b] 1983–1990.
[c] 1991–1998.
Source: UNCTAD *World Investment Report 1999*; IMF *World Economic Outlook* (May 1999); Hirst, P. and G. Thompson *Globalization in Question* (Cambridge: Polity Press, 1996).

exceptionally high rates of FDI outflow expansion over the 1980s can be attributed to the relaxation by several governments of effective controls on overseas investment during this period. Once restrictions were lifted (in 1981 in the case of the UK) there was almost certain to be something of a surge in FDI activity as firms took advantage of the freedoms and business opportunities newly available to them in overseas markets.

There can be little doubt then that MNCs are important: collectively they produce one quarter of the world's output, and their sales in foreign markets are much higher than the total value of world trade. At the same time their significance is increasing compared with other interests in the world economy: most obviously, they are growing faster than individual nation states. This means that the largest MNCs are leaving most of the world's nations, whose incomes they already eclipse, further and further behind. Measured by the ratio of total sales to GDP, General Motors is now 'bigger' than Denmark, more than 10 times 'bigger' than Guatemala and 100 times 'bigger' than Armenia, and the gaps between them and it are on present trends likely to continue to increase.

Having established the significance of MNCs in the world economy, the remainder of this chapter concentrates on three main issues:

- The changing patterns of MNC activity: what are the principal locations of MNCs, and in which industries are they most heavily represented?

- Why do MNCs exist, and what are the specific economic forces that give rise to them?

- What, if anything, should governments do about MNCs? Do MNCs need to be encouraged as a source of investment and jobs, or is there a need to try to exercise a degree of control over such large concentrations of private economic power?

15.2 Patterns of multinational activity

Regional distribution

We saw from Table 15.1 that MNC activity as represented by FDI flows has been one of the fastest-growing forms of international economic activity since the early 1980s.

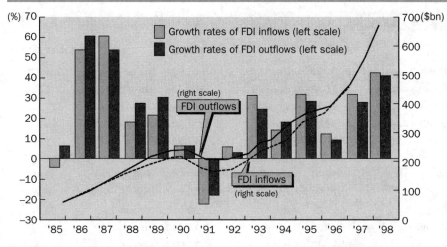

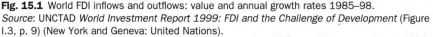

Fig. 15.1 World FDI inflows and outflows: value and annual growth rates 1985–98.
Source: UNCTAD *World Investment Report 1999: FDI and the Challenge of Development* (Figure I.3, p. 9) (New York and Geneva: United Nations).

Fig. 15.1 allows us to reflect on FDI flows in more detail over the period 1985–98. The right-hand scale of Fig. 15.1 indicates the *absolute size* of FDI inflows and outflows measured in $ billion. In principle, world FDI inflows and outflows measured on an annual basis should be equal, but differences in methodologies and measurement conventions mean that in practice they are not.[3] Except for 1991, when inflows and outflows fell, the figure shows that FDI has consistently expanded year on year since 1985, with particularly marked increases in 1986, 1987 and 1998. The left-hand scale indicates that the percentage increases in inflows for these years were 55, 60 and 39 per cent respectively. The pause in FDI expansion at the beginning of the 1990s can be accounted for by the slower growth rates experienced in some of the major MNC 'home' nations at this time – the United States, the UK, France and Canada in particular (see Table 9.1).

Fig. 15.1 (right-hand scale) indicates that FDI inflows and outflows in the world economy reached $644 billion and $649 billion respectively in 1998. Of total inflows, 71.5 per cent went to the world's developed economies, while of total outflows 91.6 per cent came from the developed economies. On this evidence, the world's richest economies clearly both *host* and *sponsor* most of the world's MNC activity. This might surprise some readers, given the popular impression that multinationals have been steadily forsaking the developed countries in favour of investment in alternative developing country locations; and, indeed, that economic progress amongst many developing nations has allowed them to begin to challenge the developed countries on their own terms – for example, by fostering their own MNC activity. We have more to say about MNCs and developing countries below, but for the present let us elaborate further upon the developed country experience.

Table 15.2 describes cumulative FDI flows for the OECD countries between 1990 and 1998. The table allows us to discern which countries, amongst the group already responsible for by far the biggest share of the world's MNC activity, are the 'most senior players' in this respect. Several countries appear near the top of each of the three columns in Table 15.2. The USA and the UK are the world's top two recipients

---

[3] Note, however, that the two series move in close parallel.

Table 15.2 Cumulative FDI flows involving OECD countries, 1990–98 ($ million)

	Inflows		Outflows		Net outflows (+)
United States	605 052	United States	662 652	Germany	258 379
United Kingdom	240 513	United Kingdom	364 733	Japan	214 353
France	178 323	Germany	318 640	United Kingdom	124 220
Belgium-Luxmbg.	105 859	France	257 407	Netherlands	79 836
Netherlands	101 028	Japan	227 984	France	79 085
Spain	84 039	Netherlands	180 864	Switzerland[a]	61 584
Mexico	68 576	Canada	93 565	United States	57 600
Sweden	67 789	Switzerland[a]	83 657	Italy	40 346
Canada	66 888	Sweden	80 010	Canada	26 677
Germany	60 260	Belgium-Luxmbg	79 540	Finland	18 942
Australia	55 603	Italy	71 624	Sweden	12 212
Italy	31 278	Spain	50 984	Korea	9 350
Greece[a]	26 823	Finland	37 736	Norway	3 021
Denmark	24 456	Australia	27 636	Denmark	210
Poland	22 909	Korea	24 931	Iceland	−75
Switzerland[a]	22 073	Denmark	24 657	Austria	−3 358
Norway	19 709	Norway	22 730	Turkey	−5 901
New Zealand	19 523	Austria	15 516	Portugal	−8 063
Austria	18 875	Portugal	8 029	Czech Republic	−9 856
Finland	18 794	New Zealand	4 079	Ireland	−10 361
Hungary	17 193	Turkey	1 442	New Zealand	−15 444
Portugal	16 091	Hungary	1 012	Hungary	−16 181
Korea	15 582	Czech Republic	500	Poland	−22 546
Japan	13 631	Poland	363	Belgium-Luxmbg	−26 319
Ireland	10 361	Iceland	310	Greece[a]	−26 823
Czech Republic	10 356	Greece[a]	na	Australia	−27 967
Turkey	7 343	Ireland	na	Spain	−33 055
Iceland	385	Mexico	na	Mexico	−68 576
OECD	**1 928 899**		**2 640 600**		**711 701**

[a] 1990–97
na: data not available
Source: OECD *Financial Market Trends*. Reproduced by permission of the OECD.

and donors of FDI activity. Over the period covered by the table, these countries were responsible for 43.8 per cent of FDI inflows and 38.9 per cent of FDI outflows involving OECD countries. The top ten places in each of the three columns in Table 15.2 are taken by the long-established industrial countries, with the exception of Mexico, which comes seventh in the list of FDI recipients. Mexico's success in attracting MNC investment in the 1990s can be explained in part by its membership of NAFTA (see Chapter 13, section 13.5). NAFTA has encouraged US and Canadian MNCs to establish production facilities in Mexico, where labour costs are lower. The output of these foreign affiliates can then be exported back to the USA and Canada

Table 15.3 Regional distribution of FDI inflows and outflows, 1995–98 (per cent)

	Inflows				Outflows			
	1995	1996	1997	1998	1995	1996	1997	1998
Developed countries	**63.4**	**58.8**	**58.9**	**71.5**	**85.3**	**84.2**	**85.6**	**91.6**
Western Europe	37.0	32.1	29.1	36.9	48.9	53.7	50.6	62.6
European Union	35.1	30.4	27.2	35.7	44.7	47.9	46.0	59.5
Other western Europe	1.8	1.8	1.9	1.2	4.2	5.8	4.6	3.1
United States	17.9	21.3	23.5	30.0	25.7	19.7	23.1	20.5
Japan	–	0.1	0.7	0.5	6.3	6.2	5.5	3.7
Other developed countries	8.5	5.3	5.6	4.1	4.4	4.6	6.4	4.9
Developing countries	**32.5**	**37.7**	**37.2**	**25.8**	**14.5**	**15.5**	**13.7**	**8.1**
Africa	1.3	1.6	1.6	1.2	0.1	–	0.3	0.1
Latin America and Caribbean	10.0	12.9	14.7	11.1	2.1	1.9	3.3	2.4
Developing Europe	0.1	0.3	0.2	0.2	–	–	0.1	–
Asia	20.7	22.9	20.6	13.2	12.3	13.6	10.0	5.6
West Asia	–0.1	0.2	1.0	0.7	–0.2	0.6	0.4	0.3
Central Asia	0.4	0.6	0.7	0.5	–	–	–	–
S, E, & S.E. Asia	20.4	22.1	18.9	12.0	12.5	13.0	9.6	5.3
The Pacific	0.2	0.1	–	–	–	–	–	–
Central and Eastern Europe	**4.3**	**3.5**	**4.0**	**2.7**	**0.1**	**0.3**	**0.7**	**0.3**
World	**100**	**100**	**100**	**100**	**100**	**100**	**100**	**100**

Source: UNCTAD *World Investment Report 1999: FDI and the Challenge of Development* (Table I.3, p.20) (New York and Geneva: United Nations).

without any trade policy hindrance, given that NAFTA guarantees free trade between its members. The other notable feature of Table 15.2 is the appearance of Germany and Japan in the top two places in the net FDI outflows column. Both Germany and Japan are major sponsors of FDI outflows (third and fifth respectively in column 2) but they are much less susceptible to FDI inflows. Japan admitted only $13.6 billion in FDI between 1990 and 1998. In 1998 its share of world FDI inflows was only 0.5 per cent (see Table 15.3). There have been claims in the USA, which has been running a significant balance of payments deficit with Japan in recent years, that the apparent inability of foreign MNCs to make investments in the affluent Japanese market reflects *inter alia* protectionist policies on the part of the Japanese authorities. For example, in 1999, the Japanese government announced a freeze on the construction of large stores for periods up to at least 18 months (*Financial Times*, 23 February 1999). This may be thought to 'target' potential retailers from the US, some of which had made inroads into the Japanese market in the 1990s (see also Chapter 14, section 14.2).

Table 15.3 describes the regional distribution of FDI inflows and outflows in the world economy between 1995 and 1998. The table confirms the noted dominance of the developed countries in MNC activity. In turn, however, the so-called 'Triad' economies of the USA, the European Union (EU) and Japan were responsible for the bulk of developed country FDI flows. In 1998, for example, the Triad hosted 66.2 per cent of world FDI inflows and sponsored 83.7 per cent of world FDI outflows. For the developing countries, Table 15.3 suggests that the mid-to-late 1990s were years in which MNC investment was rising. In 1996 and 1997, for example, FDI inflows passed the threshold of a one-third share in the world inflows total. However, in 1998 this fell back to 25.8 per cent. UNCTAD argues that the drop has much to do with the most recent increases in FDI flows to the developed countries, but the effect of the Asian crisis of 1997 must also be taken into consideration – especially when it is noted that most of the reduction in the share of FDI inflows to the developing country group is accounted for by a reduction in south, east and south-east Asian inflows. The same case can be made when the 1998 fall in the already small share of FDI outflows from the developing countries is considered.

Table 15.3 shows that the FDI performance of Latin America and the Caribbean was also checked in 1998, but here the downturn in shares has been more modest than in Asia. Indeed, UNCTAD reports that FDI inflows into Latin America and the Caribbean *increased* in 1998 by 5 per cent over 1997 to $71 billion. Here then the loss in share of world inflows is wholly accounted for by the even greater increase in developed country FDI inflows. For the OECD countries, this was estimated to be of the order of 71 per cent.

FDI inflows into Africa in 1998 were $8.3 billion, down from a record $9.4 billion in 1997 and, again from Table 15.3, Africa's share of world FDI inflows fell to 1.2 per cent in 1998. UNCTAD attributes Africa's apparent inability to 'realize its potential' to misplaced and unfortunate perceptions amongst MNCs as to the opportunities that Africa affords.

Finally, for central and eastern Europe (CEE), Table 15.3 reveals a fall in the share of FDI inflows that parallels that experienced elsewhere in the non-developed world. However, as in the Latin American and Caribbean case, there is something of a mixed message behind this statistic. While the CEE countries do lose in terms of their share of FDI inflows, much of this is again accounted for by the surge in FDI inflows into the developed countries in 1998. UNCTAD reports that, excluding the Russian Federation, which suffered its own crisis in 1997 and where foreign investor confidence evaporated, the CEE economies attracted record FDI inflows in 1998 of $16 billion – a 25 per cent increase on the previous year.

To sum up, it appears that the overwhelming developed country interest in MNCs has yet to be seriously challenged. Progress in south east Asia has recently been held up by the crisis in that region. Increasing FDI inflows into Latin America and the Caribbean and the non-Russian Federation CEE economies are welcome but modest, and in any case are vastly overshadowed by the 1998 surge in MNC activity amongst the developed countries. It is to this fervour on the part of multinationals for the developed world that we now turn.

The growing importance of mergers and acquisitions[4]

Multinational activity is increasingly driven by the process of *merger and acquisition* (M&A). The OECD estimates that more than 60 per cent of FDI in the advanced countries is based on M&A. For some important economies the equivalent figure is even higher. For example, in the United States, about 80 per cent of FDI arises from

---

[4] This section draws heavily on the OECD's *Financial Market Trends*, No. 73 (June 1999).

Table 15.4 Top 20 buyer and seller countries in world M&A, 1998

Seller	Deals	Value ($ bn)	Buyer	Deals	Value ($ bn)
United States	849	201.2	United Kingdom	658	127.7
United Kingdom	560	86.1	United States	1440	124.8
Germany	364	36.7	Germany	369	60.9
Belgium	127	26.1	Canada	403	40.7
Brazil	162	24.6	France	356	40.5
France	320	23.1	Netherlands	358	38.7
Netherlands	165	18.3	Italy	94	15.2
Canada	240	15.3	Sweden	146	14.0
Australia	143	7.4	Switzerland	145	12.1
Japan	88	6.9	Spain	65	11.6
Switzerland	83	6.3	Australia	70	7.5
Korea	76	6.3	Japan	159	7.2
Sweden	102	6.1	Finland	105	6.0
Spain	149	5.7	South Africa	36	4.9
Italy	181	5.6	Ireland	76	4.1
Finland	70	5.3	Portugal	10	3.7
China	85	5.0	Bermuda	10	2.6
New Zealand	39	3.4	Hong Kong, China	50	2.3
Austria	37	3.1	Korea	10	2.2
Argentina	54	3.1	Belgium	120	2.0

Source: OECD *Financial Market Trends*. Reproduced by permission of the OECD.

M&A. This means that to understand multinational behaviour it is also necessary to understand the imperatives that drive M&A.

Table 15.4 lists the top 20 buying and selling countries in international M&A in 1998. As for FDI flows (see Table 15.2), the top two places are again taken by the USA and the UK. As the world's largest economy, the USA is traditionally the largest cross-border buyer and seller of firms, but in 1998 the UK took the top buyer's spot by virtue of the BP-Amoco merger. This was valued at $61 billion. Given that the total value of purchases of foreign firms by MNCs with a UK base amounted to $127 billion, the influence of very large transactions on data such as those presented in Table 15.4 is apparent.

We must note, however, that there is a certain dualism in M&A processes. We have seen the rising scale of FDI activity in the world economy compared with the much more modest increases in international trade (see Table 15.1). But increases in trade are *necessarily* associated with additional real economic activity – following the Ricardian model, specialization and trade call forth net increases in world output. M&A isn't like this. It implies not an increase but a *change in ownership* of productive capacity. This means that, on the basis of the figure above, about 60 per cent of multinational activity in the advanced economies involves buying existing foreign firms, rather than setting up new foreign branches to produce more output. On the other hand, even if all FDI was based on M&A, it would still mean the increasing internationalization of existing productive capacity, with all the implications that would necessarily follow. We discuss some of these implications in section 15.4 of this chapter.

The question arises: *why* has M&A activity increased in recent years? As UNCTAD notes, it appears to have yielded relatively poor results in profitability terms, particularly in certain industries, but the appetite of MNCs for foreign firms remains sharp. Part of the explanation for the popularity of M&As can be found in the continuing climate of market liberalization present in many advanced economies and regions. Trade and investment regimes have become more open, and processes of privatization and deregulation in formerly state owned or controlled sectors have presented MNCs with new opportunities for acquisition. At the same time, more intensive competition between MNCs has forced them to seek out new economies of scale and points of entry into important markets. Finally, in the new 'knowledge-based' international economy, MNCs have been forced to re-evaluate the technological environments in which they operate. M&A activity may be an effective way for MNCs to ensure that they do not lose ground in leading-edge technologies.

Box 15.1 describes M&A activity during the 1990s by *Lear Seating*, a car components manufacturer that illustrates some of the noted pressures behind this process. Lear Seating purchased the seating business of the Ford Motor Company in 1993 and was retained by Ford as a 'first tier supplier'. This gave Lear Seating a platform from which to develop similar relationships in new markets in other parts of the

---

Box 15.1

Lear Seating: becoming a preferred first tier supplier

In 1993 Lear Seating secured its position in the United States seat systems business by acquiring the North American seat cover and seat systems business of the Ford Motor Company. As part of the deal, Ford entered into a five-year supply agreement with Lear, and the latter assumed primary engineering responsibility for Ford's seating systems. Three years later Lear and Ford opened a joint research centre in Dearborn, Michigan. In 1994, a similar process enabled Lear to gain entry into the Italian market and to obtain preferred first tier supplier status with Fiat around the world. It also acquired a research centre in Turin. As the market advanced, Lear purchased Dunlop Cox Ltd (United Kingdom) for its ability to design and manufacture automobile electronic and manual seat adjusters.

A series of M&As and greenfield investments in South America in 1996 and 1997 further established Lear as a global player in the seating system market, reinforcing its links to Ford and Fiat. At the same time, its acquisition of Keiper, a leading automotive vehicle seat systems supplier on a just-in-time basis for the VW group, Porsche and Mercedes-Benz, opened new markets in Brazil, South Africa, Germany, Hungary and Italy.

As modularized production of whole sub-assemblies became increasingly the norm, Lear Seating also moved to acquire assets in cockpit-related components. In 1995 it bought Automotive Industries Holding, thus acquiring the design and manufacturing capability to produce high-quality interiors. In 1996 it took over the Masland Corporation primarily for its floor and acoustic system technologies and its technical centre in Plymouth, Michigan, for acoustics testing, design, product engineering, systems integration and production management and Borealis A.B. for its ability to design and manufacture instrument and door panels. Today, Lear is able to fill the role of systems integrator and to manage the design, purchasing and supply of the total automotive interior.

Source: UNCTAD *World Investment Report 1999: FDI and the Challenge of Development* (Box III.6, p. 111) (New York and Geneva: United Nations).

world with the likes of Fiat, VW, Porsche and Mercedes-Benz. Again, M&A was the key to expansion. The box emphasizes in particular that Lear Seating was buying not just firms but also the technological knowledge they possessed. Ultimately, this MNC's acquisition strategy has enabled it to become a major designer and supplier of 'total automotive interiors' in the international economy.

Who are the multinationals?

Having examined some of the salient trends in contemporary MNC activity, it is useful to round off this section with a brief review of the relative characteristics of actual multinationals from the developed and developing regions of the world, together with those in the transition economies. As noted, UNCTAD's 1999 *World Investment Report* lists the world's 100 largest MNCs, ranked by foreign assets. It is interesting to note that of these giant firms, all but two originate in developed economies. UNCTAD also publishes lists of the largest 50 MNCs from the developing countries and the largest 25 from those based in central Europe. None of the central European MNCs is large enough to make it into the developing countries list. The top 10 MNCs from each list are given in Table 15.5.

From Table 15.5, Daewoo and Petroleos Venezuela are the two developing country MNCs that feature in UNCTAD's list of the world's largest 100 MNCs. Note the fairly dramatic change in MNC scale as we move down the table. The developed country MNCs each have foreign assets of at least $30 billion.[5] Foreign sales for this group vary from $24.5 to $104.8 billion and at least five firms have in excess of 100 000 overseas employees. Amongst the developing country top ten, overseas assets range from $3.2 to $10.5 billion, overseas sales from $1.5 to $32.5 billion, and at least six firms have fewer than 12 000 overseas employees. Finally, amongst the central European MNCs, the largest firm has foreign assets of only $400 *million*, foreign sales of $200 *million* and 1600 overseas employees.

Table 15.6 describes the industry composition of the world's top 100 MNCs for 1996 and 1997. In 1997, the first four industries in the table – chemicals and pharmaceuticals, electronics/electrical equipment, automotive and petroleum refining/distribution, and mining – accounted for 66 of the 100 largest MNCs. Unsurprisingly, these industries are typified by the presence of very significant *economies of scale*. To compete effectively in car making for example, it is usually necessary to produce a range of models at high volume. In Chapter 3, section 3.3, we discussed the important productivity gains achieved by Henry Ford when he introduced the large scale 'flow-line' method of assembly to the car industry. Ford's innovation demonstrated that cars could be made more cheaply when they were produced in large numbers. Although the detail of car production has changed since Ford's time, this basic principle has not. If you wish to compete in the volume car market, you must achieve scale economies to match those enjoyed by your rivals. This helps to explain the pressures for merger and acquisition in the car industry that have been evident for some time. A recent example is the purchase of Nissan by Renault.

Transnationals

We referred earlier to the issue of the transnational corporation (TNC). There is an unfolding debate over the existence of large numbers of TNCs: there are certainly

[5] General Motors excepted. The zero entry here may be an error or an unknown.

Table 15.5 The world's top ten non-financial MNCs, developed countries, developing countries and central European countries, ranked by foreign assets in 1997

Top ten developed country MNCs

Rank	Firm	Country	Industry	Assets ($ bn)		Sales ($ bn)		Employment ('000)	
				Foreign	Total	Foreign	Total	Foreign	Total
1	General Electric	United States	Electronics	97.4	304.0	24.5	90.8	111	276
2	Ford	United States	Automotive	72.5	275.4	48.0	153.6	174	364
3	Shell	Netherlands/UK		70.0	115.0	69.0	128.0	65	105
4	General Motors	United States	Automotive	0.0	228.9	51.0	178.2	–	608
5	Exxon	United States	Petroleum	54.6	96.1	104.8	120.3	–	80
6	Toyota	Japan	Automotive	41.8	105.0	50.4	88.5		159
7	IBM	United States	Computers	39.9	81.5	48.9	78.5	135	269
8	Volkswagen	Germany	Automotive	...	57.0	42.7	65.0	134	279
9	Nestlé	Switzerland	Food	31.6	37.7	47.6	48.3	219	226
10	Daimler Benz	Germany	Automotive	30.9	76.2	46.1	69.0	75	300

Top ten developing country MNCs

Rank	Firm	Country	Industry	Foreign	Total	Foreign	Total	Foreign	Total
1	Daewoo	Korea	Diversified	10.5	22.9	7.3	18.8	11	15
2	Petroleos Venezuela	Venezuela	Petroleum	9.0	47.1	32.5	34.8	11.8	56.6
3	Jardine M.	Hong Kong	Diversified	6.7	12.0	8.0	11.5	–	175
4	First Pacific	Hong Kong	Other	6.3	11.4	7.4	8.3	40.5	51.3
5	Cemex	Mexico	Construction	5.6	10.2	2.2	3.8	10.7	19.1
6	Hutchison Whampoa	Hong Kong	Diversified	5.0	15.1	1.9	5.6	17	37.1
7	Sappi Ltd	South Africa	Other	3.8	5.0	2.4	3.6	9.5	23.5
8	China State Construction	China	Construction	3.7	7.2	1.5	5.4	5.5	258
9	China Chemicals	China	Other	3.5	5.8	11.2	17.9	0.6	8.9
10	LG Electronics	Republic of Korea	Electronics	3.2	15.4	5.2	17.6	32.5	80.4

Top ten European MNCs

Rank	Firm	Country	Industry	Foreign	Total	Foreign	Total	Foreign	Total
1	Latvian Shipping Co.	Latvia	Transportation	0.4	0.5	0.2	0.21	1.6	2.3
2	Pdravka Group	Croatia	Food	0.29	0.48	0.12	0.4	0.5	6.9
3	Gorenje	Slovenia	Domestic appliances	0.26	0.66	0.64	1.1	0.6	6.7
4	Motokov	Czech Rep.	Trade	0.16	0.26	0.26	0.35	0.6	1.0
5	Atlanska	Croatia	Transport	0.15	0.17	0.05	0.05	–	0.5
6	Pliva Group	Croatia	Pharmaceuticals	0.14	0.86	0.33	0.46	1.6	6.7
7	Skoda	Czech Rep.	Diversified	0.14	1.0	0.15	1.2	1.1	19.8
8	Adria Airways	Slovenia	Transportation	0.13	0.14	0.98	0.98	–	0.6
9	Hungarian Gas & Oil	Hungary	Petroleum and natural gas	0.13	2.9	0.2	3.0	0.6	20
10	VSZ	Slovakia	Iron and Steel	0.72	1.4	0.0	0.9	0.06	26.7

Source: UNCTAD *World Investment Report 1999: FDI and the Challenge of Development* (Table III.1, p. 78; Table III.8, p. 86; Table III.12, p. 90) (New York and Geneva: United Nations)

Table 15.6 Industry composition of top 100 MNCs, 1996 and 1997

Industry	1996	1997
Chemicals and pharmaceuticals	16	21
Electronics/electrical equipment	17	18
Automotive	14	14
Petroleum refining/distribution and mining	14	13
Food and beverages	12	9
Diversified	4	7
Telecommunication/utilities	5	4
Trading	4	3
Machinery and engineering	2	2
Metals	3	–
Construction	3	3
Media	2	1
Other	4	5
Total	**100**	**100**

Source: UNCTAD *World Investment Report 1999: FDI and the Challenge of Development* (Table III.5, p.83) (New York and Geneva: United Nations)

more and more internationally oriented firms, and they are becoming larger. Does this mean that a 'critical mass' of stateless firms has emerged or not? While we do not have the space to fully develop an answer to this question in a book of this sort, we can at least briefly set out the terms of the debate. UNCTAD for one appears to accept that transnationalism has arrived. Its publications habitually refer to TNCs rather than MNCs, and it has developed a means of measuring the extent of the 'transnationality' of individual firms. Table 15.7 lists UNCTAD's top ten transnationals for 1997 as defined by its *transnationality index*. This figure is calculated as the average of three ratios: a firm's foreign assets to total assets; its foreign sales to total sales; and its foreign employment to total employment. In the table, *Nestlé* emerges with a transnationality index of 93.2 per cent, making it the fourth most transnational firm in the world. Referring back to Table 15.5, we can see how this figure emerges. Of Nestlé's total assets of $37.7 billion, $31.6 billion (83.8 per cent) are held abroad. Of its total sales of $48.3 billion, $47.6 billion (98.6 per cent) are made abroad. Finally, of its 226 000 employees, 219 000 (96.9 per cent) work abroad. The average of these three percentages yields the transnationality index.

Before making explicit criticism of the notion of transnationalism, we should consider two additional points that emerge from Table 15.7. First, although it appears to consider the firms listed here as transnationals, UNCTAD still concedes that they have some national affiliation; Nestlé is a *Swiss* firm, Seagram a *Canadian* one and so on. Second, note that most of the firms in the list are associated with smaller advanced economies: Switzerland, the Netherlands, Sweden and Belgium. UNCTAD itself recognizes that international firms that originate in small domestic markets will have a higher average transnationality. This is because smaller markets reach commercial saturation before larger ones. For example, a Swiss international firm will exhaust the possibilities afforded by its domestic market faster than an American firm will in the much larger US market.

Table 15.7 The world's top MNCs in terms of degree of transnationality, 1997

Transnationality rank	Corporation	Country	Industry	Transnationality index (%)
1	Seagram Company	Canada	Beverages	97.6
2	Asea Brown Boveri	Switzerland	Electrical equipment	95.7
3	Thompson Corp.	Canada	Printing and publishing	95.1
4	Nestlé	Switzerland	Food	93.2
5	Unilever	Netherlands	Food	92.4
6	Slovay	Belgium	Chemicals/pharmaceuticals	92.3
7	Electrolux	Sweden	Electrical appliances	89.4
8	Philips Electronics	Netherlands	Electronics	86.4
9	Bayer	Germany	Chemicals	82.7
10	Roche Holding	Switzerland	Pharmaceuticals	82.2

Source: UNCTAD *World Investment Report 1999: FDI and the Challenge of Development* (Table III.6, p. 83) (New York and Geneva: United Nations)

An explicit critique of the notion of transnationalism, while recognizing the potential importance of the breadth of foreign interests of an international firm, would take issue with the view that this *necessarily* makes it a TNC. The more telling point is not the breadth of foreign assets, sales or employment but their *depth*. If it could be conclusively demonstrated, for example, that many international firms have substantial overseas assets that include executive decision-making, research and development and higher administration, *then* it might be possible to make a stronger argument for transnationalism, but in the absence of such information the case must remain circumstantial.

15.3 Why multinationals exist

It is helpful to begin this section with an example. Budweiser and Becks are two of the most popular bottled beers in the UK. Budweiser is brewed by the Budweiser Stag Brewing Company in London. It is the product of a multinational enterprise: the Budweiser parent company is Anheuser-Busch in the United States. Becks, on the other hand, is, as its advertising stresses, 'Only ever brewed in Bremen, Germany'. Becks is imported into the UK from Germany, and its production is *not* multinational. Why the difference? A number of theoretical possibilities suggest themselves:

- Transport costs might be an issue. It is cheaper to ship beer to the UK from Germany than it is from the United States. While this means that Becks can be exported, relatively high transport costs may make it more efficient for Budweiser to be actually brewed in the distant market for which it is intended.

- It may be desirable for beer producers to have a presence in the market in which their product is sold. Putting transport costs to one side for a moment, Budweiser could be shipped from the United States to the EU. Wholesalers in the EU would then distribute it. Instead, it is brewed in the UK and distributed in the EU by

Anheuser-Busch affiliates. This may be because Anheuser-Busch is of the view that it is better placed to judge the nature of the market by being in it, instead of servicing the market remotely through foreign distributors. In addition, Anheuser-Busch may reduce its costs by 'internalizing' the transaction that it would other-wise undertake with foreign distributors. Simply, foreign distributors charge more than Anheuser-Busch is prepared to pay, so it does the job itself. This issue does not arise for Becks as it sells into the EU market in which it is already located.

- Finally, assuming that it wishes Budweiser to be sold in the EU, Anheuser-Busch could license a British brewer to produce the beer on its behalf. This would bring in licence revenue, while an unrelated company undertook all the actual work. In such a case, there would be no multinational dimension to the enterprise. That this *doesn't* happen may be a testament to the value that Anheuser-Busch places on the Budweiser brand image. It claims an 'exclusive beechwood aging process' for its beer. Such exclusivity might be undermined if Budweiser was also produced by someone else. Again, this is a non-issue for Becks: it does not need any other enterprise, affiliate or non-affiliate, to assist its EU operations.

So although Budweiser *could* be exported from the United States to the EU, there are several reasons that help to explain its production in the EU by a multinational enterprise. In fact, our three bullet points above are *generalizable*. They can be help us to understand the basis not just of the multinational production of beer where this arises, but of much wider forms of multinational activity.

The bullet points corresponds to generally recognized principles that underpin the multinational process. These principles are known as *location*, *internalization* and *ownership*. We shall consider each in turn.

Location

Multinational activity may arise as a result of a number of 'locational' influences. In our beer example, it was the distant location of the large EU market that we argued could help to explain why Budweiser is not produced in the United States for ship-ment to the EU. Relatively high transport costs make local production in the EU the more efficient option. There are other possibilities. Refer back to Box 13.2 for a moment. The box reveals that 'up to 50 000 textile jobs' might be lost in the UK as textile firms shift production to North Africa. Why *this location*? The answer is that textile production can be carried out more efficiently in North Africa because it is cheaper to employ labour there than in the UK. The multinational process in this instance is driven by the production advantages offered by another (foreign) loca-tion. One final example. John West, itself part of the Heinz group, is a producer of canned tuna fish. John West is based in Liverpool, but it has production plants in West Africa and the Seychelles. John West is engaged in multinational activity at least in part for the simple reason that the River Mersey and Irish Sea are not prime fishing grounds for tuna. Part of its business has to be conducted where the fish are – hence its decision to operate production plants overseas.

Internalization

Continuing with our tuna fish theme for a moment, notice that *location* need not be decisive in the decision to operate multinationally. John West contracts some fishing work to local communities in West Africa. It could also contract out fish processing and canning – the 'factory' end of its business. If it did this it could cease to operate multinationally (discounting, for the sake of argument, that John West is a subsidiary of Heinz); everything could be contracted from Liverpool to unrelated businesses overseas. In these circumstances, John West would be managing its business through a network of *market* relationships. Such an approach might sound a little cumbersome but it *is* possible. Why doesn't this happen? Instead of using the market in this way, John West *internalizes* many of these market relationships by virtue of its decision to act multinationally. By operating its own canning plants, John West is presumably advantaged; otherwise it would use the market to contract this work out, as it does with some of the fishing. The advantages that it derives from investing in its own canning plants might be based on its experience of the tuna business, or better technology, or simply that there are few potential contractors near the fishing grounds. The point is that, in this instance, the multinational process works better than extended and distant market relations. The reader may recognize a parallel between this discussion and one conducted in Chapter 3, section 3.3, which considered why firms exist. We saw that the alternative to organizing production through firms was to use the market, but that firms offered a number of advantages, which centred on *internalizing* market relations. This is exactly the same principle. It operates both at the domestic and international levels.

Notice finally that John West's multinational activities as we have described them are 'upstream' in the production process – near its origin in tuna fishing. This is in contrast with some of Anheuser-Busch's distribution work in the EU – 'downstream' of the main activity of brewing. Upstream and downstream business connections are sometimes referred to as *vertical integration*. This may be contrasted with *horizontal integration*, which, in multinational terms, involves buying or setting up foreign businesses that undertake the same kind of activity as the parent company. The purchase by Heinz of John West in 1997 is an example of horizontal integration. Heinz is a large American MNC which has an established reputation for the production of canned foods. A canned tuna firm therefore sits easily in its portfolio. Heinz clearly understands the canned food business, and the John West acquisition may again be understood by reference to the principle of internalization. Heinz perhaps sees 'synergies' between its existing activities and those of John West.

Ownership

Our earlier beer examples suggest that both Becks and Budweiser have jealously guarded reputations. These brands are *owned* by their respective firms. In the case of Budweiser, it may be that the decision to go multinational was based on the twin desires to access the lucrative EU market *and* preserve brand integrity. Recall from Chapter 5, sections 5.7 and 5.9, that the establishment of brand loyalties by a firm imply that it is a *price maker*. The firm can then earn supernormal profit, at least in the short run. If, however, brand loyalties are particularly strong, and perhaps brands are protected by patents, then there may be limits to the extent to which rival firms can compete in the market. In such circumstances, supernormal profits can be earned beyond the short run. The ownership of a powerful brand or patent may therefore explain why some firms become multinational. Coca-Cola and McDonald's are examples of brand names that are recognized throughout the world. This means that their owners have an incentive to exploit and enhance these brands through multinational activity.

The ownership of raw materials might similarly explain multinational production. Table 15.5 shows that Petroleos Venezuela is the second largest of the MNCs from developing countries. This firm has substantial overseas sales and assets. It need not maintain such foreign interests in order to stay in the business of selling fuel in foreign markets. That it chooses to do so is probably a reflection of the view that it can best exploit the resources it owns through a business network under its direct control.

15.4 Multinationals and government policy

MNCs are a major force in the international economy. They embody significant concentrations of economic power, and they are enjoying particularly rapid growth relative to the growth rates of nation states. All this makes MNCs an issue for other agencies with which they coexist and interact: most obviously governments but also (non-multinational) firms, trade unions and single-interest groups such as those concerned with the environment. In this section, we concentrate on the relationship between MNCs and government policy. Given that MNCs are increasingly important, should governments try to control or condition their behaviour? If the answer to this question is yes, we must reflect upon the means by which governments might seek to influence MNCs. It may be that the scale and economic power of MNCs place them increasingly beyond the reach of state sanction.

For *host* countries the arrival of MNCs may be disruptive economically, politically and environmentally. This is especially so where the MNCs and the investments they make are significant in relation to the size of the host economy. We might then generally expect MNC activities to have particularly pronounced impacts upon *developing* countries. As we have seen, though, most investment by MNCs does not flow to the developing countries: it is retained by the developed countries. Here the 'scale of host versus scale of MNC' issue is less likely to arise. Even so, MNCs still have the potential to significantly alter established patterns of economic activity in developed countries. For example, 40 years ago the UK had a vibrant *UK-owned* car industry; now it has none. The reasons for the change are complex, but at least part of the explanation lies in increased multinational investment in car production in the UK. We are not arguing here that foreign ownership of the UK's car industry is regrettable – indeed, the alternative might have been *no* UK car industry – merely that there has been a major change, and that it is 'MNC related'.

If the arrival of MNCs may presage important developments in host economies, their *departure* is likely to be even more significant. As we shall see, MNCs are widely regarded as a source of jobs, skills, technology and much else for host countries, whether developed or less developed. This means that, in a competitive international economy, few if any countries can actually afford to shun MNCs on the basis of some *a priori* principle. There is a famous line, modified from Oscar Wilde, that encapsulates this point: *'There is only one thing worse than being "exploited" by multinationals – not being "exploited" by them.'* The conclusion is clear enough: MNCs offer net economic attributes to which host countries cannot remain indifferent.

What of those countries that *provide* multinational investment? The first point to make here is that, in the developed world at least, investing and host countries are often one and the same. This means that much MNC activity is a broadly *even* process, in which FDI inflows find some counterbalance in outflows. For example, over the period 1990–98 (see Table 15.2), the USA and UK taken together accounted for 44 per cent of FDI inflows to OECD countries and 39 per cent of FDI outflows from OECD countries. However, as we have seen, for some countries FDI flows are much less symmetrical. From Table 15.2, FDI net outflows for 1990–98 were particularly marked for Germany and Japan. The question remains: are significant FDI net outflows an issue or problem for investing countries? The conventional answer is a simple *no*. This is really an old debate concerning the possibility of investment lost to the domestic economy – it flows abroad instead. The potential cost here is a lower level of domestic economic activity, with consequent losses in output and employment. Against this, most governments would now accept that MNCs know what they're doing. While investment abroad may take on the *appearance* of loss to the domestic economy, in the longer term, productive assets overseas will yield a continuous stream of profit (an alternative form of monetary inflow). Thus, when MNCs choose to invest abroad, it is not for governments to second-guess them and gainsay such commercial decisions. To do so would put at risk the international competitiveness of one's 'own' MNCs. As noted, in policy terms this attitude has translated into the abolition of restrictions on capital movements that had been in place in many of the developed economies prior to the 1980s.

National policies towards multinationals

Our discussion would seem to suggest that, while governments might have concerns about the implications of some aspects of multinational investment, the potential economic advantages they bring are too important to ignore. This view is not uncommon. For example, the late Susan Strange has argued that, in their quest for improved shares in world markets, states must seek to attract MNCs as these firms have:

first, command of technology; second, ready access to global sources of capital; and third, ready access to major markets in America, Europe and, often, Japan.[6]

Strange raises the intriguing prospect that the foreign policy of governments may become an adjunct to the forms of industrial policy that have traditionally been used to raise competitiveness. The object of foreign policy here would be to persuade MNCs that the country in question is a suitable location for investment. Similarly, Hirst and Thompson (1996) consider that FDI offers the best prospect for the improvement of the economic prospects of the world's poor countries. In their view the big challenge is to identify forms of *governance* that will encourage FDI to flow in appropriate directions. Hirst and Thompson favour the general term 'governance' above the more specific 'government' as a means of indicating that the articulation of economic policy at the international level is the province of a *range of agencies* such as the Triad, the G7, the WTO and the EU, as well as individual nation states. We shall return to the issue of *international policies* towards MNCs later, but for the present we concentrate on the broad policy stance of national governments.

Undoubtedly there *is* a broad policy shared by most governments in the international economy: it is to attract FDI. Whatever problems might be associated with the arrival of multinationals, there appears to be a general consensus that these are sometimes illusory, often relatively minor and in any case far outweighed by the

[6] Strange, S. 'States, firms and diplomacy', in R. Stubbs and G.R.D. Underhill (eds), *Political Economy and the Changing Global Order* (Basingstoke: Macmillan, 1994).

benefits that MNCs bring.[7] In the context of a discussion of the benefits of FDI to developing countries, UNCTAD offers a representative summary of the benefits which flow from multinational activity. These are summarized under the following headings:

- capital
- technology
- market access
- skills and management techniques
- environment.

Capital

Clearly, multinational investment will usually mean an inflow of capital to a host economy. However, UNCTAD stresses that FDI is likely to represent a *long-term* commitment to a host economy and is therefore more stable than other sources of foreign capital.

Technology

MNCs are an important means for the international transmission of technology. This is clearly the case for developing countries, where the level of technological achievement is usually relatively low. However, the influence of MNCs on technology diffusion is not confined to the developing world. Refer briefly back to the example in Box 15.1. Here we can see that the growth of one multinational automotive parts manufacturer has built up a technology network that encompasses the United States and countries in Europe and South America. In other words, this MNC is spreading technology across developed *and* developing economies.

Market access

Because they have established market networks, MNCs are able to provide new exporting possibilities for host economies. This is particularly important for developing countries and countries in transition as they may not have strong traditions in many foreign markets. As we saw in Chapter 13, the richest and fastest-growing nations in the international economy have been those that have performed well in export terms. Because MNCs can be instrumental in helping countries join or stay in this elite group, they will be actively courted by most nations, regardless of their stage of development.

Skills and management techniques

In the same way that they contribute to the diffusion of technology, MNCs can help to spread skills and effective management techniques across international borders. Again, although it may be developing and transition economies that will benefit most from this kind of process, similar benefits may be realized in the developed countries too. For example, when Japanese car manufacturers started to build production plants in the UK in the 1980s, the British government welcomed such investment partly for the 'lessons' Japanese manufacturers might impart to British industry in terms of working practices, labour relations and management.

[7] Note that this perception of MNCs is held by governments. Other interest groups have contrary views. We are making no claims here as to the validity of either position.

Environment

UNCTAD asserts that MNCs 'are in the lead in developing clean technologies and modern environmental management systems', and that their good practice can improve environmental care in other firms in host economies.

As noted, given these attributes, the general policy position towards MNCs of most governments is one of encouragement. There is a realization that, if *you* do not attract multinational investment, then others who are more receptive will be in a position to gain a competitive edge. Evidence for this liberal policy stance is provided by UNCTAD and reproduced in Table 15.8. The table indicates that of the regulatory changes affecting FDI that were introduced by individual governments between 1991 and 1998, the majority were consistently favourable to MNCs.

Table 15.8 National regulatory changes 1991–98

	1991	1992	1993	1994	1995	1996	1997	1998
No of countries changing investment regimes	35	43	57	49	64	65	76	60
Number of regulatory changes of which:	82	79	102	110	112	114	151	145
More favourable to FDI[a]	80	79	101	108	106	98	135	136
Less favourable to FDI[b]	2	–	1	2	6	16	16	9

[a] Including liberalizing changes aimed at strengthening market functioning, as well as increased incentives.
[b] Including changes aimed at increasing control as well as reducing incentives.
Source: UNCTAD *World Investment Report 1999: FDI and the Challenge of Development* (Table IV.1, p. 115) (New York and Geneva: United Nations)

Many countries supplement an 'open door' position on FDI with active pursuit of MNCs. For example, the UK government sponsors an agency – the Invest in Britain Bureau (IBB)[8] – that seeks to market Britain as a location for multinational investment. A brief inspection of the IBB's website (see Internet links at the end of this chapter) will confirm that the government has only one real concern over MNCs – to get more of them in. Box 15.2 contains an example of what might not unkindly be termed the 'boosterism' of the IBB. In this instance, it is Britain's successful record and apparently bright prospects for attracting FDI that are being trumpeted.

Finally, let us return to the question of the agency of MNCs in relation to the authority of sovereign governments. We noted earlier that, in some developing economies at least, it might be argued that the economic importance of MNCs permits them certain immunities and levels of influence over host governments determined not to risk losing these prized assets. A recent case in the UK suggests that this issue might also arise for developed economies. In Chapter 14, section 14.9, we saw that the British government chose not to adopt the euro when it was launched at the beginning of 1999. However, Britain is committed in principle to joining a successful euro zone. Unsurprisingly, this position has created some degree of uncertainty. If the present government remains in power, *when* will Britain join? If there is a change in government, will Britain *ever* join? There may also be a referendum to help

[8] The IBB has recently evolved into *invest uk*.

Box 15.2

Britain stays favourite for future global FDI

The UK will remain attractive for worldwide foreign direct investment for years ahead, the latest business environment rankings from the Economist Intelligence Unit (EIU) have confirmed.

In a comparison of 60 countries, Britain's favourable disposition to private enterprise and foreign investment, the size and sophistication of its capital markets, and the flexibility of its labour markets are all cited as features likely to continue attracting investment. A further improvement in the UK's score over the period 1999–2003 is expected to come from a more stable macroeconomic environment marked by lower inflation, a less volatile exchange rate, and stronger

public finances than in the period 1994–98.

The benefits of macroeconomic stabilization are expected to offset the costs of more regulated labour markets arising from Britain's closer links with the rest of the single European market. Although the UK has attracted a much higher level of foreign investment than other EU states in the past, periods of high inflation, currency volatility and sharp macroeconomic policy reversals in the 1980s and early 1990s were 'not the UK's most attractive features as a business location', says the EIU.

The British government has now devoted much attention to improving the

prospects for macroeconomic stability over the medium term with new frameworks for monetary and fiscal policy. The EIU says these should help to reduce instability.

Labour market reforms are not expected to have a large adverse impact on Britain's attractiveness for business. While representing a move towards the social models in much of the rest of the EU, even after their introduction the EU says 'the UK's labour market should remain among the more flexible in the world'.

Source: Invest in Britain Bureau website, accessed on 18 January 2000

decide the issue. In an open society, we would also expect other interest groups to make their voices heard on the question of the single currency; most obviously the business community and trade unions will contribute to the debate. However, what if some voices are louder than others? Box 15.3 reveals that 'big business' is determined that Britain should adopt the euro, and that some MNCs at least will review

Box 15.3

Toyota threat to quit UK over euro
By Jonathan Watts in Tokyo

The head of one of the world's biggest car companies reignited the debate over the single currency yesterday with a warning to the government that its £1.5bn investment in the UK would be at risk if Britain stayed out of the euro.

Executives of Japan's biggest car manufacturer, Toyota, which employs thousands of workers at plants in Derbyshire and Clwyd, said they could no longer sit on the fence as Britain decides whether or not to enter EMU.

'Waiting for a decision is really hurting us and it is time to state very clearly to the British public that we want Britain to join the single currency,' said Shoichiro Toyoda, honorary chairman and former chief executive of Toyota.

The comments are sure to increase the pressure on the government and come days after the trade and industry secretary, Stephen Byers, admitted that

big business was telling ministers that they must make a decision on the euro early in the next parliament.

Toyota's broadside echoes earlier calls by senior figures from industry to sign up to the single currency. The chairman of Rover Group, Prof W. Samann, told reporters recently that full membership of the euro would 'consolidate BMW's investment' in Britain.

Naoyuki Akikusa, the president of Fujitsu, went further last year. 'If the UK were to join in 2002, that would be OK. But if 2020 – that would pose a big problem.'

Toyota managers said yesterday that its UK operations . . . would be at risk if the strong pound continued to push its British operations deep into the red. The company said its British operation had suffered its worst performance ever last year as a result of the sharp strengthening of sterling against the euro. This currency

fluctuation hurts the competitiveness of the 200 000 Toyota cars produced each year in the UK, 70 per cent of which are sold elsewhere in Europe.

'The figures are not yet available, but we posted a very significant loss in the UK last year,' said Shinro Iwatsuki, director in charge of European operations. 'I would imagine that Ford and Vauxhall are in a similar position.'

He said Toyota sent a senior delegation to Mr Byers last month to express its concerns.

'We told him that if the present situation continues, then at the very least it will be impossible to expand our operations in the UK. If there is no change in the long term, then we will have to decide whether even our existing operations should continue.'

Source: *Guardian* 18 January 2000

their British operations if this does not happen soon. Toyota, the latest MNC to air this possibility, has investments in the UK worth £1.5 billion. The implication is clear enough: if the British government does not want to risk the commitment of its MNCs, of which, recall, it has a substantial number, it must clarify its euro timetable. While this example does not conclusively demonstrate that MNCs can *impose* their preferences on governments, it does at least suggest that the economic importance of these firms makes their views difficult to ignore.

International policy towards multinationals

There is certainly *implicit* international regulation of MNCs. For example, the EU undoubtedly gains some measure of influence over even the largest firms simply because none can afford to be isolated from the world's single largest market over which the EU presides. This applies *a fortiori* in the case of the Triad, given that its sphere of influence extends to markets covering most of the developed world. However, there have been few serious attempts *explicitly* to articulate international policy on MNCs. A recent initiative, under the auspices of the WTO, floundered partly in the face of opposition from developing countries. The 1986–94 Uruguay Round of international trade negotiations (see Chapter 13, section 13.5) had at one stage included an ambitious agenda for *Trade Related Investment Measures* (TRIMs). These measures were intended to open up markets in Japan, east and south-east Asia and Latin America to FDI. The argument was that these regions should be as accessible to MNCs as Europe and North America. Furthermore, international investors wished to be rid of the restrictions and requirements that were sometimes imposed on them by developing countries. For example, MNCs are sometimes obliged by host governments to set export targets or establish 'local content' thresholds. In the latter case, the MNC agrees to use local suppliers for a given proportion of its inputs; this is meant to provide a direct demand stimulus in the host economy. Export targets, on the other hand, help to secure scarce foreign exchange. The developing countries did not wish to see an end to their right of negotiation with MNCs, and their opposition helped to ensure that the TRIMs agenda was narrowed to the extent that it merely confirmed certain existing GATT/WTO principles in an investment context. An attempt to resurrect the spirit of TRIMs was made under the auspices of the OECD in 1995. However, this – the *Multilateral Agreement on Investment* (MAI) – was mothballed in 1998 following disagreements amongst the OECD countries and in the face of growing opposition from pressure groups concerned at the implications of an 'MNCs' charter'.

Reflecting on policies towards multinationals

There appears to be a certain ambivalence in the attitudes of policy-makers towards MNCs. Individually, governments appear receptive. They like the technologies, the jobs, the skills and the exports that MNCs can offer. Collectively though, there is no agreed framework for accommodating FDI; indeed, the developing countries in particular are clearly resistant to initiatives such as TRIMs and the MAI. How can we account for this? One possibility might be that, individually, governments retain the *right* to negotiate with MNCs. In certain circumstances, at present or in the future, they may feel the need to assert such rights. Governments cannot do this if they collectively agree to a borderless world for multinational investors.

Summary

◆ MNCs are worthy of particular attention because they are among the most important and fastest-growing agents in the international economy. They currently account for a quarter of world output, and their annual sales exceed the value of world trade. Over the last 20 years, the growth of FDI outflows has exceeded both the growth of world trade and growth in world output.

◆ The developed economies, especially the Triad, are responsible for most of the world's FDI outlows, and they receive most of the world's FDI inflows. Multinational activity largely remains a developed country preserve. Some developed economies such as Germany and Japan are responsible for significant net FDI outflows. Others, such as the USA and UK, maintain more balanced FDI inflows and outflows. Although FDI inflows to parts of the developing world have increased in recent years, their *share* of total world inflows has simultaneously declined because of much greater new inflows to the developed countries.

◆ Multinational activity is increasingly driven by the process of merger and acquisition (M&A). Firms in the USA and the UK are the world's major buyers and sellers of firms internationally. M&A appears to be a good way of maintaining a technological edge in competitive international markets.

◆ While multinational activity is commonplace, it is debatable whether or not there are large numbers of transnational firms in the world economy. Even the largest MNCs appear to maintain definitive national affiliations.

◆ Some MNCs exist for reasons similar to those that give rise to the existence of firms. It would be possible to conduct international transactions through the market, but MNCs make it possible to internalize such transactions and conduct them more efficiently.

◆ The policies of individual governments towards MNCs are usually favourably liberal. FDI inflows offer a jobs, technology and access to overseas markets. FDI outflows promise income streams for the future. However, the world's governments appear unable to agree a collective policy for dealing with MNCs. The two most recent attempts – TRIMs and the MAI – have failed.

Key terms

◆ Multinational corporation (MNC)
◆ Foreign direct investment (FDI)
◆ Transnational corporation (TNC)
◆ Mergers and acquisitions (M&A)
◆ Location
◆ Internalization
◆ Ownership
◆ Host economy
◆ Investing economy

◼ Questions for discussion

◆ What is the difference between an MNC and a TNC?

◆ What are the principal sources of FDI outflows and locations of FDI inflows?

◆ Why has M&A activity contributed more to multinational activity in recent years?

◆ Why do MNCs exist?

◆ What are the potential attractions of MNCs to host economies?

◆ What forms of policy have countries adopted towards MNCs?

◼ Further reading

The best single source on trends in the activities of MNCs is UNCTAD's annually published *World Investment Report*. Details of the latest issue can be found on the UNCTAD website (address below). Parts of the document may be downloaded without charge.

Hirst, P. and G. Thompson *Globalization in Question* (Cambridge: Polity Press, 1996). For an excellent and accessible discussion of multinational issues see especially Chapters 1 and 3.

Dunning, J.H. *Globalization, Trade and Foreign Direct Investment* (Oxford: Elsevier, 1998). Provides an overview of FDI issues in a contemporary context.

◼ Internet links

UNCTAD's website is at: **http://www.unctad.org/en/enhome.htm**

The *Siemens* website gives a good *sense* both of the international orientation of this firm and of its distinctly German roots. The site can be found at: **http://www.siemens.com/en2/flash/**

The *Invest in Britain Bureau* has recently evolved into *invest uk*. Its website is at: **http://www.invest.uk.com/index_flash.html**

General Electric, the world's largest MNC in terms of overseas assets, has a site at: **http://www.ge.com/**

International or Global Economy?

CHAPTER 16

Key issues

▶ What is meant by globalization?

▶ Is there a global economy?

▶ What are the origins of the globalization thesis?

Contents

16.1 Introduction

In Chapters 13 and 14 we introduced the 'open economy' concepts of the balance of payments and exchange rates. Our discussion in part concentrated on the problems and issues that such concepts pose for *national* economies. For example, we saw that, because a country cannot ignore a persistent balance of payments imbalance, it may choose to confront potential balance of payments problems by (say) allowing its currency's exchange rate to float freely against other currencies. Alternative measures to promote balance of payments adjustment are, of course, also possible. In this final chapter we move beyond national economic concerns of this nature to further explore perhaps the key *international* economic issue of the new millennium: *globalization* and the supposed recent emergence of a new '*global*' *economy*. This concept is often invoked, but what exactly does it mean and what is its basis in reality? The chapter then moves on to consider the implications of our analysis of globalization for business. As will become clear, we in fact share the view expressed most forcefully by Hirst and Thompson (see guide to further reading) that *something rather less developed than globalization* currently underpins the world's economic arrangements. However, this is not to deny that important changes have indeed taken place in the international economy, or that these pose both significant problems and opportunities for business.

We begin by justifying our preference for the continuing validity of the *international* economy. This term may of course be contrasted with the alternative and increasingly popular conceptualization of the *global economy* and the purported '*globalization*' of economic processes. Our major concern about the invocation of the 'global' is that it is often too glibly done, with insufficient thought for what the term actually means, or what the implications of its use might be. For example, in our view, too many discussions of multinational corporations (MNCs) as a dimension of

the 'globalization process' find a neat correspondence between, on the one hand, their immense financial, industrial and geographical scales and, on the other, their (asserted) 'globalized' immunity from *national* concerns. A recognition that some firms are big and powerful is transformed into an assessment that, collectively, these same firms are now free to, *literally*, roam the globe without so much as a passing interest in the aspirations of sovereign nations or even supranational bodies such as the EU. There are two major problems with this kind of approach. The first is that *at the outset* it prescribes clear limits to the competence and authority of policymakers. It does not matter what you, I or the President of France think about the activities of MNCs – they are apparently so powerful and globally unconstrained that we cannot deal or reach accommodations with them. The second problem is that the very presence of MNCs appears sufficient to 'prove' the globalization thesis. Against this, in our view, it is important to begin by thinking carefully about how, in several important respects, the international economy has evolved in the last 30 or so years. As we shall argue, as far as MNCs are concerned, there have been changes, but their development also betrays some significant continuities, and it is by no means certain that these firms are either now beyond sovereign influence, or that their presence validates notions of the 'global'.

16.2 The globalization debate

Let us develop this theme by posing an apparently simple question. What is an economy?

- Economies can be *local*, operating at, say, the level of a city, as in: 'Berlin's economy has been transformed by the removal of the Berlin Wall.'
- They can be *regional*: 'The economic prospects for the north west of England have been improved by the decision to extend Manchester airport.'
- They can be *national*: 'The French economy grew by 3 per cent last year.'
- They can encompass *groups of nations*: 'The European economy has become much more closely integrated since the introduction of the euro.'
- Finally, there is the *international* or '*global*' economy.

This list suggests that in one sense an economy is really a conceptual device: a way to parcel up and think about economic processes, which in capitalism, as we know, are articulated by markets. But as well as a means of analysis, economies are also very real structures, which decide the central economic questions introduced in Chapter 1: what is produced, how is it produced and for whom. *Economies therefore can be interpreted both as vehicles for understanding and as concrete frameworks of production.* In both cases, however, note that our interest is in the levels at which *markets are articulated and cohere* (from the local through to the international/global).

Now, which is the more helpful as an aid to understanding *and* accurate as a representation of actual market processes: an international or a global economy? To resolve this issue we need to reflect a little more carefully on the precise meanings of the terms 'international' and 'global'. International means *between nations*. The international economy is therefore one in which markets have become generalized beyond the national level but, crucially, *the relevance of individual nation states is retained in important ways*. By contrast, global means *worldwide*. A strong definition of a global economy might then refer to a situation in which markets have transcended national boundaries to the extent that individual nation states lose much of their economic and even cultural significance (see Box 16.1). This view is clearly radical: it implies that the most important economic decisions are now taken not by sovereign governments or their agents but by rootless transnational corporations, currency speculators, those who operate in stateless markets in finance capital and so on. There is, however, also a *softer* definition of globalization. This suggests that, while markets have become increasingly global, and do therefore threaten national sovereignty, it is still possible for states, recognition of their resultant growing interdependence, to work *collectively* to solve common economic problems through institutions such as the World Trade Organization and the G7. Indeed, given the immense power of globalizing market forces, collective action is, on this definition, now deemed necessary if economic instability is to be avoided.

Box 16.1

A global culture

Normally, globalization refers to the international flow of trade and capital. But the international spread of cultures has been at least as important as the spread of economic processes. Today a global culture is emerging. Through many media – from music to movies to books – international ideas and values are being mixed with, and superimposed on, national identities. The spread of ideas through television and video has seen revolutionary developments. There are now more than 1.2 billion TV sets around the world. The United States exports more than 120 000 hours of programming a year to Europe alone, and the global trade in programming is growing by more than 15 per cent a year.

Popular culture exerts more powerful pressure than ever before. From Manila to Managua, Beirut to Beijing, in the East, West, North and South, styles in dress (jeans, hair-dos, T-shirts), sports, music, eating habits and social and cultural attitudes have become global trends. Even crimes – whether relating to drugs, abuse of women, embezzlement or corruption – transcend frontiers and have become similar everywhere. In so many ways the world has shrunk.

Source: United Nations Development Programme, *Human Development Report 1997*
(Oxford: Oxford University Press, 1997)

We have then three approaches to the international/global economy:

- an *internationalist* perspective, which recognizes that important changes have taken place in the international economy over recent years (we shall have more to say on the question of the timing of change in a moment), but which also argues that such changes have *not* rendered nation states irrelevant as economic actors or indeed as discrete economic spaces

- a *strong globalization* thesis, which argues that the worldwide – to all intents *borderless* – articulation of market forces *has* undermined the economic sovereignty of states

- a *softer globalization* position, which contends that, while markets have become much more generalized and beyond the meaningful influence of many individual states, it is both possible and necessary for states collectively to influence the new global economic forces.

As noted, our preference is for the first approach. We shall now explain the reasons for this choice in more detail. *The crucial issue in our view remains market coherence*: can we really say that markets are now organized on a global basis and, if we can, has the course of globalization been consistent only with our softer definition or with the strong version? Alternatively, is the long-standing international coherence of these markets still prevalent? To explore such questions, let us think about the recent developments in:

- international trade
- foreign exchange markets
- foreign direct investment.

16.3　International trade: a global process?

As discussed in previous chapters, during the postwar boom (1945–70) most advanced nations enjoyed a combination of sustained economic growth, low unemployment and low inflation. In this period, flourishing international trade, especially in manufactured goods, served to open up markets and stimulate demand (see Chapter 13, section 13.4). However, it is true that during the boom most trade took place between the advanced countries. Although some less developing countries managed to gain a foothold in the markets for internationally traded manufactured goods and thereafter successfully industrialized – especially the Asian 'tiger' economies such as South Korea – most of the developing group remained on the periphery of the trade boom. Now, the key question is: *have things changed significantly since the end of the postwar boom*? One might expect the hypothesized process of globalization to have embraced the formerly peripheral parts of the world, unevenly and hesitantly at first perhaps, but there should be some evidence that trade is now less dominated by the developing countries and, as a corollary, that it is increasingly articulated at a global level. In fact, little appears to have changed; *trade in the international economy remains segmented largely along old lines*. Referring back to the top half of Table 13.5, recall that in 1998 the developing countries' share of world merchandise exports was 69.85 per cent, compared with 63.13 per cent almost 20 years earlier. In other words, the developing countries have actually enjoyed an *increase* in their share of export trade. Over the same period, the Asian economies maintained their remarkable progress, but again not at the expense of the established industrial countries. From the bottom half of the table, those countries that have lost ground in export markets are in Africa, the Middle East and the transitional category. According to a recent United Nations' estimate, the world's least developed economies, with 10 per cent of the world's population, now have only a 0.3 per cent share in world trade – and this is half their share two decades ago. When we consider trade in services, similar conclusions are reached. As Table 13.6 indicates, the combined share of North America and western Europe in world service exports fell only slightly between 1980 and 1998 (from 70.49 to 68.3 per cent – calculated from the table). On this evidence then globalization has simply not happened; rather, there appears to be a decisive continuity in general patterns of international trade.

Of course, there remains the *expectation* of change. Box 16.2 summarizes a recent World Bank report that anticipates that a new 'big five' group of countries (Brazil, China, India, Indonesia and Russia) will 'become a dominant force in global trade'

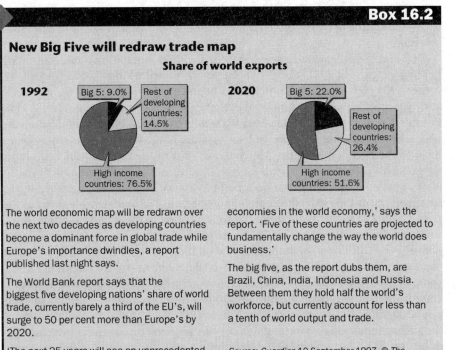

Box 16.2

New Big Five will redraw trade map

Share of world exports

1992

Big 5: 9.0%

Rest of developing countries: 14.5%

High income countries: 76.5%

2020

Big 5: 22.0%

Rest of developing countries: 26.4%

High income countries: 51.6%

The world economic map will be redrawn over the next two decades as developing countries become a dominant force in global trade while Europe's importance dwindles, a report published last night says.

The World Bank report says that the biggest five developing nations' share of world trade, currently barely a third of the EU's, will surge to 50 per cent more than Europe's by 2020.

'The next 25 years will see an unprecedented boost in the prominence of developing economies in the world economy,' says the report. 'Five of these countries are projected to fundamentally change the way the world does business.'

The big five, as the report dubs them, are Brazil, China, India, Indonesia and Russia. Between them they hold half the world's workforce, but currently account for less than a tenth of world output and trade.

Source: *Guardian* 10 September 1997. © *The Guardian* 1997.

at the expense of the established industrial countries by 2020. We would make two comments on forecasts of this kind. First, they are clearly not evidence of change now, and therefore cannot be used to *currently* validate the globalization thesis. This argument applies *a fortiori* in the case of the recession-bound Russian economy. Second, recent developments in trade policy suggest that change will be fiercely resisted by the advanced nations. As noted in Chapter 13, section 13.5, the developing countries have typically responded to shifting comparative advantage and the exposure of certain industries to new sources of competition by introducing protectionist trade policy in an attempt to hold on to market share. This indicates that any nascent globalization imperatives will not unfold unchallenged.

16.4 A globalized foreign exchange market?

On the face of it, here the evidence for globalization appears more compelling. In Chapter 14, sections 14.7 and 14.8, we discussed the growing importance of currency speculation as a source of exchange rate instability, and noted in this context the ERM crises of 1992 and 1993. Recall that, in 1992, speculative pressures on sterling forced the suspension of British participation in the ERM. In 1993, speculation, primarily against the French franc, resulted in a significant widening of the ERM target zones for most participant currencies. Crises such as these are taken as indicative of the *new* powers of currency speculators to 'take on' and defeat the collective will of sovereign governments to set exchange rates for their own currencies. Remember that the ERM was a system jointly sponsored by several of the world's most advanced industrial economies (four of the G7). If nations such as these are rendered impotent then – the argument runs – this is clear evidence of the power of agents in new *global* markets.

But again what exactly is new here? Sterling and destabilizing speculation are hardly strangers. In 1931 speculation forced the pound off the Gold Standard (an earlier fixed exchange rate regime). In 1949 and 1967 British governments reluctantly conceded devaluations inside the Bretton Woods system. Indeed, in 1971 the Bretton Woods system itself collapsed as a result of a loss of market confidence in the US dollar. Speculation was an established feature of the international economy for most of the twentieth century! Moreover, in each of the cases to which we refer, adverse market sentiment towards a currency arose not because omnipotent speculators 'fancied having a go' but because of *legitimate* underlying doubts about the sustainability of the established parity and/or because of irredeemable faults in the fixed exchange rate system at issue. As we explained in Chapter 14 (section 14.7), sterling's suspension from the ERM was predicated both on unfavourable conditions in the UK economy at the time and on the fragility of the ERM itself. In this context, currency speculators were bound to take a dim view of sterling, and the outcome can hardly be taken as evidence of the emergence of a wholly new 'globalized' currency market. Moreover, Chapter 14 also provided evidence that currency markets can be conditioned by purposeful state intervention. Recall the successful efforts of the leading industrial nations in the mid 1980s to engineer a depreciation of the US dollar (the Plaza Agreement) and their adoption of undisclosed target zones outside which their currencies would not be allowed to float (the Louvre Accord). There is little doubt that currency speculators are better resourced now than they have been in any previous era, but this is not a sufficient condition for the validation of the globalization thesis.

16.5 Multinationals and globalization

For MNCs, the globalization thesis implies a *new openness* in the world economy: they should be free to use the planet as a borderless space in which to organize production. Traditional affinities to countries of origin or particular markets will disappear as these firms adjust to the new locational discretion they enjoy. However, as we saw in Chapter 15, when we look for evidence of such change little is readily apparent, and one is again struck by the *continuities* that can be observed instead.

In the 1930s, approximately two-thirds of FDI was accounted for by developing countries, with the remaining third concentrated in the developed part of the world. This distribution reflected the general form of MNC activity prior to the Second World War. At that time, multinational investment was driven primarily by *commodity production*: that is, the production of food and raw materials. The natural resource endowments of developing countries encouraged them to specialize in commodity production, but without foreign investment they often lacked sufficient capital to do so competitively. Many developing countries were also locked into subservient relationships with colonial powers. For these reasons, MNCs from the developed and imperial countries were ideally placed to invest in and organize commodity production in less developed parts of the world. However, a glance back to Table 15.3 shows that, now, the distribution of FDI flows in the world economy has been radically altered with the dominant share (71.5 per cent in 1998) now going to the developed countries. The reason for the shift is a change in the form of MNC activity. From the 1950s onwards, FDI in the production of *manufactured goods* increased sharply, and most of this activity was retained in the more developed parts of the world. Moreover, in what we might term the new 'era' of hypothesized globalization – the 1980s, 1990s and the start of the new millennium – it is clear from the table that MNC preferences for the developed world are actually *strengthening*. The United Nations (UN) estimates that, currently, North America, Europe and Japan – together with the coastal provinces of China – receive 90 per cent of the world's FDI. Thus the rest of the world (comprising 70 per cent of its population) gets only 10 per cent. Moreover, again according to the UN, a third of all developing countries have seen their levels of FDI *fall* in relation to GDP over the last ten years. These trends run completely against one of the most popular implications of globalization: that MNCs are forsaking developed areas of the world in order to take advantage of cheap labour or lax environmental controls, or whatever, elsewhere. Of course, we do not deny that the developing countries do indeed hold such 'attractions' for MNCs. Indeed, Box 13.2 provides a specific example of the link between shifting comparative advantage in the clothing industry and relatively low wages in Morocco. But what is clearly in dispute is that this is part of any *new and decisive trend* in globalization.

16.6 Origins of the globalization thesis

The question then arises: if the notion of globalization is really so contentious, how can we account for its popularity? A recent study by Hirst and Thompson (1996) – see guide to further reading at the end of this chapter – links the ascent of the globalization thesis to the uncertainties of the international economy since the end of the postwar boom. Their argument is that a number of widely experienced economic problems, together with important forms of structural economic change, have fostered the perception that individual nations are increasingly at the mercy of destabilizing 'globalized' market forces. Hirst and Thompson suggest that the collapse of the Bretton Woods system, the OPEC oil price shocks (1973–74 and 1979) and the emergence of worldwide inflation in the early 1970s caused a crisis of confidence in what had been long-standing policy regimes of the advanced countries. As economic growth slowed and unemployment re-emerged as a significant problem in many nations for the first time since the 1930s, a clear need arose for an *explanation* of this new period of turbulence. At the same time, structural changes in both the developed and developing parts of the world and, indeed, in the relations between the two, made 'globalization' a convenient way to conceptualize what was going on.

One of the key structural changes cited by Hirst and Thompson is the industrialization of some developing countries. They note the coincidence of this process and the emergence of *deindustrialization* in several of the advanced nations such as the UK and the USA. Deindustrialization refers to the absolute loss of jobs in manufacturing industry. In the UK, deindustrialization has accelerated since the end of the postwar boom as British industry has cut jobs in an attempt to improve its domestic and international competitiveness. The temptation is, of course, to explicitly link developing country industrialization and deindustrialization in the advanced economies: the former 'causing' the latter. While in *some* industries this might be a valid connection to make (see again Box 13.1), as we have argued, the general case (for most industries and most countries) is much harder to sustain. Beyond the noted exception of Asian industrialization, there has not been any decisive reshaping of the international division of labour in manufacturing in recent years. Hirst and Thompson's point is that such limited forms of structural economic change, coincident with the end of the postwar boom, have been improperly elevated to the status of a global process.

Finally, Hirst and Thompson argue that the popularity of the globalization thesis reflects the current difficulties of international economic policy. Over the last quarter of the twentieth century, it has clearly not been possible to re-establish the conditions for sustained expansion in the international economy. Governments, acting alone or collectively, appear less convinced than previously that they can positively affect the long-term course of economic change. Why? Part of the answer, in Hirst and Thompson's view, is that policy-makers have effectively become preoccupied with 'globalization'. The assumed presence of global market forces invalidates the underlying assumption of the Bretton Woods institutions and the GATT that there can be a managed capitalism 'without losers'. Thus the notion that the international economy can be made to function for the collective good of many nations has partly given way to a *laissez-faire* perspective that countries must engage in a process of febrile 'global' competition if they are in any way to prosper. Hirst and Thompson call this 'the pathology of over-diminished expectations' – or, to put it another way, policy-makers are effectively saying 'globalization makes it impossible for us to make the kinds of commitments in world economic affairs that we used to, so we won't try.'

16.7 Justifying the internationalist perspective

Earlier in this section we offered three approaches to the conceptualization of the international/global economy. Our preference was for the *internationalist* perspective. The intervening discussion should make the reasons for this choice apparent. In international trade, the markets in foreign exchange and in foreign direct investment flows, while there is some evidence of change, it is of insufficient magnitude to validate the notion of a new and wholly different global economy. This would, at least, seem to undermine the stronger globalization approach. But, in essence, it also negates the softer version too. The key aspect of 'soft globalization' is its recognition of the collective potency of states as necessary regulators of new *global* markets. But if there are no global markets, the entire premise may be readily dismissed. This does not mean that the *internationalist* perspective is ambivalent about collective action by states: far from it. The postwar boom was predicated on cooperation between the major industrial nations. In our view, the further such cooperation extends amongst the developed *and* less developed countries, the better are the chances of achieving widespread and sustainable economic development, and the greater is the possibility of suppressing the 'diminished expectations' of the globalization thesis.

16.8 Business and globalization

How does the globalization debate bear upon business? In order to answer this question we need to reflect back to some of the issues raised in Chapter 1, section 1.2. Here, we discussed the significance of economics itself for business. Our argument was that economics provides us with a means of understanding the interactions between consumers, firms and governments in markets. We also tried to show that government has a more pervasive interest in markets than might be popularly supposed. Our examples of the markets for clothing and textiles, cars and professional football all suggested the presence of important forms of government intervention. The point we were making is that, in modern capitalist economies, *governments matter*. If those who assert that the world economy is now composed of a set of overlapping *global* markets are right, governments would matter much less, or not at all. We hope we have offered a convincing argument that this is not the case.

For business, the central conclusion is then that markets are *still* arenas where firms and consumers interact under the conditioning influence of governments. Even the world's largest MNCs will shape their commercial strategies by factoring in relevant forms of government policy. We saw in Chapter 15, section 15.4, how Toyota is concerned about the British government's decision over whether or not to adopt the euro. If Britain stays out, Toyota may disinvest in the UK in favour of continental Europe. To the extent that it may be influential, this certainly says much about the potential agency of Toyota, but it also underscores the continuing relevance of British economic policy to the business plans of MNCs. And if the British government counts, so too does the US government, the Japanese, the German and so on. Moving up a tier, the EU, NAFTA and other collective sources of authority such as the Triad also continue to influence the development of markets.

We conclude this book as we began it: by suggesting that whether studying business or conducting it, one needs an awareness of economics in order to understand the continuing interplay between consumers, firms and government in markets at *every* level.

■ Summary

◆ While there is some evidence of change in the international economy, the case for 'globalization' has been overstated. Globalization implies the widest possible articulation of market forces, to the extent that the economic interests and capabilities of individual nation states become irrelevant.

◆ Against the globalization thesis, there appears to be a sometimes remarkable degree of continuity in the international patterns of trade and foreign direct investment. Foreign exchange markets too are by no means beyond sovereign influence.

◆ The origins of the globalization thesis appear to lie in the period of economic uncertainty that followed the end of the postwar boom. A particular focus has been change in the international division of labour and the appearance of limited forms of industrialization in less developed parts of the world. This, coupled with pronounced deindustrialization in some developed countries, has given rise to claims of the existence of new generalized 'global' market forces.

■ Key terms

◆ Globalization
◆ Global economy

◆ International economy
◆ International division of labour
◆ Industrialization
◆ Deindustrialization

■ Questions for discussion

◆ What would be the main characteristics of a 'global' economy?
◆ What evidence is there against the existence of a global economy?
◆ Why has the globalization thesis proven so popular?

■ Further reading

Hirst, P and G. Thompson, *Globalization in Question* (Cambridge: Polity Press, 1996). Offers a jaundiced view of the globalization thesis. Chapter 1 of this book provides an admirable summary of their argument.

Lechner, F. and J. Boli (eds) *The Globalization Reader* (Oxford: Blackwell, 1999).

Daniels, P.W. and W.F. Lever (eds) *The Global Economy in Transition* (Harlow: Addison Wesley Longman, 1996). Part 3 of this book sketches out the major contemporary trends in the 'globalization' of production.

Giddens, A. *Runaway World: How Globalization is Re-shaping Our Lives* (London: Profile Books, 1999).

■ Internet links

The best general sources on trends towards globalized economic processes are institutions such as:
The *International Monetary Fund*: **http://www.imf.org/**
The *OECD*: **http://www.oecd.org/**

Answers to Self-Test Questions

Chapter 1

True (t) or false (f)
1. t 2. f 3. f 4. t 5. f 6. f 7. t 8. t 9. f 10. t

Chapter 2

True (t) or false (f)
1. t 2. f 3. f 4. f 5. f 6. t 7. t 8. f 9. f 10. t
11. f 12. t 13. t 14. t 15. t 16. f

Missing word(s)
1. the quantity demanded 2. extension; contraction
3. complement 4. equilibrium 5. clear
6. intervention 7. substitutes 8. disequilibrium
9. responsiveness; price 10. unit elastic 11. close
substitutes 12. income 13. inferior 14. one

Chapter 4

True (t) or false (f)
1. t 2. t 3. f 4. t 5. f 6. f 7. t 8. t 9. f 10. f

Missing word(s)
1. production function 2. variable factor 3. fixed costs
4. marginal product of labour 5. change in scale
6. average costs 7. total revenue 8. total revenue
9. maximize profit 10. average cost

Chapter 5

True (t) or false (f)
1. t 2. t 3. t 4. f 5. t 6. f 7. t 8. f 9. f 10. t
11. t 12. t

Missing word(s)
1. concentration ratios 2. perfectly elastic
3. homogeneous 4. exceed 5. minimum
6. barriers to entry 7. $MC = MR$ 8. makers 9. kinked
10. interdependently 11. price discrimination
12. planning sector 13. revised sequence

Chapter 6

True (t) or false (f)
1. t 2. f 3. t 4. f 5. t 6. t 7. f

Missing word(s)
1. investment appraisal 2. cash outlay
3. payback period 4. ARR 5. cash flows

6. the payment of dividends in the future 7. discounted
cash flow techniques 8. internal rate of return 9. net
present value 10. acceptance of all NPV projects

Chapter 8

True (t) or false (f)
1. t 2. f 3. t 4. f 5. t 6. f 7. t 8. f 9. f 10. t

Missing word(s)
1. derived 2. marginal physical product 3. wage
4. substitution; income 5. reservation wage 6. wage
rate 7. human capital 8. normative 9. transfer
earnings 10. demand

Chapter 9

True (t) or false (f)
1. t 2. f 3. t 4. t 5. f 6. t 7. t 8. f 9. t 10. t

Missing word(s)
1. real 2. G7 3. actively 4. perfectly anticipated
5. helps; penalizes 6. hyperinflation 7. international
transactions 8. surplus 9. John Maynard Keynes
10. Keynesianism; monetarism

Chapter 10

True (t) or false (f)
1. t 2. t 3. f 4. f 5. t 6. t 7. f 8. t 9. f 10. t
11. f 12. t 13. t 14. f 15. t 16. f 17. t 18. f
19. t 20. f 21. t 22. t 23. t 24. f 25. t 26. t

Missing word(s)
1. real wage 2. frictional; structural; demand-deficient
3. autonomous 4. frictional; structural 5. aggregate
demand 6. Milton Friedman 7. microeconomic
8. labour turnover; adverse selection; shirking; fairness
9. NAIRU 10. hysteresis 11. monetary 12. stable;
predictable 13. Phillips curve 14. excess demand for
labour 15. demand-pull inflation 16. expected rate of
inflation 17. vertical; natural 18. independently
19. cost-push; sociological 20. prices and incomes
policy 21. outside

Chapter 11

True (t) or false (f)
1. t 2. f 3. f 4. f 5. f 6. t 7. f 8. t 9. t 10. t
11. t 12. t 13. f 14. f 15. f 16. t 17. f 18. t
19. f 20. f 21. t

Missing word(s)
1. diminishing 2. quality 3. diminishing returns
4. steady state 5. exogenous 6. Paul Romer; Robert
Lucas Jr 7. human capital 8. long-term trend path
9. expansionary phase; contractionary phase
10. multiplier process; accelerator 11. multiplier
12. monetary shocks 13. fixed 14. Robert Lucas Jr
15. unanticipated 16. supply-side shocks 17. Finn
Kydland; Edward Prescott 18. boom; slump

Chapter 12

True (t) or false (f)
1. t 2. t 3. t 4. t 5. f
6. t 7. t 8. f 9. t 10. f

Missing word(s)
1. fine tuning 2. passive 3. unstable 4. aggregate
demand 5. inside 6. outside 7. stable
8. unanticipated; short run 9. rational expectations
10. Lucas critique

Chapter 13

True (t) or false (f)
1. t 2. t 3. f 4. t 5. t
6. t 7. f 8. f 9. t 10. f

Missing word(s)
1. mercantilism 2. free 3. labour productivity
4. factor endowments 5. Leontief paradox
6. infant-industry 7. inter-industry 8. Multi-Fibre
Arrangement

Chapter 14

True (t) or false (f)
1. f 2. f 3. t 4. t 5. t
6. t 7. f 8. t 9. t 10. t

Missing word(s)
1. persistent 2. price 3. expenditure reduction policy;
expenditure-switching policy 4. Marshall–Lerner
5. demand; supply 6. speculators; government
7. integration argument; anchor argument 8. Triffin /
dollar dilemma 9. inflation 10. depreciation

Glossary

Absolute advantage   The ability of a country to produce more of a particular commodity than another country, using an equal quantity of factor inputs.

Accelerator principle   The theory that the level of net investment depends on the change in output.

Accommodating transaction   One undertaken for balance of payments purposes.

Activist policy rule   A pre-specified rule for the conduct of policy that is linked to the state of the economy; also known as a feedback rule.

Adaptive expectations   An approach that assumes that people's expectations of the future value of a variable are based solely on recently observed values of that variable.

Aggregate demand (AD)   The total planned expenditures of all buyers of final goods and services; composed of consumer expenditure, investment expenditure, government expenditure and net exports.

Aggregate demand management   The use of fiscal and monetary policies to influence the level of aggregate demand.

Aggregate production function   A functional relationship between the quantity of aggregate output produced and the quantities of inputs used in production.

Aggregate supply (AS)   The total planned output in the economy.

Appreciation   The appreciation of a currency involves an increase in its value in terms of other currencies when the currency in question is not part of a formal exchange rate system.

Autonomous expenditure   Expenditure that does not depend on the level of national income.

Autonomous transaction   One undertaken for its own sake.

Average cost   The total cost of producing any given output divided by the number of units produced. Average cost can be divided into average fixed costs and average variable costs.

Average product of labour   The total output produced per worker employed.

Average revenue   Total revenue divided by the number of units sold; it also equals price.

Balance of payments   A record of a country's international transactions.

Barriers to entry   Barriers or restrictions that prevent the entry of new firms into an industry.

Bretton Woods system   A fixed exchange rate system established at the end of the Second World War. The system broke down in the early 1970s.

Business cycle   Fluctuations in aggregate economic activity; in particular movements in output around its trend.

Cairns Group   Comprises Argentina, Australia, Brazil, Canada, Chile, Columbia, Fiji, Hungary, Indonesia, Malaysia, Philippines, New Zealand, Thailand and Uruguay.

Capital gains   Arise when the value of an asset, such as a share, rises above the price at which it was purchased.

Capital goods   Goods, such as plant, machinery and buildings, that are used (and eventually wear out) in making other goods and services.

Capital–labour ratio   The amount of capital per worker; the ratio of the quantity of capital inputs to the number of workers.

Capital–output ratio   The ratio of the amount of capital to the amount of output produced by it.

Capital rationing   A situation whereby a firm does not have sufficient capital available to invest in all the profitable projects in which it is interested.

Cartel   A group of firms or producers that agree to act as if they were a single firm or producer, for example with regard to pricing or output decisions.

Centrally planned economy   One in which resource allocation is organized predominantly by the state.

Ceteris paribus   All other things being equal or remaining constant.

Classical economics   A pre-Keynesian approach based on the assumption that wages and prices adjust to clear markets, and that monetary policy does not influence real variables, such as output and employment.

Cold turkey   A rapid and permanent reduction in the rate of monetary growth, aimed at reducing the rate of inflation.

Collective bargaining   Involves negotiations between a trade union and one or more employers over pay or workplace conditions.

Collective provision   The provision of goods and services by the state.

Comparative advantage The ability of a country to produce a commodity at a lower opportunity cost, in terms of other commodities forgone, than another country.

Competition policy Policy aimed at promoting competitive practices between firms in markets.

Complement A good that complements another good.

Concentration ratio A ratio that measures the total market share of the largest firms in an industry.

Conglomerate merger Arises when two firms from different industries merge together.

Constant returns to scale The proposition that a proportionate increase in all factor inputs will lead to the same proportionate increase in output.

Consumers' expenditure The aggregate purchases of goods and services by households for their own use.

Consumption function The relationship between aggregate consumer expenditure and aggregate income.

Convergence The tendency for output per worker in different countries to converge over time.

Cost-push inflation Inflation caused by cost increases even though there are no shortages of goods and services and the economy is below full employment.

Credibility The degree to which people believe the authorities' announcements about future policy.

Crowding out The reduction in private sector expenditure that results following an increase in government expenditure.

Cyclical unemployment See *demand-deficient unemployment*.

Debentures Documents that are issued by a firm in order to borrow funds. The document entitles the lender of funds to an annual interest payment during the period of the loan.

Debt finance Arises when a firm borrows in order to obtain the necessary funds for investment.

Demand The quantity of a good or service that consumers wish to purchase at each conceivable price, *ceteris paribus*.

Demand-deficient unemployment Unemployment that results because aggregate demand is insufficient to provide employment for everyone who wants to work at the prevailing real wage; also known as cyclical unemployment.

Demand-pull inflation Inflation caused by an excess demand for goods and services when the economy is at, or above, full employment.

Depreciation The depreciation of a currency involves the lowering of its value in terms of other currencies when the currency in question is not part of some formal exchange rate system.

Depression A very severe and prolonged recession.

Derived demand Arises for a factor of production because of the demand for the output the factor helps to produce. The factor in itself does not generate demand.

Devaluation The devaluation of a currency involves the lowering of its value in terms of other currencies when the currency in question is part of some formal exchange rate system.

Diminishing marginal utility The decline in marginal utility that occurs as more and more of a good or service is consumed.

Diminishing returns A situation in which successive increases in the use of a factor input, holding other factor inputs constant, eventually results in a fall in the additional output derived from a unit increase in that factor input.

Dirty flexible/floating exchange rate See *managed exchange rate*.

Discretionary policy A situation in which the authorities are free to vary the strength of fiscal and/or monetary policy, in any way they see fit, in order to achieve their desired objectives.

Diseconomies of scale A situation in which long-run average costs rise as output increases.

Disinflation A decrease in the rate of inflation.

Disposable income Income that households have at their disposal after the payment of tax.

Dividends Sums of money paid by a firm to shareholders; each shareholder receives a dividend for each share held.

Dominant strategy A strategy that is best for one firm whatever the other firm decides to do.

Dumping Involves the export of goods to foreign markets with prices set at or below the costs of production.

Eclectic approach One that combines themes and policies from different schools of thought.

Economic growth An increase in real GDP over time.

Economic rent Payment to a factor of production above that necessary to retain it in its present use.

Economically active Economically active individuals are those people of working age who are either in work or actively seeking it.

Economies of scale Economies that arise when a larger output is produced without a proportionately equal increase in the costs of production.

Efficiency wage A real wage paid by firms, above the market-clearing real wage rate, because it is both profitable and rational for them to do so.

Elasticity of labour supply   Measures the responsiveness of the quantity of labour supplied to changes in the wage rate.

Endogenous variable   A variable that is explained within a particular model.

Entrepreneur   The risk-taking individual producer who perceives a demand in the market and organizes resources to meet that demand in the anticipation of profit.

Equilibrium price   The price at which the quantity demanded equals the quantity supplied.

Equilibrium quantity   The amount of a good that is bought and sold at the equilibrium price.

Equity finance   Arises when a firm obtains investment funds by issuing shares.

European Free Trade Association (EFTA)   A free trade area that was formed under British leadership to rival the EEC; created in 1960 it has more recently been absorbed by the EU single market.

Eurosclerosis   A term used to describe the belief that Europe suffers from excessive labour market rigidities.

Excess demand   Occurs when the quantity demanded exceeds the quantity supplied at some given price.

Excess supply   Occurs when the quantity supplied exceeds the quantity demanded at some given price.

Exchange rate   The price of one currency expressed in terms of another.

Exchange rate mechanism (ERM)   The fixed but adjustable exchange rate element of the European Monetary System (EMS).

Exogenous variable   A variable that is not explained within a particular model; its value is taken as given.

Expenditure reduction policy   Involves a reduction in the level of aggregate demand in the domestic economy in order to improve the balance of payments position on the current account.

Expenditure-switching policy   Switches domestic and foreign demand away from foreign goods and towards home produced goods.

Externalities   The costs incurred by, or benefits received by, other members of society not taken into account by consumers or producers. Externalities are also known as third-party effects.

Factor inputs   Any goods and services used in the process of production.

Factor intensity   The emphasis in production towards the use of one particular factor of production above others.

Factor markets   Markets in which factors of production – land, labour and capital – are bought and sold.

Feedback rule   See *activist policy rule*.

Final output   Goods and services that are sold to their ultimate users.

Fiscal policy   Measures that alter the level and composition of government expenditure and taxation.

Fixed costs   Costs that do not change with the output level; also referred to as overhead costs or unavoidable costs.

Fixed exchange rate   An exchange rate that is fixed at a predetermined level by intervention by the country's central bank in the foreign exchange market.

Flexible exchange rate   An exchange rate that is determined in the foreign exchange market by the forces of demand and supply; also known as a floating exchange rate.

Floating exchange rate   See *flexible exchange rate*.

Foreign exchange reserves   Stocks of foreign currencies held by central banks.

Free market economy   One in which resource allocation is predominantly market based.

Free trade   An absence of government regulation in the international market for goods and services.

Frictional unemployment   Unemployment that results because it takes time for workers to search for suitable jobs; also known as search unemployment.

Full employment   A situation in which all unemployment is frictional and structural, and cannot be reduced by increasing aggregate demand.

Full employment output   See *potential output*.

G5   The world's five leading industrial nations: the United States, Japan, Germany, France and the United Kingdom.

G7   The seven main industrial economies in the world: the United States, Japan, Germany, France, Italy, the United Kingdom and Canada.

GDP in current prices   See *nominal GDP*.

GDP in real prices   See *real GDP*.

Goods   Tangible products.

Goods markets   Markets in which goods and services are bought and sold.

Gradualism   An approach to disinflation that involves a slow and gradual reduction in the rate of monetary growth.

Gross domestic product (GDP)   The total value of goods and services produced in a country by the factors of production located in that country regardless of who owns them.

Gross national product (GNP)   The value of final goods and services produced by domestically owned factors of production; GDP plus net property income from abroad.

Herfindahl–Hirshmann index   An index that measures the degree of market power by summing the square of the market shares of each firm in the industry.

Horizontal merger   Arises when two firms in the same industry and stage in the production process merge together.

Human capital   The knowledge and skills of workers in an economy.

Human resource management   The employment, training and management of the workforce in order to ensure that the firm is able to achieve its overall objective.

Hyperinflation   A situation in which the rate of inflation is extremely high for over a year or more.

Hysteresis   The proposition that the equilibrium value of a variable depends on the history of that variable, for example, if the actual rate of unemployment remains above the natural rate for a prolonged period the natural rate will tend to increase, and vice versa.

Imperfect competition   A market structure in which there are a large number of firms selling similar but differentiated products; also known as monopolistic competition.

Imperfectly anticipated inflation   A situation in which the actual rate of inflation differs from the anticipated or expected rate of inflation.

Income elasticity of demand   The proportionate change in the quantity of a good demanded divided by the proportionate change in consumers' incomes.

Industrial policy   Policy aimed at enhancing the performance of firms in markets.

Inferior good   One for which demand decreases when income increases.

Inflation   A situation in which the overall or general level of prices rises over time.

Inflation rate   The rate at which the general level of prices increases; expressed as a percentage on an annual basis.

Inter-industry trade   The tendency for countries to trade the same kinds of goods and services.

Internal rate of return   The discount rate that generates a net present value equal to zero.

International division of labour   Patterns of specialization in the production of goods and services between nations.

International Monetary Fund (IMF)   An international agency, located in Washington, which promotes stability of member countries' exchange rates and assists them in correcting balance of payments disequilibria.

Investment appraisal   The use of techniques to ensure that all projects are consistent with the objective of the firm.

Investment expenditure   Purchases of capital goods, such as plant, machinery and buildings.

Keynesian economics   An approach based on the belief that capitalist economies are inherently unstable and can come to rest at less than full employment for prolonged periods. Keynesian economists favour the use of discretionary aggregate demand policies to stabilize the economy at, or near, full employment.

Labour market segmentation   Arises when labour faces barriers to entry to a particular labour market.

Laissez-faire   A situation in which there is little or no state interference in the market economy.

Law of diminishing returns   States that if more of a variable input is employed, holding the quantity of other inputs constant, the marginal product of the variable input will eventually decrease.

Legal monopoly   As defined in the UK, a legal monopoly arises when a firm enjoys a market share of 25 per cent or more.

Limited liability   A situation in which, in the event of losses incurred by a firm, the personal wealth of its owners is not at risk. Liability is limited to the value of the firm.

Long run   A period of time in which all inputs may be varied.

Lucas critique   The argument that traditional policy evaluation may be misleading as it fails to take into account that people may change their expectations and behaviour when policy changes.

Macroeconomics   The study of the economy as a whole.

Macroeconomic policies   Policies that governments use to try to influence overall economic performance.

Managed exchange rate   An exchange rate that is influenced by intervention of the country's central bank in the foreign exchange market; also known as a dirty flexible, or dirty floating, exchange rate.

Marginal cost   The change in total cost resulting from increasing production by one unit.

Marginal physical product   The change in total output resulting from a unit change in the variable factor.

Marginal product of labour   The increase in total production as a result of employing one more worker.

Marginal propensity to consume   The change in consumption expenditure resulting from an additional unit of income.

Marginal propensity to import   The change in import expenditure resulting from an additional unit of income.

Marginal propensity to withdraw   The fraction of an additional unit of income that is withdrawn from the circular flow of income.

Marginal revenue   The change in total revenue resulting from a one-unit change in output sold.

Marginal revenue product   The change in a firm's total revenue resulting from the sale of output produced by one more unit of the variable factor.

Marginal social benefit   The money value of the benefit from one additional unit of consumption.

Marginal social cost   The cost of producing one additional unit of output. It includes both the marginal cost incurred by the producer and any marginal costs incurred by other members of society in the form of externalities.

Marginal utility   The change in total satisfaction resulting from a one-unit change in the consumption of a good or service.

Market   A framework that brings buyers and sellers together.

Market clearing   Occurs when all goods or services supplied in a market are sold.

Market failure   Arises when the market either fails to provide certain goods, or fails to provide them at their optimal or most desirable level.

Market power   The ability of a firm to set the price of a good or service without risking the loss of its entire market share.

Market segmentation   The division of a market by the producer into a number of discrete parts between which consumers cannot easily move.

Market structure   Characterizes a market according to the degree of competition in it.

Microeconomics   The study of the behaviour of individual households and firms, and the determination of the relative prices of particular goods and services.

Mismatch unemployment   See *structural unemployment*.

Mixed economy   One that combines market and state forms of resource allocation.

Monetarism   An approach based on the belief that capitalist economies are inherently stable, unless disturbed by erratic monetary growth, and will return fairly rapidly to the neighbourhood of the natural level of output and employment when subjected to some disturbance.

Monetary policy   Measures that alter the money supply and/or interest rates.

Monopolistic competition   See *imperfect competition*.

Monopoly   A market structure in which there is a sole supplier of a good or service that has no close substitutes and for which there are barriers to entry into the industry.

Monopoly power   Arises where potential competitors can be excluded from a market.

Multinational   A firm that owns and controls assets in more than one country.

Multiplier   The ratio of the change in income to a change in autonomous expenditure.

Nash equilibrium   A situation in which both firms are doing the best they can, given what the other firm is doing.

National income   The income that originates in the production of goods and services supplied by residents of a nation.

Natural monopoly   Arises where a single firm is the most efficient structure for the production of a particular good or service.

Natural rate of unemployment   The rate of unemployment that exists when the labour market is in equilibrium; composed of frictional and structural unemployment.

Net exports   Exports minus imports.

Net present value technique of investment appraisal   Calculates whether the present value of future returns from a project are at least equal to the cost of that project.

New classical economics   An approach based on the three assumptions of continuous market clearing, incomplete information and rational expectations.

New Keynesian economics   An approach that explores a variety of reasons for wage and price stickiness that prevent market clearing.

Nominal GDP   The value of gross domestic product measured in terms of the prices prevailing at the time; also known as GDP in current prices.

Non-accelerating inflation rate of unemployment (NAIRU)   The rate of unemployment at which inflation is stable.

Non-system   The broad system of flexible exchange rates prevailing in the world economy since 1973.

Normal good   One for which demand increases when income increases.

Normal profit   The minimum amount of profit that a firm must earn to induce it to remain in the industry.

Normative issues   Those that are a matter of opinion.

North American Free Trade Agreement (NAFTA)   A free trade area that covers the US, Canadian and Mexican economies.

Oligopoly   A market structure in which there are a small number of firms.

Opportunity cost   The cost of an action measured in terms of the best forgone alternative action.

Organization for Economic Cooperation and Development (OECD)   An intergovernmental organization, based in Paris, which provides a policy forum for the major industrialized countries for the promotion of economic growth, expansion of multilateral trade and provision of foreign aid to developing countries.

Overhead costs   See *fixed costs*.

Pareto efficiency   A situation in which it is impossible to make someone better off without making someone else worse off; also known as Pareto optimality.

Participation rate   The proportion of economically active workers in a particular group of the population.

Passive policy rule   A pre-specified rule for the conduct of policy not linked to prevailing economic circumstances.

Payback   The length of time that it takes for the cash inflows from an investment project to equal the initial cash outlay.

Pay differentials   Exist where there are wage rate premiums attached to particular kinds of work.

Peak load pricing   A situation in which a firm charges higher prices during times of peak demand and lower prices at other times.

Perfect competition   A market structure characterized most notably by a situation in which all firms in the industry are price takers and there is freedom of entry into and exit from the industry.

Perfectly anticipated inflation   A situation in which the actual rate of inflation is equal to the anticipated or expected rate of inflation.

Perfectly elastic demand   Arises where the response of quantity demanded to a price change is infinitely large; price elasticity of demand is ∞ (infinity).

Perfectly inelastic demand   Arises where the quantity demanded does not respond to a change in price; price elasticity of demand is 0.

Permanent income   The average income that people expect to receive over a period of years in the future; also known as normal income and average expected income.

Phillips curve   The relationship between the inflation rate and the unemployment rate.

Policy ineffectiveness proposition   The proposition that anticipated changes in monetary policy will have no effect on output and employment.

Political business cycle   Fluctuations in the level of output and employment caused by the manipulation of the economy for electoral gains or due to partisan differences.

Positive issues   Those that are factually based.

Potential output   The maximum output that can be produced in an economy, given its factor endowments, without generating accelerating inflation; also known as full employment output.

Price discrimination   Arises when a firm sells the same good to different consumers at different prices.

Price elastic   Describes a situation in which the proportionate change in quantity demanded is greater than the proportionate change in price; elasticity is greater than 1.

Price elasticity of demand   The proportionate (or percentage) change in the quantity demanded of a good divided by the proportionate (or percentage) change in its price that brought it about.

Price elasticity of supply   The proportionate change in quantity supplied of a good divided by the proportionate change in its price that brought it about.

Price inelastic   Describes a situation in which the proportionate change in quantity demanded is less than the proportionate change in price; elasticity is less than 1.

Price index   A measure of the average level of prices of a set of goods and services relative to the prices of the same goods and services in a particular base year.

Price maker   A firm that is able to determine the price of its product.

Price taker   A firm that takes the market price of its product as given.

Prices and incomes policy   Measures that establish guidelines or controls for wage and/or price increases.

Private good   One that is wholly consumed by an individual.

Production function   A functional relationship between the total quantity of goods or services produced and the quantity of factors of production used in the production process.

Profit   The difference between total revenue and total cost.

Public good   One that, once produced, can be consumed by everyone.

Public sector borrowing requirement (PSBR)   The amount by which the expenditure of the public sector exceeds its revenue.

Pure monopoly   A market structure in which there is a sole supplier of a good or service that has no close substitutes, and for which there are barriers to entry into the industry.

Quantity demanded   The amount of a good or service that consumers wish to purchase at a particular price, other things being equal.

Quantity supplied   The amount that producers wish to sell at a particular price, *ceteris paribus*.

Quota   A quantitative limit on goods.

Random walk   The path of a variable whose changes over time are unpredictable.

Rational expectations   An approach that assumes that people make the best use of all available information to forecast the future.

Real business cycle approach   An approach in which fluctuations in aggregate output and employment are driven by persistent supply-side shocks to the economy, most notably random fluctuations in the rate of technological progress.

Real GDP   The value of gross domestic product measured in terms of the prices that prevailed in some particular base year; also known as GDP in constant prices.

Real wage   The money wage divided (or deflated) by a price index; the amount of goods and services that a money wage can buy.

Recession   A decline in real GDP that lasts for at least two consecutive quarters of a year.

Relative price   The ratio of the price of one good to the price of another good; expressed as the number of units of one good that one unit of another good will buy.

Reservation wage   The minimum rate required to induce an individual to accept a job.

Retained earnings   Funds generated internally by the firm, such as profits from previous investment projects.

Returns to scale   The percentage increase in output as a result of a percentage increase in both labour and capital in the production process.

Revaluation   An increase in the value of a currency in terms of other currencies when the currency in question is part of some formal exchange rate system.

Rights issues   Occur where a firm issues shares to the market but gives existing shareholders the option to buy the shares first.

Rules   Pre-specified guidelines that determine the conduct of policy.

Say's law   States that supply creates its own demand.

Search unemployment   See *frictional unemployment*.

Services   Intangible products.

Short run   A period of time in which some inputs such as capital are fixed, while others such as labour may be varied.

Short-run Phillips curve   The relationship between inflation and unemployment that exists for a given expected rate of inflation.

Social provision   See *collective provision*.

Stabilization policies   Policies aimed at stabilizing output and employment at, or near, their full employment or natural levels by influencing the level of aggregate demand.

Stagflation   A situation in which high unemployment and high inflation occur simultaneously; a combination of stagnation and inflation.

Steady state   A situation in which output per worker and capital input per worker are no longer changing.

Structural unemployment   Unemployment that results from a mismatch between the skills or location of existing job vacancies and the present skills or location of the unemployed; also known as mismatch unemployment.

Substitute   A good that can be substituted in place of another good.

Supernormal profits   Profits that exceed the minimum amount that a firm must earn to induce it to remain in the industry.

Supply   The quantity of a good or service that producers wish to sell at each conceivable price, other things being equal.

Tariff   A tax on traded goods.

Time inconsistency   The temptation for policy-makers to deviate from a previously announced policy once private decision-makers have adjusted their behaviour to the announced policy.

Time value of money   Arises because cash flows received today are worth more than equivalent cash flows received at a later date.

Total cost   The sum of the costs of all inputs used in producing a firm's output; can be divided into fixed costs and variable costs.

Total revenue   The amount of money that a firm receives from the sale of its output; equals the price of output multiplied by the number of units sold.

Transfer earnings   Payments to a factor that are necessary to retain it in its present use.

Transnational   A firm that owns and controls assets in more than one country, and which organizes production without regard to any particular nation state.

Unemployed   People who are available for work and are actively seeking jobs but cannot find them.

Unemployment rate   The percentage of the labour force who are unemployed.

Unit elasticity   Situation in which the proportionate change in quantity demanded is equal to the proportionate change in price; elasticity is 1.

Unlimited liability   Places the entire personal wealth of the owner of a firm at risk in respect of losses that the firm may incur.

Utility   The satisfaction that a consumer receives from the consumption of a good or service.

Valuation ratio The market valuation of a firm expressed by the price of its shares divided by the book value of its assets.

Variable costs Costs that vary with the output level; also referred to as direct costs and avoidable costs.

Vertical merger Occurs when two firms in the same industry, but at different stages in the production process, merge together.

Bibliography

Adnet, N. (1996) *The European Labour Market* (2nd ed.) (Harlow: Addison Wesley Longman).

Alt, J.E. and K.A. Chrystal (1983) *Political Economics* (Brighton: Wheatsheaf Books).

Armstrong, P., A. Glyn and J. Harrison (1991) *Capitalism Since 1945* (Oxford: Basil Blackwell).

Artis, M.J. (ed.) (1996) *The UK Economy* (14th ed.) (Oxford: Oxford University Press).

Atkinson, B., F. Livesey and B. Milward (1998) *Applied Economics* (Basingstoke: Macmillan).

Barrell, R. (1994) *The UK Labour Market* (Cambridge: Cambridge University Press).

Bassett, P. (1986) *Strike Free: New Industrial Relations in Britain* (London: Macmillan).

Begg, D., S. Fischer and R. Dornbusch (2000) *Economics* (6th ed.) (London: McGraw-Hill).

Blanchard, O. (2000) *Macroeconomics* (2nd ed.) (Englewood Cliffs, NJ: Prentice Hall).

Brealey, R.A., S.C. Myers and A.J. Marcus (1998) *Fundamentals of Corporate Finance* (2nd ed.) (London: McGraw-Hill).

Chrystal, K.A. and S. Price (1994) *Controversies in Macroeconomics* (3rd ed.) (Hemel Hempstead: Harvester Wheatsheaf).

Crafts, N. and G. Toniolo (eds.) (1996) *Economic Growth in Europe Since 1945* (Cambridge: Cambridge University Press).

Curran, J. (1999) *Taking the Fear Out of Economics* (London: Business Press).

Damodaran, A. (1999) *Applied Corporate Finance: A Users Manual* (New York: John Wiley).

Daniels, P.W. and W.F. Lever (eds) (1996) *The Global Economy in Transition* (Harlow: Addison Wesley Longman).

Dawson, G. (1992) *Inflation and Unemployment: Causes, Consequences and Cures* (Aldershot: Edward Elgar).

Denison, E.F. (1985) *Trends in American Economic Growth* (Washington, DC: Brookings Institution).

Dunning, J.H. (1998) *Globalization, Trade and Foreign Direct Investment* (Oxford: Elsevier).

Ferner, A. and R. Hyman (eds) (1998) *Changing Industrial Relations in Europe* (Oxford: Basil Blackwell).

Ferguson, C.E. (1969) *The Neoclassical Theory of Production and Distribution* (Cambridge: Cambridge University Press).

Friedman, M. (1962) *Capitalism and Freedom* (Chicago: University of Chicago Press).

Friedman, M. (1968) 'The role of monetary policy', *American Economic Review*, March, pp. 1–17.

Friedman, M. (1970) *The Counter-Revolution in Monetary Theory* (London: Institute of Economic Affairs).

Friedman, M. (1975) *Unemployment Versus Inflation* (London: Institute of Economic Affairs).

Friedman, M. and A.J. Schwartz (1963) *A Monetary History of the United States, 1867–1960* (Princeton, NJ: Princeton University Press).

Galbraith, J.K. (1973) *Economics and the Public Purpose* (Harmondsworth: Penguin).

George, K.D., C. Joll and E.L. Lynk (1992) *Industrial Organization* (4th ed.) (London: Routledge).

Gerber, J. (1999) *International Economics* (Reading, MA: Addison-Wesley).

Giddens, A. (1999) *Runaway World: How Globalization is Re-shaping Our Lives* (London: Profile Books).

Gordon, R.J. (2000) *Macroeconomics* (8th ed.) (Harlow: Addison Wesley Longman).

Griffiths, A. and S. Wall (eds) (1995) *Applied Economics* (6th ed.) (London: Longman).

Heidensohn, K. (1995) *Europe and World Trade* (London: Pinter).

Hirst, P. and G. Thompson (1996) *Globalization in Question* (Cambridge: Polity Press).

Hoekman, B. and M. Kostecki (1995) *The Political Economy of the World Trading System* (Oxford: Oxford University Press).

Jackson, P.M. and C.M. Price (eds) (1994) *Privatization and Regulation* (Harlow: Longman).

Jacobsen, J.P. (1998) *The Economics of Gender* (2nd ed.) (Harlow: Addison Wesley Longman).

Jepma, C.J., H. Jager, and E. Kamphuis (1996) *Introduction to International Economics* (Harlow: Longman).

Johnson, C. and S. Briscoe (1995) *Measuring the Economy* (Hardmondsworth: Penguin).

Jowsey, E. (1998) *100 Essay Plans for Economics* (Oxford: Oxford University Press).

Keegan, W. (1984) *Mrs Thatcher's Economic Experiment* (Harmondsworth: Penguin).

Keynes, J.M. (1936) *The General Theory of Employment, Interest and Money* (London: Macmillan).

Kindleberger, C. (1975) *The World in Depression* (Berkeley: University of California Press).

Kitson, M. and J. Michie (1995) 'Trade and growth: a historical perspective', in J. Michie and J. Grieve Smith (eds) *Managing the Global Economy* (Oxford: Oxford University Press).

Kirzner, I. (1992) *The Meaning of Market Process* (London: Routledge).

Koutsoyiannis, A. (1979) *Modern Microeconomics* (2nd ed.) (Basingstoke: Macmillan).

Krugman, P. and M. Obstfeld (1994) *International Economics* (3rd ed.) (New York: HarperCollins).

Layard, R., S. Nickell and R. Jackman (1994) *The Unemployment Crisis* (Oxford: Oxford University Press).

Lechner, F. and J. Boli (eds) (1999) *The Globalization Reader* (Oxford: Basil Blackwell).

Le Grand. J., J. Propper and R. Robinson (1992) *The Economics of Social Problems* (3rd ed.) (Basingstoke: Macmillan).

Levacic, R. (1993) 'Markets as coordinating devices' in R. Maidment and G. Thompson (eds) *Managing the United Kingdom* (London: Sage Publications).

Lipsey, R.G. (1960) 'The relationship between unemployment and the rate of change of money wage rates in the UK 1862–1957: a further analysis', *Economica*, February, pp. 1–31.

Lipsey, R.G. and K.A. Chrystal (1999) *Principles of Economics* (8th ed.) (Oxford: Oxford University Press).

Lumby, S. (1994) *Investment Appraisal and Financial Decisions* (5th ed.) (London: Chapman & Hall).

McDonald, F. and S. Dearden (eds) (1998) *European Economic Integration* (3rd ed.) (London: Longman).

Mankiw, N.G. (2000) *Macroeconomics* (4th ed.) (New York: Worth).

Marin, A. (1992) *Macroeconomic Policy* (London: Routledge).

Martin, S. and D. Parker (1997) *The Impact of Privatization* (London: Routledge).

Moon, B.E. (1996) *Dilemmas of International Trade* (Boulder, CO: Westview Press).

Odell, P.R. (1987) 'The world petroleum market: the current situation and prospects', in K.I.F. Kahn (ed.) *Petroleum Resources and Development* (London and New York: Belhaven Press).

Ormerod, P. (1998) *Butterfly Economics* (London: Faber & Faber).

Parkin, M., M. Powell and K. Matthews (2000) *Economics* (4th ed.) (Harlow: Prentice Hall).

Penn, R., M. Rose and J. Rubery (eds) (1994) *Skill and Occupational Change* (Oxford: Oxford University Press).

Peston, M.H. (1984) *The British Economy: An Elementary Macroeconomic Perspective* (2nd ed.) (Oxford: Philip Allan).

Phillips, A.W. (1958) 'The relation between unemployment and the rate of change of money wage rates in the United Kingdom, 1861–1957', *Economica*, November, pp. 283–99.

Pike, R.H. (1983) 'The capital-budgeting behaviour and corporate characteristics of capital-constrained firms', *Journal of Business Finance and Accounting*, Vol. 10, No. 4, pp. 663–71.

Pike, R.H. (1988) 'An empirical survey of the adoption of sophisticated capital budgeting practices and decision-making effectiveness', *Accounting and Business Research*, Vol. 18, No. 72, pp. 341–51.

Pike, R.H. (1996) 'A longitudinal study of capital budgeting practices', *Journal of Business Financing and Accounting*, Vol. 23, No. 1, pp. 79–92.

Pindyk, R. and D.L. Rubinfield (1998) *Microeconomics* (4th ed.) (Englewood Cliffs, NJ: Prentice Hall).

Pratten, C.F. (1988) 'A survey of the economics of scale', in *Research on the Costs of Non-Europe* (Office for Official Publications of the European Communities).

Putterman, L. and R.S. Kroszner (eds) (1996) *The Economic Nature of the Firm* (London: Cambridge University Press).

Ricardo, D. (1817) *The Principles of Political Economy and Taxation* (1948 reprint) (London: J.M. Dent and Sons).

Scherer, F.M., A. Beckenstein, E. Kaufer and R.D. Murphy (1975) *The Economics of Multiplant Occupation: An International Comparisons Study* (Cambridge, MA: Harvard University Press).

Shackleton, J.R. (ed.) (1990) *New Thinking in Economics* (Aldershot: Edward Elgar).

Shaw, G.K. (1984) *Rational Expectations* (Brighton: Wheatsheaf Books).

Shepherd, W.G. (1990) *The Economics of Industrial Organization* (Englewood Cliffs, NJ: Prentice Hall).

Sloman, J. (2000) *Economics* (4th ed.) (Harlow: Prentice Hall).

Smith, A. (1776) *An Inquiry into the Nature and Causes of the Wealth of Nations* (1930 reprint) (London: Methuen).

Smith, D. (1987) *The Rise and Fall of Monetarism* (Harmondsworth: Penguin).

Snowdon, B. and H.R. Vane (eds) (1997) *Reflections on the Development of Modern Macroeconomics* (Cheltenham: Edward Elgar).

Snowdon, B., H.R. Vane and P. Wynarczyk (1994) *A Modern Guide to Macroeconomics: An Introduction to Competing Schools of Thought* (Aldershot: Edward Elgar).

Stewart, M. (1986) *Keynes and After* (3rd ed.) (Hardmondsworth: Penguin).

Stubbs, R. and G.R.D. Underhill (eds. (2000) *Political Economy and the Changing Global Order* (2nd ed.) (Basingstoke: Macmillan).

United Nations Conference on Trade and Development (1999) *World Investment Report* (New York and Geneva: United Nations).

United Nations Development Programme (1997) *Human Development Report 1997* (Oxford: Oxford University Press).

Vane, H.R. and J.L. Thompson (1993) *An Introduction to Macroeconomic Policy* (4th ed.) (Hemel Hempstead: Harvester Wheatsheaf).

Index